The HUB

The HUB

BOSTON PAST AND PRESENT

Thomas H. O'Connor

NORTHEASTERN UNIVERSITY PRESS

Boston

Northeastern University Press

Library of Congress Cataloging-in-Publication Data

O'Connor, Thomas H., 1922–
The hub : Boston past and present / Thomas H. O'Connor.
p. cm
Includes bibliographical references and index.
ISBN 1-55553-474-0 (acid-free paper)
1. Boston (Mass.)—History. I. Title.

F73.3 .O26   2001
974.4'61–dc21   00-068974

Designed by Gary Gore

Composed in Minion by Bookcomp, Inc., Grand Rapids, Michigan. Printed and bound by Edwards
Brothers, Inc., Ann Arbor, Michigan. The paper is Frasier Odyssey Book, an acid-free stock.

Manufactured in the United States of America
05 04 03 02 01   5 4 3 2 1

*To my students, who have always given
back much more than they received*

CONTENTS

ILLUSTRATIONS

ILLUSTRATIONS

PREFACE

There must be thousands of books about Boston.

Boston is a city with such a long, fascinating, and often controversial history that it could not help spawning innumerable histories and biographies, novels and essays, monographs and journals, usually concentrating on some particular time period, some unusual personality, or some special event. A great many writers have focused their attention on Boston's unique colonial heritage as well as its celebrated role in the struggle for American independence, as evidenced by the throngs of visitors and tourists who travel the city's Freedom Trail. Other scholars have immersed themselves in the celebrated works of Boston's distinguished list of literary figures, often pointing out their important contribution to the cultural renaissance called the "Flowering of New England." Still others have chronicled the heroic efforts of those men and women who worked tirelessly to achieve the social demands of liberated women, or who committed themselves to the moral imperatives of the movement to free the slaves.

The changing character of Boston's economic fortunes is a phenomenon that has intrigued a number of writers who have watched the city constantly reinvent itself in the face of changing times and revolutionary technologies. Boston's experience as a city of immigrants has also been a subject of studies by authors who have analyzed the efforts of an old city to retain its original character and its cherished traditions in the face of overwhelming social, cultural, and ethnic change. And in more recent years, the increasing and pervasive impact of racial diversity and multicultural differences on Boston's traditional networks of ethnic communities has occupied the time and attention of historians and social scientists.

Despite the number and variety of these specialized studies, however, there is really no single, one-volume history that provides either the general reader or the specialist with an overall survey of the three-hundred-year history of Boston—something that is essential in order to appreciate Boston's distinctive qualities as a truly special place. In the course of its history, Boston has undergone extensive topographical transformations, survived serious economic revolutions, experienced major social upheavals, and absorbed massive population changes—all without losing its essential character and personality. For more than three hundred years, Boston has demonstrated an unusual ability not only to survive, but to assimilate the old with the new, the traditional with the progressive, blending the past with the present in a style all its own. I become particularly aware of this juxtaposition of historical images whenever I stop along Tremont Street in downtown Boston, just beyond the cemetery at King's Chapel, and look eastward. I can actually see three centuries of Boston architecture at a single glance: in the center background is the eighteenth-century Faneuil Hall; to the right in the foreground is the nineteenth-century redbrick Sears Crescent; and to the left is the twentieth-century City Hall. And on a clear day, perhaps you can catch a glimpse of Boston Harbor, where John Winthrop's small fleet arrived in the early seventeenth century. It's all there, and it's all uniquely Boston.

It is this long view, this broad view, that makes it possible to better appreciate the many different and significant changes that have taken place during the city's long history. These transformations didn't just happen by accident, nor did they take place in a historical vacuum. To fully appreciate the many ways Boston has changed over the course of three hundred years, grasp the full meaning of each critical turning point, understand the forces driving the responses, and evaluate the conditions shaping the consequences, a larger historical perspective is absolutely essential. The story of Boston is not merely a classic example of immediate challenge and response; it is a unique example of long-range and remarkably effective adaptation to the kinds of cosmic changes that have reduced some communities to ghost towns and caused others to seek survival by transforming themselves into historical theme parks.

One of the oldest cities in North America, Boston has demonstrated a remarkable degree of toughness, resiliency, and ingenuity in not only adjusting to each crisis, but in most cases coming out stronger than before. It continually adapted to new political ideas, adjusted to new cultural forms, reorganized its economic structure, rebuilt its streets, filled in new lands, expanded its limits, absorbed new people, and experimented with new social patterns without losing that indefinable but recognizable quality that makes it so distinctive. Not that change comes easily to Boston—it never did. Indeed, it was when confronted with change that Boston all too often displayed a mean and selfish spirit that belied its reputation as the Cradle of Liberty and the Athens of America. Proud of its intellectual accomplishments and conscious of its cultural preeminence, Boston seldom welcomed any sort of change that would threaten what it had so carefully built. Whether it was political intolerance against those who protested the Puritan establishment in the eighteenth century, religious bigotry against Roman Catholics in the nineteenth century, or displays of racial hatred against African Americans in the twentieth century, Boston was capable of frequently disillusioning even those friends who most admired it.

By eventually adapting to change and accommodating itself to modern ways—although at times grudgingly, often angrily, and almost always slowly—Boston has continued to be a live, functioning urban community that has not given into the nostalgic impulses that can so often turn a once-famous city into a lifeless historical shrine. It is certainly true that Boston is one of the great historical attractions in the United States, and the famous colonial monuments are there to prove it—the Old North Church, Faneuil Hall, the Old South Meeting House, and the Old Granary Burying Ground, plus many others. But the city did not become frozen in time; it continued to be a place where people live and work and study and play. Having survived generations of political struggle, industrial change, and social turmoil, Boston recovered from a period of debt and deterioration to become a prosperous commercial metropolis, a capital of banking, a leading city of computer technology, a major center of medical research and higher education, and a vital urban community that is in the process of even further expansion and development.

The most serious challenge Boston faces in the future, however, is no longer confined to the construction of high-rise buildings, multilane highways, or extravagant commercial developments. The current challenge is the extent to which Boston will be able to retain its own distinctive identity as a city whose moral standards, civic virtues, and intellectual accomplishments once inspired a nation. The degree to which it will be able to restore and reinvigorate these special qualities and effectively transmit them to new generations of immigrants, as it did to past generations of those who came to share in the blessings of John Winthrop's "City upon a Hill," will largely determine whether or not, at the end of the next millennium, Boston will again deserve to be hailed as the "Hub of the Universe."

THOMAS H. O'CONNOR
CHESTNUT HILL, MASSACHUSETTS

ACKNOWLEDGMENTS

I would like to express my appreciation to William Frohlich, director at Northeastern University Press, for his personal friendship and professional encouragement in this undertaking. As always, John Weingartner, senior editor, has been unfailingly helpful in his careful direction and wise counsel throughout the entire process. Yvonne Ramsey, copyeditor, provided the careful overview that saves the author from many embarrassing errors. In the selection of photographs and illustrations for this volume, I am grateful to Douglas Southard of the Bostonian Society and to Aaron Schmidt of the Boston Public Library's Print Department for the kindness and courtesy with which they responded to my requests.

BOOK ONE
Cradle of Liberty

Chapter

1

A Wilderness Zion

I N EARLY April 1630, a line of vessels cleared the Isle of Wight in the English Channel, caught the prevailing winds, and set sail across the stormy waters of the Atlantic Ocean. In the lead was the flagship *Arbella*, a sturdily built ship of 350 tons, followed by three more vessels—the *Talbot*, the *Ambrose*, and the *Jewel*—with seven other emigrant ships departing in their wake to America. Crowded below deck, where the overhead was so low that a man could not stand erect, passengers were often sick from eating tainted beef, cheese, or butter, and terrified by the rolling and pitching of the vessel. "The winds blew mightily, the sea roared," wrote Francis Higginson, "and the waves tossed us horribly."

The men and women aboard the small flotilla headed for the New World were members of an English Protestant group called Puritans. They were leaving behind them a country where they felt they could no longer enjoy religious freedom, social harmony, or financial prosperity. Following the break with the Roman Catholic Church during the early part of the sixteenth century because the pope refused to annul Henry VIII's marriage to Catherine of Aragón, Lutherans, Calvinists, Baptists, and other members of different Protestant sects appeared in various parts of the kingdom, vying for power and appealing for followers. Frustrated by the turmoil created by so many conflicting religious factions, Henry's daughter, Queen Elizabeth I, set out to rid England of what she described as "foolish theological quibbling." With the support of Parliament, Elizabeth established a single national church, the Church of England (the Anglican Church); provided the Thirty-Nine Articles as its official creed; and instituted the Penal Laws to enforce conformity and compliance. This powerful combination of religious faith and national loyalty proved an effective establishment that satisfied most English citizens.

There were some, however, for whom the Elizabethan Settlement was by no means a satisfactory resolution of the religious conflicts. This was especially true of English Protestants who wished to carry the Reformation to its logical conclusion, and who refused to accept the vestiges of Catholic rituals and ceremonies they still found in the Anglican Church. A large number of these nonconformists held views very similar to those of the European theologian John Calvin, who preached a wrathful God of terrible judgment, a humankind born into sin and corruption, and a doctrine of predestination wherein God alone had already determined who would be saved (the "elect," the "saints") and who would be sent to eternal damnation. Convinced that outstanding moral virtue and exemplary personal behavior were outward signs of salvation, those who considered themselves members of the elect self-imposed the strictest standards of personal conduct, with an emphasis on the serious, sober, and frugal aspects of life. Denouncing all ornamentation as sinful frivolity, they refused to support the Church of England until it was purified of distasteful papist rituals and practices. Some moderate dissenters, professing themselves to be loyal and law-abiding citizens, agreed to obey the letter of the law. They officially became members of the Anglican Church but made no secret of the fact that they intended to work from within to purify that church. As a result, they became known as Puritans. Other, more radical members of the Puritans refused to join the Anglican Church at all and separated themselves from the new state religion completely. These dissenters became known as "Separatists."

With the death of Queen Elizabeth I in 1603, the position of religious dissenters in general—and Puritans in particular—became increasingly precarious. Leaving behind neither husband nor children, the Virgin Queen was succeeded by King James VI of Scotland, son of the late Mary Stuart—Mary, Queen of Scots. Taking up residence in London as James I, the penniless young Scotsman proved as politically tactless as he was personally arrogant. As a staunch advocate of the philosophy of the divine right of kings—which held that the monarch was absolute, answerable only to the laws of God and not the laws of men—King James demanded the unquestioning obedience of his subjects. In the process, he also insisted that every English subject subscribe to the doctrines and practices of the Church of England. He made it clear that as head of both state and church, he would brook neither political disloyalty nor religious dissent.

Many Protestant dissenters found this kind of royal absolutism totally unacceptable. They reacted strongly against the idea of the king forcing them to acknowledge the Church of England, which they refused to recognize as a truly Protestant religion. King James was adamant, however, and insisted that either the dissenters conform to the regulations of the Anglican Church or he would "harry them out of the land." Indeed, the king and his agents made life so miserable for the Separatists that in 1608 one congregation in Nottinghamshire fled England to seek asylum in Holland. Some twelve years later, in 1620, a group of these Separatists sailed across the Atlantic Ocean as Pilgrims and created an independent settlement of their own at Plymouth Plantation on the shores of Cape Cod.

In 1625, King James I was succeeded by his son, Charles I, who was equally committed to the divine-right-of-kings philosophy and just as strongly opposed to religious dissenters in any form. In his determination to enforce strict political and religious conformity, Charles I was supported actively by the archbishop of Canterbury, William Laud. Working together, they renewed the punitive measures and harassing tactics against various Puritan groups whose insistence upon substantial reforms in the Anglican Church were regarded by the king as both dangerous and treasonous.

The mounting pressures of royal persecution were made even worse by the discouraging economic conditions in sections of England where many Puritans were located. East Anglia, for example, was in the midst of a serious depression after the importation of silk from France and other European countries caused a decline in the local cloth trade. This affected the farmers who raised sheep, the spinners, weavers, and dyers who worked the cloth, and the clothiers who were forced to discharge their workers when they could not sell their goods. Faced with the failure of a land that "grows weary of its inhabitants," as John Winthrop wrote in his "General Observations," and the official disapproval of a government that subjected them to constant humiliations, a number of middle-class Puritan dissenters began to chafe under the pressure. Persuaded that "evil times were coming upon us," they were convinced that there was little or no

John Winthrop was a prosperous country squire whose dissenting Puritan views caused him to despair of a future in England. On March 22, 1630, he led a small fleet across the Atlantic to eventually establish a settlement on the Shawmut peninsula. Winthrop was regularly elected governor of the Puritan colony until 1634, when he was turned out of office in favor of Thomas Dudley. Winthrop was returned to office in 1638, and after 1645 was elected governor annually until his death in 1649. *Courtesy of the Bostonian Society/Old State House.*

future in England for themselves or for their children. It had become painfully obvious that they would have to find some other place where they could earn a living, organize their own kind of society, and worship God in the ways they thought appropriate.

Late in the summer of 1629, a gentleman by the name of John Winthrop, lord of the manor of Groton, in East Anglia, and a justice of the peace, met at Cambridge, England, with John Humphrey, Isaac Johnson, Thomas Dudley, and several other well-to-do Puritan colleagues from Lincolnshire to discuss plans for leaving England. Realizing that the hostile authorities in London would never give Puritans a piece of land for themselves, they investigated a grant of land in America that King Charles had given the previous year to a merchant named Matthew Craddock. The grant was a substantial strip of territory extending from the Merrimack River south to the Charles River, and extending (as most colonial charters did at that time) "from sea to sea." Craddock represented a group of merchant-adventurers who were looking forward to making their fortunes by establishing a string of mines and trading posts along the Atlantic seacoast. The members had elected Craddock head, or "governor," of what was called the New England Company, whose corporate rights were spelled out in a document known as the "Charter of the Colony of the Massachusetts Bay in New England." Before Craddock and his associates could launch their commercial enterprise, however, the company's powers were taken over by Winthrop and his Puritan supporters who had bought up the controlling shares of the corporation, and who prepared to use it as a ready-made means of creating their own kind of social experiment in the New World.

Appreciating the necessity of establishing some kind of barrier between themselves and the hostile English authorities, Winthrop and the other Puritan leaders insisted that the company transfer its government from London to America and to those "that shall inhabit there." Having observed the way in which English-based stockholders had manipulated the operations of other enterprises, the Puritans did not want their Massachusetts company to become one of those colonies where the settlers made the difficult crossing and then endured all the hardships of frontier living, while others stayed home in England, made all the important decisions, and then enjoyed the lion's share of the profits.

As part of their "Cambridge Agreement," Winthrop and the other Puritan leaders decided that only those people who were willing to leave England and actually make the journey to America would be allowed to become stockholders. Persons who did not want to emigrate would be required to sell their stock in the company to those who were prepared to become part of the overseas settlement. On the basis of this agreement, John Winthrop was elected governor of the association now known as the Massachusetts Bay Company. To further ensure that the company would be free of English interference, and that all future meetings of the stockholders would take place in Massachusetts, not in London, the Puritan leaders took the original copy of the company charter with them. This was quite unusual, and exactly how it was accomplished even the eminent historian Samuel Eliot Morison admits was a mystery, but the Puritans insisted that it had been done legally before a court in England. Under the leadership of John Winthrop in East Anglia, Sir Richard Saltonstall in the London area, and John White in the West Country, small groups of Puritans moved ahead with their plans with remarkable speed during February and March of 1630. Winthrop's people from the Midlands and London embarked from the port of Southampton; those from the West Country sailed out of Bristol and Plymouth. Setting out in relays, by early April the first eleven vessels, with Winthrop and the *Arbella* in the lead, were on their way across the Atlantic Ocean.

In the course of the voyage, Governor Winthrop delivered to his fellow Puritans on board the *Arbella* an eloquent address called "A Modell of Christian Charity," in which he outlined the spirit of the enterprise and the importance of its mission. The immediate objective, he said, was to seek out a new home "under a due forme of Government, both civill and ecclesiasticall," a community in which concern for "the publique" must outweigh all private interests. To accomplish this, a spirit of brotherly love was absolutely essential, he emphasized, one in which "we must bear one another's burdens. . . . We must be willing to abridge ourselves of our superfluities, for the supply of other's necessities. We must uphold a familiar commerce together in all meekness, gentleness, patience, and liberality." If the members of the Puritan community acted in such a manner, Winthrop assured them, then they would have God on their side, and He would bless them and protect them in their undertaking. And then people everywhere would compare the Puritan community with their own settlement and say: "The Lord make it like that of New England." Winthrop concluded, "For we must consider that we shall be as a City upon a Hill. The eyes of all people are upon us. So that if we shall deal falsely with our God in this work we have undertaken, and so cause Him to withdraw His present help from us, we shall be made a story and a byword throughout the world."

After making landfall near Cape Ann, Winthrop's small fleet moved down along the coastline of Maine until on June 12, 1630, the first ships finally anchored in the North River near Salem. This was not the first time that Englishmen had set foot on the coast of the "Northern Parte of Virginia," as they originally called New England. But the earlier landings had all been small, temporary, and commercial. Bartholomew Gosnold's voyage in 1602 to the northern fishing banks was financed by English entrepreneurs, as was Captain Martin Pringle's search for sassafras and furs the following year. In 1604, George Weymouth visited the shores of New England near the mouth of the

Kennebec River and returned to England with glowing reports of the region's commercial possibilities. Most leaders in such overseas expeditions were sea captains and merchant-adventurers who were out to establish the kinds of trading posts and fisheries that would turn up sizable profits for their English backers. The leaders of the Massachusetts Bay Colony, however, were set on a different mission, with an entirely different objective. Once John Winthrop had taken the company away from Matthew Craddock, observes historian Bernard Bailyn, "the leadership of the company was securely in the hands of men whose main occupation was not trade." One by one, the rest of the Puritan fleet put in either at Salem or farther south at Charlestown, until by the end of the summer nearly a thousand settlers had arrived. Although at first Winthrop and most of the other Puritan leaders decided to settle on the Charlestown peninsula, the lack of fresh drinking water and the outbreak of various illnesses such as scurvy and "hectic fever" caused them to reconsider their location.

It was this point that Winthrop was approached by a rather reclusive Anglican clergyman, the Reverend William Blackstone (Blaxton), who had built a home for himself on the Shawmut peninsula on the opposite side of the Charles River.* Blackstone told the governor about an excellent spring that would furnish plenty of fresh drinking water, and urged him to leave Charlestown and bring his settlers across the river to the new location. Winthrop accepted the friendly invitation, others followed, and by the middle of October of 1630 the new settlement had a population of some 150 persons. By the end of the year, the congregation that originally gathered in Charlestown had made the move across the Charles River and became the First Church of Boston. "Boston" was the name chosen, after the town in Lincolnshire, England, from which many of the Puritans had come. Originally known as St. Botolph's Town, its minister, John Cotton, delivered a farewell sermon to the first group of settlers as they left; later he also moved to America to become a teacher in the First Church of Boston.

The Puritans who had moved across to the Shawmut peninsula found their home to be very small, roughly two miles long and only a mile wide at its most extreme points. It was, in fact, almost an island, joined to the mainland by a narrow strip of land ("Boston Neck") so low-lying that the waters of the harbor swept over it completely during stormy weather. The settlers would

---

* Today there is a plaque at 50 Beacon Street, on the corner of Spruce Street, indicating the approximate location of the Reverend Blackstone's original house.

have appreciated the description set down in 1634 by a visiting Englishman named William Wood as he stood in the prow of a ship in Boston Harbor and surveyed the town's shoreline in a broad sweep, from the 80-foot Fort Hill on the south side looking out on Roxbury Bay, across to the windmill that stood atop the 50-foot rise known as Windmill Hill overlooking the Charles River. "This necke of land is not above four miles in compasse, in form almost a square, having on the south in one corner a great broad hill whereon is planted a fort," he wrote. "On the north side is another hill equal in bigness whereon stands a windmill." Between these two landmarks, forming the backbone of the small peninsula, he called attention to perhaps one of the peninsula's most prominent features—"a high mountain with three little rising hills on the top of it, whereof it is called 'Tramount.'" These were the three peaks that crowned the central ridge—the 80-foot Cotton Hill on the eastern side; the West Hill, which balanced it off on the Charles River side to the west; and in the middle Beacon Hill, or Sentry Hill, which rose to a height of some 150 feet. This central hill served as a strategic point from which lookouts could survey the ocean and set fire to a beacon light (originally a barrel of pitch atop a large pole) to alert the citizens of the town in the event of an attack by some French man-of-war.

THE TRAMOUNT.

Certainly the most prominent topographical feature of early Boston was the high elevation of land in the center of the Shawmut peninsula, with three distinctive hills or peaks referred to as Trimountain—eventually Tremont. The easternmost peak was Pemberton Hill, called Cotton Hill; the westernmost peak was known as Mount Vernon Hill. The central hill, rising some 138 feet above sea level, was originally called Sentry Hill, and later named Beacon Hill. *Courtesy of the Bostonian Society/Old State House.*

This was colonial Boston, an isolated, independent, jagged fragment of land, whose irregular coastline was broken up by numerous coves, inlets, creeks, and marshes. It was around one of these coastal landing places on the south side, known as the Town Dock, where most of the early settlers congregated, close to sources of fresh water and not far from Cotton Hill. It was in this part of the peninsula that the early town slowly began to take shape, growing from about two hundred people in 1631, to nearly three hundred the following year, to over four hundred in 1633. At first the town was little more than a motley collection of branch huts and turf cottages, arranged in two rough semicircles around the Town Dock. In 1641, the Boston settlers purchased from the Reverend Blackstone a parcel of forty-five acres of land that they set aside for what they called the "Common use." This phrase was clarified in 1649 by a law of the General Court stating: "There shall be no land granted either for house plott or garden out of ye open ground or Common field." On this common land, against the backdrop of the town's three towering hills, the townspeople pastured and exercised their horses, grazed their cattle, and drilled their militia. Despite the legend that wandering cows were responsible for the town's notoriously crooked maze of streets, the urban historian Lawrence Kennedy points out in *Planning the City upon a Hill* that Boston was actually laid out on the pattern of a medieval English village, with the focus on the market area off the Town Dock. The question now was whether this small settlement would be able to survive in a new land and a strange environment, so far away from all that was safe and familiar.

In at least one respect, the first settlers of the Massachusetts Bay Colony were fortunate in their initial permanent outpost. They were able to begin their American enterprise in a section of the North American continent that was surprisingly devoid of native inhabitants. The size of the original Indian population of the New England area before the Puritans arrived in 1630 is estimated to have been about twenty-five thousand, most of them branches of the Algonquin family. During 1616–1617, however, some strange and still-undiagnosed epidemic decimated the local Indian tribes, wiping out at least two-thirds of their people and reducing their total population to somewhere between fifteen thousand to eighteen thousand in all New England. As a result of this plague, as well as previous losses suffered in wars with the Abenaki Indians to the north, the number of Indians located along the Massachusetts seacoast dropped from about three thousand to a mere five hundred, mostly scattered along the seacoast and the river valleys. The Wampanoag Indians, too, located farther south in the general vicinity of the Plymouth Colony, suffered heavy losses from the epidemic of 1616–1617 and were forced to abandon large portions of their lands. To make matters worse, in 1633, only three years after the establishment of the Massachusetts Bay Colony, a smallpox epidemic broke out among the local Indians, who had no immunity to most European diseases, and reduced their numbers even further.

Although the first years of settlement in Boston took place without serious conflict, the movement of white settlers into the Connecticut River valley resulted in clashes with the native Pequots in the region. In 1636, after the Pequots killed two Massachusetts merchants, the General Court sent John Endecott and nine men to burn several Indian villages. The following year, a combined force of ninety colonists from Massachusetts and Connecticut, supported by several hundred Indian allies, surprised the main Pequot stronghold and ruthlessly massacred four hundred men, women, and children.[*]

Without having to face the immediate prospect of conflict with native peoples, therefore, early settlers had the relative leisure of examining the advantages and disadvantages of their location on the Shawmut peninsula. Availability of fresh drinking water was perhaps their greatest asset, along with the possibility of grazing their cattle safely and securely within the narrow confines of the peninsula. This was an important consideration since the absence of trees on the small neck of land made it extremely difficult to obtain lumber not only for buildings and fences, but also for fuel to take the settlers through the cold winter months. During most of the colonial period, wood would have to be lugged in from the mainland, or brought in from one of the numerous islands that dotted Boston Harbor.

The economic future of Boston, however, did not lie in fresh water, trees, or rocky soil; it lay in the salt waters of the harbor. Boston was situated in a location ideal for it to become a major shipping center, very similar to the role the old town of Boston in Lincolnshire, England, had played in medieval times.

---

[*] The English continued to push south and west until in 1675, under the leadership of a Wampanoag chief called King Philip, Indians began attacking English settlements. The New England Confederation—combined colonial militia forces organized out of Boston—found the mobile Indian warriors difficult to pin down. By the late summer of 1676, however, the militia had subdued most of the warriors and on August 12 it was reported that King Philip had been killed. The cost of King Philip's War for white settlers was enormous, but for the Indians the cost was much greater. In addition to the destruction of their villages and the deaths of thousands of their people, the Indians suffered the loss of their lands and the erosion of their native culture.

The Shawmut peninsula was central to the whole Boston Harbor, the center for all traffic that went on between the towns to the north and those to the south. The port itself, safely sheltered behind the harbor islands, was deep enough to accommodate the largest ocean-going vessels from across the sea, yet shallow enough to allow effective construction of wharves and piers. Almost as soon as they had settled in their new homes, merchants of Boston and nearby Salem were busy building ships and beginning a maritime trade that would radiate outward like spokes of a wheel. They supplied manufactured goods to the inland towns; they sent their vessels out to the fishing banks and brought back fish for their own consumption; they exported their products to the Jamestown Colony and to the West Indies. Before long, they were exporting fish to England as well as to such Catholic countries as Spain and Portugal, whose religious days of fast and abstinence made them profitable customers. Within a year of his arrival in Boston, Governor John Winthrop had ordered the construction of the thirty-ton bark *The Blessing of the Bay*, which he used to carry valuable furs he acquired from the Indians to be sold in England. Even at this early stage, the small Puritan colony was showing signs of unusual enterprise and prosperity.

Once securely settled, the first serious concern of Governor John Winthrop was to establish a suitable "civill and ecclesiasticall" government for the new Puritan community. With the original copy of the Charter securely in hand, and with company headquarters located in Boston, the Massachusetts Bay Company was practically independent of England, and proceeded to regulate its own affairs through a relatively simple form of government. Stockholders in the company were called "freemen" and were required to meet together four times a year as "one, great, generall, and solemn Assemblie." It was up to them to admit additional freemen, and to "make, ordeine, and establishe all manner of wholesome and reasonable orders, laws, statutes, and ordinances, directions, and instructions" for the colony—with the proviso that such laws could not be "contrarie to the lawes of this our realme of England." Once a year, at the spring session of this general assembly, the freemen were responsible for electing from among their own numbers a governor, a deputy governor, and a court of fifteen assistants. The original idea of an overseas company was that the president and directors would remain in England and deal with the settlers in America through an agent who would reside in the colony. In the case of the Massachusetts Bay Colony, the president and directors became the on-site executives of the company located in America, as well as members of the upper branch of a legislative assembly and the judicial officers of a Puritan commonwealth. Since it soon became inconvenient for many of the freemen to attend all the meetings of the assembly, or the "General Court," as it came to be known, a representative system was devised to lessen the burden of attendance.

While the General Court was content to legislate for the Bay Colony as a whole, it delegated powers over such local matters as mending fences, establishing weights and measures, maintaining militia watches, and appointing town constables to the residents of Boston and to the other communities that gradually came into being. According to historian G. B. Warden, the first settlers had "no single precedent in mind" when they first organized town meetings to settle such matters. In all probability, the Puritan concept of the "godly community" helped promote the idea of a general body in which most adult males could elect their own town officials and settle their own local problems. And, indeed, this seemed to be the case. At first, all free male residents took part in the town meetings, and although most were members of the church, the town had not yet made a clear distinction between freemen and general inhabitants. It was not until March 1636 that the General Court formally defined the parameters of town government, giving the "freemen of every towne" the power to carry out most of the local responsibilities. Women and servants, even though they may have been church members, according to historian Darret Rutman, were excluded from town affairs.

Upon the initiative of the General Court, or upon popular petition, the town constables would notify the inhabitants when a town meeting was scheduled to convene and what the general agenda would be. At the appointed time, the voters and other residents would assemble at the Town House in Boston at the head of King Street (later State Street). After a moderator was chosen to see that the bylaws and orders of the town were followed correctly, a prayer was delivered by a local minister, after which the gathering would turn to the business at hand. At the March and May meetings, the duly qualified freemen would cast secret ballots for their own town officers as well as for the town representatives who would serve in the General Court. Other town meetings were held throughout the year to deal with ongoing concerns or special issues, with decisions made by a voice vote in which many inhabitants in attendance usually joined their voices with those of the official voters, regardless of the rules. All town officials, with the exception of schoolteachers and watchmen, were part-time amateurs without any fixed salary or any organized bureaucracy. After an examination of contemporary letters and documents, G. B. Warden has concluded that there is little record of what actually went on behind the scenes at these early town meetings. Those people involved in public life rarely put down in writing what they did, how they did it, how they politicked, or what techniques they used in deciding the fate of the town—an early example of the secrecy for which the conduct of local political affairs in Boston would later become famous.

Through this somewhat informal and often spontaneous system of participatory government, Governor John Winthrop was determined not only to preserve the liberties of "free born Englishmen" in the Massachusetts Bay Colony, but also to foster the kind of education and learning that would ensure that the religious and moral principles of the Puritan colony would be carried well into the future. As early as 1642, every town was instructed by the General Court to see that parents were training their children in "learning & labor & other imployments." Five years later, in 1647, the General Court ordered every town in the colony with fifty householders to pay someone to teach children to "write & reade." If a town had grown so large that it had "one hundred Families or Housholders [sic]," then it was required to set up a "grammer schoole" supported by public funds. It was hardly a coincidence that having created the Boston Latin School in 1635, the Puritans established Harvard College the following year, only six years after they had landed on the desolate shores of Massachusetts Bay. One of the primary considerations in establishing this college was, to be sure, to guarantee an adequate supply of wise and learned ministers when the present ones—as the anonymous pamphlet of 1643 entitled *New England's First Fruits* put it—"shall lie in the dust." But the founders of Boston also wanted to "advance learning and perpetuate it to posterity," not only through the ministers themselves, but also through those future political and financial leaders of the colony who would have available to them the classical education of an English university like Cambridge, where John Winthrop and so many of his Puritan colleagues had studied.

The establishment of civil government and the promotion of higher learning were very important to the future of the new Puritan commonwealth, but these two goals were essentially subordinate to an even higher objective—the establishment of a true religion. As governor and leader of the enterprise, John Winthrop had a responsibility to establish the truly "godly city" that he and his colleagues envisioned as a proper place for the communion of the elect. This would include not only the formulation of a distinctly Puritan form of Protestant worship, the kind that had been denied them in England, but also a markedly recognizable way of life that personified their spiritual values.

Increase Mather was born in Dorchester, Massachusetts, in 1639, graduated from Harvard College in 1656, and received his M.A. degree from Trinity College, Dublin, in 1658. In 1664 he became teacher of Boston's Second Church and later refused to leave to become president of Harvard. Although he protested the withdrawal of the Massachusetts Charter in 1683, he accepted a new charter framed by William and Mary, and became politically influential. *Courtesy of the Bostonian Society/Old State House.*

An insistence on sobriety of manners, purity of morals, and a form of social community that would neither "exalt the rich nor degrade the poor" were characteristics designed to make Boston the "City upon a Hill" for all to see and admire. Strictly speaking, the Puritans who had followed Winthrop from

England to the shores of Massachusetts Bay were members of the Anglican Church. Indeed, they insisted upon their devotion to England and their loyalty to the Church of England even as they waved goodbye to their families and their friends at the dock. "Forget not Old England!" cried the Reverend John Cotton, vicar of St. Botolph's Church, as he preached a farewell sermon to the voyagers at Southampton. "Forget not the wombe that bore you and the breasts that gave you sucke." And the Reverend Francis Higginson brought his children to the stern of the ship to take a last look at their native land and bid a fond farewell to "Dear England! . . . We do not go to New England as Separatists from the Church of England," he reminded them, in obvious contrast to the Pilgrims who had sailed to Plymouth ten years earlier, "but we go to practice the positive part of church reformation, and propagate the gospel in America."

By the time they arrived on this side of the Atlantic, however, the differences between the Puritans and their Separatist brethren seem to have narrowed considerably. Almost as soon as they landed, they began to establish the type of religious worship the authorities had prevented them from having back in England. They organized their churches on the basis of the Congregational model, with each church virtually an independent unit. Each congregation, once it was approved, managed its own affairs and elected its own pastor, who derived his power from the consent of the congregation. There were no bishops and no hierarchical structure of any kind, except for periodic meetings of ministers sitting in synods. Stripped of every outward sign or symbol reminiscent of Catholicism or Anglicanism—stained-glass windows, holy water, incense, statues, candles, crucifixes, vestments, robes, and surplices—their places of worship were stark and simple meetinghouses where the congregations gathered to conduct religious services on the Sabbath, or to transact matters of civic and political importance during the remainder of the week.

A Puritan congregation usually came together three times a week to worship, in the morning and afternoon on Sunday, and again for a midweek lecture. These gatherings normally included the entire community, although only the so-called "visible saints" were considered full members and participated in the Lord's Supper. A church member, at that time, did not mean a mere believer, a churchgoer, or a member of a parish, as it might mean today. Membership was not conferred automatically by birth, or sacramentally by baptism or confirmation later in life, as in most other Christian denominations. Membership was a trial, a personal ordeal, the successful passage of which involved new obligations of "mutual watchfulness, helpfulness, and rigorous conduct," according to historian Samuel Eliot Morison. A Visible Saint, therefore, was someone who was admitted to the body of communicants only after rigorous examination by himself and by the elders concerning his conversion to the faith and his ability to walk with God.

Once gathered, the congregation sat in rigidly defined ranks, according to their places in the spiritual and social hierarchy. For hours they would listen to a sermon, a highly logical and intellectual unfolding of the meaning and application of a particular scriptural passage. Although women were formally admitted to church membership—where they were, for the most part, what historian Darret Rutman called "mute observers"—they were denied all political rights, as were many men who either were not church members or did not own any property. Leaders of the Bay Colony made it clear that they did not really welcome those who did not accept Puritan religious views. As the Reverend John Cotton later observed: "The design of our first planters was not toleration, but [they] were professed enemies of it. . . . Their business was to settle . . . and secure Religion to Posterity according to the way which they believed was of God." Those who did not subscribe to Congregationalism, therefore, were permitted to reside in the Bay Colony as long as they did not cause any disturbances, but they were not allowed to take an active role in the governance of the colony. Furthermore, although such persons were not members of the established church, they were obliged to have it oversee their public and private lives. This was to be a colony based on Puritan ideals and governed according to strict Puritan principles. The community would be controlled by Puritan leaders who were conscious of having created what John Winthrop called a "City upon a Hill," a shining beacon that would attract "the eyes of all people" upon it.

With the laws of the Bible, especially the Old Testament, providing the overall source of faith and the rule of life, the Puritan clergy, headed by the Reverend John Cotton, worked in close cooperation with the political leadership, headed by Governor John Winthrop. Together they developed a Bible commonwealth that they were certain would become a model for the ages. In the early stages of Boston's history, however, it was always the rule of the Bible that came first. As chief political magistrate Winthrop might govern and Winthrop might execute the laws, but always Winthrop and the laws had to be in accordance with a higher law, the law of Divine Authority, that encompassed all things. Precisely what that authority was would be explained by the priestly teacher, the Reverend John Cotton. According to his Calvinistic views, the elders of the community were responsible to God for the spiritual welfare of the people entrusted to their care. The state, therefore, must always aid, and never hinder, the church leaders in the exercise of their spiritual leadership. Under this arrangement, Winthrop was the divine student exercising what appeared to be absolute legislative and judicial power. It was his duty to determine; it was the duty of the people to obey. But Winthrop's almost divinely inspired authority was always understood to be a sacred stewardship subordinate to the precepts of the Bible as interpreted by the Reverend Cotton. Puritanism was a powerful influence, writes historian Edmund Morgan, that created a tension "at best painful and at worst unbearable." It required that a person rest his whole hope in Christ, but at the same time taught that Christ would utterly reject him unless, before he was born, God had foreordained his salvation. As a result, many persons lived in "an agony of uncertainty," wondering whether God had singled them out "for eternal glory or eternal torment."

Despite what seemed to be an ideal interrelationship between church and state in the Bay Colony—a model of what an ideal Christian community would look like under God's revealed law as interpreted by his leadership of Saints—it was not long before this ideal structure began to show signs of breaking down. In a dramatic example of what historian Edmund Morgan has called the "Puritan Dilemma," the conflict between Rule and Reason soon became apparent. While Puritan leaders assumed that there would be a natural political and religious conformity in the community, the Puritan (and Protestant) ideal of individual interpretation led to a growing multiplicity of beliefs and convictions that often conflicted with the official teachings of the established Puritan leadership. Although the resulting theological disputes usually led to swift and decisive action on the part of the authorities, the conflicts continued.

There was the case, for example, of a young minister in Salem named Roger Williams, who believed that the Church of England was beyond redemption and who felt that reforms from within were totally ineffective. In conflict with Puritan policy, he argued that the law requiring everyone to attend church services was wrong, if only because it brought unregenerate sinners into the house of worship. As far as he was concerned, only those who had been "born again" into God's love should be allowed to attend services. The young minister's political ideas caused even greater consternation among the members of the Puritan establishment in Boston. He felt that the claims of the king of England to the continent of America were completely unsound, since the English neither owned the land nor had discovered it. Properly speaking, he said, the land belonged to the Indians, from whom the English should have purchased it. Williams also questioned whether people should have to pay taxes to support ministers, indicating that he could find nothing in the Bible to justify such procedures. Williams's outspoken criticism of the Puritan commonwealth threatened to disrupt the colony and weaken the control of the Puritan leaders. The magistrates, therefore, ordered Williams banished from the Bay Colony in 1635, causing him to flee south into the wilderness until he finally reached safety on the shores of Narragansett Bay. There he purchased some land from the local Indians and established a settlement he called Providence Plantation.

At just about the same time, another dissenter from Puritan thinking was also banished from Boston. Anne Hutchinson and her family had settled in Boston in 1634, and before long she began holding weekly prayer meetings in her home, where she discussed matters of religious doctrine. Her meetings became so popular that she soon attracted a large following. Contrary to the prevailing views of the Puritan leadership, Hutchinson taught that divine revelation was a continuing process and that truths gained through revelation should supplant biblical authority. To the Puritans, this was nothing short of heresy, and they grew more disturbed when they learned that she was denying that good conduct could be taken as a sign of salvation (as the Puritans taught), while insisting that the Holy Spirit in the hearts of true believers relieved them of the responsibility of obeying the laws of God (which the Puritans denied). This was too much! Such teachings, along with the fact that as a woman she should not be speaking out in public on religious matters, caused the male-dominated leadership to move against her. In November 1636, the woman whom Governor Winthrop described as being of "haughty and fierce carriage" was brought before the magistrates and charged with the civil offense of acting in disruptive ways inappropriate for a woman. After a spirited trial in which Hutchinson defended herself with embarrassing effectiveness, the magistrates ordered her banished from the Bay Colony. A few months later, this civil punishment was followed by formal excommunication from the church. Anne Hutchinson fled with her family to found Portsmouth, Rhode Island, and became a member of a small but growing number of religious dissenters from Massachusetts who sought refuge in what would later become the colony of Rhode Island. After her husband died, Hutchinson and her fourteen children moved to Long Island, where they were killed in 1643 by Indians who were quarreling with the region's Dutch settlers.

Only a few years later, in 1649, another woman suffered the consequences of public disapproval for similar inappropriate behavior. Anne Hibbens was

Anne Hutchinson arrived in Boston with her husband and children in 1634. She became well known for the weekly meetings she held at her home to discuss religious topics. She so vigorously expounded her ideas of a "covenant of grace" that within three years she was put on trial by the Puritan magistrates for "traducing the ministers and their ministry." Banished from the church and the colony, in 1638 she emigrated to Rhode Island, and in 1642 moved to Pelham Bay in the Bronx where she was killed by Indians. *Courtesy of the Boston Public Library, Print Department.*

a housewife who was taken to court by a carpenter who complained that she had publicly accused him of doing shoddy work. In the course of the trial, the magistrates reprimanded the woman for not being submissive enough, and for speaking out publicly against a man instead of having her husband do it. Hibbens was excommunicated from the church for breaking God's law calling for wives to be "subject to your husbands in all things."

The incidents involving Anne Hutchinson and Anne Hibbens dramatically portray the position of woman in colonial Boston. Boston men were continually on the defense, warning women of the dire consequences of failing to fulfill the properly submissive and basically nonintellectual role of the female they believed to be prescribed by God. Women were to keep house, raise the children, fear God, and serve the needs of their husbands. Women were considered spinsters if they had not married by their mid-twenties or early thirties and viewed as outcasts for not fulfilling the proper womanly duty of marriage. In sermons and speeches, the male authorities continued to emphasize that, as the weaker sex, women should be submissive to men, who were stronger and considered to be the closest to God in the chain of superiority.

A married woman was not allowed to hold property or to maintain an income of her own. All she possessed on entering marriage was turned over to her husband, who became, in effect, her overseer. If she became a widow, a wife was entitled to one-third of her late husband's estate (enough to subsist on), but the remainder was either disposed of according to her husband's wishes or given to sons, who then became responsible for the care of their mother. Women were not allowed to share pews with men in the church and usually had to enter the meetinghouse through separate doors. In addition, women were not allowed to speak in church or to ask questions; in keeping with the admonitions of St. Paul, they were instructed to "ask their husbands at home, for it is a shame for women to speake in the church."

Although Boston prided itself on the education it provided for its male members, only the most basic education was available to females. Little girls were allowed to join little boys at "dame schools" at a penny a week, where they were trained in good manners, the alphabet, penmanship, and a bit of reading. Beyond that, girls were excluded from book learning and thoroughly grounded in whatever arts they would need to become housewives. Often young girls were sent out as apprentices to other people's homes to learn the household tasks of domesticity. Mothers were not trusted with this task because it was believed that they would not be strict enough with their own daughters. Anything like higher education was not considered suitable for women, in the belief that women were not strong enough mentally to endure the difficult educational process.

In addition to unsettling religious controversies, there were other internal difficulties that added to the changing character of the original Bay Colony. At first, the ruling authority of the General Court consisted only of the governor, his assistants, and the dozen or so original stockholders of the company— the "freemen." This ensured a tightly controlled political system, and for the first few years, while the number of settlers in the Shawmut peninsula was still small, this was an acceptable arrangement. Within a short space of time, however, the population of the Massachusetts Bay Colony began to grow rapidly. King Charles I persisted in his persecution of the Puritans, with the result that thousands of dissenters continued to flee England in search of peace and security. The decade from 1630 to 1640 saw some seventy-five thousand people leave England because of religious persecution and economic hardship. One of the largest waves of this "Great Migration" swelled the population of Massachusetts to over fifteen thousand by the year 1643. As the colony grew increasingly larger, the inhabitants began to resent the idea that a mere handful of men should be governing a settlement that was already approaching twenty thousand people. They organized their protests and put pressure on the General Court to expand its very limited membership.

Puritan leaders grudgingly agreed to admit over a hundred new "freemen" to the General Court, but in order to ensure future political control they stipulated that only members of the Congregational Church would be allowed to hold the title of freemen. "No man shall be admitted to the freedom of this body politic," ruled the General Court, "but such as are members of the church." The freemen, it was agreed, would elect the assistants; the assistants, in turn, would elect one of their number as governor. Under this arrangement, only the governor and the assistants were empowered to make the laws of the commonwealth. Here was a political structure in which membership in the General Court was restricted on the basis of religious affiliation, and the powers of the legislative body further restricted to the governor and his assistants.

Several towns quickly expressed dissatisfaction with such a close-knit system of legislative power, and when the assistants began levying taxes without consulting with local town meetings, the towns began agitating for further changes in the political structure. In April 1634, representatives from several towns forced Governor Winthrop to show them an actual copy of the well-guarded corporate Charter they had brought with them from England. It was then discovered that not only were the governor and the officers of the company supposed to present themselves for general elections once a year, but also that the laws of the colony were to be made by all freemen—not just by the governor and his assistants. Accordingly, when the General Court met the following month, representatives from the various localities expanded the size of the legislative body to include deputies from every town, and after that proceeded to participate in the legislative process. They also established the rule that elections in which all freemen would take part would be held every year—and then promptly showed their displeasure with what they felt were Winthrop's questionable tactics by voting him out of office and electing Thomas Dudley as their new governor.

The idea of an annual election, an election held on a specific date, of all officers—governors and members of the upper branch as well as deputies from the towns—became so popular in the American colonies that it was imitated wherever the king could be persuaded to give his royal consent. The process became an integral feature of the various state constitutions that were drawn up during the later Revolutionary years and appeared even later in the Federal Constitution, which called for the election of the president, senators, and representatives on the same day. This was a very early indication of the ways in which the American approach to representative government would differ from the traditional English parliamentary model.

For the next ten years, the General Court of Massachusetts contained a troublesome mixture of argumentative factions. The assistants were loyal to the governor and generally sympathetic to the Puritan leadership in Boston. The growing number of deputies, on the other hand, were generally responsive to the lower classes who lived in the surrounding towns. Finally, in 1644, a two-house legislature was established, permitting each group to form its own separate chamber, organize its own rules, and conduct its own affairs. This development marked the complete transition of the Massachusetts Bay Colony from a mere overseas trading company to a bona fide commonwealth in its own right.

The basic tenets of Puritanism may have been confined to a relatively tiny segment of the New England seacoast during the first half of the seventeenth century, but they were to have an impact on American society and culture that would extend far beyond their immediate geographical surroundings. Although still a small, isolated, seafaring community with less than twenty-five years of history behind it, the town of Boston had already developed certain basic themes that not only were characteristic of its colonial origins, but also may be considered an essential part of its present-day distinctiveness.

In spite of a close association between church and state that drove some dissenters such as Roger Williams and Anne Hutchinson into exile and others into prison, the conservative Congregational establishment contained within itself the seeds of revolutionary democratic forms that would have surprised even its Puritan originators. By cultivating a system of separate churches and independent congregations, the leaders of the Puritan community conditioned their colonists in their town meetings to think in terms of limited government, individual interpretation, civil liberties, and the power of the people. And by emphasizing the existence of divine law and a supreme authority to which all man-made laws must conform—"the bounds which the Lord hath set," as John Cotton expressed it—they impressed upon the public conscience its right, and even its obligation, to question the precepts of human rulers whenever they conflicted with the eternal morality of the "higher law." The element of reformism, too, was an integral part of Puritanism from the very beginning; after all, the movement was started to reform and purify the Anglican Church. That commitment to critical analysis and constructive change would continue as an essential ingredient of the Boston mentality well into the future.

Above all, from the very beginning of their enterprise, Bostonians were firmly convinced that the community they had established was truly something unique, something really special. Puritan leaders such as John Winthrop considered themselves more than simply political refugees, homeless emigrants, or religious exiles seeking temporary relief from royal persecution or economic depression. Instead, they saw themselves engaged in a permanent and long-range mission of cosmic proportions, offering to lead the whole world to the new freedom and fulfillment of the Reformation. Every moment of their lives, they were conscious of building their tiny outpost on the Shawmut peninsula into the "City upon a Hill" that would become the veritable hub of the universe and the inspiration for all mankind. Times would change and circumstances would differ tremendously, but future generations of Bostonians would continue to view Boston not just as "another" city, but as a city set apart by its origins, its history, and its dedication to excellence, destined to accomplish great and unusual things for the glory of God and the benefit of the community.

2

Loyalty Versus Liberty

THE European colonial process in the Americas during the seventeenth and eighteenth centuries, whether conducted by the Spanish, the French, or the English, was·based on certain common assumptions. The most basic of these was that a colony existed primarily for the political prestige and financial prosperity of the mother country—not the other way around. Colonies were expected to pay taxes, furnish manpower for the imperial armies, and produce valuable natural resources: gold and silver, hides and furs, lumber and tobacco. These products would not only enrich the royal coffers of the colonizing power, but also make the colony itself a more valuable part of the colonial network. Commercial nations like England would have their trading companies carry many of these products throughout the world for sale, while the colonies that had produced the raw materials in the first place would buy them back as finished goods at much higher prices. The colonial relationship was essentially a complementary one, with colonies in undeveloped areas occupying a subordinate political and economic position in relation to the imperial authority across the ocean.

By the middle of the seventeenth century, it had become all too clear to many persons in the English government that the Massachusetts Bay Colony was not conducting itself in accordance with the basic assumptions of the English colonial system. For a period of some thirty years, from 1630 to 1660, the Bay Colony ran its own affairs and pretty much "did its own thing." It operated its own government, conducted its own religious establishment (from which even members of the Church of England were excluded), created its own educational system, built its own ships, conducted its own trade, evaded the payment of taxes, and generally behaved in a manner that was remarkably independent of the supervision and regulation of the authorities in England.

For the most part, England had virtually ignored the imperial shortcomings of the Massachusetts Bay Colony. This was certainly not because it approved of what was happening, but because conditions at home were in such turmoil that the government was in no position to do anything about the colony. A long train of bitterness and conflict between King Charles I and the Puritan leaders of Parliament had finally led to an outbreak of bloody civil war that lasted from 1642 to 1646 and ended with the trial and execution of King Charles I in 1649. For the next decade, political power was assumed by Oliver Cromwell, leader of the Puritan forces, who abolished the monarchy entirely, dismissed Parliament, and ruled the nation as a virtual military dictator under a commonwealth form of government until his death in 1658. These were years of constant change and upheaval, when Englishmen had little or no inclination to concern themselves with colonial problems far across the Atlantic Ocean. In the face of political anarchy following Cromwell's death, English military leaders finally invited the eldest son of the late king to return from exile in France and assume the throne of England as Charles II.

Although he was in power only a short time after his restoration to the throne in 1660, King Charles II undertook an aggressive colonial policy in North America. In 1663, he rewarded a group of eight friends and cavaliers with a huge grant of land for the "Carolina" region, and the following year he authorized his brother, James, Duke of York, to take away from the Dutch the lands between the Connecticut and Delaware Rivers, which subsequently became the English colonies of New York and New Jersey. In the space of only a few years, the new monarch had extended the boundaries of the English colonies in North America in one unbroken line along the Atlantic coast, from the southern borders of French Canada in the north to the northern borders of Spanish Florida in the south.

Charles also moved vigorously against the New England colonies with the intention of making them a much more loyal, productive, and cooperative part of the empire. First, he struck out sharply at the practice in the Massachusetts Bay Colony of restricting voting powers to members of the Congregational Church and denying the right to vote to all others—especially members of the Church of England. He ordered the Bay Colony to extend the suffrage to all persons of "good estate," regardless of church membership—except Catholics, Jews, and infidels.

Perhaps a more serious issue concerned the question of foreign markets and overseas trade. King Charles II and his administrators were well aware that many of the American colonies were developing their own trade routes with nations outside the empire. Much of the tobacco produced in colonies such as Virginia and Maryland, for example, was reported to be going to foreign markets, while numerous New England merchants were apparently seeking out their own customers all over the world. Of all the regions in colonial North America, New England was perhaps the least suited to the mercantilist concept that the major function of a colony was to supply raw materials to the mother country. Most of New England, with its rocky soil and small farms, produced very few raw materials or staple products that England wanted—with the notable exception of lumber and such lumber products as pitch, tar, resin, and turpentine, which were in great demand by the shipyards of the royal navy. In order to supplement their meager farm incomes, New Englanders had turned to the sea. They built and manned their own ships and developed an extensive transatlantic network that was referred to as the "triangular trade" because of the configuration of its lanes. Perhaps the best known of these overseas routes was that by which Boston merchants exported fish, livestock, hay, flour, and lumber to various parts of the West Indies; in return their ships would bring back cargoes of sugar, coffee, cocoa, and molasses. Converting much of the molasses into rum in local distilleries, these same Boston merchants would carry their cargoes across the Atlantic on the second leg of the journey, which brought them to the west coast of Africa. There the rum would be exchanged for Africans, who were then transported across the ocean to be sold into slavery in the West Indies.

But there were many other routes that also fit into the informal triangular pattern. Some ships sailed from New England to the West Indies carrying food, horses, lumber, and fish, which were exchanged for great amounts of sugar. The sugar was then shipped to England, where it was traded for manufactured goods that were then brought back across the Atlantic to markets in North America. Still other ships from New England carried fish, food, furs, and timber to various countries in southern Europe, where the raw materials were exchanged for such commodities as wine, silk, spices, and tropical fruit. These products were then transported to England, where they were traded for manufactured goods that were shipped back to America for sale. In this way, Yankee ships sailed back and forth from one continent to another, doing an active business and making many Boston merchants incredibly wealthy, while contributing substantial amounts to the English economy.

Once King Charles II had been restored to the throne and the government stabilized, English authorities became determined to exercise more control over the colonial trade and make sure that more of the profits from that trade went directly into the royal coffers. With this idea in mind, Parliament

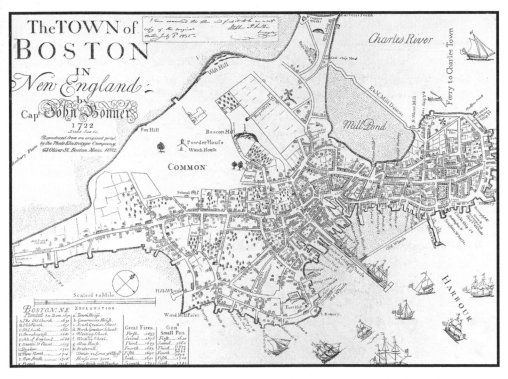

The first printed plan of Boston, titled *The Town of Boston in New England*, was done in 1722 by Captain John Bonner, a navigator and shipwright. It points out the location of the Boston Common, and demonstrates that well into the eighteenth century most of Boston's population still congregated along the docks and wharves at the south side of the peninsula. *Courtesy of the Boston Public Library, Print Department.*

passed a series of Navigation Acts in 1660 and expanded them in 1663. Among other things, these laws insisted that colonials use only English-built ships and man them with predominantly English crews, in order to maintain a high level of employment among English sailors and shipbuilders at home. They also forbade colonial merchants to sell their raw materials to other nations, especially such "enumerated" commodities as tobacco, sugar, indigo (a blue vegetable dye), and cotton, which were to be channeled exclusively to English markets. By means of such regulations, the English clearly set out to reestablish the supremacy of the home government over all economic activities within the empire, and to subordinate private profits to imperial prosperity. It was obvious to King Charles II and his ministers that in order to make the mercantilist system work properly, it was necessary for the authorities to maintain continuous and effective supervision of colonial activities.

For the next ten years or so, however, the new Navigation Acts were honored much more in breach than in observance. England was still far away across the Atlantic Ocean, and Puritan leaders in the Massachusetts Bay Colony were able to circumvent the new regulations fairly easily, to a great extent because the English government had become so deeply involved with complex foreign problems involving France and Holland that it had little opportunity to exercise the kind of supervision and control necessary to ensure compliance. Things began to change in 1674, however, after an imperial customs officer named Edward Randolph (a mean-spirited spy and revenue collector, according to Thomas Boylston Adams) visited America and conducted an on-site inspection of the Bay Colony. Randolph returned to England with a blistering indictment of conditions in Massachusetts. He accused the colonials of continuing to defy the authority of the king, of violating the trade and navigation laws, of coining their own money, and of using religion to enforce a restricted suffrage in direct defiance of the king's specific orders to the contrary. He urged King Charles II to bring Massachusetts directly under royal control, even if it was necessary to use English troops to "reduce Massachusetts to obedience."

After a period of prolonged and fruitless negotiations, in October 1684 England finally decided to annul the old Massachusetts Charter. Not only was the Bay Colony transformed into a royal colony, under the direct supervision of the Crown, but King Charles II also set in motion a plan to consolidate Massachusetts with all the other New England colonies into a single major colony to be known as the Dominion of New England. This plan was designed to accomplish two objectives: First, it would establish a much more unified and effective military defense zone in the northeast in the event of a war with the French in Canada; second, it would provide a better opportunity for English authorities to enforce the rules and regulations concerning foreign trade. Although King Charles II died in 1685 before his plan could be put into effect, his brother, King James II, formerly Duke of York, quickly followed through with the design for this new political-military province. A year after succeeding to the throne, James II sent a boyhood friend, Sir Edmund Andros, to Boston to assume his new position as governor general of the Dominion of New England. Known as "Tyrant Andros" because of the unpopular reputation he acquired while serving as governor in New York and New Jersey, Andros arrived in Boston with great pomp and ceremony, escorted by a company of sixty red-coated guardsmen, in a display designed to intimidate the local inhabitants. This group of Englishmen sparked considerable animosity among the local citizenry and was described by some of the local clergy as "a crew that began to teach New England to drab [use prostitutes], drink, blaspheme, curse, and damn, committing insufferable riots amongst a quiet and peaceable people."

Governor Andros almost immediately made himself completely obnoxious with a series of tactless and provocative measures that were totally at odds with the traditions of the Puritan commonwealth. He placed the militia under his direct control and issued a declaration that town meetings would be limited to one a year. He further announced that taxes would be set and levied by executive fiat, not voted on annually by elected representatives as had been the custom. Money for the support of schools was cut off. The oil from stranded whales was declared the king's property as a gift from God and confiscated for the welfare of the Crown. Old land titles were declared to be "of no more worth than the scratch of a bear's paw," with the result that all persons holding title to land and property of any sort were required to come to offices in Boston and there revalidate their deeds and titles—for a price, of course. On March 25, 1687, Andros flew in the face of the town's Congregational establishment when he ordered that the Old South Meeting House be converted into an Anglican Church. Edmund Andros had made himself the most hated man in Boston.

Fortunately for the inhabitants of Boston, the detested rule of Governor Andros proved to be short-lived as a result of events across the ocean. In England, the high-handed tactics of King James II led his political opponents to drive him off the throne and out of the country in 1688; he was replaced with his daughter, Mary, and her Dutch husband, William of Orange.* Once the Puritans in Boston heard the news about this "Glorious Revolution," they conducted their own insurrection. The people of Boston rose up in revolt, seized and imprisoned Governor Andros and the members of his council, restored the old government, and then waited to see what would happen when William and Mary finally took over the reins of government in England. Indeed, the Bay Colony's most eminent minister, the Reverend Increase Mather, had sailed to London the previous year to plead the colony's case against Governor Andros. Now that King James II had been ousted, Mather was hard at work trying to persuade the new monarchs to forget about the plan to create a Dominion of New England, and to let Massachusetts go back to its former political life under its original charter.

William and Mary had serious objections about allowing the Bay Colony to resume its former semi-independent status; at the same time, however, the new sovereigns were hesitant about alienating an important segment of their North American colonies. In 1691, therefore, they agreed to a new compromise charter for Massachusetts. On the one hand, they insisted that the governor of the colony would henceforth be appointed by the Crown; on the other hand, they agreed to allow the members of the governor's council to be chosen by the members of the elected lower house. On one point, however, William and Mary were particularly insistent: representatives of the General Court were to be elected by voters of the colony on the basis of *property*— not on the basis of their religious affiliation. Members of the Massachusetts government would no longer be required to be members of the established Congregational Church. Although King Charles II had tried unsuccessfully to accomplish this some thirty years earlier, this time the provision proved effective and would have significant long-range results on the town's future. For the time being, of course, most of the old clerical leaders continued to exercise considerable power and influence in the colony, and for many years they would be regularly consulted about things like the appointment of the governor and the election of his councilors. But the abolition of the religious requirement for holding office and participating actively in the affairs of the Bay Colony clearly set the stage for the gradual decline of Boston's "Aristocracy of Saints."

* In 1707, England and Scotland were united as Great Britain (or the United Kingdom) by the Act of Union. From here on in the text, reference will be made to Great Britain instead of England.

Even without this constitutional change, however, it seems highly unlikely that the old church oligarchy would have been able to sustain itself as the central focus of power in the face of the religious and social changes that were taking place in the Massachusetts Bay Colony toward the end of the seventeenth century. For one thing, the very nature of Congregationalism contained a natural self-destruct mechanism. Its strongly independent nature and essentially separatist character worked against any kind of permanent authoritarian hierarchy—another instance of such Protestant concepts as self-reliance and individual interpretation proving to have subtle but significant political ramifications. Then, too, the system of landholding prevalent in the New England region had a definite influence on the forms of political representation that developed in the area. In other parts of colonial North America, large patroonships or sprawling plantations often made it possible for a handful of landholders to emerge as the self-appointed spokesmen for the laboring classes. Because the freeholds in the Boston area were usually small and highly independent family units, there emerged a grass-roots yeomanry that was almost impossible to control, and that demanded individual representation in the political process. But it was the new charter's substitution of property qualifications for religious qualifications that struck the final blow to clerical supremacy in the Bay Colony. The new charter supplied the impetus for the gradual emergence of a new kind of oligarchy whose power would be based not so much upon religious orthodoxy as upon material prosperity and financial success.

Many orthodox Puritans were painfully aware of the changing religious and cultural patterns in their colony, and were fearful of the movement away from what they regarded as the divine protection of the Almighty. It may well be that the atmosphere of fear and tension that prevailed in Massachusetts during the early 1690s contributed in no small way to the brief but frightening outburst of hysteria in 1692 over the presence of witches and witchcraft in the colony. The decade from 1690 to 1700, especially with the new century approaching—an event that many feared might be the Apocalypse, the end of the world—proved to be a period of great change and considerable instability for the Bay Colony. After all, in only a short time the citizens of Massachusetts had seen the revocation of their revered old charter and the loss of their political autonomy. They had suffered through the creation of the Dominion of New England, the revolution against the king of England, and their own revolution against Governor Andros and his administration. Now, they were being forced by the new charter to allow all kinds of religious sects to worship as they pleased in what they had once assumed was the exclusive domain of the Puritan faith. In 1709, even the Quakers were given permission to construct a meetinghouse in Boston. Everything the Puritans had always believed in was changing before their very eyes.

To make matters worse, there were terrifying rumors at this particular time that the dreaded Roman Catholics were plotting to return to power and overthrow the Protestant religion. Puritan Boston might have to extend a certain degree of tolerance to other Protestant denominations, but it had made no change in its hostile attitude toward Roman Catholics. Hatred of Catholicism was something the Puritans brought with them from England, where Catholics, commonly referred to as Papists, were regarded not only as members of a blasphemous religion, but also as subversive enemies committed to the overthrow of the government. "Rome was Babylon," writes historian James Hennesey, "the pope the anti-Christ of the Apocalypse." Puritans took every precaution to prevent Catholics from coming into the Bay Colony, and in 1700 the General Court passed a law forbidding any Catholic priest to reside in Massachusetts, under penalty of death. Indeed, in 1688, in the midst of a Catholic "scare," an elderly woman named Ann Glover was accused of being a secret Catholic and hanged as a witch on Boston Common.

Puritans looked upon Quakers—members of the Society of Friends who followed the teachings of George Fox in seventeenth-century England—with similar fear and loathing. The religious views of these "Children of the Light," who rejected established creeds and formalized doctrines, and refused to accept the intermediary of anything like an organized church in their private and highly personal relationship with the Almighty, made them immediately suspect as a Christian sect. The fact that they also refused to pay tithes to the established church and repudiated the leadership of those they called a "hireling ministry" made them also appear a clear and present danger to the Puritan establishment. Considered to be evil influences on the young, Quakers were usually whipped out of town at the end of a wagon, and were put to death if they returned. In 1659, two members of the sect were hanged on Boston Common, and on June 1, 1660, a woman named Mary Dyer went to the gallows for coming to Boston and spreading the doctrines of Quakerism.

With rumors of Catholic uprisings in the air, and with Puritan ministers such as Increase Mather and his son, Cotton Mather, warning the members of their congregations that "Satan was walking the streets," one of the most extreme forms of emotional hysteria broke out in the nearby town of Salem Village (now Danvers). The strange and unusual behavior of a group of young girls in that town raised charges of witchcraft that quickly whipped people into a frenzy of fear and recrimination. Hundreds of people were accused of being witches, many of them were sentenced to death, and nineteen were executed before the witchcraft trials ran their course. Instead of reinforcing the old religious standards, however, the overall effect of the witchcraft hysteria appears to have further diminished the prestige of the established church and weakened the political authority of the old Puritan leaders in the Bay Colony.

After 1700, there emerged a group of men of wealth and property who began replacing the men of religion as the determining force in the life of Boston. Not that Bostonians rejected their religious heritage, forgot about their idealistic mission, or discarded their traditional moral principles. The tendency in Boston, even in colonial times, is never to destroy old things, but to build new things over old things. This new emphasis on wealth, property, and material success in old Boston did not, however, develop at the expense of morality. It was constructed on the solid foundation of the traditional Puritan ethic. In his perceptive biography of Thomas Hutchinson, Bernard Bailyn described the life of the future governor's father, Colonel Thomas Hutchinson, who became rich from trading and shipping investments. "He was industrious, . . . charitable, unaffected, unworldly, and clannish," writes Bailyn. "A strait-laced, pious provincial, he read the scriptures to his family mornings and evenings, and devoted himself to trade and to the welfare of his kin and community." In Boston, at least, it was clear that money and morality would have no difficulty walking hand in hand for many generations.

During the first ten years of the small colony's existence, Bostonians had been able to make a fairly comfortable living providing foodstuffs, meat, fish, dairy products, and personal services for the large number of immigrant Puritans escaping the rigors of English persecution during the reign of the Stuart kings. The first generation of Puritans generally continued to follow the types of occupations they had worked at back in England, serving as cobblers, carpenters, blacksmiths, masons, shopkeepers, tradesmen, and craftsmen. When the heavy migration from England dropped off sharply during the late 1640s, however, a serious economic crisis took place in the town, and new sources of income had to be found. Some colonists sought out new and more fertile lands for more extensive agricultural production; others embarked on a wide variety of diversified economic enterprises, setting up ironworks and leather tanneries;

in the late 1660s, they expanded the manufacture of rum and the smuggling of slaves; by the early 1700s, they were busily engaged in importing from Holland. The colonists learned quickly, and by the first half of the eighteenth century, Boston was leading all other towns in shipbuilding, the leather trades, meat-packing, hat-making, the manufacture of axes and hardware of all kinds, cheap export furniture, the distilling of rum, and the construction of such vehicles as chaises, sedans, and coaches.

With their various triangular networks well established, Boston merchants continued to use their own ships and their own seamen, ignored the Navigation Acts, kept their own profits, and participated in ventures that brought them wealth and position. A typical example of Boston's new men of wealth was Thomas Hancock, whose grandfather, Nathaniel, had started out as a simple shoemaker with a family of thirteen children to support. Young Thomas began his own career as a bookbinder's apprentice, but he scraped together enough capital to go into his own bookselling business and soon expanded into a substantial trade with England. By the early 1700s he had branched out into a variety of import-export activities with Nova Scotia, the West Indies, England, Holland, and Spain. After building himself a handsome mansion on the slope of Beacon Hill, he was able to bequeath to his nephew and adopted son, John, the modern equivalent of a million dollars. Through thrift, hard work, imagination, shrewdness, and an increasing amount of illegal evasion of the navigation laws, men like Thomas Hancock, John Amory, and James Bowdoin—the last of whom increased his own standing by marrying Elizabeth Erving, daughter of another Boston merchant—assumed positions of respectability and influence. Thomas Boylston acquired the reputation of being the richest man in Massachusetts, and Peter Faneuil, the son of a French Huguenot (Protestant), became such a successful businessman that he offered to build what he called "a noble and complete structure . . . for the sole use and benefit and advantage of the town." Constructed in 1742, directly behind the Town Dock, Faneuil Hall combined facilities for both commercial transactions and political activities—a dramatic illustration of the close relationship between politics and business in mid-eighteenth-century Boston.

At the turn of the century, the town of Boston also began to take on a design and permanency more in keeping with the affluence of its merchants than the penury of its ministers. In 1691, the selectmen had been authorized to assign and fix the names of the streets. By 1708 the job was done, and Boston was given the names of streets that are still familiar today—Summer, Milk, Beacon, Water,

Tremont, Brattle, Salem, and scores of others. A number of public buildings originally made of wood were replaced by brick structures, especially after a disastrous fire in 1711. The wooden Town House, for example, was replaced by a more permanent brick structure (today's Old State House) that would house both the town government and the provincial government, and furnish the central exchange for the town's merchants as well. In 1729, the Old South Church replaced its wooden building with the present Old South Meeting House, and in 1754 the present King's Chapel on Tremont Street was erected on the site of the original church. Although the original Faneuil Hall was consumed by fire in 1761, it was soon rebuilt as a two-story brick structure that continued to dominate the waterfront. Instead of the wooden dwellings of an earlier generation, the new men of wealth and influence were now able to construct handsome two- and three-story brick mansions, surrounded by sumptuous gardens and impressive walls, in quiet locations like Hanover Street, Bowdoin Square, Tremont Street, Beacon Street, and Summer Street, conveniently distant from the hustle and bustle of the waterfront.

The town's ministers greatly feared that this constant preoccupation with conducting business, discussing prices, building mansions, and accumulating wealth would cause families to turn away from religion and forget the moral mission of the Bay Colony. "My fathers and brethren," John Higginson had said, addressing the members of his congregation, "this is never to be forgotten, that New England is originally a plantation of religion, not a plantation of trade." In 1706, Cotton Mather published *The Good Old Way,* decrying the lessening of old-time Puritan influences throughout the American colonies, and bemoaning the way in which a new generation of colonists had lost respect and reverence for members of the clergy.

In addition to their concern over the growing preoccupation with financial matters, the town's ministry was also concerned about many of the new ideas and secular opinions that were creeping into the Bay Colony. America was proving hospitable to science and scientists, and in Massachusetts many people involved themselves in such disciplines as astronomy and mathematics because of their obvious importance to the study of navigation. John Winthrop, Jr., for example, had been the outstanding scientist of the early colonial period. In 1631, the governor's son imported a telescope from England through which he observed a fifth satellite of Jupiter. Winthrop also embraced the Copernican system of astronomy, which taught that the sun was the center of the universe, at a time when most authorities still held to the old Ptolemaic system, which

Cotton Mather, son of Increase Mather, was born in Boston in 1663 and graduated from Harvard College in 1678. He was ordained in 1685 and served with his father at the Second Church until the elder Mather's death, and thereafter as sole pastor for the rest of his life. A scholar and author as well as a Puritan clergyman, his *Magnalia Christi Americana* (1702) is considered the greatest American literary accomplishment up to that time. *Courtesy of the Bostonian Society/Old State House.*

placed the earth at the center of things. By the turn of the century, there were also signs of a new "natural" philosophy beginning to appear in America, strongly influenced by the scientific theories of Sir Isaac Newton, which had been introduced into the colonies as early as 1708. Although Newton accepted that God had created the universe, he also believed that God had laid down the natural laws that governed that universe. Newton said that human beings, through their rational powers and scientific observations, could come to understand the natural and scientific laws (such as gravity) that controlled the universe. Based on these theories, some of Newton's followers (called deists) concluded that God—often referred to as the First Cause or the Grand Architect—no longer "interfered" in the affairs of man after the initial act of creation. As a result of these ideas, they argued that Divine Revelation was unnecessary, and the Bible was not the literal word of God.

To the Puritan leaders of the colony, these were truly disturbing ideas that not only challenged the validity of the Holy Scriptures and the authority of the established church, but also brought into question the very existence of God. This was a time when Satan was blamed for almost all forms of illnesses, from melancholy to madness. Any extraordinary events that were unexplainable—such as lightning, hurricanes, and shipwrecks—were signs of the Lord's displeasure. When a farmer had a poor crop, or if his cow broke a leg, it was the work of the devil. In a sermon entitled "Heaven's Alarm to the World," Increase Mather stated his belief that the comet of 1680 was a precursor of some terrible calamity. As early as 1681, the New England clergy had met to discuss the dangers of losing church membership as a result of the growth of new "rational" ideas that were beginning to appear in the colony even before Newton's theories arrived. They decided to combat the problem with proof from the supernatural by documenting all unexplained phenomena such as drought, famines, floods, earthquakes, witchcraft, and diabolical possession. In 1684, Increase Mather wrote a widely discussed document called *An Essay for the Recording of Illustrious Providences*, which spoke of magicians, witches, and "imps," and which some historians suggest may well have planted the seed that sprouted into the witchcraft hysteria of the 1690s.

No less confusing to the old Puritan establishment than the growth of materialism and the appearance of rationalism was the way in which women were becoming more of a visibly public presence in the colony. As merchants amassed great wealth through their overseas trading, they formed a new leisure class in which their wives played a more prominent role. More and more women cast off the old Puritan ideal of the industrious woman in favor of the more pleasurable pursuits of high tea, card parties, and parlor games. They could now afford to hire domestic servants from the lower classes to handle domestic duties. Although the underlying social structure of male dominance still remained intact, the women of Boston's new leisure class experienced a great deal more freedom to socialize, to engage in charitable activities, and to choose their own clothes. By 1700, the women of Boston were beginning to forgo the virtue of modesty in dress in favor of more modern fashions. Women were baring their backs, exposing their shoulders, and ornamenting themselves in ways that were heretofore unimaginable. Corsets, elaborate hairpieces, and all kinds of new designs were being brought from Europe through the extensive trade that Boston men were carrying on, and women lost little time in trading in their homespun for the glamour of international fashion. While this plunge into fashion helped facilitate the tendency of men to view women as objects of beauty, it was also an expression of individualism that the women had never before experienced.

As an increasing number of Boston men went to sea, traveled to other parts of the colonies, or spent more time at their places of business during the late 1600s and early 1700s, many women began to take over their husband's affairs, supervise their accounts, and become more knowledgeable about financial matters and world affairs. A number of Boston women also began operating inns and boardinghouses, coffee shops, grocery stores, and bakeries, in order to keep families going while their husbands were away. Even after their husbands returned from sea, however, many women continued to operate their various enterprises, often using their shops to sell goods the men had obtained during their travels. Widows, too, continued the occupations of their deceased husbands or operated shops of their own in Boston to earn a living and keep the family together. In 1754, Mary Salmon advertised in Boston that she would continue operating the blacksmith shop that her deceased husband had owned; another widow, Mary Jackson, advertised that in her foundry shop she could turn out all kinds of pots and kettles. In the face of women's increasing visibility, male authorities continued to express their traditional views about the submissive and essentially inferior nature of the female. In 1692, for example, the Reverend Cotton Mather published his *Ornaments for the Daughters of Zion,* advising young women to learn "all the affairs of housewifry and besides a good skill at her needle, as well as in the kitchen." The Reverend John Cotton also urged wives to stay at home, educate their children, and assist the industry of their husbands. But it was too late. By the 1690s, at least twenty-one women were listed as innkeepers in Boston, over half the total number of innkeepers in the town at that time. In addition, six women were awarded liquor licenses and allowed to serve alcoholic beverages at the inns they operated.

By the mid-1700s, there was no question that many individual merchants such as Hancock, Bowdoin, Boylston, and Faneuil had made a great deal of money through their financial enterprises, and had risen to positions of social prominence in the Boston community. After about 1743, however, the overall financial status of the town itself began to decline in a disturbing manner. For one thing, a number of new colonial towns had come into existence throughout America during the hundred years that had passed since Boston's founding. New urban centers such as Philadelphia and New York City were now giving the old Yankee capital a run for its money. In 1760 Philadelphia, with a population of 23,750, and New York City, with a population of 18,000, had already moved ahead of Boston, whose population was recorded at only 15,631 that year. And both these capital cities were continuing to expand, while the population of

BOSTON'S FIRST TOWN-HOUSE
1657~1711

In 1657, the first Town House was built at the head of King Street to serve as the meeting place for the General Court. Constructed entirely of wood in the English medieval style, with gables and overhanging upper stories, it burned to the ground in the "great fire" of 1711. It was replaced by a handsome brick colonial structure now known as the Old State House. *Courtesy of the Bostonian Society/Old State House.*

the Bay Colony remained discouragingly stagnant. Boston had also felt the effects of competition from other towns within New England itself. Secondary seaports such as Newburyport and Portsmouth were fast becoming rivals in shipbuilding; Salem and Newport were cutting sharply into the West Indies traffic; Lynn and neighboring villages on the North Shore were taking the butchering and leather trades away from Boston workmen; and Medford was drawing off a greater portion of the rum industry every year. Boston's local economy was suffering, unemployment was rising, and able-bodied workers were heading off to other towns in search of jobs.

To make matters worse, the town's municipal expenses and tax demands began to rise at an abnormal rate—much of this as a result of a series of costly imperial wars between England and France that had erupted after the succession of William and Mary in 1689. These wars were fought not only in continental Europe, but also as far east as India, where French rivals were trying to dislodge powerful English trading companies, and as far west as North America, where French colonial efforts in Canada competed with the buildup of English colonies along the Atlantic coast. The worldwide conflicts between England and France over colonial supremacy began with King William's War in 1689, which ended with the Peace of Ryswick in 1697. Fighting broke out again in 1701 in what was called Queen Anne's War, which concluded with the Treaty of Utrecht in 1713.[*]

After a quarter century of peace, a third conflict, known as King George's War, broke out in 1740, during which the Massachusetts Bay Colony was called upon to make greater sacrifices in men and money than any of the other American colonies. On the high seas, in actions in the waters of the West Indies, and in the various overland expeditions to invade French Canada, Boston suffered crippling losses of young soldiers and sailors. It also incurred the largest debts and levied the highest taxes, and was forced to support numerous widows and orphans at public expense. Increasing numbers of workmen abandoned Boston and went off to Lynn, Salem, Newburyport, and other Massachusetts towns in search of more favorable sources of income for themselves and their families.

The Treaty of Aix-la-Chapelle that ended King George's War in 1748 proved to be so inconclusive that before half a dozen years had passed, Great Britain and France were at each other's throats again. Conflict between French and

---

[*] In order to satisfy Mary's insistence that her husband be named king, instead of prince consort, Parliament agreed to make them joint sovereigns. They would reign as William and Mary.

Peter Faneuil, son of a French Huguenot refugee, became so successful in his business enterprises that in 1740 he offered the town of Boston the necessary funds to construct a large building that could be used both for commercial activities and for political meetings. Erected in 1742, Faneuil Hall stood on the waterfront of the Town Dock. *Courtesy of the Bostonian Society/Old State House.*

American settlers over possession of the fertile lands of the Ohio Valley led to an outbreak of fighting in North America in 1754, which became known as the French and Indian War. This was nearly two years before the conflict in the American wilderness expanded into a global struggle for colonial supremacy—the Seven Years' War. Events of the ensuing years subjected Americans in general, and Bostonians in particular, to a long and painful emotional ordeal that once again took a heavy toll on the town's manpower and resources. A stunning series of French military victories—on the European continent, in far-off India, and in North America—weakened the British defenses so severely that most colonials everywhere anticipated a humiliating English surrender at any moment. It was in the midst of this period of insecurity and anxiety that the town of Boston suffered an even more immediate and traumatic experience. An early morning earthquake in November 1755 tumbled thousands of terrified residents out of their beds and brought them running into the streets, just in time to see a number of large brick buildings come crumbling down. It was almost an omen of more terrible disasters to come, as reports carried the news of one British defeat after another.

Slowly, however, especially after the appointment in 1757 of William Pitt as war minister, Great Britain's military prospects began to improve. A popular member of Parliament with a reputation for honesty, Pitt replaced incompetent old commanders with aggressive young officers. Using British gold to subsidize England's ally, Frederick of Prussia, to conduct military operations on the continent, Pitt shipped British troops to India and to North America as fresh reinforcements. Almost immediately the fortunes of war began to shift in favor of the British and their colonial forces. Starting with the capture of the French stronghold at Fort Louisburg in July 1758, British military and naval forces took the offensive and started pushing the French back on all fronts. By the time the fortress city of Quebec had fallen to General James Wolfe and his force of redcoats in the fall of 1759, and General Jeffrey Amherst had captured Montreal the following spring, the mood of the colonials had swung from deepest depression to wild rejoicing—except that most Bostonians could not join fully in the celebrations. In March 1760, a terrible fire erupted in the center of town near Cornhill, just west of the Town House on King Street, and swept eastward to Dock Square and the waterfront area. By the time the flames had been extinguished and the smoke had cleared, townspeople could see that more than three hundred buildings lay in ashes, stores and ships had been destroyed, and more than a thousand people were left homeless. It was at the time the most disastrous fire in Boston's history.

The effects of this catastrophe were made worse by the long-term effects of Great Britain's seventy-five-year struggle with France. The nine years of the French and Indian War in America, from 1754 to 1763, played havoc with the already unstable Boston economy. Scores of valuable merchant ships had been sunk or captured by the French on the high seas, and income from the Atlantic fisheries had dropped to an all-time low. As a result of the town's peninsula location, winter firewood sold at what seemed a prohibitive figure to inhabitants of moderate and low incomes. Too often, when skilled young workers and their families migrated to nearby towns in search of work, they left behind them those poor, disabled, elderly, and homeless people who contributed little to the tax base, but who put great strains on the local welfare system. Food prices inside the town continued to be high and uncertain compared with those in the countryside, and bankruptcies reached a record high in 1758. Total economic collapse was averted only because, as long as the war was in progress, Great Britain was forced to subsidize the wholesale importation of military materiel and the transport of troops. Once the war was over, however, this artificially sustained economic system had to be replaced by normal peacetime competition for markets. The question was: Could Boston regain its economic underpinnings and increase its share of the empire's trade?

The Treaty of Paris in 1763 was the official end of the Seven Years' War. It was a total victory for Great Britain and a humiliating defeat for France, marking the end of France as an imperial power in North America. Britain swept the board, receiving undisputed possession of all territories in North America east of the Mississippi River, including the disputed Ohio Valley region; all of the former French territory in Canada; and all of Spanish Florida. Although the end of the fighting ushered in a period of peace and prosperity for most of the American colonies, Boston's economy failed to show any substantial improvement. In fact, things actually went from bad to worse. Mounting taxes for the care of the poor and the relief of widows and orphans caused grave delinquencies among taxpayers. Many residents were forced to sell off their property in order to pay their taxes and meet their debts, but with so many people still leaving town for better opportunities elsewhere, tenants were hard to come by. And all the while, the town fathers were looking desperately for additional funds with which to maintain their public school system, to straighten and resurface their notoriously crooked streets, and to make the repairs necessary to restore homes, warehouses, and docks after the disastrous fire that had devastated the town only three years earlier.

While other towns in America were expanding rapidly during the years of prosperity following the end of the Seven Years' War, Boston was suffering from depression, unemployment, heavy taxation, a declining population, and a shrinking tax base. The one thing that kept Boston going during the later half of the eighteenth century was the fact that it could still make a brisk livelihood from the sea. Of all the colonial seaports, Boston was still the most active in shipbuilding, cod fishing, and seaborne commerce in general. It still contained some of the most productive distilleries in North America, an industry that depended on a regular supply of molasses from the West Indies. Boston lived on its ships, its wharves, its shipyards, its ropewalks, and its sail lofts. Even for its regular supply of food, it required access by water to the grazing grounds located on the cluster of small islands in the outer harbor, where many Bostonians pastured their cattle and sheep.

But even this life-giving source of support was destined to disappear all too soon, as relations between the American colonies and their mother country began to break down, and as the specter of separation and independence began to loom in the background. The war had been won. The prolonged conflict between Great Britain and France was now a thing of the past; the French would never return. The results of the peace, however, were destined to bring about consequences that few people on either side of the Atlantic had ever anticipated.

Chapter

3

From Colony to Commonwealth

W ITH the fall of Quebec," wrote the eminent Boston historian Francis Parkman, "began the history of the United States." The end of the French and Indian War set in motion a series of events that would eventually lead to a breakdown in civil relations between the American colonies and the British authorities. This disruption was based, in great part, on a total misunderstanding—by each side—of what their transatlantic relationships would be like in a postwar world.

For its part, Great Britain saw the end of the war as a heaven-sent opportunity to reorganize its colonial system, reestablish financial accountability, and bring the colonists themselves under strict imperial control. For generations, Americans had boldly mistreated British officials, ignored official rules and regulations, and openly ridiculed the mercantile system. Political problems at home and conflicts with France abroad persuaded the British to adopt a policy of "let sleeping dogs lie," the kind of attitude that prevented them from supervising their colonies properly. Now, however, with the conflict between Crown and Parliament a thing of the past, with the Protestant succession safely established, and with France subjected to ignominious defeat, Britain felt free at last to give the American colonies the attention they deserved.

The newly established monarch, King George III, through the agency of his prime minister, Sir George Grenville, had Parliament pass a series of laws designed to make the recalcitrant colonials observe the letter of the law and help contribute to paying off the enormous war debt that had virtually bankrupted the nation. The Proclamation Act of 1763 prevented the Americans[*] from crossing the Appalachian Mountains and moving west into the Ohio Valley. At the same time, a permanent garrison of ten thousand British redcoats was established at colonial expense to patrol the Proclamation Line to fend off a bloody war between the native Indians and the incoming settlers, which would ruin the valuable fur trade. The Currency Act of 1764 prohibited Americans from coining and issuing their own forms of money; the Sugar Act, the same year, assigned elements of the royal navy to patrol North American waters and established special Vice Admiralty courts, instead of local colonial courts, to try all cases involving smuggling and illegal trade. The British regarded these Grenville Acts as reasonable and responsible measures by which the colonial system could be restructured, reorganized, and properly financed for the future.

On the other side of the Atlantic, the American colonists responded angrily and defiantly to this series of restrictive laws, which they regarded as absolutely unnecessary and totally unwarranted. Every one of the statutes collided head-on with the hopes and expectations of American settlers in the postwar era. With the imperial wars over and France gone forever as a tangible threat to the security of the North American colonies, colonists could see no reason for not being able to cross the Appalachians and move west into the fertile lands of the Ohio Valley. And they certainly could see no reason for keeping a permanent garrison of redcoats in North America—especially since the haughty disdain displayed by British regular troops toward the rustic colonial militiamen during the war had earned them the title of "lobsterbacks." The Sugar Act was seen by Americans as a particularly spiteful and unnecessary piece of legislation that threatened to cut deeply into their smuggling activities and bypass their local court system. The act provoked especially strong reaction throughout the town of Boston, where the political atmosphere was becoming dangerously charged.

During the early 1690s, the new Massachusetts Charter promulgated by William and Mary had had the effect of creating a new and more fashionable royal establishment for the province. From their headquarters in the Town House in Boston, Governor Francis Bernard, Lieutenant-Governor Thomas

[*] The British began referring to the colonial settlers as "Americans" at about this time.

Hutchinson, and Secretary Andrew Oliver set the proper tone for the younger members of their staffs. Living in stately homes, dressed in elegant clothing, riding in ornate carriages to their country estates, they displayed the lofty affectations of the English court. Although it was true that the governor and other officials were dependent on the General Court for their salaries, the royal establishment could still exercise considerable influence over provincial affairs. During time of war, for example, the governor's control over army and navy contracts was an important force in keeping the town's influential financial leaders in line. The awarding of judgeships and other choice appointments in county government was still another important consideration in assessing the strength of royal power in Massachusetts.

Without the kind of internal organization to provide direction for policy or pressure for appointments, the local town meeting system found it increasingly difficult to stand up for the interests of local inhabitants in the face of royal influence in the General Court. As a result, by 1720 a caucus had appeared in the town—an attempt, says colonial historian G. B. Warden, to provide a "coherent political management for the somewhat loose town meeting." In the smoke-filled backrooms of local taverns and coffeehouses, gathered together over "punch, wine, pipe and tobacco, biscuit, cheese, etc.," caucus members laid their plans to make sure that "certain persons" were selected as town meeting members. They also arranged for tax rebates, cultivated occupational groups such as the caulkers and the sail-makers, drew upon social organizations such as the Masons, and instructed the fire and militia companies in how to operate as communications and action networks. In organizing these local associations along political lines, caucus members saw themselves promoting the popular interest in the face of what they viewed as the selfish interests of privileged groups in the royal establishment.

As conflicting interests between the town and the province began to multiply, and as an increasing number of Boston's leaders came from outside the town—John Adams, John Hancock, and Josiah Quincy from Braintree; James Otis from West Barnstable; Joseph Warren from Roxbury—political activists looked for other forms of political organization beyond the town meeting and the caucus to express their views and protect their interests. Groups of Bostonians from all walks of life formed a variety of clubs and associations— the Loyal Nine, the Merchants Club, the Body of the People—through which townspeople could gather in an informal manner to discuss important matters of the day. In this way, they created an unofficial but powerful "third force" in

Boston politics, somewhere between the functions of the General Court and the operations of the town meeting.

By the time the news of the new British imperial policies reached the colonies, therefore, Boston had more than its share of political groups, ready to debate the relative advantages and disadvantages of Parliament's latest actions. At first, the British Coffee House, located on King Street, was a popular place where Crown officers, military men, merchants, lawyers, and men of all points of view met, before differences over British policies divided the town into the Whigs and the Tories. On the south side of King Street was the Bunch of Grapes, which was frequented by the more prosperous members of the local patriot factions, while the Green Dragon on Union Street near Faneuil Hall and the Salutation in the North End were the taverns where the less well-to-do members of the local opposition met to air their grievances. Like Samuel Adams, an emerging political organizer, many people dropped into several of these popular locations in the course of a single day and night, participating in the discussions and carrying the various arguments from one group to another.

It took very little time before the discussions and debates generated in these taverns became known to the general public. By 1764, there were already a number of weekly newspapers published in Boston, but it was the *Boston Gazette*, published each Monday by Benjamin Edes and John Gill, that quickly became the favorite of the town's patriot leaders. In his diary for September 3, 1769, John Adams described how he spent a Sunday evening with his cousin, Samuel Adams, along with James Otis, William Davis, and John Gill, "cooking up paragraphs, articles, occurrences, etc.—working the political engine." Although Samuel Adams had been one of the leaders of the patriot cause for some time, it was not until April 4, 1768, that his first article appeared in the *Gazette*, signed, "A Puritan." From that time on, he used the local newspapers constantly to attack the actions of the governor and Parliament, using such Latin pseudonyms as "*Candidus*," "*Vindex*," "*Populus*," and "*Poplicola*."

In almost every way and in every form, therefore, Boston residents were prepared to protest the ways in which they felt the Grenville Acts were threatening their livelihoods and depriving them of their traditional liberties. The passage in 1764 of the Sugar Act, claimed James Otis, "set the people thinking, in six months, more than they had done in their whole lives before." Otis had already established a reputation for defiant oratory. Four years earlier, in an impassioned four-hour speech, he had denounced the British use of general search warrants, called Writs of Assistance, as a violation of "the immunity of

Samuel Adams displayed an unusual flair for political organization and patriotic agitation. In his Circular Letter he denied the authority of Parliament over the colonies; in his Committee of Correspondence he exchanged vital information with other patriots; and he stirred up popular hatred against British troops that later climaxed with the Boston Massacre of 1770. He served in the Continental Congress and after the war was elected lieutenant-governor of Massachusetts 1789–1793; he then served as governor 1794–1797. *Courtesy of the Boston Public Library, Print Department.*

an English home" and a transgression of basic constitutional principles. Now, with the passage of the Sugar Act, Otis renewed his denunciations, and even Governor Francis Bernard was forced to admit that this latest Grenville Act had caused a greater alarm among the citizens of Boston "than the taking of Fort William in 1757." Boston merchants, convinced that the act would destroy their lucrative trade in sugar and molasses with the West Indies, formally petitioned Parliament for its repeal.

But colonial reaction to the Sugar Act was nothing compared to the outrage that greeted the passage of the Stamp Act in March 1765, requiring colonists to pay special taxes on all legal and commercial documents. Wills, licenses, contracts, newspapers, almanacs, pamphlets—even playing-cards and dice— were required to bear the tax stamp in order to be considered legal property. The tax itself was designed to raise some £60,000 annually in additional revenue that would be used to offset the expenses involved in colonial defense. Colonials were furious at this latest move by the British Parliament, and local agitators such as James Otis echoed the sentiments expressed by Patrick Henry in the Virginia House of Burgesses that taxation without representation was tyranny. Boston merchants banded together to institute a boycott of British goods, while mobs of angry citizens stoned and looted the homes of Andrew Oliver, the local tax agent; Benjamin Hallowell, the customs collector; and even Thomas Hutchinson, the lieutenant-governor.

With a vigilante organization called the Sons of Liberty whipping up public excitement and threatening effective reprisals, by the fall of 1765 no government official dared distribute the hated tax stamps. The women of the town, too, demonstrated their annoyance at the Stamp Act. They formed their own organization called the Daughters of Liberty, responded to the call for a boycott on all British goods, and called for patriotic Americans to abstain from drinking English tea. They brewed their own home-grown version of "liberty tea" out of local leaves, herbs, and berries. At the suggestion of Massachusetts, delegates from nine other colonies met together in New York City in October 1765. Calling themselves the Stamp Act Congress, they respectfully called upon King George III and the British Parliament to repeal the Stamp Act. Although they professed to acknowledge the overall authority of Parliament in external matters, the Americans denied that Parliament had any right to tax the colonies since the colonists had no specific representation in that body.

Yielding to the growing pressure from English merchants who were now suffering the effects of the American boycott, Britain repealed the obnoxious

Stamp Act in March 1766. When one of John Hancock's ships brought Boston the news of the repeal on Friday, May 16, 1766, it touched off one of the greatest celebrations in the town's history. At the Brattle Street Congregational Church the following Sunday, the Reverend Samuel Cooper preached from the text: "The Lord reigneth: let the earth rejoice," and the citizens prepared to do just that. Although the selectmen designated the next day, Monday, May 19, as the official day of celebration, the townspeople could not wait for the sun to come up. At one o'clock in the morning, they began to ring the church bells, and within a short time almost every bell in town was pealing out the good news. Bands began to play in the darkness, drums started to bang, muskets were discharged into the air, and by the time daylight came, the Liberty Tree, public buildings, and private homes were decorated with flags and bunting. People celebrated all through the day and, according to the diary of town clerk William Cooper, when evening came John Hancock gave a grand "Entertainment" for the "genteel Part" of the town, while treating "the Populace" to pipes of Madeira wine out on his front lawn on the Beacon Hill side of the Common. In front of his house, he erected a staging for an elaborate "illumination," which he touched off every now and then in response to fireworks set off by the Sons of Liberty on the opposite side of the Common. Most Americans felt that the crisis had passed, the confrontation was over, the English had learned their lesson, and the colonies could again live in a kind of peaceful coexistence with the mother country.

And, indeed, for two years after the repeal of the Stamp Act, relations between the American colonies and Great Britain followed what most observers agreed was a fairly peaceful and routine pattern. In 1767, however, Parliament came out with a new series of laws, directed by King George III's recently appointed prime minister, Charles Townshend. This was a new attempt to raise revenue by placing import duties on such imported products as glass, lead, paper, paint, and tea. Since these were regarded as "external" taxes, outside the structure of colonial assemblies, Townshend argued that they had to be accepted by the Americans, who apparently objected only to "internal" taxes. In addition to bringing in more revenue, the Townshend duties would also pay the salaries of most royal government officials in North America, thus freeing them from their longtime dependence on the colonial assemblies, which usually paid their salaries.

For a second time, however, the attempt of Great Britain to raise revenue without going through the wishes of the settlers in their colonial assemblies produced a storm of protest. Following Boston's lead, in March 1768 merchants in colonial ports, ranging all the way from Maine to Georgia, formed associations to boycott British goods. Housewives in villages and towns promised not to purchase any of the articles on the Townshend list; the weaving of homespun cloth was promoted as a patriotic enterprise; many communities celebrated public tea-burnings; and Americans everywhere were encouraged to devise local substitutes to replace products they had formerly imported from England. What products they couldn't replace, enterprising Boston merchants smuggled in from such European nations as France, Holland, and Spain.

Once again, Massachusetts was the storm center around which swirled the powerful currents that would move the colonies even further away from the influences of the mother country. Already forty-six-year-old Samuel Adams was moving to the forefront as one of the most energetic and imaginative political leaders in Boston, making a forceful case against the authority of the Crown. He organized committees of correspondence that quickly spread to other colonies and, under his direction, in February 1768 the Massachusetts House of Representatives issued a Circular Letter to the other colonial legislatures denouncing the Townshend Acts as unconstitutional violations of the principle of no taxation without representation. In response to the letter, merchants in New York and Philadelphia organized nonimportation agreements. When the local legislators defiantly refused to obey an order by Lord Hillsborough, the British secretary of state, to rescind the Circular Letter, Governor Francis Bernard promptly dissolved the Massachusetts assembly. In the absence of this representative body, angry mobs of Bostonians moved into the streets to terrorize customs officials, harass royal authorities, and generally make known their displeasure at what they considered illegal and high-handed tactics on the part of British officials.

Convinced that Massachusetts was now in the grip of anarchy, Lord Hillsborough ordered two regiments of British troops stationed in Ireland to embark for North America to establish law and order. When these troops arrived in Boston in early October 1768, marching down King Street in all their impressive glory, the tension between the colonies and the British government escalated to dangerous levels. With nearly four thousand armed redcoats in the small seaport town of only fifteen thousand inhabitants (roughly four soldiers for every civilian), Boston was a powder keg ready to explode. The eruption came on March 5, 1770, a cold, snowy Monday night, when a crowd of locals began throwing snowballs and pieces of ice at a British sentry outside the Custom House on King Street. When Captain Thomas Preston and seven of his men came to the aid of the sentry with muskets and bayonets, an angry scuffle ensued between the soldiers and the civilians. Somebody cried "Fire!" and the troops fired into the menacing crowd. When the smoke had cleared, three Boston men lay dead, eight others had been wounded, and two more died a short time later.*

With the town in an uproar over the killings, Lieutenant-Governor Hutchinson sent the British regulars out to Castle Island to avoid further trouble and promised the residents that "the full course of justice" would determine responsibility for the tragedy. When Captain Preston and his men were brought to separate trials for murdering unarmed civilians, John Adams of Braintree agreed to serve as defense counsel. As a result of his capable defense, the British captain was found not guilty of having given the command to fire. The soldiers were also freed, after Adams was able to use the self-defense argument to show that they had been in fear of their lives. Upholding the English common-law tradition of trial by jury, the patriot lawyers had saved the lives of those responsible for the Boston Massacre.†

In an ironic twist of fate, on the very day of the Boston Massacre, Lord North, the newly appointed British prime minister, had moved to repeal the Townshend Acts that had caused so much trouble over the past three years. The colonial boycott of English goods had proved extremely effective, and once again British merchants had exerted pressure on Parliament to make the necessary concessions. Most of them could not justify the cost and inconvenience of enforcing the duties; by 1769–1770, North American nonimportation policies had cut British sales to the colonies by two-thirds. The royal treasury had collected less than £21,000 from its duties, but British businessmen had lost an estimated £1,700,000 in trade. The British government, therefore, agreed to repeal the Townshend Acts—except for the duty on tea. That was retained as a symbol of the "supremacy of Parliament" and a declaration of its right "to govern the colonies."

Although the British did a great deal to reduce colonial tensions when they repealed the Townshend Acts in March 1770, their stubborn insistence on

---

* The three men slain that night were Sam Gray, James Caldwell, and Crispus Attucks, an African-American worker from Framingham. The two men who died later were Samuel Maverick and Patrick Carr.

† The "Boston Massacre" got its name from Paul Revere's cleverly designed engraving that showed British troops deliberately firing into a peaceful group of colonials at the command of an officer's sword.

In a variation on Paul Revere's famous engraving of the Boston Massacre, in 1856 J. H. Bufford produced a popular and widely distributed lithograph that focused on Crispus Attucks as an African-American patriot and one of the five men who died in the melee on King Street. As the Civil War approached, black residents of Boston hailed Attucks as a model of heroic resistance and a symbol of black liberation. *Courtesy of the Bostonian Society/Old State House.*

keeping the tax on tea made it possible for local radicals like Samuel Adams to keep their agitation alive, and to wait for the next opportunity to strike a blow for independence. They did not have long to wait. In 1773, the ministry of Lord North passed the Tea Act in an attempt to rescue the British East India Company from bankruptcy, the result of a combination of poor management and an enormous surplus of unsold tea. This act would allow the company to ship its tea directly to North America without paying the usual English export taxes, and then sell the high-grade tea directly to the colonials without going through American middlemen. This meant greater profits for the company and the maintenance of the its power in India; it also meant lower prices for the American consumer and a reduction in the amount of widespread tea smuggling. Even though colonials would be required to pay the threepence

Townshend tax, the selling price of the tea in North America would still be half the price paid in England.

Lord North had badly misjudged the colonial temper, however, and his Tea Act provided exactly the kind of provocation for which the radicals were waiting. American merchants suspected a British plot to establish a monopoly on tea and thereby undermine the rising American merchant class. The average colonist saw it as a British trick to seduce Americans into paying the detested Townshend duty on tea. Reactivating the committees of correspondence, Samuel Adams and other radical leaders in seacoast towns along the Atlantic seaboard circulated petitions, organized public opinion, and made preparations to prevent British tea from being brought ashore in North America. Under orders from King George III, however, three ships loaded with tea headed for the Massachusetts colony. The first to arrive was the *Dartmouth*, which docked at Griffin's Wharf on November 28, 1773. A second ship, the *Eleanor*, arrived on December 2; a third, the *Beagle*, was sighted on December 7. This brought matters to a head.

During early December, local patriots held stormy meetings at the Old South Meeting House, demanding that the tea be shipped back to London. When Governor Thomas Hutchinson refused to order the return of the tea ships, Samuel Adams and his supporters took matters into their own hands. On the night of December 16, 1773, after a packed meeting at the Old South, some fifty Bostonians, crudely disguised as Mohawk Indians to prevent any later attempts at identification, led a mob of inhabitants down to Griffin's Wharf where the *Dartmouth* and the *Eleanor*, each carrying 114 chests of tea, were anchored; anchored nearby was the *Beagle* with 112 chests. Altogether the three vessels had more than ninety thousand pounds of dutied tea, worth about £9,000. After boarding the ships and forcing the customs officers ashore, the patriots hauled the chests onto the deck, smashed them open, and poured the loose tea into the waters of Boston Harbor. All the while, a large crowd gathered along the waterfront, watching in silent approval.

British reaction to the Boston Tea Party was both immediate and decisive. It was one thing for the colonials to defy the government in speeches, broadsides, and public demonstrations. It was quite another thing, however, to lay violent hands on property aboard one of His Majesty's ships. In the spring of 1774, Parliament passed a series of measures known as the Coercive Acts, singling out Boston as the chief culprit and moving to destroy both the political and economic leadership of that troublesome town. The Boston Port Bill closed Boston

Harbor to all commerce and trade; the Massachusetts Government Act brought in a military governor, established martial law, and moved the colonial capital from Boston to Salem. The Administration of Justice Act established that all British officials would henceforth be tried in English courts, and the Quartering Act made it possible for British troops to be quartered in private homes. What the Americans called the "Intolerable Acts" were to remain in effect at least until the loss of the valuable tea was paid for, and until the culprits responsible for the Boston Tea Party were apprehended and punished. Defiance had turned to rebellion in Boston; after the Tea Party things would never be the same.

Compounding an already dangerous situation was the fact that in developing plans for the reorganization of its worldwide empire after the defeat of France, the British Parliament passed the Quebec Act in 1774—the same year it passed the Coercive Acts, leading one historian to call it "a good law in bad company." The Quebec Act reestablished the rights of the Roman Catholic Church, not only in Canada but also in the Ohio Valley territory it had taken from France, as a means of making the process of imperial integration much easier and more humane. Colonists in Boston and throughout New England, however, were infuriated at the idea that the detested papist religion their Puritan forebears had fled England to escape should be allowed to exist in the New World. Many Americans saw the Quebec Act as one more deliberate conspiracy to undermine their religious liberties. In her study *The Old Revolutionaries,* historian Pauline Maier suggests that subsequent colonial demands for independence were based as much on their reaction against Britain's "softness" on Catholicism as on their opposition to unfair tax laws or the closing of the port of Boston.

The tolling of church bells, the wearing of black mourning bands, the long days of prayer and fasting did nothing to avert or even delay the imperial anger. Precisely at the stroke of noon on June 1, 1774, the Boston Port Act went into effect. From that moment on, Boston Harbor was sealed off from the rest of the world by a tight blockade that would not even allow residents to row their boats across the harbor to the islands where their cattle were pastured. General Thomas Gage, the newly appointed military governor, had been instructed to compel "a full and absolute submission" to the letter of the law. Ships were tied up at the piers, shipyards suspended operations, carpenters were idle, wharves were deserted, and sailors walked the streets of Boston with nothing to do. Porters and stevedores were thrown out of work, mechanics departed to find work in other towns, the great warehouses were shut, mercantile houses had no more business, and the clerks of the town went without pay.

The population of Boston dropped by the thousands, going from sixteen thousand down to ten thousand, and then to as low as about six thousand, as young patriots left to join the rebel forces in other colonies and family men looked for more promising livelihoods in other parts of the commonwealth. Those who remained in the town, however, showed no signs of remorse and little inclination to change their defiant ways. They would not sell food to Gage's troops, burned up straw that the army could have used for bedding, and refused to construct barracks for the additional regiments that had been sent into Boston to enforce the Coercive Acts. All in all, the local populace more than justified General Gage's frustrated complaint that Bostonians were absolutely "unmanageable."

Hopes faded for a peaceful settlement between the American colonials and British authorities, as both sides became more fixed in their respective positions. In September 1774, American leaders convened a Continental Congress in Philadelphia, where radical delegates such as Samuel Adams called for a showdown with Great Britain. They condemned the Coercive Acts as "unjust, cruel, and unconstitutional," demanded stronger economic reprisals against the mother country, and called for the creation of a continental army. Samuel's cousin, John Adams of Braintree, was also a member of the Continental Congress and was active in working on a statement declaring the reasons that led the American colonies to separate from Great Britain. His wife, Abigail, far from the submissive housewife of the previous century, urged her husband to "remember the ladies" in the statement of rights he was preparing. If congress did not, she warned, then the ladies were prepared to "foment a Rebelion, and will not hold ourselves bound by any laws in which we have no voice or Representation." On July 18, 1776, a copy of the Declaration of Independence was read from the balcony of the Town House to a crowd of jubilant Bostonians. When the reading was concluded, wrote Abigail to her husband, the cannon was discharged and all the people shouted, "God save our American states!"

The British, for their part, were equally determined not to back down. "We must not retreat," insisted King George III in September 1774, while leaders in Parliament agreed that this time Great Britain must remain firm in the face of the latest incident of colonial defiance. As tensions increased during the winter of 1774–1775, General Gage began receiving unsettling reports that colonials in and around Boston were collecting muskets, cannons, ammunition, and all kinds of other military supplies. Gage decided to move quickly and nip any possible full-scale rebellion in the bud. After notifying British authorities and receiving permission to use his own discretion, on the night of April 18, 1775, he sent a force of some eight hundred men to seize a store of military supplies at the town of Concord, about twenty miles northwest of Boston. Alert townspeople, however, closely watching the activities of the British troops stationed on Boston Common, had arranged a system of signals to be flashed by lanterns from the belfry of the town's Old North Church. If the troops marched southward toward Dorchester and Braintree, one lantern would be lit, and if the troops marched toward the Charles River heading for Cambridge, two lanterns would be lit, sending riders ahead to warn the countryside.

The British had hardly reached Lechmere Point when the two-lantern signal sent William Dawes and Paul Revere riding through Charlestown, Medford, and Menotomy, alerting local militia groups that the "regulars" were on their way. By the time the British reached the town of Lexington about daybreak the next morning, they found a small group of seventy armed minutemen drawn up on the green. The British commander ordered the colonials to disperse, shots rang out, and when the smoke had cleared eight Americans lay dead and ten wounded on the Lexington green—the opening shots in what was to become America's war for independence. As the British columns continued their march to Concord, the countryside swarmed with colonial minutemen from all parts of the region who had heard reports about the fighting at Lexington and were waiting for the British to march back from their raid at Concord. There was only one road back to Boston, and the returning British were subjected to a harassing gauntlet of fire from New England farmers lined up behind rocks, fences, trees, and bushes. The British troops barely made it back to the safety of their barracks in Boston, suffering nearly three hundred casualties before the day was over.

Colonials everywhere were outraged by reports (often greatly exaggerated) of the British attacks at Lexington and Concord. They held protest meetings, conducted public demonstrations, and began drilling their local militias. On May 10, 1775, a Second Continental Congress assembled in Philadelphia, and one of its first actions was to appoint a Virginian, George Washington, as commander-in-chief of the colonial forces, which by that time were encamped around Boston.

A month later, on June 17, 1775, General William Howe used the British fleet to land a force of regulars on nearby Charlestown, sweep through the peninsula, and overrun the colonial positions. Learning about the British plans, several American regiments moved into Charlestown Neck and set up fortifications atop Breed's Hill. Furious at the patriots' actions, Howe ordered a frontal assault, sending some fifteen hundred British troops marching up the hill against the Americans entrenched at the top. Warned not to fire until they could see "the whites of their eyes," the Americans inflicted heavy casualties on the first two assaults. Although the third assault was successful, and the British overwhelmed the defenders, the Battle of Bunker Hill (as it was incorrectly labeled) demonstrated that the clashes at Lexington and at Concord two months earlier had been no accident. This latest confrontation was the tragic prelude to an all-out war. Boston found itself no longer the controversial center of a parliamentary dispute over constitutional issues; it was now an occupied enemy town in the midst of a bitter international conflict between a group of rebellious colonies and their mother country.

The winter of 1775–1776 was severely cold in British-occupied Boston, and the need for fuel was almost as great as the need for food. More than a hundred buildings were pulled down and used for firewood, and the handsome trees that lined Boston Common all had to be sacrificed to the desperate need for fuel. Milk was impossible to obtain; the cost of such items as cheese, bread, butter, and potatoes rose to staggering heights; and meat was generally unavailable at any price. Most of the foodstuffs were brought in by ships of the royal navy—the only vessels allowed to come in and out of Boston Harbor. The provisions were almost immediately consumed by the British soldiers in the town—but not always with happy results. Because of the bad weather, the long journey across the Atlantic, and considerable graft among the British contractors, most of the incoming supplies were not fit to eat. The bread was moldy, the butter rancid, the flour insect-infested, the peas worm-eaten, and the beef crawling with maggots. Hundreds of British soldiers suffered from malnutrition and scurvy, exacerbating the troops' numerous casualties in the Battle of Bunker Hill. To make matters worse, an epidemic of smallpox raged through the town to such an extent that British authorities looked upon the terrible disease as an actual deterrent to any possible attack by the Americans.

While Bostonians and their British overseers were suffering through their winter ordeal, General George Washington arrived to take over his responsibilities as commander-in-chief and was trying to decide the best way of driving the British troops out of Boston. His determination to force an evacuation was further strengthened when Colonel Henry Knox, a Boston bookseller turned artilleryman, arrived with a number of heavy cannons he had dragged through the deep snowdrifts all the way from Fort Ticonderoga in upstate New York.

With the arrival of these guns in Cambridge on January 24, 1776, Washington began planning his strategy. His first idea was to launch a series of direct assaults against the town across the bay while the winter ice was still deep and hard. Washington's generals would not approve such a risky plan, however, arguing that gaining control of Dorchester Heights on the nearby South Boston peninsula (then called Dorchester Neck) would be safer and more effective. Planting the cannons atop the heights would either force the British to come out of their defenses and fight in the open or evacuate the town completely.

Bowing to the decision of his military council ("I must suppose it to be right," he told John Hancock), Washington began preparations to seize and fortify Dorchester Heights. Under cover of diversionary bombardments from several positions around Boston (Abigail Adams complained that she could hardly get any sleep) on the night of March 4, 1776, General John

General George Washington used the arrival of heavy cannon from Fort Ticonderoga in January 1776 as an opportunity to fortify Dorchester Heights on the nearby South Boston peninsula and force the British to evacuate the town. Transports carrying the 9,000-man British garrison, along with nearly 1,100 American loyalists, sailed away for Nova Scotia. On March 17, 1776, Washington's troops marched into the liberated town, which they found a tragic shambles after the period of British occupation. *Courtesy of the Bostonian Society/Old State House.*

Thomas commanded a long train of some two thousand American soldiers through Dorchester and across the neck of land that led into the peninsula of South Boston. Working swiftly and silently through the night, by daybreak the colonists had constructed two substantial fortifications on the crest of Dorchester Heights overlooking the town of Boston. To the consternation of the British across the bay, the American cannons menaced not only the British forces in the town itself, but also the numerous British ships riding helplessly at anchor in the harbor. Although Sir William Howe considered launching a counterattack, he thought better of it and decided that evacuation was the only alternative. In return for a British promise not to burn the town, Washington agreed not to fire on the British vessels as they left Boston Harbor. A fleet of 125 warships and transports left Boston Harbor bound for Halifax, Nova Scotia. Aboard were General Howe, some nine thousand officers and men, and more than one thousand loyalists and their families.

On March 17, 1776, General Washington's troops, spearheaded by a contingent of soldiers who had already had smallpox, marched into the liberated town of Boston only to find it a tragic shambles. Trees had been cut down everywhere, fences had been ripped up, and barns and warehouses had been razed to supply the townspeople with firewood. Churches and meetinghouses had been used for stables, private homes had been turned into hospitals, and monuments and public buildings had been shockingly defaced. Slowly and painfully, however, the town began to pull itself together after the ordeal of siege, occupation, and plunder. Houses were repaired, the streets were swept of debris, the churches and meetinghouses were restored to their original uses, the wharves were reclaimed, and the coffee shops were opened again. But the war was still on, and times were still hard. Boston's population, which before the war had reached nearly twenty thousand, had dropped to less than six thousand at the time of the siege. People still lived from hand to mouth, and jobs were so scarce that able-bodied men were forced to earn a living by carrying wood and vegetables into town from the outlying villages. The most the old town could do was look forward to the day when the war would end, the wharves would hum, and the ships would go out to sea once again.

After General Washington's defeat of British forces under the command of General Cornwallis at the Battle of Yorktown on October 19, 1781, Great Britain finally acknowledged the inevitable and negotiated for peace. The Treaty of Paris, recognizing the independence of the United States of America, was formally signed on September 3, 1783. The town of Boston, however, did not immediately acquire the profits or enjoy the prosperity it hoped would follow the end of the fighting. Money was scarcer then ever; wages and prices skyrocketed in an inflationary spiral that showed no signs of leveling off. Skilled workers were impossible to find. And rents rose to triple their prewar levels. The loss of ships, the lack of manpower, the broken-down state of the shipyards, and the obsolescence of gear that had not been used in seven years made it extremely questionable whether the Bay State would ever again be able to resume its former prominence in such enterprises as fishing, shipping, and overseas commerce.

Many of the economic difficulties afflicting Boston, however, were duplicated in other parts of the commonwealth, and this helped convince many political leaders that the postwar framework of government called the Articles of Confederation would have to be revised and strengthened. Some people felt that if more power were given to the central government, the nation's economy would be more effectively stabilized. After the Revolution ended, a period of deflation set in, forcing down prices and greatly reducing personal incomes. In the western parts of Massachusetts particularly, farmers who had purchased goods, livestock, and farmlands when times were good and money plentiful found themselves in serious trouble now that times were bad and incomes low. The number of mortgage foreclosures and business failures rose to new heights, and many people were imprisoned for failing to pay their debts. Instead of issuing paper money to alleviate the problem, however, the state legislature in Boston ignored the farmers' protests and proceeded to levy even heavier taxes in an attempt to pay off the war debt. By the summer of 1786, mob action had broken out as bands of hard-pressed farmers, headed by Daniel Shays, a former captain in the Continental Army, marched on various courts throughout the western sections of the state and prevented the judges from sitting to hear their cases.

Shays' Rebellion, as it was called, was promptly put down by Governor James Bowdoin, who sent General Benjamin Lincoln with a force of forty-four hundred troops to crush the insurgents. The uprising had important repercussions, however, not only throughout the commonwealth but also throughout the nation. This insurrection, along with many similar disorders among farmers and debtors in other rural sections of the country, had come as a frightening shock to the propertied classes and the well-to-do interests of the newly organized republic. This was precisely the type of "bloody anarchy" they greatly feared. And it helped convince many delegates to the upcoming convention in Philadelphia that a much stronger central government was needed. It was only a few months later, on May 25, 1787, that the convention in Philadelphia finally opened, after a sufficient number of delegates had arrived to form the necessary quorum.

In many ways, the four delegates who arrived from Massachusetts reflected the social and economic attitudes that divided the Bay State. Nathaniel Gorham, the most recent president of the Continental Congress, together with the eloquent Rufus King, urged a stronger central government, a vigorous chief executive, and a prosperous national economy. The other two members, however, took much different positions. Caleb Strong, a Northampton lawyer, and Elbridge Gerry, a merchant from Marblehead, spoke out strongly in favor of keeping more power in the hands of the states and of maintaining a greater degree of local autonomy. Although Strong was eventually persuaded to support the new Constitution, Gerry refused to sign the final document, predicting that Massachusetts citizens, "devoted to democracy," would rise up in revolution against the new Constitution.

At the end of seventeen long, hot weeks—from May 25 to September 17, 1787—only forty-two of the original fifty-five delegates still remained in Philadelphia to put their signatures on the new Constitution of the United States. Three members, including Gerry of Massachusetts, had declined to do so and had returned to their respective states to fight against ratification. Special elections were held in each of the states to elect members of the ratifying conventions. Candidates—Federalists or Antifederalists—were chosen on the basis of their pledges to support the new Constitution or oppose it. At the first session of the General Court during his second administration, Governor John Hancock ordered the secretary to lay this "momentous affair" before the legislators for their consideration. It was then decided that Massachusetts would hold a ratifying convention, which would open in Boston on January 9, 1788. By that date, five states had already voted to ratify the new Constitution. The vote of Massachusetts was considered by many observers to be crucial in deciding the votes of the remaining seven states.

From all parts of the commonwealth, including Maine, 364 delegates made their way to Boston to take part in the convention that many felt would decide the fate of the new Constitution.* The delegation from Boston consisted of

---

* The colony of Maine had been annexed by Massachusetts in 1677 and continued to remain a political part of the Bay State until the Compromise of 1820. In that year, Maine was admitted to the Union as a free state to balance Missouri, which came in as a slave state.

five members. Three of them—Governor John Hancock, former governor James Bowdoin, and Judge William Sullivan—were known to support the new framework of government; the other two—Samuel Adams and Stephen Higginson—were critical of Hancock and opposed to ratification. Complaining of the gout, Hancock kept to his bed and did not attend the early sessions.

A sharp division of opinion among the delegates was immediately apparent as Antifederalists, representing farmers and former Shaysites from the western counties, continued to blame eastern Federalists for their problems. They expressed their fears that a more powerful national government would diminish the rights of the states and endanger the liberties of the people. Greatly concerned about the numbers and the arguments of their rural opponents, Federalist leaders finally persuaded John Hancock to leave his sickbed and come to the convention hall in person. Helped out of his house and driven across town by coach, the ailing governor made a dramatic entrance "wrapped in his flannels" and carried bodily into the hall.

Taking over as chairman of the convention, Hancock made an effort to bridge the gap between Federalists and Antifederalists, well aware of the Bay State's strategic importance in the struggle for ratification. If Massachusetts, the second most populous state in the Union at that time, should fail to ratify the Constitution, with New York and Virginia still undecided, then the entire movement to create a new national government might well collapse. Hancock, therefore, proposed a compromise: a "conciliatory proposition" in the form of nine amendments, a sort of Bill of Rights, that he promised would be added to the Constitution after it had been ratified. One amendment would prohibit Americans from accepting offices or titles from foreign governments; another would allow direct taxes only when there were no other sources of revenue available; still another would allow Congress to regulate elections only when the states had neglected to do so. But perhaps the most important—one that would later appear in slightly different form in the Tenth Amendment—was Hancock's proposal calling for powers not expressly delegated to the national government to be reserved to the states.

Hancock's proposals, together with their public support by Samuel Adams, shifted the balance of power within the convention. Support for the new Constitution, with the understanding that amendments protecting the rights of the states would be added later, gradually built up among the delegates. When the final vote was called late in the afternoon of February 6, 1788, the vote was 187 yes, 168 no. By the narrow margin of 19 votes, Massachusetts

John Hancock was born in Braintree, Massachusetts, in 1737, and after graduating from Harvard in 1754 became a successful merchant. Hancock became actively involved in political activities against the Crown and was president of the Continental Congress when he signed the Declaration of Independence. He supported the ratification of the new Constitution of the United States, and in 1780 he was elected first governor of the state of Massachusetts, serving nine terms in that post until his death in 1793. *Courtesy of the Bostonian Society/Old State House.*

had become the sixth state to ratify the Constitution of the United States, and was now a member of what everyone hoped would truly be a more perfect Union.

The announcement that the convention had voted in favor of ratification produced a wave of jubilation and good fellowship throughout Boston. Bells in public buildings and churches pealed out the good news, and for several days the town of Boston resounded to the noise of booming cannon-fire and other "demonstrations of joy." At the call of the local Committee of Tradesmen, large numbers of laborers, craftsmen, tradesmen, and mechanics showed up at nine o'clock the next morning in front of Faneuil Hall to begin a "Grand Procession" through the streets of Boston. There were bands of foresters with their axes, followed by yokes of oxen and clusters of horse-drawn harrows. Sowers, mowers, and winnowers marched along carrying hoes, spades, and scythes, while blacksmiths, shipwrights, rope-makers, painters, carvers, and riggers testified to the maritime character of the town. Midway in the procession came a large float of the good ship *Federal Constitution,* drawn by thirteen horses and followed by ship captains, sailors, and merchants. A little farther on came another float, the old ship of state *Old Confederation,* symbolically hauled up for repairs, with carpenters working on its crippled hull.

It was a gala parade that stopped every now and then in front of the house of some distinguished citizen of the town to give three cheers and fire a salute. As the marchers reached the vicinity of the Old State House about two o'clock, they halted and proclaimed that Long Lane, the site of the ratifying convention, would henceforth be called Federal Street. About four o'clock, the procession arrived back at its starting point in front of Faneuil Hall, where refreshments were liberally provided. Later that evening, the vessel *Old Confederation* was hauled up to Boston Common, officially declared to be "unfit for further service," and set afire. A huge bonfire lit up the night sky and brought the day's celebrations to what the spectators all agreed was a fitting conclusion.

While Boston was making the transition from the excitement of revolution to the stability of nationhood under a new Constitution, a new cluster of leaders took over the direction of state and local affairs. With the disappearance of British administrators and Tory bureaucrats, a political vacuum had been created that was quickly filled by a group of well-known Bostonians, who now moved up from levels of financial wealth and social influence to positions of political power and legislative prominence. After the war, for example, John

Hancock, one of the town's most successful merchants and entrepreneurs, became governor of the state from 1780 to 1793, except for the years 1785–1787, when James Bowdoin served two terms. Thomas Cushing, a close friend of Hancock and a former member of the town's Merchants Club, served as lieutenant-governor from 1780 to 1788. Samuel Adams, who had failed in a number of business ventures before the Revolution, found political fulfillment as lieutenant-governor from 1789 to 1793, and then as governor from 1794 to 1797, after Hancock's death. James Bowdoin, who was active in postrevolutionary politics, and served briefly as governor from 1785 to 1787, came from a distinctly mercantile background, as did Stephen Higginson and James Warren, who regularly opposed the Federalist policies of John Hancock. Elbridge Gerry had started out in the family shipping business on the North Shore before making politics his career, and Thomas Handasyd Perkins continued to pursue his profitable commercial enterprises while becoming active as a Federalist legislator in the postwar era.

A number of small-town lawyers of local repute, too, found the postwar years a time of unparalleled opportunity for moving up into positions of greater power and influence after British jurists left the scene. Josiah Quincy of Boston and Fisher Ames of Dedham found seats in the new U.S. Congress. Harrison Gray Otis, a young lawyer whose father had been ruined by the Revolution, now went on to political prominence in both the House and the Senate. Theophilus Parsons of Newburyport left his law practice in Boston to become Chief Justice of the Massachusetts Supreme Judicial Court. And John Adams, after serving as America's first minister to Great Britain, would shortly reach the pinnacle of success, first as vice-president, and then as president of the United States in 1796.

By the time the national elections had been held in the fall of 1788, and the new government of President George Washington was under way in the spring of 1789, a new political oligarchy had firmly established itself in power. In line with the orderly process of Federalism created by Alexander Hamilton at the national level, a new Federalist aristocracy in Boston was content to retain the class structure that had characterized its society over the past century and a half. Once Bostonians had driven out their British overlords and achieved national independence, they were satisfied that for all practical purposes the rebellion was over—their "revolution" was complete. Assuming that their colonial traditions—religious orthodoxy, social integrity, and political responsibility—would remain intact, they anticipated no further surprises. Hamilton's policy of government by "the wise, the well-born, and the good," combined with his stake-in-government principle that wedded the stability of the new nation to the prosperity of its financial leaders, was perfectly consistent with the views of local Federalists. Boston's new political leaders were satisfied that God was in His Heaven, and that all was right with His world—and with theirs.

BOOK TWO
Athens of America

Chapter

4

From Town to City

WITH the Revolution over, independence won, a new Constitution in place, and a federal aristocracy in charge of things, by the 1790s the town of Boston began to regain an air of confidence and assume a spirit of achievement. Already many of the town's streets had been named after such patriotic leaders as John Hancock, Benjamin Franklin, James Bowdoin, James Warren, and Thomas Cushing, while others were changed to more appropriate titles. King Street, for example, now became State Street, Queen Street was changed to Court Street, Long Lane had become Federal Street, and the wide road that ran through the main part of town across the Neck was now called Washington Street. Boston, it was quite clear, was becoming thoroughly Americanized.

Fortunately for Boston, economic conditions began to improve once political stability had been established. The period of runaway prices and foreign rivalry that had characterized the immediate postwar period proved only a temporary setback to the town's maritime prosperity. Yankee skippers found ways to evade British trade regulations and renew their valuable trade with the West Indies. The Caribbean Islands supplied large quantities of cocoa, sugar, tobacco, and molasses, so greatly in demand throughout the Bay State. In return,

Yankees supplied badly needed outlets for the codfish, whale oil, lumber, and rough manufactured goods of the entire New England region. One enterprising young man, Frederick Tudor, pioneered the business of shipping thousands of tons of ice annually from Boston to Charleston, Savannah, and New Orleans, and then on to the tropical countries of the West Indies and the Far East. For the first time in many years, money started to become available in large enough amounts to revive old industries, expand new ones, and adjust the balance of payments that had drained Massachusetts of almost all its specie.

As the town's economy began to revive during the late 1790s and early 1800s, local entrepreneurs began to branch out into more ambitious overseas activities. In addition to the valuable West Indies trade, Yankee whalers and fur traders found the eastern waters of South America a most lucrative source of commercial profits. When the outbreak of the Napoleonic wars between England and France in the early 1800s made a normal traffic with Europe too hazardous, many Americans opened up markets at Rio de Janeiro and along the River Plate for the exchange of such commodities as hides and lumber. More enterprising skippers made their way even farther down the South Atlantic, through the Straits of Magellan, and then up along the western shores of South America and into the waters of the Pacific to explore the rich China market.

By 1800, too, Boston vessels, loaded with copper, cloth, trinkets, and clothing of all sorts, were making regular voyages to the Columbia River, along what is now the Washington-Oregon border. After bargaining their wares with the Indians in exchange for otter skins and furs, they would sail across the Pacific, with frequent stops at the Hawaiian Islands and the Sandwich Islands, to finally dispose of their goods in China. Then they made their way home around the southern tip of Africa (there was no Suez Canal then) and across the stormy Atlantic with cargoes of Chinese teas, colorful silks, and delicate porcelains so much in demand by the well-to-do families back in Boston. The aromas of exotic spices wafted through parts of town, little monkeys became stylish as household pets, and new fabrics were available for personal adornment.

The growing prosperity of the town in the late 1790s and early 1800s was reflected in both the growth of its citizenry and the expansion of its living space. From an all-time low of six thousand during the period of British occupation, by 1790 the population of Boston had risen to eighteen thousand. In 1800 it was recorded at twenty-five thousand, and by 1810 it had gone well beyond thirty thousand—a fivefold increase in only thirty-five years. Considering the fact that the old town still looked like a small, half-inflated balloon attached

After the American Revolution was over and the new Constitution established, Bostonians returned to the sea in an effort to restore the town's badly shattered economy. During the early 1800s, Yankee skippers sought out more ambitious overseas activities, exploring the shores of South America, venturing out into the Pacific, and arriving at the ports of China. The growing prosperity of the town was reflected in a growing population that passed the thirty thousand mark in 1810. *Courtesy of the Bostonian Society/Old State House.*

to the mainland only by a thin stretch of mudflats, this remarkable increase forced a series of changes, not only to accommodate the rising numbers, but also to make up for the deteriorating conditions in the older parts of town. What had once been a small, pleasant, somewhat rustic colonial town was fast becoming an uncomfortably crowded and congested urban metropolis. A number of well-to-do merchants, businessmen, lawyers, and retired sea captains had already started to move away from the cluttered and unsightly district around the waterfront and the Town Dock. They were building new homes farther away in such areas as the South End and the West End, which soon became fashionable residential districts with substantial brick buildings and carefully cultivated gardens.

A young architect who was most instrumental in effecting many of the changes that came about during the late 1790s and early 1800s was Charles Bulfinch. Son of a prominent Boston physician and a graduate of the Boston Latin School and Harvard College, Bulfinch worked in a countinghouse before making a two-year tour of Europe. While in France, he was struck by the beauty of town planning in Paris, with its public parks and its tree-lined boulevards. In England, he was impressed by the work of Sir Christopher Wren in London, as well as the stylistic designs of the Adam brothers in the town of Bath. Returning to Boston in 1787, he began to apply his ideas to the architecture of his hometown in such an enthusiastic manner that he came close to transforming the whole tone and character of Boston almost single-handedly.

Young Bulfinch first made his mark by designing handsome mansions for well-known citizens who were anxious to move out of the old parts of town and settle in the open spaces of the West End. In 1792, he built a three-story brick house between Temple and Bowdoin Streets for his relative Joseph Coolidge; four years later, he built another three-story mansion at the corner of Cambridge and Lynde Streets for Harrison Gray Otis, a successful lawyer and real estate investor. In 1815, Bulfinch built a handsome set of double houses made of granite for Samuel Parkman between Cambridge and Green Streets, near Bowdoin Square. The young architect did not restrict himself to the West End area, however; he made his influence felt in other parts of the town as well. In 1804, for example, he designed a large four-story mansion for the wealthy merchant Thomas Amory on the corner of Park and Beacon Streets. The following year, he built a row of four uniform, attached townhouses along Park Street, with a long wrought-iron balcony under the second-floor dining room windows.

In addition to private homes, Charles Bulfinch also involved himself with several local commercial enterprises. In 1805, he designed a series of warehouses, wharves, and stores along the waterfront district in the area of Long Wharf at the end of State Street. The same year, he rebuilt and enlarged old Faneuil Hall, doubling the width of the building, adding a third story, and moving the cupola from the middle of the building to the front. In 1810, he built the new Boylston Market on the corner of Washington and Boylston Streets for the residents of the South End; the same year, he designed a large market building on the corner of Cambridge and Green Streets to accommodate residents of the West End.

Bulfinch also turned his hand to the construction of churches. After building the Hollis Street Church, with its two domed towers and domed ceiling, in 1800 he went on to design free of charge for Boston's first Catholic bishop, Jean Cheverus, the first Catholic church in New England. Located on Franklin Street, it was made of red brick with white Italian-classic details, and was completed in 1803 to serve the town's small Catholic population. In 1804, he built another church on Hanover Street in the North End. Made of red brick, with white pilasters on the façade and topped by a clock tower and a belfry, it was originally designed for the New North Religious Society but later passed into the hands of Catholics, who transformed it into St. Stephen's Church.

Of more long-range significance than Bulfinch's efforts at designing individual structures were his imaginative plans regarding real estate development and urban planning. In 1793, in an area behind Summer Street, Bulfinch set about building the first block of connected townhouses in a project called the Tontine Crescent.* The curved unit, five hundred feet long and containing sixteen houses, was erected on Franklin Street. The handsome houses were brick, painted gray, with recessed arches framing the first-floor windows and pilasters on the faces above. The crescent rose to a slightly higher level in the center and had a large arch that spanned a passageway, which passed entirely through the structure. In front of the crescent was a small tree-shaded park, enclosed by a wrought-iron fence, with a large urn in the center in honor of Benjamin Franklin.

While the Tontine Crescent was an exciting experiment in urban development, and perhaps a forerunner of the modern condominium, in the short run it proved to be a costly venture. Lack of investors in the project brought bankruptcy to Charles Bulfinch and his family, and even caused the young architect to spend some time in jail for debt. He was not discouraged, however, and continued to explore new undertakings. In 1810, for example, he built a row of attached townhouses, known as Colonnade Row, that extended along Tremont Street from West to Mason Streets, directly across from Boston Common. This imposing structure had a Doric colonnade, with a delicate wrought-iron balcony under the long dining room windows of the second floor, from which residents could look out across the Common to see the sun setting in the west.

But perhaps the most distinctive and permanent additions Bulfinch made to the Boston landscape were his design of the new State House and his architectural influence on the subsequent development of the whole Beacon

---

* The name Tontine was used because the money for the enterprise was to be raised by selling shares of stock to members of the public, who would later share in the profits from the sale of the homes. Lorenzo Tonti, an Italian banker, gave his name to this kind of arrangement, which he introduced in France in the seventeenth century.

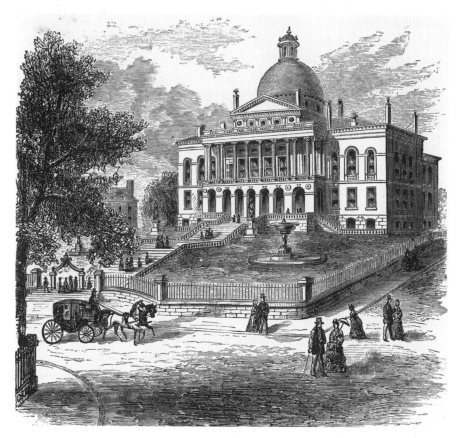

Once free of British rule, Bostonians wanted their own seat of government. Charles Bulfinch, a young Boston architect, was commissioned to design and construct a new State House on the crest of Beacon Hill. This new structure helped stimulate a wave of housing construction that created an entirely new and fashionable residential district for many of Boston's more prosperous families in the center of the town. *Courtesy of the Bostonian Society/Old State House.*

Hill area. Bulfinch had sketched designs for a new state capitol as early as 1787— only four years after America had won its independence from Great Britain. After the war, Bostonians continued to use the old provincial Town House for the conduct of state business, but it was clear that they wanted a new state house of their own, not one to which memories of British authority were still painfully attached. In 1795, two years after John Hancock's death, the town purchased Hancock's pastureland on the slope of Beacon Hill as the site for a new state office building. Charles Bulfinch, already well known for the houses he had built for prominent merchants, was selected as the appropriate architect for the project. In 1798 he completed his new State House, providing the town with an impressive redbrick building with white marble trim, a long flight of stone steps, and an imposing golden dome that would eventually become a distinctive landmark of the city.

News that the new capitol would be constructed on the crest of Beacon Hill immediately produced other changes in the rustic surroundings of nearby Park Street and Tremont Street, where hay carts rumbled and cattle still grazed. Within a dozen years, the whole area was in the midst of rapid development, transforming the old Puritan town of wood and thatch into a new Federal-style capital of stone and granite. One particularly dramatic change came when a group of investors, calling themselves the Mount Vernon Proprietors, bought up the extensive Beacon Hill farmlands belonging to the well-known portrait painter John Singleton Copley, who had gone off to England during the Revolution. Using that parcel of land, they began to transform the southwest slope of the hill into a new residential district. Hilly pastureland that had not been especially valuable until the new State House was built now became prime real estate. After laying out a system of streets to accommodate blocks of townhouses, in the summer of 1799 the Proprietors lopped off fifty or sixty feet from the top of Mount Vernon with the use of small gravity cars, which dumped the fill from the top of the hill into the waters at the foot of Charles Street. This made more usable land for the Proprietors at the top, created new property for the town at the bottom, and provided an enjoyable pastime for spectators who gathered regularly to watch the operations.

As the houses began to go up in the new Beacon Hill development, the architectural influence of Charles Bulfinch once again became apparent. Earlier houses had been built by some of the Mount Vernon Proprietors for their own use, and probably to stimulate further construction in the neighborhood as well. Between 1806 and 1812, fifteen houses were built on the old Copley property, giving the new area a distinctive atmosphere. One of the first of these houses was the second mansion designed by Bulfinch, in 1802, for Harrison Gray Otis—a brick house with white classical trim—on what is now Mount Vernon Street. Four years later, Bulfinch designed a third mansion for the Otis family at 45 Beacon Street, a four-story brick house with white trim, on the slope of Beacon Hill overlooking the Common. In addition to providing a mansion for Stephen Higginson, Jr., at 87 Mount Vernon Street, Bulfinch also constructed several townhouses on Chestnut Street, with brick stables in the rear.

Besides Bulfinch, there were several other architects who contributed to the changing character of the town. Asher Benjamin, for example, was another well-known Federalist architect who, like Bulfinch, had been influenced by the classical style of late Georgian England. He worked first in western Massachusetts, but lived and worked in Boston from 1803 until his death in 1845. Benjamin added to the new buildings going up in the West End with his construction in 1809 of the West Church on Cambridge Street. This was a lovely Federal-style church, constructed of red brick, that had a triple portal and a belfry that terminated in a dome topped by a weather vane. Not too far away, Benjamin built another church, on lower Mount Vernon Street at the corner of Charles Street—the Charles Street Meeting House. This was also a redbrick structure with arched doorways, a belfry, a cupola, a dome, and a weather vane. One of the most distinctive churches erected at this time was the work of Peter Banner, an Englishman who worked in Boston from 1806 to 1828. This was the Park Street Church, constructed in 1809 on the corner of Park and Tremont Streets, next to the Old Granary Burying Ground on one side, and overlooking Boston Common on the other. The graceful white steeple of this Congregational church quickly became a landmark of the new residential area of the town, and a permanent feature of Boston's architectural renaissance on the western side of Tremont Street.

These new private residences, public buildings, marketplaces, warehouses, townhouses, and churches not only provided the town with new, bright, modern, and substantial structures, but they also helped emphasize the fact that the center of gravity in the town had shifted perceptively. Before the Revolutionary War, the political, financial, and religious focus of the town had centered on the area bounded by the waterfront, the market district, Faneuil Hall, the Old South Meeting House, and the Old State House. By the early 1800s, however, the center of power was already beginning to move across Tremont Street to Park Street, Beacon Hill, and the new State House. Whether this would be a permanent change, or only a temporary fluctuation, only time would tell.

Members of Boston's Federalist aristocracy may have been pleased with their improving financial status and delighted with the physical improvements taking place in their town, but they were greatly disturbed about the political changes taking place in the nation's capital. In November 1800, Thomas Jefferson and his Democratic-Republican supporters defeated John Adams of

Massachusetts and the members of the conservative Federalist party. The results of this political turnover had devastating effects on the immediate mood and the future prospects of the Boston oligarchy. Before 1800, Massachusetts had been in the forefront of American affairs—articulating the defiance, organizing the rebellion, fighting the Revolution, forming the Confederation, designing the Constitution, implementing the new Federal republic. After 1800, however, it quickly became evident that the Bay State was having much less influence on national policies at home or abroad. Massachusetts congressmen spoke out regularly in opposition to Jefferson's restrictive fiscal policies, opposed his purchase of the Louisiana territory in 1803, condemned his ill-advised Embargo of 1807 that put an end to overseas shipping, and took a strong public stand against his foreign policy measures that they feared would eventually lead to war. But their objections were regularly voted down by Republican supporters from the South and the West, or scornfully rejected out of hand. After 1800, with the single exception of John Quincy Adams, no Bay State figure would play an influential role on the national scene until Daniel Webster emerged as a prominent Washington statesman a quarter of a century later.

Even worse than the states-rights political agenda of the new Jefferson Democrats in Washington were the social and economic principles enunciated by the Virginia leader, which conservatives believed would bring ruin to the Federal establishment. Federalists feared that Jefferson would surely dismantle Alexander Hamilton's centralized authority and orderly political structure, and hand power back to the states and to the masses of the people. Jefferson's strong belief in the superiority of yeoman farmers and the values of the agrarian way of life would undoubtedly cause commerce to suffer, banks to fail, and property values to tumble. The Virginian's sympathy for revolutionary France and its bloodthirsty leaders might well involve the United States in a war with Great Britain. What were regarded as his "atheistic" views, his liberal political attitudes, and his "radical" philosophies, drawn in great part from suspiciously foreign and decidedly "alien" sources, caused Boston Federalists to bemoan the loss of all moral standards and despair of the future of the republic. To most Federalists, as one historian put it, Thomas Jefferson was "the political devil incarnate."

Already, anxious conservatives could see the unsettling results of liberal ideas and secular philosophies in the changing religious trends taking place within the Bay State. Old Calvinistic views concerning the vengeance of God, the depravity of man, and the salvation of none but the "elect" had not been able to keep pace with the democratic spirit of the nation and the natural optimism of people who had carved a civilization out of the wilderness and then secured their own independence. Americans were extremely proud of what they had accomplished and could no longer conceive of themselves as depraved sinners, doomed to eternal damnation by a vengeful God. Surely in the new American Republic there must be a more enlightened road to salvation for everyone. Without questioning either the existence of the Almighty or the authority of the Bible, a new religious group called the Unitarians had begun to attract attention as they placed greater emphasis on the beneficence of God, the innate goodness of man, and the availability of salvation to all souls. At a time, too, when Newtonian science was having a significant impact on the thinking of intelligent men and women, the Unitarians accepted the importance of human reason and conceived of a truly Godly community that would operate in a rational, orderly manner in accordance with the natural laws designed by the Almighty.

Some indication of the speed with which Unitarianism took hold can be seen in the fact that by the early 1800s, nearly all Congregational pulpits in and around Boston had been taken over by Unitarian preachers. Nathaniel Frothingham was at the First Church; John Gorham Palfrey, historian and future Dexter Professor of Sacred Literature, served at the Brattle Street Unitarian Church. Francis Parkman held forth at the New North; the eloquent William Ellery Channing enunciated his gospel of the "adoration of goodness" at the Federal Street Church. When Henry Ware, who preached at the Second Church, was named Hollis Professor of Divinity at Harvard College, it was clear that the preeminence of Congregationalism as an intellectual and theological force was a thing of the past. At this point, many old-line Federalists, most of them Harvard graduates, withdrew in disgust from active political involvement. Convinced that the godless were in the ascendancy, and that the nation was doomed beyond all hope of redemption, a number of them retired to the seclusion of their mansions to read the classics, cultivate their roses, and reflect on the folly of mankind.

The worst fears of the New England Federalists were realized on June 18, 1812, when, at the urging of Jefferson's successor, President James Madison, both houses of Congress voted in favor of war against Great Britain. With the start of the War of 1812, political activity in the Northeast came alive once again and took on new vehemence in its attacks on the Republican administration. Federalist leaders throughout New England publicly opposed what they contemptuously called "Jimmy Madison's War" from the very start. They refused to supply either men or money for a conflict they considered unjust and immoral. The lower house of the Massachusetts General Court issued an address urging the people of America to organize a new peace party and "let all other party distinctions vanish." Governor Caleb Strong followed up by proclaiming a public fast in order to atone for a declaration of war "against a nation from which we are descended, and which for many generations has been the bulwark of the religion we profess." Most of the old Boston families supported the governor's opposition, and members of the Harvard Corporation—President Kirkland and Treasurer Davis, together with fellows Lathrop, Lowell, Phillips, Gore, and Chauncy—announced themselves in agreement with the "ANTI-WAR POSITION" of the Federalist party.

There were other New Englanders, however, who felt that words alone were not enough to head off disaster. In Massachusetts, a group of determined Federalists, headed by Senator Timothy Pickering of Salem and known as the Essex Junto, decided that the only recourse was for Federalists to secede from the Union and form a separate "Northern Confederacy" made up of New York, New Jersey, Pennsylvania, and the New England states. However, this extreme solution found little support among most rank-and-file members of the Federalist party, who preferred to remain in the Union and work through established political channels. But with the continued victories of British men-of-war on the high seas, the success of the British naval blockade along the Atlantic seacoast, and the shocking attack on the nation's capital in late August 1814, Federalists were finally persuaded to take more drastic action. On December 15, 1814, the Massachusetts legislature called for a convention of the New England states at Hartford, Connecticut, to protest the continuation of the war and to consider actions against the Madison administration. For three weeks, delegates at this Hartford Convention debated whether to secede from the Union or make a separate peace with Great Britain. Although moderates finally overruled those who wanted secession, they decided to present the Madison administration with a series of constitutional amendments designed to end the war, restore the dominance of New England, and advance its commercial interests. Their recommendations included the repeal of the three-fifths compromise and a requirement that a two-thirds majority in Congress would be necessary to declare war, restrict foreign trade, and admit new states to the Union.

Just as the delegates from the Hartford Convention reached Washington, D.C., to present their proposals to the administration, however, they learned that the war had ended. News had just arrived that on January 8, 1815, General Andrew Jackson and his frontier troops had inflicted a disastrous defeat on the British forces at the Battle of New Orleans. This was followed by reports that a peace treaty between the United States and Great Britain had been concluded two weeks earlier (December 24, 1814) at the Belgian town of Ghent. President Madison paid no attention to the malcontents from New England, who were regarded with derision, and the entire country now turned against the Federalist party, which was labeled "the party of treason" because of the way in which it refused to assist the nation in its hour of peril. From this point on, it was difficult for any New Englander to admit to being a card-carrying member of a political party that had worked so openly against the national government, and that had refused to supply money or men for the national defense. Although there would always be a handful of crusty old Bostonians who would insist to their dying day that they were dyed-in-the-wool Federalists, for all practical purposes the party was dead. Officially, the old Federalist party passed into obscurity, and an important phase of Boston history came to an abrupt, and some would have said an ignominious, end.

The collapse of the Federalist party and the disappearance of the old Puritan ideology were not the only important changes to come about in Boston during the early 1800s. The Federalists' traditional sources of economic power and financial prosperity—shipping and commerce—were also drastically altered by America's second war with Great Britain. During the course of the war, enemy blockading squadrons swept the seas clean of American shipping, so that by 1813 Boston Harbor was clogged with hundreds of empty vessels, swinging idly on their anchor chains with no place to go. Now that maritime activities were no longer profitable sources of investment, Yankee merchants were forced to look elsewhere for new enterprises in which to invest the capital they refused to give the government to fight the war.

The financial salvation of New England proved to be not in wooden hulls or captains' cabins, but rather in hastily constructed textile factories. Yankees quickly diverted their idle capital into manufacturing, instead of into mercantile enterprises that no longer paid dividends. The long period of embargoes and sinkings had forced interior sections of the country to go so long without manufactured goods that they were crying out for commodities at any price. Yankee enterprise was only too happy to respond. If there was a demand, New England would furnish the supplies. This was especially true with regard to the production of cotton textiles with which New Englanders had been experimenting in recent years. In spite of some false starts and early setbacks, the cotton textile industry expanded rapidly during the war years, most of it backed by Boston money and sparked by Yankee ingenuity.

What started as a temporary wartime expedient turned into a permanent addition to the Bay State economy once the War of 1812 was over. The introduction of the power loom by Francis Cabot Lowell at his Waltham plant in 1810 provided the means for increasing the production of woven fabrics, as well as bringing together under one roof all the processes of spinning and weaving. In 1821, Francis Lowell, Nathan Appleton, and Patrick Tracy Jackson moved out from Waltham and established new plants about forty miles north of Boston, where powerful falls were located along the Merrimack River. Here they set up a distinctive type of company-town called Lowell, which included boardinghouses for the workers and elaborate supervision of the young women (the "Mill Girls") who came from nearby farms to work in the factories.

The War of 1812 and the subsequent British naval blockade encouraged the growth of the textile industry when New England shipping went into serious decline. The early textile mills in Waltham and later in Lowell operated by water power and depended upon the labor of young women, known as the "Mill Girls," who came from neighboring farms to work in the factories. *Courtesy of the Boston Public Library, Print Department.*

The acceptance of manufacturing as a permanent feature of the American economy was accomplished not only because of the profits it generated, but also because of its significance to the national security. Letting our workshops "remain in Europe," as Thomas Jefferson had argued for so long, sounded wonderful—as long as there was peace. Once the country found itself at war for a second time with a major European power like Great Britain, however, it was evident that the United States needed its own manufacturing system to provide the goods necessary to defend itself. The War of 1812 had been a frightening demonstration of how national security was directly related to an independent industrial system. Even Jefferson was forced to admit, somewhat grudgingly, that "manufactures are now necessary to our independence as well as to our comfort."

The new factory system, which fast expanded from a small, localized enterprise in the early 1800s to a multimillion-dollar industry by the 1830s, also helped create a new aristocracy of wealth and power. Many of the old mercantile families of Boston had grown rich on the commercial profits of Europe and the Far East. They had built spacious mansions in Boston, provided their wives and daughters with the latest fashions from London and Paris, and for generations had sent their sons to sea at an early age to learn the family business. Now, the members of this "codfish aristocracy" began to merge with the new manufacturers of cotton cloth and fancy fabrics, many of whom had moved into Boston from other areas of New England. Nathan Appleton, for example, had originally come down from New Hampshire as a merchant before going into textiles. Two brothers, Amos and Abbott Lawrence, had moved in from Middlesex County to set up in the import-export business before engaging in manufacturing. Every day, new families were moving in from Salem, Newburyport, Worcester, and New Bedford to blend their social and economic fortunes with those of the Boston group in what Samuel Eliot Morison has described as a marriage between "the wharf and the waterfall." The Lowells, already associated with such prominent merchant families as the Cabots, the Higginsons, and the Russells, now linked up with the Jacksons through the marriage of Francis C. Lowell to Hannah Jackson, sister of Patrick Tracy Jackson; John Amory's son, Augustus, married Abbott Lawrence's daughter, Katherine; and in 1842 Abbott's nephew, Amos Adams Lawrence, married Sarah Elizabeth Appleton, the niece of Nathan Appleton.

Not only were the Lowells, the Lawrences, and the Appletons partners in industry and colleagues in business, but they further integrated their interests through the powerful agency of kinship and marriage. It is generally agreed that it was Oliver Wendell Holmes who first applied the term "Brahmins" to the members of this new Boston aristocracy. In his novel *Elsie Venner*, Holmes wrote of a young Bostonian: "He comes of the Brahmin caste of New England. This is the harmless, inoffensive, untitled aristocracy." Expanding upon the description even further, Holmes painted a fascinating portrait of the "Boston Brahmins" with their "houses by Bulfinch, their monopoly of Beacon Street, their ancestral portraits and Chinese porcelains, humanitarianism, Unitarian faith in the march of the mind, Yankee shrewdness, and New England exclusiveness." Like the priestly Brahmin class of the ancient Hindus, who performed the sacred rites and set the moral standards, the new leaders of Boston society emerged as the self-styled Brahmins of a modern caste system in which they were clearly and indisputably the superior force.

One practical result of this revival of Boston's fortunes, and especially this influx of new young blood into old Yankee veins, was a renewed sense of obligation on the part of older families to the welfare of "their" town, and a new determination to participate actively once again in local political affairs. Just because the rest of the nation had lost its bearings and lowered its standards was no reason that Boston could not be saved, if members of the "better class" took over their responsibilities and regained positions of social and political leadership in the community. Once they had survived the initial shock of Jeffersonianism, Unitarianism, and Industrialism, the old families discovered that things had not turned out quite as badly as they had anticipated. They found ways of acclimating themselves to the new realities of Boston life, without losing their traditional characteristics.

They saw that manufacturing, for example, did not necessarily spell the end of commerce and shipping—indeed, it could actually be seen as a definite asset. By diversifying their investments and buying into new textile companies, old mercantile families found that they could not only use their commercial outlets for marketing their own manufactured goods, but they could also use the profits from their industrial activities to tide over their commercial enterprises when times were slow. Indeed, as Robert Dalzell observed in *The Enterprising Elite*, many Boston merchants found that manufacturing offered a much more steady income than the uncertainties of trade, as well as more time and leisure to pursue a political career, to patronize the arts, or to engage in all sorts of philanthropic and humanitarian enterprises.

Bostonians also found that the end of Congregationalism did not necessarily mean the end of moral principles or ethical standards. The new and more liberal theology of Unitarianism was soon accepted as a happy medium between the old hellfire-and-brimstone approach of Calvinism, and the more science-oriented views of deists who saw no need of organized religion at all. After a while, Unitarianism was regarded as the best of two worlds—a religion that accepted the lessons of scientific reason, while still acknowledging the traditions of Boston's Puritan religious heritage. Rather than continuing to fight against the new "Boston religion" any longer, the upper classes of the town decided to accept it as a comfortable and rational approach to the Christian message.

In much the same spirit, rather than continuing to engage in a life-and-death struggle against the "new politics" of Jeffersonian democracy and popular government, a younger generation of Federalists, such as Harrison Gray Otis and Josiah Quincy, decided to adopt a more realistic attitude and appeal to the mass electorate in the new democratic fashion. Although there is little doubt that they still believed in the leadership of "the wise, the well-born, and the good," they had come to accept universal suffrage as regrettable but inevitable. They concentrated their efforts, therefore, on convincing lower- and middle-class voters that the upper classes, with their high ideals, exalted virtues, and substantial incomes, could contribute far more to the social and economic well-being of the working people of the town than the Johnny-come-lately Jeffersonian Democrats, who were seeking only political power and financial profit.

In contrast to their elders, many of whom still refused to engage in the distasteful give-and-take of political campaigning (a proper Bostonian did not "run" for public office—he "offered himself" for the position), the younger breed of Federalists showed a keen appreciation for the importance of party politics, the power of the popular vote, and the influence of public opinion. Pitching their appeals to the Boston's working class, the young Federalists emphasized the responsibility of the "happy and respectable classes" to watch over those laws that affected "the less prosperous portions of the community." Their obvious desire for political control of Boston carried with it a sense of responsibility for the prosperity of the town and the welfare of its less fortunate classes—a sort of moral stewardship, a form of *noblesse oblige*—that would continue to be an integral part of Boston's political heritage. This arrangement not only would help the upper classes stay in power, but would condition the lower classes to emulate the moral, social, and political values of the Brahmins, and thus become an unconscious part of the tradition itself. Conservative leaders might not be able to control national politics and save the people in the rest of the country from "democratic" claptrap and egalitarian nonsense, but they could still fight to keep Boston a model of excellence—their cherished "City upon a Hill."

As part of their new effort to position themselves at the head of local government, the young Federalists actively supported what had been for many years an on-and-off movement to change Boston from a town to a city. It had become increasingly obvious that with an expanding economic structure and a rising population, the old town-meeting system was no longer capable of dealing with the demands of what was clearly a growing urban center. Old buildings needed to be razed and new ones erected. The lighting and paving of streets required municipal attention, and a fresh-water supply was desperately called for, as was a more adequate system for cleaning the streets and disposing of garbage. Even more important, the recent growth in Boston's population pointed up the serious lack of adequate police and fire protection for the general public.

During the early 1800s, Boston had a total of twenty-four constables who served as "Captains of the Watch," supervising the activities of the town's "watchmen." All males over eighteen years of age were required to serve as watchmen to patrol the streets from ten o'clock at night until sunrise, to keep an eye out for fires and to see that good order was maintained. Under the direction of the constables, thirty-six watchmen worked each night in two shifts of eighteen men each, operating out of four watch stations in different parts of the town. While the system looked effective on paper, in actual practice it left much to be desired. Most of the watchmen were young men from the lower classes of the town who needed part-time jobs. Armed only with a rattle for summoning help and a long hook that was practically useless for collaring troublemakers, they did not go out of their way to look for danger on a job that paid only fifty cents a night. The responsibility of the watchmen was simply to report infractions of the law—not to look for trouble, detect crime, or seek out violent situations.

The conditions of fire prevention in the town were not much better. After a disastrous fire in 1711, Boston had been divided into several fire districts, administered by officers, called "Firewards," who were given special badges and a five-foot-long red staff topped with a brass spire. These men headed up groups of several hundred young residents who enrolled in volunteer fire companies, elected their own officers, designed their own uniforms, held an annual supper, and became a powerful political force in the town. In addition to performing their civic duty, many volunteers were also motivated by the cash prizes regularly awarded to the first company to appear at a fire, as well as by the opportunities for slipping into burning buildings and walking off with valuable loot. Not only were these colorful volunteer fire companies highly inefficient, they were also likely to turn the scene of a fire into an occasion for a bloody brawl with rival volunteer companies. Clearly, steps had to be taken to change these haphazard arrangements as soon as possible. The old town-meeting system, however, seemed incapable of addressing any of these urban challenges.

Despite bitter and highly emotional arguments against changing the hallowed name of the "Towne of Boston," which had produced "our glorious revolution" and which had seen its narrow streets "died with blood," the vote in favor of incorporation passed on January 7, 1822. On February 23, Governor John Brooks officially approved "an act establishing the City of Boston." This act provided that the administration of all the "fiscal, prudential, and municipal concerns" of the city be vested in "one principal officer" called the Mayor, a committee of eight persons called the Board of Aldermen, and a council of forty-eight persons called the Common Council. A city seal, showing a view of the city from South Boston point, was adopted, as was a motto from the Book of Kings: "*Sit Deus nobiscum sicut fuit cum patribus nostris.*" Adapted for the city seal, the motto reads: "*Sicut Patribus Sit Deus Nobis.*"

Once the formalities were out of the way, the city turned to the task of electing its first mayor. At that point, the political influence of the "new" Federalists became immediately evident. One branch of the local Federalist leadership put up fifty-seven-year-old Harrison Gray Otis as its candidate, while the "Middling Classes" of the town favored the more popular fifty-year-old Josiah Quincy. When neither side could claim the required majority, the voters settled on John Phillips, a graduate of Harvard College and a member of an old Boston mercantile family. After Phillips completed his single year in office, Josiah Quincy secured the nomination and seized the reins of government with a vigor and determination that eventually won him the title of the "Great Mayor." Born in Braintree into a distinguished family, Quincy graduated from Harvard in 1790 and served in Washington, D.C., as a Federalist congressman from 1805 to 1813. After the War of 1812, he returned to Boston, served in the Massachusetts senate from 1813 to 1820, and then moved to a single term in the lower house before taking a seat on the Boston municipal bench. Elected as mayor to six consecutive one-year terms, serving from 1823 to 1828, Quincy established a program of urban planning and city development that few mayors have been able to duplicate.

In Josiah Quincy's day, Boston was still an impressive city to look at—especially coming into the harbor by ship. The great wharves that stretched far out into the water were surmounted by large four-story brick storehouses. All were uniform in height, with streets on either side for unloading the commercial cargoes that came into the city from all parts of the world. The visitor's eyes would be immediately attracted to the lofty dome of the new State House high atop Beacon Hill, and then be drawn to the irregular cluster of church spires that rose above the pointed gables and jutting chimney tops. The cupola of Faneuil Hall, the outline of the Old State House, and the peaks of a dozen other public buildings, together with the graceful white steeples of the numerous churches scattered throughout the city, gave the low-lying seaport town an appearance of height and spaciousness.

Once ashore, however, closer inspection would reveal that the passage of time had taken its toll on this venerable town, now more than two centuries old. There were, to be sure, many charming reminders of the colonial past—along the tree-lined avenues of Pearl Street, High Street, and Summer Street, where handsome residences were landscaped with colorful bushes and lovely gardens. With the reclaiming of the land around the new State House, blocks of elegant mansions had gone up on the north side of Beacon Street, and along Tremont Street the attractive houses of Colonnade Row provided attractive quarters for the city's well-to-do merchants and businessmen.

Within the heart of the old city itself, however, things had deteriorated over the years. With a total population of nearly forty-three thousand—already twenty-five thousand more than in 1790—Boston's limited confines were showing the strains. Its meandering streets had always been notoriously crooked and narrow, but now they were hedged in by four- and five-story houses that blocked out the sunlight and obscured the view. Pedestrians were in constant danger of being knocked down by stagecoaches, or bowled over by droves of pigs being hustled to market. On "high market days," the congested Faneuil Hall market district was a compressed, discordant mass of people, with butchers cutting their meat along the first floor of the hall itself, vendors of fruits and vegetables lined up under wooden sheds along the outside walls, and fishmongers stationed behind long wooden benches with large tubs full of all kinds of seafood.

One of the most notable achievements of Mayor Josiah Quincy was the construction of a new market district directly behind Faneuil Hall. A large granite market house, executed by Alexander Parris in the Greek Revival style, was flanked by four-story granite warehouses that stored incoming cargo from all parts of the world. *Courtesy of the Boston Public Library, Print Department.*

What was new about this market scene—an integral part of Boston's life for generations—was the abominable stench that rose above it all. Not only were there the oily smells from the docks, the briny tang of salt water, and the sickening odor of the mudflats at low tide, but there was also the repulsive reek of uncollected street refuse and untended garbage. To make matters worse, the city's sewage system emptied out into the Town Dock, which was located directly behind Faneuil Hall. This body of water became the stagnant receptacle for every sort of filth, rubbish, and waste. Indeed, a note in the log of one Boston constable for April 1805 complained: "The Mill Pond is a nuisance, full of putrid fish and dead dogs and cats." But the stench of the city was not confined to the market district. All through the inner parts of the city, the obvious lack of any effective system for cleaning the streets had produced piles of rubbish, garbage, "house dirt," and "street dirt" that went uncollected for long periods of time. Open privies, contaminated wells, and pools of rancid water created such a dreadful condition that many of the more prosperous residents had given up on any possibility of saving the old part of the city and were already moving into the West End or across Tremont Street into the Beacon Hill area.

Almost as soon as Josiah Quincy was sworn into office as Boston's second mayor, he announced his determination to take action against this "generated pestilence." Rich people, he observed in his inaugural address, could always move out of town during the hot summer months and seek refuge in "purer atmospheres." Poor people, on the other hand, were forced to remain in the city and inhale the "noxious effluvia." In a dramatic demonstration of how an upper-class Federalist mayor could work for the welfare of the "less prosperous" classes of the city, Quincy set to work rescuing the oldest part of the city from decay and ruin. Refusing to be handcuffed by the obstructionist tactics of old town board members who objected to the new mayor stepping on their administrative toes, Josiah Quincy took whatever municipal powers he needed to accomplish his purposes. By appointing himself chairman *ex officio* of all executive committees, he assumed a controlling voice in all municipal activities and decisions. By appointing professional administrators who reported to him personally, he established a system of direct accountability. Less than two weeks after taking office, for example, he appointed Benjamin Pollard, a Harvard graduate and a practicing lawyer, as city marshal. In addition to his duties as chief police officer, Pollard was also authorized by Mayor Quincy to act as the city's chief health officer.

Always, however, Josiah Quincy made it evident that he was in charge of things. He customarily conducted tours of inspection on horseback at five o'clock in the morning, and on one occasion, during the summer of 1825, he led a posse of burly truckmen into one of the city's scandalous red-light districts to break up disturbances that had been going on for a week. In a remarkably short time, the new mayor was having the streets cleaned by teams of sweepers, had the refuse collected on a regular basis, and brought the sewers under public control. By the end of his first year in office, he could boast of having collected six thousand tons of street dirt (he had it weighed!), making Boston reputedly one of the healthiest and safest cities in the United States.

A definite spirit of civic reform was in the air in Boston during the mid-1830s, directed by members of the "happy and respectable classes" who obviously saw themselves as high-minded and responsible stewards of the city. Members of old Boston families, like Josiah Quincy, were intent on using their powers of political leadership to refashion and renew the urban community in which they lived—not only for themselves, but also for all the people of the community. This reform impulse, however, was destined to go far beyond physical concerns and material benefits of the city, gradually influencing the moral and intellectual standards by which the ordinary people of Boston lived and the heights to which they might eventually aspire.

Chapter

5

The Reform Impulse

I T IS easy to ascribe the extensive physical changes and material improvements that took place in the city of Boston during the late 1820s to the extraordinary energies of a single individual like Josiah Quincy. In many ways, however, this desire for reform, this striving for perfection, was symptomatic of a much broader social commitment on the part of the city's Brahmin aristocracy. There had always been, of course, the regular philanthropic support for good and noble causes—generous contributions to Harvard College, to the Massachusetts Historical Society, to Massachusetts General Hospital, to the Boston Athenaeum, to the building of the Bunker Hill monument, to the restoration of George Washington's home at Mount Vernon. For the most part, however, these acts of generosity were directed toward projects with which the prosperous classes themselves were concerned.

What was striking about events in the late 1820s and early 1830s, however, was that conservative Bostonians extended their reform activities to include humanitarian concerns that affected the less fortunate members of the community. Assistance for the poor and homeless of the city, for example, was one area of concern that attracted the attention of Mayor Quincy and his associates. They were concerned about what they regarded as the ineffective methods used by old "Overseers of the Poor" and now wanted to handle the problem at the municipal level in a much more equitable and efficient manner. If the inspiration for the reform impulse in Boston came out of the Protestant ideal of perfectionism, its newer approaches reflected the rational spirit of the Enlightenment era. City authorities were content to extend municipal charity to those they termed the "impotent poor"—infants, the elderly, the sick, and the disabled. They strenuously objected, however, to the "able poor"—persons who were apparently able-bodied and capable of doing manual labor—getting free handouts without doing any work. When Mayor Quincy sold off the old Almshouse in March 1825, therefore, he replaced it with a new building he called, appropriately enough, the House of Industry. At this location, all able-bodied recipients of public relief would be required to work for their keep. In this way, Quincy boasted, he could separate the "respectable and honest poor" from the "idle and vicious" elements of the community.

In seeking other ways to improve the city, community leaders were also concerned about the increase in intemperate drinking, especially its influence on the growth of crime and pauperism among the poorer classes. After 1824, with the election of Dr. John Collins Warren as president, the Massachusetts Society for the Suppression of Intemperance became much more active. Its members worked with Mayor Quincy and the aldermen to prohibit the sale of alcoholic beverages in all theaters and public places. Dr. Warren also persuaded the Massachusetts Medical Society to adopt resolutions urging all doctors to refrain from prescribing alcoholic medications whenever possible. When the powerful sermons of the Reverend Lyman Beecher helped awaken public conscience to the moral implications of intemperate drinking, the movement became more militant and turned to total abstinence in an effort to conquer the immoral temptations of the "Demon Rum." In 1833, various elements of the crusade for "teetotalism" came together in what became known as the Massachusetts Temperance Society.

Prison reform was still another humanitarian effort that drew heavy support from the upper classes of the city. Mayor Quincy was appalled when he saw nearly four hundred persons crammed into the thirty-two-room county jail at Leverett Street, and he agitated strongly for immediate change. Members of the Boston Prison Discipline Society, formed in 1825 by the Reverend Louis Dwight, took the lead in denouncing the deplorable conditions they found in the old state prison in Charlestown. Largely as a result of the efforts of these upper-class men and women, in 1826 the state legislature authorized the construction of a new prison along the more humane lines of New York's Auburn system. Individual cells now separated hardened criminals from first offenders, and provisions were made for inmates to learn new occupations and to engage in recreational activities.

In exploring other ways by which criminals could be rehabilitated, officials agreed that henceforth the treatment of juvenile offenders would take place at a different location. While fully convinced that society had the obligation to punish young people for criminal offenses, Josiah Quincy also felt that society had no right to confine young people to a "moral pest house, out of which nothing good can ever issue." In 1828, therefore, following the strong urging of the mayor, a new House of Reformation was constructed on the nearby South Boston peninsula. Here, at what later would be called the Reform School, juvenile offenders were not only separated from older and more hardened criminals, but they were also provided with work training for their eventual rehabilitation.

Even the question of slavery caused many Brahmins to have bouts of conscience during the 1820s and 1830s. A number of prominent Bostonians became active in the work of the American Colonization Society, which proposed purchasing slaves to free and resettle them in Africa. Many businessmen regarded the colonization plan as a sensible and highly rational solution that would eventually remove all blacks and bring an eventual end to slavery.*

In these and in many other philanthropic and humanitarian enterprises, the Brahmins displayed a consistent belief that it was their moral obligation to use their time, talents, and money for the benefits of all the citizens of the city, poor as well as rich. Although wedded to tradition, Brahmins were by no means opposed to progress. And if progress could come about in a gradual manner, directed by the "better classes," without any serious threat to the existing order, then surely Boston could continue to be a model of excellence. Already they felt that their civic achievements—a more effective police department, a better fire department, urban renewal, cleaner streets, aid for the poor, temperance programs, more humane prisons—guaranteed a healthy, law-abiding city; a gradual improvement in the lot of the "less fortunate" classes; and an upgrading of the whole moral tone of the community.

There were other Bostonians, however, who felt that there had to be an even more ambitious effort to raise the overall cultural and intellectual tone of

---

* Many white people believed that colonization would also help Christianize the "dark continent" by sending back to Africa former slaves who had been exposed to Christianity in America.

the city, an effort that would go beyond modernizing its politics and cleaning its streets. If the town of Boston had now become a city, then it must be a great city—not only in the stability of its political institutions and the prosperity of its commercial activities, but also in the brilliance of its intellects and the creativity of its artists. Nothing would do but for Boston to become not merely the "Athens" of America but, indeed, as Dr. Oliver Wendell Holmes would have it, the "Hub" of the entire universe.

The dream of universal renown for Boston in the world of letters suddenly became a reality as the region experienced one of the most creative periods in all of American literature. Out of Puritan New England's "stern and rockbound" environment came a number of artists who turned the rugged terrain into a veritable garden of delights. During what Van Wyck Brooks has aptly called "The Flowering of New England," those who had complained that Americans had contributed little to the world of letters now had more literary works than they had ever imagined. Boston writers soon won international distinction with a flood of works epitomizing the optimistic and progressive spirit of the day. It is significant that most literary works of the period had certain features in common: they emphasized the theme of "America," accentuated the democratic spirit, and placed great store in the innate goodness of all people and their natural ability to rise to great heights. In almost every respect, America's famous literary renaissance echoed precisely the same ideals that were found in the political rhetoric of Jacksonian democracy during the very same period.

The best-known spokesman for the new intellectual movement was Ralph Waldo Emerson, who had left the Unitarian ministry to gain considerably more fame as a writer, lecturer, and philosopher. Making his home in the town of Concord, Massachusetts, Emerson gathered about him a small band of devoted disciples, many of whom would become famous authors in their own right. In his famous Phi Beta Kappa address delivered at Harvard College in 1837, Emerson issued a ringing declaration of American intellectual independence by calling on American scholars to stop imitating "the courtly muses of Europe." He urged young writers to forget about dusty archives and ancient sources, and derive their inspiration from the creativity of their own minds and the scenes of natural beauty right around them. Emerson had already suggested, in an essay entitled "Nature," that people must learn the lessons of the universe firsthand if they were ever to understand the complete workings of the world of eternal truth. In a series of essays, he emphasized the virtues of individualism,

Ralph Waldo Emerson left the Unitarian ministry to pursue a career as an essayist and philosopher, becoming a highly regarded public figure. Emphasizing individualism and self-reliance, and expounding upon the inspirational beauties of nature, Emerson became the focal center of a group of creative men and women who became known as the Transcendentalists. *Courtesy of the Bostonian Society/Old State House.*

self-reliance, and self-improvement, accentuating the optimism of the age and the unlimited opportunities available to the American people.

One of Emerson's close friends was Henry David Thoreau—poet, writer, and incurable nonconformist. For two years, Thoreau lived in a small shack beside Walden Pond near Concord, without any of the then-modern conveniences. He provided a memorable record of those two years in his book *Walden* (1854), in which he not only described the beauties of nature during the changing seasons of the year, but also philosophized about the importance of the individual and the desperate need for simplifying the innumerable details that complicate life. A rugged individualist himself, Thoreau spent a night in jail for refusing to pay his taxes to support the Mexican War, and then justified his position with his "Civil Disobedience" (1849), an essay on passive resistance and civil disobedience that was destined to have lasting influence throughout the world.*

Almost every conceivable phase of the American experience was explored by a host of writers who were friends and acquaintances of Emerson. Nathaniel Hawthorne reached back into the early New England past to write with biting criticism about the old Puritans in his *Scarlet Letter* (1850) and *House of the Seven Gables* (1851). Certainly one of the most popular poets of the day was Henry Wadsworth Longfellow, whose "Voices in the Night" (1838) ranked him as one of the great American poets. His best-known works came later, however, as he delved into the American past and produced such memorable works as "Evangeline" (1847), "The Song of Hiawatha" (1855), and "The Courtship of Myles Standish" (1858). His "Midnight Ride of Paul Revere" (1860) became an instant popular classic and a permanent part of American folklore. The gentle Quaker poet John Greenleaf Whittier first gained attention with his *Voices of Freedom* (1848), a volume of antislavery verse. Later, however, he won a much wider audience with such nostalgic poems as "The Barefoot Boy" (1856) and "Snow-Bound" (1866), tenderly reminiscent of his New England boyhood. During the same period, Oliver Wendell Holmes—essayist, poet, and novelist, as well as an eminent medical authority—achieved wide literary fame with his witty and urbane series of essays entitled "The Autocrat of the Breakfast-Table" in the *Atlantic Monthly* (1857).

At the same time that scores of Boston writers were producing brilliant works of creative literature, other scholars were searching the American past to uncover the tangled roots of the democratic experience. Starting in 1834, George Bancroft (who also found time to serve as a Cabinet member and a foreign minister) began producing his ten-volume *History of the United States.* Heavily nationalistic and profoundly democratic, Bancroft's history was

---

* Thoreau's essay "Civil Disobedience" was the inspiration for Mahatma Gandhi's struggle against British colonialism in India, and for the Reverend Martin Luther King, Jr.'s, struggle for civil rights in the United States.

extremely popular with the American public. His patriotic history books were the kind that American families were only too happy to purchase for edification of their children.

Jared Sparks, a Unitarian minister and Harvard professor, was another prodigious worker who, in addition to editing the *North American Review,* managed to publish the twelve-volume *Diplomatic Correspondence of the American Revolution* (1829–30) and equally long sets entitled *The Writings of George Washington* (1834–37) and *The Works of Benjamin Franklin* (1836–40). William Hickling Prescott interested himself in the history of Spain, especially where it concerned the origins of American history. In 1838 he published his *Ferdinand and Isabella,* followed by colorful studies entitled *The Conquest of Mexico* (1843) and *The Conquest of Peru* (1847). A friend of Prescott, John Lothrop Motley, felt that the saga of freedom in Holland offered an interesting prelude to the struggle for American independence and won fame with his *The Rise of the Dutch Republic* (1856). Superior to both Prescott and Motley, though most of his works would not appear until just after the Civil War, was Francis Parkman. Overcoming the disabilities of terrible health and virtual blindness, Parkman produced a series of historical works dealing with French exploration in North America over the course of a century and a half. With *Pioneers of France in the New World* (1865), *The Jesuits in North America* (1867), *The Conspiracy of Pontiac* (1851), and many other works, Parkman established a model of scholarly history and excellent literature.

The creative imagination that produced this remarkable American literary renaissance was further intensified by a new philosophical movement called Transcendentalism. Although the term was borrowed from the German philosophy of Immanuel Kant, which insisted that objective reality existed only in the mind, the American version corresponded only vaguely to its original German meaning. Some of the most active adherents of the new philosophy were Ralph Waldo Emerson and his literary friends, who met regularly in Concord at the Transcendental Club, and from 1840 to 1844 published a journal called *The Dial* to immortalize their ideas. At one time or another, membership in this group included Thoreau, William Ellery Channing, Theodore Parker, Bronson Alcott, and Margaret Fuller. During their sessions of the Transcendental Club, they discussed a philosophy that held that the innate qualities of individuals transcended their actual experiences, and that the soul had the inherent power to grasp the truth. By relying on instinct and intuition, rather than reason and science, they held that man and society could be renovated.

Many of these celebrated lecturers and writers made their homes in Boston or resided there for a time. The British traveler Alexander MacKay observed that if one met a gentleman in the vicinity of Washington Street "with a decent coat and a clean shirt," chances were that he was "either a lecturer, a Unitarian minister, or a poet; possibly the man might be all three at once." Beacon Hill was a favorite location where many of the literati made their homes. George Ticknor, professor of Romance languages at Harvard College, moved into the old Amory House on the corner of Park and Beacon Streets; William Prescott worked on his histories at 55 Beacon Street overlooking Boston Common. The Parkman House stood just a little down from the new State House on Beacon Hill; Longfellow lived for a while on Cedar Street; William Dean Howells at Louisburg Square; Thomas Bailey Aldrich on Mount Vernon Street; and Oliver Wendell Holmes first on Bosworth Street, then on Charles Street. Julia Ward Howe and her husband, Dr. Samuel Gridley Howe, lived for a while on Chestnut Street; Louisa May Alcott lived first on Pinckney Street and then moved to Louisburg Square.

It was customary for many of these writers to walk to the Old Corner Book Store, on the corner of Washington and School Streets. They would browse through the books on sale on the ground floor of the old building managed by William Ticknor, and then wander over to the "curtained corner" to discuss their works in progress. Later in the afternoon, they would often dine at the home of Ticknor's partner, James T. Fields, continue their conversations, and occasionally meet visiting British authors like Charles Dickens.

Another favorite gathering place for the Boston literati during this same period was the nearby Boston Athenaeum. Over the years, prominent Boston citizens had built up substantial private collections of books. The Athenaeum was established in 1808 in order to bring these private collections together under one roof and to provide an institution—"a place of social intercourse"—where members could read and study in quiet and comfortable surroundings. At first the Athenaeum was located in the Perkins estate on Pearl Street, but it was later moved to an impressive sandstone Italian Renaissance–style building at 10½ Beacon Street. It continued to be financed by its private members and was open only to them and to qualified scholars.

Not content associating only with their own limited circle of friends, the Boston writers looked for outlets through which to make their views known to a wider audience. In 1815, members of the Monthly Anthology Club began what would eventually become a famous Boston magazine called the *North American Review*. Its articles, essays, and works of poetry cut across a whole range of the thinking going on in Boston literary circles during the 1830s and 1840s. Noted Harvard professors like Jared Sparks, Edward Everett, Charles Eliot Norton, James Russell Lowell, and Henry Adams charted the direction of this influential publication for many years to come. Although the Transcendental publication *The Dial,* under the direction of Margaret Fuller, appeared only from 1840 to 1844, it provided still another opportunity for Boston writers to express their literary ideas and philosophical views. In 1857, the *Atlantic Monthly* made its appearance, breaking new ground in American literary expression with Holmes's "Autocrat of the Breakfast-Table" and Lowell's "Biglow Papers."

The printed page alone could not confine the vigorous energies of the Boston writers, however. They missed few opportunities to take to the lecture platform, not only to expound upon their special fields of knowledge, but also to air their personal opinions on the public issues of the day. At a time when Josiah Holbrook's Lyceum lecturing system was becoming popular in other parts of the country, the Boston writers were using a number of local organizations to establish lecture programs all over the city. Edward Everett, Daniel Webster, and Nathan Hale created the Useful Knowledge Society, and within a short time other groups followed. The Boston Lyceum, the Mercantile Library Association, and the Mechanics Association were among the best-known groups that emphasized the importance of self-education and made the "lecture habit" a prominent feature of Boston society. In 1836 John Lowell, Jr., founded the Lowell Institute, which offered free lectures on science, religion, history, and literature. The Lowell lectures proved to be extremely popular in their day, with as many as eight to ten thousand people applying for tickets to a particular series of lectures by some prominent scholar such as Benjamin Silliman discussing chemistry, James Russell Lowell examining poetry, or Ralph Waldo Emerson, Henry David Thoreau, or Oliver Wendell Holmes speaking on a variety of topics.

Raised from childhood in the belief of "the infinite capacity of human nature," the leaders of Boston's cultural revival were not satisfied with merely raising the intellectual standards of their own small circle of upper-class and highly educated friends. They were also determined to open new horizons for every citizen of Boston, regardless of class or station. Not only did George Ticknor build up the greatest personal library in Boston, but he also threw himself into the ambitious task of creating a circulating library that would be free and open to all citizens of the city. Working with Edward Everett, he persuaded city authorities to build a public library that would serve the less-favored classes of the community. Founded in 1848 as the first large municipal public library in America, the Boston Public Library originally shared rooms with the Massachusetts Historical Society above the archway in Bulfinch's Tontine Crescent in Franklin Square. Later, in 1895, it would move to its present location in Copley Square, to occupy a new Renaissance-style building designed by McKim, Mead, and White.

Those who set the standards for excellence in the city, like George Ticknor and his fellow Brahmins, were seriously concerned that even those people who occupied the lowest rungs of Boston's socioeconomic ladder should have more "useful knowledge" in order to raise themselves up and improve the quality of their lives. On a visit to Boston, British author Matthew Arnold observed a barefoot newsboy reading quietly in the public library. "I do not think I have been so impressed with anything else I have seen since arriving in the country," he wrote. The writer Van Wyck Brooks later observed, "Boston, all New England, respected learning. No New England boy was allowed to question that he was destined to succeed in life, provided he knew enough; and Boston was determined that the boys and girls, and the blind and the insane as well, should have the opportunity to know enough."

Making sure that everybody in Boston "knew enough" meant doing something about the educational system of the day. During the early years of the Republic, there were some excellent private schools available for those young people whose parents could afford the tuition; colleges were reserved for those who had the proper academic preparation, social background, and financial income. As early as 1647 the General Court had ordered all townships with more than a hundred families to establish grammar schools. The results, however, had been usually uneven and mostly unsatisfactory. The very few "free schools" that did manage to exist—usually single-room, little red schoolhouses with ungraded classes—stayed open only a few months out of the year. They offered little more than the fundamental three R's, a pot-bellied stove, and a cranky schoolteacher who usually worked on a part-time basis.

With more Americans voting and taking part in the political process during the Jacksonian years of the 1830s and 1840s, however, it seemed absolutely necessary to extend educational benefits to as many people as possible. The haphazard and completely unprofessional educational system that existed seemed not only undemocratic, but actually dangerous to the interests of a republic whose future was based on the voting power of an informed electorate. The only answer, obviously, was a system of free, public education.

One of the outstanding leaders in the fight to change the educational system of the day was Horace Mann, the son of a poor farmer, who gave up a promising political career to work at educational reform. Appointed secretary of the Massachusetts Board of Education in 1837, he set out to establish an efficient and reputable school system. He demanded better schools, a uniform curriculum, more modern equipment, and the establishment of "Normal Schools" for the professional training of teachers.

The struggle to establish public education was not won without overcoming stubborn opposition, however. Taxpayers complained about the high costs of free education; childless property-owners objected to paying taxes to educate "other folks'" children. Wealthy parents preferred a more exclusive educational system; private schools condemned the introduction of unfair government competition. Influential church-related institutions protested against the "godless atheism" of people like Horace Mann, who retained the general moral principles of Protestantism in the form of Bible-reading, prayers, and hymns, but who also insisted that individual sectarianism (Congregationalism, Unitarianism, Presbyterianism, etc.) be kept out of public education.

Slowly, however, the advocates of free public education won out, supported by the views of a growing popular electorate. Urban workers and rural farmers now demanded a proper education for their children, and labor organizations soon found that compulsory education was an effective means of keeping children out of the labor market. Newly arrived immigrants welcomed the opportunity to provide their children with an education they themselves could never hope to obtain. And politically conscious Americans from all walks of life saw the value of an educational system that would provide the nation with literate voters. Gradually the tide began to turn. By 1860 the principle of free, public, tax-supported education was generally accepted throughout the northern sections of the country, although the implementation of this principle would take some time.

But this was not enough. There were children in Boston who were blind, who could not be accommodated in regular schools, and yet who also deserved their chance to "know enough." And so, with characteristic thoroughness, the leaders of Boston undertook a task that still challenged both medical science and professional education. Education of blind people was something new in the United States when a number of schools for the blind were established during the early 1830s in New York, Philadelphia, and Boston. By far the best known of these schools was the one established in Boston by Dr. Samuel Gridley

Julia Ward Howe worked with her husband, Dr. Samuel Gridley Howe, developing programs for the benefit of young persons who were blind and disabled. During the Civil War, Julia became a national figure as the author of "The Battle Hymn of the Republic" and was in the forefront of the struggle for women's rights during the rest of the nineteenth century. *Courtesy of the Bostonian Society/Old State House.*

Howe, husband of Julia Ward Howe and a close friend of Horace Mann. Howe established his Perkins Institution for the Blind with the financial assistance of Colonel Thomas Handasyd Perkins, a prominent Boston merchant. Perkins was persuaded to donate his huge estate on Pearl Street after the Boston community put on a vigorous fund-raising campaign that matched his gift of $50,000. Moving into the rural peninsula of South Boston in 1839, the Perkins Institution soon became world famous as a result of Howe's experiments with musical instruments, raised alphabets, and other novel techniques for educating blind persons. European visitors constantly marveled at the progress Howe made with Laura Bridgman, a child born without hearing or sight. Inspired by the work of Howe, similar schools were soon established in many other parts of the United States.

If Bostonians were concerned about the plight of poor children who were unable to get a proper education, or blind children who could get only a limited education, their hearts were moved by the conditions of mentally handicapped children who could get no assistance at all. These were times when persons who were mentally retarded, feeble-minded, or mentally ill suffered from shameful neglect and callous brutality. Usually such persons were left either to roam around by themselves and become the butt of cruel jokes, or else were locked away and left to be forgotten.

Early reforms in handling the mentally handicapped were begun by the Quakers of Philadelphia, but by far the most dramatic advances came in the late 1840s through the heroic efforts of Dorothea Lynde Dix. A frail woman who ran a school for girls in Boston, Miss Dix went to teach Sunday school at the Cambridge House of Correction in 1841 and was appalled by the conditions of the "insane" inmates she found there who had committed no crimes. Shocked beyond words, she traveled the length and breadth of Massachusetts, visiting as many local jails and asylums as possible, taking detailed notes and carefully documenting the terrible conditions she found. In 1843, Miss Dix presented to the General Court of Massachusetts a "Memorial" in which she summarized the most repulsive brutalities inflicted on the insane men and women of the commonwealth, and demanded immediate action be taken to improve such conditions. Despite the attacks of those who dismissed her as nothing more than a sentimental female, Dorothea Dix was supported by reformers like Dr. Samuel Gridley Howe and Horace Mann. Eventually the state legislature appropriated funds to build a large addition to the Worcester hospital for the insane, thereby sparking campaigns in other northern states for state-supported hospitals for the treatment of the insane.

To a number of younger Bostonians, however, all these social projects and humanitarian efforts, though well-intentioned, did not get to the heart of what they regarded as some of the more pressing issues of the day. These

Dorothea Lynde Dix was one of a large number of women in the mid-nineteenth century who became active in social and humanitarian reforms. A vigorous and articulate advocate who demanded special facilities for people with mental illnesses, Dorothea Dix succeeded in setting up several hospitals and asylums for their care and treatment. *Courtesy of the Bostonian Society/Old State House.*

young people were convinced that there were more significant injustices in society that required immediate attention. Promoting temperance, improving prisons, upgrading education, and assisting the handicapped certainly provided immediate help to individual persons, but they did not go far enough. Such efforts lent a helping hand to a few hapless victims of an oppressive society but made no attempt to force basic changes in the social system itself. They assisted paupers but did nothing about poverty. They improved prison conditions but did nothing about an environment that fostered crime. And, they would send a few slaves back to Africa but did not denounce the institution of slavery.

In many eastern cities, and most prominently in Boston, a number of people began to engage in activities designed to bring about substantial changes in the existing social structure—if not to overturn it completely. The spirit of radical reform was in the air. Young men started growing beards; took up the wearing of robes and sandals; ate fruits, nuts, berries, and other natural foods; gathered in rustic communes; and came up with utopian plans for a brave new world. "We are all a little wild here with numberless projects of social reform," Ralph Waldo Emerson told the English historian Thomas Carlysle in the fall of 1840. "Not a reading man but has a draft of a new Community in his waistcoat pocket." All this was disturbing to members of the conservative establishment, and occasionally frightening, when groups of these young radicals gathered together, as they did in November 1840 to attend a convention on "universal reform" at Boston's Chardon Street Church. Addressing themselves to such controversial issues as perfectionism, pacifism, communitarianism, socialism, birth control, civil disobedience, and the repeal of the Sabbath Laws, they formed what Edmund Quincy called "the most singular collection of strange specimens of humanity that was ever assembled." Emerson was even less charitable in his description of the radicals who rushed to the podium to sound off for their particular causes: "Mad-men and mad-women, men with beards, Dunkers, Muggletonians, Come-outers, Groaners, Agrarians, Seventh-Day Baptists, Quakers, Abolitionists, Calvinists, Unitarians, and Philosophers, all came successively to the top and seized the moment, if not the hour, wherein to chide, or pray, or preach, or protest."

Alternately regarded as well-meaning zealots, demented crackpots, or dangerous extremists, the emotional young radicals were clearly viewed as a disruptive influence in a conservative community that believed that true reform could be achieved only through calm, gradual, and rational procedures. To make matters worse, the young Boston reformers were often led by ministers who had traded their quiet Unitarian pulpits for soap boxes and noisy lecture halls. Indeed, as historian Henry Commager has pointed out, these were the only major reform movements in American history—at least until the civil rights movement of the 1960s—in which the clergy not only provided spiritual inspiration, but also took a physical part in the activities themselves.

The attainment of universal peace and the rejection of war as an instrument of national policy were idealistic goals to which a number of the young Boston reformers turned their attention. In 1845, a thirty-four-year-old Harvard graduate and a promising young lawyer named Charles Sumner gave the annual Fourth of July address at Faneuil Hall before a distinguished gathering of political officials and military representatives. Having announced the title of his oration as "The True Grandeur of Nations," Sumner surprised and stunned his unsuspecting audience by elaborating on the evils of war, the wastefulness of national defense, and the uselessness of the U.S. military academy as nothing more than a "seminary of idleness and vice." Decorated generals and admirals walked out of the hall in complete disgust, while old Boston families whose ancestors had fought at Lexington and Bunker Hill were shocked beyond words by such treasonous views. Mayor Samuel Eliot summed up the opinion of Beacon Hill quite accurately when he sputtered: "That young man has cut his own throat!"

Similar outrage from the conservative Brahmin establishment greeted the sudden and public emergence of females as outspoken crusaders for the cause of women's rights. According to traditional English legal customs that still operated in the United States, women had few, if any, legal, political, or civil rights. When they married, they became the wards of their husbands, who assumed title over their property and their earnings. Women could neither vote nor hold public office, nor were they allowed to speak before "mixed audiences," deliver sermons, attend college, or enter any of the professions. They received an elementary education in the three R's, which enabled them to handle the simple accounts of the kitchen, the markets, and other parts of their carefully restricted "sphere of influence." Beyond that, advanced studies were considered much too dangerous for the delicate female mind.

In the age of the "Common Man," however, when the ideals of equality were so frequently emphasized, it seemed nothing short of heresy that women should be ranked as second-class members of American society, especially at a time when illiterate foreign immigrants were allowed to become naturalized citizens. There were many females, and some sympathetic males, who were highly indignant over the outright discrimination that prevented women from having the same legal, political, and educational opportunities as men. Buoyed by the spirit of universal democracy that permeated the age, women began to agitate for equal rights at all levels of American society.

No longer displaying the meekness and submissiveness expected of them by the male-dominated society of the day, women demanded the right to vote, the right to work, the right to hold money and property in their own names, and the right to a higher education. And they demonstrated their ability to achieve great things, even in what was still considered a man's world. Margaret Fuller, for example, a close friend of Emerson and other intellectuals, worked at an incredible pace. Teacher, translator, and public lecturer, she was the editor of the Transcendental journal *The Dial,* as well as the author of a controversial best-selling book called *Woman in the Nineteenth Century* (1845). Lydia Maria Child, another leading Boston feminist, served for many years as executive secretary of the American Anti-Slavery Society, and in 1841 assumed the editorship of *The National Anti-Slavery Standard.* Women like Elizabeth Cady Stanton of New York, Sarah and Angelina Grimké of Philadelphia, and Lucretia Mott of Philadelphia joined their Boston associates in taking to the lecture circuit and pouring out their feelings in books and magazines. Lucy Stone, a graduate of Oberlin College who later settled in Dorchester, had her husband sign a protest in which he renounced all the laws that had given him injurious and unnatural superiority over his wife. Not only did she keep her maiden name as a symbol of her legal equality, but she founded Lucy Stone Leagues to encourage other women to follow her emancipated example.

The sight of females working, writing, lecturing, and engaging in all sorts of "vulgar" enterprises far beyond the familiar confines of hearth and home evoked hostile reaction from the conservative Boston community. Some residents were openly scornful of the attempts by "liberated women" to tamper with the established norms of society and undermine the fundamental teachings of Christianity. Others poked fun at those women who had pretensions to professional careers or literary futures as nothing more than frustrated "bluestockings." But perhaps the most poignant insult came from those very men who were supposed to be dedicating themselves to the eradication of discrimination. In 1840, several American women traveled to London to attend a meeting of the World Anti-Slavery Congress, only to find themselves excluded from the proceedings simply because they were women. Infuriated at being treated as inferiors, they returned to America and in 1848 held the first Women's Rights Convention at Seneca Falls, New York. Here they issued a ringing paraphrase of the Declaration of Independence, announcing that "all men and women" were created equal, and demanding that women be given "immediate admission to all the rights and privileges which belong to them as citizens of the United States."

William Lloyd Garrison, operating out of a small, hole-in-the-wall office on Washington Street, published *The Liberator* on January 1, 1831, as the organ of the abolition movement in Boston. He was responsible for transforming a gradualist humanitarian reform movement into a powerful immediatist moral crusade. Regarding slavery as a moral evil, Garrison demanded the total and immediate abolition of slavery without compensation to slave owners. *Courtesy of the Bostonian Society/Old State House.*

But if the movement for women's rights caused the Brahmin establishment to raise an eyebrow in astonishment, it was the new antislavery movement begun by William Lloyd Garrison in January 1831 that caused the Brahmin establishment to shake its fist in anger. Harrison Gray Otis was halfway through his third term as mayor of Boston—having succeeded Josiah Quincy in 1829—

when he began receiving explosive letters from the governors of Virginia and Georgia demanding that he take action against some "incendiary" newspaper called *The Liberator*, published in his city, that was inciting the slaves of the South to riot and revolt. Nat Turner's abortive slave uprising in August 1831 struck terror in the hearts of Southerners everywhere, and many slaveholders blamed the Yankee publication for having caused it. Senator Robert Y. Hayne of South Carolina demanded legal action against the editor, and the *National Intelligencer* publicly inquired of "the worthy mayor of the city of Boston" whether there were any laws that could prevent the publication of such "diabolical papers."

Mayor Otis was at a complete loss. Although *The Liberator* had been circulating for almost a year, neither he nor any of his conservative friends and acquaintances had heard of it. He ordered an investigation of the offending publication, and in due time he was informed that the paper was indeed called *The Liberator* and was being published by a man named Garrison. His office was described as nothing but an "obscure hole" on Washington Street, and his staff was reported as consisting only of a few "insignificant persons of all colors."

Mayor Otis breathed a sigh of relief—only a tempest in a teapot. He wrote to his friends in the South and assured them that this unfortunate incident was of no serious concern. This new "fanaticism," he wrote, had no influence at all among persons of consequence in the Bay State. Nor was it likely, he emphasized, "to make proselytes among the respectable classes of our people." Some years later, a bewildered Harrison Gray Otis sighed, "In this I was mistaken."

Just *how* mistaken he had been even Mayor Otis himself would never know. This "obscure" little newspaper and its "fanatical" editor were destined to revolutionize completely the antislavery movement in the United States, tear apart the great "conspiracy of silence," and accelerate the sectional confrontation leading to the great crisis of the Union.

Chapter

6

Liberty and Union

THERE had been concern about the issue of slavery long before America had ever heard of William Lloyd Garrison. During the early 1800s, discussions about slavery had generally been rational, the demands moderate, and the approach gentlemanly. One of the most popular of all early emancipation programs was the American Colonization Society, which proposed to purchase the freedom of so many slaves a year and "colonize" them back to Africa. Boasting a membership that included such prominent Southerners as Judge Bushrod Washington, President James Monroe, and Senator Henry Clay, the experiment also attracted a great deal of interest in the North. Conservative Boston businessmen like Amos Lawrence saw the movement as a way by which to rid the United States of slavery in a gradual, reasonable, and nonthreatening manner.

There were other Americans, however, who regarded the institution of slavery with the utmost horror, and who demanded nothing less than its total and immediate abolition. The uncompromising attitude of such people was translated into action on January 1, 1831, when William Lloyd Garrison ran off the first issue of *The Liberator*. Although Garrison was by no means the first abolitionist, he was certainly the most articulate spokesperson for an immediate resolution of the problem. He rudely thrust aside the traditional quiet and genteel approach by publicly declaring that he would not use moderation "in a cause like the present." He insisted that in working toward the goal of total abolition he would be "as harsh as truth" and "as uncompromising as justice." Garrison and his followers based their new crusade on the premise that slavery was a sin, a moral evil, and a crime against humanity. They refused to accept any resolution of the slavery question that did not call for total and immediate abolition, without payment or compensation.

At first, Garrison's new movement seemed to be getting nowhere. Looked upon as agitators, cranks, and crackpots who were involving themselves in dangerous and unsavory racial matters that were best left alone, members of the abolition movement were not socially acceptable in most respectable circles. Furthermore, the early issues of *The Liberator* caused hardly a ripple on the placid surface of Boston. Garrison himself complained that he found "contempt more bitter, detraction more relentless, prejudice more stubborn, and apathy more frozen" in the city of Boston than "among the slave owners themselves." With implacable determination, however, Garrison gradually gathered a small band of devoted followers about him and created the New England Anti-Slavery Society to formulate policy and gather new adherents.

For a while, conservative Bostonians could afford to laugh at Garrison and sneer at his little newspaper. But by the mid-1830s, Garrison's followers had increased in number to the point that they could not be tolerated much longer. They were causing unsettling effects in the Boston community with their literary attacks on leading citizens of the city who had been supporting the colonization that Garrison dismissed as "White-Manism." Garrison publicly charged the American Colonization Society with being a secret agency for slaveholders because of its pledge not to interfere with a system "unfathomly deep in pollution" and "encrusted with corroding evil." To accuse upstanding Brahmin families of complicity with organized slavery was no way to gain acceptance and support in Boston.

There was also the matter of Garrison's outspoken attacks against the local churches. Insisting that emancipation ought to be "the work of Christianity and the churches," Garrison was appalled by the lack of support his movement received from organized religion. Since the slavery issue was potentially divisive, most churches tended to either ignore the issue completely or support the moderate goals of colonization. As a result, according to the Transcendentalist minister Theodore Parker, the American pulpit had become "the sworn ally of slavery." Abolitionists attacked the churches for their silence on slavery and often staged "speak-ins" during church services to make their point. They encouraged African Americans to conduct "pray-ins" in all-white churches and to refuse to sit in separate "Negro pews" in those churches that were racially mixed. In addition, they demanded that all Christian churches should not only refuse to accept slaveholders as ministers, but also exclude all slaveholders from communion. Such disruptive tactics were considered outrageous by the conservative community, which felt that Garrison and his followers were undermining organized religion and contributing to the breakdown of moral standards.

Perhaps even more serious was the dangerous rift Garrison was creating between the cotton-producing South and the textile-manufacturing North— between what Charles Sumner labeled the "Lords of the Lash" and the "Lords of the Loom." Profitable cotton textile plants in places like Waltham, Lowell, and Lawrence had now become an integral part of the Bay State economy and were completely dependent on the plantations of the South for a regular supply of cotton. Acutely aware of their financial leverage, angry Southerners were already threatening serious economic reprisals if their associates in the North did not put an end to this bothersome abolition agitation. "The people of the North must go to hanging these fanatical wretches if they would not lose the benefit of Southern trade," threatened one Southern newspaper, while another journal conjured up the frightening picture of grass growing in the streets of Lowell. The extensive economic investments of the Brahmin community were clearly much too important to allow this group of radical reformers to go unchallenged and unchecked.

It was not long before denunciation turned to violence. On the afternoon of October 21, 1835, an angry mob burst into a meeting of the Boston Female Anti-Slavery Society on Washington Street, caught hold of Garrison, and dragged him at the end of a rope through the streets toward Boston Common. Although he was rescued from the mob and put in protective custody at the Leverett Street jail, he was advised to leave town. Of the nature of the mob that attacked him, Garrison had no doubt: "It was planned and executed," he charged, "not by the rabble, or the workingmen, but by 'gentlemen of property and standing, from all parts of the city.' " Wendell Phillips described the assault as being carried out "in broadcloth and in broad daylight"; T. L. Nichols, a visitor from Baltimore, reported that the attack had been organized by "merchants and bankers of Boston, assembled on 'Change in State Street." Clearly, persons close to Boston's leading merchants and businessmen had decided to demonstrate their goodwill to their friends and "brethren" in the South.

Garrison and the abolitionists refused to be intimidated; indeed, the violence that flared up during 1835–36, in Boston as well as in other cities throughout the North, actually provided more sympathy than the original antislavery movement had ever been able to muster. The list of new converts grew alarmingly, as persons of wealth and position joined Garrison's cause. Wendell Phillips (Harvard class of 1831), son of Boston's first mayor, joined the ranks of the insurgents, as did Edmund Quincy (Harvard class of 1827), son of Boston's second mayor. The prominent Dr. Henry Ingersoll Bowditch became an abolitionist after witnessing the attack on Garrison. And even the influential merchant John Murray Forbes, long indifferent to the problem of slavery, said that "I changed my whole feeling with regard to it" after learning of the murder in Alton, Illinois, of the abolitionist publisher Elijah Lovejoy. James Russell Lowell and Ralph Waldo Emerson added their literary talents to those of the poet John Greenleaf Whittier and soon became influential participants in the drive for emancipation. Abolitionist membership was increasing every day, and by 1840 there were over two hundred antislavery societies in Massachusetts alone.

Local abolitionists became even more unpopular with the conservative community when they began to focus their moral outrage on the discrimination being practiced by white people against black residents of Boston itself. African Americans had a rich social and cultural history in Massachusetts, especially in Boston. The first black community in Boston was settled in the North End during the seventeenth century on what became known as Copp's Hill. The area was called "New Guinea," after that part of the west coast of Africa from which many of them had come. In the Copp's Hill Burial Ground today are the remains of more than a thousand African Americans, both slaves and free persons, including Prince Hall, founder of the black Masonic Lodge in Boston.

Slavery was a fact of life in North America, and during colonial times some of the most respected white citizens were slaveholders. Although the town never had a formal slave market, in 1737 a Boston newspaper carried an advertisement from a man who offered to sell blacks at "six pence a pound on all he sells, and a reasonable price if he does not sell." The Reverend Cotton Mather's congregation gave him a slave worth fifty pounds as a gift. Peter Faneuil, the town's leading merchant, ordered a house slave from the West Indies in 1739, paying for him with a shipment of fish. And Paul Revere's grandmother owned a piece of a slave; in her will she bequeathed to her son "all of my part of and in my negro boy, Nulgar." Escaped slaves were regularly hunted down by their masters through "wanted" advertisements in colonial newspapers, usually describing the missing slave as a "Congoman," a "Madagascar boy," or a "Guinyman."

In 1761, Mrs. Susanna Wheatley, the wife of a prosperous tailor with a large house on King Street, purchased a sickly eight-year-old black girl who had been transported to Boston as a slave. The child took the name Phillis Wheatley, and within two years she had not only learned to speak and write English, but by the age of fourteen she was publishing poems. She was honored by royalty in England for her literary accomplishments, and in America she received a personal note from General George Washington, for whom she had written a complimentary piece of verse. In 1778 Wheatley married John Peters, described as "a respectable colored man of Boston," and had three children, all of whom died young. Wheatley's own poor health continued to deteriorate, and she died in 1784 at the age of thirty-one, the first African-American slave to publish a book of poetry, and the second woman in America to be recognized as a literary figure.[*]

As the number of African Americans in Boston increased, blacks gradually moved inland, away from the extreme tip of the North End, toward what would become known as the West End. They settled on the north side of Beacon Hill, in a section north of Pinckney Street running from Joy Street down to the Charles River. In 1809, the founding of the first all-black church, originally called the African Meeting House, at 8 Smith Court off Belknap Street drew even more African Americans into this section of town. The church had a decisive influence within Boston's black community, serving as a gathering place for religious observances as well as becoming a center for the exchange of ideas and information. By 1820, members of Boston's African-American population were living along most of the north slope of Beacon Hill, in Wards 6 and 7 (called "Nigger Hill"); by 1840 their numbers had reached nearly two thousand.

Although they formed a long-established and proud community, Boston's African Americans were subject to various forms of economic and social discrimination. Few black artisans could get enough patronage to stay in business on their own, and custom forbade any white merchant or mechanic from

---

[*] Anne Bradstreet, the daughter of Governor Thomas Dudley, was an accomplished poet. A collection of her early poems was published in London in 1650 under the title *The Tenth Muse Lately Sprung Up in America.*

An eight-year-old African girl from Senegal arrived in Boston in 1761 as the property of Mrs. John Wheatley. Taking the name Phillis Wheatley, the young girl quickly learned English and in 1767 published her first poem. In 1773 she traveled to London, where a collection of her poems was published. Back in America, she later received a personal note from General George Washington, for whom she had written a complimentary piece of verse. *Courtesy of the Bostonian Society/Old State House.*

taking on a colored apprentice. Members of the black population, therefore, were relegated to such service occupations as laborers, waiters, caterers, clothing salesman, stevedores, barbers, hairdressers, and laundresses. A Massachusetts law prohibited marriages between blacks and whites, and railroad companies operating out of Boston normally set aside a Jim Crow car for black travelers. It was customary for theaters, restaurants, and lecture halls to refuse admission to persons of color, and on one occasion even the well-known black orator Frederick Douglass was informed by one restaurant owner: "We don't allow niggers in here." And until African Americans finally built their own church, many of Boston's white churches still provided separate "Negro pews" in remote corners of their structures. One of the most flagrant examples of racial discrimination in nineteenth-century Boston was the segregated school system that prevented black children from attending any of the city's all-white schools. Back in 1789, when they could get no support from the town fathers, Boston's black citizens had set up a small school of their own in the home of Prince Hall. In 1808, a new school was finally constructed as the result of the legacy of a wealthy merchant named Abiel Smith, who had been an admirer of the black schoolmaster Prince Sanders. The Smith School, as it was called, came under the jurisdiction of the Boston Primary School Board, which established it as a primary school exclusively for colored children.

Starting in 1844, a group of Boston's African-American residents began petitioning the school board to remove the racial designation of the Smith School and allow black children to enroll in the other schools of the city. They were encouraged in this effort by the agitation of William Lloyd Garrison and the local Boston abolitionists, as well as by a resolution of the Massachusetts Anti-Slavery Society informing all black people of their legal rights. The Society also offered them all possible aid in securing "the full and equal enjoyment of the public schools." Consistently, however, the majority of the votes of the school board went against the black petitioners, arguing that it was the board's responsibility to keep apart the two races that "the All-Wise Creator had seen fit to establish." The black citizens and their white supporters, however, kept up the fight through community organizations, public petitions, and legal activities.

In the fall of 1849, a resident named Benjamin F. Roberts brought suit against the city of Boston on behalf of his five-year-old daughter. Sarah Roberts had been denied admission to a nearby white school solely on the basis of her color. The resulting case was argued before the Supreme Judicial Court of Massachusetts, with Charles Sumner representing Sarah Roberts, and Robert Morris, the only black member of the Massachusetts Bar, serving as assistant counsel. Despite Sumner's eloquent plea for "equality before the law" and his arguments that both white children and black children suffer from attending separate schools, Chief Justice Lemuel Shaw decided against the plaintiff.

Even though they had lost the Roberts case, black and white abolitionists renewed their efforts for integrated education in Boston. Switching their attacks from the judicial chamber to the political arena, they were able to bring enough public pressure to bear to persuade state legislators to repudiate the decision of the court. On April 18, 1854, the Great and General Court of Massachusetts passed a law stating that no child, on account of "race, color, or religious opinions," could be excluded from any public school in the commonwealth. Following passage of this statute, a number of boys from the all-white Phillips School were transferred to the all-black Smith School, and a corresponding number of black boys from the Smith School walked over to take their seats at the Phillips School.

Despite their growing numbers and their occasional victories, however, William Lloyd Garrison and the other reformers of Boston continued to remain a small, almost infinitesimal part of the city's total population. Most residents never really accepted the radical theories of Garrison and his followers or approved of their disruptive tactics. There were times during the late 1840s and early 1850s, to be sure, when certain incidents created periods of greater sympathy for the antislavery cause. In 1850, for example, to secure passage of the Compromise of 1850, the U.S. Congress passed a new Fugitive Slave Law that allowed federal marshals to apprehend alleged runaway slaves in any state of the Union. Several Northern states, including Massachusetts, demonstrated their opposition to this federal law by enacting their own Personal Liberty Laws. These were state measures that guaranteed a fugitive slave the writ of habeas corpus and trial by jury, and prohibited the use of any state or county jail for the detention of fugitives. Even conservative Boston lawyers who still rejected abolitionism were outraged by violations of the Constitution that allowed human beings to be hunted like animals through the streets of their city.

It was only a year later, in 1851, when the first chapters of Harriet Beecher Stowe's explosive novel, *Uncle Tom's Cabin*, began to appear in serial form; it went into publication as a book the following year. In skillfully personalizing the issue of human bondage, Beecher Stowe took slavery out of the lecture hall and the senate chamber and brought it into the living room and kitchen of every home in America. In book form, and a short time later in numerous stage performances, *Uncle Tom's Cabin* reached millions of Americans and kept the issue of slavery in the forefront of the national consciousness.

Despite all the tears that were shed for Uncle Tom, however, the Compromise of 1850 still held firm. Political leaders on both sides of the aisle refused to allow the slavery issue back into national politics where it could divide parties and endanger the Union. And back in Boston, conservative businessmen continued to correspond with their "Southern brethren," assuring them that the abolition movement was still getting nowhere and that the slavery question was no longer an issue of consequence. The "conspiracy of silence" was still in effect, but not for long.

The event that shook conservative Bostonians out of their lethargy concerning slavery and sent the nation down the slippery slope to civil war came in January 1854, when Senator Stephen A. Douglas of Illinois proposed his Kansas-Nebraska Bill. By erasing the 36°-30' line established by the Missouri Compromise of 1820, and by allowing slavery to move north of that line, Douglas made slavery a red-hot political issue once again. The Kansas-Nebraska Bill (often referred to at the time as simply the "Nebraska Bill") set North against South, paved the way for the collapse of the old Whig party, and set the stage for the creation of the new Republican party. Old-time Bostonians who had

Bostonians were outraged when escaped slaves were taken into custody by federal authorities and returned to their owners under the terms of the Fugitive Slave Act of 1850. Seventeen-year-old Thomas Sims was apprehended, spent nine days in the federal courthouse, and on the morning of April 11, 1851, under heavy guard, was marched down to Long Wharf and placed aboard a ship for his return to Georgia and to slavery. *Courtesy of the Bostonian Society/Old State House.*

remained aloof from the unsavory controversy over slavery because of their close financial relations with Southern cotton planters were shocked beyond words by what had happened. "We went to bed one night, old-fashioned, conservative, compromise, Union Whigs," wrote Amos A. Lawrence, "and waked up stark mad Abolitionists."

Business interests throughout the Northeast, for the first time, added their considerable influence to the groundswell of angry public opinion. "We regard the Nebraska movement of Douglas and his backers as one of measureless treachery and infamy," exploded Horace Greeley in his *New York Tribune,* while the *New York Post* observed: "The City of New York is awake at last," as great numbers of bankers and businessmen held mass meetings calling for the defeat of the bill. And in Boston, some three thousand "solid men" of the city gathered at Faneuil Hall on February 3, 1854, to protest the Nebraska Bill and to demand that the nation return to the compromise spirit of 1850. The *Boston Times* reported that a number of prominent merchants, "who had never before given their influence on the anti-slavery side," had signed a public petition calling for the repeal of the Fugitive Slave Act.

One dramatic example of this new sense of outrage in the city came in May 1854 when authorities seized a black man named Anthony Burns as a fugitive slave and prepared to return him to the South. On the day that Burns was marched down State Street to the ship waiting to take him back to slavery, all business was suspended, the buildings were draped in black, and the mood of the city was so menacing that authorities feared mob action. More than two thousand uniformed men—marines, regular army troops, state militia, and city police—lined the streets to prevent a rescue. "The commercial class have taken a new position on the great question of the day," observed the *Boston Times.* But the political skills of Senator Douglas proved more than a match for the irate protests of his Eastern opponents. Supported by President Franklin Pierce and sustained by jubilant Southerners of both parties, the Kansas-Nebraska Act was signed into law by the president on May 30, 1854.

Although they had failed to defeat Douglas in the senate, anti-Nebraska Northerners were determined to beat him on the plains of Kansas. To frustrate the doctrine of popular sovereignty, the Boston textile magnate Amos A. Lawrence organized the New England Emigrant Aid Society as a means of sending a flood of free-soil settlers westward to settle Kansas. Similar emigrant aid societies were soon established by businessmen in other Northern states, and by the winter of 1854–55 there were over five hundred free-soilers clustered along the Kansas River in such settlements as Lawrence (named after their Boston patron), Manhattan, and Topeka. Insisting that they were now the legally constituted government, the free-soilers were convinced they had ensured the freedom of Kansas. The settlers from the East, however, had not considered the hostile reaction of the pro-slavery settlers just across the border in western Missouri. When the time came for territorial elections, large numbers of "Missouri ruffians" flooded into Kansas, elected a pro-slavery governor, and then elected a pro-slavery territorial legislature. Furious at what they considered a violation of the democratic process, in October 1855 the free-soilers drew up their own free-state constitution, with their own governor and their own legislature. At that point Kansas had two separate and hostile governments, and it was not long before ballots turned into bullets. On May 21, 1856, an armed pro-slavery posse rode into the "Boston abolition town" of Lawrence, Kansas, arrested "treasonous" free-state leaders, and sacked the town. Three days later, John Brown and his free-state followers hacked to death five pro-slavery settlers at Pottawatomie Creek.

As blood started to flow in the Kansas Territory, in May 1856 Senator Charles Sumner of Massachusetts delivered a blistering two-day oration on what he called "The Crime against Kansas." He denounced all those who had conspired to turn Kansas into slave territory; he condemned the "slavocracy" of the South for supporting slavery; he attacked Senator Douglas for giving slavery a chance to spread. Sumner went on to question the loyalty of South Carolina and blackened the reputation of Andrew P. Butler, that state's elderly senator. Infuriated at this insult to his state and the assault on his uncle, Representative Preston Brooks of South Carolina came upon Sumner in the senate chambers on the afternoon of May 22, 1856, viciously beat the Bay State senator with a heavy cane, and left him lying unconscious and bleeding on the senate floor.

The attack on Charles Sumner was a dramatic demonstration of how far apart the two sections of the United States had grown. Except for semi-official statements from the South, expressing regret that the incident had taken place in the senate, most Southerners felt that the arrogant abolitionist had received the horsewhipping he deserved. In the North, however, Sumner was hailed as a hero and a martyr to the cause of freedom. Even those Bostonians who did not approve of Sumner (and there were many), turned out to meet the bandaged statesman at the railroad station and invited him to recuperate at their homes. Harvard College provided the finishing touch by conferring upon him the honorary degree of Doctor of Law.

Each year after that, one incident followed another, forcing the two sections of the country even further apart. In 1857, the Dred Scott decision, denying African Americans the right to citizenship and declaring that Congress had no right to legislate on matters concerning slavery, created even more turmoil between the North and the South. And in 1858, the highly publicized debates in the Illinois senate race between the Democratic candidate, Stephen A. Douglas, and the Republican candidate, Abraham Lincoln, focused national attention on the controversial issues of slavery, popular sovereignty, and territorial expansion. Any hopes that sectional relations might improve with the passage of time, however, were dashed for good on October 16, 1859. On that day, John Brown and a small band of followers crossed into Virginia and attacked a federal arsenal at Harpers Ferry, with the intention of sparking a slave uprising throughout the South. Although the invasion was quickly suppressed, and Brown promptly executed, the dramatic raid made the split between North and South all but final. In the North, antislavery spokesmen hailed John Brown as a Christian martyr and viewed his death as the start of a new era in human rights. Henry Thoreau called him an "angel of light," while Ralph Waldo Emerson claimed that he had made "the gallows glorious like the cross." The South, on the other hand, saw John Brown as a symbol of the hatred of the entire North. With the national conventions in anticipation of the presidential election of 1860 approaching, Southern political leaders began making elaborate preparations to ensure that the "Black Republicans" did not win. They could not afford to have the kind of people who had sent a terrorist like John Brown into the South take over the government of the United States.

The election of 1860 was a hotly contested battle between antislavery Republicans in the North, who nominated Abraham Lincoln as their candidate, and a Democratic party that suffered a fatal split between the moderate forces of Stephen A. Douglas and the secessionist supporters of John C. Breckinridge. When Abraham Lincoln was finally elected president of the United States in November 1860, without an electoral vote from a single slave state, the South refused to remain in a Union in which it saw itself no longer represented. The secession of South Carolina the next month was followed by the secession of six more states from the lower South. This proved a deadly prelude to open warfare, which erupted on April 12, 1861, only a month after the inauguration of President Lincoln, when Confederate shore batteries opened fire on Fort Sumter, a federal fort in Charleston harbor.

On April 15, three days after the fall of Fort Sumter, President Lincoln called upon the states to supply seventy-five thousand militia to suppress "combinations" in seven states that were "too powerful to be suppressed by the ordinary course of judicial proceedings." Among the first to respond to the call to arms were the well-trained militia units of Massachusetts. As soon as he was contacted, Governor John A. Andrew called upon four regiments, numbering over three thousand men, to report for active duty. The very next morning, April 16, three companies of the Massachusetts 8th Regiment from Marblehead pulled into Boston by train, in the teeth of a howling blizzard. The following day, April 17, the 6th Regiment, equipped with new rifles, came marching down Beacon Street and halted before the broad steps of the State House. Governor Andrew presented them with their regimental colors and then sent them off to Washington, D.C., to defend the nation's capital. The 6th Regiment boarded the trains for Baltimore, and two days later their railroad cars were drawn by horses across the city to the depot where they would entrain for Washington.

Maryland was one of those states that lay exactly between the North and the South—one of the "border states" whose loyalties were divided throughout the war. The city of Baltimore had been in a constant state of turmoil ever since the attack on Fort Sumter. One moment, crowds of Confederate sympathizers would be marching through the streets singing "Dixie"; the next moment, Union sympathizers would be chanting "The Star-Spangled Banner." When they arrived at the Baltimore station, seven companies of the 6th Regiment were taken to the depot on the other side of the city without incident. As the last three Massachusetts companies were being drawn across the city, however, an excited group of Confederate sympathizers spotted them and began pelting the soldiers with rocks and stones as they got out of their cars and formed their ranks. Pistol shots rang out, one of the soldiers crumpled to the ground, and then the troops fired into the crowd and cleared a path with their bayonets. Rejoining the rest of their regiment on the other side, the 6th Massachusetts Regiment continued its determined journey to the nation's capital.

In the meantime, reports had reached Washington about the clash at Baltimore. Since the final outcome was not yet known, people in the capital did not know if the troops had been able to get across the city to the Washington trains. At this point, with all the railroad bridges destroyed and the telegraph wires cut, Washington, D.C., was in a state of panic. With rioting Maryland on one side and Confederate troops under General Beauregard on the other, Washington was desperate to know the whereabouts of the Massachusetts 6th— the only Northern force that could offer the U.S. capital any protection.

A short time after five o'clock that evening, a special train came puffing into the Washington station. With a great cheer, the citizens of Washington recognized the men in the dark-gray overcoats as members of the 6th Massachusetts Regiment. These were the first armed volunteers to come to the defense of the capital, and the residents rushed to take care of the wounded. The rest of the regiment wearily made its way to the senate chamber, where the soldiers dropped to the floor, wrapped themselves in their blankets, and gathered what rest they could in preparation for an uncertain tomorrow. At a moment when everything about him was tinged with gloom and despair, President Abraham Lincoln greatly appreciated this gesture from Massachusetts. Washington had been abandoned; the South was in rebellion; Maryland was in revolt; everything seemed lost. Yet the boys from Massachusetts had arrived—they were there. "You are the only Northern realities," a grateful Lincoln told them. They were the only single Union regiment on hand that could have confronted a Confederate attack on the capital during its six days of complete isolation.

Fortunately, the Confederates did not cross the Potomac, and on April 25 the crack troops of the New York 7th Regiment, smartly dressed in their new gray uniforms, came marching to the relief of the capital. Next came the men of the 1st Rhode Island, clad in gray pants and dark-blue shirts. And, as the 8th Massachusetts Regiment arrived from Annapolis, where they had been repairing railroad lines, the men of the 6th Massachusetts let out a cheer. After handshaking and backslapping, they all went over to the Capitol, where the 8th Regiment was quartered in the huge Rotunda next to their comrades from the 6th, laughing and cheering well into the night.

Back in Massachusetts, the citizens were of one mind and one spirit, mobilized first by the attack on Fort Sumter, and then by the news that their own boys had been fired upon. This unity was especially true when it was realized that the attack on the 6th Massachusetts Regiment had taken place on April 19—the very day that Massachusetts celebrated the anniversary of the shots heard 'round the world at Lexington and Concord. Party differences were put aside for the moment, and old enmities were forgotten, as the Bay State gave its undivided allegiance to President Lincoln and Governor Andrew. Young men rushed to join the colors, older men offered their money and their services to the cause, and women hastened to tend the wounded. No one in the

Bay State could possibly know how long the war would last or what the coming months would bring. But of one thing the people of the commonwealth were certain—Massachusetts had kept the faith.

The Civil War proved to be long, costly, and bitter. Unfortunately, there were very few opportunities for Bostonians to celebrate during the first two years of the conflict when the Confederates seemed to be winning everywhere. The Union defeat at Bull Run in July 1861 came as a terrible shock to those Northerners who were expecting a quick and easy Union victory—the "peace in ninety days" they had talked about. The failure of General George McClellan to capture the Confederate capital at Richmond during the spring of 1862, in his highly touted peninsula campaign, brought local morale even lower during the summer months. Despite a change of command, Northern forces continued to suffer depressing setbacks, and in August 1862 General Robert E. Lee defeated another Union force at the Second Battle of Bull Run. Although the Union army managed to stop Lee's invasion of the North at the Battle of Antietam the next month, the victory was not at all satisfactory. Not only had the casualties been appalling, but the elusive Confederate general had been allowed to escape with his army into the relative security of northern Virginia.

In addition to the obvious effects the Civil War was having on the battle-fields, the conflict was also producing substantial but unintended changes in the social and economic life of Boston. The city's Irish immigrant community, for example, which now composed nearly one-third of the city's total population, became a visible and highly desirable part of the war effort. Although a great many of the Irish had little interest in fighting for the freedom of slaves, they had no hesitation in offering their lives to preserve the Union and to support their "adopted country." Within a few days after the attack on Fort Sumter, Irish-born Thomas Cass, former commander of a local Irish militia group called the Columbian Artillery, offered his services to Governor Andrew, who authorized him to recruit the all-Irish 9th Regiment, Massachusetts Volunteer Infantry. After a State House ceremony at which the governor presented the colors to "this splendid regiment," the 9th Regiment marched off to join the other Massachusetts regiments fighting at the front. So successful was the record of the "Fighting Ninth" in battle that Governor Andrew obtained permission to raise another Irish regiment. This time it was the 28th Regiment, which went off to New York, where it joined four other Irish regiments from New York and Pennsylvania to form the Irish Brigade, under the command of Thomas Francis Meagher.

The impressive patriotism displayed by Boston's Irish immigrants, their heroism on the battlefield, and the financial contributions from prominent Irish Americans in the city brought both recognition and respect from native Bostonians. In July 1861, Boston-born John Bernard Fitzpatrick, the Roman Catholic bishop of Boston, was awarded an honorary doctor of divinity degree from Harvard College, a highly unusual distinction for a prelate of this denomination. In addition, the state legislature modified an earlier ruling that had required Irish-Catholic children to read the Protestant version of the Bible in public schools. These may have been small measures, but in retrospect they were symbols of a change of attitude that would bring about changes in the social and economic status of the Boston Irish once the war was over.

The course of the Civil War also produced significant changes in the traditional lifestyles and expectations of the city's female population. From the moment the fighting started, Boston women immediately rallied to the Union cause and began doing all those things women did, and were expected to do, in time of war. In the quiet of their homes, or in large groups in schoolrooms or church parlors where they formed what became known as "sewing circles," they turned out bandages, blankets, and quilts, as well as such knitted goods as socks, mittens, scarves, gloves, and caps. On many occasions, they attached a personal note or an encouraging message to the boys at the front.

As the tempo of the fighting increased, however, and especially as the number of casualties began to rise beyond all expectations, it became clear that women would be needed in many other wartime roles—especially nursing and hospital care for the wounded. Except for the nursing care provided in a few urban hospitals by the Catholic order of the Sisters of Mercy, there was no organized, professional nursing care available. Into this vacuum moved two Bay State women. One was sixty-year-old Dorothea Lynde Dix, already famous for her work with the mentally ill, who in April 1861 was asked by the Lincoln administration to become superintendent of women nurses for the Union Army and undertake the formation of the nation's first organized nursing corps. Despite opposition from doctors, disagreements with nurses, and controversies with army officers who viewed females as meddlers and obstructionists, Dix remained at her post until the end of the war, when she returned to her work helping the mentally ill.

The other notable woman who responded to the needs of wounded servicemen was Clara Barton. A native of western Massachusetts who had been working in the U.S. Patent Office in Washington, D.C., Barton was appalled at the terrible suffering of soldiers as they waited to be transported from the battlefield to the hospital. Determined to bring relief to wounded troops as soon as possible, Barton arrived at the front lines late in August 1862, while the Second Battle of Bull Run was still raging. Barton and her helpers gave water, coffee, and sandwiches to the wounded troops, tending their wounds until the ambulances arrived to take them to hospital trains. Barton went on to nurse the sick and tend the wounded at Harpers Ferry and then at Antietam in early September, becoming famous as the "Angel of the Battlefield"—the woman who would "follow the cannons."

But however heroic and self-sacrificing the individual acts of courage, the expansion of the war and the enormity of the casualties made it increasingly obvious that larger, more professional and more effectively organized responses were needed to cope with the demands of the conflict. One major support group grew out of the Young Men's Christian Association of New York, which organized the Christian Commission to coordinate the wartime efforts of hundreds of individual church volunteer groups throughout the United States. Seeking to help as much with spiritual solace as with physical recovery, commission

The extent of the Civil War and the size of the Union Army gave American women unusual opportunities for a greater range of work experience and financial incomes in jobs hitherto reserved for men. This contemporary engraving from *Harper's Weekly* shows Boston women filling cartridge shells on an assembly line at the Watertown Arsenal. *Courtesy of the Boston Public Library, Print Department.*

members, relying heavily on the contributions of women, visited the sick, comforted the wounded, wrote letters, read the Bible, and conducted prayer services for wounded soldiers.

The second major organization dedicated to medical relief work was the U.S. Sanitary Commission, started in New York City by Frederick Law Olmsted, who would later design Boston's park system. The purpose of the commission was to promptly and efficiently distribute clothing, food, and medicine to Union soldiers. John Murray Forbes of Boston put together his own committee of twenty local businessmen, lawyers, ministers, and physicians to form a local chapter of the Sanitary Commission. Although the executive officers of the commission were men, the most active members were women, who worked to provide troops with essential medical and hospital services not furnished by the army. They worked to get medical equipment to the battlefields, used wagon trains and hospital ships to transfer wounded soldiers to military aid stations, and arranged transportation for disabled troops to permanent hospitals or convalescent stations. By the end of the war, hundreds of women had moved far beyond the limited confines of their traditional "spheres of domesticity," with results that would influence the course of women's history well into the future.

It was upon Boston's small and long-established African-American community, still concentrated on the northern slope of Beacon Hill, that the Civil War had perhaps its deepest and most significant impact. Despite numerous appeals that they be accepted into military service, blacks were not allowed to fight for their own freedom—not even after war had become a reality. But change came with great suddenness. The Battle of Antietam in September 1862 had not provided the decisive victory for which Abraham Lincoln had hoped. It did, however, provide President Lincoln with the opportunity to issue his Emancipation Proclamation, declaring that as of January 1, 1863, all slaves in seceded states would be "then, thenceforward, and forever free." To members of Boston's African-American community, as well to Garrison and the abolitionists, this was the great moment they had anticipated. "Prophets and kings have waited for this day, but died without the sight," said Governor John Andrew. Bells rang and people rejoiced when the proclamation was first announced in September, and then everyone waited for the edict to go into effect three months later.

On the evening of January 1, 1863, there was a gala at the Boston Music Hall, where both blacks and whites gathered to await the great moment. When the telegraph lines reported that President Lincoln had actually put his signature on the historic document, the auditorium erupted into cheers for Lincoln and Garrison. Ralph Waldo Emerson stepped forward to recite the "Boston Hymn" as an ode to justice and liberation:

> To-day unbind the captive.
> So only are ye unbound;
> Lift up a people from the dust.
> Trump of their rescue, sound!

After a singing of the Hallelujah Chorus from Handel's *Messiah*, the emotional evening of celebration came to an end, with most of the participants feeling that they had ushered in a new era of American life.

Since the terms of the Emancipation Proclamation provided that former slaves were now authorized to be "received into the armed forces of the United States," Governor Andrew and other state leaders felt it appropriate that an African-American regiment should be established to highlight the new status of black persons. The 54th Massachusetts Regiment was the first black regiment raised by any Northern state, although men were recruited from other states to fill the ranks of the unit. Indeed, so many men came pouring into the Bay State that another black regiment, the 55th, was later organized. Believing that the leader of the 54th Regiment should be an officer of "the highest tone and honor," Governor Andrew offered the command to Robert Gould Shaw, a member of one of Boston's oldest and most respected families. An abolitionist since his student days at Harvard, and already a veteran of several battles, young Shaw accepted the command. Later that summer, Colonel Shaw died leading his courageous regiment in a charge against an almost impregnable earthwork at Fort Wagner, at the gates of Charleston, South Carolina. After the war, Boston would commemorate the gallantry of Robert Gould Shaw and the 54th Regiment of African-American troops with a magnificent bronze plaque by the noted American sculptor Augustus Saint-Gaudens, placed opposite the State House on the crest of Beacon Hill.

Slowly the tide of conflict began to turn, and after the Union victories at Gettysburg and Vicksburg in July 1863, the news from the battlefront became more encouraging. Once General Ulysses S. Grant assumed overall command, there was a new sense of direction and determination to the Union war effort. Although the costs were still high, and the casualties still terrible, by the close of 1864 there were indications that the end could not be too far away.

Once President Abraham Lincoln's Emancipation Proclamation went into effect in January 1863, African-American citizens had their first opportunity to serve in the armed forces. Private Abraham F. Brown (above) was one of many volunteers who joined the 54th Massachusetts Regiment when it was established. The heroism of this all-black regiment was later commemorated with the memorial to Colonel Robert Gould Shaw by Augustus Saint-Gaudens, located on Beacon Street directly opposite the State House. *Courtesy of the Massachusetts Historical Society.*

General William Tecumseh Sherman completed his devastating march from Chattanooga to Atlanta by September 1864, and then pushed on all the way to the seaport of Savannah by December. And early in 1865, his great war machine was turning around and preparing to march up through the Carolinas. Out in the Shenandoah Valley, General Philip Sheridan's hard-riding cavalry had destroyed most of the Rebel fighting units and put the torch to the once-fertile valley. And General Grant himself, despite frightful losses, was now entrenched at Petersburg, hammering on the door of the Confederate capital of Richmond.

After the first of the year in 1865, the people of Boston read their morning newspapers with a definite sense of anticipation as the Union ring grew tighter around the hard-pressed Confederates. In mid-February, General Sherman captured Charleston, South Carolina, and Boston's 54th Massachusetts Regiment was one of the first federal contingents to enter the city. Three days later, troops from the 55th Regiment marched into the stricken city, with Lieutenant George Thompson Garrison, son of the Boston abolitionist, commanding one of the companies. The immense irony of the situation was not lost on the Boston abolitionist Wendell Phillips, who was beside himself with joy. "Can you conceive a bitterer drop that God's chemistry could mix for the son of the Palmetto State than that a Massachusetts flag and a colored regiment should take possession of Charleston?" he asked. On April 3, the news that General Grant had finally taken the Rebel capital of Richmond, Virginia, sent the city into wild rejoicing. Flags went up all over town, bells pealed for a solid hour at noon, and at one o'clock a hundred-gun salute was fired on Boston Common. Six days later, the joy turned to absolute delirium with the news that General Lee and his entire army had surrendered to General Grant at Appomattox Court House. Once again, the flags appeared everywhere, people fired guns off in public, buildings were decorated, and schools, banks, and offices were closed. Impromptu celebrations were held all over town, bands played patriotic music, and at night the city was treated to displays of fireworks. The war was finally over! It seemed that nothing could possibly happen to dampen the city's joy and enthusiasm.

Less than a week later, however, the once-joyful city was in deep mourning. On Saturday morning, April 15, 1865, Boston received the shocking news that President Abraham Lincoln had been assassinated—a catastrophe that came, as one newspaper put it, "like a thunderbolt from a clear sky." Those flags that only the day before had fluttered joyously over the city in celebration of victory now drooped silently at half-mast, while bells tolled out their mournful dirge. The faces of men and women that only the day before had been radiant with joy were now bathed with tears and twisted in anguish. "As one passes along the street," noted the *Boston Journal*, "strong men are met with their eyes dimmed with tears." On Wednesday, April 19, the funeral of Abraham Lincoln took place in the nation's capital. On that day, everything in Boston was closed down in solemn tribute to the occasion. Horsecarts were withdrawn from service, and the operations of the steam railroads were suspended between noon and two o'clock. Churches throughout the city held special services that were attended by overflow throngs of people; every house displayed some public mark of mourning. Later in the day, several thousand people held an impromptu ceremony on Boston Common to express their grief.

At the end of the year, late in December 1865 on Forefathers' Day, commemorating the landing of the Pilgrims at Plymouth 245 years earlier, a "Return of the Flags" ceremony was held in Boston. In a procession that included all divisions in which every Bay State regiment was represented, the regimental flags of each unit were carried through the streets of Boston to the State House. As each formation came to a halt, a color bearer stepped forward from the ranks, marched up the steps, and presented the colors to Governor John Andrew. The banners, many of them tattered and bloodied, were taken into the State House, where they were draped around the pillars in Doric Hall. Later, they were all placed in Memorial Hall, or the Hall of Flags, where they continue to give silent testimony to the role Massachusetts played in the preservation of the Union. The Civil War marked the end of one era in Boston's history, and would clearly mark the beginning of another.

BOOK THREE
Melting Pot

Chapter

7

Winds of Change

T HE four years of the Civil War had changed the shape and direction of American history, and had also brought many changes for the Boston community. Some changes were welcome, exciting, and anticipated; others were discouraging, disappointing, and unexpected. One thing was certain: things would never be the same again—for Boston or for the nation.

No other war in the history of the United States had ever had such a direct and personal effect on so many people as did the Civil War. By the time the fighting had stopped, over half a million Americans were dead—out of a population of about thirty-one million. This conflict between the states killed more Americans in four years than all the wars fought in the twentieth century; and, because the total population was so much smaller in 1860, the Civil War had a far greater impact on the nation. This was truly a war that touched every city, every town, every family in America.

The Civil War had taken a generation of young Boston men out of their isolated, insular, and parochial surroundings and sent them far away from home for as long as three or four years. This disruptive experience obviously produced sociological as well as psychological effects on young soldiers. They had seen other places, talked with different people, experienced unfamiliar events, faced danger, suffered wounds, confronted death—and then, after all that, returned to their homes in Boston and Cambridge to a rapidly changing America.

A great many of the Boston women who had been involved in the Civil War had also gone through remarkable and stimulating experiences that gave them new skills and proficiencies. What they had done in the war dramatically changed the way they saw themselves as women and provided new outlooks on their purpose in the world. The war had given many Boston women the opportunity to travel freely, to speak publicly before mixed audiences, to assume managerial positions in national wartime relief agencies, to engage in active politics, and to hold their own with government officials and military bureaucrats. These experiences gave women the kind of confidence and self-assurance that they would carry into professional activities, educational careers, and social reform movements well into the twentieth century.

For Boston's African-American community, on the other hand, the Civil War had perhaps raised higher expectations but delivered fewer substantial results. The coming of the war, the issuance of the Emancipation Proclamation, the end of slavery assured by the Thirteenth Amendment, and the guarantee of full civil and political rights guaranteed by the Fourteenth Amendment all seemed to offer black Americans a full and equal share in the promise of America. Soon, though, it was clear that the inspiring rhetoric would produce few meaningful results—even in Boston. Black Bostonians were still confined to their back-of-the-hill community along the slopes of "Nigger Hill," still prevented from becoming apprentices in the skilled professions, and still denied the kind of social acceptance that was consistent with their political rights. Although the Republican party had succeeded in eradicating the institution of slavery as a direct result of the war, during the postwar years it soon tired of its role as the champion of equal rights and failed to transform the social structure of the South. For the sake of political survival in the disputed election of 1876–1877, the Republicans agreed to allow African Americans to be deprived of their constitutional rights and reduced to the category of second-class citizens. From then on, the disease of racism was allowed to fester silently and secretly under the surface of the American body politic like a deadly cancerous growth. It would erupt a century later to engulf the nation in racial strife and bitter, violent, and deadly social confrontation.

For the members of Boston's business community who had become loyal Republicans and supported the Lincoln administration's efforts to preserve the

Union, the Civil War had provided substantial prosperity during wartime and seemed to promise unlimited financial prospects in the future. The secession of the South and the departure of Southern congressmen had opened up the national legislative system to a stream of Republican economic programs that changed the face of America well into the twentieth century. In the absence of Southern opposition, the Republicans were able to create a national currency system and to organize a national banking system. The Homestead Act offered free public land to settlers who wanted it; the Morrill Act created a system of land-grant colleges; and the Pacific Railroad Act provided thousands of acres of public land for the construction of transcontinental railroads. Taking advantage of secession, the Republican congress had drafted, in effect, what one historian called "a blueprint for modern America" by endorsing an industrialized, capital-intensive, national business structure.

Ironically, however, the very industrial system the Boston businessmen endorsed so enthusiastically at war's end was one that quickly left a parochial and outmoded Bay State economy in the lurch. The war, according to Harvard's Charles Eliot Norton, proved to be "a cataclysm" that deepened the breach between the "old period" and the new, between the past and the present. Before the Civil War, much of the nation had looked to Boston, the "Hub of the Universe," as a leading center of diversified industrial investment and ingenious capital enterprise. By the 1870s, however, the nation's "Age of Big Business" was in full swing, with more railroads, larger factories, more sophisticated machinery, greater production, and higher profits than ever before. In almost no time, the Bay State's financial efforts rapidly faded into insignificance compared with the gigantic corporate structures and incredible personal fortunes being accumulated by such new entrepreneurial giants as Cornelius Vanderbilt, John D. Rockefeller, and Andrew Carnegie. The fortunes being made in new enterprises dwarfed the incomes derived from old New England shipyards, traditional family businesses, and deteriorating textile factories. It was clear that the old Yankee dollar was no longer what it used to be. "We are vanishing into provincial obscurity," moaned Barrett Wendell of Boston. "America has swept from our grasp. The future is beyond us."

Not only had the nation changed industrially and technologically, but the tone and flavor of postwar American society had also been transformed. In an age characterized more and more by material forces and secular philosophies, Puritan Christianity's old moral concepts seemed alarmingly out of place. Many of the old Boston families viewed the postwar industrial period as completely alien, in contrast to the prewar society in which they had lived and flourished. Traditional moral principles, ethical practices, and cultural standards suddenly seemed to have completely degenerated. The gentlemanly and democratic *laissez-faire* system espoused by Thomas Jefferson had become a highly competitive dog-eat-dog jungle where only "the fit" were entitled to survive. The idealistic doctrine of self-reliance preached by Ralph Waldo Emerson and his Transcendental followers had been reduced to mere self-aggrandizement by the new giants of industry. Jefferson's "spirit of independence" was now interpreted as Vanderbilt's "The Public Be Damned." "The leaders of Massachusetts sixty, seventy, eighty years ago were men who had *done* something," asserted Edward Everett Hale. "The leaders of society now," he scoffed, were those whose "most prominent business is to unlock a safe in a safety deposit vault, cut off coupons from their bonds, and carry them to be cashed." The lavish and often vulgar display of personal wealth, gaudy mansions, and the all-pervading influence of big business in the corrupt affairs of the nation during the Grant administration convinced many Bostonians that the "new" America was not their America. It would have been better, Charles Eliot Norton told his class in the history of the fine arts at Harvard College, "had we never been born in this degenerate and unlovely age."

To make matters worse, not only was the nation as a whole changing, but so was the traditional old city of Boston itself. In terms of the size, the shape, the scope, and the very character of the venerable old town, Boston was going through such remarkable changes that it was hardly recognizable anymore. Despite the pressures and sacrifices of the Civil War, Boston had continued with an expansive building boom that had been going on since the nation had secured its independence. During the early 1800s, the construction of Bulfinch's new State House had stimulated development of a fashionable residential district in the Beacon Hill area. This community was further expanded when nearby Pemberton Hill was reduced to provide residences for wealthy businessmen and retired sea captains.

To provide even more living space for the city's increasing population, developers dumped tons of gravel into the muddy waters along the south side of the thin strip of land (the "Neck") that connected the old Shawmut Peninsula to the Roxbury mainland. As early as the 1840s, the South End began to take shape as an attractive and well-designed community into which wealthy Boston families could move when there was no more room on Beacon Hill. Architect Gridley Bryant chose "the modern style of Renaissance architecture" when

This nineteenth-century view shows the South End's Blackstone Square, with the spire of the Shawmut Avenue Universalist Church in the background. This was one of a series of attractive squares and fountains that developers hoped would attract wealthy patrons to the new South End. The subsequent creation of the Back Bay, however, put an end to optimistic expectations for the future of the South End. *Courtesy of the Bostonian Society/Old State House.*

he designed the new City Hospital on the South End's Harrison Avenue in 1861. The main administration building, with its impressive dome and portico, was flanked by mansard-roofed pavilions, creating what historian Walter Muir Whitehill later called "the handsomest development in the South End."

When the city's rapidly growing Roman Catholic population became too large for its modest church on Franklin Street in downtown Boston, it was the South End that Bishop John Fitzpatrick selected as the place to build a much larger Gothic cathedral. The members of the Society of Jesus (the Jesuits) also chose the South End for their imposing granite Church of the Immaculate Conception, which the architectural historian Douglass Shand-Tucci has described as a splendid example of how mid-century American architects "translated the Classical tradition into the idiom of their own time." Two years later, in 1863, the South End was also the site for the first structure to house Boston College, designed to provide a higher education for the sons of Irish immigrants. The Jesuits believed that the South End, with its "better class of houses," would be a promising part of the city for such an institution. A similar conviction also persuaded a number of Protestant denominations to seek out locations in the South End. A new Unitarian church was built on West Newton Street; the South Congregational Church constructed a new building on Union Park Street in 1862; a building for a Methodist church was completed the same year on Tremont Street; the First Presbyterian Church went up on Columbus Avenue; and a new structure for the Evangelical Lutheran Zion Church was erected at the corner of Shawmut Avenue and Waltham Street.

But the bright and promising future of the South End as the city's most promising and lucrative real estate venture was suddenly and unexpectedly eclipsed by spectacular developments across the way in Boston's Back Bay. Motivated by the private impulse for immense real estate profits, as well as by the public desire to clear up a serious health hazard, a major effort was undertaken to fill in the waters along the north side of Boston Neck. For years the ebb and flow on the tidal flats had left the sewage dumped into the basin exposed to the sun and open air. This produced what one city health report called "nothing less than a great cesspool" that acted as a giant receptacle for "all the filth of a large and constantly increasing population." To alleviate this disgusting condition, as well as to provide additional housing space near the city's center, in 1857 a special state commission recommended the "Filling up and sale of [Back Bay] lands." The project was begun in 1858, when earth from the Needham sand hills and gravel pits, nine miles to the west, was carried to Boston in railroad cars to begin creating what would eventually become 580 acres of brand new land.

In developing the vast acreage of the new Back Bay, the commissioners followed an impressive design, usually credited to the architect Arthur Gilman, that conveyed a distinctively Parisian flavor. In looking to the city's postwar development, observes Douglass Shand-Tucci, "Boston suddenly surrendered to a passion for things French." Letters and memoirs from many traveling Bostonians during the 1850s reflected their admiration for the ways in which Emperor Napoleon III had beautified the city of Paris—the expansive new boulevards; the magnificent public buildings; the new Louvre, housing the nation's art collection; the imposing new opera house, with its ornate decorations and brilliant gaslights—and made Boston planners want to emulate the City of Lights. In laying out the Back Bay, therefore, architect Arthur Gilman envisioned long vistas, residences fashioned in the Second-Empire style, and a broad central boulevard reminiscent of the Champs Elysées. The main thoroughfare, Commonwealth Avenue, was two hundred feet wide, running west from Arlington Street at the foot of the Public Garden. Beacon Street and Boylston Street extended westward on either side of the boulevard, and two new streets, Marlborough and Newbury, also ran parallel to Commonwealth Avenue. From the very start, the Back Bay was clearly to be the most fashionable and luxurious residential section in the expanding city. The extensive French influence consciously reflected a Parisian elegance that wealthy Bostonians were convinced would make their city, as one modern analyst expressed it, "the cultural center of the United States, and one of the greatest cities in the world."

During the 1860s, despite the crisis of the Civil War, Bostonians went ahead with their plans to fill in the Back Bay and create a fashionable new neighborhood that would rival the boulevards and buildings of Paris. With Commonwealth Avenue serving as the city's Champs Elysées and the mansions done in Second French Empire style, the Parisian influence was very much in evidence as Boston sought to become a "world city." *Courtesy of the Bostonian Society/Old State House.*

The filling-in of land on either side of the Neck had caused the old Shawmut peninsula to become an integral and, as time went on, an almost indistinguishable part of the mainland. But it was with the annexation of a number of adjoining towns that Boston suddenly experienced a tremendous physical growth. During the postwar years, large numbers of Boston residents, many of them Irish immigrants, abandoned the congested waterfront districts and moved into the nearby suburbs. Very soon they were raising demands for such services as water, sewers, streets, schools, hospitals, police security, and fire protection. As a result, several towns sought to annex themselves to the City of Boston in order to obtain the vital municipal services they were unable to provide for themselves.

In those days, annexation required the approval of the state legislature and voter approval in both Boston and the town seeking annexation. Roxbury was the first to vote for annexation in 1866 and formally became a part of Boston in 1868. Dorchester followed two years later, while in 1873 Charlestown and Brighton agreed to annexation, as did West Roxbury, whose residents had debated the issue for several years. Largely as a result of this remarkable annexation movement, Boston's population jumped from 140,000 in 1865 to 341,000 ten years later—an increase of more than 200,000 people in only ten years. Once a small community of some 780 acres of land, Boston now spread over almost 24,000 acres—nearly thirty times its original size. Boston had definitely changed. It was no longer the "tight little island" that had always made it so distinctive, so aloof, so parochial. It was something else entirely.

If the postwar changes had been limited to those of a financial and topographical nature, perhaps most native Bostonians would have made the necessary adjustments with a certain amount of grace, if not good humor. But the changes went much deeper than that, and their obvious consequences provoked a sense of impending doom. Especially alarming was the way in which the flood of European immigrants, which had started during the decades before the Civil War, was picking up again and threatening to inundate the whole city with strange faces and even stranger ways. The fact that a large percentage of these newcomers were from Ireland increased even further the feelings of fear and anxiety spreading through a native population whose staunch Puritan background made them ill-equipped to deal with outsiders.

For generations it had been comforting for the "better elements" of Boston to reflect upon the purity of their culture and the homogeneity of their race. They could take pride in the fact that no persons of Irish birth, or members of any other of the "lesser breeds," had intruded upon their illustrious heritage. Successions of Harvard-trained, New England–bred historians had assured their readers quite categorically that no Irish were to be found in North America much before 1830. The inhabitants of New England at the time of the Revolution, according to John Gorham Palfrey in his *History of the Revolution* (1865), were "wholly English." Not a single county in all England, he wrote, had "purer English blood than theirs." Some twenty-five years later, the eminent historian John Fiske, writing in *The Beginnings of New England* (1889), also agreed that the Puritan exodus to America had been "purely and exclusively English." A short time later, in *The Story of the Revolution* (1898), Henry Cabot Lodge agreed that those American colonials who had fought for independence were "almost of pure English blood, with a small infusion of Huguenots and a slight mingling, chiefly in New Hampshire, of Scotch-Irish from Londonderry."

In fact, however, many immigrants from Ireland had come to New England as early as the seventeenth century. Contemporary shipping records, passenger lists, town records, minutes of town meetings, church registers, and graveyard epitaphs list family names that are distinctively Irish. On the basis of such sources, as well as on data taken from the 1790 federal census, modern historians estimate that the total number of those persons who had come from all parts of Ireland to America by the time of the Revolution was somewhere between 350,000 and 400,000. At first, during the early 1600s, it was Catholics who left Ireland from such southern ports as Cork and Kinsale. As indentured servants, they were pledged to complete several years of bonded labor in return for free passage either to the West Indies or to such early American colonies as Virginia and Maryland.

During the later decades of the 1600s, however, the number of non-Catholics emigrating from ports in northern Ireland greatly exceeded that of Catholics leaving from southern ports. By the start of the 1700s, Protestants constituted the major source of Irish emigration to the New World. Most of these northern Protestants were the descendants of original Scottish settlers who had been "planted" on confiscated Irish lands in rebellious Ulster by King James I. Their numbers were augmented later in the 1600s by some 50,000 additional families, which also came from Scotland. Life in Ireland was difficult for these transplanted Scots, who had settled on lands that had been taken away from the native Irish peoples. Because they were not Roman Catholics, and because they were seen as an overseas arm of English oppression, the Ulster

Irish were hated and despised by the Catholic majority. That was to be expected. What was not expected, however, was the shabby treatment they received from an English government to which they were loyal. As fundamentalist Protestants, mainly Presbyterians, they found themselves subject to many of the same kinds of punitive laws the Church of England leveled against Roman Catholics. As landowners, artisans, small businessmen, and enterprising merchants, they struggled against high rents, repressive taxes, and discriminatory trade laws that unfairly benefited the English economy.

Disillusioned and disheartened about their prospects for the future, by the early 1700s the Protestants of northern Ireland sought greater religious freedom, political independence, and economic opportunity across the Atlantic. During 1715–1720, high rents, bad weather, and crop failures produced heavy emigration from Ulster; another wave followed from 1725 to 1729. Between 1730 and 1769, perhaps as many as 70,000 Presbyterians sailed to the colonies, while in the next five years, from 1770 to 1775, emigration from northern Ireland reached a peak, with some 30,000 Ulster Presbyterians escaping high rents and wholesale evictions. Scholars estimate that during the colonial period, between 200,000 and 250,000 Ulster Irish emigrated to North America, with about half that number arriving during the sixty years between 1717 and 1776.

The earliest immigrants from Ireland generally stayed clear of the Boston area, where residents were predominantly Anglo-Saxon and decidedly hostile to the Irish, whom they considered members of a barbaric and inferior race. The first arrivals from Ireland, therefore, tended to settle in the less populated regions of New England—places like Bangor, Belfast, and Limerick in Maine; Dublin, Londonderry, and Hillsboro County in New Hampshire; and Orange County in Vermont. Gradually, however, the Ulster Irish were accepted into the Boston community, especially after the new Massachusetts charter of 1691 specified that political representation be based not on religious affiliation but on income and property. The fact that most of the Ulster Irish spoke English rather than Gaelic made them more acceptable, as did the fact that as merchants, commercial farmers, and enterprising businessmen their lifestyle seemed to be compatible with the traditional Puritan work ethic.

As early as 1657, a Scots Charitable Society was formed in Boston to assist the poorer members of the community, and in 1724 the Irish Charitable Society was created for similar purposes, insisting that members be "natives of Ireland," "Protestants," and "inhabitants of Boston." Three years later, the Ulsterites established the Irish Presbyterian Church in an old building not far from the waterfront, and in 1744 moved to more spacious quarters on Long Lane, only a short distance from the Town House. By vigorously supporting the colonial rebellion against acts of British oppression—similar to the restrictive laws that had forced them to leave Ireland—and then by taking an active role in the subsequent American Revolution, the Irish Presbyterians finally won recognition as loyal and patriotic Americans. The political ascendancy of the first wave of Irish Protestants was perhaps most dramatically illustrated in 1807 when an Ulster Protestant named James Sullivan, an influential lawyer whose father had emigrated from Ireland in the mid-1700s, was elected governor of Massachusetts. His brother, John Sullivan, had risen to the rank of brigadier general in the Continental Army and had served as an aide to General George Washington during the evacuation of Boston.

While Protestant Irish from the northern counties dominated the exodus from Ireland during the 1700s, the number of Catholics emigrating from the southern counties, by contrast, was decidedly small. The modern historian Kerby Miller suggests that during the period from 1700 to 1776, Roman Catholics constituted only one-fifth to one-fourth of the immigrants from Ireland. The reasons for this obvious reluctance to emigrate are fairly obvious. For one thing, oppressive English land policies had reduced most Irish Catholics to the level of impoverished tenant farmers, migratory workers, and unskilled laborers. They were often seen roaming the countryside in search of land, food, and work. Very few of them had money enough to afford the long and hazardous passage across the stormy Atlantic.

Then, too, many were discouraged by the pessimistic reports coming back from North America describing the extent and intensity of anti-Irish and anti-Catholic feelings among the predominantly Anglo-Saxon colonials. Centuries of bitter political conflict and savage military struggles between English invaders and Irish defenders had caused the English to regard Irish Catholics not only as members of a blasphemous and heretical religion, but also as political subversives engaged in a conspiracy to destroy the monarchy and overthrow the English government. These convictions were carried to America, where they conditioned the responses of Puritan political and religious leaders. Throughout New England, Papists (as Catholics were called) were not only excluded from liberties extended to most other settlers, but were also subjected to specific penalties similar to the Penal Laws then already in force throughout the British Isles. In Massachusetts, especially, Catholics were placed under unusually severe limitations, and according to a law passed by the General

Court in 1700, Catholic priests were subject to imprisonment and possible death if found in the colony.

In most cases, those Irish Catholics who did come into Boston from the southern parts of Ireland during the mid-1700s were a poor, hardworking class. Since money was scarce and most Irish Catholics were unable to pay for their transportation across the Atlantic, many were "bound out" as indentured servants under an agreement to work out the cost of their passage when they arrived in America. Among those recorded on passenger lists were artisans, masons, bricklayers, carpenters, cabinetmakers, tailors, shoemakers, stonecutters, hatters, weavers, and blacksmiths, as well as husbandmen, farmhands, and common laborers. Some of the women were described as cooks, dressmakers, seamstresses, and household servants. Those who had the temerity to display any public evidence of their papist beliefs were usually regarded with fear and suspicion by members of a Puritan community that continued to regard Catholicism as both a subversive political menace and a fearsome religious heresy.

It was not until the outbreak of the War for Independence that New Englanders began to exhibit some measure of tolerance for Europeans in general, and for Roman Catholics in particular. In November 1775, when he arrived in Cambridge to take official command of the Continental Army, General George Washington ordered his officers and men to refrain from taking part in that "ridiculous and childish" custom known as "Pope's Night." This was a popular anti-papist celebration held annually on November 5 that commemorated the gunpowder plot, parodied various Catholic rituals, and climaxed with a public burning of the pope in effigy.* Since he hoped to secure an alliance with France and with French Canadians in the colonial rebellion against Great Britain, Washington pointed out the "impropriety" of insulting the religious beliefs of those people in such a "monstrous" and inexcusable fashion.

Unofficial but invaluable assistance from the French court of King Louis XVI in the early stages of the fighting also helped make Catholicism a little more acceptable in the colonies. And when the government of France agreed to recognize the United States and make a formal treaty of military and commercial

---

* On November 5, 1606, a group of disgruntled Catholics, among them Guy Fawkes, made an unsuccessful attempt to blow up King, Lords, and Commons in one spectacular explosion. After the attempt failed, English Protestants celebrated the end of the "gunpowder plot" with an annual demonstration on Guy Fawkes Day.

alliance early in 1778, many Americans showed a willingness to adopt a more tolerant attitude toward the beliefs and practices of their traditional enemy. On a visit to Boston in 1778, the French admiral Comte Charles-Henri d'Estaing and members of his fleet were hospitably received and graciously honored by leading citizens of the town, and were later invited to dine at the Beacon Street home of John Hancock. And when one of d'Estaing's young officers was accidentally killed ashore while attempting to break up a fight between local ruffians and some French bakers, apologetic Bostonians allowed the lieutenant the extraordinary honor of a burial in the town's venerable King's Chapel.

By the time the United States had finally secured its independence from Great Britain in 1783, therefore, there was a sufficient atmosphere of forbearance in Boston to accommodate a handful of Roman Catholics, who had begun to practice their religion openly. Numbering fewer than a hundred, mostly French and Irish, they attended Mass in a small brick structure that had formerly been a French Huguenot chapel, located on the south side of School Street a few doors down from Washington Street. For their spiritual direction, they had to make do with several transient French clerics until the arrival of two French priests—Fr. François Antoine Matignon in 1792, and Fr. Jean-Louis Lefebvre de Cheverus in 1796—whose charm, kindliness, and priestly devotion captured the hearts of most Bostonians. When the lease on the old church was about to expire in 1799, the Catholics of the town purchased a site on nearby Franklin Street where, on March 17, 1800, the ground was broken for the first Catholic church in Boston. Many of the town's Protestant residents contributed generously to the undertaking, and young Charles Bulfinch furnished the architectural plans free of charge for the new Church of the Holy Cross, which was finally dedicated in September 1803. The report, five years later, that Pope Pius VII had created Boston as a separate episcopal see, and had named the popular Cheverus as its first bishop, was welcome news to the residents of the town who had come to love and respect the hardworking French priest.

Although the number of Catholics in the town continued to increase slightly every year, the newcomers were still manageable enough in size, and useful enough in the services they provided, to ensure their continued toleration. Many of the French, for example, served as skilled watchmakers, candy makers, cooks, caterers, waiters, musicians, and dancing instructors; the Irish functioned as blacksmiths, glassblowers, grocers, clothiers, and tailors. A number of unskilled laborers had been brought over from Ireland to do the pick-and-shovel work involved in various major construction projects during the early

1800s—the filling in of coves and inlets, the cutting down of old Beacon Hill to make way for the new State House, and the construction of the Mill Dam at the outer end of the town to increase the land area for new real estate developments.

It was not long, however, before larger numbers of Irish began to cross the Atlantic and join their friends and relatives in America. With the end of the War of 1812, and especially after the collapse of grain prices that followed in the wake of Napoleon's defeat in 1815, the landlords of Ireland made a major effort to sustain their prosperous wartime incomes. They either raised rents on their property to unrealistic levels or else converted their fields into pastureland for the grazing of sheep and cattle. One result of this preemptive postwar land policy was a marked acceleration of large-scale emigration of bankrupt farmers and displaced laborers from all parts of Ireland, but especially from the rural counties in the south and west. From 1825 through 1830, approximately 125,000 people emigrated from Ireland to the United States—an average of 20,000 a year. Over 30,000 of these arrivals came to the Commonwealth of Massachusetts, with the result that by 1830 there were over 8,000 Irish Catholics living in Boston.

The dramatic growth in the number of Irish Catholics in Boston during the late 1820s and early 1830s was disturbing to native Bostonians simply as a religious phenomenon. Taken in conjunction with the numerous social and economic problems the Catholics helped to intensify, their arrival was now viewed with great alarm by the older inhabitants of the city. During the late 1820s, there were sporadic outbreaks of violence against persons and property along Ann Street, Broad Street, and other Irish neighborhoods near the waterfront. Throughout the summer months of July and August 1825, for example, the *Boston Advertiser* reported "disgraceful riots" taking place almost every night by gangs who broke windows, damaged furniture, and destroyed several small houses. The mayor and aldermen finally had to station six constables in the Irish district from ten o'clock at night until morning in order to keep the peace.

Tensions persisted, however, and the continued presence of so many Roman Catholics in the old Puritan city conjured up the old fears of a Catholic menace. The Boston Sunday School Union constantly predicted the dangers of a papist revival in America, the Reverend Lyman Beecher called upon "Native Americans" to be on their guard against a "Catholic conspiracy" on this side of the Atlantic, and in 1834 an angry mob burned down the Ursuline Convent in Charlestown while hundreds stood around and cheered. Three years later, in June 1837, violence broke out in the very heart of the city when a company

During the mid-1840s, a deadly fungus ruined Ireland's entire potato crop, the food upon which the poor families of the rural areas depended for sustenance. Faced with a devastating famine, unprecedented numbers scraped together whatever money they could and booked passage to America. Often they left in vessels so poorly constructed they were called "coffin ships." *From the* Illustrated London News, *May 10, 1851.*

of firemen, returning from a call, clashed with an Irish funeral procession traveling along the same street. In moments, what started out as a fistfight had mushroomed into a full-scale riot, reportedly involving some fifteen thousand persons, as residents from both sides spilled out of their houses and into the streets to participate in the battle. The "Broad Street Riot" was finally brought to a halt only when Mayor Samuel Eliot called in the state militia, complete with cavalry, to disperse the rioters and restore order to the city.

But if "Native Americans" were alarmed at this first wave of Irish-Catholic immigration during the 1820s and 1830s, they were thunderstruck at what took place during the 1840s and 1850s, when the catastrophic potato blight—known as the Great Famine—brought death and starvation in Ireland and sent a new wave of emigrants seeking shelter and safety on the shores of the New World. By the hundreds of thousands, the Irish poured into America during the "Black Forties," huddled together in the dark stinking holds of cargo ships. Their small savings completely used up by the price of passage, they landed sick and destitute at Boston and at other East Coast ports—too poor to move on, too desperate to care. Living in squalor, herded together in the congested streets of the North End or in the dilapidated houses of the once-fashionable Fort Hill district, they clung to the wharves and struggled to survive in their new environment.

Americans must have expected a substantial increase in Irish immigration as a result of the Great Famine, but they certainly did not anticipate the sudden tidal wave that threatened to engulf them. In 1847, for example—in a single year—the city of Boston, which had been absorbing immigrants at the rate of about four or five thousand a year, was inundated by over thirty-seven thousand new arrivals, most of whom were officially listed as "Irish labourers." Upwards of one thousand immigrants landed at the port of Boston in a single day—April 10, 1847—and although many of them moved on through the city to find homes in other parts of the state, a sufficient number remained to increase the urban population substantially.

In contrast to other American cities, Boston had never really accepted Irish immigrants, but at least those who had come over during the 1820s and 1830s had been physically robust and sturdy—strong enough to swing the picks and shovels on construction jobs and lug heavy cargo on the docks. And for this reason, they had been tolerated for their contributions to the community's economic development. Most of the newly arrived "Famine Irish," however, came ashore pallid and weak, half-starved, disease-ridden, and impoverished, with no skills at all except a rudimentary knowledge of farming. There was little they could offer to the community in which they found themselves. Perhaps more to the point, there was almost nothing the community could do for them. Boston offered few economic opportunities to those without skills and without tools. At a time when other American cities were developing industrial centers, manufacturing outlets, and railroad concentrations capable of employing large numbers of unskilled workers, Boston's capital investments had long been dispersed into such outlying areas as Waltham, Lowell, and Lawrence, where waterpower sites had been available for textile production. Within the city itself, therefore, there was little call for the abundant supply of cheap Irish labor now at hand. Without the schooling to become clerks, the training to become craftsmen, or the capital to become shopkeepers, the Boston Irish became, as Oscar Handlin expressed it in his classic study *Boston's Immigrants,* "a massive lump in the community, undigested, undigestible." Most men were forced to rely on the meager earnings of their womenfolk—their wives, their sisters, their daughters—working as domestic servants in the hotels and private homes of the city, in order to tide them over until they could scrape up temporary jobs as day laborers sweeping streets, tending horses, cleaning stables, unloading ships, cutting fish, and lugging crates.

In addition to a bleak economic picture, Irish Catholics also confronted the problem of a social climate that was decidedly hostile. At the time the immigrants were fleeing pestilence and famine, Boston was already an old city, with more than two centuries of history and tradition behind it. The city's Brahmin aristocracy was inordinately proud of its distinctive past and was, therefore, fiercely determined to fight against any changes that could possibly threaten its future. Then, too, Boston had retained its distinctively Anglo-Saxon-Protestant character long after other East Coast cities like New York and Philadelphia had become metropolitan centers, and newer western cities like St. Louis and Chicago were absorbing frontiersmen and immigrants alike. The possibility that Irish Catholics, with their alien culture and their detested religion, would ever be welcomed or even admitted into the exclusive ranks of such a long-established and highly self-conscious social system was extremely unlikely.

Because of such attitudes, newcomers who once may have been looked upon merely as nuisances or inconveniences were regarded as menaces to the city and obvious threats to democratic institutions everywhere. "Foreign paupers are rapidly accumulating on our hands," warned Mayor John Prescott

Bigelow in 1850, telling sympathetic taxpayers about the large numbers of "aged, blind, paralytic, and lunatic immigrants who have become public charges on our public charities." The extent of their drinking was exaggerated, and their inclination for brawling became almost legendary. The vile and congested slums in which they were forced to live were cited as evidence of their essentially lazy character. Native Bostonians were appalled at the unsanitary living conditions of the newcomers and complained that they were turning Massachusetts into a "moral cesspool." When, in spite of their supposed laziness, they took jobs of the most menial sort, they were accused of taking work away from deserving local Yankees and further denounced for driving down the standard of living. Their Catholic religion was looked upon as a permanent obstacle to social assimilation, and when they began showing a flair for political organization, they were denounced as a danger to the American political system.

In the face of this new and greatly enlarged "Catholic Menace" after the Great Famine of 1847, native-born Americans felt that more effective measures were needed to control what appeared to be a crisis of national proportions. During 1852–1853, a number of local patriotic and "nativist" organizations combined to form the "American Party," a national political organization designed to protect the United States from the "insidious wiles of foreigners." The party was highly secret, complete with handshakes and passwords, and was commonly referred to as the "Know-Nothing Party" because its members were pledged not to give out a single word about the organization, its activities, or its membership. Their stock response to any such question was: "I know nothing." The object of the new party was to keep recent immigrants in an essentially subservient position while the party worked to develop legislation that would put strict controls on further Catholic immigration.

Political power in such East Coast cities as Boston, New York, Philadelphia, and Baltimore took a sudden swing to the new party. In Massachusetts, the American Party succeeded in electing the governor, all the state officers, the entire state senate, and all but one member of the house of representatives. Once they took office, the members of the Know-Nothing legislature pushed forward a program of "Temperance, Liberty, and Protestantism" in the name of the people of Massachusetts who, according to one house member, were ready to eliminate "Rome, Rum, and Robbery." In addition to proposing a Twenty-One-Year Law that would have prevented any immigrant from voting until he had been a resident of the commonwealth for twenty-one years, the legislature dissolved all Irish militia companies and confiscated their military

THE FIERY CROSS!

An anti-Catholic cartoon of the early nineteenth century shows how Nativists saw the Catholic hierarchy, here personified by Paul Cullen, archbishop of Armagh, moving aggressively across the Atlantic Ocean from the various counties in southern Ireland. Fearing a papal conspiracy to establish the power of the Catholic Church in the United States, Protestants organized various political organizations to defend the nation against the inroads of foreigners.

equipment. The legislature also made the reading of the Protestant version of the Bible (the King James version) compulsory in all public schools and deprived diocesan officials of all control over church property. In February 1855, a joint committee of the state legislature was formed to inquire into "certain practices" alleged to be taking place in nunneries and in Catholic schools. This "Nunnery Committee" undertook a series of visitations at several Catholic schools with such insensitivity and heavy-footed boorishness, however, that the legislature was quickly forced to dissolve it.

So great was the power of the American Party as it swept through all the other states of the Union that by 1856 it was preparing to take over the conventions, make a victorious sweep of the national elections, and put a Know-Nothing president in the White House. But the triumph of the American Party, although swift and impressive, was remarkably short-lived. During the spring of 1856, the violence in the Kansas Territory, the news of John Brown's bloody raid, and the savage beating of Senator Charles Sumner were enough to convince most Americans that slavery was the overriding issue of the day. There was little chance that something as nebulous and contrived as a "Catholic Menace" would distract the nation's attention from the problem of slavery, the reality of national expansion, and the growing crisis of the Union. The fact that the Know-Nothings' presidential candidate, Millard Fillmore, received the electoral votes of only a single state (Maryland) was clear evidence that its moment of glory had passed. Bigotry had proved a poor cement for the foundation of a truly national political organization.

Despite its collapse, the Know-Nothing movement was a dramatic and tangible demonstration of the fear with which nativists, in Boston and in other parts of the country, regarded the influx of immigrants and the lengths to which many nativists would go to keep outsiders in their place. By 1850, there were already some 35,000 persons of Irish extraction living in Boston, and five years later that number had grown to more than 50,000. Considering the fact that the city's total population in 1855 was about 160,000, this meant that even before the outbreak of the Civil War the Irish already constituted almost one-third of Boston's population—clearly a force to be reckoned with.

For the time being, however, the nation was caught up in the incredible events that followed the election of Abraham Lincoln in November 1860. For a brief period of time, the Civil War neutralized the tensions between the Yankee and the Celt, as the problem of controlling the immigrant became secondary to the task of saving the Union. For the first time, immigrants had an opportunity to demonstrate their loyalty to their adopted country. "We Catholics have only one course to adopt, only one line to follow," stated the local Irish newspaper, *The Pilot*, on January 12, 1861. "Stand by the Union; fight for the Union; die by the Union." Almost without exception, the Irish came out in support of the Lincoln administration, although they made it clear that they were willing to fight to save the Union but not to free the slaves. Many joined the all-Irish 9th Regiment and went off to the battlefields, where their green banners were always in the forefront of the fighting.

The loyalty demonstrated by the Irish during the Civil War caused native Bostonians to relax their defensive posture for a time and show a greater degree of tolerance and understanding. In 1861, for example, Harvard College conferred an honorary doctor of divinity degree upon John Bernard Fitzpatrick, the Catholic bishop of Boston, and a short time later the City Hospital announced that patients could be attended by a clergyman of their own choosing. While it lasted, the Civil War seemed to have provided a kind of watershed in relations between native Bostonians and the immigrants, with a sense on the part of local Bostonians that the immigrant flood had reached its highest level and would gradually recede once the war was over. It was hoped that future generations of Irish Catholics would quietly withdraw into the background, become orderly and obedient citizens, and leave the running of the city of Boston to those old and established families who had done it so well in the past.

Chapter

8

Clash of Cultures

AFTER the Civil War, the future seemed much more promising for the members of the city's Irish community. For one thing, the war provided a sudden and unexpected opportunity for Irish Catholics to gain a measure of acceptance that would have seemed unthinkable only a few years earlier, when they had been regarded as a barbarous and totally unreliable people who could never be assimilated into the American way of life.

With the Rebel attack on Fort Sumter, however, Boston's large Irish-Catholic population became an invaluable human resource that had to be brought to bear on the struggle at hand. The loyalty to the Union that the Irish community displayed and the gallantry with which they fought on the battlefields did much to erase, or at least greatly reduce, the troublesome old questions about their ability to become loyal and responsible Americans. The honorary degree awarded to the Catholic bishop by Harvard College as a gesture of civic friendship was soon followed by similar concessions. Local school committees modified the requirements of Bible reading and the recitation of Protestant prayers; Catholic priests were allowed to visit patients in the Boston City Hospital and perform religious rites; and the law requiring a two-year waiting period for naturalization was repealed.

The Civil War also marked a significant transition in the depressed economic circumstances of the Boston Irish. By joining the Union Army, by replacing a local conscript and getting a generous bonus, or by gaining employment in nearby armories, factories, or shipyards, many Irishmen had their first real opportunity to make a little money and gain more acceptance in a community that had hitherto regarded them as little more than lazy loafers.

Ambitious construction projects such as laying out the South End, building the new City Hall, putting up the City Hospital, hauling in the gravel, and filling in the Back Bay furnished additional employment for Irish laborers. The work was hard and the hours long, but this combination of war work and city construction gave many Irish workers their first real opportunity to bring home a day's pay on a regular basis. With this first step up on the rung of economic success, the Irish began moving out of the old, congested waterfront sections of downtown Boston into such nearby neighborhoods as Charlestown, South Boston, East Boston, and Dorchester. Then, in the late 1860s and early 1870s, using new forms of transportation such as the horse-drawn streetcar, many were able to move out into more suburban neighborhoods such as Roxbury, Brighton, and West Roxbury, as Sam Bass Warner, Jr., showed in his study entitled *Streetcar Suburbs*. With immigrant families creating whole new residential neighborhoods, new schools, churches, hospitals, and businesses had to be constructed. Police and fire departments had to be organized, roads and streets paved, water mains and sewer lines constructed, and municipal services developed, all of which not only accommodated the needs of new families, but also provided full-time jobs for many able-bodied Irish-American workers.

Along with these municipal services, a series of new public utilities were incorporated during the 1880s—the New England Telephone and Telegraph Company, the Edison Electric Illuminating Company, the Massachusetts Electric Company, the Boston Consolidated Gas Company—to bring in the gas, the electricity, and the telephone lines needed to service the new communities. These new public utility companies, together with a vast array of municipal service projects, offered badly needed employment on a scale never before seen in Boston. These were new opportunities that did not take jobs away from native-born Bostonians, and for which Irish Americans considered themselves eminently qualified. In large numbers they rushed to fill the enormous labor vacuum. At first, of course, most of them worked at the more menial jobs working as ditch diggers, hod carriers, pile drivers, cement mixers, and common laborers. But those with shrewder minds, quicker reflexes, or better political connections soon became successful public-works contractors, owners of trucking companies, managers of construction corporations, or real estate investors.

Despite their improved social status and their better economic standing during the postwar period, there were few signs that the Boston Irish would be able to significantly improve their political influence. Indeed, for a time it was questionable whether Democrats in general could continue to exist as a bona fide political party after 1865. The Republican party—as the party of Abraham Lincoln, the advocate of emancipation, and the architect of victory—was riding high at the end of the war. The Democrats, by contrast, were viewed as the supporters of Jefferson Davis, the defenders of slavery, and the champions of states' rights. In the full flush of postwar nationalism, it was difficult for anyone to admit to being a card-carrying Democrat.

This was discouraging to the Irish, who had been loyal supporters of the Democratic party since the days of Jefferson and Jackson although, despite their growing numbers, they had been unable to move into the higher echelons of party influence. Before the Civil War, there had never been a single Irishman on Boston's eight-man Board of Aldermen, and only one man with an Irish name (Edward Hennesy) was recorded on the city's forty-eight-man Common Council. The fire department was clearly reserved exclusively for "American" candidates, and the only Irishman to become a member of the city's police department (Barney McGinniskin) lasted only one year on the force. In the postwar surge of patriotic solidarity, there seemed little indication that things would get any better.

There were a number of influential Yankee Democrats, too, who were equally disheartened at the dismal prospects for their party. Boston still had a solid core of old-time lawyers, bankers, merchants, and shippers who had seen their earlier influence in the Federalist and Whig parties eclipsed by the antislavery Republicans. Their numbers had been augmented by younger, native-born, Harvard-educated Brahmins like Nathaniel S. Shurtleff, a prominent physician; Frederic Octavius Prince, class poet at Harvard, active in law and Democratic politics; Nathan Matthews, Jr., lecturer in government at Harvard; and Josiah Quincy, a dedicated Democrat and last in Boston's long line of famous Quincys. They saw themselves as providing a necessary bulwark against the radical social experiments of Republican politicians who were engaging in an unholy alliance with corrupt businessmen. They looked to the traditions of the Democratic party to restore the old-fashioned virtues of personal integrity and self-reliance by emphasizing states' rights, low taxes, limited expenditures, and restricted powers for the federal government.

In order to get the kind of numbers they needed to make any kind of political impact during the postwar era, Yankee Democrats would have to form alliances with the loyal Irish stalwarts who, for more than three decades, had made up the silent rank and file of the Democratic party. The Irish, meanwhile, saw the advantages of such an unlikely coalition and moved quickly to take a leadership role in reestablishing the Democratic party as a vital force in the city's political structure. A major figure in this undertaking was a young Irishman named Patrick Collins, who had emigrated to America with his mother after his father had died at the height of the Great Famine. Living in Chelsea in the midst of the Know-Nothing turmoil, the Collins family moved to Chicago for two years, where young Patrick worked in the fields and the coal mines before returning to Boston, where he worked as an upholsterer's apprentice. In 1867, Collins joined the local Democratic party and soon became known for his abilities as a public speaker. He won election to the state legislature, where he used his energies to remove many of the restriction against Catholics in various penal and charitable institutions.*

On August 18, 1868, while serving as one of only nineteen Democrats in the state legislature, Collins held a meeting with a number of young Irish political colleagues at Boston's Parker House. Included in the group were Thomas Gargan, a lawyer who had served in the Civil War; Michael Cunniff, a young immigrant who had gone into banking and land development; and Patrick Maguire, who had moved from the printing business into real estate. The Parker House meeting was the start of the Young Men's Democratic Club, which chose twenty-five-year-old Collins as its first president and proceeded to hold weekly meetings to promote voter registration and plan campaign strategy. On October 20, 1868, the club held a mammoth rally at Faneuil Hall, with Collins presiding at a gathering that included such prominent Brahmin Democrats as John Quincy Adams, Jr., Reuben Noble, William Gaston, and Edward Avery—public evidence of the new coalition between the Yankees and the Celts. Collins announced that the Democrats of Massachusetts were now

---

* While serving in the state legislature, Collins attended Harvard Law School, from which he received a law degree in 1871. He passed the Massachusetts bar examination the same year and built up a lucrative law practice in the city.

"organized and at work" and called upon all young men to join in a "ballot revolution" to rescue the state from Republican control.

During the presidential election of 1872, Collins and the Democrats were joined by local Liberal Republicans who had become so disgusted with the corruption of the Grant administration that they agreed to support the Democratic candidate, Horace Greeley. Although Greeley was soundly defeated by the Grant Republicans, the state's new Democratic coalition acquired new visibility and respect. Hoping to organize the power of the Irish on a statewide basis, in 1874 Collins organized a Democratic City Committee and worked to get Democrat Samuel J. Tilden of New York into the White House in 1876. Once again, however, the Democrats went down to defeat as Republican Rutherford B. Hayes of Ohio beat Tilden in a close and bitterly contested victory.

Discouraged but still hopeful, Collins, Gargan, Cunniff, and the others held their statewide Brahmin-Irish coalition together with the continued support of Josiah Abbott, Frederic O. Prince, and Leverett Saltonstall. In 1881, Collins himself won a seat in the U.S. Congress and worked for the candidacy of Grover Cleveland, who won the presidency in November 1884—the first Democrat to occupy the White House in twenty-eight years.

As Collins moved into national affairs in Washington, political leadership in the city of Boston was taken over by Patrick J. Maguire, an Irish immigrant who spent his youth in the printing business until he went into real estate at the age of twenty-seven. By 1882, he had become successful enough to establish a local Irish newspaper called *The Republic,* which was designed to champion "all things Irish" and to attack "all things Republican." With their substantial growth in numbers and their extraordinary movement into the neighborhoods in the course of a single generation, the Boston Irish now formed a larger political constituency than ever before. The population increase meant that old wards would have to be subdivided; the addition of new land meant that entirely new wards had to be created. In 1854, there had been only twelve wards in the city; the number increased to twenty-four by 1875 and then to twenty-five in 1876. With his keen political sense, and through his membership on the Democratic City Committee, Patrick Maguire decided that the time had come to elect an Irish mayor and picked a successful, self-made businessman named Hugh O'Brien as his candidate. O'Brien had come from Ireland in 1832, when he was five years old, and worked at the printer's trade until he established his *Shipping and Commercial List,* an invaluable source of financial information for the city's merchants. He also served seven years on the Board of Aldermen, where he distinguished himself by what the *Boston Advertiser* called his "conscientious hard work." The Democratic City Committee endorsed Hugh O'Brien for the office of mayor, Maguire's *Republic* supported his candidacy, and in December 1884 the City of Boston elected its first Irish-born, Roman Catholic mayor. Nearly two decades of effort to create a citywide Democratic party that would move the Irish into political power had finally produced tangible results.

To many native Bostonians, Hugh O'Brien came as something of a pleasant surprise. Businesslike, sober, and cautious, he displayed none of the disturbing characteristics Yankees usually associated with immigrants from Ireland. He dressed appropriately, spoke correctly, was cordial to the Brahmins, and was deferential to the traditions of the city they personified. Indeed, O'Brien proved such a popular and efficient executive that he was elected to four consecutive terms as mayor. O'Brien, like Patrick Collins, was perceived to be an Irishman of the "better sort," an "acceptable" Irishman, the kind of Irishman Yankees would seek out and encourage to eventually become leaders of the city.

But these "better sort" of conciliatory Irishmen were few and far between as far as most Yankees were concerned, based on the Yankee perception of the way in which so many of the "other sort," the confrontational kind, took over control of their own local districts for selfish purposes. As the number of Irish immigrants increased during the 1870s, first in the downtown wards of the West End, the North End, and the South End, and later in the neighborhoods of Charlestown, South Boston, Dorchester, and Roxbury, a number of local politicians emerged who set themselves up as "bosses" of their particular districts. Immigrants, or the sons of immigrants, they had usually worked their way up from jobs (grocers, bartenders, funeral directors) that enabled them to meet a wide variety of people and hone their talents at influence and persuasion. As they elbowed out their political rivals, these bosses solidified their power through a political system that soon became an accepted pattern throughout the city. Once a local boss took over, his ward was divided into precincts, each with a captain in charge. Each captain supervised perhaps a dozen lieutenants who, in turn, supervised workers assigned to specific streets. Comparing census lists with voting lists, these workers were expected to check each house on the street to make sure that every party member voted in every election. Shrewd, ambitious, and manipulative, the bosses acquired a reputation for turning out the votes of "their people" with machinelike precision.

In the West End's Ward 8, Martin Lomasney, known to his followers as "the Mahatma," exercised extraordinary influence. He arrived early every morning,

MARTIN
LOMASNEY

The "massive dome," the dark mustache, the gold-rimmed spectacles, and the prominent jaw of Martin Lomasney did not escape the clever pen of "Norman," the cartoonist of the *Boston Post*. Legendary boss of the West End's Ward 8, Lomasney was known as "the Mahatma" as he worked day and night for the interests of the people in his district. *Courtesy of the Bostonian Society/Old State House.*

365 days a year, at his headquarters at the Hendricks Club, where he cared for the people in his ward in all phases of their lives, relieving thousands, as he liked to put it, of "the inquisitorial terrors of organized charity." To the people of the West End, wrote Doris Kearns Goodwin, "he was a god." In the nearby North End (Ward 6), an energetic young man named John F. Fitzgerald had risen to

a position similar to that of Lomasney. A bright son of immigrant parents, he had been forced to leave college when his father died and quickly moved into the exciting world of politics. When the local ward boss died unexpectedly, it was the twenty-nine-year-old Fitzgerald who took his place as the boss of the North End. Fitzgerald's counterpart across the harbor in East Boston was Patrick J. Kennedy, who had also left school to help his widowed mother run the family grocery store. By the time he was thirty, Kennedy had not only acquired his own liquor-importing business, but was also regarded as the political boss of East Boston. In Charlestown, Joe Corbett was the kingpin; in Dorchester's sprawling Ward 20, Joseph O'Connell was the acknowledged political leader; "Smiling Jim" Donovan controlled the immigrants moving into the tenements and boardinghouses of the South End's Ward 9; and P. J. ("Pea Jacket") Maguire (not to be confused with Patrick J. Maguire) ruled Roxbury's Ward 17 until he was ousted by a young, up-and-coming politician named James Michael Curley. When they arrived in America, the Irish had found most avenues for rapid economic advancement closed to them, especially in a city like Boston whose financial establishment was so rigidly controlled by family ties and corporate boards. Politics, therefore, provided one of the few ready-made roads to power and success for those who were quick enough, shrewd enough, and tough enough to seize the opportunity.

But for many an Irish boss, politics was not merely a means for personal advancement. It was also an invaluable opportunity to provide effective assistance to his own people at a time when they could not obtain what they needed from any other source. Their needs were largely basic—food and clothing, dentures and eyeglasses, jobs and pardons, medical care and legal advice—but mostly unattainable at that time; political support of their ward boss brought assurance that he would supply those needs. As Martin Lomasney once philosophized: "The great mass of people are interested in only three things—food, clothing, and shelter. A politician in a district such as mine sees to it that his people get these things. If he does, then he doesn't have to worry about their loyalty and support." It was as simple as that. Power and patronage went hand in hand in the Irish neighborhoods and pointed up the fact that the basic political philosophy of the Irish differed substantially from that of the old Yankees.

---

* Patrick Kennedy's son, Joseph, would later marry John Fitzgerald's daughter, Rose. Joe and Rose would raise a large family that would eventually produce a son, John Fitzgerald Kennedy, the first Irish-Catholic president of the United States.

Carrying out the requisite functions of a typical Irish ward boss, John F. Fitzgerald personally hands out Christmas turkeys and groceries to his loyal constituents in the North End while supplying dolls, blackboards, and toys for their children. The political survival of a ward boss depended on his ability to provide for the basic needs of the people in his particular district. *Courtesy of The John F. Kennedy Library.*

For generations, the Yankees and the Brahmins had held fast to a strain of political thinking that the historian John William Ward once labeled "rational politics." This is an essentially bureaucratic view of politics that conceives of government as establishing the rule of law for the community as a whole in a rational and equitable manner. Under this system, political leaders of integrity and experience are chosen to resist selfish interests and individual concerns so that they can govern for the "public interest" and the "common weal." By contrast, the immigrant strain of political thinking that Ward calls "ethnic politics" emphasizes family and friendship, the personal and the individual, rather than the general or the universal. Newly arrived immigrants took it for granted that the major function of government was to look to the interests of individuals and their families—to provide them with safety and sanctuary, furnish them with the basic necessities of life, and offer them practical opportunities for social and economic advancement. After all, what was government for, if not to help people in this way? "I think that there's got to be in every ward somebody that any bloke can come to—no matter what he's done—and get help," Martin Lomasney is reported to have told the writer and social critic Lincoln Steffens. "Help, you understand; none of your law and justice, but help."

Seen in the light of rising Irish-Catholic political power, both in the wards as well as throughout the city, prospects for Yankee Protestants in Boston were poor—especially as demographics predicted an even more dismal future. "New England Protestants will do well to remember that the Catholic population gains on them every year, as well by natural increase as by emigration," observed Francis Parkman from his Beacon Street home. He bemoaned the fact that the size of Yankee families had "dwindled in numbers generation after generation through [the nineteenth] century." Clearly, the prospect of having their traditional Puritan town, their cherished "City upon a Hill," taken over by hordes of Irish Catholics, with no appreciation of the city's distinctive past or of the outstanding virtues of its distinguished families, was depressing enough for any Boston Brahmin.

Even worse, however, was the fact that at almost the very moment that the Irish were electing their own mayor and moving into other positions of political power, a whole new wave of immigration was bringing in people from different parts of Europe who had even less in common with the traditions of Boston and, as far as most native Bostonians were concerned, practically nothing to contribute to the city's future.

For the greater part of the nineteenth century, most immigrants arriving in America had come from northern and western Europe—from the British Isles, the northern parts of France and Germany, and various Scandinavian countries. By the 1880s, however, the national character of immigration had begun to change dramatically, and by the 1890s most immigrants were coming from the countries of southern and eastern Europe—Italy, Austria-Hungary, Greece, and the various Balkan countries, as well as Poland, Lithuania, and Russia. Fleeing from high taxes, low wages, drought, famine, political oppression, religious persecution, and military conscription, the members of this "new immigration" were no longer the easily assimilable groups whose cultural traditions and political institutions were similar to those of the United States. But these people, too, had been drawn by America's celebrated image as a nation of freedom and a land of opportunity, and they were determined to build for themselves a new and more hopeful future. Together with other northeastern states such as New York, New Jersey, and Pennsylvania, Massachusetts also received its share of the new European immigrants. In the decade between 1900 and 1910, over 150,000 Italians entered the Bay State, along with some 80,000 Poles and nearly 25,000 Lithuanians. Most of these newcomers headed for major urban centers like Boston, Lowell, Lawrence, and Brockton in search of jobs and a place to call home.

The flood of Italian immigrants came, in great measure, because of their desperate desire to escape the natural disasters that ruined their lands and destroyed their lives. In the southern parts of Italy, particularly, there was a drastic shortage of rain, and every year the lands, without access to large rivers and without effective systems of irrigation, were plagued by drought. Generations of chopping down forests on the slopes of the mountains made those slopes so barren that when it did rain, landslides came down to ruin the farms and build up the marshes where mosquitoes flourished. In Sicily, in the provinces around Naples, and in the recesses of the Po Valley, thousands of *braccianti* (landless men) wandered from farm to farm looking for work, weakened by malaria and other debilitating diseases.

In 1880, an estimated 109,000 Italians left their homes and their farms. By 1881, the average number of emigrants was up to 154,000; by 1886 it had reached 222,000. By the mid-1880s, more than half were going to America, many of them lured by North American industrialists and shipping concerns who found it profitable to import cheap, unskilled labor. In the years that followed, Italian men, often referred to as "birds of passage," traveled back and forth across the Atlantic, bringing home anywhere from $4 million to $30 million a year to their families in Italy, and then returning to make more money at their jobs in America. Only a fifth of the more than 300,000 Italians migrating to America in the 1880s were women. After the turn of the century, however, the number of females increased, the men became permanent residents, and families grew rapidly on this side of the Atlantic.

The vast majority of Italian immigrants to Boston arrived during the late 1880s and 1890s. At first they congregated along the waterfront of Boston's North End, where the Italian population grew from one thousand in 1880 to seven thousand in 1895—almost a thousand more Italians in the North End

New sights and sounds accompanied the arrival of the wave of immigrants from Southern and Eastern Europe as they brought their food and their clothing, their habits and their customs, from the Old World to the shores of the New World. Here a hurdy-gurdy man turns the handle of his instrument and plays his tunes for an appreciative audience of young newcomers in Boston's North End. *Courtesy of the Bostonian Society/Old State House.*

that year than Irish. Gradually they moved into East Boston as well as other neighborhoods that had once been predominantly Irish. Before long, Italians became an important part of all Boston neighborhoods, working as barbers, and hairdressers, cobblers, and leather workers, and also operating nearly all the fruit stores and groceries in the districts. Invariably they were hailed familiarly as "Mickey," "Sully," and "Pat" by the Irish residents who were never able to pronounce names like Minichiello, Solimini, or Pasqualucci.

Mostly poor and illiterate, the Italians depended on their *paesani* (friends from the same village in Italy) to help them get settled, and they sought out a *padrone* (a labor contractor) to find them their first jobs—for a fee, of course.

Because most of them were unskilled workers, the jobs available to them were decidedly limited. They worked on the docks, in the granite quarries, and on the railroads, or they left the city in large groups early each morning to build a sewer system in Brockton or Beverly, or to pour concrete for the sidewalk construction in Arlington and Belmont. Almost all single Italian women worked, and nearly a quarter of all married women worked at least part-time in some local garment factory or confectionery works.

Although the Italians were mostly Catholic, as were the Irish, they preferred to attend their own churches where they could hear Italian priests give sermons in their own language. St. Leonard's Church was founded in the North End in 1873, and in 1888 the Sacred Heart Church was established for the benefit of the newcomers. Out of these churches came a host of benevolent societies, schools, and social clubs. One of the customary responsibilities of these societies was to honor their patron saint with a yearly festival. In 1903, for example, former villagers from San Sossio Baronia began celebrating the feast of *La Madonna delle Grazie;* Sicilian fishermen, on the other hand, honored *La Madonna de Soccorso* each year for her help in protecting the men at sea. Similar festivals for St. Joseph, St. Anthony, St. Rocco, and many other favorite saints were always a colorful part of the North End's religious and social life.

The structure of the North End itself gradually reflected the villages, the provinces, and the regions of these parts of southern Italy from which these people had come. As William De Marco has shown in *Ethnics and Enclaves,* the North End was divided—almost on a street-by-street basis—into separate enclaves of Avilanese, Calabrese, and Abruzzeze; Neapolitans and Sicilians; and a small group of Genoese from Northern Italy. Each group had its own dialect; its own customs, foods, and patron saints; and its own way of following "*la via vecchia*"—the old way of life. Residents not only defined themselves as living "on North Street," or "near St. Mary's," or "from lower Prince Street," but they also identified the part of Italy from which their family had come, the church they attended, the societies to which they belonged, and the occupation they pursued.

Another immigrant group that arrived in large numbers during the 1880s and 1890s was the Jews, whose numbers had reached four thousand by 1890 but soared to forty thousand by 1910. Before the Civil War, Boston had only a small Jewish population that had grown from less than forty in 1840 to about a thousand by 1860. The majority of these early Jews were more Polish than German in origin, the majority coming from the Polish region of Posen. Within the first synagogue, Ohabei Shalom, on Warrenton Street in the South End, the members followed the Polish-Jewish rite known as *Minhag Polin*. The minority that preferred the German rite, known as *Minhag Ashkenaz*, broke away in 1853 and established what was later called Temple Israel.

It was during the 1880s and 1890s, however, that Jews began to arrive in much greater numbers, coming from the Eastern European ghettoes of Lithuania, Poland, and Russia, escaping the vicious pogroms that destroyed their homes, wrecked their businesses, and threatened their lives. In the 1880s, an average of twenty thousand Jews left Russia each year; during the 1890s, the figure rose to forty thousand a year. Sometimes, as with the Italians, the men came first, made a little money, and later brought over their wives and children. The newcomers would come ashore with little more than the clothes on their backs, perhaps a little money, and a cloth bag containing two candlesticks, a samovar, and some feather pillows. "When we arrived in Boston," wrote Anne Goldberg of Brighton, "I remember being taken from a boat to Scollay Square in a surrey. As we came along Hanover Street, I saw the Star Theater and the Olympia. It was Christmas time, and their signs lit up the sky. To a little girl from a village in Poland, this was a fairyland." Into the North End they moved, along with the Italians who were arriving at the same time, crowding in on the remnants of the equally poor Irish who still lived along the waterfront.

At first, the Jews congregated in a small triangular section of the North End, bounded by Hanover, Endicott, and Prince Streets. "It resembled a Russian fair," one visitor recalled. "Men, women, and children in multi-colored garb jostled each other on sidewalk and street. Pushcarts loaded with fruit and vegetables, fish and crabs, and edibles of every description pre-empted the sidewalk, the gutters, and most of the street." As their numbers increased, many of the Jews moved into East Boston, the South End, and Roxbury, and then across the harbor on a three-cent ferry boat ride to the neighboring city of Chelsea. This was where the family of little Mary Antin first settled when they came over from Russia in the early 1890s. Later they moved to the South End, not far from Dover Street, where there was little except "meals in the kitchen and beds in the dark." Seeing how their neighbors gave their children "boundless liberty," Mary later wrote in her autobiography, *The Promised Land,* her parents turned their children loose, "never doubting but that the American way was the best way."

As time went on, Jews moved into the West End in such impressive numbers, and formed such a significant part of that congested neighborhood, that Martin Lomasney would not, and could not, ignore them. "When our boat landed in East Boston, we were met by a welcoming committee," recalled Edgar Grossman, founder of the Massachusetts Envelope Company. "They were shouting: 'Welcome to America. The Democratic Party welcomes you to America. Martin Lomasney welcomes you to Boston.'" The Jews quickly became an integral part of the political constituency of the West End. Within their tightknit community, they established health clinics, orphanages, sewing circles, lending libraries, free-loan societies, labor groups, and even a baseball team. In 1910, when the Jewish population had swelled to eighty thousand, Boston boasted seven Yiddish-language newspapers, while an active Yiddish theater flourished in the vicinity of Dover and Washington Streets in the South End.

Since many of them had come from rural villages and small towns in Eastern Europe, many Jews turned to peddling or operating small shops in order to make a living. One elderly Jewish woman recalled that "Everyone who came to Boston would take a basket." The immigrants would fill these baskets with bits of inexpensive merchandise from a store that extended them credit. They would then set out—if they were lucky, with a horse and cart—to sell their goods in a neighborhood that had not yet been visited by many peddlers. Those newcomers who were not yet able to speak English had been taught to say: "Look in the basket." Those Jews who did not work in trade or sales looked for jobs in other lines of work. Some used the streetcar to travel to Boston's suburbs, where they found work as rag men, junk dealers, shoemakers, tailors, or garment workers. A number of Jews drove horse-drawn cabs in many parts of the city; others moved around, taking whatever jobs they could find. It was hard, but for most of them it was far better than what they had left behind in the ghettoes of Eastern Europe. "It was a beautiful time for the Jews," insisted Miriam Rogers, whose parents arrived in the West End in 1906. "Poverty? There's no doubt. But you didn't see anybody starving. The mothers did what they had to do to feed their children. It was just great!"

Immigrants from Poland were another sizable group to come to America during the 1880s and 1890s, and by the turn of the century there were, by some estimates, approximately ten thousand people from Poland already located in the Boston area. Most of them settled near the boundary line that separated South Boston and Dorchester, just off Andrew Square. It was in this area that they established a site for a national church, and in November 1894 a wooden church was dedicated to Our Lady of Czestochowa. The Polish population in the area continued to grow and quickly became a small but active part of

The closing years of the nineteenth century brought a new flood of immigrants from Southern and Eastern Europe to Boston and other East Coast cities. Newcomers from Italy settled into the North End and across the harbor in East Boston; Jewish peddlers sold fruit from their pushcarts in the West End; and everywhere signs of European influence could be seen throughout the city. *Courtesy of the Bostonian Society/Old State House.*

the peninsula district. At about the same time, some one thousand Lithuanian immigrants arrived in Boston, and most of them also made their homes in South Boston. Reflecting the strong national impulse of the 1880s that called upon Lithuanians everywhere to preserve their own traditional ways and customs, the newcomers settled in the lower end of the South Boston peninsula, along C and D Streets, directly across town from where the Polish immigrants had settled.

The continent of Asia was also represented in the "new immigration" that brought peoples to Boston from unfamiliar parts of the world. For almost a century, Boston had maintained commercial relations with the Chinese mainland, carrying on a valuable China trade that contributed to the personal fortunes of many local merchants. It was not until the 1890s, however, that the city had its first permanent Chinese community. During the 1850s and 1860s, many Chinese had come to the West Coast of the United States, where they served as a source of cheap labor, first during the gold rush and later during the building of the transcontinental railroad tracks. Once the tracks were completed, jobless laborers began drifting to the big cities of the East Coast. In 1875, a group of Chinese was brought in to break a strike at a shoe factory in North Adams. After the strike was settled, the workers continued on to the Boston area in search of jobs. Arriving at the South Station, they settled in a low-rent area at the edge of the downtown business district known as the South Cove. By 1890, the whole South Cove area was clearly established as a settlement of some two hundred Chinese residents, in a neighborhood that was soon called Chinatown.

Many old-time Yankees of Boston, as the historian Barbara Solomon perceptively observed in *Ancestors and Immigrants,* were at a complete loss to comprehend the magnitude of this sudden and completely unexpected inundation of strange foreigners into their ancient and honorable city. The Irish Catholics who had arrived half a century earlier had been bad enough, but at least they had been able to speak English and usually had some acquaintance with basic Anglo-Saxon social customs and political traditions. But these *new* people—swarthy Italians, black-bearded Jews, a motley collection of Poles, Lithuanians, Greeks, and Chinese—spoke a babel of tongues, followed entirely different social customs, and lacked any firsthand experience with the democratic process. Things had reached a point, Dr. Oliver Wendell Holmes told a friend, where a New Englander felt much more at home "among his own people" in London, England, than "in one of our seaboard cities."

Those Brahmins who had always hoped that they could gradually absorb or "acculturate" the immigrants into the Boston way of life began to see the hopelessness of the situation. The birth rate of the immigrants was continuing to rise, too many new immigrants were still coming into the city each year, and there were already disturbing signs that the newcomers would soon dominate the entire city. The announcement in 1880 by the Catholic archbishop, John Williams, that there would be a separate parochial school system for Catholic boys and girls came as an additional blow. The Yankees had always counted on the public school system as a way to bridge the gap between the "old" and the "new," to unify the various races and nationalities, to serve as what Stanley K.

Schultz has called a "culture factory" by which immigrants could be gradually absorbed into the Boston culture. Now they faced the prospect of having future generations of young Catholics growing up beyond their supervision, guidance, and control.

Some Brahmins reacted to these alarming developments the way some old-time Federalists had done in the early 1800s when the radical Jeffersonian Democrats had come to power. They simply threw up their hands in despair, withdrew completely from active political involvement, and moved out of the city to seek the more rustic atmosphere of such places as Dover, Gloucester, Marblehead, and Prides Crossing.

There were others, however, who felt that drastic measures were necessary to save Boston from being overrun by mobs of ignorant and inferior foreigners. The only effective solution, they believed, was to cut off all further immigration altogether, taking especially strict measures to prevent the admission of any more undesirable elements from southern and eastern Europe. In 1894, three young Brahmins—Charles Warren, Robert DeCourcy Ward, and Prescott Farnsworth Hall, all recent Harvard graduates, members of old Boston families, and terrified by the prospects of continued immigration— founded the Immigration Restriction League of Boston. Their movement attracted immediate encouragement and support from many reform-minded Bostonians, and before long they could boast of having such influential persons as Henry Lee, Robert Treat Paine, Henry Parkman, and Leverett Saltonstall as vice-presidents in their organization. The League acquired an important ally when Henry Cabot Lodge, then only forty-four years of age, added his voice to the cause of immigration restriction. As a congressman, he had already made his views known when he introduced a bill calling for a literacy test, designed to exclude members of those races whom he considered "most alien to the body of the American people." There was a limit, he said, to the capacity of any race to assimilate an "inferior race," and when you begin to bring in, in unlimited numbers, people of "alien or lower races of less social efficiency and less moral force," you are running the most frightful risk that a people can run. "The lowering of a great race," concluded Senator Lodge, "means not only its decline, but that of civilization."*

---

* The Immigration Restriction League continued to function actively until World War I. In the aftermath of anti-foreign sentiments during the 1920s, federal legislation established restrictive quotas that accomplished most of the League's objectives.

Despite the cries of alarm and the prophecies of doom, there were still Bostonians who felt it necessary to maintain the high standards of taste and excellence they had always associated with Boston leadership. In the midst of all this demographic change, they dutifully worked to extend the cultural benefits of "old" Boston into the more recently constructed sections of the "new" parts of the city, which had been created out of filled land. From the fashionable environs of the Back Bay, through the Copley Square district, down Huntington Avenue westward toward Brookline, Bostonians became extraordinarily active in creating new architectural structures and cultural institutions for the aesthetic enrichment of the city and its people.

In 1871, when the Brattle Square Unitarian Church sold its old colonial meetinghouse in favor of a new Romanesque church, designed by Henry Hobson Richardson, at the corner of Commonwealth Avenue and Clarendon Street, it set the tone for a remarkable series of architectural accomplishments west of Beacon Hill. The following year, the exotically ornate Museum of Fine Arts went up in Copley Square, just about the same time that a disastrous fire practically wiped out the city's entire downtown business district. On the evening of November 9, 1872, fire broke out in a building on the corner of Summer and Kingston Streets, not far from where the South Station would later be located. In a matter of minutes, both sides of Summer Street were ablaze as the fire roared through the canyon of five- and seven-story granite buildings, and then swung east down Otis, Arch, and Devonshire Streets, shooting sparks, brands, and hot cinders in all directions. While one part of the conflagration fanned northeast up Milk Street toward Washington Street, another part raced south through Federal and High Streets toward the waterfront. By the time the catastrophe was over the following day, the Great Fire of 1872 had gutted sixty-five acres of Boston's business and commercial district, destroying property valued at some $75 million. Most of the entire downtown area had to be rebuilt and modernized, while the city's fire department was reorganized to make it professional and efficient.

In the meantime, the Great Fire of 1872 helped finalize the decision by a number of churches, public institutions, and commercial establishments to move out of the old part of town and take up residence in the new Back Bay area. Members of Trinity Church, for example, the Episcopal parish of the colonial South End, moved from their Summer Street location to the Back Bay and purchased a lot on the east side of what would become Copley Square. In 1877, work was finally completed on Richardson's famous Trinity Church, a massive masonry structure, designed in the French Romanesque style, that dominated most of the east end of Copley Square. The Boston Public Library, located in downtown Boston on Boylston Street since 1858, also moved to the Back Bay, and in 1880, plans were begun for the construction of the magnificent new library. A handsome Renaissance-style building was designed by the firm of McKim, Mead, and White, and was ready for occupancy in 1895. The Old South Church also moved at that time from its original location at the corner of Washington and Milk Streets to the Back Bay. The New Old South Church, on the corner of Boylston and Dartmouth Streets, directly across from the new public library, was dedicated in 1875. Designed in a North Italian Gothic style, the new church featured a striking campanile that still dominates the site.

In 1899, the Massachusetts Historical Society moved from its Tremont Street location to a handsome new Georgian Revival building on Boylston Street at the corner of the Fenway. The following year, Symphony Hall, designed by McKim, Mead, and White in a splendid Renaissance-classic style, was constructed on the corner of Huntington and Massachusetts Avenues as an appropriate home for the world-famous Boston Symphony Orchestra that Colonel Henry Lee Higginson had created in 1881. Farther west along Huntington Avenue, Northeastern University began a series of buildings that would gradually expand over the years, and in the same area Eben Jordan, whose father had founded the Jordan Marsh Company, built a beautiful opera house at his own expense to provide further adornment to an area of the city that was already becoming famous for its cultural institutions. It was Huntington Avenue, near the Fenway marshes, that was chosen as the new site for Boston's Museum of Fine Arts, with its Ionic temple portico, when it was moved from its original Copley Square location in 1909. Not far away was the dazzling "Palace" that Mrs. Isabella Stewart Gardner ("Mrs. Jack") had built for her own pleasure. This was a structure that was an *objet d'art* in itself, a transplanted Florentine *palazzo* that became in turn a repository for her own impressive collection of fine art, a showplace for innumerable concerts, and a cultural center for the public of Boston to visit and enjoy.

This was a period in American history, too, when there was growing interest in the outdoors and in nature, in health and in exercise, in conserving natural resources and preserving the natural landscape. It was a time when the leaders of Boston were experimenting with their own ways of recapturing the natural greenery of the city, as the expansion of roads and the multiplication of buildings were fast destroying the natural environment. Many prominent civic leaders developed the Franklin Park area in Dorchester, laid out the beautiful Arnold Arboretum in Jamaica Plain, cultivated the Fenway district, and created a series of parks, playgrounds, and recreation centers throughout the city. The city of Boston also brought in the famous landscape architect Frederick Law Olmsted, designer of New York's Central Park, to establish a natural boundary around the city. Olmsted eventually created a plan for a string of sparkling ponds and sylvan parks—eventually called Boston's "Emerald Necklace"—that was designed to run from the Public Garden down Commonwealth Avenue to the Fens, along the Jamaicaway to Franklin Park, and then down Columbia Road and along the South Boston strandway to Marine Park at City Point. It was a staggering project that not only provided the city with a natural boundary of exceptional beauty, but also provided a place where the working people of the city could come with their families to enjoy the beauties of nature.

While providing the immigrant population with edifices of great culture to inspire their minds, and parks of great beauty to improve their bodies, many Bostonians felt that more immediate and practical solutions should be found to help the newcomers assimilate into the American way of life. Some means had to be found to help transform those immigrants already living in the city into useful and responsible citizens. Prominent civic leaders, many of whom had previously been active as Liberal Republicans during the 1870s (known as "Mugwumps"), fighting against the corrupt politics of the Grant administration in Washington, now turned their efforts to civic improvements and good government in Boston. By the mid-1880s, they had established a number of clubs, societies, and associations with such names as the Massachusetts Society for Promoting Good Citizenship, the American Institute of Civics, the Citizens Association, and the Citizens Club of Boston. Ostensibly designed to eliminate graft and corruption in government, these associations also attempted to promote among newcomers a proper understanding of the democratic process and to indoctrinate them into the basic principles of Anglo-Saxon law. The associations published books and pamphlets on American history, held classes on the meaning of the Constitution, sponsored public lectures on current events, and promoted programs to acquaint newcomers with the numerous patriotic sites and historical monuments in the Boston area.

During this same period, social reformers became aware of the effectiveness of neighborhood centers, called settlement houses, functioning in such cities as Chicago, where Jane Addams's Hull House (established in 1889) offered a wide range of social and educational services to slum dwellers. A number of civic leaders promoted the creation of similar centers in Boston. They felt that more direct and personal contact between members of the upper class and people who were poor and disadvantaged would help produce friendlier relations among the different classes of the city. Robert A. Woods, for example, a well-known professional social worker, established a number of settlement houses in the poorer sections of the city, the most famous of which were South End House and West End House. Through this method, he encouraged the "better classes" of the city—often young men and women from Harvard and Radcliffe—to put their talents and education to good use by helping young immigrants—Irish, Italians, Jews—discover more acceptable roads to personal success and economic prosperity than resorting to crime or turning to politics. "Here was an institution which spoke to them in their own tongue, and made them feel at home in their solution to their problems," wrote Philip Davis, a Russian-born Harvard student, who returned to teach classes at the Civic Service House on Salem Street in the North End. "Instead of having to reach out for it blindfolded, America was brought to them." Another prominent Bostonian, Joseph Lee, later known as the Father of American Playgrounds, took a slightly different approach as he encouraged the construction of numerous parks and playgrounds for the underprivileged children of the city. He hoped in this manner not only to provide youngsters with opportunities for wholesome play and recreation, but also to make them better citizens by building up their health, their character, and their vitality, in accordance with the old Roman maxim: "A sound mind in a sound body."

Among its other accomplishments, the settlement movement gave a number of Boston women the opportunity to create what the historian Sarah Deutsch, in her book *Women in the City*, describes as "female urban space" in a city whose public spaces, up to that point, were almost totally and unequivocally male-dominated. The first incursion of women into the immigrant neighborhoods had come during the 1870s and 1880s, and consisted largely of wealthy, upper-class matrons from Beacon Hill and the Back Bay. They set out to perform what they saw as their Christian duty to relieve the suffering of the poor and the disadvantaged, and, in the process, hoped to help mitigate what they regarded as the dangers of "European-style class hatred." Increasingly, however, younger professional and college-educated women began replacing the generation of what Deutsch calls "elite transcendental volunteers." In 1892, the establishment of Denison House in the crowded South End marked the movement of a number of Wellesley graduates into the congested immigrant neighborhood, in the belief that the "influence of ladies" might be a good thing. Trying to compete with what they saw as the unsavory influence of the ward boss and the local political machine, the women not only offered courses in Shakespeare and Dante in their settlement house, but also set up kindergartens, day nurseries, boys' clubs, men's clubs, and reading rooms where the examples of clean living and neighborliness would enrich the lives of working-class families and improve their prospects for the future.

The women who came to work at Denison House were mostly college-educated professionals who tended to support themselves as professors, music teachers, artists, and writers. As time went on, they encouraged the brighter young women in the neighborhood to liberate themselves from the confining influences of the home, as well as from the stultifying routines of domestic service or factory labor. They urged them to go out into the competitive world of the city where they could live on their own, assume greater personal independence, and become "self-supporting and self-respecting." In this regard, their efforts were supported by the opening in 1904 of the Boston Trade School for Girls in the South End, which was taken over by the Boston School Committee in 1909 as the first state-aided industrial school for females. Girls of high-school age learned typing, bookkeeping, shorthand, stenography, accounting, and other business subjects at the Trade School as well as at Boston Girls High School, which soon expanded its own clerical programs. As a result, an increasing number of young women, many of them second-generation Irish Catholics, were getting jobs at much higher wages as typists, stenographers, telephone operators, bookkeepers, accountants, salespersons, and buyers in departments stores. With the Women's Educational and Industrial Union creating a "union consciousness" among the rising tide of semiprofessional women, and with the Boston League of Women Voters promoting a greater sense of political entitlement as the prospects of woman's suffrage came closer, Boston women began to assume a much more visible and independent role in the affairs of the city.

With greater interaction among members of the city's various classes, and serious interest among older Bostonians to promote the physical and financial welfare of the newer and less prosperous residents, there were encouraging signs by the end of the nineteenth century that with continued patience and understanding, the Yankee and the Celt might be able to work out a more friendly and cooperative relationship. Hugh O'Brien, for example, proved to be surprisingly popular as the city's first Irish-Catholic mayor. His ability to hold down the tax rate and repair the streets made him almost indistinguishable from the procession of Yankee mayors who had preceded him. And in the world of letters, John Boyle O'Reilly captured the attention and admiration of the Yankees. An exiled Irish nationalist who had escaped from an English penal colony in Australia, O'Reilly made his way to Boston and by the 1880s established himself as one of the city's most respected literary figures. Owner and editor of the Boston *Pilot*, O'Reilly argued for an independent Ireland, championed the cause of African Americans as well as American Indians, and in 1889 was invited to give the main address at the dedication of the Pilgrim Monument at Plymouth.

And there was Patrick Collins, another notable Irish immigrant who had lifted himself up by the bootstraps to earn a law degree from Harvard, establish a successful law practice, become a state legislator, and reorganize the state's Democratic party before going to Washington to serve in the U.S. Congress. Because of Collins's support for the Democratic party, President Grover Cleveland appointed him to the prestigious post of consul general at London, where he remained until 1896, when William McKinley and the Republicans regained the White House. After returning to Boston, Collins was persuaded to run for the office of mayor and in November 1901 defeated Republican Thomas N. Hart by the largest majority in the city's history. During his first two-year term as mayor, Collins ran a businesslike administration that so greatly impressed the city's financial leaders that he was reelected to a second two-year term in 1903, the first Democrat ever to carry every ward in the city. The triumphant reelection of Patrick Collins, with his ability to establish good relations with Protestants and Catholics alike, seemed to promise a long-lasting *pax politica* as Boston moved into the twentieth century.

It was, therefore, with the greatest of anguish that Bostonians reacted to the startling news that on September 14, 1905, only two months before the end of his second term, Mayor Patrick Collins had died suddenly at the Homestead Resort in Hot Springs, Virginia, where he had gone for a rest. The entire city was thrown into mourning as citizens of all races, creeds, and political affiliations praised the virtues of Patrick Collins and lamented his passing.* Clearly an era had come to an end, and the city faced an uncertain future. Almost all

---

* A committee of prominent citizens raised funds for a granite monument—declaring Patrick Collins to be "a talented, honest, generous, serviceable man"—that was placed on the Commonwealth Avenue Mall.

the members of the older generation of citywide Irish political leaders who had believed in maintaining a harmonious relationship with the Yankee Democrats were now dead. John Boyle O'Reilly had died in 1890; Hugh O'Brien passed away in 1895; Patrick Maguire expired in 1896; Thomas Gargan would meet his end in 1908. The passing of this cycle of Democratic stalwarts meant not only the loss of a number of dedicated public servants, but also a significant change in the overall direction of political philosophy. Coming along was a younger generation of Irish politicians who were, for the most part, pragmatic in their approach and parochial in their outlook, concerned almost exclusively with what was happening in Boston and its neighborhoods. The new young leaders showed little interest in the Yankee community and displayed much less enthusiasm for maintaining the traditional alliance with the old Yankee Democrats. What the political future of Boston would be like, now that Patrick Collins was gone, was a matter of serious concern and anxious reflection.

Chapter

9

A City Divided

WHEN he was a little boy growing up in Boston's North End, John Francis Fitzgerald could not engage in contact sports because of his short stature and frail constitution. Instead, he determined to become a championship runner. "He devoted his whole mind to the task of propelling his body forward as swiftly and smoothly as an animal in pursuit of prey," writes Doris Kearns Goodwin in *The Fitzgeralds and the Kennedys*.

John Fitzgerald was forty-two years old and the ward boss of the North End when he heard the shocking news of Patrick Collins's death on September 14, 1905. Like the champion sprinter he had always wanted to be, the scrappy young man was off the mark in an instant. Actually, he had been promoting his own candidacy for several years. He spoke regularly at churches and civic groups throughout the neighborhoods, and in 1902 took over control of Maguire's weekly newspaper, *The Republic*. Bright, bouncy, and energetic, Fitzgerald was a product of the boss system and accepted the system as he found it. He made his arrangements with as many of the other ward bosses as possible while forming temporary, uneasy, but indispensable alliances with conservative businessmen of the city. With the news of Collins's death, Fitzgerald swung into action. Mobilizing his supporters and organizing his machine, he caught everyone off guard as he campaigned vigorously for the Democratic primary that was scheduled for November 14, 1905. Despite last-minute attempts by rival ward bosses to upend the young upstart, Fitzgerald defeated Martin Lomasney's man in the Democratic primary and then went on to defeat his Republican opponent in the December general election. On January 1, 1906, John Francis Fitzgerald was sworn into office as the city's first Boston-born Irish-Catholic mayor.

Fitzgerald had promised Boston voters that his administration would function in an efficient and "businesslike" manner, and that there would be no graft or corruption during his term of office. However, the traditions of ethnic friendship and neighborhood loyalty proved stronger than the new mayor's idealistic promises. City Hall became so crowded with throngs of cronies and lobbyists, pensioners and office-seekers, salesmen and contractors, newspaper reporters and city workers, that Fitzgerald was forced to put off all city business until after business hours. He spent his regular office hours talking with visitors and tourists; after five o'clock he met with his department heads. Evenings were an endless round of parties, banquets, wakes, athletic events, and public functions.

Boston newspapers expressed shock at the reports of scandalous behavior going on at City Hall by Fitzgerald and his "wanton mercenaries," and complained about the extensive payroll padding that allowed the hiring of "scores of men who did not labor." Boston's Brahmin community found its worst fears finally realized. The situation had been bad enough when the Irish had grown so numerous that they virtually monopolized the municipal services, but the upper classes of the city could still put one of their own in the mayor's office—or at least select an accommodating and "acceptable" Irishman like Hugh O'Brien or Patrick Collins to serve as occasional representatives for their ethnic constituencies. The challenge from the likes of Fitzgerald, however, was something else again. Not only was he regarded as a brash opportunist and vulgar upstart but, more important, his role as a representative of the neighborhood ward system would provide him with the opportunity to centralize control of Boston's Democratic machine. It was this frightening prospect of a complete Irish-Democratic takeover that prompted Yankee Republicans to even greater efforts to save their city from the evils of what they were already calling "Fitzgeraldism."

For several years, the upper classes of Boston had been working seriously on various methods of reforming city management and improving the quality of candidates for public office. In many respects, this was part of a nationwide "progressive" movement taking place at the turn of the century that called for more professional and efficient approaches to the mechanics of city government. By selecting "clean" candidates without ties to either crooked political machines or corrupt business corporations, reformers were certain they could return the blessings of "good government" to the people. Political reformers hoped that such a movement would encourage greater citizen participation and promote a more dedicated spirit of civic responsibility. In such large cities as Toledo, Detroit, and Milwaukee, reform mayors ousted powerful bosses, broke up corrupt political machines, fostered municipal ownership of public utilities, and experimented with special commissions and city-manager forms of government. Educational reformers, too, were proclaiming the virtues of democracy and the benefits of academic excellence. At Harvard, A. Lawrence Lowell took over the presidency in 1908 and immediately called for an end to the traditional admissions system. By placing too much emphasis on the social distinctions of wealth and family, he said, Harvard was failing to fulfill its mission of bringing together "youths of promise of every kind from every part of the country." At the same time, Princeton's new president, Woodrow Wilson, was eliminating the exclusive "eating clubs" in order to bring democracy to the campus and upgrade the university's standards.

There were many reform-minded Bostonians who felt that their city would also benefit from taking the direction of such city departments as fire, police, finance, and public works out of the hands of untrained politicians and placing them into the more capable hands of professional experts without deference to party politics. Many of these same Bostonians, however, also saw these institutional reforms as effective means of keeping the less desirable elements of the Irish population out of political life in favor of those middle-class professionals—lawyers, bankers, financiers—who were more acceptable to the local advocates of good government.

One of the first organized efforts of old Bostonians to translate the theoretical ideas of "progressivism" into a more practical way of controlling the political future of the city came when various business groups banded together in 1903 to form the Good Government Association (GGA). Calling for political reform, an end to organized corruption, efficiency in administration, and a lower tax rate, these men represented the conservative financial interests of the community. Almost entirely Yankee, composed of property owners, bankers, financiers, lawyers, and real estate men, the membership of the GGA saw it as their responsibility to support for public office candidates who possessed background, breeding, education, experience, and integrity. They made it clear that they would support "good" Irishmen for public office—the "better kind" who possessed the qualities they had in mind. At the same time, however, they believed it their duty to oppose the type of Irish politicians who were more interested in jobs, contracts, and personal favors than in good government and honest administration.

The activities of John Francis Fitzgerald during his first two-year term as mayor, 1906–1907, caused the GGA to increase its efforts at reform, especially after the Republican-dominated state legislature created a special Finance Commission to investigate "all matters pertaining to the finances of the city." The report of this watchdog agency, consisting of seven prominent citizens, was highly critical of Fitzgerald's spending and contract policies, and was undoubtedly instrumental in the defeat of Fitzgerald in 1907 by Republican George Albee Hibbard.

Having achieved their initial goal in removing Fitzgerald from office, the reformers took immediate steps to make certain that neither Fitzgerald nor any other machine Democrat out of the wards would get back into the mayor's office again. Members of the Finance Commission asked the state legislature to authorize a new city charter that would change the basic structure of Boston's government. The eight-man Board of Aldermen would be completely abolished; the seventy-five-member Common Council, whose members represented each of the twenty-five wards in the city, would be replaced by a single city council, whose nine members would be elected at large. The members of this greatly reduced body would serve terms of two years, while the term of the mayor would be expanded to four years. The new mayor would become a much stronger figure, with veto power over all acts of the city council, and with all of his department heads certified by the Civil Service Commission. In a further effort to take municipal administration out of party politics—and obviously to cripple the growing Democratic machine in Boston—the Finance Commission stipulated that city elections would be conducted on a nonpartisan basis. A new city charter, incorporating the proposed changes, was passed by the Massachusetts state legislature in 1909. With the vigorous support of the members of the GGA, the new charter was adopted by the voters of Boston in November 1909, just in time for the special mayoral election of January 1910.

The passage of the new city charter made progressives, reformers, Mugwumps, and good-government advocates more optimistic than ever before about their chances of putting one of their own "clean" candidates in the mayor's office. For some time they had been grooming a public-spirited banker named James Jackson Storrow, whose credentials were impeccable, whose integrity was unquestioned, and who seemed unbeatable. To supply Storrow with experienced political workers and an effective campaign strategy, the GGA organized the Citizens Municipal League, composed of representatives of the GGA and the Finance Commission, as well as members of the Yankee political establishment. Once Fitzgerald announced his plans to run for a second term, Storrow's supporters plastered the walls and lampposts with posters denouncing the "evils of fitzgeraldism" in hopes of capturing enough respectable middle-class Irish voters to tip the scales in Storrow's favor.

But prim, proper, polished Storrow didn't have a chance. Never an effective public speaker, he was no match for the aggressive, two-fisted attack of his blustery Irish opponent. Fitzgerald launched a whirlwind campaign with a spectacular motorcade that took him into every ward in the city. Perched high on the backseat of a large touring car, he denounced Storrow as a tool of the "merchants of Boston," called for "manhood against money," and promised his supporters "a bigger, better, busier Boston." Before he left each neighborhood gathering, he would sing "Sweet Adeline" at the top of his lungs to the delight of his partisans, who nicknamed him "Honey Fitz." To the Yankees' chagrin, they saw Fitzgerald win the election of 1910 by a plurality of 1,402 votes, becoming the first Boston-born Irish-Democrat to hold a four-year term as mayor of Boston—an honor the Yankees had so carefully designed for one of their own.

The only ray of hope left to the frustrated downtown establishment was that when Fitzgerald finally completed his term as mayor, he would not try for another. As the end of his second term approached, "Honey Fitz" was suggesting that he was getting bored with the office and was ready to move on to greener pastures—perhaps a run for U.S. Senate. Since neither the Democratic City Committee nor the local ward bosses appeared to be grooming any other Irish candidate, the Yankees had every reason to believe they could take back the office again. It came as a complete surprise, therefore, when early in 1913, thirty-nine-year-old James Michael Curley of Roxbury announced that he would attempt to succeed Fitzgerald in the upcoming mayoral election.

Born in 1874 to immigrant parents, Curley grew up in the mudflats behind the City Hospital in Boston's South End. When his father died suddenly, the ten-year-old Jim worked at a variety of jobs—delivering groceries, peddling newspapers, working at a local drug store—while attending public school. He spent most of his evenings at a local tobacco shop, where he listened

Thanks to his new touring car, "Honey Fitz" was able to campaign in every city ward during the course of a single evening. As mayor, Fitzgerald organized massive civic celebrations for the 1912 championship Boston Red Sox team. Here he poses (center) with fast-ball pitcher Smoky Joe Wood (back with bow tie) and other members of the Sox team that won the 1912 World Series. *Courtesy of Northeastern University.*

to old-timers swap yarns about the fascinating world of politics in Ward 17. Reading voraciously and cultivating his remarkable speaking voice, young Curley worked his way up in local party politics and in 1899 won a seat on the Common Council. A year later, he ousted "Pea Jacket" Maguire for the leadership of Ward 17 and became the youngest ward boss in the city. Setting up his headquarters in the South End with his own version of the Tammany Club, Curley solidified his control in the ward while he continued to move up the political ladder by serving a term as a state representative. In 1903, however, while running for a seat on the city's Board of Aldermen, his promising political career almost came to an abrupt end. Curley and a friend were caught taking a Post Office civil service examination for two young Irish immigrants. Curley and his friend were found guilty by federal judge Francis Cabot Lowell of "defrauding" the U.S. government and sentenced to two months in the Charles Street jail. Instead of apologizing for what he had done, Curley explained to his constituents that he "did it for a friend." He won his seat on the Board of Aldermen, where he remained until 1909, and then moved on to the city council. A year later, Curley ran successfully for a seat in the U.S. Congress and moved his family to Washington, D.C., where he served two uneventful terms.

Never feeling at home in the nation's capital, James Michael Curley took the news of John Francis Fitzgerald's impending retirement as the signal for his own announcement that he would be a candidate for the office of mayor of Boston. In making this unilateral announcement, Curley made it quite clear from the outset that he was acting on his own. He refused to seek the blessings of the city's influential Democratic machine, which he ridiculed as a pack of "empty eggshells" incapable of delivering the votes, and he publicly dismissed the Irish ward bosses as parasites and hypocrites—a "collection of chowderheads." At the same time, he ridiculed the members of the prestigious GGA as a bunch of simple-minded "Goo Goos," referred to the business leaders of the city as the "State Street wrecking crew," and characterized the distinguished Boston aristocracy as "clubs of female faddists, old gentlemen with disordered livers, or pessimists croaking over imaginary good old days and ignoring the sunlit present." Instead, he appealed directly and personally to voters in the city's various ethnic neighborhoods, on his own terms. He created his constituency through a political plebiscite of his own making—claiming the people as his only source of power and legitimacy.

With considerable natural intelligence, determined application, and a remarkable photographic memory, young Curley had devoured books on law, politics, literature, the fine arts, and a host of other subjects. By the time he had become a public figure, he dressed impeccably, attended the symphony, talked knowledgeably on oriental jade, quoted the classics, and cited appropriate passages from Shakespeare, Tennyson, and Kipling whenever the occasion provided an opportunity for him to display the cultivated trappings of a learned Bostonian. Unlike former Irish mayors Hugh O'Brien and Patrick Collins, however, Curley never failed to reassure his working-class supporters in the neighborhoods that with all his pomp and elegance, he had not abandoned his roots. He continued to make his home in Jamaica Plain, attended Sunday Mass regularly with his wife and children, and appeared regularly and prominently at such important functions as wakes, weddings, christenings, and St. Patrick's Day parades. He may have cultivated a rich and mellifluous Oxonian accent with which to delight his audiences and enthrall his listeners, but none of his followers—scrubwomen, teamsters, dockworkers, streetcar conductors, policemen, firemen, housewives—ever doubted for a minute that "Young Jim" was still "one of us." Curley was clearly ready to take over the office of mayor.

There was a moment of uncertainty, however, when Fitzgerald changed his mind about retiring and announced that he would try for another term. Curley, in turn, announced that he planned to give a series of public lectures, including one called "Great Lovers, from Cleopatra to Toodles." Since this would obviously bring up Fitz's well-known dalliance with a blonde cigarette girl from the Ferncroft Inn named Toodles Ryan, Fitzgerald apparently decided that discretion was the better part of valor and withdrew from the race "for reasons of health." In a panic-stricken attempt to prevent this irreverent upstart from taking office, the Democratic City Committee and the GGA joined forces in an unlikely coalition. They put their combined support behind Thomas J. Kenny of South Boston, a successful Irish-Catholic attorney, president of the city council, and a candidate they hoped would take the middle-class Irish vote away from Curley. But Curley's superb political showmanship, his grandiloquent speeches, his biting wit, his gigantic outdoor rallies, and his glowing promises of a more prosperous future turned the trick. He defeated Kenny by six thousand votes, carrying sixteen of the twenty-six wards and running ahead in all the lower-income neighborhoods of the city—even in Kenny's own home district of South Boston.

The new mayor captured public attention by breaking with precedent right away. Instead of the customary swearing-in ceremony held in the quiet chambers of City Hall, attended by family members and a few friends, Curley held his inauguration in Tremont Temple, where some twenty-five hundred of his loyal supporters had an opportunity to salute their champion—"the people's mayor"—in grand fashion. Once installed in office, Curley more than met the expectations of his gleeful supporters, and the fears of his disgruntled opponents. The day after he was sworn into office, he sent Yankees into fits of apoplexy by proposing to sell the Public Garden for $10 million. He would put half the money into the city coffers, he blandly suggested, and use the other half to purchase a series of smaller public gardens out in the neighborhoods where they would be "more easily accessible to the general public." Even while the Yankees were sputtering at this "outrageous" and "preposterous" suggestion, the newly elected mayor further horrified the guardians of the city's traditions by proposing that a water-pumping station be installed under the sacred grounds of Boston Common, and that a public comfort station be provided for the convenience of tourists and visitors.

Although it seems that Curley was acting more out of mischief than spite, the battle lines were clearly drawn. If there had been any prospect of even a temporary alliance between Curley and the conservative elements of Boston society, it was gone now. The Brahmin aristocracy and the conservative elements of Boston society would never cooperate with a political leader who openly mocked their institutions and trifled with their proud sense of family heritage. Curley understood this perfectly and made it clear that he was not at all intimidated by what he regarded as the outworn power of the local bluebloods. What Boston needed now, he boldly proclaimed, were "men, and mothers of men, not gabbing spinsters and dog-raising matrons in federation assembled." The Brahmins must learn, said the new mayor, that "the New England of rum, codfish, and slaves is as dead as Julius Caesar."

During his first months in office, Mayor Curley surprised many observers by putting on a great display of reform as he slashed salaries of city employees, fired many of Fitzgerald's appointees, and canceled a number of his predecessor's "sweetheart" contracts. Local progressives expressive pleasure at this turn of events, and the Republican *Boston Herald* praised the new mayor for his reform measures. In reality, however, Curley was using the pretense of cleaning house as a means of replacing Fitzgerald's people with his own appointees and establishing himself as the central focus of patronage in Boston. In short order, the corridors and staircases of City Hall teemed with constituents looking for jobs and favors of every description. Curley proceeded to make his own arrangements with a whole new army of contractors, vendors, and lobbyists who paraded through his office at all hours of the day and night.

More than personal showmanship or political demagoguery, this new routine was actually a basic realignment of power in the city—the start of the "Curley machine." The local ward bosses had always wielded extraordinary power because of their ability to dispense patronage directly to their constituents. Curley now stripped the ward bosses of this prerogative, cutting their political legs out from under them. A few, such as Martin Lomasney in the West End, were able to withstand the force of Curley's attacks and maintain some semblance of control in their local districts, but most others simply withered

Proud of his title as "the people's mayor," James Michael Curley poses with a jackhammer to publicize his efforts at large-scale construction projects in the city, which provided benefits and jobs for his grateful supporters in the various ethnic neighborhoods of the city. For nearly forty years Curley dominated the Boston political scene, appealing to ethnic voters in the city's various neighborhoods. *Courtesy of the Bostonian Society/Old State House.*

on the vine. Day and night, fifty-two weeks of the year, James Michael Curley alone would dispense favors to his citywide constituents, either from his desk at City Hall or from the elegant new home he had built on the Jamaicaway.

Curley had been in office scarcely six months when a general European war broke out in August 1914 and threatened to engulf the world. At first, most Americans tended to follow President Woodrow Wilson's admonition to remain neutral "in thought as well as in deed." As time went on, however, public sentiment gradually shifted against the Germans. The startling announcement that after February 1, 1917, German submarines would follow a "sink on sight" policy made hostilities almost inevitable as a series of unarmed American merchant vessels were sent to the bottom of the ocean the following month. On the evening of April 2, 1917, President Wilson went before a joint session of Congress, reviewed the hostile actions of the German government, and asked for a declaration of war. Within the week, both the Senate and the House voted overwhelmingly in favor of a war with Germany.

Boston suddenly became a patriotic city where the word "slacker" was used to characterize any young man who did not rush off immediately to put on the uniform. Recruiting tents went up on Lafayette Mall, "Liberty Bond" drives were launched all over the city, and thousands of young draftees traveled to nearby Ayer to receive their basic training at Camp Devens. Those who stayed at home worked with such agencies as the Red Cross, the YMCA, the YWCA, the National Catholic War Council, the Jewish Welfare Board, the Salvation Army, and the Knights of Columbus. Schoolchildren raised money to send "comfort kits" to soldiers; "Victory boys" tended victory gardens; women's organizations held dances to raise funds for surgical dressings that went to the local Red Cross. Families put up with "wheatless Mondays," "meatless Tuesdays," and "porkless Saturdays," and because of a lack of coal some schools had to be closed on a temporary basis. Boston became the military and naval headquarters of New England, as well as the principal wartime shipping port to Europe. Mines were placed in the harbor, and a wire net was stretched across the channels to keep out German submarines.

The people of Boston followed the news of the fighting overseas very closely but paid particular attention to reports concerning the 26th Division—the "Yankee Division"—that had been formed from the national guard of New England. The 26th was one of the first four American divisions to arrive in France, the first to go into the trenches, and the first to take part in major engagements at Belleau Woods, Château-Thierry, Saint-Mihiel, and the

Argonne Forest. But the exciting news of the fighting in Europe was suddenly overshadowed by the frightening specter of illness and disease at home. Late in August 1918, Boston newspapers reported that sailors aboard a training ship at Commonwealth Pier had come down with what was called "Spanish influenza." By early September, readers were informed that thousands of soldiers at Fort Devens had come down with the disease. Boston found itself one of many American cities in the grip of a mysterious epidemic. By the end of September, the flu was racing through the city and the death rate was accelerating at an alarming pace. Theaters, clubs, lodges, and other gathering places were shut down, and at the end of the first week in October all the Boston schools were ordered closed until further notice. Deaths were happening so fast, and gravediggers were so scarce, that circus tents were used to cover stacks of coffins in local graveyards until funeral and burial arrangements could be made. On October 1, 1918, the epidemic reached its frightening peak with 206 deaths reported.

Fortunately, by the first part of November, the worst of the epidemic began to diminish, although people continued to suffer for many months from the effects of influenza and pneumonia. Schools were allowed to reopen; boxing matches started up again; schoolboy football games resumed; saloons, billiard parlors, and soda fountains were permitted to resume business. When the Yankee Division returned home from Europe on April 25, 1919, people flocked into downtown Boston to line the streets and greet the war heroes as they marched down Tremont Street to the blare of brass bands and the cheers of the crowd.

At just about the same time the war was coming to an end, so was the term of James Michael Curley, mayor of Boston. At that point, his political fortunes looked none too bright. Wartime business was still booming, employment was high, voters continued to make money, and most people were fairly content. There were no burning issues Curley could hammer away at; there were no controversial issues he could stir up. The ward bosses stepped in quickly and seized the opportunity to oust the young upstart who had embarrassed them so shamefully. They came out in support of Andrew J. Peters, a trustworthy Republican of "unquestioned integrity," and prevented Curley from being reelected. In January 1919, Curley walked down the steps of City Hall into private life and a brief period of political obscurity.

Whether or not it was an omen for the future, only a short time later Boston's North End was rocked by a terrifying explosion. Shortly after noon on

January 15, 1919, a giant molasses storage tank on Commercial Street, opposite Copp's Hill, exploded and sent some fourteen thousand tons of liquid molasses cascading down the streets of the North End. Twenty-three people lost their lives, and more than 150 were injured. Horses were swallowed up, houses were destroyed, and warehouses were smashed to pieces. Although the sticky mess was finally cleaned up, for many years Bostonians insisted they could smell the sweet odor of molasses on hot summer days.

Once wartime production began to decline, people all over the United States found that their incomes were falling behind as the cost of living in 1919 rose to double what it had been only five years earlier. The frustration of workers broke out in a flood of public demonstrations that spawned some thirty-six hundred strikes during 1919. In New York, harbor workers walked off the job; in Seattle, shipworkers conducted a work stoppage; in Boston, fishermen went on strike, elevated railroad workers walked off their jobs, and female telephone operators struck for better hours and higher wages. It was in the fall of 1919, too, that some nine hundred Boston policemen joined the American Federation of Labor in an effort to obtain higher wages and improved working conditions. When police commissioner Edwin Upton Curtis dismissed the patrolmen he considered responsible for organizing the union, fellow patrolmen responded by walking off their jobs on September 9, 1919.

Left without organized police protection, the city of Boston found itself virtually defenseless against the senseless violence of vandals and trouble-makers. On the first night, trouble broke out in the downtown area as mobs smashed windows, looted clothing stores, and broke into jewelry shops along Washington, Tremont, and Boylston Streets. Quickly the violence spread to the neighborhoods, where rioters took advantage of the absence of police protection to start bonfires, break streetcar windows, and ransack grocery stores. In an effort to prevent another night of violence, the next morning Mayor Andrew Peters called out the state guard, although he was already being assisted by a makeshift volunteer militia force made up of prominent Back Bay Brahmins, old-time Beacon Hill residents, and about fifty Harvard underclassmen. Late that afternoon, Governor Calvin Coolidge proclaimed that "There is no right to strike against the public safety anywhere, anytime," called up additional regiments of the national guard, and ordered them to duty in Boston.

While the senseless vandalism continued for several more nights, the arrival of helmeted national guard units, equipped with rifles and bayonets, clearly turned the tide. Taking up positions in the heart of the downtown business

Demands for higher pay, better hours, and more sanitary working conditions led some nine hundred members of the Boston police department to leave their stations and go out on strike on September 9, 1919. City and state officials denounced the actions of the patrolmen and used national guard troops to restore order in the city. No striking policeman was ever rehired by the City of Boston. *Courtesy of the Boston Public Library, Print Department.*

district, as well as in the various neighborhoods, the troops quickly restored order in the streets; except for sporadic incidents, the troubles gradually ceased. On December 21, 1919, the last units of the state guard were finally relieved of their patrol duties. No striking policeman was ever rehired, and an entirely new Boston police force was recruited, in large part from young men recently discharged from military service.

By the time the aftereffects of the police strike had died down, the postwar economy was beginning to even out as Calvin Coolidge prepared to go to Washington as Warren G. Harding's vice-president. It was also time for another Boston election. Preoccupied with the leisurely pursuits of golf and yachting, as well as with the charms of an eleven-year-old girl with the improbable name of

Starr Faithfull, Andrew J. Peters in his administration from 1918 to 1922 proved to be a major disappointment. He left the details of city government to underlings who sold jobs, gave out promotions, and assigned municipal contracts in a prodigal manner. Charging wholesale graft and corruption in the Peters administration, James Michael Curley reappeared as a "reform" candidate and called on voters to "turn the rascals out." Realizing that they would be unable to stop the new Curley bandwagon, members of the Republican-dominated state legislature passed a bill making it illegal for a mayor of Boston to succeed himself. Despite the objections of ward bosses, city bankers, and Republican businessmen, in 1922 James Michael Curley won a second term by a slight margin. After a victorious inauguration at Mechanics Hall before twelve thousand cheering spectators, the new mayor prepared to launch the city into a new era of building and expansion that would benefit the poor, the elderly, and the disadvantaged—all in keeping with his prideful boast that he was, indeed, "the people's mayor."

The devotion of Curley's followers and the magnetism of his hold on the voters could be sustained, however, only as long as the mayor delivered the two things his constituents needed most—benefits and jobs. And this was precisely what Curley set out to do, with a zest and efficiency that exhausted newspaper reporters who tried to dog his footsteps and unravel the financial knots that held together his numerous operations. Using the force of his office, Curley produced all kinds of social, medical, and recreational facilities for his low-income supporters in the neighborhoods that fringed the central city. He enlarged the City Hospital, created a series of local health units, constructed branch libraries, developed extensive beaches and bathhouses, and built playgrounds, stadiums, and recreational facilities in different parts of the city. He extended the harbor tunnel to East Boston, expanded the subway system, tore down slums, paved streets, built bridges, and widened roads. Not only did Curley provide extensive benefits for his grateful constituents through these ambitious construction projects, but the projects themselves provided the necessary jobs upon which his whole system of patronage depended.

This rash of citywide construction projects cost a great deal of money, however, and in almost no time conservative businessmen and bankers expressed horror at the way in which evaluations and taxes were climbing to astronomical heights. Curley simply brushed aside their objections and protestations with a careless wave of his hand. Tax money was supposed to be used to help the people, not hoarded away in bank vaults, he insisted. Whether the bills were paid or the budget balanced was immaterial to Curley as long as his credit was good and he could borrow more money. When there were no funds left in the city treasury to pay bills or cover salaries, he went before the state legislature to borrow additional money until he was able to bring in more revenue by raising the tax rate a notch higher. If there was insufficient money on hand to meet operating expenses until the tax money came in, he went to the bankers of the city for a loan. Over 90 percent of the banking resources of the entire city of Boston at the time was in the hands of the two largest international banking houses—Lee, Higginson and Company, and Kidder, Peabody and Company—as well as the two largest banks in the city—the National Shawmut Bank and the First National Bank of Boston—along with the twenty-one other banks and trust companies whose directors had such distinguished names as Amory, Choate, Gaston, Lawrence, Lyman, Saltonstall, Sears, Shaw, and Storrow. Although such conservative bankers were not at all sympathetic to Curley or his harebrained schemes to raise more money that would enable him to launch more projects that would inevitably push the tax rate even higher, the mayor usually had ways of getting the loans he needed. A gentle reminder that some city inspector might well order a certain bank closed because of "faulty wiring" or "improper plumbing" was often enough to open the reluctant Brahmin pocketbook.

But the mayor's high-handed tactics also helped widen the breach between the "inner city" and the "outer city," between the Yankee and the Celt, between the Boston of the Protestants and the Boston of the Catholics. Well-defined neighborhoods, with distinctive ethnic characteristics and identifiable boundaries, had been a feature of Boston's history since the early part of the nineteenth century. What Curley had done was to weld these disparate elements together into a powerful political force capable of offsetting the opposition of those Yankees who submitted to his power but continued to deny him the legitimacy he sought as mayor of the entire city. Curley left the residents of the inner city, therefore, to wallow in their Puritan self-righteousness and turned his attention and his municipal favors during the 1920s and 1930s to the people of that "other" Boston, who never failed to give him their devotion—and their votes. While he built playgrounds in Dorchester and Roxbury, Scollay Square turned into a place where ugly tattoo parlors and sleazy burlesque houses blighted the historic landscape. While he planned extensive bathhouses in South Boston, the docks along Atlantic Avenue's waterfront section rotted on their pilings. While he laid out miles of paved sidewalks in Charlestown and East Boston, the cobblestones of Beacon Hill fell apart and the lampposts came tumbling down. The idea of improving "new" Boston with money extracted from "old" Boston struck Curley as a particularly appropriate way of balancing the scales that had, for so long, been weighted against the people he represented.

Because the new state law made it impossible for the sitting mayor to succeed himself, Curley's inability to run again in 1926 opened the door to an amazing number of candidates, including Frances Curtis, the first woman to run for mayor in Boston's history. The record of women candidates in Boston elections during the first two decades after women were granted suffrage in 1920 was "hardly stellar," according to the historian Sarah Deutsch. Despite the fact that at the beginning of the 1920s Boston women outnumbered men by nearly ten thousand, and at the end of the decade by nearly twenty thousand, only three women were elected to the school committee, and only one woman managed to get elected to the city council. In 1937, Mildred Gleason Harris of the South End, whose "brilliant blue eyes" and "ready smile" seemed to have captivated the *Boston Globe* political reporter, won a special election to take over the council seat of her brother Richard, who died in office. Women seeking the more exalted office of mayor, however, would have to wait much longer even to get on the ballot. Frances Curtis was a longtime member of the Boston School Committee who saw Curley's absence in 1926, along with the large number of male candidates, as an opportunity to capitalize on the women's vote. Having brought up nine brothers and sisters, Curtis felt fully qualified to run the city, which she saw as little more than a large household. "With women in office," she declared, "there will be no graft. Women will not stand for graft." By the time the ballots were printed, however, Curtis had been dropped from the list because she failed to gather the required number of signatures. In the subsequent voting, the election was won by Malcolm E. Nichols of Jamaica Plain, a Harvard-educated lawyer, former state legislator, and federal tax collector who was supported by the GGA. As the city's last Brahmin mayor, Nichols served from 1926 to 1930 but was unable to succeed himself (unfortunately for the Republicans, their state law cut both ways) and had to give way to James Michael Curley, who returned in 1930 to try for a third four-year term. Curley's opponent this time was fifty-two-year-old Frederick W. Mansfield, an Irish-Catholic Democrat, president of the Massachusetts Bar Association, and former state treasurer. Not only did the dignified and impressive Mansfield (whom Curley once described as "colorful as a lump of mud") receive the backing of the GGA, but he was also rumored to have the blessing of His Eminence Cardinal William Henry O'Connell.

William Henry O'Connell assumed the post of archbishop of Boston in 1907 and was a powerful force in Boston for the first half of the twentieth century. Elevated to the post of Cardinal in 1911, O'Connell exerted a strong personal influence not only in the management of church affairs, but also on the character of Catholicism throughout the archdiocese of Boston. *Courtesy of the Archdiocese of Boston.*

The fact that Curley beat Mansfield by a margin of some twenty-one thousand votes certainly did nothing to improve the already strained relations between the wily and manipulative mayor and the distinguished prelate who wanted to raise the standards of his flock. When he first took over in 1907 as archbishop of Boston at the age of forty-four, O'Connell saw that Irish

Catholics were no longer the powerless and oppressed minority they had been half a century earlier. Already they had begun to move up into positions of considerable power and influence. John F. Fitzgerald, for example, a Boston-born Irish Catholic, had been elected mayor of Boston in 1906, and in 1914 David I. Walsh had become the commonwealth's first Irish-Catholic governor. Cardinal O'Connell urged the members of his flock to become independent of Anglo-Saxon social and cultural standards, and focus on their own distinctive cultural heritage. The prelate established what historian Paula Kane called a "triumphalist, separatist Catholic subculture" throughout the archdiocese, deliberately designed to free Catholics from all forms of Yankee influence.

Catholics were warned never to set foot in a Protestant church, or to participate in non-Catholic rituals and ceremonies—even in semisocial occasions such as marriages and funerals. Youngsters were cautioned not to join Boy Scout or Girl Scout troops, not to participate in YMCA or YWCA activities, and not to attend social gatherings at local neighborhood clubs. Instead, church leaders organized a series of parallel and exclusively Catholic social activities for young people, such as Catholic Boy Scout and Girl Scout troops, as well as the Catholic Youth Organization (CYO). Men enrolled in the Holy Name Society and women joined the Legion of Mary as a way of dramatizing the unity of their religious purpose and the impressive size of their numbers. Wittingly or unwittingly, Cardinal O'Connell supplied an additional socioreligious dimension to the political and fiscal policies of Mayor James Michael Curley that effectually divided Boston into two entirely separate and often antagonistic camps. "The new assertive mood in the Church," observes Curley's biographer Jack Beatty, "closely paralleled the new ethnic politics."

It was as the leader of an increasingly divided city that James Michael Curley dominated the Boston political landscape for more than thirty years, from before World War I to after the close of World War II. After his first term as mayor of Boston from 1914 to 1918, he served three more terms as the city's chief executive—from 1922 to 1926, from 1930 to 1934, and finally from 1946 to 1950. In addition to his duties as mayor, he also served two terms in the U.S. Congress, first from 1911 to 1914, and later from 1943 to 1946. In 1935, he served a single two-year term as governor of the commonwealth, earning him the flattering title of "Governor" wherever he went for the rest of his days. After that, however, he began to find it more and more difficult to maintain his hold on the electorate. In 1936, for example, he was beaten in a race for the U.S. Senate by Henry Cabot Lodge, Jr., and the following year he suffered a particularly disappointing defeat in a bid for mayor of Boston, losing to Maurice J. Tobin, a handsome young Irish-Catholic politician from Roxbury's Mission Hill district.

Curley's loss to Tobin was all the more bitter because he had become the victim of the kind of dirty trick he had used so often and so successfully against others. Election day, November 2, 1937, fell on All Soul's Day, and as thousands of the faithful left morning Mass, they saw below the masthead of the *Boston Post* a statement by Cardinal O'Connell declaring: "The walls are raised against honest men in civic life." Below this statement was a ringing endorsement of Maurice J. Tobin as "an honest, clean, and competent young man." Most readers failed to notice that the endorsement of Tobin was not part of the Cardinal's statement (actually made six years earlier), but had been cleverly appended by the editors of the *Post.* Voters went to the polls and apparently voted the way they thought His Eminence had directed, and Curley's try for a fourth term was doomed. Although he managed to win the Democratic nomination for governor in 1938, he lost the general election to the Republican candidate, Leverett Saltonstall, who captured a surprising number of Irish votes by capitalizing on what he laughingly called his "South Boston face." And in November 1941, in another effort to regain the office of mayor, Curley was once again defeated by Maurice Tobin.

The excitement over the 1941 Boston mayoral election was hardly over when, on December 7, 1941, the Japanese attacked the American fleet at Pearl Harbor. As a big-city mayor in a nation at war, Maurice Tobin became almost totally preoccupied with the innumerable details of civilian defense and home-front activities. Not only did he have to set aside any plans he had for reducing expenditures and balancing the budget, but in the face of wartime inflation, he had to modify his program of fiscal controls.

Wartime prosperity gave a much-needed jolt to the city's sagging economy. A global conflict of this magnitude brought an end to more than a decade of depression and provided welcome jobs for men and women in war plants, factories, armories, and shipyards. The Bethlehem shipyards in East Boston and the Fore River shipyards in Quincy were operating around the clock, while the huge army base in South Boston offered additional employment opportunities. Walworth Manufacturing Company, United Carr Fastener, the Commercial Filters Company, Linde Air Products, and many other private industries in the Greater Boston area geared up for wartime demands. Service-men and -women on weekend passes or two-week furloughs, together with civilian visitors traveling on official business, provided a thriving commerce for hotels, restaurants, and nightclubs throughout the city. Scollay Square, because of its proximity to the Charlestown Navy Yard, became a favorite haunt for thousands of sailors, who frequented the tattoo parlors, the photo studios, the burlesque houses, and the hot dog stands for which the district had become world famous.

Because of the scarcity of essential raw materials, the government issued books of ration stamps for hard-to-get products such as sugar, coffee, butter, cheese, gasoline, and fuel oil. Civic groups and youth organizations turned in heaps of scrap metal to be recycled, or collected piles of old automobile tires for scrap-rubber drives. Fears of espionage and fifth-column activities caused city officials to station armed military guards along the beaches and waterfront districts to defend against possible German submarine attacks. Small red-white-and-blue service flags hung in the windows and doorways of houses all over the city—a blue star on the flag for every member of the family on active duty, a gold star for any family member who had been killed in action.

With the nation at war and people consumed with the great struggle between the Allies and the Axis Powers, the complex problems of Boston politics were temporarily obscured by the exigencies of national survival. And yet the deteriorating condition of the city was too critical to be completely overlooked. With a growing deficit, an unbalanced budget, alarmingly high taxes, an inability to attract either government funding or private investment, and a constant state of warfare between the Irish-Catholic political system and the Yankee-Protestant financial establishment, Boston was clearly in trouble. Even the most optimistic observer would have to conclude that once the terrible war was over, the city's future did not look very promising.

BOOK FOUR
A New Boston

Chapter

10

Building a New City

IN THE midst of the climactic events
of World War II, Boston politics went through some bewildering convolutions.
Maurice Tobin, in the third year of his second four-year term as mayor of
Boston, suddenly announced that he intended to enter the 1944 race for
governor. After defeating the Republican candidate in November, he moved
from City Hall on School Street to the State House on Beacon Hill, leaving the
mayor's office to be filled by city council president John E. Kerrigan as acting
mayor until a regular election could he held in November 1945. While these
bizarre events were taking place, James Michael Curley suddenly reappeared
on the local scene. In 1942 he had won a seat in the U.S. Congress from
the Charlestown-Cambridge eleventh district. Halfway through his term in
Washington, however, he announced that he would return to Boston to become
a candidate for mayor in the 1945 election.

By the time the Allies defeated Germany in April 1945 and the explosion
of the atomic bombs ended the war with Japan in August, preparations for the
Boston mayoral election were taking place against the backdrop of a collapsing
fiscal structure. The Bethlehem shipyards in East Boston and the Fore River
shipyards in Quincy were already closing down; the South Boston army base

was cutting back operations. War contracts were being canceled; the machine and tooling industries were conducting substantial layoffs; inflation kept rising higher and higher. Without effective municipal leadership, imaginative coalitions, or outside assistance of any kind, the city's aging infrastructure continued to crumble, and the housing stock deteriorated at a rapid pace. Boston's once-famous seaport facilities had fallen into disuse, its rolling stock rusted on abandoned railroad yards, and a discouraging number of businesses were leaving the city for other parts of the country where taxes were lower, labor cheaper, and the political climate more congenial. According to the *Boston Globe*, Boston had become "a hopeless backwater, a tumbled-down has-been among cities." John Collins, a future mayor, recalled that there was a kind of "malaise of spirit" at the time. "We were all kind of ashamed."

It was this overwhelming sense of anxiety and insecurity that brought so much attention to Boston politics as the war came to an end. True to his word, James Michael Curley left Washington, returned to Boston, and defeated Johnny Kerrigan in November 1945 to embark on his fourth term as mayor of Boston. Curley's victory was all the more remarkable because it took place while he was under indictment by a federal grand jury on charges of using the mails to defraud. Taking more than a year to exhaust all his judicial appeals, in June 1947 Curley was finally sentenced to a term of six to eighteen months in the federal penitentiary at Danbury, Connecticut—once again putting Boston in the awkward position of having a vacant office in City Hall. In an effort to maintain a semblance of administrative continuity, Republican governor Robert Bradford appointed the city clerk, John B. Hynes, as temporary mayor until Curley returned from prison.

One day before Thanksgiving 1947, five months after he first entered Danbury prison, James Michael Curley's sentence was commuted by President Harry S Truman. After receiving a hero's welcome at Boston's Back Bay Station, Curley spent Thanksgiving day with his family at their Jamaicaway home, and then showed up the next day at City Hall, where he was greeted by hundreds of friends and well-wishers. Ready to pick up where he left off, Curley spent the next several hours in his office reviewing correspondence, interviewing job candidates, and signing contracts. When his day's work was done, he emerged from his office and boasted expansively to the waiting reporters: "I have accomplished more in one day than has been done in the five months of my absence." With a wave of his hand, he was out the door.

While Curley undoubtedly considered his offhand remark typical of the kind of humorous response the media expected, John B. Hynes regarded Curley's parting comment as an insulting reflection on his hard work as acting mayor. In a blaze of anger, the usually mild-mannered city clerk decided to put his name in for the next mayoral race, in November 1949. Calling upon his many friends and associates, he began creating a political organization to challenge one of the most charismatic big-city mayors in the United States. From all points of view it looked like an unlikely David-and-Goliath contest, with a challenger who had never run for elective office in his life, had no political machine, and had no war chest at all. Even Curley himself could not take it seriously, scoffing at the idea that he could be beaten by a contender he referred to as "that little city clerk."

There are several historical factors, however, that help explain why Hynes's seemingly Quixotic challenge was not quite as reckless as it first appeared. For one thing, Curley's days were already numbered. "Young Jim," as his devoted followers like to call him, was now in his mid-seventies, showing the unmistakable ravages of illness and old age. The golden voice had lost its vibrancy, and one had only to look at the rheumy eyes and sunken cheeks to recognize the fact that he would not be on the political scene much longer. It was a time, too, when Curley's centralized and highly personalized system of patronage had been severely undermined by the legacy of Franklin D. Roosevelt's New Deal legislation. Such measures as social security, unemployment compensation, workmen's compensation, and the extensive benefits provided by the G.I. Bill of Rights encouraged citizens to become much more dependent on the bottomless largesse of federal agencies than on the limited handouts of city bosses. All over America, big-city bosses like James Michael Curley were becoming political dinosaurs.

Finally, by 1948, many of the old Boston neighborhoods, which had supplied such solid and unwavering support for men like Curley, were losing both their political clout and their ethnic distinctiveness. Sons and daughters of families that had now been in America for two or three generations had lost touch with their ethnic roots and were all but impervious to old neighborhood appeals. In ever-increasing numbers, young families were leaving three-deckers in such communities as Charlestown, Dorchester, East Boston, and South Boston and moving to new split-level ranch houses in the suburbs. Statistics showed clearly that the population of Boston was declining at an alarming rate. In 1950, the population of the city was recorded at over eight hundred thousand; over the course of the next ten years, it would drop to less than seven hundred thousand—with no sign of leveling off.

But Curley's weaknesses were not the only reason the upcoming election of 1949 would be much closer than expected. Hynes, too, had certain political advantages that became clearer as the campaign progressed. Not only could he call upon his old friends, neighbors, and cronies, but he could also draw upon the support of a wide range of city employees, newspaper reporters, and local politicians he had come to know during his many years as city clerk. Former backers of Maurice Tobin, particularly, saw in Hynes a political figure with many of the more urbane characteristics they had admired in their former candidate, who was now Secretary of Labor in the Truman administration. Especially noticeable among those who gathered around the Hynes banner were a number of young war veterans, many of whom were participating in a city election for the first time. Better educated, less parochial, and more sophisticated in their political idealism, they were clearly ready for a new style of political leadership that would bring honesty and integrity to a city that had acquired a reputation for graft and corruption. Seeing the advantage of cultivating a whole new generation of Boston voters, Hynes persuaded a young law school graduate named Jerome Rappaport to organize Students for Hynes, a group that drew in young men and women from neighboring colleges and universities. Although they might not be able to vote in the 1949 election, after writing newsletters, handing out leaflets, and registering voters, they might well become dedicated "Hynes people" by the time the next election came around.

There were other voting blocks, too, that Hynes was able to use in order to help distinguish his campaign from that of Curley. Capitalizing on a groundswell of dissatisfaction among elements of the community that had been generally neglected by the prevailing system, Hynes drew together a broad-based coalition of reform-minded, middle-class Irish, Jewish, and Italian voters, as well as a number of representatives of the African-American community in the South End–Roxbury district who also felt ignored by the Curley machine. The woman's vote, too, became a conscious factor in the new organization's planning, as it had three years earlier, in 1946, when young Jack Kennedy ran for a seat in the U.S. Congress from the famous eleventh district. "Women compose the majority of votes now," he told a meeting of the League of Catholic Women. "Women not only have political power, but they have financial power." And the Kennedy women played it to the hilt. At VFW posts, at Legion halls, at house parties, at tea parties in hotels, and at receptions in churches, his sisters Eunice and Pat proved resourceful and effective campaigners. And Jack's mother, Rose Kennedy, was always in demand wherever she went. "Rose was so important to Jack in 1946," recalled Dave Powers, "because she was better known than anyone else in that district." Following a similar pattern, John Hynes and the members of his family held Sunday afternoon tea parties in the parlors of private homes and small public halls to cultivate the interests of young housewives and working women, promising them that he would "restore Boston's good name and reputation." And even members of the downtown Yankee business and financial establishment showed tentative signs of support for Hynes. Few of them would ever lift a finger on behalf of their old nemesis, James Michael Curley, but several of them who had earlier supported Maurice Tobin—people such as Robert Cutler, Henry Shattuck, Stuart Rand, and Henry Parkman—could certainly see Hynes as the lesser of two evils.

The election of 1949, therefore, proved to be a hard-fought contest, and one that was much closer than observers had originally predicted. Curley continued to emphasize his long political experience, his ability to get things done, and his promises to rebuild the city. Hynes, on the other hand, played cleverly on Curley's age and the inability of his "tired and forlorn" administration to accomplish anything. He called upon voters to come over to his side and end the division in the city that had proved to be a "dismal failure." Curley reminded voters that "CURLEY GETS THINGS DONE"; Hynes urged voters to "RESTORE BOSTON'S GOOD NAME."

As the newspapers predicted, the turnout on November 8, 1949, was large, the race close, and the contest fought right down to the wire. When the final vote was tallied, Hynes had 138,700 votes—the largest ever won by any mayoral candidate in the city's history—while Curley came in second with 126,042, the largest vote in the old warrior's long political career. Despite the closeness of the outcome, many people sensed that something significant had taken place. "The decision rendered yesterday by the voters of the city of Boston," commented the *Boston Globe*, "marks the end of one era and the beginning of another."

Throughout his campaign against Curley, Hynes had emphasized the theme of a reformed and reconstructed "New Boston." He promised to restore Boston's "good name and reputation," and he assured voters that he would eliminate the "arrogance, waste, and inefficiency" that had for so long characterized operations at City Hall. In light of the Curley legacy, however, the question was whether the new mayor would be able to carry out his campaign promises. Could he possibly break down the social and religious rivalries that had divided the city for generations? Could he form new alliances between the city's political leaders and its business executives? Could he bring in funding from the federal government and investments from outside corporations? Could he renew the infrastructure of an old and battered city? In short, was such a thing as a "New Boston" possible?

At first glance, the odds seemed decidedly against the fifty-three-year-old Hynes. Despite his carefully groomed white hair, rimless glasses, good manners, and bankerlike appearance, there was little indication that he was different from any other typical Irish-Catholic politician. He had been born in Boston's South End, of immigrant parents, and later moved to Dorchester, where he spent

Mayor John B. Hynes poses at the controls of a wrecking crane at Seneca Street to start a $4.3 million project to convert the New York Streets area of Boston's South End into light industrial and commercial use. Congressman John W. McCormack stands by the mayor's side, while members of the Boston City Council and representatives of the city's business community look on. *Courtesy of the Boston Public Library, Print Department.*

the rest of his life. At the age of fourteen John went to work for the telephone company and attended night school at Dorchester High, where he learned stenography and other business subjects. After serving briefly in World War I, he received an appointment as a stenographer at City Hall, then gradually worked his way up to become chief clerk in the office of Mayor Curley. After taking courses at Suffolk Law School, Hynes passed the bar in 1927, got married, and began raising a family. After he returned from a brief period of service in World War II, he was appointed to city clerk. A quiet, gentle, and compassionate man who attended Mass every morning and telephoned his wife every noon, he met regularly with members of the press every afternoon at four o'clock. A virtually unknown bureaucrat who had never held elective office, the new man inherited an entrenched municipal bureaucracy perpetuated for decades by personal power and extensive patronage. It was very difficult to see how Hynes could possibly emerge from the shadow of Curley and become his own man.

Gradually, however, John B. Hynes began to acquire a standing and a reputation in his own right that brought him respect and recognition. Among the growing number of middle-class and upper-middle-class Irish-American families in the city who were ready to dispense with the steady diet of ethnic rivalry and class animosity that had been served up to them for so long by their older political leaders, Hynes seemed like a voice of reason. Young people graduating from college and servicemen returning from military life were often embarrassed by the boisterous rhetoric and outmoded antics of the old-time bosses. The time had come for a new man to bring a new respectability to Boston politics and do something to restore the city's battered reputation.

After his inauguration, Hynes also impressed members of the city's business community by making a number of highly publicized changes in the city's overgrown administrative structure. Drawing on his long experience with the municipal bureaucracy, he was able to eliminate a number of departments and substantially reorganize several others. Slowly, conservative business leaders became aware of the fact that Hynes was much more in the "accommodationist" tradition of such earlier Irish mayors as Hugh O'Brien and Patrick Collins than in the "confrontationist" mode of "Honey Fitz" and Jim Curley. This might well be the type of "acceptable" Irish politician with whom they could work. Furthermore, there were no signs that Hynes was anxious to rekindle old ethnic antagonisms, to set the needs of the neighborhoods against the interests of the central city, or to employ the old divisive political tactics of pitting Catholics against Protestants. His political appeal was for a new coalition in which the formerly diverse and hostile elements could somehow be brought together to work for the benefit of the city as a whole.

Demonstrating that his initial victory in 1949 was no political accident, Hynes defeated Curley a second time in a special election in 1951, after the old 1909 charter had been changed by what was called the Plan A system. The size of the city council was reduced to only nine members, elected at large, and a September primary was established, which would reduce the number of mayoral contestants to two with a final election in November. Hynes won a third term in 1955 in a hard-fought campaign in which he beat the first attempt by state senator John E. Powers of South Boston to move into the mayor's office. John B. Hynes would serve a total of ten years as mayor of Boston, the longest continuous tenure in the city's history up to that point.

Certainly a factor that must also have played an important but subtle role in changing the political atmosphere in the city at this particular time was the emergence in 1945 of Archbishop Richard J. Cushing as the spiritual leader of Boston's substantial Catholic population. A crusty and completely unpredictable cleric from South Boston—gruff, affable, and down-to-earth—Cushing contrasted sharply with his rather pompous and autocratic predecessor, Cardinal William H. O'Connell, who had dominated the local religious scene for the past thirty years. Breezy and extroverted, the new archbishop welcomed publicity, courted photographers, played with children, mingled with all sorts of people from the very rich to the very poor, and generally showed a remarkable grasp of the potential of the modern media to dramatize his policies and publicize his goals.

But Cushing was more than just a new man in town with a charismatic personality and an effective public relations campaign. He was genuinely interested in defining a new level of human and spiritual relations in an archdiocese that heretofore had not been particularly tolerant toward those who were new or "different." Attuned to the interests of second- and third-generation Americans of Irish, Italian, and German descent who were born, raised, and educated in the United States, he worked in the current spirit of ecumenism, pledging to refrain from "all arguments with our non-Catholic neighbors and from all purely defensive talk about Catholics." Cushing unceremoniously knocked aside many of the barriers that, for so long, had separated his Catholic parishioners from their non-Catholic neighbors. By the time he was raised to the rank of Cardinal by Pope John XXIII in 1958, Cushing had already anticipated many of the changes that would come with the Second Vatican Council. He was preaching to Protestant gatherings, speaking before Jewish audiences, and generally working to promote feelings of fellowship and good will among large numbers of ethnic and religious groups in the Greater Boston area.*

Coincidentally, but significantly, the new archbishop's ecumenical approach during the 1950s and 1960s was also clearly in tune with the political exhortations of Mayor Hynes, who was urging the citizens of Boston to put aside their differences and work together for the renewal and reconstruction of the city. To have the prestigious religious leader of the community voicing the same humanitarian ideals and moral sentiments as the city's political leader could not help creating a new and healthier climate in which fundamental improvements could finally take place.

By managing to convey an air of personal integrity and administrative ability, John Hynes established closer and more familiar ties with members of the downtown Republican community. He made some carefully calculated appointments of well-known Bostonians to boards of trustees, to planning boards, and to professional commissions. For the first time in most people's memory, the mayor met with business executives, consulted with financiers, listened to bankers, and formed special committees to give him advice about difficult decisions. "Building bridges with the local business community was one area where Hynes really made a contribution to the city's future development," one municipal director later recalled. In this way, Hynes was gradually able to pull together into a working coalition the two most hostile elements of Boston politics. Protestant-Brahmin Republicans now indicated a willingness to extend to Hynes both the political legitimacy and the financial cooperation they had so long denied James Michael Curley. Irish-Catholic Democrats, in turn, demonstrated a willingness to work with the Yankee establishment on the basis of equality and respect.

Anxious to display his capacity for dealing with urban reconstruction, as well as responding to the city's pressing need for low-income housing, Mayor Hynes directed the Boston Housing Authority (BHA) to create a number of public housing projects in several working-class neighborhoods. The Fidelis Way project in Brighton (1950), the Cathedral project in the South End (1951), the Bromley-Heath project in Jamaica Plain (1954), the Franklin Field project

---

* Cardinal Cushing developed close personal friendships with members of Boston's Jewish community and boasted that his own brother-in-law, a man he praised as "a devoted husband" and "a great example to me," was Jewish.

in Dorchester (1954), and the enormous Columbia Point project just outside South Boston (1954) were only a few of the dozen new housing projects that were calculated to reduce both demographic pressures and social tensions. Although most of these socially isolated and racially segregated projects would later be judged as unmitigated disasters, at the time they were welcomed as much-needed housing for poor and low-income families.

Evidence of how the changing image of the new mayor produced tangible results came in the spring of 1952, when Hynes learned that the Prudential Insurance Company was looking for a site, somewhere in the northeast, for a regional office. The mayor immediately offered Prudential the twenty-eight acres of abandoned Boston & Albany railroad yards in the Back Bay section, between Boylston Street and Huntington Avenue, as a site for its prospective office building. Although negotiations between the city and Prudential would drag on interminably for many years over questions of location, property valuation, and tax assessments, the very fact that an outside corporation would even think of coming to Boston was the first tangible sign that the city's new image was beginning to attract positive attention.

For the first time, too, Hynes was able to elicit the support and cooperation of several leading colleges and universities in the Greater Boston area that had contributed painfully little to the city's progress and well-being. Specialists from Harvard began working on a variety of economic studies and financial reports; engineers and urban planners from MIT involved themselves in architectural designs and much-needed transportation reports; and in 1954 Boston College, under the direction of the Reverend W. Seavey Joyce, S.J., established a series of Boston Citizen Seminars that provided a valuable forum for the public discussion of many of Boston's most pressing problems. Indeed, it was at a Citizen Seminar on October 26, 1954, that Hynes delivered the opening address, "Boston, Whither Goest Thou," in which he laid out his remarkable vision of a completely transformed and modernized "New Boston." If the city could form an effective coalition of government and business leaders, readjust its tax system, and put its economy on a solid footing, said Hynes, then it could clear its slums, revitalize its neighborhoods, rebuild its downtown business district, and build a modern highway system. With those things accomplished, Boston could then go on and create a Back Bay Center to rival New York City's Rockefeller Center; construct a major "convention hall-auditorium" to attract large conventions to Boston; establish a World Trade Center that would restore the city's commercial legacy; construct a Government Center with a new municipal office building; and build a second harbor tunnel to East Boston and Logan Airport.

Encouraged by the positive responses he received to his ideas about urban renewal, Hynes and his advisors used Pittsburgh as a model of how a working coalition—consisting of an active big-city mayor (David L. Lawrence) and a group of determined business leaders—could work together to plan a successful urban reconstruction program. Returning to Boston after a visit to Pittsburgh, Hynes worked with Boston banks and a variety of federal funding agencies during the prosperous years of the Eisenhower administration to begin renewing the face of a badly scarred city. He established an Auditorium Commission to undertake the design of a multipurpose auditorium and convention center; a short time later he created a Government Center Commission to plan an expansive area in the old Scollay Square district for municipal office buildings. After inaugurating programs of slum clearance in several neighborhoods, in 1957 Hynes established the Boston Redevelopment Authority (BRA), which undertook the demolition of old tenement houses in the New York Streets area of the South End to make way for light industrial and commercial uses.

In 1958, Hynes launched an even more ambitious program of urban renewal, this time directed at the West End, one of Boston's oldest communities. Consecutive waves of immigrants—Irish, Italians, Jews, Greeks, Armenians, Poles, Russians—had turned the neighborhood into a seething and colorful melting pot that at one point was home to as many as twenty-three thousand residents. Despite the congestion, or perhaps because of it, most inhabitants of the West End regarded their neighborhood as a warm, friendly, and familiar community in which to live and raise their children. "The West End was beautiful and unique," recalled one former resident. "One of the city's crimes against itself is that the West End's narrow and mysterious European streets and alleys are not there for the old men to walk, for me to walk, for everyone else to walk."

As far as younger, more liberal, and more professional observers were concerned, however, the West End was an impoverished, overcrowded, and dangerous slum area that should be wiped out as soon as possible. With a closely packed population that was susceptible to contagious epidemics such as polio, and with those "mysterious European streets" so narrow that fire engines could not reach a conflagration, social scientists regarded the West End as a disaster waiting to happen. The BRA declared that the area was "so clearly substandard" that the only solution was a "sweeping clearance of buildings."

A photograph by Robert Severy in 1963 shows the extensive demolition taking place in the West End, with the Hotel Madison and the Boston Garden in the background. Except for the Old West Church, the first Harrison Gray Otis house, Saint Joseph's Church, the Charles Street jail, and the Massachusetts General Hospital, no other building was left standing in the entire fifty-two-acre neighborhood. *Courtesy of the Bostonian Society/Old State House.*

Despite belated protests and last-minute appeals, the wrecking crews were soon demolishing houses, tearing down tenements, bulldozing entire city blocks, and thoughtlessly evicting residents. Most of them were poor, many of them immigrants and refugees, and the city had made no adequate provisions for alternative housing for them. Although a few important historic sites such as the Old West Church and the first Harrison Gray Otis House were fortunately rescued from destruction at the last minute, the rest of the West End was completely obliterated. It was sacrificed to the misplaced technology of those who believed that this part of Boston would be better off with high-rise luxury apartments, modern shopping centers, massive garages, and sprawling parking lots that would attract "quality shoppers" back from the suburbs to a new and modernized downtown Boston.

Although the West End Development Plan had become an accomplished fact, the totality of the destruction and the ruthlessness with which it had been carried out engendered such bitter feelings that the future of any further urban renewal projects in Boston was very much in doubt. Residents of other sections of the inner city and of the outlying neighborhoods became so terrified at what had happened to the people of the West End that they determined not to allow the bureaucrats, the technocrats, and the real estate developers destroy their communities and displace their people. "Not in my neighborhood!" became the battle cry of those who opposed any more urban renewal programs.

By the time Mayor John B. Hynes's final administration was coming to an end in 1959, it was clear that any further urban renewal plans would either have to be given up completely or radically redesigned with greater concern for the welfare of the residents of the communities. There were many Bostonians, however, who felt that the results of the upcoming mayoral election might well bring an end to urban renewal completely. With the clear understanding that Hynes would not run for another term in November 1959, it was generally conceded that John E. Powers, then president of the Massachusetts Senate, would succeed Hynes. A short, energetic, and widely recognized political leader from South Boston's Ward 6, Powers was a well-known expert on parliamentary procedure who had the labor vote solidly behind him, the support of most of the Boston newspapers, and the personal friendship of Cardinal Cushing. Powers's only serious opposition came from John Collins of Jamaica Plain, who had served in the house and the senate as well as on the Boston city council before being appointed Suffolk County Register of Probate, virtually a lifetime position that ordinarily offered few opportunities for political advancement. At first glance, Collins appeared to be a political lightweight and a career bureaucrat who offered little competition; Powers's election seemed assured.

There were, however, several factors that operated in Collins's favor. First, there is little doubt that his courageous comeback from a crippling bout with polio in 1955, much in the tradition of Franklin Delano Roosevelt, created a measure of both sympathy and respect that worked to his political advantage. Second, at a time when television was becoming an influential factor in American politics (the famous Kennedy-Nixon television debates were less than a year away), Collins was able to convey to the voters a clean-cut, wholesome, nonpolitical image. As one commentator expressed it, Collins came across with "the carefree sunny charm of a curly-haired parochial choir boy grown older." Powers, by contrast, came across to the viewing public as a tough, arrogant, old-time machine politician out of the Curley era. And last, Collins and his campaign managers were able to capitalize effectively on this contrast of personalities, presenting Collins as an honest, efficient, nonpartisan manager in the style of John B. Hynes, while attacking Powers as a "little Napoleon" and a tool of the worst elements of Boston's political and criminal society. No better indication of the Collins approach can be found than the cleverly designed posters and newspaper advertisements that called on the voters to "STOP POWER POLITICS" while holding out the prospect of what Collins labeled a "New Boston."

In perhaps the biggest upset in Boston's political history, John Collins defeated Johnny Powers for mayor by twenty-four thousand votes. Since neither economic, ethnic, nor religious considerations played a part in the eventual outcome (both Powers and Collins were white, middle-class, Irish-Catholic Democrats), one can only assume that the Boston electorate continued to favor an essentially "nonpolitical" candidate who had no visible attachments to any machine organization, as opposed to a clearly "political" candidate whose candidacy smacked too much of the old Curley regime.

In his inaugural address on January 4, 1960, John Collins emphasized that his goal was not simply to keep the city alive, but to revitalize it. "We must restore, rebuild, and redevelop," he said. As a basis for such a program, he emphasized two particular issues that confronted his administration: the rising costs of city government, and the rising property tax rates. Both these problems had to be dealt with before he could turn to the subject of urban renewal.

In preparing to undertake extensive financial decisions and cost-cutting techniques, Collins turned to a small but powerful group of Boston business leaders who had formed an organization known as the Boston Coordinating Committee, more familiarly known as "The Vault." During the final year of Hynes's term, the business community feared that the growing tax rate, increased expenditures, and ambitious bond issues would force the city into bankruptcy and receivership. To prepare for such an eventuality, Ralph Lowell of the Boston Safe Deposit and Trust Company, Charles Coolidge of Ropes and Gray, Gerald Blakely of Cabot Cabot and Forbes, Lloyd Brace of the First National Bank, Paul Clark of John Hancock, Carl Gilbert of Gillette's, and several other prominent businessmen met in a boardroom near the vault (hence "The Vault") of Lowell's bank on Franklin Street to prepare emergency measures. Although the finances of the city proved to be in better shape than expected, the group continued to hold its meetings even after the mayoral election. Once he took office, John Collins consulted with members of The

Vault for professional advice concerning such technical matters as reorganizing the city's assessing department and computerizing complicated tax records. As time went on, however, every two weeks at four o'clock, the mayor would meet with the members of The Vault for advice and assistance concerning the broader issues involving urban renewal. The close association that developed between the mayor of Boston and influential leaders of the city's business and financial establishments would go far in providing the kind of stability needed for any further progress on the physical development of the city.

From the outset, John Collins was determined to develop a successful program of urban renewal that would create a truly "New Boston" for which he would become famous. The lessons from the West End debacle were not lost on Collins, and it was clear that if he expected public support he would have to come up with a plan that was professionally engineered, adequately funded, and humanely administered. It was with these goals in mind that he selected as his director a thirty-nine-year-old man named Edward J. Logue, who had shown energy and imagination in running the urban renewal program in New Haven, Connecticut. Logue arrived in Boston in March 1960 as a consultant and, after an initial survey of the city, concluded that except for several individual projects, there was, for all practical purposes, "no overall plan or program to change the city, and certainly no public or civic organization equipped to do it." On the basis of his studies, Logue presented to the mayor a comprehensive development plan, which Collins publicly announced on September 22, 1960, as his "Ninety Million Dollar Development Program for Boston." This was an ambitious program to rebuild the city under ten separate plans encompassing not only downtown Boston, but also most of the surrounding neighborhoods. Conscious of the frightening West End experience, Collins assured voters that the program would be planned in consultation "with the people who live in these communities." He would take a "rehabilitation" approach, he promised, instead of resorting to the "bulldozer."

For the next three months, Logue and his staff organized plans, studied documents, compiled statistics, and made out applications to the federal government for enough money to get the large-scale operation off the ground "at one crack." The work paid off: the Urban Renewal Administration agreed to allocate nearly $30 million for Collins's development program. On January 25, 1961, after a bitter fight among board members, Edward J. Logue was chosen administrator of the BRA and given extraordinary powers. He was responsible only to the mayor and to the BRA board, could develop and execute comprehensive plans for the city, and could hire and fire his own staff members. Collins had the man he wanted, invested with all the powers necessary to put his urban renewal program into effect.

Before launching any new programs of his own, however, Logue pushed for completion of such pending projects as the Prudential Center, the Convention Center, and the Government Center, whose effective completion, he felt, would not only put the new Collins administration on a sound footing, but also inspire public confidence in developing future projects. "Getting Prudential Center built," he later wrote, "was essential if any of our other plans were to go forward."

At the time Collins took office in January 1960, plans for the Prudential Center had become stalled after an agreement by Mayor Hynes granting Prudential special tax considerations was struck down as unconstitutional by the state's Supreme Judicial Court. For the next few months, city and state agencies worked feverishly but ineffectually to come up with a tax arrangement that would satisfy Prudential but still pass constitutional muster with the court. Logue finally cut the knot by declaring that the Back Bay site qualified as a "blighted area" under the federal definition and could be placed under the authority of the BRA as a public project, instead of being handled as a private enterprise. Once the Court agreed that the new arrangement was not unconstitutional, construction of the new Prudential complex proceeded rapidly. Designed by architect Charles Luckman and heavily influenced by the work of Swiss architect Le Corbusier, the main tower of the Prudential building, constructed of glass and steel, sat on a concrete platform and rose some 743 feet—fifty-two stories—into the air. As one BRA official later reflected: "The Prudential Center was conceived in the fifties to give a new, slick, shiny image that would attract new developers."

It was during the same early months of 1960 that another long-standing project—an underground garage—came back to life. Although it had been agreed back in 1950 that a garage would be constructed underneath Boston Common, the work was just getting under way when John Collins took office as mayor. Despite protests from the residents of Beacon Hill and Charles Street about the noise, the dust, and the "earthquake tremors" of the pile drivers, the three-level structure was finally completed just before Thanksgiving 1961. The new garage not only added some much-needed parking spaces in the city, but also provided more convenient access to the downtown retail district. In the months following construction, Boston newspaper readers were treated to colorful and juicy scandals involving charges of graft and corruption in the construction process.

While the Prudential Center and the underground garage were under construction, the Collins administration turned its attention to the Government Center project slated for the Scollay Square area. After prolonged negotiations succeeded in persuading federal and state agencies to commit themselves to the construction of administration buildings on the site, BRA director Edward Logue acquired the property rights to the Scollay Square district. In February 1962, the bulldozers came rumbling in, property owners were moved out, and the wrecking ball smashed down one block after another. Only at the last minute were prominent Bostonians like Walter Muir Whitehill able to rescue the historic Sears Crescent from demolition, persuading Logue to incorporate the building's curved, redbrick structure into the overall design of the project.

From the outset, the centerpiece of the Government Center was to be a new $30 million City Hall, set prominently in a broad open space. In November 1960, a national competition for the design of this structure was announced, and a unanimous decision was made in favor of three young members of the Columbia University architectural school—Gerhard Kallman, Noel McKinnell, and Edward Knowles. With great ceremony, the public unveiling of the new design took place on May 3, 1962, at the Museum of Fine Arts. When the curtain was lifted, viewers saw not the traditional, colonial-type structure many had expected, but instead a strikingly modernistic design, low and huge, with what Whitehill described as "Mycenaean or Aztec overtones" in its soaring massiveness. Neither then, nor since, have there been any neutral feelings about Boston's new City Hall. People either love it fervently or hate it passionately. It looks like "the crate that Faneuil Hall came in," remarked one disappointed observer. But there was no turning back. Despite the storm of controversy, Collins and Logue accepted the new design for City Hall and pushed ahead with their plans for the Government Center.

Although disagreements over the new structure's architectural shape would continue well into the future, the decision to create a Government Center in the heart of the city had important ramifications. With Boston serving as the location not only of its own city hall, but also of the state capital, as well as the federal government's New England regional headquarters, government increased its role as the region's major employer. The creation of a special Government Center in Boston assured that billions of dollars of economic

The design for Boston's new City Hall was unveiled on May 3, 1962, at the Museum of Fine Arts. Developed by architects from the Columbia University Graduate School of Architecture, the structure immediately provoked a storm of controversy. Supporters insisted that it was a major work of design, symbolizing the transformation of Boston from a colonial seaport town to a modern metropolis. Critics complained that the extreme modernistic design was totally inappropriate for a city with Boston's historical past. *Courtesy of the Bostonian Society/Old State House.*

activity would not be scattered across the commonwealth. According to Boston economist Barry Bluestone, no other city had such a wide range of government employment concentrated in such a way as to drive the whole regional economy.

There was a rising tide of excitement in response to Boston's urban renewal projects that led a number of private investors to begin participating in the process. In December 1959, New York real estate developer Jerome Rappaport was awarded the contract to build on the demolished forty-six-acre site of the old West End. With the construction of the fashionable Charles River Park complex—featuring expensive townhouses and luxury apartments designed expressly to attract well-to-do tenants from the suburbs—the ethnic working-class character of the old West End was changed forever. As the Prudential tower and the massive War Memorial Auditorium (later renamed the Hynes Auditorium) went up on the site of the old railroad yards along lower Boylston Street, the Sheraton Corporation began construction of a twenty-nine-story hotel. Located directly behind the Prudential project, the First Church of Christ Scientist also caught the "contagion of improvement" and in 1963 sought assistance from the BRA in improving its surroundings. The church launched an ambitious construction program that included administration buildings, apartment complexes, merchandise marts, and a seven hundred-foot-long reflecting pool that lit up the approaches to Massachusetts Avenue and Symphony Hall. In the old South Cove area below Chinatown, the Tufts–New England Medical Center transformed a rundown section of the city into a major center of medical and dental research; in Copley Square, the John Hancock Insurance Company erected a spectacular glass-faced sixty-story office building across from Trinity Church. And in the new Government Center area, developer Norman B. Leventhal's Beacon Construction Company started work on a three-part, crescent-shaped commercial structure (One, Two, and Three Center Plaza) that separated Government Center from the Suffolk County Courthouse in Pemberton Square. One by one, a number of banks, trust companies, law firms, and insurance agencies constructed a series of expensive, high-rise office buildings in the area of Washington Street and State Street, bringing both money and confidence to the "New Boston."

The new construction in downtown Boston, substantial funding from Washington, and serious investment by outside companies—all tangible signs of progress and prosperity—gave Mayor Collins great personal satisfaction as well as professional pride. In June 1963, he announced that he would be a candidate for reelection to a second term as mayor of Boston and called on voters to retain him in office for another four years "so that together we may complete the job we have started." On November 5, 1963, Collins swept the boards, taking nineteen of the city's twenty-two wards, and defeating his rival, Gabriel Piemonte, by a plurality of 34,775 votes. With such an obvious vote of confidence, it seemed as though John Collins could look forward to another four years in office, during which he could complete his comprehensive program for a truly "New Boston."

The initial focus of Collins's Ninety Million Dollar Development Program was on projects in the downtown area—the Prudential Center, the War Memorial Auditorium, the Government Center—attracting federal funds, encouraging local investment, and bringing in outside developers. The long-range ambition of the program, however, was to extend many of the same urban renewal techniques into the various neighborhoods that surrounded the central city. It would be awkward for Collins to boast about his beautiful

Determined to make the New Boston the centerpiece of his administration, Mayor John F. Collins brought young Edward J. Logue up from New Haven, Connecticut, to take over the planning and execution of the city's urban renewal program. Collins (seated) watches Logue use a pointer to describe to a group of professional builders the plans for a hundred-acre waterfront development project. In the left foreground is the Fan Pier, which is currently under development. *Courtesy of the Boston Public Library, Print Department.*

"New Boston" when the refurbished downtown area was still hemmed in by a series of old neighborhoods, generally populated by blue-collar families living in two- and three-story wooden houses and by people of color occupying run-down tenements and shabby rooming houses. The city's new program was designed to transform these valuable locations into clusters of attractive and income-producing communities with the kind of shiny new townhouses and modern apartments that would bring middle-class families and well-to-do professionals back to the city.

The question, of course, was where to begin. Appalled by what had happened to the poor residents of the old West End, neighborhood leaders were on guard against similar intrusions by politicians, real estate developers, and "social engineers" who would knock down their houses, displace their people, and disrupt their traditional way of life. For this reason, Collins and Logue did not attempt to bring their urban renewal program into either South Boston or East Boston, both of which had vocal representatives in the Boston city council who were openly hostile to the idea of urban renewal. Taking the path of least political resistance, therefore, Logue and the BRA directed their efforts to areas like Charlestown and Allston-Brighton, neither of which had a representative on the city council. In both cases, however, longtime residents—"townies" as they were called—rose up in angry protest against the plans of "outsiders" to tear down their old houses and replace them with fashionable housing developments with rents the locals could never afford. Although Collins, Logue, and the BRA eventually succeeded in accomplishing many of their projects, the result was a growing and bitter antagonism between Irish-Catholic residents of the neighborhoods and the Irish-Catholic politicians who ran city government.

Feeling themselves caught between the influence of municipal authorities and the greed of urban developers, neighborhood residents responded by taking over control of their own districts. They organized political action groups to plan their own civic improvements and to force city authorities to consult with neighborhood representatives before taking any action that might endanger their communities. Local groups defeated plans to construct a multilane "Southwest Corridor" through Roxbury, fought against plans to expand Logan Airport, and prevented the increase of medical institutions in the Mission Hill district. As Mayor Collins's second four-year term drew to a close, community-based groups were well on their way to becoming an important political force that would have to be reckoned with by candidates in the 1967 mayoral election.

Growing conflict between local political groups in the white ethnic neighborhoods was not the only political complication facing John F. Collins in the last two years of his term as mayor. A rising tide of anger and discontent in the African-American community also presented the beginnings of a new political force in Boston's history. At first, a number of the city's prominent African-American leaders—such as Otto and Muriel Snowden, political representative Royal Bolling, Jr., and attorney Clarence Elam—welcomed the revitalization and modernization of their multiracial South End community that they felt urban renewal would bring. In a very short time, however, as the BRA moved in with bulldozers and steam shovels to smash their old wood-frame houses to splinters and reduce many of their brick houses to what one resident called "clouds of rubble," residents quickly became disenchanted with the process. They concluded that the real object of the BRA program was to take their property, evict their multicultural people—African Americans, Puerto Ricans, Hispanics, Eastern Europeans, and poor people—and build high-rent, fashionable apartments for those members of the "white gentry" who wanted to live close to the city.

Resolved to take matters into their own hands, during the mid-1960s a diverse group of ministers, poverty-program employees, social workers, and community organizers formed political action groups to oppose the BRA, halt further demolition, and push for more subsidized housing. At the same time, a new wave of younger and more assertive black community activists began speaking out against Mayor Collins, accusing his administration of ignoring the basic needs of poor black people living in what the local black newspaper called "the worst slum conditions in Massachusetts." Early in 1966, a group of Roxbury welfare mothers staged a sit-in at Mayor Collins's office at City Hall on School Street, demanding action against the unsanitary conditions in which they were forced to live. On another occasion, a group of Roxbury residents dumped a huge pile of trash and garbage on the front steps of City Hall to protest inadequate sanitation services in the black community. As Mayor John B. Collins was preparing to leave office after his two terms as mayor, Boston's African-American residents were making it clear that they were not convinced city government was doing enough to meet their basic needs: health care, low-income housing, employment opportunities, and better schools. The opening years of the new mayoral administration in Boston were already being shaped by political forces in white ethnic neighborhoods as well as in the black community that were generated during the final two years of the Collins administration.

11

Race and Ethnicity

WITH the announcement by John Collins that he would not seek a third term as mayor of Boston, the 1967 election became a wide-open contest with many more candidates than usual, all hoping to move into the new City Hall that had gone up at Government Center: BRA director Edward Logue; Barry Hynes, son of the previous mayor; Kevin White, four-term Massachusetts secretary of state; school committee member Mrs. Louise Day Hicks; at least three city councilors; and longtime Republican John Winthrop Sears.

These were not good times for either the nation or the city. Halfway through Collins's second term, the steady flow of federal funds that had fueled the city's ambitious urban renewal program began to dry up at an alarming rate. This was due in large part to the costs of the Vietnam War, which had begun to rise significantly during the mid-1960s. With the total U.S. military budget rising from $51.6 billion in 1964 to $82.5 billion in 1969, Congress was forced to cut appropriations for all kinds of domestic programs. This not only affected Boston's renewal programs and housing projects, but also caused local colleges and universities to discontinue many of the bureaus, institutes, and planning centers that had been providing valuable assistance to municipal authorities.

It was already clear that Collins's successor in 1967 would take on extensive commitments to continue projects and social welfare programs without the necessary federal funds to adequately support them.

The late 1960s, too, was a period when the social fabric of the nation seemed to be coming apart at the seams. In 1965, devastating riots in the Watts district of Los Angeles touched off a wave of racial conflict that erupted in violence during 1966 and 1967 in major northern cities such as Chicago, Detroit, and Newark. In the wake of civil rights activities, student rebellions broke out on college campuses across the country, with sit-ins, teach-ins, marches, and demonstrations protesting the oppression of the nation's corporate establishment. The formation of the National Organization for Women (NOW) in 1966 led to public rallies and vocal demonstrations by feminists demanding equal rights for women. Escalating American involvement in the Vietnam War further expanded the student agenda, with even more violent demonstrations against President Johnson, the draft, and the expansion of the fighting. Whoever was elected mayor of Boston in November 1967 would be confronted not only with serious financial cutbacks, but also with major social disruptions. By this time, too, city authorities were being confronted with the demands of an increasingly active African-American population that, for the first time in Boston's history, was becoming a tangible political force in its own right.

After the Civil War came to a victorious conclusion in 1865, there had been every reason for members of Boston's African-American community to expect a much brighter future. On January 1, 1863, President Lincoln had put his signature on the Emancipation Proclamation announcing that all slaves were "then, thenceforward, and forever free." For the first time, too, during the Civil War, African Americans were admitted into the armed forces to serve their country like all other American citizens, achieving a record of battlefield heroism that Boston later recognized with Saint-Gaudens's stirring monument to the 54th Massachusetts Regiment on the crest of Beacon Hill. And when the end of the conflict brought the Thirteenth Amendment, and then the Fourteenth Amendment, to ratify in peacetime what had been proclaimed in wartime, the postwar years for African Americans seemed promising indeed.

And immediately after the Civil War, black citizens, especially those in Boston, had even greater reason to expect a brighter tomorrow. Massachusetts Senator Charles Sumner sponsored the abolitionist black lawyer John Rock as the first African American to practice law before the U.S. Supreme Court. In the General Court of Massachusetts, Republican legislators took steps to reward black veterans who had fought for the Union with federal jobs in post offices and customhouses. In 1866, two African Americans were elected to the Massachusetts House of Representatives and, until the end of the century, one or two black men were regularly elected each year to serve in the state legislature, where they voted solidly Republican in keeping with the spirit of the Great Emancipator. And in the city of Boston itself, each ward elected two representatives to sit on the Common Council; between 1876 and 1895, a black resident from the West End (then Ward 9) filled at least one of those seats.

Beneath the surface, however, things were by no means as encouraging as they appeared. For one thing, even though the number of black residents increased substantially after the war, there were few changes either in their traditional housing patterns or in their living conditions. Between 1866 and 1868, over a thousand former slaves moved up from the South to live in the Boston-Cambridge area, raising the black population from 2,261 in 1860 to 3,496 in 1870, despite complaints by Governor John Andrew that the lack of opportunities and social services for these newcomers would create a race of "homeless wanderers." And despite the high-sounding phrases in the state's 1854 school desegregation law that followed the Sarah Roberts case, the public schools continued to reflect the city's segregated housing patterns. Elementary schools in predominantly white neighborhoods such as Charlestown, Roxbury, and Dorchester, for example, had no black students at all. By contrast, more than a third of the city's black children were enrolled in two elementary schools in the city's West End. Still confined to their highly segregated district on the north side of Beacon Hill, black adults were effectively excluded from the modern and commercial parts of Boston where jobs in business, banking, and retailing usually required more education and more sophisticated skills. Despite efforts by a small liberal labor group in Boston to integrate African-American workers into the white labor force during the postwar period, black people continued to function in their traditional capacities as laborers and stevedores, waiters and caterers, barbers and hairdressers, bootblacks and laundresses. Most black Bostonians essentially served the needs of the white community and brought in enough income to sustain their families in modest fashion. But they were seldom able to acquire the training, instruction, or experience that would enable them to move up the economic ladder.

Boston's African-American community continued to live a quiet and self-contained existence in the West End until 1895, when the Democrats in the state legislature redistricted the old black Republican neighborhood. Not only were the African-American residents stripped of what little political influence they possessed, but they also felt jeopardized by the new wave of European immigrants, with their strange ways and indecipherable languages, as they rapidly filled up large sections of the North End and the West End.

Soon after 1895, therefore, the black residents abandoned their homes in the old West End and began moving into the lower South End, between Washington Street and Columbus Avenue, taking up residence in the old brownstone apartments that had been originally intended for well-to-do whites before the construction of the Back Bay upset real estate predictions. For a time, the only way black residents retained any political visibility was through the efforts of their local church leaders and the activities of individual spokesmen such as William Monroe Trotter. Son of a Mississippi slave who moved his family north, Trotter grew up in Boston's Hyde Park section, graduated from Harvard, and became a prosperous real estate broker. Despite his own financial security, Trotter was conscious of the insidious forms of racial discrimination in the North and in 1901 began publishing *The Guardian* as a means of pressing for civil rights. Although his hopes to create a Boston-based national civil rights movement were eclipsed by the more powerful National Association for the Advancement of Colored People (NAACP), he continued his fight for freedom. In 1915 he campaigned against the showing in Boston of D. W. Griffith's movie *Birth of a Nation,* and until Trotter's death in 1934 *The Guardian* regularly reported on racial violence, police brutality, and other issues of significance to members of the city's black community.

By the early part of the twentieth century, black residents had spread along Columbus Avenue and Tremont Street into the upper part of the South End, settling along Northampton and Lenox Streets; the African-American population grew to nearly fourteen thousand by 1910. The size of the city's original black community was augmented by a fairly steady stream of black sharecroppers from rural southern states such as Georgia and Alabama who moved into Boston and took jobs as railroad porters in the Boston & Albany Railroad yards on Boylston Street or served as waiters in the various hotels around Copley Square and Park Square. After World War I, newcomers from Jamaica, Barbados, and other parts of the West Indies formed yet another part of the city's growing black population, which was still much lower (never more than 2 percent in the nineteenth century) than that of most other major American cities. Because of their small numbers even into the twentieth century, Boston blacks lacked the "critical mass" necessary for effective political or social action, wrote J. Anthony Lukas in *Common Ground,* his classic study of race relations in Boston.

Although there was still enough racial diversity in the South End to promote considerable interaction among black residents and their white immigrant neighbors, the district was fast taking on the social and cultural characteristics of an African-American community. A variety of church groups, social clubs, and fraternal lodges and their female auxiliaries flourished throughout the South End as places where active-minded citizens could gather to enrich their own social lives as well as to benefit those less fortunate members of the community who were in need of food, housing, and financial assistance. The district's black churches still offered the best place to meet friends, exchange views, display new clothes, hear music, and gain both emotional and spiritual sustenance. The church offered a place where black women especially could take on important responsibilities, participate regularly in social affairs, and provide monetary contributions to support the church and sustain its programs of charity and relief.

During the 1920s, black society in the South End centered around club meetings and elegant gatherings, usually at the homes of prominent club women. "Smart sets" of younger people, as the historian Sarah Deutsch has described them, tried to outdo each other in their social clubs, many of which included a small intelligentsia of professional social workers and creative writers. Eugene Gordon of the *Boston Post* edited Boston's black literary magazine *The Saturday Evening Quill,* which boasted among its contributors the playwright and Boston teacher Alvira Hazzard; novelist Gertrude Schalk; Josephine St. Pierre Ruffin's daughter, Florida Ruffin Ridley, a former Boston schoolteacher and editor of *Social Service News;* and Dorothy West, who described the experience of southern black visitors to Boston in her novel *The Living Is Easy,* and who later left Boston to participate in New York's Harlem Renaissance.

By the 1930s, after its population had passed the twenty-thousand mark, the African-American community had moved beyond its original limits and extended down to Dudley Street in lower Roxbury. "In 1936 this community was almost completely black," Amanda Houston remembered of her early years as a resident of the South End. "It sustained two weekly newspapers, *The Chronicle* and *The Guardian,* and at least four profitable restaurants, black-owned and -operated, that catered to both black and white customers. There were two Slade restaurants across the street from each other, Estelle's and Jobil's. There were

During the 1940s and 1950s, Boston's African-American population was concentrated mainly in the South End of the city. The South End was an active and exciting community where black residents developed their own lifestyle, and where restaurants, drugstores, florist shops, barbershops, hairdressing parlors, and other black-owned enterprises did a thriving business along Tremont Street and Columbus Avenue. It was a bright, lively, active neighborhood, recalls one of its residents, where "the streets were jammed, and so were the clubs." *Republished with permission of Globe Newspaper Company, Inc., from the August 7, 1964, issue of the* Boston Globe, © *1964.*

four drugstores, a florist shop, an appliance store, barbershops, hairdressing parlors, a tailor shop, and other black businesses lining Tremont Street."

It was here, in the South End–Lower Roxbury area, that the black community also developed its own distinctive political organization as a handful of local political leaders traded power for patronage, much as the Irish ward bosses had done a generation earlier. Dr. Silas F. ("Shag") Taylor, a local pharmacist, became the boss of Ward 9 with the help of his organization, the Massachusetts Colored League. During the 1930s and 1940s, Shag and his brother Balcolm ("Bal") worked with the Curley machine, exchanging votes in the black wards for jobs, housing, and an occasional Thanksgiving turkey. "Shag Taylor could get your street cleaned, fix a pothole, get a vacant lot cleared, garbage collected, an abandoned car removed," recalled attorney Thomas Atkins. "If you needed someone released from jail, needed a job—whatever. Nobody had any question he was the premier man, he was *the* person, he was the machine's man, and his power came from the Curley machine." The Taylors would set up meetings for Curley in the black community, "run ads in the papers for him, and use the favors that folks owed them to pressure people into supporting the white candidates in the Democratic party." They were among the black politicians who switched to the Democratic party during the 1930s when Roosevelt's New Deal seemed to offer poor people of every color their only chance for social and economic security.

It was during the 1930s and 1940s that the intersection of Massachusetts and Columbus Avenues, just two blocks east of Symphony Hall, became the exciting center of a Boston "Harlem." At the Hi-Hat nightclub, mixed audiences of blacks and whites gathered to enjoy the performances of such celebrated jazz musicians as Fats Waller, Lionel Hampton, Count Basie, and Duke Ellington pounding out such famous numbers as "The One O'Clock Jump" and "The Back Bay Shuffle." The crowds that thronged into the South End at night dazzled a sixteen-year-old newcomer named Malcolm Little (later known as Malcolm X) when he arrived in Boston from Michigan in 1940. "Neon lights, nightclubs, poolhalls, bars, the cars they drove!" he wrote in *The Autobiography of Malcolm X*. "Restaurants made the streets smell—rich, greasy, down-home black cooking! Juke boxes blared, Erskine Hawkins, Duke Ellington, Cootie Williams, dozens of others." The Savoy Café and the Rainbow Lounge, just up the street, attracted more jazz enthusiasts to hear the playing of Lester ("Prez") Young, Buck Clayton, and Sidney Bechet, and both the Roseland Ballroom and the Raymor-Playmor Ballroom featured the music of such "big bands" as Benny Goodman, Jimmy Lunceford, Charlie Barnett, and Woodie Herman for all-night dancing. "These sounds were heard for miles around," recalled Reginald Weems, who grew up in the South End, reveled in the music, and frequented the various barbecue restaurants in the neighborhood. It was a bright, lively, active community when "the streets were jammed, and so were the clubs." "Those of us who came out onto Massachusetts Avenue from the Savoy Café to find our various ways home occasionally walked in jazz time," recalled Nat Hentoff, a celebrated music critic, in his memoir *Boston Boy,* describing his travels from his home in Jewish Roxbury to the pleasures of Boston's black jazz scene. At the time, it was generally assumed that Boston's African-American population would remain relatively small and would confine itself to a permanent location in the South End–Roxbury area.

By the 1940s, however, Boston's isolated and generally unnoticed African-American community began to grow remarkably in size—a phenomenon that reflected the general growth of the African-American population throughout the northern states. Until International Harvester perfected its mechanical cotton picker in 1944, according to Nicholas Lemann in *The Promised Land,* nearly 77 percent of black Americans still lived in the South, with 49 percent of these people located in rural areas. The invention of the mechanical cotton picker changed all that. In the past, a good field hand had been able to pick twenty pounds of cotton in an hour; a mechanical picker, in that same hour, could pick as many as a thousand pounds (two bales). As far as most black sharecroppers were concerned, there was no more work in the cotton fields of the South. They would have to move north to look for new jobs. Between 1910 and 1970, 6.5 million black Americans moved from the South to the North; 5 million of these moved *after* 1940, replaced by mechanical farming. In sheer numbers, Lemann concludes, the black migration from the South outranks the migration of any other ethnic group to the United States—Irish, Italians, Jews, or Poles. For African Americans, the migration meant leaving what had always been their economic and social base in America and finding a completely new life in the North.

The internal mass migration of African Americans as the result of the mechanical cotton picker was further stimulated by the exigencies of World War II, which produced exactly the kinds of job opportunities the newly dispossessed black workers were looking for. Skilled and unskilled black workers from the South moved into northern cities like St. Louis, Detroit, Cincinnati, and Chicago in search of work; many also came into the New England region to work in industrial plants, army posts, armories, shipyards, naval bases, and arsenals. As a consequence, Boston's black population nearly doubled in only a single decade, rising from some twenty-three thousand in 1940 to over forty thousand in 1950. Because no new construction had taken place in the Roxbury area since 1920, the overcrowded black population was literally bulging at the seams. By the late 1960s, African Americans were starting to move beyond the confines of their traditional Roxbury boundaries, settling along the fringes of such formerly all-white neighborhoods as Dorchester, Mattapan, Jamaica Plain, Roslindale, and Hyde Park.

It was not long before the growing spread of the black population ran into a mounting wall of white resistance. Intensely proud of the distinctively ethnic characteristics that had distinguished their particular neighborhoods for more than half a century, and brought up with the strict admonition to "stay with your own kind," the Irish in South Boston and Charlestown, the Italians in East Boston and the North End, and the Jews of Mattapan, along with other residents of traditionally white areas, reacted in panic and alarm at the idea that African Americans were moving into their neighborhoods—their "turf." Racial tensions quickly mounted as whites raised fears of blacks taking their jobs, lowering the standards of their all-white schools, bringing down property values, and adding to the danger of crime in the streets. The fact that at both the national and the state levels the economic situation was showing signs of cracking only further solidified the determination of middle-class and working-class white people to keep the black people from getting "too much, too soon." At the same time, it stiffened the resolve of African-Americans residents to get their fair share of the American way of life before it was too late.

Stimulated by the successes of the civil rights movement in the South, inspired by the words of the Reverend Martin Luther King, Jr., and encouraged by the passage of the Civil Rights Act of 1964 and the Voting Rights Act of 1965, Boston's African-American community began to translate its growing numbers into a sufficient level of political power to address the needs of blacks and bring about changes in the way they saw themselves treated. As the Collins administration and the predominantly white political establishment failed to come up with reasonable or effective solutions to such issues as high unemployment, insufficient public housing, unsatisfactory health care, and inadequate schooling, the members of the black community looked with considerable interest at the outcome of the upcoming 1967 mayoral election.

With the three city councilors cutting into each other's votes in the September primaries, and with John Sears neutralizing Ed Logue's votes in the fashionable Beacon Hill district, the two finalists who emerged to battle it out in the November election were Louise Day Hicks, who came in first with about 28 percent of the votes cast, and Kevin Hagan White, who came in second with 20 percent. This meant that in two months Boston might well have a woman as mayor for the first time in its history.

Mrs. Hicks of South Boston was a former member of the Boston School Committee and an outspoken champion of local autonomy and neighborhood schools. In June 1963, the NAACP had first pointed out that in violation of the

1954 U.S. Supreme Court ruling in the case of *Brown v. Board of Education of Topeka,* many of Boston's public schools were predominantly white while other schools were predominantly black. The NAACP demanded that steps be taken to integrate the Boston schools as soon as possible in accordance with the Court's ruling. School committee chair Louise Day Hicks, however, along with the rest of the all-white school committee, denied charges of de facto segregation in their public school system. The makeup of each school, they insisted, was merely a reflection of the racial and ethnic composition of the individual neighborhood. Insisting that the *Brown* decision did not apply to Boston schools, the school committee refused to develop any comprehensive plan for integration. White voters clearly approved this position, and Mrs. Hicks had received overwhelming support from the white ethnic neighborhoods in her bids for reelection to the school committee. Now she was using her influence as the city's top vote-getter to become the city's first female mayor.

Hicks's rival in November 1967 was Kevin H. White, former secretary of state of the commonwealth, who hoped to get enough support from a broad spectrum of the Boston community to put himself in office. As a man whose father and grandfather had served as presidents of the Boston City Council, and whose father-in-law (William "Mother" Galvin) had been a power in Charlestown politics, White came from a long line of active politicians and soon established himself as a clever and resourceful campaigner. A graduate of Williams College and the Boston College Law School, he was acceptable to upper-middle-class groups in the city as a capable administrator who would continue the urban renewal programs of his predecessors. As four-time secretary of state, he was viewed by older members of the Yankee community as an appealing "nonpolitical" and accommodationist candidate in the tradition of Hynes and Collins. And as a reputed liberal-minded progressive, he was more than acceptable to members of the city's black community, who endorsed him strongly as the only viable alternative to Mrs. Hicks. "Kevin White has realistically met the issues of this campaign and the issues and problems that confront the city of Boston with a candid and believable approach," declared the black community's *Bay State Banner* in its election-eve endorsement.

Although her supporters in South Boston's Wards 6 and 7 gave Louise Day Hicks a whopping 11,335 votes to a meager 4,489 for her opponent, White was able to pile up enough votes in the city's other wards to defeat Mrs. Hicks in November 1967 by a margin of 12,000 votes. The former secretary of state began his first term of office (1968–1972) during perhaps one of the most chaotic and

Kevin White was the first Boston mayor to recognize the city's growing African-American population as a new political constituency. During times of racial tensions, he visited the city's black neighborhoods, cultivated the support of community leaders, and provided recreational outlets for young people. Here he meets with Melnea Cass (second from left) and other community leaders to help launch a drive for the construction of the Harriet Tubman House in the South End. *Courtesy of the Boston Public Library, Print Department.*

disruptive periods in American history. The nation had been shocked beyond words by the tragic assassination of President John F. Kennedy in November 1963 and suffered further anguish when the brutal murder of the Reverend Martin Luther King, Jr., in April 1968 was followed by the killing of Senator Robert F. Kennedy only two months later. In one American city after another, waves of explosive violence erupted. Protests against the war in Vietnam grew in both number and intensity; civil rights demonstrations multiplied at a prodigious rate; student upheavals paralyzed the nation's colleges and universities from one coast to the other. The city of Boston—as a major academic center, as a focal point of antiwar resistance, and as an urban community whose black population was increasingly militant—could easily have been ripped apart by the convulsive emotionalism generated by national rage and racial frustration.

Mayor Kevin White worked long and exhaustively to keep the city under control during those critical years by placating as many of the varied and often conflicting constituencies as possible. He maintained good relations with the bankers and businessmen of the inner-city financial establishment by pushing ahead with the various plans for urban renewal and commercial development in order to further modernize the city and improve its financial standing. Most of the basic planning and design for the "New Boston" had been the work of Mayors Hynes and Collins, but a great many of the projects actually came to completion during the unprecedented sixteen-year term of Kevin White. The new mayor enthusiastically sustained the momentum for construction begun by his predecessors and added his own touch by transforming the old and dilapidated Quincy Market area behind Faneuil Hall into one of the most attractive and successful tourist attractions in the city. He took advantage of the new spirit of optimism to encourage business leaders, builders, and real estate developers to become part of Boston's changing scene. A cluster of high-rise structures—banks, insurance companies, hotels—went up in the heart of the city, adding to Boston's service-oriented economy and contributing more impressive silhouettes to its emerging skyline. White used his energetic talents and charismatic personality to dramatize the "New Boston," publicizing its financial opportunities, capitalizing on its cultural advantages, and declaring it to be "livable" city.

At the same time, Kevin White set about establishing closer contact with representatives of the middle- and low-income white ethnic communities who had complained that their local interests had been ignored by the Collins administration. Assuring the neighborhoods that he would respond to their concerns, White created a series of "Little City Halls" in various localities, staffed by members of his administration, as a means of making downtown city government more responsive to the needs of the neighborhood residents. In the process, these Little City Halls also served as strategic political bases from which City Hall could send out foot soldiers and volunteers to build up greater grass-roots political support for Kevin White. White spent much more money than previous administrations on capital improvements in the neighborhoods, providing better lighting and improved fire and police protection to help reduce crime and vandalism.

Kevin White also appreciated the political realities of the racial issues that had appeared for the first time in Boston political history during the election of 1967. As mayor, he worked hard to keep things calm in the city's restive African-American community, especially after the murder of the Reverend Martin Luther King, Jr., only three months after White had begun his first term as mayor. With his jacket slung over his shoulder and his necktie loosened around the collar of his oxford-cloth shirt, White became a frequent visitor in the black neighborhoods, strolling along the streets, sauntering through the playgrounds, talking with groups of mothers, and establishing personal contacts with local black leaders. He increased the number of black policemen in the Roxbury area to counteract charges of police brutality, made an effort to include black residents as full members of the Boston community, and supported a popular mobile program called "Summerthing" to supply music and entertainment for the younger elements of the neighborhoods during the long and dangerous summer months.

Also in 1968, in a further effort to upgrade the status of black residents, Mayor White encouraged a consortium of twenty-two Boston savings banks called the Boston Banks Urban Renewal Group (B-BURG) to allocate some $50 million in mortgage money to encourage low-income black families to purchase homes in the Mattapan area. When the Hynes administration demolished the New York Streets section of the South End back in 1954, displaced tenants were forced to look for other places to live. Most white families went into housing projects in South Boston, Dorchester, and Jamaica Plain; African-American and Puerto Rican families moved to Washington Park and North Dorchester. A number of these black families moved across into northern Mattapan, a neighborhood considered to be the largest Jewish community in New England. After World War II, some younger Jewish families (many veterans taking advantage of the G.I. Bill) moved into the suburbs of Milton, Randolph, and Canton in search of larger houses and better schools. As late as the mid-1950s, however, there were still some fifty thousand Jewish residents still living in Mattapan. The availability of new mortgage money from the Boston banks changed all that. Between 1968 and 1970, some three thousand African-American families entered Mattapan, moving along Blue Hill Avenue from Grove Hall toward Mattapan Square. By 1972, the number of Jewish residents in the area had dropped to fewer than twenty-five hundred, and the subsequent flare-ups of racial fears, panic selling, and blockbusting accelerated the exodus of Jewish families to the point where a once predominantly Jewish community was transformed into an almost all-black neighborhood.

By the time Kevin White started his second term as mayor in 1972, it seemed to most observers that Boston had weathered the worst of the storm. By that time the Vietnam War had begun to wind down, the antiwar protests had begun to peter out, the colleges were settling down, and racial controversies appeared to be lessening. By the time the war in Vietnam officially came to an end early in 1973, the city showed signs of resuming a more normal and peaceful routine, with little more trouble on the horizon than deciding the most appropriate way of celebrating the bicentennial of the nation's independence. During 1975–1976, the White administration organized a spectacular series of events that caught the attention of people everywhere, including the arrival of the Tall Ships in Boston Harbor, the historic visit of Queen Elizabeth II of England, and the gigantic Fourth of July concert on the Esplanade with Arthur Fiedler and the Boston Pops playing Tchaikovsky's *1812 Overture* as fireworks lit up the summer night.

Unfortunately, however, the air of gaiety and festivity that marked the bicentennial celebrations was largely superficial—and certainly short-lived. Underneath the apparently calm and tranquil surface, there were a number of critical issues that had already divided the community into bitter factions and would eventually lead to serious confrontations with city government. One complex issue was the changing character of the national economy and its numerous repercussions at the local levels. During the mid-1970s, national production began declining alarmingly. Before long, runaway inflation began to send prices for food, clothing, heating fuel, gasoline, and rent soaring to incredible heights. In 1977 the inflation rate was up to 6 percent; by 1979 it was over 10 percent; by 1980 it had passed 12 percent. The resulting recession worked its most distressing effects on the New England region, where unemployment rates climbed to levels not seen since the days of the Great Depression. In view of the complex financial needs of a big city like Boston, with a large blue-collar white population and rising unemployment among its growing black population, the already uneasy relationship between low-income blacks and low-income whites became even more precarious. Basic racial antagonisms resulting from the movement of blacks into white neighborhoods were transformed into a life-and-death struggle for economic survival as both races fought desperately for a share in the meager economic benefits that seemed to be getting smaller every day. Indeed, this growing economic tension between racial groups in Boston only served to exacerbate another major problem that was to occupy much of Mayor White's time and attention during his second administration—the issue of school desegregation and the crisis of mandatory busing.

Despite their recent and quite dramatic increase in numbers, African-American citizens of Boston were still unable to translate their growing presence in the city into meaningful political clout. In 1960, they still constituted little more than 10 percent of the total population. Then, too, the postwar social problems plaguing major American urban centers like Boston now went far beyond the capacities of traditional ward bosses and local neighborhood leaders. Houses needed repair, tenements were becoming dilapidated, rents were going up all the time, unemployment was becoming endemic to black neighborhoods, and insurance companies were holding back on coverage. The black population became increasingly angry and restive as the white political establishment showed no signs of coming up with effective solutions. Despite the fact that in 1965 the Massachusetts General Court passed a Racial Imbalance Act, which stated that any school that was more than 50 percent black would be considered racially imbalanced, the Boston School Committee refused to admit charges by the NAACP that de facto segregation existed in the public schools and indicated that it had no intention of developing any plans for integration.

Frustrated by what they considered the Boston School Committee's lack of response, a number of African-American parents arranged with the NAACP to bring a class-action suit against the school committee in the name of a parent named Tallulah Morgan. Since James Hennigan was school committee chair at the time, the case became known as *Morgan v. Hennigan*. Early in 1972, the *Morgan* case was assigned by lot to federal judge W. Arthur Garrity, Jr., an Irish-Catholic from Worcester, a graduate of Holy Cross and the Harvard Law School, a campaign worker for John F. Kennedy, and a highly respected member of the Massachusetts Bar. For two years Judge Garrity read the literature and listened to the arguments in the case; on June 21, 1974, he finally handed down his decision. The Boston School Committee, he said, had "knowingly carried out a systematic program of segregation" and had "intentionally brought about and maintained a dual system." For these reasons, he concluded, "the entire school system of Boston is unconstitutionally segregated." He then went on to order a program designed to bus some eighteen thousand schoolchildren, to go into effect the following September, in order to achieve a balanced mix of white and black students in the schools.

As far as the white neighborhoods were concerned, this was the last straw. They decided to resist to the bitter end what they regarded as the latest intrusion into their private lives and local traditions. Encouraged by officials on the school committee as well as by members of the city council who called Judge Garrity's decision the "death knell of the city," they prepared to defend the sanctity of their "neighborhood schools" with every weapon at their command. In many localities, the old "neighborhood spirit," which had declined appreciably during the 1950s and 1960s, was amazingly revitalized by the busing issue; it provided

Louise Day Hicks was the first woman in the history of Boston to be a candidate for the office of mayor. In 1961, Mrs. Hicks had won a seat on the Boston School Committee, where she became a vocal critic of plans to desegregate the city's public school system. She later won widespread support in her own neighborhood of South Boston, as well as in other ethnic communities, for her opposition to court-ordered busing and her support of local neighborhood schools. *Courtesy of the Boston Public Library, Print Department.*

a common danger and a common enemy against which residents could unify their efforts and direct their attacks. Strikes, boycotts, harassment, and outright violence attended the start of the city's busing program during 1974–1975, to the extent that hundreds of city and state police officers were called in to patrol the streets, monitor the schools, and protect the yellow buses that carried black students to schools in white neighborhoods and white students to schools in black neighborhoods. Because of their traditional roles as leading Irish-Catholic neighborhoods, and because of their strategic geographical locations as virtually isolated peninsulas, South Boston and Charlestown became the storm centers of white protest, and the high schools in these districts the focal points of the most serious racial disturbances.

Despite the noise and tumult that attended the enforcement of mandatory busing, Judge Garrity refused to be deterred from what he regarded as the program's moral objective. When the school committee refused a direct order to develop a citywide school integration plan, the judge held the offending officials in contempt of court and put forth his own desegregation plan for September 1975, calling for the busing of three thousand more students than under his 1974 plan. On May 10, 1975, the U.S. Supreme Court gave its support to Judge Garrity by refusing to review his original decision that found the Boston schools to be unconstitutionally segregated.

Garrity's newest actions only further fanned the flames of neighborhood opposition. A coalition of neighborhood groups known as ROAR (Restore Our Alienated Rights) was formed by Louise Day Hicks to continue the fight against busing and, encouraged by sympathetic remarks by President Gerald L. Ford, the advocates of neighborhood schools pressed for a constitutional amendment to outlaw enforced busing. In this effort, however, they were discouraged by such national political leaders as Senator Edward Kennedy, Senator Edward Brooke, and Congressman Thomas ("Tip") O'Neill. A short time later, the protesters suffered another serious setback when the U.S. Attorney General refused to have the Justice Department review the Boston situation. For the time being, at least, the opponents of busing would have to rely on their own resources to maintain control of their neighborhoods and determine the composition of their schools. The next two years saw a series of ugly racial incidents—including stonings, beatings, firebombings, and even shootings—earning Boston the label of the most racist city in America. For a city that had been heralded as the "Cradle of Liberty" and the "Athens of America," this was an embarrassment from both a historic as well as a humanistic point of view.

The busing issue created a major schism in the city, not only between white people and black people, but also between working-class Irish Catholics in the neighborhoods and their more affluent friends and relatives who had moved away to the suburbs. "The federal court orders of 1974 and 1975," observes J. Anthony Lukas in *Common Ground,* "assumed that the burden of integration would fall disproportionately on the poor of both races." Blue-collar families in neighborhoods like South Boston, Charlestown, and East Boston felt they were being forced to face the full impact of racial desegregation all by themselves, while other parts of the Greater Boston area got away scot-free. These neighborhood residents were the ones who had to watch their children bused away every morning to predominantly black neighborhoods, while their friends and relatives in the affluent suburbs enrolled their children in mostly all-white schools that were unaffected by Judge Garrity's ruling. The neighborhood residents complained that they were the ones whose husbands, fathers, brothers, and uncles were denied jobs or promotions in the police, fire, and public works departments, while doctors, lawyers, and bankers in the suburbs were far removed from the effects of such liberal "social experiments." Irish and Italian working-class residents and their families felt betrayed and abandoned by "their own kind," by people they had always looked up to and counted on—political leaders, social workers, educators, lawyers, judges, even priests and bishops—who now seemed to be more concerned with the problems of newly arrived black people than with the needs of poor white people whose families had lived in Boston for generations. "For the opponents of busing," wrote Ronald Formisano in *Boston against Busing,* "the threat to their neighborhoods and lifestyles constituted a trampling on their freedom." Feeling themselves at the mercy of outside forces, and realizing that there was no one to help them, local residents took matters into their own hands and, in the long Celtic tradition of lost causes, decided to go down fighting.

At almost the same time that Mayor White was grappling with the tensions and violence generated by a busing crisis that seemed incapable of resolution, he also found his administration under attack from organized forces in the white neighborhoods that were demanding a greater role in the decision-making process of city government. In addition to their general feelings of alienation and neglect by an administration they felt catered to the business-people, the bankers, and the financiers of downtown Boston, the people in the neighborhoods had several very specific complaints. One was the way in which government agencies, private institutions, and real estate developers were moving into local communities, taking over land and housing, displacing old-time inhabitants, and polluting the environment in various ways. The continued expansion of Logan Airport in East Boston, the spread of the Harvard Medical School complex into the Mission Hill area, and the impact of the Tufts–New England Medical Center on the Boston Chinatown district were examples of the kind of encroachment feared by every neighborhood. The recollections of what had happened to the old West End were still vivid in the memories of local Bostonians.

Another complaint of local communities was the way in which banking and real estate policies affected public and private housing in the neighborhoods. In the years after World War II, many Boston banks refused to grant mortgages or home-improvement loans in areas they declared to be "blighted" or "bad"

Court-ordered busing as a method of desegregating Boston's public schools provoked a decade of controversy between those who believed it was the only way to end a racially segregated school system and those who insisted on the right of parents to send their children to neighborhood schools. Crowds of angry parents often clashed with special tactical police units in front of schools, while police motorcycles escorted the yellow school buses to ensure the safety of the children. *Republished with permission of Globe Newspaper Company, Inc., from the December 11, 1974, issue of the* Boston Globe, © *1974.*

neighborhoods. As a result of this policy of "redlining," houses could not be sold to young families, the cost of maintenance and repairs became prohibitive, and older neighborhoods began to show signs of the blight and decay predicted by the banks. Parks and playgrounds soon were neglected, streets were no longer cleaned, garbage was not collected, homes fell into serious disrepair, vandalism became commonplace, many dwellings were abandoned, and in areas like the Fenway the frightening specter of arson added to the growing sense of helplessness and despair.

Still another problem in several neighborhoods was the relatively new process called "gentrification." In an interesting reversal of the post–World War II movement of families into the suburbs, the late 1960s and early 1970s saw a movement back to the city. Well-educated and affluent young people, mostly professionals—engineers, computer specialists, architects, designers, nurses, medical technicians—single or married with few or no children, saw the obvious benefits of living in a city like Boston. They were attracted by the city's service economy, its numerous cultural and educational institutions, its proximity to rural and recreational areas, and its appeal as a walkable and "livable" city. In large numbers, this young "gentry" moved into convenient and historic locations like the North End and the South End, as well as into locations along the waterfront. With their professional incomes, however, they forced up the price of rents, raised the costs of leasing apartments, and accelerated the conversion to condominiums. This transformation caused serious financial burdens for older and poorer residents, forcing many of them to move out of old and familiar neighborhoods in which most had spent their entire lives.

Fearing that the problems with which they were confronted would escalate beyond control, and convinced that they could obtain no effective relief or protection from the ordinary channels of city government, residents at the local level took matters into their own hands. They would determine their own priorities, assess their own needs, and defend their own neighborhoods. Boston saw an example of grass-roots political power designed to force both city officials and business representatives, whenever they prepared any future plans involving the neighborhoods, to take into account the interests of the people. Drawing heavily upon the organizational techniques employed so successfully by student protesters, civil rights organizers, and feminist demonstrators, militant groups of local activists formed community organizations to prevent what they regarded as the destruction of their neighborhoods. Men and women, whites and blacks, Hispanics and Asians, longtime residents and new arrivals, housewives and laborers, amateurs and professionals—some had considerable backgrounds in community organization, but most had little experience at all.

Neighborhood residents formed their own development corporations to help them rehabilitate rundown houses, redevelop dying business districts, and even encourage light industry to come into their districts. The Codman Square Community Development Corporation (CSCDC) and the South Boston Community Development Corporation (SBCDC) were among several local agencies that worked to preserve their districts from government renewal plans; the Massachusetts Urban Reinvestment Advisory Group (MURAG) was especially influential in forcing many Boston banks to invest their money in local neighborhoods; the *Inquilinos Boricuas en Accion* (IBA) was successful in creating a Hispanic residential development in the South End called Villa Victoria. Parents fought for meaningful educational reforms through such coalitions as the Boston Home and School Association and the Federation for Children with Special Needs; Hispanic parents worked for successful programs in bilingual education with *La Grassa Mancha*. And in the Fenway area, residents formed the Symphony Tenants Organizing Project (STOP) when they became convinced that city and state authorities were not doing enough to stop the alarming amount of arson in that crowded neighborhood. Sometimes the groups succeeded; sometimes they failed; sometimes they were forced to accept compromise solutions. But in any case, these local organizations quickly became a force that could no longer be ignored by either the politicians at City Hall or the bankers in their boardrooms. Coalition politics became a new and alternative source of power in Kevin White's Boston and would have a decided influence on all decisions regarding the social and economic future of Boston's neighborhoods.

Racial disturbances that could not be resolved, a busing crisis that got worse every day, neighborhood opposition that cut into his political power, and nagging financial problems that made it more difficult to continue urban renewal cut deeply into Mayor White's image as a young, liberal, and effective big-city mayor. After his runaway victory in his second contest with Mrs. Hicks in 1972, Kevin White had begun to be viewed as an asset to the Democratic party on the national level. Indeed, during the presidential campaign of 1972 he was wooed by Senator George McGovern as a possible running mate. Although the nomination never materialized, White spent the better part of the next year touring the nation in an attempt to rebuild the hopes of the Democratic party.

Back home, however, White's personal magnetism began to fade, and his political power showed alarming signs of erosion. With city elections coming up in November 1975, he found himself forced to marshal his political forces against a surprisingly strong challenge from State Senator Joseph F. Timilty. Tall and handsome, an ex-Marine and former city councilor, Timilty claimed to speak for the people of the neighborhoods and cut deeply into the mayor's traditional sources of political support. Fighting against charges of political corruption and misuse of patronage, White managed to defeat Timilty by an embarrassingly narrow margin in an election that also returned an all-white school committee to administer what was becoming an increasingly nonwhite school system. This made it almost a certainty that as Kevin White prepared to enter his third term as mayor of Boston, he would not be able to make any substantial improvements in the city's complex racial dilemma that centered on court-ordered busing.

After his hard-fought 1975 election, Mayor White seemed to withdraw even further from personal involvement in neighborhood affairs. He found himself pummeled from all sides, caught between the demands of the black community and the fears of the white neighborhoods, between the authority of federal power and the pride of local authority, between the judicial gavel of Judge Arthur Garrity and the rosary beads of Louise Day Hicks. No amount of pleading, moderating, cajoling, or threatening could produce any sort of compromise solution. There was no middle ground—no common ground— and there was little or no support from other elected city officials. Whatever he did was wrong: blacks accused him of selling out to the white establishment; whites called him "Mayor Black" and accused him of pandering to the African-American constituency. Discouraged by repeated failures at solving the busing crisis, weary from grappling with community problems, and perhaps still fascinated by the prospects of national office, White concentrated more and more on the development of the downtown area. He intensified his efforts to publicize the attractions of the "New Boston" and continued to emphasize its new reputation as a "world-class city." Traveling to Europe and to the Far East, he created links with "sister cities" in various parts of the world in order to promote tourism and encourage investment. He associated with business leaders and banking officials, met with architects and designers, negotiated with planners and developers, greeted foreign diplomats at City Hall, and held receptions for dignitaries at the elegant Parkman House on Beacon Hill. He obviously found this kind of atmosphere much more congenial and rewarding than the thankless rough-and-tumble politics that now involved both racial fears and ethnic hatreds.

Although White and his revitalized political machine of department heads, city workers, precinct captains, and volunteers were able to defeat Joe Timilty again in 1979, the mayor's fourth term proved to be difficult and often painful. In addition to the continued pressures from both the black community and white neighborhoods, White's last years in City Hall were plagued by an increasingly troubled economy. During the administration of President Jimmy Carter, from 1976 to 1980, inflation reached double-digit figures, unemployment rose to unprecedented heights, and supplies of gasoline and heating fuels were both scarce and expensive. Things became even worse after the Republican victory in November 1980. President Ronald Reagan made severe cuts in the amount of federal money being spent for public health, education, welfare, unemployment, and similar social services. And at the local level, a state referendum called Proposition 2½ placed a ceiling on property taxes, thereby sharply curtailing appropriations and expenditures. The fact that the mayor of Boston had embarrassingly little political influence beyond the actual confines of the city—and that representatives from other parts of the commonwealth took a definitely unsympathetic view of Boston and its complicated economic problems—made it extremely difficult for White to obtain financial assistance from the state legislature on Beacon Hill.

On the one hand, the downtown sections of the city continued to show signs of progress and prosperity. Business and office space increased, new hotels multiplied, the old retail district was modernized, and the Faneuil Hall Marketplace did a thriving business as a major tourist attraction. On the other hand, average working-class residents in the neighborhoods suffered some of the worst effects of the recession, especially when Mayor White responded to fiscal restraints by laying off nearly four thousand city employees, including firefighters and police officers. According to the 1980 federal census, median family income in Boston had become one of the lowest among major cities in the United States. The report classified 22 percent of all Boston families as "low income" and stated that 20 percent of all Boston households received some form of rent subsidy, as compared to a national average of only 5–8 percent. Despite all the accomplishments of the "New Boston," as late as 1982 a respected Brookings Institution study on urban life concluded that Boston still ranked in the bottom third of all major U.S. cities, and well below such cities as Detroit, Newark, and Oakland, California. On twenty-two of the study's twenty-five indicators—which measured such things as unemployment, poverty, crime, and municipal debt—Boston was near or at the very bottom.

The anger and frustration of working-class families during this period of recession caused further erosion of Kevin White's political support in traditional white neighborhoods, and even many of the mayor's former supporters in the African-American community were now looking for new leadership from among their own people. White was characterized as a self-centered politician who was only interested in keeping himself in power, more concerned with prosperous investors and glamorous celebrities than with the everyday problems of working-class men and women. Early in White's fourth administration, the signs were becoming painfully clear that the once popular mayor might not be able to carry enough wards to win a fifth term.

Conservatives in the city complained about his spendthrift ways, and the Parkman House on Beacon Hill where he entertained close fiends and visiting dignitaries soon became a dramatic symbol of the mayor's extravagant tastes. Neighborhood leaders refused to accept his explanation for his financial cutbacks and denounced him for endangering the health and safety of their communities when he closed fire and police stations. Political opponents charged him with such flagrant misuse of political patronage as forcing city employees to contribute to his political campaigns and using city funds to defray the costs of a birthday party for his wife. And as election time drew near during 1983, federal investigations into charges of political corruption and financial irregularities further embarrassed the White administration and caused a steady deterioration of his base of support throughout the city.

Although his pollsters assured him that he could win another election, Kevin White decided not to try. On May 26, 1983, he delivered to the viewers of Boston a brief televised announcement of his retirement from political life. He had served as mayor of Boston for sixteen consecutive years, from 1967 to 1983, longer than any other person in the city's history. But they were years of incredible strain and turmoil that pitted young against old, black against white, rich against poor, police against citizens, parishioners against priests, and family members against each other. The incessant cries of protest, shouts of defiance, and screams of hatred took their toll as much on the mayor as they did on his badly divided city. It was time to go. Perhaps the passage of time, the cooling of passions, and the arrival of new personalities might finally restore some measure of peace to a city that had been under siege for so long.

Considering the extreme bitterness and unbearable tension that marked the decade following the violent beginnings of court-ordered busing in September 1974, the political campaign conducted for Boston's mayoral election in November 1983 took place with a remarkable degree of restraint and civility. Once Kevin White made it known that he would not seek a fifth term as mayor of Boston, a number of candidates announced their intentions, but in the preliminary election in October the final choice came down to two men: Raymond Flynn and Melvin King, both of whom represented the concerns of the neighborhoods as opposed to the interests of the downtown business and political establishment.

Ray Flynn, age forty-four, was a three-term member of the Boston City Council, a lifelong resident of South Boston, a devout Roman Catholic, and a spokesman for neighborhood schools. He had been a vocal opponent of court-ordered busing during the 1970s but actively engaged in peaceful activities to prevent the outbreaks of violence that marked the early years of the controversial experiment. A rather taciturn and unpretentious individual, Flynn went about the business of politicking in a steady, determined, and down-to-earth manner.

Flynn's opponent in 1983 was Mel King, age fifty-five, a former teacher, social worker, political organizer, and state representative who became the first African-American candidate in Boston's history to reach the preliminary election. Encouraged by the victories of black mayoral candidates in Chicago and Philadelphia during 1983, King formed a multiracial "rainbow coalition" to attract votes not only from the city's black residents, but also from the increasing number of immigrants who had come to Boston in recent years. In 1980, it was reported that the city had over eighty-seven thousand residents who had been born in foreign countries, and that nearly one hundred thousand residents of the city spoke a language other than English in their homes. While some of these newcomers came from more familiar European countries such as Poland, Czechoslovakia, and Russia, a great many more had arrived from the Caribbean and from several regions of Central and South America. In addition to thousands of immigrants from Puerto Rico, Jamaica, and Barbados, more recent arrivals had come from El Salvador and Honduras. Mel King worked hard to add these new residents to the numbers of his own loyal black supporters as "people of color" in order to create a substantial nonwhite voting block that would increase his chances for election.

Both Flynn and King took similar positions on the major issues of the campaign—espousing neighborhood interests, proposing liberal public

housing programs, and urging increased economic assistance for the un-
employed, the homeless, and the disadvantaged of the city. Despite the fact
that King captured an overwhelming number of the city's black votes, Flynn
won what proved to be an easy victory by sweeping the predominantly white
neighborhoods. In his victory statement, Flynn underlined the basic theme of
the election by promising to obtain for the neighborhoods a greater share of
the prosperous economic revitalization that was going on in the downtown
area of the city. It was time, he said, to tip the scales in the other direction in
order to achieve a more equitable balance between those who were prospering
as a result of urban renewal and those who had been left behind.

Chapter

12

Life in a Changing City

O N JANUARY 2, 1984, Boston's
forty-sixth mayor, Raymond L. Flynn, held the largest inauguration ceremony in the city's history at the Wang Center for the Performing Arts in order to accommodate over four thousand friends, neighbors, and campaign workers. This was in keeping with his image as the "people's mayor," representing the people of the neighborhoods in the well-known populist tradition of James Michael Curley. In his inaugural address, Flynn emphasized his determination to create racial harmony within the city and bring an end to the hatred and bitterness that had characterized the previous ten years. "The full weight of city government will be brought down," he declared, "on all those who seek, because of race or color, to deny anyone from any street, any school, any park, any home, any job, in any neighborhood of the city."

Flynn's forthright stand against racism and his assurances that he would enforce the laws guaranteeing civil liberties seemed to produce results. According to a poll conducted early in 1987 by the Kennedy School of Government, 41 percent of the respondents, most of whom lived in neighborhoods in which one race was predominant, agreed that race relations in Boston as a whole had improved in recent years. This type of positive response seemed to be borne out by the city's Community Disorders Unit, which reported that the number of civil rights investigations in 1987 showed a definite decline since the early days of busing. From a total of 607 racial incidents reported in 1978, the numbers steadily went down to 300 in 1980 to 200 in 1985, and to 157 in 1987. "This is not to suggest that we have reached the pinnacle of race relations in the city of Boston," said Mayor Flynn, "but that we're working very hard at it, and that we take this responsibility very seriously."

Conditions in Boston's schools resulting from the desegregation process also resumed a more normal pattern. On September 3, 1985, on the day Dr. Laval Wilson assumed office as the city's first African-American superintendent of schools, Judge Arthur Garrity turned control of the schools back to the city's school committee, although he retained standby jurisdiction over such things as student assignments and parental involvement. By this time, the racial makeup of Boston's schools had changed dramatically. Out of a total of 59,895 students in the system, there were now 28,551 blacks, 15,842 whites, 10,760 Hispanics, and 4,742 Asians. With the number of white students having dropped precipitously from 45,000 in 1974 to 15,842 in 1987—a loss of nearly 30,000 white students in little more than ten years—the school system had become almost 75 percent nonwhite.

In addition to addressing the city's racial tensions, Mayor Flynn also focused his attention on the needs of at least two other major constituencies in the city. First, he had to fulfill his pledges to the various neighborhoods and provide more low-cost housing, cleaner streets, additional parks and recreational areas, more effective fire and police protection, and greater opportunities for employment. Much in the old Curley tradition, Flynn adopted a high degree of visibility throughout the city as he dramatized the needs of the neighborhoods as well as his own personal energies in addressing those needs. Capitalizing on local television coverage, the mayor was shown riding on snow plows, filling in potholes, attending serious fires, visiting wounded police officers, playing basketball with children at local playgrounds, marching in parades, and involving himself in other public activities directly related to the interests of his working-class voting constituents in the neighborhoods.

On a more institutional level, at the beginning of his term, Flynn created a Mayor's Office of Neighborhood Services, appointed liaisons to each community and ethnic group, and encouraged the formation of neighborhood councils through which residents could monitor the delivery of basic services. Flynn also concerned himself with the growing problems of poverty and homelessness throughout the city. He established a Mayor's Hunger Commission to help create networks of public and private agencies for distributing meals and groceries to hungry residents. Committing more than $75 million to programs for the homeless, Flynn promised that no one would be denied "a warm bed, transportation to a shelter, food, or quality health care just because they are poor."

While he was dealing with neighborhood issues, Flynn also had to convince the downtown bankers, financiers, and real estate developers that he was not just another James Michael Curley out to "soak the rich" and turn back the tide of urban development. In order to stimulate greater interaction between the downtown business establishment and the neighborhood populations, the Flynn administration established a Linked Deposit program requiring that banks holding city funds meet certain standards of investment in minority neighborhoods, or else face the withdrawal of city deposits. The new administration also supported a $400 million neighborhood reinvestment agreement with the downtown banking community to increase below-market mortgage and business loans to minority neighborhoods. In addition to calling for increased hiring of local residents, women, and members of minority groups on publicly funded construction projects, Flynn also pressured construction companies and real estate developers to contribute one dollar per square foot to support local job-training programs. In pursuing his Linked Deposit program, Ray Flynn assured the members of the business community that they were essential to the future prosperity of the city and that he would work with them to continue the kind of construction and expansion that had already made Boston one of the leading cities in America in this respect. In several ways, the first four years of the Flynn administration appeared to give the city a much-needed period in which to catch its breath and get back on its feet again after the traumatic events of the previous decade.

On November 3, 1987, Raymond L. Flynn won reelection to a second term as mayor of Boston in a landslide victory, winning 63,412 votes to Joseph F. Timilty's 30,897 with more than 67 percent of the total vote, and taking twenty out of the city's twenty-two wards. Flynn's margins of victory were particularly impressive in the African-American sections of the city. Ironically, however, he suffered a surprising setback in his own home wards in South Boston after he announced his decision to comply with a federal order to desegregate the city's public housing projects. Flynn met personally with his outraged local critics at several noisy public hearings in the months that followed his reelection, reemphasizing his commitment to integrated housing but also offering to work out agreements that would allay the fears and apprehensions of older neighborhood residents. Gradually tensions lessened, and the Flynn administration settled down to a more normal pattern of accommodation with the complex elements of Boston's population, both in the central city as well as in the surrounding neighborhoods.

During Flynn's first administration, the Bay State economy was running high. The high-tech economy of New England was unusually strong, jobs were plentiful, wages were high, construction was booming, and real estate values shot up to incredible heights. Although there were some unsettling signs of what some economists were calling a "rolling recession" that was bringing hard times to petroleum centers in Texas and Louisiana, Bay Staters were assured that the "Massachusetts Miracle" being touted by Governor Michael Dukakis and state Democratic leaders would continue unabated. Taking advantage of the good times during his second administration, from 1988 to 1992, Mayor Flynn mended fences in his home community over the public housing issue and

Raymond L. Flynn was elected mayor of Boston in 1983, won reelection in 1987 and 1991, and in 1993 left office to accept the post of U.S. Ambassador to the Vatican. As mayor, Flynn emphasized the importance of the neighborhoods and promised to protect the civil rights and political liberties of all citizens in every part of the city. He traveled around the city, met with voters, took care of local problems, and established a reputation as "the people's mayor." *Courtesy of Boston City Hall.*

built new political alliances throughout the other neighborhoods. By energetic rounds of public appearances and civic activities, he clearly reestablished his popularity as "the people's mayor." When he ran again in November 1991, he not only won a third time, but he also captured every precinct in every ward in the city—a first in Boston's history.

As Ray Flynn embarked upon his third term as mayor of Boston in January 1992, several problems that had been simmering over the previous two years threatened to upset the social and economic stability he had been trying so hard to maintain. During the 1980s, the Reagan administration's policy of deregulation had created a high-flying economy reminiscent of the Roaring Twenties. Banks handed out loans for risky ventures, "junk bonds" achieved a new legitimacy, fast-moving speculators generated quick profits, and real estate prices went through the roof. Within a year of Republican George Bush's victory over Massachusetts Democrat Michael Dukakis in November 1988, however, the "Massachusetts Miracle" collapsed and Boston found itself in trouble. Eight years of tax-cutting, combined with soaring welfare costs and inflated medical charges, had pushed the federal debt past the $3 trillion mark, while the deficit in 1991 reached nearly $170 billion.

The national recession took a heavy toll on the Boston economy. Banks failed, the savings and loan industry collapsed, housing construction declined, major industries failed, and unemployment rose to new heights. At a time when states were forced to cut back on social services and welfare funding, the number of homeless people became larger than ever. The city of Boston, like other major urban centers with sizable minority populations and serious social commitments, felt the impact of hard times as industry continued to decline, bank failures became common, more companies declared bankruptcy, and more workers lost their jobs.

The recession of the 1990s exacerbated problems that had been festering during the 1980s, but those problems seemed to worsen with disturbing reports of guns, drugs, and violence. In poor neighborhoods where unemployment, homelessness, and poverty were prevalent, children sold drugs on street corners, teenagers carried guns and knives to school, gangs roamed the streets, and innocent bystanders were murdered in random drive-by shootings. This type of violence spilled over into the city's public school system, which threatened to become more unmanageable than ever. Having barely recovered from the prolonged trauma of court-ordered busing, the city's educational system felt the impact of both economic cutbacks and urban violence. The lack of adequate funding caused serious shortages in textbooks, laboratory equipment, instructional resources, trained personnel, and programs in arts, music, and sports. And all the while, the increasing menace of guns, knives, and drugs threatened the lives of teachers and students on a daily basis, making a proper educational atmosphere almost impossible. In an effort to balance the school department budget, reduce administrative red tape, and increase spending for classroom instruction, Mayor Flynn proposed changes in the existing forms of school government. In 1991, voters approved a referendum calling for the establishment of a seven-member school committee, whose members would serve four-year terms and be appointed by the mayor from among nominees recommended by a broad-based nominating committee. This new appointed committee officially replaced the former thirteen-member elected committee in January 1992.

From 1985 to 1991, Ray Flynn also involved himself in national affairs, serving as chair of the United States Conference of Mayors' Task Force on Hunger, Homelessness, and Poverty, and attacking the Reagan administration for neglecting the nation's cities and ignoring the needs of the poor. In 1991 Flynn was elected president of the Conference of Mayors and placed urban issues at the top of the national agenda. There can be little doubt that his involvement in national affairs and his association with prominent Washington figures opened the Boston mayor's eyes to new opportunities for higher political office. A man who had spent his entire life in city politics, Ray Flynn faced the end of his third mayoral term in 1995 with the nagging question of how he would make a living once his political career was over. He had no family income, no law practice, no real estate business, no insurance agency—and relatively little left of his campaign funds. The prospect of stepping into empty space in his early fifties was a frightening one and helps explain Flynn's almost frenetic search for a secure source of income after leaving City Hall. He worked energetically for the national Democratic party in the 1992 campaign against George Bush, clearly hoping, as a big-city mayor, to win a Cabinet post either in the Department of Housing and Urban Development or in the Department of Labor. After the election of Bill Clinton in November 1992, however, no Cabinet position was forthcoming; instead, Flynn was offered the post of Ambassador to the Vatican. After a period of indecision during the summer of 1993, Flynn finally accepted the overseas post, whereupon Thomas M. Menino, president of the Boston City Council, became temporary mayor until a mayoral election could be held in November.

Mayor Raymond Flynn was sworn in as U.S. Ambassador to the Vatican in a White House ceremony on Friday, July 9, 1993. The following Monday, he resigned as mayor and handed the reins of government to city council president Thomas Menino. The grandson of Italian immigrants who had left the village of Grottaminarda in the province of Avellino to come to America early in the century, Thomas Menino was born on December 27, 1942, and grew up in the Hyde Park district of Boston, where his parents, Carl and Susan, had lived their entire lives and where his father worked thirty-five years at the local Westinghouse plant. Young Tom acquired a serious interest in politics at the age of thirteen when he helped one of his father's friends run for state representative. After graduating from St. Thomas Aquinas High School, the young man almost immediately went into political life. From 1978 to 1983, he was a senior research assistant to the state legislature's Joint Committee on Urban Affairs; from 1983 to 1985 he served as vice-chair of the city council's Committee on Housing; in 1989 he became regional chair for the National Trust for Historic Preservation. A lifelong resident of Hyde Park, Menino represented that district in the Boston City Council for nine years. In 1993 he was elected president of the city council and, as such, became the temporary successor when Mayor Flynn departed for Rome.

At that point, the stage was set for a special preliminary election in September. Once again, with no established policy of succession and no citywide mechanism to screen prospective candidates, a number of mayoral hopefuls emerged. In addition to Menino, the list included Roxbury at-large city councilor Bruce Bolling, the only minority candidate in the race; James Brett, a state representative from Dorchester; Christopher Lydon, a public television commentator; Francis (Mickey) Roache, Flynn's friend and former police commissioner; Robert Ruffo, sheriff of Suffolk County; and Rosaria Salerno, at-large city councilor from Allston-Brighton. Menino and Brett became the two finalists after the September primary; two months later, Menino won the November election by a substantial margin. It was clear that in neighborhoods such as Charlestown, East Boston, Hyde Park, South Boston, and West Roxbury where the ethnic turnout was the greatest, most white voters preferred the blunt, plain-spoken, down-to-earth approach of Menino to Brett's more sophisticated manner that many critics associated with the polished style of Beacon Hill legislators. Apparently, the voters wanted to continue the bread-and-butter, neighborhood-oriented policies of Ray Flynn for at least another four years. And so Thomas Menino became the first Italian-American mayor in Boston's history.

Local and national newspaper columnists and television commentators raised the question of whether the victory of Tom Menino was the last hurrah for Irish politicians in Boston. Would Ray Flynn go down in history as the city's last Irish-Catholic mayor? Certainly the latest demographic figures suggested that it was a distinct possibility. During the 1970s, the city's Latin American population had shown a remarkable increase as refugees from Haiti, Cuba, El Salvador, Honduras, Colombia, and Nicaragua sought to escape the effects of organized crime and political oppression in their native countries. Then, during the 1980s, Boston received additional numbers of homeless immigrants from the war zones and refugee camps of Vietnam, Cambodia, Laos, and other parts of Southeast Asia. And the impact of this new wave of immigration was soon as evident in Boston as it was in other parts of the country. As late as 1965, some 90 percent of the immigrants coming into the United States each year were still coming from the more familiar countries of continental Europe. By 1985, however—only twenty years later—that figure had dropped to a mere 10 percent. Between 1980 and 1990 alone, the number of Asians in the United States doubled, reaching more than seven million, while the Latino population reached twenty million that same year. Demographers estimate that by the year 2030, Americans of European origin will be in a decided minority.

These dramatic national statistics were certainly reflected in the demographic changes taking place in Boston. Between 1980 and 1990, the city's white population dropped more than 11 percent to constitute only 59 percent of the total. By contrast, the African-American population in the city rose by 11.4 percent, the Latino population by 39 percent, and the Asian population by 45 percent. The long-range impact of these demographic changes was perhaps most dramatically evident in the makeup of the city's public school system. Although in 1980 the total population of the city was still nearly 60 percent white, the number of school-aged children who were white had already dropped to 52 percent. By 1990, that figure had declined to 40 percent, making the number of white school-aged children much lower than the combined number of African-American, Haitian, Hispanic, and Asian youngsters. Concrete evidence of this change came in August 1999 when the Boston School Committee decided it would no longer use race as a basis for assigning children to the public schools. The main reason given was that parents now wished to focus on educational equity and quality rather than race. The reality was, however, that using race as a yardstick for assignments hardly mattered anymore. With the Boston school population now 84 percent minority, more than 97 percent of the city's sixty-four thousand students would be assigned to their first-choice schools. "Busing is being abandoned," wrote Orlando Patterson in the *New York Times*, "because there is nothing for busing to do, there being hardly any white students left in the system for minorities to integrate with." Patterson commented on the irony that what started out as a program to integrate minorities into a predominantly white school system back in the 1970s ended up by creating a school system with a "minority majority."

With school desegregation no longer a major consideration, by the 1990s greater attention was given to raising academic standards and improving the conditions of the schools themselves. In 1993, the state Department of Education established the Massachusetts Comprehensive Assessment System (MCAS), a series of standardized tests designed to examine the effectiveness of the teaching process and the ability of students to meet the standards of promotion in various subjects. Despite charges that the tests were unfair, that students would be denied diplomas, and that teachers were treated badly, the MCAS test scores provided valuable information regarding the level of teaching effectiveness in various parts of the commonwealth. In Boston, Mayor Thomas Menino announced he would place a high personal priority on raising academic standards in the public schools and improving the physical conditions of the schools throughout the city. As city councilor he had actively supported policies and programs to advance educational reform. He took advantage of state legislation to establish the City of Boston Scholarship Fund, through which qualified students could apply for scholarship money—collected through property and excise tax bills as well as from corporate donations—to attend local colleges and universities. After his election as mayor, Menino worked out an important contract between the Boston School Department and the Boston Teachers' Union that paved the way for some systematic reforms, and he continued to work closely with Superintendent Thomas W. Payzant and the appointed members of the school committee. In a November 1996 referendum, Boston voters chose to retain the appointed school committee rather than return to the thirteen-member elected committee that had been voted out four years earlier. Two months later, delivering his 1996 State of the City address at the Jeremiah E. Burke High School, which had recently lost its accreditation, the mayor expressed his belief that education was the key to creating greater economic security and asked that he be judged on how far he was able to take the Boston public schools.

Mayor Menino persisted in his concern for an improved educational system, and in his 1998 inaugural address he announced the Boston 2:00–6:00 After-School Initiative, which supported partnerships between youth-serving

Thomas M. Menino, whose grandparents emigrated from Italy, became the first mayor of Italian ancestry in Boston's history. Governing a city whose population was rapidly becoming more diverse and multicultural, Menino promised to emphasize education, ensure safety, and promote economic development. This photograph shows Mayor Menino on one of his many visits to the city's schools, taking a personal interest in the worksheets of one of the students as she grapples with the problems of arithmetic. *Courtesy of Carla Osberg.*

organizations to offer after-school programs in elementary and middle schools throughout the neighborhoods. As of the fall of 1999, a total of fifty-seven schools—more than 30 percent of the city's elementary and middle schools— were operating after-school programs that served over 2,750 children. Each of these programs offered a diversity of recreation, academic enrichment, and arts and cultural programming.

The influence of the "new" Bostonians was not confined to the population of Boston's school system. In a remarkably short time, many new immigrants had moved into parts of Boston's neighborhoods that once had been over-whelmingly Irish. Everywhere one could hear strange voices and unfamiliar tongues: Vietnamese, Laotian, Cambodian, Chinese, French, Haitian Creole, Czech, Slovak, Greek, Polish, Russian, Lebanese, Italian, and others, while signs and symbols of these changes were apparent throughout the city. On one stretch of Brighton Avenue in Allston, there was a Russian restaurant, a Southeast Asian food store, and a Middle Eastern restaurant, while across the street was the Sons of Greece social club with a Vietnamese food store only a short distance away. Allston-Brighton Free Radio announced that it would include programs in Spanish, Portuguese, Ethiopian, and Eritrean music. In Jamaica Plain, grocery stores, clothing shops, and hairdressing salons with signs in Spanish along the stretch of Washington Street from Eggleston Square to Forest Hills showed how the old Irish neighborhood had changed; in Hyde Park, hundreds of African-American youngsters made their way to the Academy of the Pacific Rim in the old Westinghouse building where Mayor Menino's father had once worked. And similar changes could be seen along Dorchester Avenue, the six-mile-long road that runs through the spine of Boston's largest neighborhood from the outskirts of South Boston to the suburb of Milton. Signs in Spanish and Vietnamese were posted in the windows of the bank in Fields Corner; the ATM machine on the corner of Dorchester Avenue offered instructions in English and Spanish as well as in Braille; the voice-mail system at Dorchester House greeted callers in English, Spanish, and Vietnamese. In the Field's Corner section, where solid three-decker houses still stood as a reminder of the Irish-Catholic families who had once dominated the neighborhood, new ethnic groups had changed the character of the community. St. Matthew's Church, built with the savings of Irish immigrants, held liturgies in French for the benefit of its mostly Haitian immigrant parishioners. And at nearby St. Peter's Church, also originally Irish, three Vietnamese priests ministered to the Vietnamese con-gregation. In so many ways, these new waves of immigrants are transforming

Boston into a city where the traditional white, ethnic population is fast being outnumbered by people of color from different and largely unfamiliar parts of the world.

Despite the fact that the "new" Bostonians made up a new majority in Boston, however, the city's voting population, particularly in municipal elections, continued to remain older, white, and distinctly ethnic. Throughout the 1990s, members of the new majority did not play much of a role in the city's continuing political drama, largely because they did not make use of the traditional political processes. Many of the newcomers are not eligible to vote, it is true, but many who are eligible are not politically active. In the words of one *Boston Globe* columnist, they constitute an essentially "passive audience." According to one study of the voter turnout in the 1991 mayoral election, for example, nearly half the voters in that election, as well as about 40 percent of the registered voters in the city, lived in six neighborhoods: South Boston, West Roxbury, Roslindale, Charlestown, South Dorchester, and Hyde Park. Although these six neighborhoods contained only 29 percent of the voting-age residents of the city, they made up 46 percent of the votes cast in the election. Significantly, these six neighborhoods were overwhelmingly white and composed of working- and middle-class residents. According to the same study, the least powerful wards in terms of voting power contained 28 percent of the voting-age residents, but only 13 percent of its voters. These wards were Chinatown, the South End, Roxbury, the Back Bay and Fenway areas, and Allston-Brighton—neighborhoods composed of minority group members, students, or affluent young professionals. How long a major urban center such as Boston, whose overall population is increasingly nonwhite, can continue to have its political institutions and municipal policies dominated by a minority of white voters is a matter of serious concern, not only for the stability of the city, but also for the continuance of the representative political process.

The 1990s was not only a decade of significant demographic change, but also remarkable social change as well. Numerous international cultural reforms, sexual revolutions, social upheavals, and religious changes during the 1970s and 1980s were having a substantial impact on everyday life and society in the United States by the 1990s. In Boston, as well as in other major cities throughout the nation, defiance of established authority, rebellion against the generally accepted norms of civilized behavior, and rejection of long-accepted moral values showed the many ways in which such institutions as religion, the family, and law are no longer receiving the same measure of respect, or exerting the

The recent history of Boston has been marked by the rapid influx of people from Puerto Rico, Haiti, Cuba, Colombia, Honduras, and other parts of Latin America, as well as immigrants from various regions of Asia. Bringing in different languages, customs, foods, and festivities to diversify the life and society of Boston, the newcomers are quickly adding an even greater measure of multiculturalism to a city that had earlier adjusted to the influx of people from many parts of Europe. *Republished with permission of Globe Newspaper Company, Inc., from the July 23, 1995, issue of the* Boston Globe, © *1995.*

same degree of influence, that formerly distinguished their recognized presence in the Boston community.

It is clear, for example, that the once-dominant and unquestioned authority of the Catholic Church in a predominantly Irish-Catholic city such as Boston has lost a good deal of its earlier force, and that the once-pervasive influence of pastors, priests, and nuns in the daily lives of parishioners has all but disappeared. And disturbing statistics indicate that the problem will probably become even more complex as time goes on. Throughout the United States, new vocations to the priesthood were a fraction of what they had once been—9,000 seminarians in 1966, for example, down to only 3,000 in 1990—while the number of young people choosing to go into religious life continued to decrease at an alarming rate. Between 1960 and 1978, attendance at Mass by Catholics in the Greater Boston area was reported to have declined from 75 percent to 55 percent; older priests were dying off or retiring at a rate of 25–30 a year; the number of seminarians at St. John's Seminary had declined from an all-time high of 418 in 1960 to only 126 in 1975. At a convocation of clergy and laity in March 1998, Boston's Cardinal Bernard Law reported a projected 22 percent decline in the number of diocesan priests by the year 2005, and predicted the closing of 40 to 60 parishes by the year 2008.

None of this suggests that the Catholic Church will disappear from the scene, or that it will cease to be an important influence in Boston. But it does seem clear that it will have to direct that influence in different ways, toward different objectives and with different personnel. In view of changing economic conditions, for example, the church will probably devote more of its funds and energy to pressing social and charitable needs, ranging from family counseling and care for the elderly to pregnancy assistance and AIDS ministries. Archdiocesan resources will also be channeled toward the interests of new apostolates of Asian, Hispanic, Haitian, and Irish immigrants who now make up the membership of many parishes. In meeting these demands, an increasing number of lay people—men and women—will have much greater roles in church affairs, taking over more and more functions previously considered the sole prerogative of the clergy. These will include not only areas such as property advisement and financial management, but also spiritual direction and pastoral counseling. As the traditional limits of old parish boundaries give way to the much newer concept of area clusters and regional groupings, church leaders will be called upon to meet the new challenges of a changing society in a much more flexible and imaginative manner.

In addition to responding to a variety of social and institutional changes, the Catholic Church in Boston has also been affected by the kind of demographic changes that have affected so many other aspects of modern city life. The influx of new immigrants, for example, has contributed to the changing ethnic composition of the church in general while helping to transform traditional parish boundaries in areas where new highway construction, industrial projects, and commercial developments forced out the original residents. Old gothic churches in depopulated urban areas where former congregations had either died off or moved away are often practically deserted. Pews that once were filled to overflowing at Sunday morning Mass are painfully empty; devotional services that had once drawn thousands of faithful communicants now go largely unattended. In the lower end of South Boston, for example, the absence of a substantial congregation made it necessary for the archdiocese to close SS. Peter and Paul's Church, one of the oldest parishes in Boston. Issues of nationality and language, too, presented challenges involving both financial management and public relations. With second and third generations of young English-speaking families growing up and moving out to the suburbs, and with a diminishing number of priests competent in languages other than English, a number of the "old" German, French, Italian, Portuguese, Polish, and Lithuanian churches fell into serious disrepair and had to be closed down. These were always sad and painful experiences for original parishioners from the "old countries" who had expected their churches to continue to reflect their special ethnic and cultural characteristics. At the same time, however, as we have already seen in Dorchester, a number of comparatively new ethnic and racial populations, largely Latino and Asian, are rapidly moving into the various neighborhoods of Boston, replacing white ethnic groups who had replaced previous immigrant groups during earlier generations.

Along with the declining influence of religion as a major force in Boston society, the institution of the family and the traditional character of family values are also undergoing substantial change. The sexual revolution of the 1970s and 1980s, the prevalence of birth control, the frequency of divorce and subsequent marriages, the rise in the number of single-parent families, the increase in the number of unwed mothers, and the openness of same-sex unions have produced such an amazing array of alternative and unconventional lifestyles that "normal family" became almost impossible to define. Traditional family values, the rules of parental authority, the standards of juvenile behavior and the norms of appropriate discipline in many cases became either nonexistent or totally irrelevant. In an age of television, motion pictures, radio talk shows, rap music, MTV, and Internet chat rooms, young people are much more apt to draw their models and their values from the Cult of the Celebrity that worships fast cars, high fashion, big money, and promiscuous behavior than from older institutions that sought to inculcate the old-fashioned virtues of moderation, self-restraint, polite manners, and good taste. Writing in the *Wall Street Journal*, Nancy Ann Jeffrey decries an "e-culture" that glorifies "speed over decorum and innovation over tradition," while national columnist George Will laments the extent to which incivility has become almost normal in today's world. The vulgarity and self-absorption of the "high-tech barbarians," he says, have created a generation that is "electronically disassociated" from the society in which they exist. As a leading American city whose reputation has always been based on its historical traditions, its literary preeminence, and its high cultural standards, Boston—once hailed as the Athens of America—must take these considerations seriously if it is to retain its position as a recognized arbiter of manners and taste.

In the course of this decade of social and cultural change, Mayor Menino had the extreme good fortune of presiding over the City of Boston during one of the most prosperous periods in the nation's history. With the destruction of the Berlin Wall in November 1989, the collapse of the Soviet Union, and the end of the threat of world communism, the United States entered into what Yale economist Robert Shiller called an "Age of Triumphalism" that produced an exuberant confidence in American capitalism. The great bull market began its ceaseless upward climb in 1990, as stock market prices, combined with the transistor, the microchip, and the microprocessor—those "minute dynamos" as *Time Magazine* called them—generated a new era of commercial growth. This combination of a "hot" economy and a brand new technology created an unprecedented level of prosperity in Boston, which became the nation's largest source of venture capital. The city had $1.5 trillion in equity funds under management, the third highest amount in the world after London and New York. It also controlled one-quarter of the country's $5.5 trillion mutual fund business, prompting *Boston Magazine* to exclaim in May 2000: "The city is swimming in money!" The same journal reported that the combined wealth of the twenty richest people in the town actually exceeded the gross domestic product of New Zealand.

It was during this same period of prosperity, however, that the city's economic base also underwent a subtle but considerable transformation. Economic change is certainly not something entirely new in the three and a half centuries of Boston's existence. During the nineteenth century, for example, the shipping traditions of commerce and trade gave way to the water wheels and power looms of textile factories that greatly diversified the city's early economic development. Investments in banking and speculation in railroading provided additional sources of wealth to the local economy until after World War II, when the new electronics industry spawned a network of new corporate enterprises along Route 128. A demand for consumer products after the war, combined with Cold War demands for advanced air defense systems, helped feed the new electronics boom. MIT created the Lincoln Laboratory to develop radar, radio communications, and digital computing, later spinning off the Mitre Corporation as another research component. Boston became what the economist

Barry Bluestone has called a "hotbed of innovations," including the computer architecture designed by the region's "big four" high-tech companies—Digital Equipment, Data General, Prime, and Wang—along with the microwave oven developed by Raytheon. And in downtown Boston itself, the First National Bank (now Fleet) steered wealthy investors toward high-tech entrepreneurs, while Fidelity, Puritan, Putnam Investors, and Keystone joined other global financial companies operating out of the city. But throughout it all, whether it was shipping, textiles, electronics, or computer chips, the economy was always in the hands of persons who either lived in the city of Boston or commuted from nearly suburbs and bedroom communities on the North Shore. Most of them felt a personal and individual loyalty to their city and participated regularly in civic occasions, community programs, fund-raising activities, and cultural enterprises.

As the nature of the high-tech economy changed, however, so did the character of local ownership. In an age of corporate mergers, multinational enterprises, and international headquarters, during the 1980s and 1990s fewer and fewer Boston companies were privately owned or managed by directors, presidents, and executives who claimed Boston as their place of birth or their permanent home. Such well-known Boston institutions as the New England Telephone Company, the Shawmut Bank, Beacon Properties, Jordan Marsh, and Filene's were sold, merged, or moved out of state. The *Boston Globe* was taken over by the *New York Times,* and even the Boston Safe Deposit and Trust Company—the original home of The Vault—was bought by a Pennsylvania concern. Although the Boston Coordinating Committee (The Vault) continued to function for a time, in 1997 it officially announced its discontinuance. Fleet Bank financial chief Terrence Murray, Bank of Boston chief Chad Gifford, Boston Edison head Thomas May, and others decided that The Vault no longer served its original purpose. It was a dramatic symbol of a significant change in Boston's economic life whose long-range consequences have yet to be fully appreciated.

For the moment, however, times were good and money was plentiful. The post–World War II shift from traditional mill-based occupations to what recent economists have called "mind-based" occupations produced some dramatic shifts in the nature of the city's service industry. During the 1980s, Boston was enjoying a high rate of employment in "pink-collar" service industries. Suppliers of electronic components and accessories had already expanded rapidly, as had a number of supporting business and professional services such as software design, computer and data processing, management consulting, advertising, marketing, and public relations. By 1990, however, these services had given way to even more sophisticated white-collar occupations, including those provided by professional men and women in such fields as law, medicine, education, and business. This substantial upgrading had paid off in terms of higher wages for those with advanced schooling but resulted in lower earnings for those without such educational advantages. The prosperous economy, the availability of investment opportunities, and now the lowest jobless rate in the country were undoubtedly factors that encouraged the development of two major construction projects that promised to change forever the size and character of Boston's downtown area: the Central Artery/Tunnel Project and the Waterfront Project.

During the 1950s, in the early stages of Boston's postwar urban renewal, a six-lane elevated highway had been built through the city's waterfront section. Known as the Central Artery, it was designed to permit motorists to travel from the South Shore to the North Shore without driving through the notoriously crooked and congested streets of downtown Boston. Two problems quickly emerged from this highway project: First, the Central Artery effectively cut off the waterfront area, especially the historic North End, from the rest of the city of Boston. Second, by the time it was completed, the Central Artery had already become obsolete. Originally designed to handle about seventy-five thousand vehicles a day, the highway was eventually carrying more than two hundred thousand vehicles a day, producing horrendous traffic jams through the heart of the city and back into the neighboring suburbs.

In an attempt to solve both these problems, during the 1980s state transportation officials came up with an ambitious, complicated, and highly expensive project that became known to locals as the "Big Dig." The state decided to put the existing Central Artery underground, eventually creating over the depressed artery an attractive area of natural parks and walkways along Atlantic Avenue that would not only beautify the city but also unify some of the oldest and most historic parts of downtown Boston.

From the very outset of its original consideration, the Central Artery/Tunnel Project was the subject of continuous political arguments and financial recriminations because of the length of time it would take to complete the job, the serious disruptions of downtown traffic, and the amount of money the project would involve. According to initial plans, the Big Dig, the largest civil-engineering construction job in U.S. history, was supposed to take eighteen years to complete. It was projected for completion in the year 2004, and the total cost of construction was set at $11 billion. At first, the Reagan administration refused to allocate any federal funds at all for the ambitious project. Later, when the money was finally forthcoming, many unforeseen technical difficulties made the project seem impossible. Much of the original landfill in the old waterfront area, for example, proved much too soft to work with, and some of the existing bridges were too low to accommodate the tall cranes and construction equipment. All these difficulties were further complicated by the fact that the eight-mile-long project had to be undertaken while all parts of the city continued to function at normal capacity.

The first phase of the extensive construction project that tore up acres of land along the harbor front of South Boston and tunneled under Boston Harbor all the way to East Boston was opened in December 1995. This was the Ted

The largest civil-engineering construction project in U.S. history, the Central Artery/Tunnel Project, known popularly as the Big Dig, is managed by the Massachusetts Turnpike Authority. The goal of the project is to replace the existing Central Artery, which cuts through the heart of the city, with an underground expressway. The depression will eventually be covered over with an attractive area of parks and buildings that will unify some of the oldest and most historic parts of downtown Boston. *Republished with permission of Globe Newspaper Company, Inc., from the December 23, 1999, issue of the* Boston Globe, © 2000.

Williams Tunnel, named after the famous Red Sox home-run hitter, providing a new access under Boston Harbor directly to Logan Airport. In October 1999, a four-lane span across the Charles River, called the Leverett Circle Connector Bridge, also opened on schedule, taking traffic out of Boston from the Leverett Circle to Route I-93 north. A much larger ten-lane bridge is under construction that will give the North End, the Sumner Tunnel, and the Government Center direct access to Route I-93 north. The widest cable-stayed bridge in the world, it will have 300-foot towers to provide the fulcrum for cables that anchor the weight of the main span of the bridge to land-based back spans. Unfortunately, however, significant overruns in scores of multimillion-dollar contracts caused the initial cost estimates to skyrocket with the result that in February 2000, Big Dig officials announced that the project would cost at least $12.1 billion—a $1.4 billion revision in the original figure. Despite this fiscal miscalculation, state authorities insisted that the project would be completed early in the year 2005.

At the same time that the Big Dig was under construction, city authorities decided to enlarge financial opportunities by expanding into the only area where open land was available for commercial development—eastward across the Fort Point Channel into the lower end of the South Boston peninsula. A district dominated by wharves, ship terminals, fish-processing plants, and warehouses, its convenient location—only a ten-minute walk from Boston's downtown financial district and a six-minute drive to Logan International Airport—made it a prime target for "New Boston's" next move. Already the federal government had selected a strategic corner of land called the Fan Pier as the site for a modernistic new federal courthouse that looked out onto Boston Harbor; in 1998, only a short distance away, the World Trade Center opened a Seaport Hotel on land leased from Massport. The focal point of the city's plans for the district, however, was a major convention center large enough to attract the kinds of national and international meetings that had been bypassing Boston.

For a project of its size and complexity, the convention center actually went from concept to construction in a relatively short period of time. Over the course of three years, a group of politicians and business leaders shepherded enabling legislation through the state legislature and agreed on a site and design, and then the city took the sixty-two acres by eminent domain. Financed by $700 million in state and municipal bonds and taxes, the convention center is a modernistic structure 120 feet long and six stories high. The center itself is likely to lose money (about $15 million annually) but is expected to generate some $500 million a year in direct economic activity. "The convention center is a loss leader to fill the hotels and restaurants," explained Alan D. Reid, the center's chief financial officer. In addition to the center, eight other projects, valued at $3 billion, are being developed nearby, including luxury hotels, office buildings, and twelve hundred residential units to be constructed within the next five years.

The increased real estate costs generated by the Waterfront Project have already raised housing prices in many of the surrounding residential areas but are expected to have a special impact on the neighborhood of South Boston. "The waterfront," said Dean Stratouly, a Cambridge developer directing the convention project, "is going from lunch boxes to briefcases." Acutely aware of the effects the project would have in gentrifying the traditionally blue-collar, working-class neighborhood of South Boston and creating difficulties for low-income residents, in April 1999 political representatives from South Boston worked out a "memorandum of understanding" with the Menino administration agreeing that moneys would be used for the benefit of their community. The "linkage" part of this agreement, whereby linkage payments from developers would be distributed among the various neighborhoods, was fairly well defined in city zoning laws. Other payments in the form of "community benefits," however, which could divert $65–75 million for the exclusive use of South Boston, were challenged by the mayor as well as by representatives of other neighborhoods, who claimed that all communities should share more equitably in the dispersal of linkage funds.

The dispute between the mayor and the South Boston representatives was seen by some observers as a potential Achilles' heel in the mayor's otherwise impenetrable political armor. For nearly seven years, since he took over after Ray Flynn's departure in 1993, Menino had relatively smooth sailing and in 1997 was reelected without any opposition at all. Governing during a time of economic prosperity and diminished voter interest, he was credited with running the city effectively, cutting back on serious crime, and working hard to improve the city's public schools. In the matter of development, however, his critics pointed to a number of inconsistencies that raised questions about his administrative decisions. Some complained that he bullied his opponents and intimidated personnel who disagreed with him; others claimed that he tended to be unpredictable in his decisions and secretive in his procedures. He strongly supported a convention center, for example, and yet opposed a new runway at Logan Airport; he encouraged the Red Sox to plan a new ballpark in the

Fenway area but sent out mixed signals about their actual proposals; he worked out an ill-advised "memorandum of understanding" with South Boston leaders and then refused to honor the agreement. These kinds of shortcomings caused several commentators to raise questions about Menino's political prospects for the future.

A great many of the controversies between city leaders and private investors, however, were not merely local political feuds or trivial personal animosities. More often than not, they reflected serious and longstanding differences of opinion about the way in which the city will expand its boundaries and the manner in which various interests will benefit by the extraordinary expansion of land and profits at a time of critical change. Forty years earlier, when the postwar urban renewal projects of mayors John B. Hynes and John F. Collins set out to rescue an old, dilapidated city from financial collapse and physical deterioration, the resulting "New Boston" rose on the ashes of a city whose general size and configuration had not changed much in the course of a century, and whose population continued to reflect the social and cultural patterns of white European immigration. The present expansion of the downtown area of the city across the Fort Point Channel into the seaport area of South Boston, however, not only extends the territorial limits of the city well beyond the downtown area, but also dramatizes conflicting visions of what Boston is going to look like in the twenty-first century. Some Bostonians would prefer the old forms and the traditional boundaries that made Boston well-known as a "city of neighborhoods," retaining the insular nature and colorful character of the various ethnic groups. Others, however, would prefer a newer and more unified city, in which old boundaries would no longer provide either geographical division or social separation.

These are considerations that must be taken seriously, because although Boston's past is certainly rich, colorful, and fascinating, its future has yet to be defined. As we stand at the opening of the twenty-first century, it is important to recognize the fact that the "Old Boston"—the Boston as we have known it in history and in literature—no longer exists. Some time ago it ceased to be the Boston of John Winthrop, Josiah Quincy, or James Jackson Storrow—the Boston of *The Autocrat of the Breakfast-Table* or *The Late George Apley*. But at this point, it is equally clear that it is no longer the Boston of John Francis Fitzgerald, James Michael Curley, or John F. Kennedy—the Boston of *The Last Hurrah* or *The Friends of Eddie Coyle*. All that may be wonderfully romantic and nostalgic, but it is now part of the city's past, not of its future. Instead of Yankees,

Irish, and Italians, Boston is increasingly populated by African Americans, Hispanic Americans, and Asian Americans—these are our "new Bostonians." Instead of a small, close-knit coterie of Brahmins who made their money in old family businesses and sat quietly on their trust funds, the city is populated by a younger generation of high-tech entrepreneurs who generate the kind of profits previously reserved for New York and Chicago. Businesses formerly owned for generations by prominent Boston families have been taken over by national enterprises and international conglomerates. And booming real estate prices have transformed the old blue-collar neighborhoods like Charlestown and South Boston into condominium communities where young newcomers can travel to work on their bicycles after they have had their morning latte at Starbuck's. Boston has become a city in the midst of remarkable social, cultural, and economic changes that could well homogenize the unique and distinctive character of the old city and turn it into just another urban center, almost indistinguishable from most other American cities.

Not that change itself is anything new in Boston's history, although it has always been regarded with some degree of suspicion and a definite sense of apprehension. In the course of three hundred years, however, Boston has actually succeeded in adapting to a number of substantive changes without losing that sense of history that is so much a part of its special identity, and without giving up on a commitment to excellence that has characterized its social and cultural life. It succeeded in replacing colonial rule with national statehood, substituting an industrial technology for its former commercial supremacy, expanding a basically elitist establishment to offer a remarkable range of humanitarian institutions, adjusting a rigid and homogeneous soci- ety to include an increasing amount of both ethnic and racial diversity—all without losing those distinctive characteristics that make it quaint, colorful, and decidedly different.

And that is Boston's challenge for tomorrow. It must continue to combine the old with the new, the past with the present, the advances of the new technologies with the traditions of academic excellence, the profits of business with the pleasures of the fine arts. While expanding its geographical boundaries, it should strive to preserve its reputation as a livable city, a small town where everybody can still get everywhere by walking. It would do well to maintain its reputation as a city of distinctive neighborhoods, but work to prevent the kinds of racial conflicts and turf battles that have marked so much of its recent history. It is important for Boston to restore the preeminence of a public school system whereby all citizens are determined that every boy and girl, regardless of background, has the opportunity to "know enough" in order to achieve great things. And it is essential for the city to create the kind of open and welcoming society that provides social and economic opportunities for newcomers from various lands and different cultures. After all, in a city where colonial churches, federal townhouses, and Greek Revival markets can exist alongside Victorian mansions, Gothic cathedrals, and high-rise skyscrapers of glass and steel, it seems entirely possible for Boston's inhabitants to live together in a similar spirit of tolerance and harmony. If the lessons of the past can be brought to bear on the challenges of the future, then the new millennium could be one of considerable promise and opportunity for the City of Boston.

BIBLIOGRAPHY

GENERAL WORKS

Amory, Cleveland. *The Proper Bostonians.* New York, 1947.

Buni, Andrew, and Alan Rogers. *Boston: City on a Hill.* Woodland, Calif., 1984.

Chiang, Yee. *The Silent Traveler in Boston.* New York, 1959.

Early, Eleanor. *And This Is Boston.* Boston, 1938.

Forbes, Esther, and Arthur Griffin. *The Boston Book.* Boston, 1947.

Formisano, Ronald, and Constance Burns, eds. *Boston, 1700–1980: The Evolution of Urban Politics.* Westport, Conn., 1984.

Herlihy, Elizabeth, ed. *Fifty Years of Boston.* Boston, 1932.

Howard, Brett. *Boston: A Social History.* New York, 1976.

Jones, Howard Mumford. *The Many Voices of Boston: A Historical Anthology: 1630–1975.* Boston, 1975.

Kay, Jane Holtz. *Lost Boston.* Boston, 1980.

Kennedy, Lawrence W. *Planning the City upon a Hill: Boston since 1630.* Amherst, 1992.

Koren, John. *Boston, 1822–1922: The Story of Its Government and Principal Activities during One Hundred Years.* Boston, 1923.

Krieger, Alex, and David Cobb, eds. *Mapping Boston.* Cambridge, Mass., 1999.

McCord, David. *About Boston: Sight, Sound, Flavor, and Inflection.* New York, 1948.

O'Connor, Thomas H. *Bibles, Brahmins, and Bosses: A Short History of Boston,* 3d ed. Boston, 1991.

Seaburg, Carl. *Boston Observed.* Boston, 1971.

Shand-Tucci, Douglass. *Built in Boston: City and Suburb, 1800–1950.* Amherst, 1988.

Snow, Edward Rowe. *The Romance of Boston Bay.* Boston, 1946.

Weston, George F. *Boston Ways: High, By, and Folk,* 3d ed. Boston, 1974.

Whitehill, Walter Muir, and Lawrence W. Kennedy. *Boston: A Topographical History,* 3d ed. Cambridge, Mass., 2000.

Wilkie, Richard, and Jack Tager. *Historical Atlas of Massachusetts.* Amherst, Mass., 1991.

Winsor, Justin, ed. *The Memorial History of Boston, Including Suffolk County, Massachusetts, 1630–1880.* 4 vols. Boston, 1880.

BIBLIOGRAPHY

CHAPTER 1: A WILDERNESS ZION

Anderson, Virginia. *New England's Generation: The Great Migration and the Formulation of a Society and Culture in the Seventeenth Century*. New York, 1991.

Bailyn, Bernard. *The Peopling of British North America: An Introduction*. New York, 1986.

Battis, Emery. *Saints and Sectaries: Anne Hutchinson and the Antinomian Controversy in the Massachusetts Bay Colony*. Chapel Hill, N.C., 1962.

Berkin, Carol. *First Generations: Women in Colonial America*. New York, 1996.

Demos, John A. *A Little Commonwealth: Family Life in Plymouth Colony*. New York, 1970.

Dunn, Richard S. *Puritans and Yankees: The Winthrop Dynasty of New England, 1630–1717*. Princeton, 1962.

Graham, Judith S. *Puritan Family Life: The Diary of Samuel Sewall*. Boston, 2000.

Jennings, John H. *Boston: Cradle of Liberty, 1630–1776*. New York, 1947.

Kawashima, Yasuhide. *Puritan Justice and the Indian: White Man's Law in Massachusetts, 1630–1763*. Middletown, Conn., 1986.

Labaree, Benjamin W. *Colonial Massachusetts: A History*. Millwood, N.Y., 1979.

Lepore, Jill. *The Name of War: King Philip's War and the Origins of American Identity*. New York, 1998.

Middlekauff, Robert. *The Mathers*. New York, 1971.

Miller, Perry. *The New England Mind: The Seventeenth Century*. New York, 1939.

———. *Orthodoxy in Massachusetts, 1630–1650*. Cambridge, Mass., 1933.

———. *Roger Williams: His Contribution to the American Tradition*. Indianapolis, 1953.

Morgan, Edmund. *The Puritan Dilemma: The Story of John Winthrop*. Boston, 1958.

———. *The Puritan Family: Essays on Religion and Domestic Relations in Seventeenth-Century New England*. Boston, 1944.

———. *Visible Saints: The History of a Puritan Idea*. New York, 1963.

Morison, Samuel Eliot. *Builders of the Bay Colony*. Boston, 1930.

Murdock, Kenneth B., *Increase Mather: The Foremost American Puritan*. Cambridge, Mass., 1925.

Porterfield, Amanda. *Female Piety in Puritan New England*. New York, 1992.

Reiss, Oscar. *Blacks in Colonial America*. Jefferson, N.C., 1997.

Rutman, Darrett. *Winthrop's Boston: Portrait of a Puritan Town*. Chapel Hill, N.C., 1965.

Treckel, Paula A. *To Comfort the Heart: Women in Seventeenth-Century America*. New York, 1996.

Vaughan, Alden T. *New England Frontier: Puritans and Indians, 1620–1675*. Boston, 1965.

Vaughan, Alden T., and Edward Clark. *Puritans among Indians: Accounts of Captivity and Redemption, 1676–1724*. Cambridge, Mass., 1981.

Wall, R. E. *The Massachusetts Bay: The Crucial Decade, 1640–1650*. New Haven, 1972.

Wendell, Barrett. *Cotton Mather: The Puritan Priest*. Cambridge, Mass., 1926 [1891].

Westerkamp, Marilyn J. *Women and Religion in Early America, 1600–1850*. New York, 1999.

BIBLIOGRAPHY

CHAPTER 2: LOYALTY VERSUS LIBERTY

Andrews, Charles M. *The Boston Merchants and the Nonimportation Movement.* New York, 1968 [1917].

Ayer, Mary F. *Boston Common in Colonial and Provincial Days.* Boston, 1903.

Bailyn, Bernard. *The New England Merchants in the Seventeenth Century.* Cambridge, Mass., 1955.

Baxter, William T. *The House of Hancock, 1724–1775.* Cambridge, Mass., 1945.

Brown, Robert E. *Middle-Class Democracy and the Revolution in Massachusetts, 1691–1780.* Ithaca, 1955.

Bruchey, Stuart, ed. *The Colonial Merchant: Sources and Readings.* New York, 1966.

Conkin, Paul K. *Puritans and Pragmatists.* New York, 1968.

Crawford, Mary C. *Romantic Days in Old Boston.* Boston, 1910.

Dow, George. *Every Day Life in the Massachusetts Bay Colony.* New York, 1967 [1935].

Gaustad, Edwin S. *The Great Awakening in New England.* New York, 1957.

Greven, Philip J. *The Protestant Temperament: Patterns in Child-Rearing, Religious Experience, and the Self in Early America.* New York, 1977.

Hall, Michael G., ed. *The Glorious Revolution in America.* Chapel Hill, N.C., 1964.

Harper, Lawrence A. *The English Navigation Laws: A Seventeenth-Century Experiment in Social Engineering.* New York, 1939.

Johnson, Richard R. *Adjustment to Empire: The New England Colonies in the Era of the Glorious Revolution, 1675–1715.* New Brunswick, 1981.

Leach, Douglas E. *Roots of Conflict: British Armed Forces and Colonial Americans.* Chapel Hill, N.C., 1986.

Pares, Richard. *Yankees and Creoles: The Trade between North America and the West Indies before the American Revolution.* London, 1956.

Peckham, Howard H. *The Colonial Wars, 1689–1762.* Chicago, 1964.

Piersen, William D. *Black Yankees: The Development of an Afro-American Subculture in Eighteenth-Century New England.* Amherst, 1988.

Seybolt, Robert F. *The Public Schools of Colonial Boston, 1635–1775.* Cambridge, Mass., 1935.

Warden, Gerard B. *Boston, 1689–1776.* Boston, 1970.

Weisman, Richard. *Witchcraft, Magic, and Religion in Seventeenth-Century Massachusetts.* Amherst, 1984.

Zuckerman, Michael. *Peaceable Kingdoms: New England Towns in the Eighteenth Century.* New York, 1970.

CHAPTER 3: FROM COLONY TO COMMONWEALTH

Alden, John R. *A History of the American Revolution.* New York, 1969.

Allan, Herbert. *John Hancock: Patriot in Purple.* New York, 1948.

Bailyn, Bernard. *Ideological Origins of the American Revolution.* Cambridge, Mass., 1967.

——. *The Ordeal of Thomas Hutchinson.* Cambridge, Mass., 1974.

BIBLIOGRAPHY

Bridenbaugh, Carl. *Cities in Revolt: Urban Life in America, 1743–1776.* New York, 1955.

Brown, Richard D. *Revolutionary Politics in Massachusetts.* Cambridge, Mass., 1945.

Cash, Philip. *Medical Men at the Siege of Boston: April 1775–April 1776.* Philadelphia, 1973.

Fischer, David Hackett. *Paul Revere's Ride.* New York, 1994.

Fleming, Thomas J. *The Story of Bunker Hill.* New York, 1960.

Forbes, Esther. *Paul Revere and the World He Lived In.* Boston, 1942.

Fowler, William M. *Rebels under Sail: The American Navy during the Revolution.* New York, 1976.

Hosmer, James K. *Samuel Adams: Man of the Town Meeting.* Baltimore, 1884.

Kaplan, Sidney, and Emma Nagrady Kaplan. *The Black Presence in the Era of the American Revolution,* rev. ed. Amherst, 1989.

Labaree, Benjamin. *The Boston Tea Party.* New York, 1964.

Maier, Pauline. *American Scripture: Making the Declaration of Independence.* New York, 1997.

———. *From Resistance to Revolution: Colonial Radicals and the Development of American Opposition to Britain, 1765–1776.* New York, 1972.

Morgan, Edmund, and Helen Morgan. *The Stamp Act Crisis: Prologue to Revolution.* Chapel Hill, N.C., 1953.

Norton, Mary Beth. *Liberty's Daughters: The Revolutionary Experience of American Women, 1750–1800.* Boston, 1980.

O'Connor, Thomas H., and Alan Rogers. *This Momentous Affair: Massachusetts and the Ratification of the Constitution of the United States.* Boston, 1987.

Quarles, Benjamin. *The Negro in the American Revolution.* Chapel Hill, N.C., 1961.

Schlesinger, Arthur M., Sr. *The Colonial Merchants and the American Revolution.* New York, 1918.

Szatmary, David P. *Shays' Rebellion: The Making of an Agrarian Insurrection.* Amherst, 1980.

Wallace, Willard. *Appeal to Arms: A Military History of the American Revolution.* New York, 1951.

Zobel, Hiller. *The Boston Massacre.* New York, 1970.

CHAPTER 4: FROM TOWN TO CITY

Allen, Katherine G. *Sketches of Some Historic Churches of Greater Boston.* Boston, 1918.

Baltzell, E. Digby. *Puritan Boston and Quaker Philadelphia: Two Protestant Ethics and the Spirit of Class Authority and Leadership.* New York, 1979.

Banner, James. *To the Hartford Convention: The Federalists and the Origins of Party Politics in Massachusetts.* New York, 1970.

Brown, Abram. *Faneuil Hall and Faneuil Hall Market.* Boston, 1900.

Chamberlain, Allen. *Beacon Hill: Its Ancient Pastures and Early Mansions.* Boston, 1925.

Current, Richard. *Daniel Webster and the Rise of National Conservatism.* Boston, 1955.

BIBLIOGRAPHY

Dalzell, Robert F., Jr. *Enterprising Elite: The Boston Associates and the World They Made.* Cambridge, Mass., 1987.

Darling, Arthur B. *Political Changes in Massachusetts, 1824–1848.* New Haven, Conn., 1925.

Greenslet, Ferris. *The Lowells and Their Seven Worlds.* Boston, 1946.

Kirker, Harold. *Bulfinch's Boston, 1787–1817.* New York, 1964.

Knights, Peter. *The Plain People of Boston, 1830–1860: A Study in City Growth.* New York, 1971.

Lane, Roger. *Policing the City: Boston, 1822–1885.* Cambridge, Mass., 1967.

Livermore, Shaw. *The Twilight of Federalism: The Disintegration of the Federalist Party.* Princeton, N.J., 1962.

McCaughey, Robert. *Josiah Quincy: The Last Federalist.* Cambridge, Mass., 1974.

Morison, Samuel Eliot. *Maritime History of Massachusetts.* Boston, 1921.

O'Connor, Thomas H. *Lords of the Loom: The Cotton Whigs and the Coming of the Civil War.* New York, 1968.

Place, Charles. *Charles Bulfinch: Architect and Citizen.* Boston, 1925.

Porter, Kenneth W. *The Jacksons and the Lees: Two Generations of Massachusetts Merchants, 1765–1844.* 2 vols. Cambridge, Mass., 1937.

Seaburg, Carl, and Stanley Paterson. *Merchant Prince of Boston: Colonel T. H. Perkins, 1764–1854.* Cambridge, Mass., 1971.

Story, Ronald. *The Forging of an Aristocracy: Harvard and the Boston Upper Class, 1800–1870.* Middletown, Conn., 1980.

Tharp, Louise Hall. *The Appletons of Beacon Hill.* Boston, 1973.

Tyack, David B. *George Ticknor and the Boston Brahmins.* Cambridge, Mass., 1967.

CHAPTER 5: THE REFORM IMPULSE

Bartlett, Irving. *Wendell Phillips: Brahmin Radical.* Boston, 1961.

Berg, Barbara J. *The Remembered Gate: Origins of American Feminism: The Woman and the City, 1800–1860.* New York, 1978.

Blanchard, Paula. *Margaret Fuller: From Transcendentalism to Revolution.* Cambridge, Mass., 1978.

Brooks, Van Wyck. *The Flowering of New England.* New York, 1936.

Chadwick, John W. *William Ellery Channing.* Boston, 1903.

Commager, Henry Steele. *Theodore Parker: Yankee Crusader.* Boston, 1936.

Epstein, Barbara L. *The Politics of Domesticity: Women, Evangelism, and Temperance in Nineteenth-Century America.* Middletown, Conn., 1981.

Filler, Louis. *The Crusade against Slavery, 1830–1860.* New York, 1960.

Freedman, Estelle B. *Their Sisters' Keepers: Women's Prison Reform in America, 1830–1930.* Ann Arbor, Mich., 1981.

Gatell, Frank O. *John Gorham Palfrey and the New England Conscience.* Cambridge, Mass., 1963.

Ginzberg, Lori D. *Women and the Work of Benevolence: Morality, Politics, and Class in the Nineteenth-Century United States*. New Haven, 1990.

Green, Martin. *The Problem of Boston*. New York, 1966.

Griffin, Clifford S. *Their Brothers' Keepers: Moral Stewardship in the United States, 1800–1865*. New Brunswick, N.J., 1960.

Hersh, Blanche. *The Slavery of Sex: Feminist Abolitionists in Nineteenth-Century America*. Urbana, Ill., 1978.

Horton, James O., and Lois E. Horton, *Black Bostonians: Family Life and Community Struggle in the Antebellum North*. New York, 1979.

Howe, Helen. *The Gentle Americans, 1864–1960*. New York, 1965.

Korngold, Ralph. *Two Friends of Man: The Story of William Lloyd Garrison and Wendell Phillips and Their Relationship with Abraham Lincoln*. Boston, 1950.

Lader, Lawrence. *The Bold Brahmins: New England's War against Slavery*. New York, 1961.

Marshall, Helen E. *Dorothea Dix: Forgotten Samaritan*. Chapel Hill, N.C., 1937.

Nye, Russel B. *William Lloyd Garrison and the Humanitarian Reformers*. Boston, 1955.

Richards, Leonard L. *"Gentlemen of Property and Standing": Anti-Abolition Mobs in Jacksonian America*. New York, 1970.

Schlesinger, Arthur M., Sr. *The American as Reformer*. Cambridge, Mass., 1950.

Schultz, Stanley K. *The Culture Factory: Boston Public Schools, 1789–1860*. New York, 1973.

Schwartz, Harold. *Samuel Gridley Howe*. Cambridge, Mass., 1956.

Sterling, Dorothy. *Ahead of Her Time: Abby Kelley and the Politics of Anti-Slavery*. New York, 1991.

Thomas, John L. *The Liberator: William Lloyd Garrison*. Boston, 1963.

Tyack, David B. *George Ticknor and the Boston Brahmins*. Cambridge, Mass., 1967.

Tyler, Alice Felt. *Freedom's Ferment: Phases of American Social History to 1860*. Minneapolis, 1944.

CHAPTER 6: LIBERTY AND UNION

Abbott, Richard H. *Cotton and Capital: Boston Businessmen and Antislavery Reform, 1854–1868*. Amherst, 1991.

Burchard, Peter. *One Gallant Rush: Robert Gould Shaw and His Brave Black Regiment*. New York, 1965.

Burton, William L. *Melting Pot Soldiers*. Ames, Iowa, 1988.

Conyngham, David P. *The Irish Brigade and Its Campaigns*. New York, 1994 [1869].

Donald, David. *Lincoln*. New York, 1995.

———. *Charles Sumner and the Coming of the Civil War*. New York, 1960.

Duberman, Martin. *Charles Francis Adams, 1807–1886*. Stanford, Calif., 1968 [1960].

Emilio, Luis F. *A Brave Black Regiment: History of the Fifty-Fourth Regiment of Massachusetts Volunteer Infantry, 1863–1865*. Boston, 1891.

Fite, Emerson D. *Social and Industrial Conditions in the North during the Civil War.* New York, 1963 [1930].

Foner, Eric. *Free Soil, Free Labor, Free Men: The Ideology of the Republican Party before the Civil War.* New York, 1970.

Fredrickson, George M. *The Inner Civil War: Northern Intellectuals and the Crisis of the Union.* New York, 1965.

Gienapp, William E. *The Origins of the Republican Party, 1852–1856.* New York, 1987.

Giesberg, Judith. *Civil War Sisterhood: The U.S. Sanitary Commission and Women's Politics in Transition.* Boston, 2000.

Holt, Michael F. *The Political Crisis of the 1850s.* New York, 1978.

Leonard, Elizabeth D. *Yankee Women: Gender Battles in the Civil War.* New York, 1994.

Levesque, George A. *Black Boston: African-American Life and Culture in Urban America, 1750–1860.* New York, 1994.

MacNamara, Daniel G. *History of the Ninth Regiment.* Boston, 1899.

Massey, Mary Elizabeth. *Bonnet Brigades: American Women and the Civil War.* New York, 1966.

Maxwell, William Q. *Lincoln's Fifth Wheel: The Political History of the U.S. Sanitary Commission.* New York, 1956.

McPherson, James M. *Battle Cry of Freedom: The Civil War Era.* New York, 1988.

——. *The Negro's Civil War.* New York, 1965.

——. *Struggle for Equality: Abolitionists and the Negro in the Civil War and Reconstruction.* Princeton, 1964.

Merrill, James M. *The Rebel Shore: The Story of Union Sea Power in the Civil War.* Boston, 1957.

Murdock, Eugene. *One Million Men.* Madison, Wis., 1971.

Oates, Stephen B. *To Purge This Land with Blood: A Biography of John Brown.* New York, 1970.

——. *A Woman of Valor: Clara Barton and the Civil War.* New York, 1994.

O'Connor, Thomas H. *Civil War Boston: Home Front and Battlefield.* Boston, 1997.

——. *Lords of the Loom: The Cotton Whigs and the Coming of the Civil War.* New York, 1968.

Paludan, Phillip S. *A People's Contest: The Union and Civil War, 1861–1865.* New York, 1988.

Pearson, Henry G. *The Life of John A. Andrew, Governor of Massachusetts, 1861–1865.* Boston, 1904.

Schouler, William. *A History of Massachusetts in the Civil War.* Boston, 1868.

Silbey, Joel. *A Respectable Minority: The Democratic Party in the Civil War Era.* New York, 1977.

Stewart, James B. *Holy Warriors: The Abolitionists and American Slavery.* New York, 1976.

Trefousse, Hans. *The Radical Republicans: Lincoln's Vanguard for Racial Justice.* New York, 1969.

Von Frank, Albert J. *The Trials of Anthony Burns: Freedom and Slavery in Emerson's Boston.* Cambridge, Mass., 1998.

Ware, Edith. *Political Opinion in Massachusetts during the Civil War and Reconstruction.* New York, 1916.

West, Richard S., Jr. *Lincoln's Scapegoat General: A Life of Benjamin F. Butler, 1818–1893.* Boston, 1965.

Williams, T. Harry. *Lincoln and the Radicals.* Madison, Wis., 1941.

CHAPTER 7: WINDS OF CHANGE

Billington, Ray Allen. *The Protestant Crusade, 1800–1860.* New York, 1938.

Cullen, James. *The Story of the Irish in Boston.* Boston, 1889.

Diner, Hasia. *Erin's Daughters in America: Irish Immigrant Women in the Nineteenth Century.* Baltimore, 1983.

Foley, Albert. *Bishop Healy: Beloved Outcaste.* New York, 1954.

Frawley, Mary A. *Patrick Donahoe.* Washington, D.C., 1946.

Gallagher, Thomas. *Paddy's Lament: Ireland, 1846–1847.* New York, 1982.

Ginger, Ray. *The Age of Excess: The United States from 1877 to 1914.* New York, 1965.

Handlin, Oscar. *Boston's Immigrants, 1790–1865.* Cambridge, Mass., 1941.

Hansen, Marcus Lee. *The Atlantic Migration.* Cambridge, Mass., 1940.

Hofstadter, Richard. *The Paranoid Style in American Politics.* Chicago, 1979 [1965].

Holloran, Peter C. *Boston's Wayward Children: Social Services for Homeless Children, 1830–1930.* Rutherford, N.J., 1989.

Huggins, Nathan. *Protestants against Poverty: Boston's Charities, 1870–1900.* Westport, Conn., 1971.

Lord, Robert H., John E. Sexton, and Edward Harrington. *History of the Archdiocese of Boston.* 3 vols. Boston, 1945.

Miller, Kerby. *Emigrants and Exiles: Ireland and the Irish Exodus to North America.* New York, 1985.

Mulkern, John R. *The Know-Nothing Party in Massachusetts: The Rise and Fall of a People's Movement.* Boston, 1990.

O'Connor, Thomas H. *Boston Catholics: A History of the Church and Its People.* Boston, 1998.

———. *Fitzpatrick's Boston, 1846–1866.* Boston, 1984.

Potter, George. *To the Golden Door: The Story of the Irish in Ireland and America.* Boston, 1960.

Schneider, Eric. *In the Web of Class: Delinquents and Reformers in Boston, 1810s–1930s.* New York, 1992.

Schultz, Nancy L. *Fire and Roses: The Burning of the Charlestown Convent, 1834.* New York, 2000.

Tager, Jack, and John Ifkovic, eds. *Massachusetts in the Gilded Age.* Amherst, 1985.

Taylor, Philip. *The Distant Magnet: European Emigration to the United States of America.* New York, 1971.

BIBLIOGRAPHY

Walsh, James B. *The Irish: America's Political Class.* New York, 1976.

Wittke, Carl. *The Irish in America.* Baton Rouge, 1956.

Woodham-Smith, Cecil. *The Great Hunger: Ireland, 1845–1849.* New York, 1962.

CHAPTER 8: CLASH OF CULTURES

Ainley, Leslie. *Boston Mahatma: Martin Lomasney.* Boston, 1949.

Blodgett, Geoffrey. *The Gentle Reformers: Massachusetts Democrats in the Cleveland Era.* Cambridge, Mass., 1966.

Brown, Thomas N. *Irish American Nationalism, 1870–1890.* Philadelphia, 1966.

Curran, Michael. *The Life of Patrick Collins.* Norwood, Mass., 1906.

Evans, A. G. *Fanatic Heart: A Life of John Boyle O'Reilly, 1844–1890.* Boston, 1999.

De Marco, William M. *Ethnics and Enclaves: Boston's Italian North End.* Ann Arbor, Mich., 1980.

Deutsch, Sarah. *Women and the City: Gender, Space, and Power in Boston, 1870–1940.* New York, 2000.

Green, James, and Hugh Donahue. *Boston's Workers: A Labor History.* Boston, 1979.

Hardy, Stephen. *How Boston Played: Sport, Recreation, and Community, 1865–1915.* Boston, 1982.

Keating, Suzanne. *Illuminations: The History of the Boston Gas Company, 1822–2000.* Rockland, Mass., 1999.

Levine, Edward M. *The Irish and Irish Politicians: A Study of Cultural and Social Alienation.* Notre Dame, 1966.

Mann, Arthur. *Yankee Reformers in an Urban Age.* Cambridge, Mass., 1954.

Marchione, William P. *The Bull in the Garden: A History of Allston-Brighton.* Boston, 1986.

Marquand, John P. *The Late George Apley.* Boston, 1937.

Morison, Samuel Eliot. *One Boy's Boston, 1887–1901.* Boston, 1962.

O'Connor, Thomas H. *The Boston Irish: A Political History.* Boston, 1995.

———. *South Boston, My Home Town: The History of an Ethnic Neighborhood.* Boston, 1988.

Pleck, Elizabeth. *Black Migration and Poverty: Boston, 1865–1900.* New York, 1979.

Ryan, Dennis. *Beyond the Ballot Box: A Social History of the Boston Irish, 1845–1917.* Rutherford, N.J., 1983.

Rybczynski, Witold. *A Clearing in the Distance: Frederick Law Olmsted and America in the Nineteenth Century.* New York, 1999.

Sarna, Jonathan, and Ellen Smith. *The Jews of Boston.* Boston, 1995.

Schneider, Mark. *Boston Confronts Jim Crow, 1890–1920.* Boston, 1997.

Shand-Tucci, Douglass. *The Art of Scandal: The Life and Times of Isabella Stewart Gardner.* New York, 1997.

———. *Boston Bohemia, 1881–1900: Ralph Adams Cram: Life and Architecture.* Amherst, 1995.

Solomon, Barbara. *Ancestors and Immigrants: A Changing New England Tradition.* Cambridge, Mass., 1956.

Von Hoffman, Alexander. *Local Attachments: The Making of an American Urban Neighborhood, 1850–1920.* Baltimore, 1994.

CHAPTER 9: A CITY DIVIDED

Beatty, Jack. *The Rascal King: The Life and Times of James Michael Curley, 1874–1958.* Reading, Mass., 1992.

Curley, James Michael. *I'd Do It Again: A Record of All My Uproarious Years.* Englewood Cliffs, N.J., 1957.

Cutler, John H. *Honey Fitz: Three Steps to the White House.* Indianapolis, 1962.

Dinneen, Joseph F. *The Purple Shamrock: The Honorable James Michael Curley of Boston.* New York, 1949.

——. *Ward Eight.* New York, 1936.

Goodwin, Doris Kearns. *The Fitzgeralds and the Kennedys: An American Saga.* New York, 1987.

Huthmacher, J. Joseph. *Massachusetts People and Politics, 1919–1933.* Cambridge, Mass., 1959.

Kane, Paula. *Separatism and Subculture: Boston Catholicism, 1900–1920.* Chapel Hill, N.C., 1994.

Merwick, Donna. *Boston Priests, 1848–1910: A Study of Social and Intellectual Change.* Cambridge, Mass., 1973.

O'Connor, Edwin. *The Last Hurrah.* Boston, 1956.

O'Toole, James M. *Militant and Triumphant: William Henry O'Connell and the Catholic Church in Boston, 1859–1944.* Notre Dame, 1992.

Pearson, Henry G. *Son of New England: James Jackson Storrow.* Boston, 1932.

Russell, Francis. *City in Terror, 1919: The Boston Police Strike.* New York, 1975.

——. *The Great Interlude: Neglected Events and Persons from the First World War to the Depression.* New York, 1964.

——. *The Knave of Boston and Other Ambiguous Massachusetts Characters.* Boston, 1987.

Sullivan, Robert E., and James M. O'Toole, eds. *Catholic Boston: Studies in Religion and Community, 1870–1970.* Boston, 1985.

Thernstrom, Stephan. *The Other Bostonians: Poverty and Progress in the American Metropolis, 1880–1970.* Cambridge, Mass., 1973.

Trout, Charles. *Boston, the Great Depression, and the New Deal.* New York, 1977.

Wayman, Dorothy. *Cardinal O'Connell of Boston: A Biography of William Henry O'Connell, 1859–1944.* New York, 1955.

CHAPTER 10: BUILDING A NEW CITY

Banfield, E. C., and M. Myerson. *Boston: The Job Ahead.* Cambridge, Mass., 1966.

Dever, Joseph. *Cushing of Boston: A Candid Biography.* Boston, 1965.

BIBLIOGRAPHY

Fisher, Sean, and Carolyn Hughes, eds. *The Last Tenement: Confronting Community and Urban Renewal in Boston's West End.* Boston, 1992.

Fried, Marc. *The World of the Urban Working Class: Boston's West End.* Cambridge, Mass., 1973.

Frieden, Bernard, and Lynne B. Sagalyn. *Downtown, Inc.: How America Rebuilds Cities.* Cambridge, Mass., 1989.

Galvin, John T. *The Gentleman Mr. Shattuck: A Biography of Henry Lee Shattuck, 1879–1971.* Boston, 1996.

Gamm, Gerald. *Urban Exodus: Why the Jews Left Boston and the Catholics Stayed.* Cambridge, Mass., 1999.

Gans, Herbert. *Urban Villagers.* 2nd ed. New York, 1982.

Gelfand, Mark I. *A Nation of Cities: The Federal Government and Urban America, 1933–1965.* New York, 1975.

——. *Trustee for a City: Ralph Lowell of Boston.* Boston, 1998.

Ginsberg, Yona. *Jews in a Changing Neighborhood: The Study of Mattapan.* New York, 1975.

Hentoff, Nat. *Boston Boy.* New York, 1986.

Kenny, Herbert. *Newspaper Row.* Chester, Conn., 1987.

Keyes, Langley, Jr. *The Boston Rehabilitation Program: An Independent Analysis.* Cambridge, Mass., 1970.

Kozol, Jonathan. *Death at an Early Age.* Boston, 1967.

Krieger, Alex, and Lisa Green. *Past Futures: Two Centuries of Imagining Boston.* Cambridge, Mass., 1985.

Kruh, David. *Always Something Doing: A History of Boston's Infamous Scollay Square.* Boston, 1989.

Levin, Murray. *The Alienated Voter: Politics in Boston.* New York, 1960.

Levine, Hillel, and Lawrence Harmon. *Death of an American Jewish Community: A Tragedy of Good Intentions.* New York, 1992.

Logue, Edward J. *Seven Years of Progress: A Final Report.* Boston, 1967.

Mollenkopf, John F. *The Contested City.* Princeton, 1983.

O'Connor, Thomas H. *Building a New Boston: The Politics of Urban Renewal, 1950–1970.* Boston, 1993.

O'Donnell, Kenneth, et al. *Johnny, We Hardly Knew Ye.* Boston, 1972.

Rosenblum, J. W. *The Boston Redevelopment Authority.* Cambridge, Mass., 1969.

Rubin, Morton. *Organized Citizen Participation in Boston.* Boston, 1971.

Schrag, Peter. *Village School Downtown.* Boston, 1967.

Stack, John F., Jr. *International Conflict in an American City: Boston's Irish, Italians, and Jews, 1935–1944.* Westport, Conn., 1979.

Stainton, J. *Urban Renewal and Redevelopment in Boston.* Boston, 1972.

Teaford, Jon. *The Rough Road to Renaissance: Urban Revitalization in America, 1940–1985.* Baltimore, 1990.

Whitehill, Walter Muir. *Boston in the Age of John F. Kennedy.* Norman, Okla., 1966.

Whyte, William. *Street Corner Society: The Social Structure of an Italian Slum.* Chicago, 1943.

CHAPTER 11: RACE AND ETHNICITY

Carden, Lance. *Witness: An Oral History of Black Politics in Boston, 1920–1960.* Chestnut Hill, Mass., 1988.

Cone, James H. *Black Theology and Black Power.* New York, 1969.

Cromwell, Adelaide. *The Other Brahmins: Boston's Black Upper Class, 1750–1950.* Fayetteville, Ark., 1994.

Daniels, John. *In Freedom's Birthplace: A Study of the Boston Negroes.* Boston, 1914.

Formisano, Ronald. *Boston against Busing: Race, Class, and Ethnicity in the 1960s and 1970s.* Chapel Hill, N.C., 1991.

Fox, Stephen R. *The Guardian of Boston: William Monroe Trotter.* New York, 1970.

Fraser, James W., et al. *From Common School to Magnet School: Selected Essays in the History of Boston's Schools.* Boston, 1979.

Friedland, Michael B. *Lift Up Your Voice Like a Trumpet: White Clergy and the Civil Rights and Antiwar Movements, 1954–1973.* Chapel Hill, N.C., 1998.

Hayden, Robert C. *African-Americans in Boston: More than 350 Years.* Boston, 1991.

Higgins, George V. *Style Versus Substance: Boston, Kevin White, and the Politics of Illusion.* New York, 1984.

Hillson, Jon. *The Battle of Boston.* New York, 1977.

Jackson, Kenneth. *Crabgrass Frontier: The Suburbanization of the United States.* New York, 1985.

Jennings, J., and Mel King. *From Access to Power: Black Politics in Boston.* Cambridge, Mass., 1986.

King, Mel. *Chain of Change: Struggles for Black Community Development.* Boston, 1981.

Lemann, Nicholas. *The Promised Land: The Great Black Migration and How It Changed America.* New York, 1991.

Lukas, J. Anthony. *Common Ground: A Turbulent Decade in the Lives of Three American Families.* New York, 1985.

Lupo, Alan. *Liberty's Chosen Home: The Politics of Violence in Boston.* Boston, 1977.

Malloy, Ione. *Southie Won't Go: A Teacher's Diary of the Desegregation of South Boston High School.* Urbana, Ill., 1986.

McGreevy, John T. *Parish Boundaries: The Catholic Encounter with Race in the Twentieth-Century Urban North.* Chicago, 1996.

Osborne, William. *The Segregated Covenant: Race Relations and American Catholics.* New York, 1967.

Roediger, David R. *The Wages of Whiteness: Race and the Making of the American Working Class.* London, 1991.

Roessner, Jane. *A Decent Place to Live: From Columbia Point to Harbor Point. A Community History.* Boston, 2000.

BIBLIOGRAPHY

Ross, J. Michael, and William M. Berg. *I Respectfully Disagree with the Judge's Order: The Boston School Desegregation Controversy.* Washington, 1981.

Schabert, Tilo. *Boston Politics: The Creativity of Power.* Berlin, 1989.

CHAPTER 12: LIFE IN A CHANGING CITY

Bluestone, Barry, and Mary Huff Stevenson. *The Boston Renaissance: Race, Space, and Economic Change in an American Metropolis.* New York, 2000.

Brooks, David. *Bobos in Paradise: The New Upper Class and How They Got There.* New York, 2000.

Howe, Neil, and William Strauss. *Millennials Rising: The Next Generation.* New York, 2000.

McNichol, Dan. *The Big Dig.* Boston, 2000.

INDEX

INDEX

INDEX

Boston Boy (Hentoff), 235
Boston Citizen Seminars, 216
Boston City Council, 181, *212*, 238, 253, 261
Boston City Hall. *See* City Hall (new); City Hall (old)
Boston City Hospital, 141, 158, 159, 187, 197
Boston College, 142, 216
Boston College Law School, 238
Boston Common, 11, *29*, 34, 53, 60, 61, 68, 77, 80, 115, 133, 134, 191; garage under, 222–23
Boston Consolidated Gas Company, 159
Boston Coordinating Committee (The Vault), 220–21, 271
Boston Female Anti-Slavery Society, 115
Boston Garden, *218*
Boston Gazette, 50
Boston Girls High School, 180
Boston Globe, 199, 208, 211, 266, 271
Boston Harbor, 10, 13, 57, 61, 242, 273–74
Boston Herald, 191
Boston Home and School Association, 249
Boston Housing Authority (BHA), 215–16
"Boston Hymn, The," 131
Boston Journal, 134
Boston Latin School, 15, 75
Boston League of Women Voters, 180
Boston Lyceum, 102
Boston Magazine, 270
Boston Massacre, 54–55
Boston Music Hall, 130–31
Boston Neck, 9, 140, 142, 144
Boston police strike, 195, *196*, 196
Boston Pops orchestra, 242
Boston Port Bill, 57–58
Boston Post, 202, 233
Boston Primary School Board, 119
Boston Prison Discipline Society, 95
Boston Public Library, 103, 177
Boston Red Sox, *188*, 274, 275
Boston Redevelopment Authority (BRA), 217, 221–22, 225, 227–28
Boston Safe Deposit and Trust Company, 220, 271
Boston School Committee, 180, 199, 243, 260, 262
Boston Sunday School Union, 150
Boston Symphony Orchestra, 177
Boston Tea Party, 57, 58
Boston Teachers' Union, 263
Boston Times, 122
Boston Trade School for Girls, 180

Boston's Immigrants (Handlin), 153
Bowditch, Henry Ingersoll, 116
Bowdoin, James, 36, 41, 64, 66, 69, 73
Boy Scouts, 201
Boycott, colonial, 54, 55
Boylston, Thomas, 36, 41
Boylston Market, 76
Boylston Street, 143, 177, 195, 216
Brace, Lloyd, 220
Bradford, Robert, 208
Bradstreet, Anne, 117n
Brahmins, 86–87, 88, 96, 103, 114, 174, 184, 191, 198, 199
Braintree, Massachusetts, 49, 60, 90
Branch libraries, 197
Brattle Street Church (Congregational), 53
Brattle Street Church (Unitarian), 82, 176
Breckinridge, John C., 124
Breed's Hill, 61
Brett, James, 261
Bridgman, Laura, 106
Brighton, Massachusetts, 144, 159
Bristol, England, 8
British Coffee House, 50
British East India Company, 56
British regulars, 48
Broad Street, 150
Broad Street Riot, 151–52
Brockton, Massachusetts, 168, 170
Bromley-Heath housing project (Jamaica Plain), 215
Brooke, Edward, 245
Brooks, John, 90
Brooks, Preston, 123
Brooks, Van Wyck, 97, 103
Brown, Abraham F., *132*
Brown, John, 123, 124, 156
Brown v. Board of Education of Topeka, 238
Bryant, Gridley, 140
Bufford, J. H., 56
Bulfinch, Charles, 75–80, 103
Bull market (1990s), 270
Bull Run, First Battle of, 127
Bull Run, Second Battle of, 127, 129
Bunch of Grapes Tavern, 50
Bunker Hill, Battle of, 94
Bunker Hill monument, 94
Burns, Anthony, 122
Bush, George, 260
Busing, court-ordered, 243–46, *247*
Butler, Andrew P., 123

INDEX

INDEX

INDEX

INDEX

Know-Nothing party. *See* American Party
Knowles, Edward, 233
Knox, Henry, 61

La Grassa Mancha, 249
Labor unrest after World War I, 195–96
Lafayette Mall, 193
Laos, immigrants from, 262
Last Hurrah, The (O'Connor), 276
Late George Apley, The (Marquand), 276
Latino population, Boston, 267
Laud, William, archbishop of Canterbury, 5
Law, Bernard, 268
Lawrence, Abbott, 86
Lawrence, Amos, 86
Lawrence, Amos Adams, 86, 122
Lawrence, David, 217
Lawrence, Kansas, 123
Lawrence, Katherine, 86
Lawrence, Massachusetts, 115, 153, 168
Le Corbusier, 222
League of Catholic Women, 210
Lee, Henry, 175
Lee, Higginson and Company, 198
Lee, Joseph, 179
Lee, Robert E., 127, 133
Legion of Mary, 201
Lemann, Nicholas, 236
Lenox Street, 232
Leventhal, Norman B., 225
Leverett Circle, 274
Leverett Circle Connector Bridge, 274
Leverett Street Jail, 95
Lexington, Massachusetts, 60, 109, 126
Liberal Republicans, 162, 178, 186
Liberator, The, 111, 112, 113
Liberty Bonds, 193
"Liberty tea," 52
Liberty Tree, 53
Limerick, Maine, 146
Lincoln, Abraham, 124, 125, 126, 130–31, 133–34, 156, 230
Lincoln, Benjamin, 64
Lincoln-Douglas debates, 124
Lincoln Laboratory, 270
Lincolnshire, England, 6, 9, 12
Linde Air Products, 202
Linkage program, 257
Linked deposit program, 257
Lithuania, immigrants from, 168, 171, 173
Little, Malcolm, 235

"Little city clerk." *See* John B. Hynes
Little City Halls, 240
Living Is Easy, The (West), 233
"Lobsterbacks." *See* British regulars
Lodge, Henry Cabot, 145
Lodge, Henry Cabot, Jr., 201
Logan International Airport, 217, 227, 247, 274, 275
Logue, Edward J., 221–22, *226,* 227, 229, 237
Lomasney, Martin, 163–64, *164,* 165, 167, 171–72, 184, 191
London, England, 174, 181
Londonderry, Maine, 146
Long Lane, 68, 73, 147
Long Wharf, 76
Longfellow, Henry Wadsworth, 99, 101
"Lords of the Lash," 115
"Lords of the Loom," 115
Louis XVI, 148
Louisbourg, Fort, 44
Louisburg Square, 101
Louisiana, 258
Louisiana Purchase, 81
Louvre, the, 142
Lovejoy, Elijah, 116
Lowell, A. Lawrence, 185
Lowell, Francis Cabot, 85, 86, 189
Lowell, James Russell, 102, 116
Lowell, John, Jr., 102
Lowell, Massachusetts, 85, *85,* 115, 153, 168
Lowell, Ralph, 220
Lowell Institute, 102
Loyal Nine, 49
Luckman, Charles, 222
Lucy Stone Leagues, 110
Lukas, J. Anthony, 233, 246
Lunceford, Jimmy, 235
Lutherans, 3
Lyceum lecturing system, 102
Lydon, Christopher, 261
Lynn, Massachusetts, 42

McClellan, George, 127
McCormack, John W., *212*
McGinniskin, Barney, 160
McGovern, George, 249
MacKay, Alexander, 101
McKim, Mead, and White, 103, 177
McKinley, William, 181
McKinnell, Noel, 223
Madison, James, 82, 84

302

INDEX

INDEX

INDEX

INDEX

INDEX

INDEX

Woods, Robert A., 179
Worcester, Massachusetts, 86
Workmen's compensation, 209
Works of Benjamin Franklin, The (Sparks) 100
World Anti-Slavery Congress, 110
World Trade Center, 216, 274
World War I, 193–94
World War II, 202–3, 207, 236
Wren, Christopher, 76
Writings of George Washington, The (Sparks), 100
Writs of Assistance, 50–51

Yankee Democrats, 160–61
Yankee Division. *See* 26th Division
Yorktown, Battle of, 63
Young, Lester ("Prez"), 235
Young Men's Christian Association (YMCA) 129, 193, 201
Young Men's Democratic Club, 161
Young Women's Christian Association (YWCA), 193, 201

p. 41   1657 day 1 Bristol

The Panda's Thumb

More
Reflections
in Natural
History

By the same author

Ever Since Darwin: Reflections in Natural History
Ontogeny & Phylogeny

The Panda's
Thumb

More
Reflections
in Natural
History

Stephen Jay Gould

W · W · NORTON & COMPANY
NEW YORK   LONDON

Copyright © 1980 by Stephen Jay Gould
Published simultaneously in Canada by George J. McLeod Limited,
Toronto. Printed in the United States of America.
ALL RIGHTS RESERVED
FIRST EDITION

Library of Congress Cataloging in Publication Data
Gould, Stephen Jay.
    The panda's thumb.
    Bibliography: p.
    Includes index.
    1. Evolution—History. 2. Natural selection—
History. I. Title.
QH361.G66 1980   575.01'62   80–15952
ISBN 0–393–01380–4

W. W. Norton & Company, Inc. 500 Fifth Avenue, New York, N.Y. 10110
W. W. Norton & Company Ltd. 25 New Street Square, London EC4A 3NT

1 2 3 4 5 6 7 8 9 0

FOR

JEANETTE McINERNEY
ESTER L. PONTI
RENE C. STACK

Three dedicated and compassionate teachers of my primary years, P.S. 26, Queens.

A teacher . . . can never tell where his influence stops.

—Henry Adams

Contents

The Panda's Thumb

More Reflections in Natural History

Prologue

ON THE TITLE PAGE of his classic book, *The Cell in Development and Inheritance,* E.B. Wilson inscribed a motto from Pliny, the great natural historian who died in his boots when he sailed across the Bay of Naples to study the eruption of Mt. Vesuvius in A.D. 79. He suffocated in the same vapors that choked the citizens of Pompeii. Pliny wrote: *Natura nusquam magis est tota quam in minimis*—"Nature is to be found in her entirety nowhere more than in her smallest creatures." Wilson, of course, commandeered Pliny's statement to celebrate the microscopic building blocks of life, minute structures unknown perforce to the great Roman. Pliny was thinking about organisms.

Pliny's statement captures the essence of what fascinates me about natural history. In an old stereotype (not followed nearly so often as mythology proclaims), the natural history essay restricts itself to describing the peculiarities of animals—the mysterious ways of the beaver, or how the spider weaves her supple web. There is exultation in this and who shall gainsay it? But each organism can mean so much more to us. Each instructs; its form and behavior embodies general messages if only we can learn to read them. The language of this instruction is evolutionary theory. Exultation *and* explanation.

I was lucky to wander into evolutionary theory, one of the most exciting and important of all scientific fields. I had

11

never heard of it when I started at a rather tender age; I was simply awed by dinosaurs. I thought paleontologists spent their lives digging up bones and putting them together, never venturing beyond the momentous issue of what connects to what. Then I discovered evolutionary theory. Ever since then, the duality of natural history—richness in particularities and potential union in underlying explanation—has propelled me.

I think that the fascination so many people feel for evolutionary theory resides in three of its properties. First, it is, in its current state of development, sufficiently firm to provide satisfaction and confidence, yet fruitfully undeveloped enough to provide a treasure trove of mysteries. Second, it stands in the middle of a continuum stretching from sciences that deal in timeless, quantitative generality to those that work directly with the singularities of history. Thus, it provides a home for all styles and propensities, from those who seek the purity of abstraction (the laws of population growth and the structure of DNA) to those who revel in the messiness of irreducible particularity (what, if anything, did *Tyrannosaurus* do with its puny front legs anyway?). Third, it touches all our lives; for how can we be indifferent to the great questions of genealogy: where did we come from, and what does it all mean? And then, of course, there are all those organisms: more than a million described species, from bacterium to blue whale, with one hell of a lot of beetles in between—each with its own beauty, and each with a story to tell.

These essays range broadly in the phenomena they treat —from the origin of life, to the brain of Georges Cuvier, to a mite that dies before it is born. Yet I hope that I have avoided that incubus of essay collections, diffuse incoherence, by centering them all upon evolutionary theory, with an emphasis on Darwin's thoughts and impact. As I stated in introducing my previous collection, *Ever Since Darwin:* "I am a tradesman, not a polymath. What I know of planets and politics lies at their intersection with biological evolution."

I have tried to weld these essays into an integrated whole

by organizing them into eight sections. The first on pandas, turtles & anglerfish, illustrates why we can be confident that evolution occurred. The argument embodies a paradox: the proof of evolution lies in imperfections that reveal history. This section is followed by a club sandwich—three sections on major themes in the evolutionary study of natural history (Darwinian theory and the meaning of adaptation, the tempo and mode of change, and the scaling of size and time), and two intervening layers of two sections each (III and IV, and VI and VII) on organisms and the peculiarities of their history. (If anyone wants to pursue the metaphorical sandwich and divide these seven sections into supporting structure and meat, I will not be offended.) I have also impaled the sandwich with toothpicks—subsidiary themes common to all sections, and intended to prick some conventional comforts: why science must be embedded in culture, why Darwinism cannot be squared with hopes for intrinsic harmony or progress in nature. But each pinprick has its positive consequence. An understanding of cultural bias forces us to view science as an accessible, human activity, much like any form of creativity. An abandonment of the hope that we might read a meaning for our lives passively in nature compels us to seek answers within ourselves.

These essays are lightly edited versions of my monthly columns in *Natural History* Magazine, collectively titled "This View of Life." I have added postscripts to a few: additional evidence of Teilhard's possible involvement in the Piltdown fraud (essay 10); a letter from J Harlen Bretz, controversial as ever at 96 (19); confirmation from the southern hemisphere for an explanation of magnets in bacteria (30). I thank Ed Barber for persuading me that these essays might be less ephemeral than I thought. *Natural History*'s editor in chief Alan Ternes and copy editor Florence Edelstein have greatly helped in deconvolution of phrase and thought and in devising some good titles. Four essays would not have been, without the gracious help of colleagues: Carolyn Fluehr-Lobban introduced me to Dr. Down, sent me his obscure article, and shared her insights and writing with me (essay 15). Ernst Mayr has urged the importance of folk taxonomy for years and had all the references on hand (essay 20). Jim Kennedy introduced me to Kirkpatrick's work (essay 22); otherwise I would never have penetrated the veil of silence surrounding it. Richard Frankel wrote me an unsolicited four-page letter explaining lucidly to this physical dunce the magnetic properties of his fascinating bacteria (essay 30). I am always cheered and delighted by the generosity of colleagues; a thousand untold stories overbalance every eagerly recorded case of nastiness. I thank Frank Sulloway for telling me the true story of Darwin's finches (essay 5), Diane Paul, Martha Denckla, Tim White, Andy Knoll, and Carl Wunsch for references, insights, and patient explanation.

Fortunately, I write these essays during an exciting time in evolutionary theory. When I think of paleontology in 1910, with its wealth of data and void of ideas, I regard it as a privilege to be working today.

Evolutionary theory is expanding its domain of impact and explanation in all directions. Consider the current excitement in such disparate realms as the basic mechanics of DNA, embryology, and the study of behavior. Molecular evolution is now a full-fledged discipline that promises to provide both strikingly new ideas (the theory of neutrality as an alternative to natural selection) and resolution of many classical mysteries in natural history (see essay 24). At the same time, the discovery of inserted sequences and jumping genes reveals a new stratum of genetic complexity that must be pregnant with evolutionary meaning. The triplet code is only a machine language; a higher level of control must exist. If we can ever figure out how multicellular creatures regulate the timing involved in the complex orchestration of their embryonic growth, then developmental biology might unite molecular genetics with natural history into a unified science of life. The theory of kin selection has extended Darwinian theory fruitfully into the realm of social behavior, though I believe that its more zealous advocates misunderstand the hierarchical nature of explanation and try to extend it (by more than permissible analogy) to realms of human culture where it does not apply (see essays 7 and 8).

Yet, while Darwinian theory extends its domain, some of its cherished postulates are slipping, or at least losing their generality. The "modern synthesis," the contemporary version of Darwinism that has reigned for thirty years, took the model of adaptive gene substitution within local populations as an adequate account, by accumulation and extension, of life's entire history. The model may work well in its empirical domain of minor, local, adaptive adjustment; populations of the moth *Biston betularia* did turn black, by substitution of a single gene, as a selected response for decreased visibility on trees that had been blackened by industrial soot. But is the origin of a new species simply this process extended to more genes and greater effect? Are larger evolutionary trends within major lineages just a further accumulation of sequential, adaptive changes?

Many evolutionists (myself included) are beginning to challenge this synthesis and to assert the hierarchical view that different levels of evolutionary change often reflect different kinds of causes. Minor adjustment within populations may be sequential and adaptive. But speciation may occur by major chromosomal changes that establish sterility with other species for reasons unrelated to adaptation. Evolutionary trends may represent a kind of higher-level selection upon essentially static species themselves, not the slow and steady alteration of a single large population through untold ages.

Before the modern synthesis, many biologists (see Bateson, 1922, in bibliography) expressed confusion and depression because the proposed mechanisms of evolution at different levels seemed contradictory enough to preclude a unified science. After the modern synthesis, the notion spread (amounting almost to a dogma among its less thoughtful lieutenants) that all evolution could be reduced to the basic Darwinism of gradual, adaptive change within local populations. I think that we are now pursuing a fruitful path between the anarchy of Bateson's day and the restriction of view imposed by the modern synthesis. The modern synthesis works in its appropriate arena, but the same Darwinian processes of mutation and selection may operate in strikingly different ways at higher domains in a hierarchy of evolutionary levels. I think that we may hope for uniformity of causal agents, hence a single, general theory with a Darwinian core. But we must reckon with a multiplicity of mechanisms that preclude the explanation of higher level phenomena by the model of adaptive gene substitution favored for the lowest level.

At the basis of all this ferment lies nature's irreducible complexity. Organisms are not billiard balls, propelled by simple and measurable external forces to predictable new positions on life's pool table. Sufficiently complex systems have greater richness. Organisms have a history that constrains their future in myriad, subtle ways (see essays of section I). Their complexity of form entails a host of functions incidental to whatever pressures of natural selection superintended the initial construction (see essay 4). Their intricate and largely unknown pathways of embryonic development guarantee that simple inputs (minor changes in timing, for example) may be translated into marked and surprising changes in output (the adult organism, see essay 18).

Charles Darwin chose to close his great book with a striking comparison that expresses this richness. He contrasted the simpler system of planetary motion, and its result of endless, static cycling, with the complexity of life and its wondrous and unpredictable change through the ages:

> There is grandeur in this view of life, with its several powers, having been originally breathed into a few forms or into one; and that, whilst this planet has gone cycling on according to the fixed law of gravity, from so simple a beginning endless forms most beautiful and most wonderful have been, and are being, evolved.

1 | Perfection and Imperfection: A Trilogy on a Panda's Thumb

1 | The Panda's Thumb

FEW HEROES LOWER their sights in the prime of their lives; triumph leads inexorably on, often to destruction. Alexander wept because he had no new worlds to conquer; Napoleon, overextended, sealed his doom in the depth of a Russian winter. But Charles Darwin did not follow the *Origin of Species* (1859) with a general defense of natural selection or with its evident extension to human evolution (he waited until 1871 to publish *The Descent of Man*). Instead, he wrote his most obscure work, a book entitled: *On the Various Contrivances by Which British and Foreign Orchids Are Fertilized by Insects* (1862).

Darwin's many excursions into the minutiae of natural history—he wrote a taxonomy of barnacles, a book on climbing plants, and a treatise on the formation of vegetable mold by earthworms—won him an undeserved reputation as an old-fashioned, somewhat doddering describer of curious plants and animals, a man who had one lucky insight at the right time. A rash of Darwinian scholarship has laid this myth firmly to rest during the past twenty years (see essay 2). Before then, one prominent scholar spoke for many ill-informed colleagues when he judged Darwin as a "poor joiner of ideas . . . a man who does not belong with the great thinkers."

In fact, each of Darwin's books played its part in the grand and coherent scheme of his life's work—demonstrating the fact of evolution and defending natural selection as its pri-

19

mary mechanism. Darwin did not study orchids solely for their own sake. Michael Ghiselin, a California biologist who finally took the trouble to read all of Darwin's books (see his *Triumph of the Darwinian Method*), has correctly identified the treatise on orchids as an important episode in Darwin's campaign for evolution.

Darwin begins his orchid book with an important evolutionary premise: continued self-fertilization is a poor strategy for long-term survival, since offspring carry only the genes of their single parent, and populations do not maintain enough variation for evolutionary flexibility in the face of environmental change. Thus, plants bearing flowers with both male and female parts usually evolve mechanisms to ensure cross-pollination. Orchids have formed an alliance with insects. They have evolved an astonishing variety of "contrivances" to attract insects, guarantee that sticky pollen adheres to their visitor, and ensure that the attached pollen comes in contact with female parts of the next orchid visited by the insect.

Darwin's book is a compendium of these contrivances, the botanical equivalent of a bestiary. And, like the medieval bestiaries, it is designed to instruct. The message is paradoxical but profound. Orchids manufacture their intricate devices from the common components of ordinary flowers, parts usually fitted for very different functions. If God had designed a beautiful machine to reflect his wisdom and power, surely he would not have used a collection of parts generally fashioned for other purposes. Orchids were not made by an ideal engineer; they are jury-rigged from a limited set of available components. Thus, they must have evolved from ordinary flowers.

Thus, the paradox, and the common theme of this trilogy of essays: Our textbooks like to illustrate evolution with examples of optimal design—nearly perfect mimicry of a dead leaf by a butterfly or of a poisonous species by a palatable relative. But ideal design is a lousy argument for evolution, for it mimics the postulated action of an omnipotent creator. Odd arrangements and funny solutions are the proof of evolution—paths that a sensible God would never tread but that a natural process, constrained by history, follows perforce. No one understood this better than Darwin. Ernst Mayr has shown how Darwin, in defending evolution, consistently turned to organic parts and geographic distributions that make the least sense. Which brings me to the giant panda and its "thumb."

Giant pandas are peculiar bears, members of the order Carnivora. Conventional bears are the most omnivorous representatives of their order, but pandas have restricted this catholicity of taste in the other direction—they belie the name of their order by subsisting almost entirely on bamboo. They live in dense forests of bamboo at high elevations in the mountains of western China. There they sit, largely unthreatened by predators, munching bamboo ten to twelve hours each day.

As a childhood fan of Andy Panda, and former owner of a stuffed toy won by some fluke when all the milk bottles actually tumbled at the county fair, I was delighted when the first fruits of our thaw with China went beyond ping pong to the shipment of two pandas to the Washington zoo. I went and watched in appropriate awe. They yawned, stretched, and ambled a bit, but they spent nearly all their time feeding on their beloved bamboo. They sat upright and manipulated the stalks with their forepaws, shedding the leaves and consuming only the shoots.

I was amazed by their dexterity and wondered how the scion of a stock adapted for running could use its hands so adroitly. They held the stalks of bamboo in their paws and stripped off the leaves by passing the stalks between an apparently flexible thumb and the remaining fingers. This puzzled me. I had learned that a dexterous, opposable thumb stood among the hallmarks of human success. We had maintained, even exaggerated, this important flexibility of our primate forebears, while most mammals had sacrificed it in specializing their digits. Carnivores run, stab, and scratch. My cat may manipulate me psychologically, but he'll never type or play the piano.

So I counted the panda's other digits and received an even greater surprise: there were five, not four. Was the "thumb" a separately evolved sixth finger? Fortunately, the giant panda has its bible, a monograph by D. Dwight Davis, late curator of vertebrate anatomy at Chicago's Field Museum of Natural History. It is probably the greatest work of modern evolutionary comparative anatomy, and it contains more than anyone would ever want to know about pandas. Davis had the answer, of course.

The panda's "thumb" is not, anatomically, a finger at all. It is constructed from a bone called the radial sesamoid, normally a small component of the wrist. In pandas, the radial sesamoid is greatly enlarged and elongated until it almost equals the metapodial bones of the true digits in length. The radial sesamoid underlies a pad on the panda's forepaw; the five digits form the framework of another pad, the palmar. A shallow furrow separates the two pads and serves as a channelway for bamboo stalks.

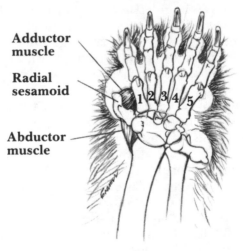

Adductor muscle

Radial sesamoid

Abductor muscle

D. L. CRAMER

The panda's thumb comes equipped not only with a bone to give it strength but also with muscles to sustain its agility. These muscles, like the radial sesamoid bone itself, did not arise *de novo*. Like the parts of Darwin's orchids, they are familiar bits of anatomy remodeled for a new function. The abductor of the radial sesamoid (the muscle that pulls it away from the true digits) bears the formidable name *abduc-*

tor pollicis longus ("the long abductor of the thumb"—*pollicis* is the genitive of *pollex,* Latin for "thumb"). Its name is a giveaway. In other carnivores, this muscle attaches to the first digit, or true thumb. Two shorter muscles run between the radial sesamoid and the pollex. They pull the sesamoid "thumb" towards the true digits.

Does the anatomy of other carnivores give us any clue to the origin of this odd arrangement in pandas? Davis points out that ordinary bears and raccoons, the closest relatives of giant pandas, far surpass all other carnivores in using their forelegs for manipulating objects in feeding. Pardon the backward metaphor, but pandas, thanks to their ancestry, began with a leg up for evolving greater dexterity in feeding. Moreover, ordinary bears already have a slightly enlarged radial sesamoid.

In most carnivores, the same muscles that move the radial sesamoid in pandas attach exclusively to the base of the pollex, or true thumb. But in ordinary bears, the long abductor muscle ends in two tendons: one inserts into the base of the thumb as in most carnivores, but the other attaches to the radial sesamoid. The two shorter muscles also attach, in part, to the radial sesamoid in bears. "Thus," Davis concludes, "the musculature for operating this remarkable new mechanism—functionally a new digit—required no intrinsic change from conditions already present in the panda's closest relatives, the bears. Furthermore, it appears that the whole sequence of events in the musculature follows automatically from simple hypertrophy of the sesamoid bone."

The sesamoid thumb of pandas is a complex structure formed by marked enlargement of a bone and an extensive rearrangement of musculature. Yet Davis argues that the entire apparatus arose as a mechanical response to growth of the radial sesamoid itself. Muscles shifted because the enlarged bone blocked them short of their original sites. Moreover, Davis postulates that the enlarged radial sesamoid may have been fashioned by a simple genetic change, perhaps a single mutation affecting the timing and rate of growth.

In a panda's foot, the counterpart of the radial sesamoid, called the tibial sesamoid, is also enlarged, although not so much as the radial sesamoid. Yet the tibial sesamoid supports no new digit, and its increased size confers no advantage, so far as we know. Davis argues that the coordinated increase of both bones, in response to natural selection upon one alone, probably reflects a simple kind of genetic change. Repeated parts of the body are not fashioned by the action of individual genes—there is no gene "for" your thumb, another for your big toe, or a third for your pinky. Repeated parts are coordinated in development; selection for a change in one element causes a corresponding modification in others. It may be genetically more complex to enlarge a thumb and *not* to modify a big toe, than to increase both together. (In the first case, a general coordination must be broken, the thumb favored separately, and correlated increase of related structures suppressed. In the second, a single gene may increase the rate of growth in a field regulating the development of corresponding digits.)

The panda's thumb provides an elegant zoological counterpart to Darwin's orchids. An engineer's best solution is debarred by history. The panda's true thumb is committed to another role, too specialized for a different function to become an opposable, manipulating digit. So the panda must use parts on hand and settle for an enlarged wrist bone and a somewhat clumsy, but quite workable, solution. The sesamoid thumb wins no prize in an engineer's derby. It is, to use Michael Ghiselin's phrase, a contraption, not a lovely contrivance. But it does its job and excites our imagination all the more because it builds on such improbable foundations.

Darwin's orchid book is filled with similar illustrations. The marsh Epipactus, for example, uses its labellum—an enlarged petal—as a trap. The labellum is divided into two parts. One, near the flower's base, forms a large cup filled with nectar—the object of an insect's visit. The other, near the flower's edge, forms a sort of landing stage. An insect alighting on this runway depresses it and thus gains entrance to the nectar cup beyond. It enters the cup, but the

Marsh *Epipactis,* lower sepals removed

a. Runway of labellum depressed after insect lands.

D. L. CRAMER

b. Runway of labellum raised after insect crawls into cup below.

D. L. CRAMER

runway is so elastic that it instantly springs up, trapping the insect within the nectar cup. The insect must then back out through the only available exit—a path that forces it to brush against the pollen masses. A remarkable machine but all developed from a conventional petal, a part readily available in an orchid's ancestor.

Darwin then shows how the same labellum in other orchids evolves into a series of ingenious devices to ensure cross-fertilization. It may develop a complex fold that forces an insect to detour its proboscis around and past the pollen masses in order to reach nectar. It may contain deep channels or guiding ridges that lead insects both to nectar and pollen. The channels sometimes form a tunnel, producing a tubular flower. All these adaptations have been built from a part that began as a conventional petal in some ancestral form. Yet nature can do so much with so little that it displays, in Darwin's words, "a prodigality of resources for gaining the very same end, namely, the fertilization of one flower by pollen from another plant."

Darwin's metaphor for organic form reflects his sense of wonder that evolution can fashion such a world of diversity and adequate design with such limited raw material:

> Although an organ may not have been originally formed for some special purpose, if it now serves for this end we are justified in saying that it is specially contrived for it. On the same principle, if a man were to make a machine for some special purpose, but were to use old wheels, springs, and pulleys, only slightly altered, the whole machine, with all its parts, might be said to be specially contrived for that purpose. Thus throughout nature almost every part of each living being has probably served, in a slightly modified condition, for diverse purposes, and has acted in the living machinery of many ancient and distinct specific forms.

We may not be flattered by the metaphor of refurbished wheels and pulleys, but consider how well we work. Nature is, in biologist François Jacob's words, an excellent tinkerer, not a divine artificer. And who shall sit in judgment between these exemplary skills?

2 | Senseless Signs of History

WORDS PROVIDE CLUES about their history when etymology does *not* match current meaning. Thus, we suspect that emoluments were once fees paid to the local miller (from the Latin *molere,* to grind), while disasters must have been blamed upon evil stars.

Evolutionists have always viewed linguistic change as a fertile field for meaningful analogies. Charles Darwin, advocating an evolutionary interpretation for such vestigial structures as the human appendix and the embryonic teeth of whalebone whales, wrote: "Rudimentary organs may be compared with the letters in a word, still retained in the spelling, but become useless in the pronunciation, but which serve as a clue in seeking for its derivation." Both organisms and languages evolve.

This essay masquerades behind a list of curious facts, but it is really an abstract discourse on method—or, rather, on a particular method widely used but little appreciated by scientists. In the stereotyped image, scientists rely upon experiment and logic. A middle-aged man in a white coat (most stereotypes are sexist), either shyly reticent, but burning with an inner zeal for truth, or else ebullient and eccentric, pours two chemicals together and watches his answer emerge in a flask. Hypotheses, predictions, experiments, and answers: the scientific method.

But many sciences do not and cannot work this way. As a paleontologist and evolutionary biologist, my trade is the reconstruction of history. History is unique and complex. It

27

cannot be reproduced in a flask. Scientists who study history, particularly an ancient and unobservable history not recorded in human or geological chronicles, must use inferential rather than experimental methods. They must examine *modern results* of historical processes and try to reconstruct the path leading from ancestral to contemporary words, organisms, or landforms. Once the path is traced, we may be able to specify the causes that led history to follow this, rather than another, route. But how can we infer pathways from modern results? In particular, how can we be sure that there was a pathway at all? How do we know that a modern result is the product of alteration through history and not an immutable part of a changeless universe?

This is the problem that Darwin faced, for his creationist opponents did view each species as unaltered from its initial formation. How did Darwin prove that modern species are the products of history? We might suppose that he looked toward the most impressive results of evolution, the complex and perfected adaptations of organisms to their environments: the butterfly passing for a dead leaf, the bittern for a branch, the superb engineering of a gull aloft or a tuna in the sea.

Paradoxically, he did just the opposite. He searched for oddities and imperfections. The gull may be a marvel of design; if one believes in evolution beforehand, then the engineering of its wing reflects the shaping power of natural selection. But you cannot demonstrate evolution with perfection because perfection need not have a history. After all, perfection of organic design had long been the favorite argument of creationists, who saw in consummate engineering the direct hand of a divine architect. A bird's wing, as an aerodynamic marvel, might have been created exactly as we find it today.

But, Darwin reasoned, if organisms have a history, then ancestral stages should leave *remnants* behind. Remnants of the past that don't make sense in present terms—the useless, the odd, the peculiar, the incongruous—are the signs of history. They supply proof that the world was not made in its present form. When history perfects, it covers its own tracks.

Why should a general word for monetary compensation refer literally to a profession now virtually extinct, unless it once had some relation with grinding and grain? And why should the fetus of a whale make teeth in its mother's womb only to resorb them later and live a life sifting krill on a whalebone filter, unless its ancestors had functional teeth and these teeth survive as a remnant during a stage when they do no harm?

No evidence for evolution pleased Darwin more than the presence in nearly all organisms of rudimentary or vestigial structures, "parts in this strange condition, bearing the stamp of unutility," as he put it. "On my view of descent with modification, the origin of rudimentary organs is simple," he continued. They are bits of useless anatomy, preserved as remnants of functional parts in ancestors.

The general point extends both beyond rudimentary structures and beyond biology to any historical science. Oddities in current terms are the signs of history. The first essay of this trilogy raised the same subject in a different context. The panda's "thumb" demonstrates evolution *because* it is clumsy and built from an odd part, the radial sesamoid bone of the wrist. The true thumb had been so shaped in its ancestral role as the running and clawing digit of a carnivore that it could not be modified into an opposable grasper for bamboo in a vegetarian descendant.

In a nonbiological musing, I found myself wondering last week why *veteran* and *veterinarian,* two words with such different meanings, should have a similar root in the Latin *vetus,* or "old." Again, an oddity suggesting a genealogical approach for its solution. Veteran presented no problem, for its root and its modern meaning coincide—no indication of history. Veterinarian turned out to be interesting. City dwellers tend to view vets as servants of their pampered dogs and cats. I forgot that the original veterinarians treated farm and herd animals (as do most modern vets, I guess—pardon my New Yorker's parochialism). The link to *vetus* is through "beast of burden"—old, in the sense of "able to take a load." Cattle, in Latin, are *veterinae.*

This general principle of historical science should apply to the earth as well. The theory of plate tectonics has led us to reconstruct the history of our planet's surface. During the past 200 million years, our modern continents have fragmented and dispersed from a single supercontinent, Pangaea, that coalesced from earlier continents more than 225 million years ago. If modern oddities are the signs of history, we should ask whether any peculiar things that animals do today might be rendered more sensible as adaptations to previous continental positions. Among the greatest puzzles and wonders of natural history are the long and circuitous routes of migration followed by many animals. Some lengthy movements make sense as direct paths to favorable climates from season to season; they are no more peculiar than the annual winter migration to Florida of large mammals inside metallic birds. But other animals migrate thousands of miles—from feeding to breeding grounds—with astounding precision when other appropriate spots seem close at hand. Could any of these peculiar routes be rendered shorter and more sensible on a map of ancient continental positions? Archie Carr, world's expert on the migration of green turtles, has made such a proposal.

A population of the green turtle, *Chelonia mydas,* nests and breeds on the small and isolated central Atlantic island of Ascension. London soup chefs and victualing ships of Her Majesty's Navy found and exploited these turtles long ago. But they did not suspect, as Carr discovered by tagging animals at Ascension and recovering them later at their feeding grounds, that *Chelonia* travels 2,000 miles from the coast of Brazil to breed on this "pinpoint of land hundreds of miles from other shores," this "barely exposed spire in mid-ocean."

Turtles feed and breed on separate grounds for good reasons. They feed on sea grasses in protected, shallow-water pastures, but breed on exposed shores where sandy beaches develop—preferably, on islands where predators are rare. But why travel 2,000 miles to the middle of an ocean when other, apparently appropriate breeding grounds are so much nearer? (Another large population of the same species breeds on the Caribbean coast of Costa Rica.) As Carr writes: "The difficulties facing such a voyage would seem insurmountable if it were not so clear that the turtles are somehow surmounting them."

Perhaps, Carr reasoned, this odyssey is a peculiar extension of something much more sensible, a journey to an island in the middle of the Atlantic, when the Atlantic was little more than a puddle between two continents recently separated. South America and Africa parted company some 80 million years ago, when ancestors of the genus *Chelonia* were already present in the area. Ascension is an island associated with the Mid-Atlantic Ridge, a linear belt where new sea floor wells up from the earth's interior. This up-welling material often piles itself high enough to form islands.

Iceland is the largest modern island formed by the Mid-Atlantic Ridge; Ascension is a smaller version of the same process. After islands form on one side of a ridge, they are pushed away by new material welling up and spreading out. Thus, islands tend to be older as we move farther and farther from a ridge. But they also tend to get smaller and finally to erode away into underwater seamounts, for their supply of new material dries up once they drift away from an active ridge. Unless preserved and built up by a shield of coral or other organisms, islands will eventually be eroded below sea level by waves. (They may also sink gradually from sight as they move downslope from an elevated ridge into the oceanic depths.)

Carr therefore proposed that the ancestors of Ascension green turtles swam a short distance from Brazil to a "proto-Ascension" on the late Cretaceous Mid-Atlantic Ridge. As this island moved out and sank, a new one formed at the ridge and the turtles ventured a bit farther. This process continued until, like the jogger who does a bit more each day and ends up a marathoner, turtles found themselves locked into a 2,000-mile journey. (This historical hypothesis does not deal with the other fascinating question of how the turtles can find this dot in a sea of blue. The hatchlings float to Brazil on the Equatorial Current, but how do they get back? Carr supposes that they begin their journey by celestial cues and finally home in by remembering the character [taste? smell?] of Ascension water when they detect the island's wake.)

Carr's hypothesis is an excellent example of using the peculiar to reconstruct history. I wish I could believe it. I am not troubled by the empirical difficulties, for these do not render the theory implausible. Can we be confident, for example, that a new island always arose in time to replace an old one—for the absence of an island for even one generation would disrupt the system. And would the new islands always arise sufficiently "on course" to be found? Ascension itself is less than seven million years old.

I am more bothered by a theoretical difficulty. If the entire species *Chelonia mydas* migrated to Ascension or, even better, if a group of related species made the journey, I would have no objection, for behavior can be as ancient and as heritable as form. But *C. mydas* lives and breeds throughout the world. The Ascension turtles represent only one among many breeding populations. Although its ancient ancestors may have lived in the Atlantic puddle 200 million years ago, our record of the genus *Chelonia* does not extend back beyond fifteen million years, while the species *C. mydas* is probably a good deal younger. (The fossil record, for all its faults, indicates that few vertebrate species survive for as many as ten million years.) In Carr's scheme, the turtles that made the first trips to proto-Ascension were rather distant ancestors of *C. mydas* (in a different genus at least). Several events of speciation separate this Cretaceous ancestor from the modern green turtle. Now consider what must have happened if Carr is right. The ancestral species must have been divided into several breeding populations, only one of which went to proto-Ascension. This species then evolved to another and another through however many evolutionary steps separated it from *C. mydas*. At each step, the Ascension population kept its integrity, changing in lock step with other separate populations from species to species.

But evolution, so far as we know, doesn't work this way.

New species arise in small, isolated populations and spread out later. Separate subpopulations of a widely dispersed species do not evolve in parallel from one species to the next. If the subpopulations are separate breeding stocks, what is the chance that all would evolve in the same way and still be able to interbreed when they had changed enough to be called a new species? I assume that *C. mydas,* like most species, arose in a small area sometime within the last ten million years, when Africa and South America were not much closer together than they are today.

In 1965, before continental drift became fashionable, Carr proposed a different explanation that makes more sense to me because it derives the Ascension population after *C. mydas* evolved. He argued that ancestors of the Ascension population accidentally drifted on the Equatorial Current from west Africa to Ascension. (Carr points out that another turtle, the west African ridley, *Lepidochelys olivacea,* colonized the South American coast by this route.) The hatchlings then drifted to Brazil in the same east-to-west current. Of course, getting back to Ascension is the problem, but the mechanism of turtle migration is so mysterious that I see no barrier to supposing that turtles can be imprinted to remember the place of their birth without prior genetic information transmitted from previous generations.

I don't think that the validation of continental drift is the only factor that caused Carr to change his mind. He implies that he favors his new theory because it preserves some basic styles of explanation generally preferred by scientists (incorrectly, in my iconoclastic opinion). By Carr's new theory, the peculiar Ascension route evolved gradually, in a sensible and predictable fashion, step by step. In his former view, it is a sudden event, an accidental, unpredictable vagary of history. Evolutionists tend to be more comfortable with nonrandom, gradualistic theories. I think that this is a deep prejudice of Western philosophical traditions, not a reflection of nature's ways (see essays of section 5). I regard Carr's new theory as a daring hypothesis in support of a conventional philosophy. I suspect that it is wrong, but I applaud his ingenuity, his effort, and his method, for he follows the great historical principle of using the peculiar as a sign of change.

I am afraid that the turtles illustrate another aspect of historical science—this time a frustration, rather than a principle of explanation. Results rarely specify their causes unambiguously. If we have no direct evidence of fossils or human chronicles, if we are forced to infer a process only from its modern results, then we are usually stymied or reduced to speculation about probabilities. For many roads lead to almost any Rome.

This round goes to the turtles—and why not? While Portuguese sailors hugged the coast of Africa, *Chelonia mydas* swam straight for a dot in the ocean. While the world's best scientists struggled for centuries to invent the tools of navigation, *Chelonia* looked at the skies and proceeded on course.

3 | Double Trouble

NATURE MARKS Izaak Walton as a rank amateur more often than I had imagined. In 1654, the world's most famous fisherman before Ted Williams wrote of his favorite lure: "I have an artificial minnow . . . so curiously wrought, and so exactly dissembled that it would beguile any sharpsighted trout in a swift stream."

An essay in my previous book, *Ever Since Darwin,* told the tale of *Lampsilis,* a freshwater clam with a decoy "fish" mounted on its rear end. This remarkable lure has a streamlined "body," side flaps simulating fins and tail, and an eyespot for added effect; the flaps even undulate with a rhythmic motion that imitates swimming. This "fish," constructed from a brood pouch (the body) and the clam's outer skin (fin and tails), attracts the real item and permits a mother clam to shoot her larvae from the brood pouch toward an unsuspecting fish. Since the larvae of *Lampsilis* can only grow as parasites on a fish's gill, this decoy is a useful device indeed.

I was astounded recently to learn that *Lampsilis* is not alone. Ichthyologists Ted Pietsch and David Grobecker recovered a single specimen of an amazing Philippine anglerfish, not as a reward for intrepid adventures in the wilds, but from that source of so much scientific novelty—the local aquarium retailer. (Recognition, rather than *machismo,* is often the basis of exotic discovery.) Anglerfish lure their dinner, rather than a free ride for their larvae. They carry a highly modified dorsal fin spine affixed to the tips of their snouts. At the end of this spine, they mount an appropriate lure. Some deep-sea species, living in a dark world untouched by light from the surface, fish with their own source of illumination: they gather phosphorescent bacteria in their lures. Shallow-water species tend to have colorful, bumpy bodies, and look remarkably like rocks encrusted with sponges and algae. They rest inert on the bottom and wave or wiggle their conspicuous lures near their mouths. "Baits" differ among species, but most resemble—often imperfectly—a variety of invertebrates, including worms and crustaceans.

Anglerfish   DAVID B. GROBECKER

Pietsch and Grobecker's anglerfish, however, has evolved a fish lure every bit as impressive as the decoy mounted on *Lampsilis*'s rear—a first for anglerfish. (Their report bears as its appropriate title "The Compleat Angler" and cites as an epigraph the passage from Walton quoted above.) This exquisite fake also sports eyelike spots of pigment in the right place. In addition, it bears compressed filaments representing pectoral and pelvic fins along the bottom of the body, extensions from the back resembling dorsal and anal fins, and even an expanded rear projection looking for all the world like a tail. Pietsch and Grobecker conclude: "The bait is nearly an exact replica of a small fish that could easily belong to any of a number of percoid families common to the Philippine region." The angler even ripples its bait through the water, "simulating the lateral undulations of a swimming fish."

These nearly identical artifices of fish and clam might seem, at first glance, to seal the case for Darwinian evolution. If natural selection can do this twice, surely it can do anything. Yet—continuing the theme of the last two essays and bringing this trilogy to a close—perfection works as well for the creationist as the evolutionist. Did not the psalmist proclaim: "The heavens declare the glory of God; and the firmament showeth his handiwork." The last two essays argued that imperfection carries the day for evolution. This one discusses the Darwinian response to perfection.

The only thing more difficult to explain than perfection is repeated perfection by very different animals. A fish on a clam's rear end *and* another in front of an anglerfish's nose—the first evolved from a brood pouch and outer skin, the second from a fin spine—more than doubles the trouble. I have no difficulty defending the origin of both "fishes" by evolution. A plausible series of intermediate stages can be identified for *Lampsilis*. The fact that anglerfish press a fin spine into service as a lure reflects the jury-rigged, parts-available principle that made the panda's thumb and the orchid's labellum speak so strongly for evolution (see the first essay of this trilogy). But Darwinians must do more than demonstrate evolution; they must defend the basic mechanism of random variation and natural selection as the primary cause of evolutionary change.

Anti-Darwinian evolutionists have always favored the *re-*

peated development of very similar adaptations in different lineages as an argument against the central Darwinian notion that evolution is unplanned and undirected. If different organisms converge upon the same solutions again and again, does this not indicate that certain directions of change are preset, not established by natural selection working on random variation? Should we not look upon the repeated form itself as a cause of the numerous evolutionary events leading toward it?

Throughout his last half-dozen books, for example, Arthur Koestler has been conducting a campaign against his own misunderstanding of Darwinism. He hopes to find some ordering force, constraining evolution to certain directions and overriding the influence of natural selection. Repeated evolution of excellent design in separate lineages is his bulwark. Again and again, he cites the "nearly identical skulls" of wolves and the "Tasmanian wolf." (This marsupial carnivore looks like a wolf but is, by genealogy, more closely related to wombats, kangaroos, and koalas.) In *Janus,* his latest book, Koestler writes: "Even the evolution of a single species of wolf by random mutation plus selection presents, as we have seen, insurmountable difficulties. To duplicate this process independently on island and mainland would mean squaring a miracle."

The Darwinian response involves both a denial and an explanation. First, the denial: it is emphatically not true that highly convergent forms are effectively identical. Louis Dollo, the great Belgian paleontologist who died in 1931, established a much misunderstood principle—"the irreversibility of evolution" (also known as Dollo's law). Some ill-informed scientists think that Dollo advocated a mysterious directing force, driving evolution forward, never permitting a backward peek. And they rank him among the non-Darwinians who feel that natural selection cannot be the cause of nature's order.

In fact, Dollo was a Darwinian interested in the subject of convergent evolution—the repeated development of similar adaptations in different lineages. Elementary probability theory, he argued, virtually guarantees that convergence can never yield anything close to perfect resemblance. Organisms cannot erase their past. Two lineages may develop remarkable, superficial similarities as adaptations to a common mode of life. But organisms contain so many complex and independent parts that the chance of all evolving twice toward exactly the same result is effectively nil. Evolution is irreversible; signs of ancestry are always preserved; convergence, however impressive, is always superficial.

Consider my candidate for the most astounding convergence of all: the ichthyosaur. This sea-going reptile with terrestrial ancestors converged so strongly on fishes that it actually evolved a dorsal fin and tail in just the right place and with just the right hydrological design. These structures are all the more remarkable because they evolved from nothing—the ancestral terrestrial reptile had no hump on its back or blade on its tail to serve as a precursor. Nonetheless, the ichthyosaur is no fish, either in general design or in intricate detail. (In ichthyosaurs, for example, the vertebral column runs through the lower tail blade; in fish with tail vertebrae, the column runs into the upper blade.) The ichthyosaur remains a reptile, from its lungs and surface breathing to its flippers made of modified leg bones, not fin rays.

Ichthyosaur
COURTESY OF THE AMERICAN MUSEUM OF NATURAL HISTORY

Koestler's carnivores tell the same tale. Both placental wolf and marsupial "wolf" are well designed to hunt, but no expert would ever mistake their skulls. The numerous, small marks of marsupiality are not obliterated by convergence in outward form and function.

Second, the explanation: Darwinism is not the theory of capricious change that Koestler imagines. Random variation may be the raw material of change, but natural selection builds good design by rejecting most variants while accepting and accumulating the few that improve adaptation to local environments.

The basic reason for strong convergence, prosaic though it may seem, is simply that some ways of making a living impose exacting criteria of form and function upon any organism playing the role. Mammalian carnivores must run and stab; they do not need grinding molar teeth since they tear and swallow their food. Both placental and marsupial wolves are built for sustained running, have long, sharp, pointed canine teeth and reduced molars. Terrestrial vertebrates propel themselves with their limbs and may use their tails for balance. Swimming fish balance with their fins and propel from the rear with their tails. Ichthyosaurs, living like fish, evolved a broad propulsive tail (as whales did later —although the horizontal flukes of a whale's tail beat up and down, while the vertical flukes of fish and ichthyosaurs beat from side to side).

No one has treated this biological theme of repeated, exquisite design more eloquently than D'Arcy Wentworth Thompson in his 1942 treatise, *On Growth and Form,* still in print and still as relevant as ever. Sir Peter Medawar, a man who eschews hype and exaggeration, describes it as "beyond comparison the finest work of literature in all the annals of science that have been recorded in the English tongue." Thompson, zoologist, mathematician, classical scholar, and prose stylist, won accolades as an old man but spent his entire professional life in a small Scottish university because his views were too unorthodox to win prestigious London and Oxbridge jobs.

Thompson was more a brilliant reactionary than a visionary. He took Pythagoras seriously and worked as a Greek geometrician. He took special delight in finding the abstract forms of an idealized world embodied again and again in the products of nature. Why do repeated hexagons appear in the cells of a honeycomb and in the interlocking plates of some turtle shells? Why do the spirals in a pine cone and a sunflower (and often of leaves on a stem) follow the Fibonacci series? (A system of spirals radiating from a common point can be viewed either as a set of left- or right-handed spirals. Left and right spirals are not equal in number, but represent two consecutive figures of the Fibonacci series. The Fibonacci series is constructed by adding the previous two numbers to form the next: 1, 1, 2, 3, 5, 8, 13, 21, etc. The pine cone may, for example, have 13 left spirals and 21 right spirals.) Why do so many snail shells, ram's horns, and even the path of a moth to light follow a curve called the logarithmic spiral?

Thompson's answer was the same in each case: these abstract forms are optimal solutions for common problems. They are evolved repeatedly in disparate groups because they are the best, often the only, path to adaptation. Triangles, parallelograms, and hexagons are the only plane figures that fill space completely without leaving holes. Hexagons are often favored because they approximate a circle and maximize area within relative to the supporting walls (minimum construction for greatest storage of honey, for example). The Fibonacci pattern emerges automatically in any system of radiating spirals built by adding new elements at the apex, one at a time in the largest space available. The logarithmic spiral is the only curve that does not change its shape as it grows in size. I can identify the abstract Thompsonian forms as optimal adaptations, but to the larger metaphysical issue of why "good" form often exhibits such simple, numerical regularity, I plead only ignorance and wonder.

So far, I have only spoken to half the issue embodied in the problem of repeated perfection. I have discoursed on the "why." I have argued that convergence never renders two complex organisms completely identical (a circumstance that would strain Darwinian processes beyond their reasonable power) and I have tried to explain close repeats as optimal adaptations to common problems with few solutions.

But what about the "how?" We may know what the fish

of *Lampsilis* and the lure of the anglerfish are for, but how did they arise? This problem becomes particularly acute when the final adaptation is complex and peculiar but built from familiar parts of different ancestral function. If the angler's fishlike lure required 500 entirely separate modifications to attain its exquisite mimicry, then how did the process begin? And why did it continue, unless some non-Darwinian force, cognizant of the final goal, drove it on? Of what possible benefit is step one alone? Is a five-hundredth of a fake enough to inspire the curiosity of any real item?

D'Arcy Thompson's answer to this problem was overextended but characteristically prophetic. He argued that organisms are shaped directly by physical forces acting upon them: optima of form are nothing more than the natural states of plastic matter in the presence of appropriate physical forces. Organisms jump suddenly from one optimum to another when the regime of physical forces alters. We now know that physical forces are too weak, in most cases, to build form directly—and we look to natural selection instead. But we are derailed if selection can only act in a patient and piecemeal way—step by sequential step to build any complex adaptation.

I believe that a solution lies in the essence of Thompson's insight, shorn of his unsubstantiated claim that physical forces shape organisms directly. Complex forms are often built by a much simpler (often a very simple) system of generating factors. Parts are connected in intricate ways through growth, and alteration of one may resound through the entire organism and change it in a variety of unsuspected ways. David Raup, of Chicago's Field Museum of Natural History, adapted D'Arcy Thompson's insight to a modern computer, and showed that the basic forms of coiled shells—from nautiloid to clam to snail—can all be generated by varying only three simple gradients of growth. Using Raup's program, I can change a garden-variety snail into a common clam by modifying just two of the three gradients. And, believe it or not, a peculiar genus of modern snails does carry a bivalved shell so like a conventional

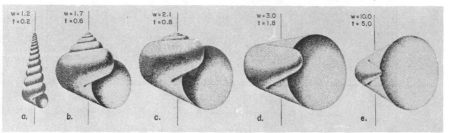

In these computer-drawn figures (they are not real snails, despite the similarities), a form (right) looking much like certain clams can be converted into a "snail" (left figures) simply by decreasing the rate at which the generating ellipse increases as the "shell" grows and by increasing the rate of translation of this ellipse down the axis of coiling. All these figures are drawn by specifying just four parameters.

PHOTO COURTESY OF D. M. RAUP

clam's that I gasped when I saw a snail's head poking out between the valves in a striking close-up movie.

This closes my trilogy on the issue of perfection and imperfection as signs of evolution. But the entire set is really an extended disquisition on the panda's "thumb," a single, concrete object that spawned all three essays, despite their subsequent wanderings and musings. The thumb, built of a wrist bone, imperfect as a sign of history, constructed from parts available. Dwight Davis faced the dilemma of potential impotence for natural selection if it must work step by countless step to make a panda from a bear. And he advocated D'Arcy Thompson's solution of reduction to a simple system of generating factors. He showed how the complex apparatus of the thumb, with all its muscles and nerves, may arise as a set of automatic consequences following a simple enlargement of the radial sesamoid bone. He then argued that the complex changes in form and function of the skull—the transition from omnivory to nearly exclusive munching on bamboo—could be expressed as consequences of one or two underlying modifications. He concluded that "very few genetic mechanisms—perhaps no more than half a dozen—were involved in the primary adaptive shift from *Ursus* [bear] to

Ailuropoda [panda]. The action of most of these mechanisms can be identified with reasonable certainty."

And thus we may pass from the underlying genetic continuity of change—an essential Darwinian postulate—to a potentially episodic alteration in its manifest result—a sequence of complex, adult organisms. Within complex systems, smoothness of input can translate into episodic change in output. Here we encounter a central paradox of our being and of our quest to understand what made us. Without this level of complexity in construction, we could not have evolved the brains to ask such questions. With this complexity, we cannot hope to find solutions in the simple answers that our brains like to devise.

2 | Darwiniana

4 | Natural Selection and the Human Brain: Darwin *vs.* Wallace

IN THE SOUTH transept of Chartres cathedral, the most stunning of all medieval windows depicts the four evangelists as dwarfs sitting upon the shoulders of four Old Testament prophets—Isaiah, Jeremiah, Ezekiel, and Daniel. When I first saw this window 'as a cocky undergraduate in 1961, I immediately thought of Newton's famous aphorism—"if I have seen farther, it is by standing on the shoulders of giants"—and imagined that I had made a major discovery in unearthing his lack of originality. Years later, and properly humbled for many reasons, I learned that Robert K. Merton, the celebrated sociologist of science from Columbia University, had devoted an entire book to pre-Newtonian usages of the metaphor. It is titled, appropriately, *On The Shoulders of Giants.* In fact, Merton traces the bon mot back to Bernard of Chartres in 1126 and cites several scholars who believe that the windows of the great south transept, installed after Bernard's death, represent an explicit attempt to capture his metaphor in glass.

Although Merton wisely constructs his book as a delightful romp through the intellectual life of medieval and Renaissance Europe, he does have a serious point to make. For Merton has devoted much of his work to the study of multiple discoveries in science. He has shown that almost all major ideas arise more than once, independently and often virtually at the same time—and thus, that great scientists are embedded in their cultures, not divorced from them. Most

47

great ideas are "in the air," and several scholars simultaneously wave their nets.

One of the most famous of Merton's "multiples" resides in my own field of evolutionary biology. Darwin, to recount the famous tale briefly, developed his theory of natural selection in 1838 and set it forth in two unpublished sketches of 1842 and 1844. Then, never doubting his theory for a moment, but afraid to expose its revolutionary implications, he proceeded to stew, dither, wait, ponder, and collect data for another fifteen years. Finally, at the virtual insistence of his closest friends, he began to work over his notes, intending to publish a massive tome that would have been four times as long as the *Origin of Species*. But, in 1858, Darwin received a letter and manuscript from a young naturalist, Alfred Russel Wallace, who had independently constructed the theory of natural selection while lying ill with malaria on an island in the Malay Archipelago. Darwin was stunned by the detailed similarity. Wallace even claimed inspiration from the same nonbiological source—Malthus' *Essay on Population.* Darwin, in great anxiety, made the expected gesture of magnanimity, but devoutly hoped that some way might be found to preserve his legitimate priority. He wrote to Lyell: "I would far rather burn my whole book, than that he or any other man should think that I have behaved in a paltry spirit." But he added a suggestion: "If I could honorably publish, I would state that I was induced now to publish a sketch . . . from Wallace having sent me an outline of my general conclusions." Lyell and Hooker took the bait and came to Darwin's rescue. While Darwin stayed home, mourning the death of his young child from scarlet fever, they presented a joint paper to the Linnaean Society containing an excerpt from Darwin's 1844 essay together with Wallace's manuscript. A year later, Darwin published his feverishly compiled "abstract" of the longer work—the *Origin of Species.* Wallace had been eclipsed.

Wallace has come down through history as Darwin's shadow. In public and private, Darwin was infallibly decent and generous to his younger colleague. He wrote to Wallace in 1870: "I hope it is a satisfaction to you to reflect—

and very few things in my life have been more satisfactory to me—that we have never felt 'any jealousy towards each other, though in one sense rivals." Wallace, in return, was consistently deferential. In 1864, he wrote to Darwin: "As to the theory of Natural Selection itself, I shall always maintain it to be actually yours and yours only. You had worked it out in details I had never thought of, years before I had a ray of light on the subject, and my paper would never have convinced anybody or been noticed as more than an ingenious speculation, whereas your book has revolutionized the study of Natural History, and carried away captive the best men of the present age."

This genuine affection and mutual support masked a serious disagreement on what may be the fundamental question in evolutionary theory—both then and today. How exclusive is natural selection as an agent of evolutionary change? Must all features of organisms be viewed as adaptations? Yet Wallace's role as Darwin's subordinate alter ego is so firmly fixed in popular accounts that few students of evolution are even aware that they ever differed on theoretical questions. Moreover, in the one specific area where their public disagreement is a matter of record—the origin of human intellect—many writers have told the story backwards because they failed to locate this debate in the context of a more general disagreement on the power of natural selection.

All subtle ideas can be trivialized, even vulgarized, by portrayal in uncompromising and absolute terms. Marx felt compelled to deny that he was a marxist, while Einstein contended with the serious misstatement that he meant to say "all is relative." Darwin lived to see his name appropriated for an extreme view that he never held—for "Darwinism" has often been defined, both in his day and in our own, as the belief that virtually all evolutionary change is the product of natural selection. In fact Darwin often complained, with uncharacteristic bitterness, about this misappropriation of his name. He wrote in the last edition of the *Origin* (1872): "As my conclusions have lately been much misrepresented, and it has been stated that I attribute the modification of species exclusively to natural selection, I may be permitted to remark that in the first edition of this work, and subsequently, I placed in a most conspicuous position—namely, at the close of the Introduction—the following words: 'I am convinced that natural selection has been the main but not the exclusive means of modification.' This has been of no avail. Great is the power of steady misrepresentation."

However, England did house a small group of strict selectionists—"Darwinians" in the misappropriated sense—and Alfred Russel Wallace was their leader. These biologists did attribute all evolutionary change to natural selection. They viewed each bit of morphology, each function of an organ, each behavior as an adaptation, a product of selection leading to a "better" organism. They held a deep belief in nature's "rightness," in the exquisite fit of all creatures to their environments. In a curious sense, they almost reintroduced the creationist notion of natural harmony by substituting an omnipotent force of natural selection for a benevolent deity. Darwin, on the other hand, was a consistent pluralist gazing upon a messier universe. He saw much fit and harmony, for he believed that natural selection holds pride of place among evolutionary forces. But other processes work as well, and organisms display an array of features that are not adaptations and do not promote survival directly. Darwin emphasized two principles leading to nonadaptive change: (1) organisms are integrated systems and adaptive change in one part can lead to nonadaptive modifications of other features ("correlations of growth" in Darwin's phrase); (2) an organ built under the influence of selection for a specific role may be able, as a consequence of its structure, to perform many other, unselected functions as well.

Wallace stated the hard hyper-selectionist line—"pure Darwinism" in his terms—in an early article of 1867, calling it "a necessary deduction from the theory of natural selection."

None of the definite facts of organic selection, no special organ, no characteristic form or marking, no peculiarities of instinct or of habit, no relations between species or between groups of species, can exist but which must now be, or once have been, useful to the individuals or races which possess them.

Indeed, he argued later, any apparent nonutility must only reflect our faulty knowledge—a remarkable argument since it renders the principle of utility impervious to disproof a priori: "The assertion of 'inutility' in the case of any organ . . . is not, and can never be, the statement of a fact, but merely an expression of our ignorance of its purpose or origin."

All the public and private arguments that Darwin pursued with Wallace centered upon their differing assessments of the power of natural selection. They first crossed swords on the issue of "sexual selection," the subsidiary process that Darwin had proposed in order to explain the origin of features that appeared to be irrelevant or even harmful in the usual "struggle for existence" (expressed primarily in feeding and defense), but that could be interpreted as devices for increasing success in mating—elaborate antlers of deer, or tail feathers of the peacock, for example. Darwin proposed two kinds of sexual selection—competition among males for access to females, and choice exercised by females themselves. He attributed much of the racial differentiation among modern humans to sexual selection, based upon different criteria of beauty that arose among various peoples. (His book on human evolution—*The Descent of Man* (1871)—is really an amalgam of two works: a long treatise on sexual selection throughout the animal kingdom, and a shorter speculative account of human origins, relying heavily upon sexual selection.)

The notion of sexual selection is not really contrary to natural selection, for it is just another route to the Darwinian imperative of differential reproductive success. But Wallace disliked sexual selection for three reasons: it compromised the generality of that peculiarly nineteenth-century view of natural selection as a battle for life itself, not merely for copulation; it placed altogether too much emphasis upon the "volition" of animals, particularly in the concept of female choice; and, most importantly, it permitted the development of numerous, important features that are irrelevant, if not actually harmful, to the operation of an organism as a well-designed machine. Thus, Wallace viewed sexual selection as a threat to his vision of animals as works of exquisite craftsmanship, wrought by the purely material force of natural selection. (Indeed, Darwin had developed the concept largely to explain why so many differences among human groups are irrelevant to survival based upon good design, but merely reflect the variety of capricious criteria for beauty that arose for no adaptive reason among various races. Wallace did accept sexual selection based upon male combat as close enough to the metaphor of battle that controlled his concept of natural selection. But he rejected the notion of female choice, and greatly distressed Darwin with his speculative attempts to attribute all features arising from it to the adaptive action of natural selection.)

In 1870, as he prepared the *Descent of Man,* Darwin wrote to Wallace: "I grieve to differ from you, and it actually terrifies me and makes me constantly distrust myself. I fear we shall never quite understand each other." He struggled to understand Wallace's reluctance and even to accept his friend's faith in unalloyed natural selection: "You will be pleased to hear," he wrote to Wallace, "that I am undergoing severe distress about protection and sexual selection; this morning I oscillated with joy towards you; this evening I have swung back to [my] old position, out of which I fear I shall never get."

But the debate on sexual selection was merely a prelude to a much more serious and famous disagreement on that most emotional and contentious subject of all—human origins. In short, Wallace, the hyper-selectionist, the man who had twitted Darwin for his unwillingness to see the action of natural selection in every nuance of organic form, halted abruptly before the human brain. Our intellect and morality, Wallace argued, could not be the product of natural selection; therefore, since natural selection is evolution's only way, some higher power—God, to put it directly— must have intervened to construct this latest and greatest of organic innovations.

If Darwin had been distressed by his failure to impress Wallace with sexual selection, he was now positively aghast at Wallace's abrupt about-face at the finish line itself. He wrote to Wallace in 1869: "I hope you have not murdered too completely your own and my child." A month later, he remonstrated: "If you had not told me, I should have thought that [your remarks on Man] had been added by some one else. As you expected, I differ grievously from you, and I am very sorry for it." Wallace, sensitive to the rebuke, thereafter referred to his theory of human intellect as "my special heresy."

The conventional account of Wallace's apostasy at the brink of complete consistency cites a failure of courage to take the last step and admit man fully into the natural system—a step that Darwin took with commendable fortitude in two books, the *Descent of Man* (1871) and the *Expression of the Emotions* (1872). Thus, Wallace emerges from most historical accounts as a lesser man than Darwin for one (or more) of three reasons, all related to his position on the origins of human intellect: for simple cowardice; for inability to transcend the constraints of culture and traditional views of human uniqueness; and for inconsistency in advocating natural selection so strongly (in the debate on sexual selection), yet abandoning it at the most crucial moment of all.

I cannot analyze Wallace's psyche, and will not comment on his deeper motives for holding fast to the unbridgeable gap between human intellect and the behavior of mere animals. But I can assess the logic of his argument, and recognize that the traditional account of it is not only incorrect, but precisely backwards. Wallace did not abandon natural selection at the human threshold. Rather, it was his peculiarly rigid view of natural selection that led him, quite consistently, to reject it for the human mind. His position never varied—natural selection is the only cause of major evolutionary change. His two debates with Darwin—sexual selection and the origin of human intellect—represent the same argument, not an inconsistent Wallace championing selection in one case and running from it in the other. Wallace's error on human intellect arose from the inadequacy of his rigid selectionism, not from a failure to apply it. And his argument repays our study today, since its flaw persists as the weak link in many of the most "modern" evolutionary speculations of our current literature. For Wallace's rigid selectionism is much closer than Darwin's pluralism to the attitude embodied in our favored theory today, which, ironically in this context, goes by the name of "Neo-Darwinism."

Wallace advanced several arguments for the uniqueness of human intellect, but his central claim begins with an extremely uncommon position for his time, one that commands our highest praise in retrospect. Wallace was one of the few nonracists of the nineteenth century. He really believed that all human groups had innately equal capacities of intellect. Wallace defended his decidedly unconventional egalitarianism with two arguments, anatomical and cultural. He claimed, first of all, that the brains of "savages" are neither much smaller nor more poorly organized than our own: "In the brain of the lowest savages, and, as far as we know, of the prehistoric races, we have an organ . . . little inferior in size and complexity to that of the highest type." Moreover, since cultural conditioning can integrate the rudest savage into our most courtly life, the rudeness itself must arise from a failure to use existing capacities, not from their absence: "It is latent in the lower races, since under European training native military bands have been formed in many parts of the world, which have been able to perform creditably the best modern music."

Of course, in calling Wallace a nonracist, I do not mean to imply that he regarded the cultural practices of all peoples as equal in intrinsic worth. Wallace, like most of his contemporaries, was a cultural chauvinist who did not doubt the evident superiority of European ways. He may have been bullish on the capability of "savages," but he certainly had a low opinion of their life, as he mistook it: "Our law, our government, and our science continually require us to reason through a variety of complicated phenomena to the expected result. Even our games, such as chess, compel us to exercise all these faculties in a remarkable degree. Compare this with the savage languages, which contain no words for abstract conceptions; the utter want of foresight of the savage man beyond his simplest necessities; his inability to combine, or to compare, or to reason on any general subject that does not immediately appeal to his senses."

Hence, Wallace's dilemma: all "savages," from our actual ancestors to modern survivors, had brains fully capable of developing and appreciating all the finest subtleties of European art, morality and philosophy; yet they used, in the state of nature, only the tiniest fraction of that capacity in constructing their rudimentary cultures, with impoverished languages and repugnant morality.

But natural selection can only fashion a feature for immediate use. The brain is vastly overdesigned for what it accomplished in primitive society; thus, natural selection could not have built it:

> A brain one-half larger than that of the gorilla would . . . fully have sufficed for the limited mental development of the savage; and we must therefore admit that the large brain he actually possesses could never have been solely developed by any of those laws of evolution, whose essence is, that they lead to a degree of organization exactly proportionate to the wants of each species, never beyond those wants. . . . Natural selection could only have endowed savage man with a brain a few degrees superior to that of an ape, whereas he actually possesses one very little inferior to that of a philosopher.

Wallace did not confine this general argument to abstract intellect, but extended it to all aspects of European "refinement," to language and music in particular. Consider his views on "the wonderful power, range, flexibility, and sweetness of the musical sounds producible by the human larynx, especially in the female sex."

The habits of savages give no indication of how this faculty could have been developed by natural selection, because it is never required or used by them. The singing of savages is a more or less monotonous howling, and the females seldom sing at all. Savages certainly never choose their wives for fine voices, but for rude health, and strength, and physical beauty. Sexual selection could not therefore have developed this wonderful power, which only comes into play among civilized people. It seems as if the organ had been prepared in anticipation of the future progress in man, since it contains latest capacities which are useless to him in his earlier condition.

Finally, if our higher capacities arose before we used or needed them, then they cannot be the product of natural selection. And, if they originated in anticipation of a future need, then they must be the direct creation of a higher intelligence: "The inference I would draw from this class of phenomena is, that a superior intelligence has guided the development of man in a definite direction, and for a special purpose." Wallace had rejoined the camp of natural theology and Darwin remonstrated, failed to budge his partner, and finally lamented.

The fallacy of Wallace's argument is not a simple unwillingness to extend evolution to humans, but rather the hyper-selectionism that permeated all his evolutionary thought. For if hyper-selectionism is valid—if every part of every creature is fashioned for and only for its immediate use—then Wallace cannot be gainsaid. The earliest Cro-Magnon people, with brains bigger than our own, produced stunning paintings in their caves, but did not write symphonies or build computers. All that we have accomplished since then is the product of cultural evolution based on a brain of unvarying capacity. In Wallace's view, that brain could not be the product of natural selection, since it always possessed capacities so far in excess of its original function.

But hyper-selectionism is not valid. It is a caricature of Darwin's subtler view, and it both ignores and misunderstands the nature of organic form and function. Natural selection may build an organ "for" a specific function or group of functions. But this "purpose" need not fully specify the capacity of that organ. Objects designed for definite purposes can, as a result of their structural complexity, perform many other tasks as well. A factory may install a computer only to issue the monthly pay checks, but such a machine can also analyze the election returns or whip anyone's ass (or at least perpetually tie them) in tic-tack-toe. Our large brains may have originated "for" some set of necessary skills in gathering food, socializing, or whatever; but these skills do not exhaust the limits of what such a complex machine can do. Fortunately for us, those limits include, among other things, an ability to write, from shopping lists for all of us to grand opera for a few. And our larynx may have arisen "for" a limited range of articulated sound needed to coordinate social life. But its physical design permits us to do more with it, from singing in the shower for all to the occasional diva.

Hyper-selectionism has been with us for a long time in various guises; for it represents the late nineteenth century's scientific version of the myth of natural harmony—all is for the best in the best of all possible worlds (all structures well designed for a definite purpose in this case). It is, indeed, the vision of foolish Dr. Pangloss, so vividly satirized by Voltaire in *Candide*—the world is not necessarily good, but it is the best we could possibly have. As the good doctor said in a famous passage that predated Wallace by a century, but captures the essence of what is so deeply wrong with his argument: "Things cannot be other than they are. . . . Everything is made for the best purpose. Our noses were made to carry spectacles, so we have spectacles. Legs were clearly intended for breeches, and we wear them." Nor is Panglossianism dead today—not when so many books in the pop literature on human behavior state that we evolved our big brain "for" hunting and then trace all our current ills to limits of thought and emotion supposedly imposed by such a mode of life.

Ironically then, Wallace's hyper-selectionism led right back to the basic belief of the creationism that it meant to replace—a faith in the "rightness" of things, a definite place for each object in an integrated whole. As Wallace wrote, quite unfairly, of Darwin:

> He whose teachings were at first stigmatized as degrading or even atheistical, by devoting to the varied phenomena of living things the loving, patient, and reverent study of one who really had faith in the beauty and harmony and perfection of creation, was enabled to bring to light innumerable adaptations, and to prove that the most insignificant parts of the meanest living things had a use and a purpose.

I do not deny that nature has its harmonies. But structure also has its latent capacities. Built for one thing, it can do others—and in this flexibility lies both the messiness and the hope of our lives.

5 | Darwin's Middle Road

"WE BEGAN TO sail up the narrow strait lamenting," narrates Odysseus. "For on the one hand lay Scylla, with twelve feet all dangling down; and six necks exceeding long, and on each a hideous head, and therein three rows of teeth set thick and close, full of black death. And on the other mighty Charybdis sucked down the salt sea water. As often as she belched it forth, like a cauldron on a great fire she would seethe up through all her troubled deeps." Odysseus managed to swerve around Charybdis, but Scylla grabbed six of his finest men and devoured them in his sight—"the most pitiful thing mine eyes have seen of all my travail in searching out the paths of the sea."

False lures and dangers often come in pairs in our legends and metaphors—consider the frying pan and the fire, or the devil and the deep blue sea. Prescriptions for avoidance either emphasize a dogged steadiness—the straight and narrow of Christian evangelists—or an averaging between unpleasant alternatives—the golden mean of Aristotle. The idea of steering a course between undesirable extremes emerges as a central prescription for a sensible life.

The nature of scientific creativity is both a perennial topic of discussion and a prime candidate for seeking a golden mean. The two extreme positions have not been directly competing for allegiance of the unwary. They have, rather, replaced each other sequentially, with one now in the ascendency, the other eclipsed.

The first—inductivism—held that great scientists are primarily great observers and patient accumulators of information. For new and significant theory, the inductivists claimed, can only arise from a firm foundation of facts. In this architectural view, each fact is a brick in a structure built without blueprints. Any talk or thought about theory (the completed building) is fatuous and premature before the bricks are set. Inductivism once commanded great prestige within science, and even represented an "official" position of sorts, for it touted, however falsely, the utter honesty, complete objectivity, and almost automatic nature of scientific progress towards final and incontrovertible truth.

Yet, as its critics so rightly claimed, inductivism also depicted science as a heartless, almost inhuman discipline offering no legitimate place to quirkiness, intuition, and all the other subjective attributes adhering to our vernacular notion of genius. Great scientists, the critics claimed, are distinguished more by their powers of hunch and synthesis, than their skill in experiment or observation. The criticisms of inductivism are certainly valid and I welcome its dethroning during the past thirty years as a necessary prelude to better understanding. Yet, in attacking it so strongly, some critics have tried to substitute an alternative equally extreme and unproductive in its emphasis on the essential subjectivity of creative thought. In this "eureka" view, creativity is an ineffable something, accessible only to persons of genius. It arises like a bolt of lightning, unanticipated, unpredictable and unanalyzable—but the bolts strike only a few special people. We ordinary mortals must stand in awe and thanks. (The name refers, of course, to the legendary story of Archimedes running naked through the streets of Syracuse shouting eureka [I have discovered it] when water displaced by his bathing body washed the scales abruptly from his eyes and suggested a method for measuring volumes.)

I am equally disenchanted by both these opposing extremes. Inductivism reduces genius to dull, rote operations; eurekaism grants it an inaccessible status more in the domain of intrinsic mystery than in a realm where we might understand and learn from it. Might we not marry the good features of each view, and abandon both the elitism of eurekaism and the pedestrian qualities of inductivism. May we not acknowledge the personal and subjective character of creativity, but still comprehend it as a mode of thinking that emphasizes or exaggerates capacities sufficiently common to all of us that we may at least understand if not hope to imitate.

In the hagiography of science, a few men hold such high positions that all arguments must apply to them if they are to have any validity. Charles Darwin, as the principal saint of evolutionary biology, has therefore been presented both as an inductivist and as a primary example of eurekaism. I will attempt to show that these interpretations are equally inadequate, and that recent scholarship on Darwin's own odyssey towards the theory of natural selection supports an intermediate position.

So great was the prestige of inductivism in his own day, that Darwin himself fell under its sway and, as an old man, falsely depicted his youthful accomplishments in its light. In an autobiography, written as a lesson in morality for his children and not intended for publication, he penned some famous lines that misled historians for nearly a hundred years. Describing his path to the theory of natural selection, he claimed: "I worked on true Baconian principles, and without any theory collected facts on a wholesale scale."

The inductivist interpretation focuses on Darwin's five years aboard the *Beagle* and explains his transition from a student for the ministry to the nemesis of preachers as the result of his keen powers of observation applied to the whole world. Thus, the traditional story goes, Darwin's eyes opened wider and wider as he saw, in sequence, the bones of giant South American fossil mammals, the turtles and finches of the Galapagos, and the marsupial fauna of Australia. The truth of evolution and its mechanism of natural selection crept up gradually upon him as he sifted facts in a sieve of utter objectivity.

The inadequacies of this tale are best illustrated by the

falsity of its conventional premier example—the so-called Darwin's finches of the Galapagos. We now know that although these birds share a recent and common ancestry on the South American mainland, they have radiated into an impressive array of species on the outlying Galapagos. Few terrestrial species manage to cross the wide oceanic barrier between South America and the Galapagos. But the fortunate migrants often find a sparsely inhabited world devoid of the competitors that limit their opportunities on the crowded mainland. Hence, the finches evolved into roles normally occupied by other birds and developed their famous set of adaptations for feeding—seed crushing, insect eating, even grasping and manipulating a cactus needle to dislodge insects from plants. Isolation—both of the islands from the mainland and among the islands themselves—provided an opportunity for separation, independent adaptation, and speciation.

According to the traditional view, Darwin discovered these finches, correctly inferred their history, and wrote the famous lines in his notebook: "If there is the slightest foundation for these remarks the zoology of Archipelagoes will be worth examining; for such facts would undermine the stability of Species." But, as with so many heroic tales from Washington's cherry tree to the piety of Crusaders, hope rather than truth motivates the common reading. Darwin found the finches to be sure. But he didn't recognize them as variants of a common stock. In fact, he didn't even record the island of discovery for many of them—some of his labels just read "Galapagos Islands." So much for his immediate recognition of the role of isolation in the formation of new species. He reconstructed the evolutionary tale only after his return to London, when a British Museum ornithologist correctly identified all the birds as finches.

The famous quotation from his notebook refers to Galapagos tortoises and to the claim of native inhabitants that they can "at once pronounce from which Island any Tortoise may have been brought" from subtle differences in size and shape of body and scales. This is a statement of different, and much reduced, order from the traditional tale of finches. For the finches are true and separate species—a living example of evolution. The subtle differences among tortoises represent minor geographic variation within a species. It is a jump in reasoning, albeit a valid one as we now know, to argue that such small differences can be amplified to produce a new species. All creationists, after all, acknowledged geographic variation (consider human races), but argued that it could not proceed beyond the rigid limits of a created archetype.

I don't wish to downplay the pivotal influence of the *Beagle* voyage on Darwin's career. It gave him space, freedom and endless time to think in his favored mode of independent self-stimulation. (His ambivalence towards university life, and his middling performance there by conventional standards, reflected his unhappiness with a curriculum of received wisdom.) He writes from South America in 1834: "I have not one clear idea about cleavage, stratification, lines of upheaval. I have no books, which tell me much and what they do I cannot apply to what I see. In consequence I draw my own conclusions, and most gloriously ridiculous ones they are." The rocks and plants and animals that he saw did provoke him to the crucial attitude of doubt—midwife of all creativity. Sydney, Australia—1836. Darwin wonders why a rational God would create so many marsupials on Australia since nothing about its climate or geography suggests any superiority for pouches: "I had been lying on a sunny bank and was reflecting on the strange character of the animals of this country as compared to the rest of the World. An unbeliever in everything beyond his own reason might exclaim, 'Surely two distinct Creators must have been at work.' "

Nonetheless, Darwin returned to London without an evolutionary theory. He suspected the truth of evolution, but had no mechanism to explain it. Natural selection did not arise from any direct reading of the *Beagle*'s facts, but from two subsequent years of thought and struggle as reflected in a series of remarkable notebooks that have been unearthed and published during the past twenty years. In these notebooks, we see Darwin testing and abandoning a number of theories and pursuing a multitude of false leads —so much for his later claim about recording facts with an empty mind. He read philosophers, poets, and economists, always searching for meaning and insight—so much for the notion that natural selection arose inductively from the *Beagle*'s facts. Later, he labelled one notebook as "full of metaphysics on morals."

Yet if this tortuous path belies the Scylla of inductivism, it has engendered an equally simplistic myth—the Charybdis of eurekaism. In his maddeningly misleading autobiography, Darwin does record a eureka and suggests that natural selection struck him as a sudden, serendipitous flash after more than a year of groping frustration:

> In October 1838, that is, fifteen months after I had begun my systematic inquiry, I happened to read for amusement Malthus on Population, and being well prepared to appreciate the struggle for existence which everywhere goes on from long-continued observation of the habits of animals and plants, it at once struck me that under these circumstances favorable variations would tend to be preserved, and unfavorable ones to be destroyed. The result of this would be the formation of new species. Here, then, I had at last got a theory by which to work.

Yet, again, the notebooks belie Darwin's later recollections—in this case by their utter failure to record, at the time it happened, any special exultation over his Malthusian insight. He inscribes it as a fairly short and sober entry without a single exclamation point, though he habitually used two or three in moments of excitement. He did not drop everything and reinterpret a confusing world in its light. On the very next day, he wrote an even longer passage on the sexual curiosity of primates.

The theory of natural selection arose neither as a workmanlike induction from nature's facts, nor as a mysterious bolt from Darwin's subconscious, triggered by an accidental reading of Malthus. It emerged instead as the result of a conscious and productive search, proceeding in a ramifying but ordered manner, and utilizing both the facts of natural history and an astonishingly broad range of insights from disparate disciplines far from his own. Darwin trod the middle path between inductivism and eurekaism. His genius is neither pedestrian nor inaccessible.

Darwinian scholarship has exploded since the centennial of the *Origin* in 1959. The publication of Darwin's notebooks and the attention devoted by several scholars to the two crucial years between the *Beagle*'s docking and the demoted Malthusian insight has clinched the argument for a "middle path" theory of Darwin's creativity. Two particularly important works focus on the broadest and narrowest scales. Howard E. Gruber's masterful intellectual and psychological biography of this phase in Darwin's life, *Darwin on Man*, traces all the false leads and turning points in Darwin's search. Gruber shows that Darwin was continually proposing, testing, and abandoning hypotheses, and that he never simply collected facts in a blind way. He began with a fanciful theory involving the idea that new species arise with a prefixed life span, and worked his way gradually, if fitfully, towards an idea of extinction by competition in a world of struggle. He recorded no exultation upon reading Malthus, because the jigsaw puzzle was only missing a piece or two at the time.

Silvan S. Schweber has reconstructed, in detail as minute as the record will allow, Darwin's activities during the few weeks before Malthus (The Origin of the *Origin* Revisited, *Journal of the History of Biology,* 1977). He argues that the final pieces arose not from new facts in natural history, but from Darwin's intellectual wanderings in distant fields. In particular, he read a long review of social scientist and philosopher Auguste Comte's most famous work, the *Cours de philosophie positive.* He was particularly struck by Comte's insistence that a proper theory be predictive and at least potentially quantitative. He then turned to Dugald Stewart's *On the Life and Writing of Adam Smith,* and imbibed the basic belief of the Scottish economists that theories of overall social structure must begin by analyzing the unconstrained actions of individuals. (Natural selection is, above all, a theory about the struggle of individual organisms for success in reproduction.) Then, searching for quantification, he read a lengthy analysis of work by the most famous statistician of his time—the Belgian Adolphe Quetelet. In the review of Quetelet, he found, among other things, a forceful statement of Malthus's quantitative claim—that population would grow geometrically and food supplies only arithmetically, thus guaranteeing an intense struggle for existence. In fact, Darwin had read the Malthusian statement several times before; but only now was he prepared to appreciate its significance. Thus, he did not turn to Malthus by accident, and he already knew what it contained. His "amusement," we must assume, consisted only in a desire to read in its original formulation the familiar statement that had so impressed him in Quetelet's secondary account.

In reading Schweber's detailed account of the moments preceding Darwin's formulation of natural selection, I was particularly struck by the absence of deciding influence from his own field of biology. The immediate precipitators were a social scientist, an economist, and a statistician. If genius has any common denominator, I would propose breadth of interest and the ability to construct fruitful analogies between fields.

In fact, I believe that the theory of natural selection should be viewed as an extended analogy—whether conscious or unconscious on Darwin's part I do not know—to the laissez faire economics of Adam Smith. The essence of Smith's argument is a paradox of sorts: if you want an ordered economy providing maximal benefits to all, then let individuals compete and struggle for their own advantages. The result, after appropriate sorting and elimination of the inefficient, will be a stable and harmonious polity. Apparent order arises naturally from the struggle among individuals, not from predestined principles or higher control. Dugald Stewart epitomized Smith's system in the book Darwin read:

The most effective plan for advancing a people . . . is by allowing every man, as long as he observes the rules of justice, to pursue his own interest in his own way, and to bring both his industry and his capital into the freest competition with those of his fellow citizens. Every system of policy which endeavors . . . to draw towards a particular species of industry a greater share of the capital of the society than would naturally go to it . . . is, in reality, subversive of the great purpose which it means to promote.

As Schweber states: "The Scottish analysis of society contends that the combined effect of individual actions results in the institutions upon which society is based, and that such a society is a stable and evolving one and functions without a designing and directing mind."

We know that Darwin's uniqueness does not reside in his support for the idea of evolution—scores of scientists had preceded him in this. His special contribution rests upon his documentation and upon the novel character of his theory about how evolution operates. Previous evolutionists had proposed unworkable schemes based on internal perfecting tendencies and inherent directions. Darwin advocated a natural and testable theory based on immediate interaction among individuals (his opponents considered it heartlessly mechanistic). The theory of natural selection is a creative transfer to biology of Adam Smith's basic argument for a rational economy: the balance and order of nature does not arise from a higher, external (divine) control, or from the existence of laws operating directly upon the whole, but from struggle among individuals for their own benefits (in modern terms, for the transmission of their genes to future generations through differential success in reproduction).

Many people are distressed to hear such an argument. Does it not compromise the integrity of science if some of its primary conclusions originate by analogy from contemporary politics and culture rather than from data of the discipline itself? In a famous letter to Engels, Karl Marx identified the similarities between natural selection and the English social scene:

It is remarkable how Darwin recognizes among beasts and plants his English society with its division of labor, competition, opening up of new markets, 'invention,' and the Malthusian 'struggle for existence.' It is Hobbes' *bellum omnium contra omnes* (the war of all against all).

Yet Marx was a great admirer of Darwin—and in this apparent paradox lies resolution. For reasons involving all the themes I have emphasized here—that inductivism is inadequate, that creativity demands breadth, and that analogy is a profound source of insight—great thinkers cannot be divorced from their social background. But the source of an idea is one thing; its truth or fruitfulness is another. The psychology and utility of discovery are very different subjects indeed. Darwin may have cribbed the idea of natural selection from economics, but it may still be right. As the German socialist Karl Kautsky wrote in 1902: "The fact that an idea emanates from a particular class, or accords with their interests, of course proves nothing as to its truth or falsity." In this case, it is ironic that Adam Smith's system of laissez faire does not work in his own domain of economics, for it leads to oligopoly and revolution, rather than to order and harmony. Struggle among individuals does, however, seem to be the law of nature.

Many people use such arguments about social context to ascribe great insights primarily to the indefinable phenomenon of good luck. Thus, Darwin was lucky to be born rich, lucky to be on the *Beagle,* lucky to live amidst the ideas of his age, lucky to trip over Parson Malthus—essentially little more than a man in the right place at the right time. Yet, when we read of his personal struggle to understand, the breadth of his concerns and study, and the directedness of his search for a mechanism of evolution, we understand why Pasteur made his famous quip that fortune favors the prepared mind.

6 | Death Before Birth, or a Mite's *Nunc Dimittis*

CAN ANYTHING BE more demoralizing than parental incompetence before the most obvious and innocent of children's questions: why is the sky blue, the grass green? Why does the moon have phases? Our embarrassment is all the more acute because we thought we knew the answer perfectly well, but hadn't rehearsed it since we ourselves had received a bumbled response in similar circumstances a generation earlier. It is the things we think we know—because they are so elementary, or because they surround us—that often present the greatest difficulties when we are actually challenged to explain them.

One such question, with an obvious and incorrect answer, lies close to our biological lives: why, in humans (and in most species familiar to us), are males and females produced in approximately equal numbers? (Actually, males are more common than females at birth in humans, but differential mortality of males leads to a female majority in later life. Still, the departures from a one to one ratio are never great.) At first glance, the answer seems to be, as in Rabelais's motto, "plain as the nose on a man's face." After all, sexual reproduction requires a mate; equal numbers imply universal mating—the happy Darwinian status of maximal reproductive capacity. At second glance, it isn't so clear at all, and we are drawn in confusion to Shakespeare's recasting of the simile: "A jest unseen, inscrutable, invisible, as a nose on a man's face." If maximal reproductive capacity is the optimal state for a species, then why make equal numbers of males and females. Females, after all, set the limit upon numbers of offspring, since eggs are invariably so much larger and less abundant than sperm in species familiar to us—that is, each egg can make an offspring, each sperm cannot. A male can impregnate several females. If a male can mate with nine females and the population contains a hundred individuals, why not make ten males and ninety females? Reproductive capacity will certainly exceed that of a population composed of fifty males and fifty females. Populations made predominantly of females should, by their more rapid rates of reproduction, win any evolutionary race with populations that maintain equality in numbers between the sexes.

What appeared obvious is therefore rendered problematical and the question remains: why do most sexual species contain approximately equal numbers of males and females? The answer, according to most evolutionary biologists, lies in a recognition that Darwin's theory of natural selection speaks only of struggle among *individuals* for reproductive success. It contains no statement about the good of populations, species, or ecosystems. The argument for ninety females and ten males was framed in terms of advantages for populations as a whole—the usual, congenial, and dead wrong, way in which most people think of evolution. If evolution worked for the good of populations as a whole, then sexual species would contain relatively few males.

The observed equality of males and females, in the face of obvious advantages for female predominance if evolution worked upon groups, stands as one of our most elegant demonstrations that Darwin was right—natural selection works by the struggle of individuals to maximize their own reproductive success. The Darwinian argument was first framed by the great British mathematical biologist R.A. Fisher. Suppose, Fisher argued, that either sex began to predominate. Let us say, for example, that fewer males than females are born. Males now begin to leave more offspring than females since their opportunities for mating increase as they become rarer—that is, they impregnate more than one female on average. Thus, if any genetic factors influence the relative proportion of males born to a parent (and such factors do exist), then parents with a genetic inclination to produce males will gain a Darwinian advantage—they will produce more than an average number of grandchildren thanks to the superior reproductive success of their predominantly male offspring. Thus, genes that favor the production of males will spread and male births will rise in frequency. But, this advantage for males fades out as male births increase and it disappears entirely when males equal females in number. Since the same argument works in reverse to favor female births when females are rare, the sex ratio is driven by Darwinian processes to its equilibrium value of one to one.

But how would a biologist go about testing Fisher's theory of sex ratio? Ironically, the species that confirm its predictions are no great help beyond the initial observation. Once we frame the basic argument and determine that the species we know best have approximately equal numbers of males and females, what do we achieve by finding that the next thousand species are similarly ordered? Sure, it all fits, but we do not gain an equal amount of confidence each time we add a new species. Perhaps the one to one ratio exists for another reason?

To test Fisher's theory, we must look for exceptions. We must seek unusual situations in which the premises of Fisher's theory are not met—situations that lead to a specific prediction about how sex ratio should depart from one to one. If change of premises leads to a definite and successful prediction of altered outcome, then we have an independent test that strongly boosts our confidence. This method is embodied in the old proverb that "the exception proves the rule," although many people misunderstand the proverb because it embodies the less common meaning of "prove." Prove comes from the Latin *probare*—to test or to try. Its usual, modern meaning refers to final and convincing demonstration and the motto would seem to say that exceptions establish indubitable validity. But in another sense, closer to its root, "prove" (as in "proving ground" or printer's "proof") is more like its cognate "probe"—a test or an exploration. It is the exception that probes the rule by testing and exploring its consequences in altered situations.

Here nature's rich diversity comes to our aid. The stereotyped image of a birder assiduously adding the rufous-crowned, peg-legged, speckle-backed, cross-billed and cross-eyed towhee to his life list gives, in unwarranted ridicule, a perverted twist to the actual use made by naturalists of life's diversity. It is nature's richness that permits us to establish a science of natural history in the first place—for the variety virtually guarantees that appropriate exceptions can be found to probe any rule. Oddities and weirdnesses are tests of generality, not mere peculiarities to describe and greet with awe or a chuckle.

Fortunately, nature has been profligate in providing species and modes of life that violate the premises of Fisher's argument. In 1967, British biologist W.D. Hamilton (now at the University of Michigan) gathered the cases and arguments into an article entitled "Extraordinary sex ratios." I will discuss in this essay only the clearest and most important of these probing violations.

Nature rarely heeds our homilies in all cases. We are told, and with good reason, that mating of brothers and sisters should be avoided, lest too many unfavorable recessive genes gain an opportunity to express themselves in double dose. (Such genes tend to be rare, and chances are small that two unrelated parents will both carry them. But the probability that two sibs carry the same gene is usually fifty percent.) Nonetheless, some animals never heard the rule and indulge, perhaps exclusively, in sib mating.

Exclusive sib mating destroys the major premise of Fisher's argument for one to one sex ratios. If females are always fertilized by their brothers, then the same parents manufacture both partners of any mating. Fisher assumed that the males had different parents and that an undersupply of males awarded genetic advantages to those parents that could produce males preferentially. But if the same parents produce *both* the mothers and fathers of their grandchildren, then they have an equal genetic investment in each grandchild, no matter what percentage of males and females they produce among their children. In this case, the reason for an equal balance of males and females disappears and the previous argument for female predominance reasserts itself. If each pair of grandparents has a limited store of energy to invest in offspring, and if grandparents producing more offspring gain a Darwinian edge, then grandparents should make as many daughters as possible, and produce only enough sons to ensure that all their daughters will be fertilized. In fact, if their sons can muster sufficient sexual prowess, then parents should make just one son and use every bit of remaining energy to produce as many daughters as they can. As usual, bountiful nature comes to our aid with numerous exceptions to probe Fisher's rule: indeed, species with sib mating also tend to produce a minimal number of males.

Consider the curious life of a male mite in the genus *Adactylidium,* as described by E.A. Albadry and M.S.F. Tawfik in 1966. It emerges from its mother's body and promptly dies within a few hours, having done apparently nothing during its brief life. It attempts, while outside its mother, neither to feed nor to mate. We know about creatures with short adult lives—the mayfly's single day after a much lengthier larval life, for example. But the mayfly mates and insures the continuity of its kind during these few precious hours. The males of *Adactylidium* seem to do nothing at all but emerge and die.

To solve the mystery, we must study the entire life cycle and look inside the mother's body. The impregnated female of *Adactylidium* attaches to the egg of a thrips. That single egg provides the only source of nutrition for rearing all her offspring—for she will feed on nothing else before her death. This mite, so far as we know, engages exclusively in sib mating; thus, it should produce a minimal number of males. Moreover, since total reproductive energy is so strongly constrained by the nutritional resources of a single thrips' egg, progeny are strictly limited, and the more females the better. Indeed, *Adactylidium* matches our prediction by raising a brood of five to eight sisters accompanied by a single male who will serve as both brother and husband to them all. But producing a single male is chancy; if it dies, all sisters will remain virgins and their mother's evolutionary life is over.

If the mite takes a chance on producing but a single male, thus maximizing its potential brood of fertile females, two other adaptations might lessen the risk—providing both protection for the male and guaranteed proximity to his sisters. What better than to rear the brood entirely within a mother's body, feeding both larvae and adults within her, and even allowing copulation to occur inside her protective shell. Indeed, about forty-eight hours after she attaches to the thrips' egg, six to nine eggs hatch within the body of a female *Adactylidium*. The larvae feed on their mother's body, literally devouring her from inside. Two days later, the offspring reach maturity, and the single male copulates with all his sisters. By this time, the mother's tissues have disintegrated, and her body space is a mass of adult mites, their feces, and their discarded larval and nymphal skeletons. The offspring then cut holes through their mother's body wall and emerge. The females must now find a thrips' egg and begin the process again, but the males have already fulfilled their evolutionary role before "birth." They emerge, react however a mite does to the glories of the outside world, and promptly die.

But why not carry the process one stage further? Why should the male be born at all? After copulating with its sisters, its work is done. It is ready to chant the acarine version of Simeon's prayer, *Nunc dimittis*—Oh Lord, now lettest thou thy servant depart in peace. Indeed, since everything that is possible tends to occur at least once in the multifarious world of life, a close relative of *Adactylidium* does just this. *Acarophenax tribolii* also indulges exclusively in sib mating. Fifteen eggs, including but a single male, develop within the mother's body. The male emerges within his mother's shell, copulates with all his sisters and dies before birth. It may not sound like much of a life, but the male *Acarophenax* does as much for its evolutionary continuity as Abraham did in fathering children into his tenth decade.

Nature's oddities are more than good stories. They are material for probing the limits of interesting theories about life's history and meaning.

7 | Shades of Lamarck

THE WORLD, UNFORTUNATELY, rarely matches our hopes and consistently refuses to behave in a reasonable manner. The psalmist did not distinguish himself as an acute observer when he wrote: "I have been young, and now am old; yet have I not seen the righteous forsaken, nor his seed begging bread." The tyranny of what seems reasonable often impedes science. Who before Einstein would have believed that the mass and aging of an object could be affected by its velocity near the speed of light?

Since the living world is a product of evolution, why not suppose that it arose in the simplest and most direct way? Why not argue that organisms improve themselves by their own efforts and pass these advantages to their offspring in the form of altered genes—a process that has long been called, in technical parlance, the "inheritance of acquired characters." This idea appeals to common sense not only for its simplicity but perhaps even more for its happy implication that evolution travels an inherently progressive path, propelled by the hard work of organisms themselves. But, as we all must die, and as we do not inhabit the central body of a restricted universe, so the inheritance of acquired characters represents another human hope scorned by nature.

The inheritance of acquired characters usually goes by the shorter, although historically inaccurate, name of Lamarckism. Jean Baptiste Lamarck (1744–1829), the great French biologist and early evolutionist, believed in the inheritance of acquired characters, but it was not the centerpiece of his evolutionary theory and was certainly not original with him. Entire volumes have been written to trace its pre-Lamarckian pedigree (see Zirkle in bibliography). Lamarck argued that life is generated, continuously and spontaneously, in very simple form. It then climbs a ladder of complexity, motivated by a "force that tends incessantly to complicate organization." This force operates through the creative response of organisms to "felt needs." But life cannot be organized as a ladder because the upward path is often diverted by requirements of local environments; thus, giraffes acquire long necks and wading birds webbed feet, while moles and cave fishes lose their eyes. Inheritance of acquired characters does play an important part in this scheme, but not the central role. It is the mechanism for assuring that offspring benefit from their parents' efforts, but it does not propel evolution up the ladder.

In the late nineteenth century, many evolutionists sought an alternative to Darwin's theory of natural selection. They reread Lamarck, cast aside the guts of it (continuous generation and complicating forces), and elevated one aspect of the mechanics—inheritance of acquired characters—to a central focus it never had for Lamarck himself. Moreover, many of these self-styled "neo-Lamarckians" abandoned Lamarck's cardinal idea that evolution is an active, creative response by organisms to their felt needs. They preserved the inheritance of acquired characters but viewed the acquisitions as direct impositions by impressing environments upon passive organisms.

Although I will bow to contemporary usage and define Lamarckism as the notion that organisms evolve by acquiring adaptive characters and passing them on to offspring in the form of altered genetic information, I do wish to record how poorly this name honors a very fine scientist who died 150 years ago. Subtlety and richness are so often degraded in our world. Consider the poor marshmallow—the plant, that is. Its roots once made a fine candy; now its name adheres to that miserable ersatz of sugar, gelatine, and corn syrup.

Lamarckism, in this sense, remained a popular evolutionary theory well into our century. Darwin won the battle for evolution as a fact, but his theory for its mechanism—natural selection—did not win wide popularity until the traditions of natural history and Mendelian genetics were fused during the 1930s. Moreover, Darwin himself did not deny Lamarckism, although he regarded it as subsidiary to natural selection as an evolutionary mechanism. As late as 1938, for example, Harvard paleontologist Percy Raymond, writing (I suspect) at the very desk I am now using, said of his colleagues: "Probably most are Lamarckians of some shade; to the uncharitable critic it might seem that many out-Lamarck Lamarck." We must recognize the continuing influence of Lamarckism in order to understand much social theory of the recent past—ideas that become incomprehensible if forced into the Darwinian framework we often assume for them. When reformers spoke of the "taint" of poverty, alcoholism, or criminality, they usually thought in quite literal terms—the sins of the father would extend in hard heredity far beyond the third generation. When Lysenko began to advocate Lamarckian cures for the ills of Soviet agriculture during the 1930s, he had not resuscitated a bit of early nineteenth-century nonsense, but a still respectable, if fast fading, theory. Although this tidbit of historical information does not make his hegemony, or the methods he used to retain it, any less appalling, it does render the tale a bit less mysterious. Lysenko's debate with the Russian Mendelians was, at the outset, a legitimate scientific argument. Later, he held on through fraud, deception, manipulation, and murder—that is the tragedy.

Darwin's theory of natural selection is more complex than Lamarckism because it requires *two* separate processes, rather than a single force. Both theories are rooted in the concept of *adaptation*—the idea that organisms respond to changing environments by evolving a form, function, or behavior better suited to these new circumstances. Thus, in both theories, information from the environment must be transmitted to organisms. In Lamarckism, the transfer is direct. An organism perceives the environmental change, responds in the "right" way, and passes its appropriate reaction directly to its offspring.

Darwinism, on the other hand, is a two-step process, with different forces responsible for variation and direction. Darwinians speak of genetic variation, the first step, as "random." This is an unfortunate term because we do not mean random in the mathematical sense of equally likely in all directions. We simply mean that variation occurs with no preferred orientation in adaptive directions. If temperatures are dropping and a hairier coat would aid survival, genetic variation for greater hairiness does not begin to arise with increased frequency. Selection, the second step, works upon *unoriented* variation and changes a population by conferring greater reproductive success upon advantageous variants.

This is the essential difference between Lamarckism and Darwinism—for Lamarckism is, fundamentally, a theory of *directed* variation. If hairy coats are better, animals perceive the need, grow them, and pass the potential to offspring. Thus, variation is directed automatically toward adaptation and no second force like natural selection is needed. Many people do not understand the essential role of directed variation in Lamarckism. They often argue: isn't Lamarckism true because environment does influence heredity— chemical and radioactive mutagens increase the mutation rate and enlarge a population's pool of genetic variation. This mechanism increases the *amount* of variation but does not propel it in favored directions. Lamarckism holds that genetic variation originates *preferentially* in adaptive directions.

In the June 2, 1979, issue of *Lancet,* the leading British medical journal, for example, Dr. Paul E. M. Fine argues for what he calls "Lamarckism" by discussing a variety of biochemical paths for the inheritance of acquired, but *nondirected,* genetic variation. Viruses, essentially naked bits of DNA, may insert themselves into the genetic material of a bacterium and be passed along to offspring as part of the bacterial chromosome. An enzyme called "reverse tran-scriptase" can mediate the reading of information from cel-lular RNA "back" into nuclear DNA. The old idea of a single, irreversible flow of information from nuclear DNA through intermediary RNA to proteins that build the body does not hold in all cases—even though Watson himself had once sanctified it as the "central dogma" of molecular biol-ogy: DNA makes RNA makes protein. Since an inserted virus is an "acquired character" that can be passed along to offspring, Fine argues that Lamarckism holds in some cases. But Fine has misunderstood the Lamarckian requirement that characters be acquired for adaptive reasons—for La-marckism is a theory of directed variation. I have heard no evidence that any of these biochemical mechanisms leads to the preferential incorporation of *favorable* genetic information. Perhaps this is possible; perhaps it even hap-pens. If so, it would be an exciting new development, and truly Lamarckian.

But so far, we have found nothing in the workings of Mendelism or in the biochemistry of DNA to encourage a belief that environments or acquired adaptations can direct sex cells to mutate in specific directions. How could colder weather "tell" the chromosomes of a sperm or egg to pro-duce mutations for longer hair? How could Pete Rose trans-fer hustle to his gametes? It would be nice. It would be simple. It would propel evolution at much faster rates than Darwinian processes allow. But it is not nature's way, so far as we know.

Yet Lamarckism holds on, at least in popular imagination, and we must ask why? Arthur Koestler, in particular, has vigorously defended it in several books, including *The Case of the Midwife Toad,* a full-length attempt to vindicate the Austrian Lamarckian Paul Kammerer, who shot himself in 1926 (although largely for other reasons) after the discov-ery that his prize specimen had been doctored by an injec-tion of India ink. Koestler hopes to establish at least a "mini-Lamarckianism" to prick the orthodoxy of what he views as a heartless and mechanistic Darwinism. I think that Lamarckism retains its appeal for two major reasons.

First, a few phenomena of evolution do appear, superficially, to suggest Lamarckian explanations. Usually, the Lamarckian appeal arises from a misconception of Darwinism. It is often and truly stated, for example, that many genetic adaptations must be preceded by a shift in behavior without genetic foundation. In a classic and recent case, several species of tits learned to pry the tops off English milk bottles and drink the cream within. One can well imagine a subsequent evolution of bill shape to make the pilferage easier (although it will probably by nipped in the bud by paper cartons and a cessation of home delivery). Is this not Lamarckian in the sense that an active, nongenetic behavioral innovation sets the stage for reinforcing evolution? Doesn't Darwinism think of the environment as a refining fire and organisms as passive entities before it?

But Darwinism is not a mechanistic theory of environmental determinism. It does not view organisms as billiard balls, buffeted about by a shaping environment. These examples of behavioral innovation are thoroughly Darwinian —yet we praise Lamarck for emphasizing so strongly the active role of organisms as creators of their environment. The tits, in learning to invade milk bottles, established new selective pressures by altering their own environment. Bills of a different shape will now be favored by natural selection. The new environment does not provoke the tits to manufacture genetic variation directed toward the favored shape. This, and only this, would be Lamarckian.

Another phenomenon, passing under a variety of names, including the "Baldwin effect" and "genetic assimilation," seems more Lamarckian in character but fits just as well into a Darwinian perspective. To choose the classic illustration: Ostriches have callosities on their legs where they often kneel on hard ground; but the callosities develop within the egg, before they can be used. Does this not require a Lamarckian scenario: Ancestors with smooth legs began to kneel and acquire callosities as a nongenetic adaptation, just as we, depending on our profession, develop writer's calluses or thickened soles. These callosities were then inherited as genetic adaptations, forming well before their use.

The Darwinian explanation for "genetic assimilation"

can be illustrated with the midwife toad of Paul Kammerer, Koestler's favorite example—for Kammerer, ironically, performed a Darwinian experiment without recognizing it. This terrestrial toad descended from aquatic ancestors that grow roughened ridges on their forefeet—the nuptial pads. Males use these pads to hold the female while mating in their slippery environment. Midwife toads, copulating on *terra firma*, have lost the pads, although a few anomalous individuals do develop them in rudimentary form—indicating that the genetic capacity for producing pads has not been entirely lost.

Kammerer forced some midwife toads to breed in water and raised the next generation from the few eggs that had survived in this inhospitable environment. After repeating the process for several generations, Kammerer produced males with nuptial pads (even though one later received an injection of India ink, perhaps not by Kammerer, to heighten the effect). Kammerer concluded that he had demonstrated a Lamarckian effect: he had returned the midwife toad to its ancestral environment; it had reacquired an ancestral adaptation and passed it on in genetic form to offspring.

But Kammerer had really performed a Darwinian experiment: when he forced the toads to breed in water, only a few eggs survived. Kammerer had exerted a strong selection pressure for whatever genetic variation encourages success in water. And he reinforced this pressure over several generations. Kammerer's selection had gathered together the genes that favor aquatic life—a combination that no parent of the first generation possessed. Since nuptial pads are an aquatic adaptation, their expression may be tied to the set of genes that confer success in water—a set enhanced in frequency by Kammerer's Darwinian selection. Likewise, the ostrich may first develop callosities as a nongenetic adaptation. But the habit of kneeling, reinforced by these callosities, also sets up new selective pressures for the preservation of random genetic variation that may also code for these features. The callosities themselves are not mysteriously transferred by inheritance of acquired characters from adult to juvenile.

The second, and I suspect more important reason for Lamarckism's continuing appeal, lies in its offer of some comfort against a universe devoid of intrinsic meaning for our lives. It reinforces two of our deepest prejudices—our belief that effort should be rewarded and our hope for an inherently purposeful and progressive world. Its appeal for Koestler and other humanists lies more with this solace than in any technical argument about heredity. Darwinism offers no such consolation for it holds only that organisms adapt to local environments by struggling to increase their own reproductive success. Darwinism compels us to seek meaning elsewhere—and isn't this what art, music, literature, ethical theory, personal struggle, and Koestlerian humanism are all about? Why make demands of nature and try to restrict her ways when the answers (even if they are personal and not absolute) lie within ourselves?

Thus Lamarckism, so far as we can judge, is false in the domain it has always occupied—as a biological theory of genetic inheritance. Yet, by analogy only, it is the mode of "inheritance" for another and very different kind of "evolution"—human cultural evolution. *Homo sapiens* arose at least 50,000 years ago, and we have not a shred of evidence for any genetic improvement since then. I suspect that the average Cro-Magnon, properly trained, could have handled computers with the best of us (for what it's worth, they had slightly larger brains than we do). All that we have accomplished, for better or for worse, is a result of cultural evolution. And we have done it at rates unmatched by orders of magnitude in all the previous history of life. Geologists cannot measure a few hundred or a few thousand years in the context of our planet's history. Yet, in this millimicrosecond, we have transformed the surface of our planet through the influence of one unaltered biological invention—self-consciousness. From perhaps one hundred thousand people with axes to more than four billion with bombs, rocket ships, cities, televisions, and computers—and all without substantial genetic change.

Cultural evolution has progressed at rates that Darwinian processes cannot begin to approach. Darwinian evolution continues in *Homo sapiens,* but at rates so slow that it no longer has much impact on our history. This crux in the earth's history has been reached because Lamarckian processes have finally been unleashed upon it. Human cultural evolution, in strong opposition to our biological history, is Lamarckian in character. What we learn in one generation, we transmit directly by teaching and writing. Acquired characters are inherited in technology and culture. Lamarckian evolution is rapid and accumulative. It explains the cardinal difference between our past, purely biological mode of change, and our current, maddening acceleration toward something new and liberating—or toward the abyss.

8 | Caring Groups and Selfish Genes

THE WORLD OF objects can be ordered into a hierarchy of ascending levels, box within box. From atoms to molecules made of atoms, to crystals made of molecules, to minerals, rocks, the earth, the solar system, the galaxy made of stars, and the universe of galaxies. Different forces work at different levels. Rocks fall by gravity, but at the atomic and molecular level, gravity is so weak that standard calculations ignore it.

Life, too, operates at many levels, and each has its role in the evolutionary process. Consider three major levels: genes, organisms, and species. Genes are blueprints for organisms; organisms are the building blocks of species. Evolution requires variation, for natural selection cannot operate without a large set of choices. Mutation is the ultimate source of variation, and genes are the unit of variation. Individual organisms are the units of selection. But individuals do not evolve—they can only grow, reproduce, and die. Evolutionary change occurs in groups of interacting organisms; species are the unit of evolution. In short, as philosopher David Hull writes, genes mutate, individuals are selected, and species evolve. Or so the orthodox, Darwinian view proclaims.

The identification of individuals as the unit of selection is a central theme in Darwin's thought. Darwin contended that the exquisite balance of nature had no "higher" cause. Evolution does not recognize the "good of the ecosystem"

85

or even the "good of the species." Any harmony or stability is only an indirect result of individuals relentlessly pursuing their own self-interest—in modern parlance, getting more of their genes into future generations by greater reproductive success. Individuals are the unit of selection; the "struggle for existence" is a matter among individuals.

During the past fifteen years, however, challenges to Darwin's focus on individuals have sparked some lively debates among evolutionists. These challenges have come from above and below. From above, Scottish biologist V.C. Wynne-Edwards raised orthodox hackles fifteen years ago by arguing that groups, not individuals, are units of selection, at least for the evolution of social behavior. From below, English biologist Richard Dawkins has recently raised my hackles with his claim that genes themselves are units of selection, and individuals merely their temporary receptacles.

Wynne-Edwards presented his defense of "group selection" in a long book entitled *Animal Dispersion in Relation to Social Behavior.* He began with a dilemma: Why, if individuals only struggle to maximize their reproductive success, do so many species seem to maintain their populations at a fairly constant level, well matched to the resources available? The traditional Darwinian answer invoked external constraints of food, climate, and predation: only so many can be fed, so the rest starve (or freeze or get eaten), and numbers stabilize. Wynne-Edwards, on the other hand, argued that animals regulate their own populations by gauging the restrictions of their environment and regulating their own reproduction accordingly. He recognized right away that such a theory contravened Darwin's insistence on "individual selection" for it required that many individuals limit or forgo their own reproduction for the good of their group.

Wynne-Edwards postulated that most species are divided into many more-or-less discrete groups. Some groups never evolve a way to regulate their reproduction. Within these groups, individual selection reigns supreme. In good years, populations rise and the groups flourish; in bad years, the groups cannot regulate themselves and face severe crash and even extinction. Other groups develop systems of regulation in which many individuals sacrifice their reproduction for the group's benefit (an impossibility if selection can only favor individuals that seek their own advantage). These groups survive the good and the bad. Evolution is a struggle among groups, not individuals. And groups survive if they regulate their populations by the altruistic acts of individuals. "It is necessary," Wynne-Edwards wrote, "to postulate that social organizations are capable of progressive evolution and perfection as entities in their own right."

Wynne-Edwards reinterpreted most animal behavior in this light. The environment, if you will, prints only so many tickets for reproduction. Animals then compete for tickets through elaborate systems of conventionalized rivalry. In territorial species, each parcel of land contains a ticket and animals (usually males) posture for the parcels. Losers accept gracefully and retreat to peripheral celibacy for the good of all. (Wynne-Edwards, of course, does not impute conscious intent to winners and losers. He imagines that some unconscious hormonal mechanism underlies the good grace of losers.)

In species with dominance hierarchies, tickets are allotted to the appropriate number of places, and animals compete for rank. Competition is by bluff and posture, for animals must not destroy each other by fighting like gladiators. They are, after all, only competing for tickets to benefit the group. The contest is more of a lottery than a test of skills; a distribution of the right number of tickets is far more important than who wins. "The conventionalization of rivalry and the foundation of society are one and the same thing," Wynne-Edwards proclaimed.

But how do animals know the number of tickets? Clearly, they cannot, unless they can census their own populations. In his most striking hypothesis, Wynne-Edwards suggested that flocking, swarming, communal singing, and chorusing evolved through group selection as an effective device for censusing. He included "the singing of birds, the trilling of katydids, crickets and frogs, the underwater sounds of fish, and the flashing of fireflies."

Darwinians came down hard on Wynne-Edwards in the

decade following his book. They pursued two strategies. First, they accepted most of Wynne-Edwards's observations, but reinterpreted them as examples of individual selection. They argued, for example, that *who* wins is what dominance hierarchies and territoriality are all about. If the sex ratio between males and females is near 50:50 and if successful males monopolize several females, then not all males can breed. Everyone competes for the Darwinian prize of passing more genes along. The losers don't walk away with grace, content that their sacrifices increase the common good. They have simply been beaten; with luck, they will win on their next try. The result may be a well-regulated population, but the mechanism is individual struggle.

Virtually all Wynne-Edwards's examples of apparent altruism can be rephrased as tales of individual selfishness. In many flocks of birds, for example, the first individual that spots a predator utters a warning cry. The flock scatters but, according to group selectionists, the crier has saved his flockmates by calling attention to himself—self-destruction (or at least danger) for the good of the flock. Groups with altruist criers prevailed in evolution over all selfish, silent groups, despite the danger to individual altruists. But the debates have brought forth at least a dozen alternatives that interpret crying as beneficial for the crier. The cry may put the flock in random motion, thus befuddling the predator and making it less likely that he will catch anyone, including the crier. Or the crier may wish to retreat to safety but dares not break rank to do it alone, lest the predator detect an individual out of step. So he cries to bring the flock along with him. As the crier, he may be disadvantaged relative to flockmates (or he may not, as the first to safety), but he may still be better off than if he had kept silent and allowed the predator to take someone (perhaps himself) at random.

The second strategy against group selection reinterprets apparent acts of disinterested altruism as selfish devices to propagate genes through surviving kin—the theory of kin selection. Siblings, on average, share half their genes. If you die to save three sibs, you pass on 150 percent of yourself through their reproduction. Again, you have acted for your own evolutionary benefit, if not for your corporeal continuity. Kin selection is a form of Darwinian individual selection.

These alternatives do not disprove group selection, for they merely retell its stories in the more conventional Darwinian mode of individual selection. The dust has yet to settle on this contentious issue but a consensus (perhaps incorrect) seems to be emerging. Most evolutionists would now admit that group selection can occur in certain special situations (species made of many very discrete, socially cohesive groups in direct competition with each other). But they regard such situations as uncommon if only because discrete groups are often kin groups, leading to a preference for kin selection as an explanation for altruism within the group.

Yet, just as individual selection emerged relatively unscarred after its battle with group selection from above, other evolutionists launched an attack from below. Genes, they argue, not individuals are the units of selection. They begin by recasting Butler's famous aphorism that a hen is merely the egg's way of making another egg. An animal, they argue, is only DNA's way of making more DNA. Richard Dawkins has put the case most forcefully in his recent book *The Selfish Gene.* "A body," he writes, "is the genes' way of preserving the genes unaltered."

For Dawkins, evolution is a battle among genes, each seeking to make more copies of itself. Bodies are merely the places where genes aggregate for a time. Bodies are temporary receptacles, survival machines manipulated by genes and tossed away on the geological scrap heap once genes have replicated and slaked their insatiable thirst for more copies of themselves in bodies of the next generation. He writes:

> We are survival machines—robot vehicles blindly programmed to preserve the selfish molecules known as genes. . . .
> They swarm in huge colonies, safe inside gigantic lumbering robots . . . they are in you and me; they

created us, body and mind; and their preservation is
the ultimate rationale for our existence.

Dawkins explicitly abandons the Darwinian concept of
individuals as units of selection: "I shall argue that the
fundamental unit of selection, and therefore of self-interest,
is not the species, nor the group, nor even, strictly, the
individual. It is the gene, the unit of heredity." Thus, we
should not talk about kin selection and apparent altruism.
Bodies are not the appropriate units. Genes merely try to
recognize copies of themselves wherever they occur. They
act only to preserve copies and make more of them. They
couldn't care less which body happens to be their temporary home.

I begin my criticism by stating that I am not bothered by
what strikes most people as the most outrageous component of these statements—the imputation of conscious action to genes. Dawkins knows as well as you and I do that
genes do not plan and scheme; they do not act as witting
agents of their own preservation. He is only perpetuating,
albeit more colorfully than most, a metaphorical shorthand
used (perhaps unwisely) by all popular writers on evolution,
including myself (although sparingly, I hope). When he says
that genes strive to make more copies of themselves, he
means: "selection has operated to favor genes that, by
chance, varied in such a way that more copies survived in
subsequent generations." The second is quite a mouthful;
the first is direct and acceptable as metaphor although literally inaccurate.

Still, I find a fatal flaw in Dawkins's attack from below. No
matter how much power Dawkins wishes to assign to genes,
there is one thing that he cannot give them—direct visibility
to natural selection. Selection simply cannot see genes and
pick among them directly. It must use bodies as an intermediary. A gene is a bit of DNA hidden within a cell. Selection
views bodies. It favors some bodies because they are
stronger, better insulated, earlier in their sexual matura-
tion, fiercer in combat, or more beautiful to behold.

If, in favoring a stronger body, selection acted directly

upon a gene for strength, then Dawkins might be vindicated. If bodies were unambiguous maps of their genes, then battling bits of DNA would display their colors externally and selection might act upon them directly. But bodies are no such thing.

There is no gene "for" such unambiguous bits of morphology as your left kneecap or your fingernail. Bodies cannot be atomized into parts, each constructed by an individual gene. Hundreds of genes contribute to the building of most body parts and their action is channeled through a kaleidoscopic series of environmental influences: embryonic and postnatal, internal and external. Parts are not translated genes, and selection doesn't even work directly on parts. It accepts or rejects entire organisms because suites of parts, interacting in complex ways, confer advantages. The image of individual genes, plotting the course of their own survival, bears little relationship to developmental genetics as we understand it. Dawkins will need another metaphor: genes caucusing, forming alliances, showing deference for a chance to join a pact, gauging probable environments. But when you amalgamate so many genes and tie them together in hierarchical chains of action mediated by environments, we call the resultant object a body.

Moreover, Dawkins's vision requires that genes have an influence upon bodies. Selection cannot see them unless they translate to bits of morphology, physiology, or behavior that make a difference to the success of an organism. Not only do we need a one-to-one mapping between gene and body (criticized in the last paragraph), we also need a one-to-one *adaptive* mapping. Ironically, Dawkins's theory arrived just at a time when more and more evolutionists are rejecting the panselectionist claim that all bits of the body are fashioned in the crucible of natural selection. It may be that many, if not most, genes work equally well (or at least well enough) in all their variants and that selection does not choose among them. If most genes do not present themselves for review, then they cannot be the unit of selection.

I think, in short, that the fascination generated by Dawkins's theory arises from some bad habits of Western scientific thought—from attitudes (pardon the jargon) that we call atomism, reductionism, and determinism. The idea that wholes should be understood by decomposition into "basic" units; that properties of microscopic units can generate and explain the behavior of macroscopic results; that all events and objects have definite, predictable, determined causes. These ideas have been successful in our study of simple objects, made of few components, and uninfluenced by prior history. I'm pretty sure that my stove will light when I turn it on (it did). The gas laws build up from molecules to predictable properties of larger volumes. But organisms are much more than amalgamations of genes. They have a history that matters; their parts interact in complex ways. Organisms are built by genes acting in concert, influenced by environments, translated into parts that selection sees and parts invisible to selection. Molecules that determine the properties of water are poor analogues for genes and bodies. I may not be the master of my fate, but my intuition of wholeness probably reflects a biological truth.

3 | Human Evolution

9 | A Biological Homage to Mickey Mouse

AGE OFTEN turns fire to placidity. Lytton Strachey in his incisive portrait of Florence Nightingale, writes of her declining years:

> Destiny, having waited very patiently, played a queer trick on Miss Nightingale. The benevolence and public spirit of that long life had only been equalled by its acerbity. Her virtue had dwelt in hardness. . . . And now the sarcastic years brought the proud woman her punishment. She was not to die as she had lived. The sting was to be taken out of her; she was to be made soft; she was to be reduced to compliance and complacency.

I was therefore not surprised—although the analogy may strike some people as sacrilegious—to discover that the creature who gave his name as a synonym for insipidity had a gutsier youth. Mickey Mouse turned a respectable fifty last year. To mark the occasion, many theaters replayed his debut performance in *Steamboat Willie* (1928). The original Mickey was a rambunctious, even slightly sadistic fellow. In a remarkable sequence, exploiting the exciting new development of sound, Mickey and Minnie pummel, squeeze, and twist the animals on board to produce a rousing chorus of "Turkey in the Straw." They honk a duck with a tight embrace, crank a goat's tail, tweak a pig's nipples, bang a cow's teeth as a stand-in xylophone, and play bagpipe on her udder.

95

Christopher Finch, in his semiofficial pictorial history of Disney's work, comments: "The Mickey Mouse who hit the movie houses in the late twenties was not quite the well-behaved character most of us are familiar with today. He was mischievous, to say the least, and even displayed a streak of cruelty." But Mickey soon cleaned up his act, leaving to gossip and speculation only his unresolved relationship with Minnie and the status of Morty and Ferdie. Finch continues: "Mickey . . . had become virtually a national symbol, and as such he was expected to behave properly at all times. If he occasionally stepped out of line, any number of letters would arrive at the Studio from citizens and organizations who felt that the nation's moral well-being was in their hands. . . . Eventually he would be pressured into the role of straight man."

As Mickey's personality softened, his appearance changed. Many Disney fans are aware of this transformation through time, but few (I suspect) have recognized the coor-

Mickey's evolution during 50 years (left to right). As Mickey became increasingly well behaved over the years, his appearance became more youthful. Measurements of three stages in his development revealed a larger relative head size, larger eyes, and an enlarged cranium—all traits of juvenility. © Walt Disney Productions

dinating theme behind all the alterations—in fact, I am not sure that the Disney artists themselves explicitly realized what they were doing, since the changes appeared in such a halting and piecemeal fashion. In short, the blander and inoffensive Mickey became progressively more juvenile in appearance. (Since Mickey's chronological age never altered—like most cartoon characters he stands impervious to the ravages of time—this change in appearance at a constant age is a true evolutionary transformation. Progressive juvenilization as an evolutionary phenomenon is called neoteny. More on this later.)

The characteristic changes of form during human growth have inspired a substantial biological literature. Since the head-end of an embryo differentiates first and grows more rapidly in utero than the foot-end (an antero-posterior gradient, in technical language), a newborn child possesses a relatively large head attached to a medium-sized body with diminutive legs and feet. This gradient is reversed through

growth as legs and feet overtake the front end. Heads continue to grow but so much more slowly than the rest of the body that relative head size decreases.

In addition, a suite of changes pervades the head itself during human growth. The brain grows very slowly after age three, and the bulbous cranium of a young child gives way to the more slanted, lower-browed configuration of adulthood. The eyes scarcely grow at all and relative eye size declines precipitously. But the jaw gets bigger and bigger. Children, compared with adults, have larger heads and eyes, smaller jaws, a more prominent, bulging cranium, and smaller, pudgier legs and feet. Adult heads are altogether more apish, I'm sorry to say.

Mickey, however, has traveled this ontogenetic pathway in reverse during his fifty years among us. He has assumed an ever more childlike appearance as the ratty character of *Steamboat Willie* became the cute and inoffensive host to a magic kingdom. By 1940, the former tweaker of pig's nipples gets a kick in the ass for insubordination (as the *Sorcerer's Apprentice* in *Fantasia*). By 1953, his last cartoon, he has gone fishing and cannot even subdue a squirting clam.

The Disney artists transformed Mickey in clever silence, often using suggestive devices that mimic nature's own changes by different routes. To give him the shorter and pudgier legs of youth, they lowered his pants line and covered his spindly legs with a baggy outfit. (His arms and legs also thickened substantially—and acquired joints for a floppier appearance.) His head grew relatively larger and its features more youthful. The length of Mickey's snout has not altered, but decreasing protrusion is more subtly suggested by a pronounced thickening. Mickey's eye has grown in two modes: first, by a major, discontinuous evolutionary shift as the entire eye of ancestral Mickey became the pupil of his descendants, and second, by gradual increase thereafter.

Mickey's improvement in cranial bulging followed an interesting path since his evolution has always been constrained by the unaltered convention of representing his head as a circle with appended ears and an oblong snout.

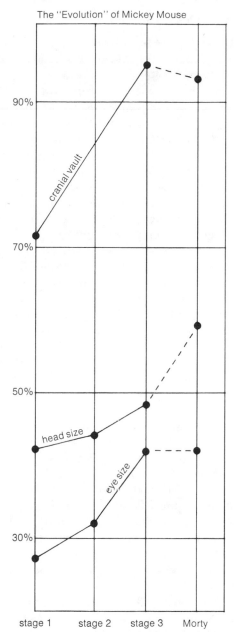

The "Evolution" of Mickey Mouse

At an early stage in his evolution, Mickey had a smaller head, cranial vault, and eyes. He evolved toward the characteristics of his young nephew Morty (connected to Mickey by a dotted line).

The circle's form could not be altered to provide a bulging cranium directly. Instead, Mickey's ears moved back, increasing the distance between nose and ears, and giving him a rounded, rather than a sloping, forehead.

To give these observations the cachet of quantitative science, I applied my best pair of dial calipers to three stages of the official phylogeny—the thin-nosed, ears-forward figure of the early 1930s (stage 1), the latter-day Jack of Mickey and the Beanstalk (1947, stage 2), and the modern mouse (stage 3). I measured three signs of Mickey's creeping juvenility: increasing eye size (maximum height) as a percentage of head length (base of the nose to top of rear ear); increasing head length as a percentage of body length; and increasing cranial vault size measured by rearward displacement of the front ear (base of the nose to top of front ear as a percentage of base of the nose to top of rear ear).

All three percentages increased steadily—eye size from 27 to 42 percent of head length; head length from 42.7 to 48.1 percent of body length; and nose to front ear from 71.7 to a whopping 95.6 percent of nose to rear ear. For comparison, I measured Mickey's young "nephew" Morty Mouse. In each case, Mickey has clearly been evolving toward youthful stages of his stock, although he still has a way to go for head length.

You may, indeed, now ask what an at least marginally respectable scientist has been doing with a mouse like that. In part, fiddling around and having fun, of course. (I still prefer *Pinocchio* to *Citizen Kane*.) But I do have a serious point—two, in fact—to make. We must first ask why Disney chose to change his most famous character so gradually and persistently in the same direction? National symbols are not altered capriciously and market researchers (for the doll industry in particular) have spent a good deal of time and practical effort learning what features appeal to people as cute and friendly. Biologists also have spent a great deal of time studying a similar subject in a wide range of animals.

In one of his most famous articles, Konrad Lorenz argues that humans use the characteristic differences in form between babies and adults as important behavioral cues. He believes that features of juvenility trigger "innate releasing mechanisms" for affection and nurturing in adult humans. When we see a living creature with babyish features, we feel an automatic surge of disarming tenderness. The adaptive value of this response can scarcely be questioned, for we must nurture our babies. Lorenz, by the way, lists among his releasers the very features of babyhood that Disney affixed progressively to Mickey: "a relatively large head, predominance of the brain capsule, large and low-lying eyes, bulging cheek region, short and thick extremities, a springy elastic consistency, and clumsy movements." (I propose to leave aside for this article the contentious issue of whether or not our affectionate response to babyish features is truly innate and inherited directly from ancestral primates—as Lorenz argues—or whether it is simply learned from our immediate experience with babies and grafted upon an evolutionary predisposition for attaching ties of affection to certain learned signals. My argument works equally well in either case for I only claim that babyish features tend to elicit strong feelings of affection in adult humans, whether the biological basis be direct programming or the capacity to learn and fix upon signals. I also treat as collateral to my point the major thesis of Lorenz's article—that we respond not to the totality or *Gestalt,* but to a set of specific features acting as releasers. This argument is important to Lorenz because he wants to argue for evolutionary identity in modes of behavior between other vertebrates and humans, and we know that many birds, for example, often respond to abstract features rather than *Gestalten.* Lorenz' article, published in 1950, bears the title *Ganzheit und Teil in der tierischen und menschlichen Gemeinschaft*—"Entirety and part in animal and human society." Disney's piecemeal change of Mickey's appearance does make sense in this context—he operated in sequential fashion upon Lorenz's primary releasers.)

Lorenz emphasizes the power that juvenile features hold over us, and the abstract quality of their influence, by pointing out that we judge other animals by the same criteria—although the judgment may be utterly inappropriate in an evolutionary context. We are, in short, fooled by an evolved response to our own babies, and we transfer our reaction to the same set of features in other animals.

Many animals, for reasons having nothing to do with the inspiration of affection in humans, possess some features also shared by human babies but not by human adults—large eyes and a bulging forehead with retreating chin, in particular. We are drawn to them, we cultivate them as pets, we stop and admire them in the wild—while we reject their small-eyed, long-snouted relatives who might make more affectionate companions or objects of admiration. Lorenz points out that the German names of many animals with features mimicking human babies end in the diminutive suffix *chen*, even though the animals are often larger than close relatives without such features—*Rotkehlchen* (robin), *Eichhörnchen* (squirrel), and *Kaninchen* (rabbit), for example.

In a fascinating section, Lorenz then enlarges upon our capacity for biologically inappropriate response to other animals, or even to inanimate objects that mimic human features. "The most amazing objects can acquire remarkable, highly specific emotional values by 'experiential attachment' of human properties. . . . Steeply rising, somewhat overhanging cliff faces or dark storm-clouds piling up have the same, immediate display value as a human being who is standing at full height and leaning slightly forwards"—that is, threatening.

We cannot help regarding a camel as aloof and unfriendly because it mimics, quite unwittingly and for other reasons, the "gesture of haughty rejection" common to so many human cultures. In this gesture, we raise our heads, placing our nose above our eyes. We then half-close our eyes and blow out through our nose—the "harumph" of the stereotyped upperclass Englishman or his well-trained servant. "All this," Lorenz argues quite cogently, "symbolizes resistance against all sensory modalities emanating from the disdained counterpart." But the poor camel cannot help carrying its nose above its elongate eyes, with mouth drawn down. As Lorenz reminds us, if you wish to know whether

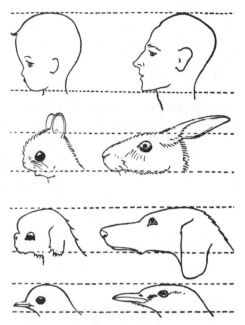

Humans feel affection for animals with juvenile features: large eyes, bulging craniums, retreating chins (left column). Small-eyed, long-snouted animals (right column) do not elicit the same response. From *Studies in Animal and Human Behavior*, vol. II, by Konrad Lorenz, 1971. Methuen & Co. Ltd.

a camel will eat out of your hand or spit, look at its ears, not the rest of its face.

In his important book *Expression of the Emotions in Man and Animals,* published in 1872, Charles Darwin traced the evolutionary basis of many common gestures to originally adaptive actions in animals later internalized as symbols in humans. Thus, he argued for evolutionary continuity of emotion, not only of form. We snarl and raise our upper lip in fierce anger—to expose our nonexistent fighting canine tooth. Our gesture of disgust repeats the facial actions associated with the highly adaptive act of vomiting in necessary circumstances. Darwin concluded, much to the distress of many Victorian contemporaries: "With mankind some expressions, such as the bristling of the hair under the influence of extreme terror, or the uncovering of the teeth under that of furious rage, can hardly be understood, except on the belief that man once existed in a much lower and animal-like condition."

In any case, the abstract features of human childhood elicit powerful emotional responses in us, even when they occur in other animals. I submit that Mickey Mouse's evolutionary road down the course of his own growth in reverse reflects the unconscious discovery of this biological principle by Disney and his artists. In fact, the emotional status of most Disney characters rests on the same set of distinctions. To this extent, the magic kingdom trades on a biological illusion—our ability to abstract and our propensity to transfer inappropriately to other animals the fitting responses we make to changing form in the growth of our own bodies.

Donald Duck also adopts more juvenile features through time. His elongated beak recedes and his eyes enlarge; he converges on Huey, Louie, and Dewey as surely as Mickey approaches Morty. But Donald, having inherited the mantle of Mickey's original misbehavior, remains more adult in form with his projecting beak and more sloping forehead.

Mouse villains or sharpies, contrasted with Mickey, are always more adult in appearance, although they often share Mickey's chronological age. In 1936, for example, Disney made a short entitled *Mickey's Rival*. Mortimer, a dandy in a yellow sports car, intrudes upon Mickey and Minnie's quiet country picnic. The thoroughly disreputable Mortimer has a head only 29 percent of body length, to Mickey's 45, and a snout 80 percent of head length, compared with Mickey's 49. (Nonetheless, and was it ever different, Minnie transfers her affection until an obliging bull from a neighboring field dispatches Mickey's rival.) Consider also the exaggerated adult features of other Disney characters—the swaggering bully Peg-leg Pete or the simple, if lovable, dolt Goofy.

Dandified, disreputable Mortimer (here stealing Minnie's affections) has strikingly more adult features than Mickey. His head is smaller in proportion to body length; his nose is a full 80 percent of head length. © Walt Disney Productions

As a second, serious biological comment on Mickey's odyssey in form, I note that his path to eternal youth repeats, in epitome, our own evolutionary story. For humans are neotenic. We have evolved by retaining to adulthood the originally juvenile features of our ancestors. Our australopithecine forebears, like Mickey in *Steamboat Willie,* had projecting jaws and low vaulted craniums.

Our embryonic skulls scarcely differ from those of chimpanzees. And we follow the same path of changing form through growth: relative decrease of the cranial vault since brains grow so much more slowly than bodies after birth, and continuous relative increase of the jaw. But while chimps accentuate these changes, producing an adult strikingly different in form from a baby, we proceed much more slowly down the same path and never get nearly so far. Thus, as adults, we retain juvenile features. To be sure, we change enough to produce a notable difference between baby and adult, but our alteration is far smaller than that experienced by chimps and other primates.

A marked slowdown of developmental rates has triggered our neoteny. Primates are slow developers among mammals, but we have accentuated the trend to a degree matched by no other mammal. We have very long periods of gestation, markedly extended childhoods, and the longest life span of any mammal. The morphological features of eternal youth have served us well. Our enlarged brain is, at least in part, a result of extending rapid prenatal growth rates to later ages. (In all mammals, the brain grows rapidly in utero but often very little after birth. We have extended this fetal phase into postnatal life.)

But the changes in timing themselves have been just as important. We are preeminently learning animals, and our extended childhood permits the transference of culture by education. Many animals display flexibility and play in childhood but follow rigidly programmed patterns as adults. Lorenz writes, in the same article cited above: "The characteristic which is so vital for the human peculiarity of the true man—that of always remaining in a state of development—is quite certainly a gift which we owe to the neote-nous nature of mankind.''

In short, we, like Mickey, never grow up although we, alas, do grow old. Best wishes to you, Mickey, for your next half-century. May we stay as young as you, but grow a bit wiser.

Cartoon villains are not the only Disney charac-ters with exaggerated adult features. Goofy, like Mortimer, has a small head relative to body length and a prominent snout. © Walt Disney Produc-tions

10 | Piltdown Revisited

NOTHING IS QUITE so fascinating as a well-aged mystery. Many connoisseurs regard Josephine Tey's *The Daughter of Time* as the greatest detective story ever written because its protagonist is Richard III, not the modern and insignificant murderer of Roger Ackroyd. The old chestnuts are perennial sources for impassioned and fruitless debate. Who was Jack the Ripper? Was Shakespeare Shakespeare?

My profession of paleontology offered its entry to the first rank of historical conundrums a quarter-century ago. In 1953, Piltdown man was exposed as a certain fraud perpetrated by a very uncertain hoaxer. Since then, interest has never flagged. People who cannot tell *Tyrannosaurus* from *Allosaurus* have firm opinions about the identity of Piltdown's forger. Rather than simply ask "whodunit?" this column treats what I regard as an intellectually more interesting issue: why did anyone ever accept Piltdown man in the first place? I was led to address the subject by recent and prominent news reports adding—with abysmally poor evidence, in my opinion—yet another prominent suspect to the list. Also, as an old mystery reader, I cannot refrain from expressing my own prejudice, all in due time.

In 1912, Charles Dawson, a lawyer and amateur archeologist from Sussex, brought several cranial fragments to Arthur Smith Woodward, Keeper of Geology at the British Museum (Natural History). The first, he said, had been unearthed by workmen from a gravel pit in 1908. Since then, he had searched the spoil heaps and found a few more fragments. The bones, worn and deeply stained, seemed indigenous to the ancient gravel; they were not the remains of a more recent interment. Yet the skull appeared remarkably modern in form, although the bones were unusually thick.

Smith Woodward, excited as such a measured man could be, accompanied Dawson to Piltdown and there, with Father Teilhard de Chardin, looked for further evidence in the spoil heaps. (Yes, believe it or not, the same Teilhard who, as a mature scientist and theologian, became such a cult figure some fifteen years ago with his attempt to reconcile evolution, nature, and God in *The Phenomenon of Man.* Teilhard had come to England in 1908 to study at the Jesuit College in Hastings, near Piltdown. He met Dawson in a quarry on May 31, 1909; the mature solicitor and the young French Jesuit became warm friends, colleagues, and coexplorers.)

On one of their joint expeditions, Dawson found the famous mandible, or lower jaw. Like the skull fragments, the jaw was deeply stained, but it seemed to be as apish in form as the cranium was human. Nonetheless, it contained two molar teeth, worn flat in a manner commonly encountered in humans, but never in apes. Unfortunately, the jaw was broken in just the two places that might have settled its relationship with the skull: the chin region, with all its marks of distinction between ape and human, and the area of articulation with the cranium.

Armed with skull fragments, the lower jaw, and an associated collection of worked flints and bone, plus a number of mammalian fossils to fix the age as ancient, Smith Woodward and Dawson made their splash before the Geological Society of London on December 18, 1912. Their reception was mixed, although on the whole favorable. No one smelled fraud, but the association of such a human cranium with such an apish jaw indicated to some critics that remains of two separate animals might have been mixed together in the quarry.

During the next three years, Dawson and Smith Woodward countered with a series of further discoveries that, in retrospect, could not have been better programmed to dispel doubt. In 1913, Father Teilhard found the all-important lower canine tooth. It, too, was apish in form but strongly worn in a human manner. Then, in 1915, Dawson convinced most of his detractors by finding the same association of two thick-skulled human cranial fragments with an apish tooth worn in a human manner at a second site two miles from the original finds.

Henry Fairfield Osborn, leading American paleontologist and converted critic, wrote:

> If there is a Providence hanging over the affairs of prehistoric men, it certainly manifested itself in this case, because the three fragments of the second Piltdown man found by Dawson are exactly those which we would have selected to confirm the comparison with the original type. . . . Placed side by side with the corresponding fossils of the first Piltdown man they agree precisely; there is not a shadow of a difference.

Providence, unbeknown to Osborn, walked in human form at Piltdown.

For the next thirty years, Piltdown occupied an uncomfortable but acknowledged place in human prehistory. Then, in 1949, Kenneth P. Oakley applied his fluorine test to the Piltdown remains. Bones pick up fluorine as a function of their time of residence in a deposit and the fluorine content of surrounding rocks and soil. Both the skull and jaw of Piltdown contained barely detectable amounts of fluorine; they could not have lain long in the gravels. Oakley still did not suspect fakery. He proposed that Piltdown, after all, had been a relatively recent interment into ancient gravels.

But a few years later, in collaboration with J.S. Weiner and W.E. le Gros Clark, Oakley finally considered the obvious alternative—that the "interment" had been made in this century with intent to defraud. He found that the skull

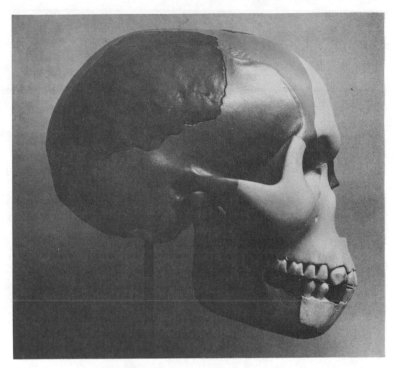

Skull of Piltdown Man.
COURTESY OF THE AMERICAN MUSEUM OF NATURAL HISTORY

and jaw had been artificially stained, the flints and bone worked with modern blades, and the associated mammals, although genuine fossils, imported from elsewhere. Moreover, the teeth had been filed down to simulate human wear. The old anomaly—an apish jaw with a human cranium —was resolved in the most parsimonious way of all. The skull *did* belong to a modern human; the jaw was an orangutan's.

But who had foisted such a monstrous hoax upon scientists so anxious for such a find that they remained blind to an obvious resolution of its anomalies? Of the original trio, Teilhard was dismissed as a young and unwitting dupe. No one has ever (and rightly, in my opinion) suspected Smith Woodward, the superstraight arrow who devoted his life to the reality of Piltdown and who, past eighty and blind, dictated in retirement his last book with its chauvinistic title, *The Earliest Englishman* (1948).

Suspicion instead has focused on Dawson. Opportunity he certainly had, although no one has ever established a satisfactory motive. Dawson was a highly respected amateur with several important finds to his credit. He was overenthusiastic and uncritical, perhaps even a bit unscrupulous in his dealings with other amateurs, but no direct evidence of his complicity has ever come to light. Nevertheless, the circumstantial case is strong and well summarized by J.S. Weiner in *The Piltdown Forgery* (Oxford University Press, 1955).

Supporters of Dawson have maintained that a more professional scientist must have been involved, at least as a coconspirator, because the finds were so cleverly faked. I have always regarded this as a poor argument, advanced by scientists largely to assuage their embarrassment that such an indifferently designed hoax was not detected sooner. The staining, to be sure, had been done consummately. But the "tools" had been poorly carved and the teeth crudely filed—scratch marks were noted as soon as scientists looked with the right hypothesis in mind. Le Gros Clark wrote: "The evidences of artificial abrasion immediately sprang to the eye. Indeed so obvious did they seem it may well be asked—how was it that they had escaped notice before." The forger's main skill consisted in knowing what to leave out—discarding the chin and articulation.

In November 1978, Piltdown reappeared prominently in the news because yet another scientist had been implicated as a possible coconspirator. Shortly before he died at age ninety-three, J.A. Douglas, emeritus professor of geology at Oxford, made a tape recording suggesting that his predecessor in the chair, W.J. Sollas, was the culprit. In support of this assertion, Douglas offered only three items scarcely ranking as evidence in my book: (1) Sollas and Smith Woodward were bitter enemies. (So what. Academia is a den of vipers, but verbal sparring and elaborate hoaxing are responses of differing magnitude.) (2) In 1910, Douglas gave

Sollas some mastodon bones that could have been used as part of the imported fauna. (But such bones and teeth are not rare.) (3) Sollas once received a package of potassium bichromate and neither Douglas nor Sollas's photographer could figure out why he had wanted it. Potassium bichromate was used in staining the Piltdown bones. (It was also an important chemical in photography, and I do not regard the alleged confusion of Sollas's photographer as a strong sign that the professor had some nefarious usages in mind.) In short, I find the evidence against Sollas so weak that I wonder why the leading scientific journals of England and the United States gave it so much space. I would exclude Sollas completely, were it not for the paradox that his famous book, *Ancient Hunters,* supports Smith Woodward's views about Piltdown in terms so obsequiously glowing that it could be read as subtle sarcasm.

Only three hypotheses make much sense to me. First, Dawson was widely suspected and disliked by some amateur archeologists (and equally acclaimed by others). Some compatriots regarded him as a fraud. Others were bitterly jealous of his standing among professionals. Perhaps one of his colleagues devised this complex and peculiar form of revenge. The second hypothesis, and the most probable in my view, holds that Dawson acted alone, whether for fame or to show up the world of professionals we do not know.

The third hypothesis is much more interesting. It would render Piltdown as a joke that went too far, rather than a malicious forgery. It represents the "pet theory" of many prominent vertebrate paleontologists who knew the man well. I have sifted all the evidence, trying hard to knock it down. Instead, I find it consistent and plausible, although not the leading contender. A.S. Romer, late head of the museum I inhabit at Harvard and America's finest vertebrate paleontologist, often stated his suspicions to me. Louis Leakey also believed it. His autobiography refers anonymously to a "second man," but internal evidence clearly implicates a certain individual to anyone in the know.

It is often hard to remember a man in his youth after old age imposes a different persona. Teilhard de Chardin became an austere and almost Godlike figure to many in his later years; he was widely hailed as a leading prophet of our age. But he was once a fun-loving young student. He knew Dawson for three years before Smith Woodward entered the story. He may have had access, from a previous assignment in Egypt, to mammalian bones (probably from Tunisia and Malta) that formed part of the "imported" fauna at Piltdown. I can easily imagine Dawson and Teilhard, over long hours in field and pub, hatching a plot for different reasons: Dawson to expose the gullibility of pompous professionals; Teilhard to rub English noses once again with the taunt that their nation had no legitimate human fossils, while France reveled in a superabundance that made her the queen of anthropology. Perhaps they worked together, never expecting that the leading lights of English science would fasten upon Piltdown with such gusto. Perhaps they expected to come clean but could not.

Teilhard left England to become a stretcher bearer during World War I. Dawson, on this view, persevered and completed the plot with a second Piltdown find in 1915. But then the joke ran away and became a nightmare. Dawson sickened unexpectedly and died in 1916. Teilhard could not return before the war's end. By that time, the three leading lights of British anthropology and paleontology—Arthur Smith Woodward, Grafton Elliot Smith, and Arthur Keith —had staked their careers on the reality of Piltdown. (Indeed they ended up as two Sir Arthurs and one Sir Grafton, largely for their part in putting England on the anthropological map.) Had Teilhard confessed in 1918, his promising career (which later included a major role in describing the legitimate Peking man) would have ended abruptly. So he followed the Psalmist and the motto of Sussex University, later established just a few miles from Piltdown— "Be still, and know. . . ."—to his dying day. Possible. Just possible.

All this speculation provides endless fun and controversy, but what about the prior and more interesting question: why had anyone believed Piltdown in the first place? It was an improbable creature from the start. Why had anyone admitted to our lineage an ancestor with a fully modern cranium and the unmodified jaw of an ape?

Indeed, Piltdown never lacked detractors. Its temporary reign was born in conflict and nurtured throughout by controversy. Many scientists continued to believe that Piltdown was an artifact composed of two animals accidentally commingled in the same deposit. In the early 1940s, for example, Franz Weidenreich, perhaps the world's greatest human anatomist, wrote (with devastating accuracy in hindsight): "*Eoanthropus* ['dawn man,' the official designation of Piltdown] should be erased from the list of human fossils. It is the artificial combination of fragments of a modern human braincase with orang-utanglike mandible and teeth." To this apostasy, Sir Arthur Keith responded with bitter irony: "This is one way of getting rid of facts which do not fit into a preconceived theory; the usual way pursued by men of science is, not to get rid of facts, but frame theory to fit them."

Moreover, had anyone been inclined to pursue the matter, there were published grounds for suspecting fraud from the start. A dental anatomist, C.W. Lyne, stated that the canine found by Teilhard was a young tooth, just erupted before Piltdown's death, and that its intensity of wear could not be reconciled with its age. Others voiced strong doubts about the ancient manufacture of Piltdown's tools. In amateur circles of Sussex, some of Dawson's colleagues concluded that Piltdown must be a fake, but they did not publish their beliefs.

If we are to learn anything about the nature of scientific inquiry from Piltdown—rather than just reveling in the joys of gossip—we will have to resolve the paradox of its easy acceptance. I think that I can identify at least four categories of reasons for the ready welcome accorded to such a misfit by all the greatest English paleontologists. All four contravene the usual mythology about scientific practice—that facts are "hard" and primary and that scientific understanding increases by patient collection and sifting of these objective bits of pure information. Instead, they display science as a human activity, motivated by hope, cultural prejudice, and the pursuit of glory, yet stumbling in its erratic path toward a better understanding of nature.

The imposition of strong hope upon dubious evidence. Before Piltdown, English paleoanthropology was mired in a limbo now occupied by students of extraterrestrial life: endless fields for speculation and no direct evidence. Beyond some flint "cultures" of doubtful human workmanship and some bones strongly suspected as products of recent interments into ancient gravels, England knew nothing of its most ancient ancestors. France, on the other hand, had been blessed with a superabundance of Neanderthals, Cro-Magnons and their associated art and tools. French anthropologists delighted in rubbing English noses with this marked disparity of evidence. Piltdown could not have been better designed to turn the tables. It seemed to predate Neanderthal by a considerable stretch of time. If human fossils had a fully modern cranium hundreds of thousands of years before beetle-browed Neanderthal appeared, then Piltdown must be our ancestor and the French Neanderthals a side branch. Smith Woodward proclaimed: "The Neanderthal race was a degenerate offshoot of early man while surviving modern man may have arisen directly from the primitive source of which the Piltdown skull provides the first discovered evidence." This international rivalry has often been mentioned by Piltdown's commentators, but a variety of equally important factors have usually escaped notice.

Reduction of anomaly by fit with cultural biases. A human cranium with an ape's jaw strikes us today as sufficiently incongruous to merit strong suspicion. Not so in 1913. At that time, many leading paleontologists maintained an a priori preference largely cultural in origin, for "brain primacy" in human evolution. The argument rested on a false inference from contemporary importance to historical priority: we rule today by virtue of our intelligence. Therefore, in our evolution, an enlarged brain must have preceded and inspired all other alterations of our body. We should expect to find human ancestors with enlarged, perhaps nearly modern, brains and a distinctly simian body. (Ironically, nature followed an opposite path. Our earliest ancestors, the australopithecines, were fully erect but still small brained.) Thus, Piltdown neatly matched a widely anticipated result. Grafton Elliot Smith wrote in 1924:

> The outstanding interest of the Piltdown skull is in the confirmation it affords of the view that in the evolution of Man the brain led the way. It is the veriest truism that Man has emerged from the simian state in virtue of the enrichment of the structure of his mind. . . . The brain attained what may be termed the human rank at a time when the jaws and face, and no doubt the body also, still retained much of the uncouthness of Man's simian ancestors. In other words, Man at first . . . was merely an Ape with an overgrown brain. The importance of the Piltdown skull lies in the fact that it affords tangible confirmation of these inferences.

Piltdown also buttressed some all too familiar racial views among white Europeans. In the 1930s and 1940s, following the discovery of Peking man in strata approximately equal in age with the Piltdown gravels, phyletic trees based on Piltdown and affirming the antiquity of white supremacy began to appear in the literature (although they were never adopted by Piltdown's chief champions, Smith Woodward, Smith, and Keith). Peking man (originally called *Sinanthropus,* but now placed in *Homo erectus*) lived in China with a brain two-thirds modern size, while Piltdown man, with its fully developed brain, inhabited England. If Piltdown, as the earliest Englishman, was the progenitor of white races, while other hues must trace their ancestry to *Homo erectus,* then whites crossed the threshold to full humanity long before other people. As longer residents in this exalted state, whites must excel in the arts of civilization.

Reduction of anomaly by matching fact to expectation. We know, in retrospect, that Piltdown had a human cranium and an ape's jaw. As such, it provides an ideal opportunity for testing what scientists do when faced with uncomfortable anomaly. G.E. Smith and others may have advocated an evolutionary head start for the brain, but no one dreamed of an independence so complete that brains might become fully human before jaws changed at all! Piltdown was distressingly too good to be true.

If Keith was right in his taunt to Weidenreich, then Piltdown's champions should have modeled their theories to the uncomfortable fact of a human cranium and an ape's jaw. Instead, they modeled the "facts"—another illustration that information always reaches us through the strong filters of culture, hope, and expectation. As a persistent theme in "pure" description of the Piltdown remains, we learn from all its major supporters that the skull, although remarkably modern, contains a suite of definitely simian characters! Smith Woodward, in fact, originally estimated the cranial capacity at a mere 1,070 cc (compared with a modern average of 1,400 to 1,500), although Keith later convinced him to raise the figure nearer to the low end of our modern spectrum. Grafton Elliot Smith, describing the brain cast in the original paper of 1913, found unmistakable signs of incipient expansion in areas that mark the higher mental faculties in modern brains. He concluded: "We must regard this as being the most primitive and most simian human brain so far recorded; one, moreover, such as might reasonably have been expected to be associated in one and the same individual with the mandible which so definitely indicates the zoological rank of its original possessor." Just a year before Oakley's revelation, Sir Arthur Keith wrote in his last major work (1948): "His forehead was like that of the orang, devoid of a supraorbital torus; in its modeling his frontal bone presented many points of resemblance to that of the orang of Borneo and Sumatra." Modern *Homo sapiens*, I hasten to add, also lacks a supraorbital torus, or brow ridge.

Careful examination of the jaw also revealed a set of remarkably human features for such an apish jaw (beyond the forged wear of the teeth). Sir Arthur Keith repeatedly emphasized, for example, that the teeth were inserted into the jaw in a human, rather than a simian, fashion.

Prevention of discovery by practice. In former years, the British Museum did not occupy the vanguard in maintaining open and accessible collections—a happy trend of recent years, and one that has helped to lift the odor of mustiness (literally and figuratively) from major research museums. Like the stereotype of a librarian who protects books by guarding them from use, Piltdown's keepers severely restricted access to the original bones. Researchers were often permitted to look but not touch; only the set of plaster casts could be handled. Everyone praised the casts for their accuracy of proportion and detail, but the detection of fraud required access to the originals—artificial sta

As I write this book in 1972 and ask myself how it was that the forgery remained unmasked for so many years, I have turned my mind back to 1933, when I first went to see Dr. Bather, Smith Woodward's successor. . . . I told him that I wished to make a careful examination of the Piltdown fossils, since I was preparing a textbook on early man. I was taken into the basement to be shown the specimens, which were lifted out of a safe and laid on a table. Next to each fossil was an excellent cast. I was not allowed to handle the originals in any way, but merely to look at them and satisfy myself that the casts were really good replicas. Then, abruptly, the originals were removed and locked up again, and I was left for the rest of the morning with only the casts to study.

It is my belief now that it was under these conditions that all visiting scientists were permitted to examine the Piltdown specimens, and that the situation changed only when they came under the care of my friend and contemporary Kenneth Oakley. He did not see the necessity of treating the fragments as if they were the crown jewels but, rather, considered them simply as important fossils—to be looked after carefully, but from which the maximum scientific evidence should be obtained.

Henry Fairfield Osborn, although not known as a generous man, paid almost obsequious homage to Smith Woodward in his treatise on the historical path of human progress, *Man Rises to Parnassus* (1927). He had been a skeptic before his visit to the British Museum in 1921. Then, on Sunday morning, July 24, "after attending a most memorable service in Westminster Abbey," Osborn "repaired to the British Museum to see the fossil remains of the now thoroughly vindicated Dawn Man of Great Britain." (He, at least, as head of the American Museum of Natural History, got to see the originals.) Osborn swiftly converted and proclaimed Piltdown "a discovery of transcendent importance to the prehistory of man." He then added: "We have to be reminded over and over again that Nature is full of paradoxes and that the order of the universe is not the human order." Yet Osborn had seen little but the human order on two levels—the comedy of fraud and the subtler, yet ineluctable, imposition of theory upon nature. Somehow, I am not distressed that the human order must veil all our interactions with the universe, for the veil is translucent, however strong its texture.

Postscript

Our fascination with Piltdown never seems to abate. This article, published originally in March, 1979, elicited a flurry of correspondence, some acerbic, some congratulatory. It centered, of course, upon Teilhard. I was not trying to be cute by writing at length about Teilhard while stating briefly that Dawson acting alone accounts best for the facts. The case against Dawson had been made admirably by Weiner, and I had nothing to add to it. I continued to regard Weiner's as the most probable hypothesis. But I also believed that the only reasonable alternative (since the second Piltdown site established Dawson's complicity in my view) was a coconspiracy—an accomplice for Dawson. The other current proposals, involving Sollas or even G.E. Smith himself, seemed to me so improbable or off-the-wall that I wondered why so little attention had focussed upon the only recognized scientist who had been with Dawson from the start—especially since several of Teilhard's prominent colleagues in vertebrate paleontology harbored private thoughts (or had made cryptically worded public statements) about his possible role.

Ashley Montagu wrote on December 3, 1979, and told me that he had broken the news to Teilhard himself after Oakley's revelation of the fraud—and that Teilhard's astonishment seemed too genuine to represent dissembling: "I feel sure you're wrong about Teilhard. I knew him well, and, in fact, was the first to tell him, the day after it was announced in *The New York Times,* of the hoax. His reaction could hardly have been faked. I have not the slightest doubt that the faker was Dawson." In Paris last September, I spoke with several of Teilhard's contemporaries and scientific colleagues, including Pierre P. Grassé and Jean Piveteau; all regarded any thought of his complicity as monstrous. Père Francois Russo, S.J., later sent me a copy of the letter that Teilhard wrote to Kenneth P. Oakley after Oakley had exposed the fraud. He hoped that this document would assuage my doubts about his coreligionist. Instead my doubts intensified; for, in this letter, Teilhard made a fatal slip. Intrigued by my new role as sleuth, I visited Kenneth Oakley in England on April 16, 1980. He showed me additional documents of Teilhard, and shared other doubts with me. I now believe that the balance of evidence clearly implicates Teilhard as a coconspirator with Dawson in the Piltdown plot. I will present the entire case in Natural History Magazine in the summer or fall of 1980; but for now, let me mention the internal evidence from Teilhard's first letter to Oakley alone.

Teilhard begins the letter by expressing satisfaction. "I congratulate you most sincerely on your solution of the Piltdown problem . . . I am fundamentally pleased by your conclusions, in spite of the fact that, sentimentally speaking, it spoils one of my brightest and earliest paleontological memories." He continues with his thoughts on "the psychological riddle," or whodunit. he agrees with all others in dismissing Smith Woodward, but he also refuses to implicate Dawson, citing his thorough knowledge of Dawson's character and abilities: "He was a methodical and enthusiastic character . . . In addition, his deep friendship for Sir Arthur makes it almost unthinkable that he should have systematically deceived his associate several years. When we were in the field, I never noticed anything suspicious in his behavior." Teilhard ends by proposing, halfheartedly by his own admission, that the whole affair might have been an accident engendered when an amateur collector threw out some ape bones onto a spoil heap that also contained some human skull fragments, (although Teilhard does not tell us how such a hypothesis could possibly account for the same association two miles away at the second Piltdown site).

Teilhard's slip occurs in his description of the second Piltdown find. Teilhard writes: "He just brought me to the site of Locality 2 and explained me (sic) that he had found the isolated molar and the small pieces of skull in the heaps of rubble and pebbles raked at the surface of the field." Now we know (see Weiner, p. 142) that Dawson did take Teilhard to the second site for a prospecting trip in 1913. He also took Smith Woodward there in 1914. But neither visit led to any discovery; no fossils were found at the second site until 1915. Dawson wrote to Smith Woodward on January 20, 1915 to announce the discovery of two cranial fragments. In July 1915, he wrote again with good news about the discovery of a molar tooth. Smith Woodward assumed (and stated in print) that Dawson had unearthed the specimens in 1915 (see Weiner, p. 144). Dawson became seriously ill later in 1915 and died the next year. Smith Woodward never obtained more precise information from him about the second find. Now, the damning point: Teilhard states explicitly, in the letter quoted above, that Dawson told him about both the tooth and the skull fragments of the second site. But Claude Cuénot, Teilhard's biographer, states that Teilhard was called up for service in December, 1914; and we know that he was at the front on January 22, 1915 (pp. 22–23). But if Dawson did not "officially" discover the molar until July, 1915, how could Teilhard have known about it *unless he was involved in the hoax*. I regard it as unlikely that Dawson would show the material to an innocent Teilhard in 1913 and then withold it from Smith Woodward for two years (especially after taking Smith Woodward to the second site for two days of prospecting in 1914). Teilhard and Smith Woodward were friends and might have compared notes at any time; such an inconsistency on Dawson's part could have blown his cover entirely.

Second, Teilhard states in his letter to Oakley that he did not meet Dawson until 1911: "I knew Dawson very well, since I worked with him and Sir Arthur three or four times at Piltdown (after a chance meeting in a quarry near Hastings in 1911)." Yet it is certain that Teilhard met Dawson during the spring or summer of 1909 (see Weiner, p. 90). Dawson introduced Teilhard to Smith Woodward, and Teilhard submitted some fossils he had found, including a rare tooth of an early mammal, to Smith Woodward late in 1909. When Smith Woodward described this material before the Geological Society of London in 1911, Dawson, in the discussion following Smith Woodward's talk, paid tribute to the "patient and skilled assistance" given to him by Teilhard and another priest since 1909. I don't regard this as a damning point. A first meeting in 1911 would still be early enough for complicity (Dawson "found" his first piece of the Piltdown skull in the autumn of 1911, although he states that a workman had given him a fragment "some years" earlier), and I would never hold a mistake of two years against a man who tried to remember the event forty years later. Still, a later (and incorrect) date, right upon the heels of Dawson's find, certainly averts suspicion.

Moving away from the fascination of whodunit to the theme of my original essay (why did anyone ever believe it in the first place), another colleague sent me an interesting article from *Nature* (the leading scientific periodical in England), November 13, 1913, from the midst of the initial discussions. In it, David Waterston of King's College, University of London, correctly (and definitely) stated that the skull was human, the jaw an ape's. He concludes: "It seems to me to be as inconsequent to refer the mandible and the cranium to the same individual as it would be to articulate a chimpanzee foot with the bones of an essentially human thigh and leg." The correct explanation had been available from the start, but hope, desire, and prejudice prevented its acceptance.

11 | Our Greatest Evolutionary Step

IN MY PREVIOUS book, *Ever Since Darwin,* I began an essay on human evolution with these words:

> New and significant prehuman fossils have been unearthed with such unrelenting frequency in recent years that the fate of any lecture notes can only be described with the watchword of a fundamentally irrational economy—planned obsolescence. Each year, when the topic comes up in my courses, I simply open my old folder and dump the contents into the nearest circular file. And here we go again.

And I'm mighty glad I wrote them, because I now want to invoke that passage to recant an argument made later in the same article.

In that essay I reported Mary Leakey's discovery (at Laetoli, thirty miles south of Olduvai Gorge in Tanzania) of the oldest known hominid fossils—teeth and jaws 3.35 to 3.75 million years old. Mary Leakey suggested (and so far as I know, still believes) that these remains should be classified in our genus, *Homo.* I therefore argued that the conventional evolutionary sequence leading from small-brained but fully erect *Australopithecus* to larger-brained *Homo* might have to be reassessed, and that the australopithecines might represent a side branch of the human evolutionary tree.

125

Early in 1979, newspapers blazed with reports of a new species—more ancient in time and more primitive in appearance than any other hominid fossil—*Australopithecus afarensis,* named by Don Johanson and Tim White. Could any two claims possibly be more different—Mary Leakey's argument that the oldest hominids belong to our own genus, *Homo,* and Johanson and White's decision to name a new species because the oldest hominids possess a set of apelike features shared by no other fossil hominid. Johanson and White must have discovered some new and fundamentally different bones. Not at all. Leakey and Johanson and White are arguing about the same bones. We are witnessing a debate about the interpretation of specimens, not a new discovery.

Johanson worked in the Afar region of Ethiopia from 1972 to 1977 and unearthed an outstanding series of hominid remains. The Afar specimens are 2.9 to 3.3 million years old. Premier among them is the skeleton of an australopithecine named Lucy. She is nearly 40 percent complete—much more than we have ever possessed for any individual from these early days of our history. (Most hominid fossils, even though they serve as a basis for endless speculation and elaborate storytelling, are fragments of jaws and scraps of skulls.)

Johanson and White argue that the Afar specimens and Mary Leakey's Laetoli fossils are identical in form and belong to the same species. They also point out that the Afar and Laetoli bones and teeth represent everything we know about hominids exceeding 2.5 million years in age—all the other African specimens are younger. Finally, they claim that the teeth and skull pieces of these old remains share a set of features absent in later fossils and reminiscent of apes. Thus, they assign the Laetoli and Afar remains to a new species, *A. afarensis.*

The debate is just beginning to warm up, but three opinions have already been vented. Some anthropologists, pointing to different features, regard the Afar and Laetoli specimens as members of our own genus, *Homo.* Others accept Johanson and White's conclusion that these older fossils are closer to the later south and east African *Aus-*

tralopithecus than to *Homo.* But they deny a difference sufficient to warrant a new species and prefer to include the Afar
and Laetoli fossils within the species *A. africanus,* originally
named for South African specimens in the 1920s. Still others agree with Johanson and White that the Afar and Laetoli
fossils deserve a new name.

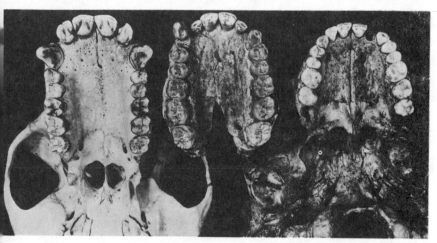

The palate of *Australopithecus afarensis* (center, compared with that of a modern
chimpanzee (left) and a human (right).

As a rank anatomical amateur, my opinion is worth next
to nothing. Yet I must say that if a picture is worth all the
words of this essay (or only half of them if you follow the
traditional equation of 1 for 1,000), the palate of the Afar
hominid certainly says "ape" to me. (I must also confess
that the designation of *A. afarensis* supports several of my
favorite prejudices. Johanson and White emphasize that the
Afar and Laetoli specimens span a million years but are
virtually identical. I believe that most species do not alter
much during the lengthy period of their success and that
most evolutionary change accumulates during very rapid
events of splitting from ancestral stocks—see essays 17 and
18. Moreover, since I depict human evolution as a bush
rather than a ladder, the more species the merrier. Johan-

son and White do, however, accept far more gradualism than I would advocate for later human evolution.)

Amidst all this argument about skulls, teeth, and taxonomic placement, another and far more interesting feature of the Afar remains has not been disputed. Lucy's pelvis and leg bones clearly show that *A. afarensis* walked as erect as you or I. This fact has been prominently reported by the press, but in a very misleading way. The newspapers have conveyed, almost unanimously, the idea that previous orthodoxy had viewed the evolution of larger brains and upright postures as a gradual transition in tandem, perhaps with brains leading the way—from pea-brained quadrupeds to stooping half brains to fully erect, big-brained *Homo*. The *New York Times* writes (January 1979): "The evolution of bipedalism was thought to have been a gradual process involving intermediate forerunners of modern human beings that were stooped, shuffle-gaited 'ape-men,' creatures more intelligent than apes but not as intelligent as modern human beings." Absolutely false, at least for the past fifty years of our knowledge.

We have known since australopithecines were discovered in the 1920s that these hominids had relatively small brains and fully erect posture. (*A. africanus* has a brain about one-third the volume of ours and a completely upright gait. A correction for its small body size does not remove the large discrepancy between its brain and ours.) This "anomaly" of small brain and upright posture has been a major issue in the literature for decades and wins a prominent place in all important texts.

Thus, the designation of *A. afarensis* does not establish the historical primacy of upright posture over large brains. But it does, in conjunction with two other ideas, suggest something very novel and exciting, something curiously missing from the press reports or buried amidst misinformation about the primacy of upright posture. *A. afarensis* is important because it teaches us that perfected upright gait had already been achieved nearly four million years ago. Lucy's pelvic structure indicates bipedal posture for the Afar remains, while the remarkable footprints just discovered at

Laetoli provide even more direct evidence. The later south and east African australopithecines do not extend back much further than two and a half million years. We have thus added nearly one and a half million years to the history of fully upright posture.

To explain why this addition is so important, I must break the narrative and move to the opposite end of biology—from fossils of whole animals to molecules. During the past fifteen years, students of molecular evolution have accumulated a storehouse of data on the amino acid sequences of similar enzymes and proteins in a wide variety of organisms. This information has generated a surprising result. If we take pairs of species with securely dated times of divergence from a common ancestor in the fossil record, we find that the number of amino acid differences correlates remarkably well with time since the split—the longer that two lineages have been separate, the more the molecular difference. This regularity has led to the establishment of a molecular clock to predict times of divergence for pairs of species without good fossil evidence of ancestry. To be sure, the clock does not beat with the regularity of an expensive watch—it has been called a "sloppy clock" by one of its leading supporters—but it has rarely gone completely haywire.

Darwinians were generally surprised by the clock's regularity because natural selection should work at markedly varying rates in different lineages at different times: very rapidly in complex forms adapting to rapidly changing environments, very slowly in stable, well-adapted populations. If natural selection is the primary cause of evolution in populations, then we should not expect a good correlation between genetic change and time unless rates of selection remain fairly constant—as they should not by the argument stated above. Darwinians have escaped this anomaly by arguing that irregularities in the rate of selection smooth out over long periods of time. Selection might be intense for a few generations and virtually absent for a time thereafter, but the net change averaged over long periods could still be regular. But Darwinians have also been forced to face the possibility that regularity of the molecular clock reflects an evolutionary process not mediated by natural selection, the random fixation of neutral mutations. (I must defer this "hot" topic to another time and more space.)

In any case, the measurement of amino acid differences between humans and living African great apes (gorillas and chimpanzees) led to the most surprising result of all. We are virtually identical for genes that have been studied, despite our pronounced morphological divergence. The average difference in amino acid sequences between humans and African apes is less than one percent (0.8 percent to be precise)—corresponding to a mere five million years since divergence from a common ancestor on the molecular clock. Allowing for the slop, Allan Wilson and Vincent Sarich, the Berkeley scientists who uncovered this anomaly, will accept six million years, but not much more. In short, if the clock is valid, *A. afarensis* is pushing very hard at the theoretical limit of hominid ancestry.

Until recently, anthropologists tended to dismiss the clock, arguing that hominids provided a genuine exception to an admitted rule. They based their skepticism about the molecular clock upon an animal called *Ramapithecus,* an African and Asian fossil known mainly from jaw fragments and ranging back to fourteen million years in age. Many anthropologists claimed that *Ramapithecus* could be placed on our side of the ape-human split—that, in other words, the divergence between hominids and apes occurred more than fourteen million years ago. But this view, based on a series of technical arguments about teeth and their proportions, has been weakening of late. Some of the strongest supporters of *Ramapithecus* as a hominid are now prepared to reassess it as an ape or as a creature near to the common ancestry of ape and human but still before the actual split. The molecular clock has been right too often to cast it aside for some tentative arguments about fragments of jaws. (I now expect to lose a $10 bet I made with Allan Wilson a few years back. He generously gave me seven million years as a maximum for the oldest ape-human common ancestor, but I held out for more. And while I'm not shelling out yet, I don't really expect to collect.*)

We may now put together three points to suggest a major reorientation in views about human evolution: the age and upright posture of *A. afarensis,* the ape-human split on the molecular clock, and the dethroning of *Ramapithecus* as a hominid.

We have never been able to get away from a brain-centered view of human evolution, although it has never represented more than a powerful cultural prejudice imposed upon nature. Early evolutionists argued that enlargement of the brain must have preceded any major alteration of our bodily frame. (See views of G.E. Smith in essay 10. Smith based his pro-Piltdown conviction upon an almost fanatical belief in cerebral primacy.) But *A. africanus,* upright and small brained, ended that conceit in the 1920s, as predicted by a number of astute evolutionists and philosophers, from Ernst Haeckel to Friedrich Engels. Nevertheless, "cerebral primacy," as I like to call it, still held on in altered form. Evolutionists granted the historical primacy of upright posture but conjectured that it arose at a leisurely pace and that the real discontinuity—the leap that made us fully human—occurred much later when, in an unprecedented burst of evolutionary speed, our brains tripled in size within a million years or so.

Consider the following, written ten years ago by a leading expert: "The great leap in cephalization of genus *Homo* took place within the past two million years, after some ten million years of preparatory evolution toward bipedalism, the tool-using hand, etc." Arthur Koestler has carried this view of a cerebral leap toward humanity to an unexcelled height of invalid speculation in his latest book, *Janus.* Our brain grew so fast, he argues, that the outer cerebral cortex, seat of smarts and rationality, lost control over emotive, animal centers deep within our brains. This primitive bestiality surfaces in war, murder, and other forms of mayhem.

---

*Jan., 1980. I just paid. Might as well start off the new decade right.

I believe that we must reassess fundamentally the relative importance we have assigned to upright posture and increase in brain size as determinants of human evolution. We have viewed upright posture as an easily accomplished, gradual trend and increase in brain size as a surprisingly rapid discontinuity—something special both in its evolutionary mode and the magnitude of its effect. I wish to suggest a diametrically opposite view. Upright posture is the surprise, the difficult event, the rapid and fundamental reconstruction of our anatomy. The subsequent enlargement of our brain is, in anatomical terms, a secondary epiphenomenon, an easy transformation embedded in a general pattern of human evolution.

Six million years ago at most, if the molecular clock runs true (and Wilson and Sarich would prefer five), we shared our last common ancestor with gorillas and chimps. Presumably, this creature walked primarily on all fours, although it may have moved about on two legs as well, as apes and many monkeys do today. Little more than a million years later, our ancestors were as bipedal as you or I. This, not later enlargement of the brain, was the great punctuation in human evolution.

Bipedalism is no easy accomplishment. It requires a fundamental reconstruction of our anatomy, particularly of the foot and pelvis. Moreover, it represents an anatomical reconstruction outside the general pattern of human evolution. As I argue in essay 9, through the agency of Mickey Mouse, humans are neotenic—we have evolved by retaining juvenile features of our ancestors. Our large brains, small jaws, and a host of other features, ranging from distribution of bodily hair to ventral pointing of the vaginal canal, are consequences of eternal youth. But upright posture is a different phenomenon. It cannot be achieved by the "easy" route of retaining a feature already present in juvenile stages. For a baby's legs are relatively small and weak, while bipedal posture demands enlargement and strengthening of the legs.

By the time we became upright as *A. afarensis,* the game was largely over, the major alteration of architecture accomplished, the trigger of future change already set. The later enlargement of our brain was anatomically easy. We read our larger brain out of the program of our own growth, by prolonging rapid rates of fetal growth to later times and preserving, as adults, the characteristic proportions of a juvenile primate skull. And we evolved this brain in concert with a host of other neotenic features, all part of a general pattern.

Yet I must end by pulling back and avoiding a fallacy of reasoning—the false equation between magnitude of effect and intensity of cause. As a pure problem in architectural reconstruction, upright posture is far-reaching and fundamental, an enlarged brain superficial and secondary. But the effect of our large brain has far outstripped the relative ease of its construction. Perhaps the most amazing thing of all is a general property of complex systems, our brain prominent among them—their capacity to translate merely quantitative changes in structure into wondrously different qualities of function.

It is now two in the morning and I'm finished. I think I'll walk over to the refrigerator and get a beer; then I'll go to sleep. Culture-bound creature that I am, the dream I will have in an hour or so when I'm supine astounds me ever so much more than the stroll I will now perform perpendicular to the floor.

12 | In the Midst of Life . . .

GREAT STORYTELLERS OFTEN insert bits of humor to relieve the pace of intense drama. Thus, the gravediggers of Hamlet or the courtiers Ping, Pong and Pang of Puccini's *Turandot* prepare us for torture and death to follow. Sometimes, however, episodes that now inspire smiles or laughter were not so designed; the passage of time has obliterated their context and invested the words themselves with an unintended humor in our altered world. Such a passage appears in the midst of geology's most celebrated and serious document—Charles Lyell's *Principles of Geology,* published in three volumes between 1830 and 1833. In it, Lyell argues that the great beasts of yore will return to grace our earth anew:

> Then might those genera of animals return, of which the memorials are preserved in the ancient rocks of our continents. The huge iguanodon might reappear in the woods, and the ichthyosaur in the sea, while the pterodactyl might flit again through the umbrageous groves of tree-ferns.

Lyell's choice of image is striking, but his argument is essential to the major theme of his great work. Lyell wrote the *Principles* to advance his concept of uniformity, his belief that the earth, after "settling down" from the effects of its initial formation, had stayed pretty much the same—no glo-

In a satirical cartoon drawn by one of Lyell's colleagues in response to the cited passage about returning ichthyosaurs and pterodactyls, the future Prof. Ichthyosaurus lectures to students on the skull of a strange creature of the last creation.

bal catastrophes, no steady progress towards any higher state. The extinction of dinosaurs seemed to pose a challenge to Lyell's uniformity. Had they not, after all, been replaced by superior mammals? And didn't this indicate that life's history had a direction? Lyell responded that the replacement of dinosaurs by mammals was part of a grand, recurring cycle—the "great year"—not a step up the ladder of perfection. Climates cycle and life matches climates. Thus, when the summer of the great year came round again, the cold-blooded reptiles would reappear to rule once more.

And yet, for all the fervor of his uniformitarian conviction, Lyell did allow one rather important exception to his vision of an earth marching resolutely in place—the origin of *Homo sapiens* at the latest instant of geological time. Our arrival, he argued, must be viewed as a discontinuity in the history of our planet: "To pretend that such a step, or rather leap, can be part of a regular series of changes in the animal world, is to strain analogy beyond all reasonable bounds." To be sure, Lyell tried to soften the blow he had administered to his own system. He argued that the discontinuity reflected an event in the moral sphere alone—an addition to another realm, not a disruption of the continuing steady-state of the purely material world. The human body, after all, could not be viewed as a Rolls Royce among mammals:

> When it is said that the human race is of far higher dignity than were any pre-existing beings on the earth, it is the intellectual and moral attributes only of our race, not the animal, which are considered; and it is by no means clear, that the organization of man is such as would confer a decided pre-eminence upon him, if, in place of his reasoning powers, he was merely provided with such instincts as are possessed by the lower animals.

Nonetheless, Lyell's argument is a premier example of an all too common tendency among natural historians—the erection of a picket fence around their own species. The fence sports a sign: "so far, but no farther." Again and again, we encounter sweeping visions, encompassing everything from the primordial dust cloud to the chimpanzee. Then, at the very threshold of a comprehensive system, traditional pride and prejudice intervene to secure an exceptional status for one peculiar primate. I discuss another example of the same failure in essay 4—Alfred Russel Wallace's argument for the special creation of human intelligence, the only imposition by divine power upon an organic world constructed entirely by natural selection. The specific form of the argument varies, but its intent is ever the same —to separate man from nature. Below its main sign, Lyell's fence proclaims: "the moral order begins here"; Wallace's reads: "natural selection no longer at work."

Darwin, on the other hand, extended his revolution in thought consistently throughout the entire animal kingdom. Moreover, he explicitly advanced it into the most sensitive areas of human life. Evolution of the human body was upsetting enough, but at least it left the mind potentially inviolate. But Darwin went on. He wrote an entire book to assert that the most refined expressions of human emotion had an animal origin. And if feelings had evolved, could thoughts be far behind?

The picket fence around *Homo sapiens* rests on several supports; the most important posts embody claims for *preparation* and *transcendence*. Humans have not only transcended the ordinary forces of nature, but all that came before was, in some important sense, a preparation for our eventual appearance. Of these two arguments, I regard preparation as by far the more dubious and more expressive of enduring prejudices that we should strive to shed.

Transcendence, in modern guise, states that the history of our peculiar species has been directed by processes that had not operated before on earth. As I argue in essay 7, cultural evolution is our primary innovation. It works by the transmission of skills, knowledge and behavior through learning—a cultural inheritance of acquired characters. This nonbiological process operates in the rapid "Lamarckian" mode, while biological change must plod along by Darwinian steps, glacially slow in comparison. I do not regard this unleashing of Lamarckian processes as a transcendence in the usual sense of overcoming. Biological evolution is neither cancelled nor outmaneuvered. It continues as before and it constrains patterns of culture; but it is too slow to have much impact on the frenetic pace of our changing civilizations.

Preparation, on the other hand, is hubris of a much deeper kind. Transcendence does not compel us to view four billion years of antecedent history as any foreshadowing of our special skills. We may be here by unpredictable good fortune and still embody something new and powerful. But preparation leads us to trace the germ of our later arrival into all previous ages of an immensely long and complicated history. For a species that has been on earth for about 1/100,000 of its existence (fifty thousand of nearly five billion years), this is unwarranted self-inflation of the highest order.

Lyell and Wallace both preached a form of preparation; virtually all builders of picket fences have done so. Lyell depicted an earth in steady-state waiting, indeed almost yearning, for the arrival of a conscious being that could understand and appreciate its sublime and uniform design. Wallace, who turned to spiritualism later in life, advanced the more common claim that physical evolution had occurred in order, ultimately, to link pre-existing mind with a body capable of using it:

> We, who accept the existence of a spiritual world, can look upon the universe as a grand consistent whole adapted in all its parts to the development of spiritual beings capable of indefinite life and perfectibility. To us, the whole purpose, the only *raison d'être* of the world —with all its complexities of physical structure, with its grand geological progress, the slow evolution of the vegetable and animal kingdoms, and the ultimate appearance of man—was the development of the human spirit in association with the human body.

I think that all evolutionists would now reject Wallace's version of the argument for preparation—the foreordination of man in the literal sense. But can there be a legitimate and modern form of the general claim? I believe that such an argument can be constructed, and I also believe that it is the wrong way to view the history of life.

The modern version chucks foreordination in favor of predictability. It abandons the idea that the germ of *Homo sapiens* lay embedded in the primordial bacterium, or that some spiritual force superintended organic evolution, waiting to infuse mind into the first body worthy of receiving it. Instead, it holds that the fully natural process of organic evolution follows certain paths because its primary agent, natural selection, constructs ever more successful designs that prevail in competition against earlier models. The pathways of improvement are rigidly limited by the nature of building materials and the earth's environment. There are only a few ways—perhaps only one—to construct a good flyer, swimmer, or runner. If we could go back to that primordial bacterium and start the process again, evolution would follow roughly the same path. Evolution is more like turning a ratchet than casting water on a broad and uniform slope. It proceeds in a kind of lock step; each stage raises the process one step up, and each is a necessary prelude to the next.

Since life began in microscopic chemistry and has now reached consciousness, the ratchet contains a long sequence of steps. These steps may not be "preparations" in the old sense of foreordination, but they are both predictable and necessary stages in an unsurprising sequence. In an important sense, they prepare the way for human evolution. We are here for a reason after all, even though that reason lies in the mechanics of engineering rather than in the volition of a deity.

But if evolution proceeded as a lock step, then the fossil record should display a pattern of gradual and sequential advance in organization. It does not, and I regard this failure as the most telling argument against an evolutionary ratchet. As I argue in essay 21, life arose soon after the earth itself formed; it then plateaued for as long as three billion years—perhaps five-sixths of its total history. Throughout this vast period, life remained on the prokaryotic level—bacterial and blue green algal cells without the internal structures (nucleus, mitochondria, and others) that make sex and complex metabolism possible. For perhaps three billion years, the highest form of life was an algal mat—thin layers of prokaryotic algae that trap and bind sediment. Then, about 600 million years ago, virtually all the major designs of animal life appeared in the fossil record within a few million years. We do not know why the "Cambrian explosion" occurred when it did, but we have no reason to think that it had to happen then or had to happen at all.

Some scientists have argued that low oxygen levels prevented a previous evolution of complex animal life. If this were true, the ratchet might still work. The stage remained set for three billion years. The screw had to turn in a certain way, but it needed oxygen and had to wait until prokaryotic photosynthesizers gradually supplied the precious gas that the earth's original atmosphere had lacked. Indeed, oxygen was probably rare or absent in the earth's original atmosphere, but it now appears that large amounts had been generated by photosynthesis more than a billion years before the Cambrian explosion.

Thus, we have no reason to regard the Cambrian explosion as more than a fortunate event that need not have occurred, either at all or in the way it did. It may have been a consequence of the evolution of the eukaryotic (nucleate) cell from a symbiotic association of prokaryotic organisms within a single membrane. It may have occurred because the eukaryotic cell could evolve efficient sexual reproduction, and sex distributes and rearranges the genetic variability that Darwinian processes require. But the crucial point is this: if the Cambrian explosion could have occurred any time during more than a billion years before the actual event—that is, for about twice the amount of time that life has spent evolving since then—a ratchet scarcely seems to be an appropriate metaphor for life's history.

If we must deal in metaphors, I prefer a very broad, low and uniform slope. Water drops randomly at the top and usually dries before flowing anywhere. Occasionally, it works its way downslope and carves a valley to channel future flows. These myriad valleys could have arisen anywhere on the landscape. Their current positions are quite accidental. If we could repeat the experiment, we might obtain no valleys at all, or a completely different system. Yet we now stand at the shore line contemplating the fine spacing of valleys and their even contact with the sea. How easy it is to be misled and to assume that no other landscape could possibly have arisen.

I confess that the metaphor of the landscape contains one weak borrowing from its rival, the ratchet. The initial slope does impart a preferred direction to the water dropping on top—even though almost all drops dry before flowing and can flow, when they do, along millions of paths. Doesn't the initial slope imply weak predictability? Perhaps the realm of consciousness occupies such a long stretch of shoreline that some valley would have to reach it eventually.

But here we encounter another constraint, the one that prompted this essay (though I have been, I confess, a long time in getting to it). Almost all drops dry. It took three billion years for any substantial valley to form on the earth's initial slope. It might have taken six billion, or twelve, or twenty for all we know. If the earth were eternal, we might speak of inevitability. But it is not.

Astrophysicist William A. Fowler argues that the sun will exhaust its central hydrogen fuel after ten to twelve billion years of life. It will then explode and transform to a red giant so large that it will extend past the orbit of Jupiter, thus swallowing the earth. It is an arresting thought—the kind that makes you stop and contemplate, or that sends shivers up and down your spine—to recognize that humans have appeared on earth at just about the halfway point of our planet's existence. If the metaphor of the landscape be valid, with all its randomness and unpredictability, then I think we must conclude that the earth need never have evolved its complex life. It took three billion years to go beyond the algal mat. It might as well have taken five times as long, if only the earth had endured. In other words, if we could run the experiment again, the most spectacular event in the history of our solar system, the explosive exhaustion of its parent, might just as well have had an algal mat as its highest, mute witness.

Alfred Russel Wallace also contemplated the eventual destruction of life on earth (though, in his day, physicists argued that the sun would simply burn out and the earth freeze solid). And he could not accept it. He wrote of "the crushing mental burthen imposed upon those who . . . are compelled to suppose that all the slow growths of our race struggling towards a higher life, all the agony of martyrs, all the groans of victims, all the evil and misery and undeserved suffering of the ages, all the struggles for freedom, all the efforts towards justice, all the aspirations for virtue, and the wellbeing of humanity, shall absolutely vanish." Wallace eventually opted for a conventional Christian solution, the eternity of spiritual life: "Beings . . . possessing latent faculties capable of such noble development, are surely destined for a higher and more permanent existence."

I would venture a different argument. The average species of fossil invertebrate lives five to ten million years, as documented in the fossil record. (The oldest may go back, though I doubt the story myself, more than 200 million years.) Vertebrate species tend to live for shorter times. If we are still here to witness the destruction of our planet some five billion years or more hence, then we will have achieved something so unprecedented in the history of life that we should be willing to sing our swan song with joy— *sic transit gloria mundi.* Of course, we might also fly off in those legions of space ships, only to be condensed a bit later into the next big bang. But then, I never have been a keen student of science fiction.

4 | Science and Politics of Human Differences

13 | Wide Hats and Narrow Minds

IN 1861, FROM February to June, the ghost of Baron Georges Cuvier haunted the Anthropological Society of Paris. The great Cuvier, Aristotle of French biology (an immodest designation from which he did not shrink), died in 1832, but the physical vault of his spirit lived on as Paul Broca and Louis Pierre Gratiolet squared off to debate whether or not the size of a brain has anything to do with the intelligence of its bearer.

In the opening round, Gratiolet dared to argue that the best and brightest could not be recognized by their big heads. (Gratiolet, a confirmed monarchist, was no egalitarian. He merely sought other measures to affirm the superiority of white European males.) Broca, founder of the Anthropological Society and the world's greatest craniometrician, or head measurer, replied that "study of the brains of human races would lose most of its interest and utility" if variation in size counted for nothing. Why, he asked, had anthropologists spent so much time measuring heads if the results had no bearing upon what he regarded as the most important question of all—the relative worth of different peoples:

> Among the questions heretofore discussed within the Anthropological Society, none is equal in interest and importance to the question before us now. . . . The great importance of craniology has struck anthropolo-

gists with such force that many among us have neglected the other parts of our science in order to devote
ourselves almost exclusively to the study of skulls.
. . . In such data, we hope to find some information
relevant to the intellectual value of the various human
races.

Broca and Gratiolet battled for five months and through
nearly 200 pages of the published bulletin. Tempers flared.
In the heat of battle, one of Broca's lieutenants struck the
lowest blow of all: "I have noticed for a long time that, in
general, those who deny the intellectual importance of the
brain's volume have small heads." In the end, Broca won,
hands down. During the debate, no item of information had
been more valuable to Broca, none more widely discussed
or more vigorously contended, than the brain of Georges
Cuvier.

Cuvier, the greatest anatomist of his time, the man who
revised our understanding of animals by classifying them
according to function—how they work—rather than by rank
in an anthropocentric scale of lower to higher. Cuvier, the
founder of paleontology, the man who first established the
fact of extinction and who stressed the importance of catastrophes in understanding the history both of life and the
earth. Cuvier, the great statesman who, like Talleyrand,
managed to serve all French governments, from revolution
to monarchy, and die in bed. (Actually, Cuvier passed the
most tumultuous years of the revolution as a private tutor
in Normandy, although he feigned revolutionary sympa-
thies in his letters. He arrived in Paris in 1795 and never
left.) F. Bourdier, a recent biographer, describes Cuvier's
corporeal ontogeny, but his words also serve as a good
metaphor for Cuvier's power and influence: "Cuvier was
short and during the Revolution he was very thin; he became stouter during the Empire; and he grew enormously
fat after the Restoration."

Cuvier's contemporaries marveled at his "massive head."
One admirer affirmed that it "gave to his entire person an
undeniable cachet of majesty and to his face an expression

of profound meditation." Thus, when Cuvier died, his colleagues, in the interests of science and curiosity, decided to open the great skull. On Tuesday, May 15, 1832, at seven o'clock in the morning, a group of the greatest doctors and biologists of France gathered to dissect the body of Georges Cuvier. They began with the internal organs and, finding "nothing very remarkable," switched their attention to Cuvier's skull. "Thus," wrote the physician in charge, "we were about to contemplate the instrument of this powerful intelligence." And their expectations were rewarded. The brain of Georges Cuvier weighed 1,830 grams, more than 400 grams above average and 200 grams larger than any nondiseased brain previously weighed. Unconfirmed reports and uncertain inference placed the brains of Oliver Cromwell, Jonathan Swift, and Lord Byron in the same range, but Cuvier had provided the first direct evidence that brilliance and brain size go together.

Broca pushed his advantage and rested a good part of his case on Cuvier's brain. But Gratiolet probed and found a weak spot. In their awe and enthusiasm, Cuvier's doctors had neglected to save either his brain or his skull. Moreover, they reported no measures on the skull at all. The figure of 1,830 g for the brain could not be checked; perhaps it was simply wrong. Gratiolet sought an existing surrogate and had a flash of inspiration: "All brains are not weighed by doctors," he stated, "but all heads are measured by hatters and I have managed to acquire, from this new source, information which, I dare to hope, will not appear to you as devoid of interest." In short, Gratiolet presented something almost bathetic in comparison with the great man's brain: he had found Cuvier's hat! And thus, for two meetings, some of France's greatest minds pondered seriously the meaning of a worn bit of felt.

Cuvier's hat, Gratiolet reported, measured 21.8 cm in length and 18.0 cm in width. He then consulted a certain M. Puriau, "one of the most intelligent and widely known hatters of Paris." Puriau told him that the largest standard size for hats measured 21.5 by 18.5 cm. Although very few men wore a hat so big, Cuvier was not off scale. Moreover, Gratiolet reported with evident pleasure, the hat was extremely flexible and "softened by very long usage." It had probably not been so large when Cuvier bought it. Moreover, Cuvier had an exceptionally thick head of hair, and he wore it bushy. "This seems to prove quite clearly," Gratiolet proclaimed, "that if Cuvier's head was very large, its size was not absolutely exceptional or unique."

Gratiolet's opponents preferred to believe the doctors and refused to grant much weight to a bit of cloth. More than twenty years later, in 1883, G. Hervé again took up the subject of Cuvier's brain and discovered a missing item: Cuvier's head had been measured after all, but the figures had been omitted from the autopsy report. The skull was big indeed. Shaved of that famous mat of hair, as it was for the autopsy, its greatest circumference could be equaled by only 6 percent of "scientists and men of letters" (measured in life with their hair at that) and zero percent of domestic servants. As for the infamous hat, Hervé pleaded ignorance, but he did cite the following anecdote: "Cuvier had a habit of leaving his hat on a table in his waiting room. It often happened that a professor or a statesman tried it on. The hat descended below their eyes."

Yet, just as the doctrine of more-is-better stood on the verge of triumph, Hervé snatched potential defeat from the jaws of Broca's victory. Too much of a good thing can be as troubling as a deficiency, and Hervé began to worry. Why did Cuvier's brain exceed those of other "men of genius" by so much? He reviewed both details of the autopsy and records of Cuvier's frail early health and constructed a circumstantial case for "transient juvenile hydrocephaly," or water on the brain. If Cuvier's skull had been artificially enlarged by the pressure of fluids early during its growth, then a brain of normal size might simply have expanded— by decreasing in density, not by growing larger—into the space available. Or did an enlarged space permit the brain to grow to an unusual size after all? Hervé could not resolve this cardinal question because Cuvier's brain had been measured and then tossed out. All that remained was the magisterial number, 1,830 grams. "With the brain of

Cuvier," wrote Hervé, "science has lost one of the most precious documents it ever possessed."

On the surface, this tale seems ludicrous. The thought of France's finest anthropologists arguing passionately about the meaning of a dead colleague's hat could easily provoke the most misleading and dangerous inference of all about history—a view of the past as a domain of naïve half-wits, the path of history as a tale of progress, and the present as sophisticated and enlightened.

But if we laugh with derision, we will never understand. Human intellectual capacity has not altered for thousands of years so far as we can tell. If intelligent people invested intense energy in issues that now seem foolish to us, then the failure lies in our understanding of their world, not in their distorted perceptions. Even the standard example of ancient nonsense—the debate about angels on pinheads— makes sense once you realize that theologians were not discussing whether five or eighteen would fit, but whether a pin could house a finite or an infinite number. In certain theological systems, the corporeality or noncorporeality of angels is an important matter indeed.

In this case, a clue to the vital importance of Cuvier's brain for nineteenth-century anthropology lies in the last line of Broca's statement, quoted above: "In such data, we hope to find some information relevant to the intellectual value of the various human races." Broca and his school wanted to show that brain size, through its link with intelligence, could resolve what they regarded as the primary question for a "science of man"—explaining why some individuals and groups are more successful than others. To do this, they separated people according to a priori convictions about their worth—men versus women, whites versus blacks, "men of genius" versus ordinary folks—and tried to demonstrate differences in brain size. The brains of eminent men (literally males) formed an essential link in their argument—and Cuvier was the *crème de la crème*. Broca concluded:

> In general, the brain is larger in men than in women, in eminent men than in men of mediocre talent, in superior races than in inferior races. Other things equal, there is a remarkable relationship between the development of intelligence and the volume of the brain.

Broca died in 1880, but disciples continued his catalog of eminent brains (indeed, they added Broca's own to the list —although it weighed in at an undistinguished 1,484 grams). The dissection of famous colleagues became something of a cottage industry among anatomists and anthropologists. E.A. Spitzka, the most prominent American practitioner of the trade, cajoled his eminent friends: "To me the thought of an autopsy is certainly less repugnant than I imagine the process of cadaveric decomposition in the grave to be." The two premier American ethnologists, John Wesley Powell and W J McGee made a wager over who had the larger brain—and Spitzka contracted to resolve the issue for them posthumously. (It was a toss-up. The brains of Powell and McGee differed very little, no more than varying body size might require.)

By 1907, Spitzka could present a tabulation of 115 eminent men. As the list grew in length, ambiguity of results increased apace. At the upper end, Cuvier was finally overtaken when Turgenev broke the 2,000-gram barrier in 1883. But embarrassment and insult stalked the other end. Walt Whitman managed to hear the varied carols of America singing with only 1,282 g. Franz Josef Gall, a founder of phrenology—the original "science" of judging mental worth by the size of localized brain areas—could muster only 1,198 g. Later, in 1924, Anatole France almost halved Turgenev's 2,012 and weighed in at a mere 1,017 g.

Spitzka, nonetheless, was undaunted. In an outrageous example of data selected to conform with a priori prejudice, he arranged, in order, a large brain from an eminent white male, a bushwoman from Africa, and a gorilla. (He could easily have reversed the first two by choosing a larger black and a smaller white.) Spitzka concluded, again invoking the shade of Georges Cuvier: "The jump from a Cuvier or a Thackeray to a Zulu or a Bushman is no greater than from the latter to the gorilla or the orang."

Such overt racism is no longer common among scientists, and I trust that no one would now try to rank races or sexes by the average size of their brains. Yet our fascination with the physical basis of intelligence persists (as it should), and the naïve hope remains in some quarters that size or some other unambiguous external feature might capture the subtlety within. Indeed, the crassest form of more-is-better—using an easily measured quantity to assess improperly a far more subtle and elusive quality—is still with us. And the method that some men use to judge the worth of their penises or their automobiles is still being applied to brains. This essay was inspired by recent reports on the whereabouts of Einstein's brain. Yes, Einstein's brain was removed for study, but a quarter century after his death, the results have not been published. The remaining pieces—others were farmed out to various specialists—now rest in a Mason jar packed in a cardboard box marked "Costa Cider" and housed in an office in Wichita, Kansas. Nothing has been published because nothing unusual has been found. "So far it's fallen within normal limits for a man his age," remarked the owner of the Mason jar.

Did I just hear Cuvier and Anatole France laughing in concert from on high? Are they repeating a famous motto of their native land: *plus ça change, plus c'est la même chose* ("the more things change, the more they remain the same"). The physical structure of the brain must record intelligence in some way, but gross size and external shape are not likely to capture anything of value. I am, somehow, less interested in the weight and convolutions of Einstein's brain than in the near certainty that people of equal talent have lived and died in cotton fields and sweatshops.

14 | Women's Brains

IN THE PRELUDE to *Middlemarch,*
George Eliot lamented the unfulfilled lives of talented
women:

> Some have felt that these blundering lives are due to
> the inconvenient indefiniteness with which the Su-
> preme Power has fashioned the natures of women: if
> there were one level of feminine incompetence as strict
> as the ability to count three and no more, the social lot
> of women might be treated with scientific certitude.

Eliot goes on to discount the idea of innate limitation, but
while she wrote in 1872, the leaders of European anthropometry were trying to measure "with scientific certi-
tude" the inferiority of women. Anthropometry, or measurement of the human body, is not so fashionable a field
these days, but it dominated the human sciences for much
of the nineteenth century and remained popular until intelligence testing replaced skull measurement as a favored
device for making invidious comparisons among races,
classes, and sexes. Craniometry, or measurement of the
skull, commanded the most attention and respect. Its
unquestioned leader, Paul Broca (1824–80), professor of
clinical surgery at the Faculty of Medicine in Paris, gathered
a school of disciples and imitators around himself. Their

152

work, so meticulous and apparently irrefutable, exerted great influence and won high esteem as a jewel of nineteenth-century science.

Broca's work seemed particularly invulnerable to refutation. Had he not measured with the most scrupulous care and accuracy? (Indeed, he had. I have the greatest respect for Broca's meticulous procedure. His numbers are sound. But science is an inferential exercise, not a catalog of facts. Numbers, by themselves, specify nothing. All depends upon what you do with them.) Broca depicted himself as an apostle of objectivity, a man who bowed before facts and cast aside superstition and sentimentality. He declared that "there is no faith, however respectable, no interest, however legitimate, which must not accommodate itself to the progress of human knowledge and bend before truth." Women, like it or not, had smaller brains than men and, therefore, could not equal them in intelligence. This fact, Broca argued, may reinforce a common prejudice in male society, but it is also a scientific truth. L. Manouvrier, a black sheep in Broca's fold, rejected the inferiority of women and wrote with feeling about the burden imposed upon them by Broca's numbers:

> Women displayed their talents and their diplomas. They also invoked philosophical authorities. But they were opposed by *numbers* unknown to Condorcet or to John Stuart Mill. These numbers fell upon poor women like a sledge hammer, and they were accompanied by commentaries and sarcasms more ferocious than the most misogynist imprecations of certain church fathers. The theologians had asked if women had a soul. Several centuries later, some scientists were ready to refuse them a human intelligence.

Broca's argument rested upon two sets of data: the larger brains of men in modern societies, and a supposed increase in male superiority through time. His most extensive data came from autopsies performed personally in four Parisian hospitals. For 292 male brains, he calculated an average weight of 1,325 grams; 140 female brains averaged 1,144 grams for a difference of 181 grams, or 14 percent of the male weight. Broca understood, of course, that part of this difference could be attributed to the greater height of males. Yet he made no attempt to measure the effect of size alone and actually stated that it cannot account for the entire difference because we know, a priori, that women are not as intelligent as men (a premise that the data were supposed to test, not rest upon):

> We might ask if the small size of the female brain de-pends exclusively upon the small size of her body. Tiedemann has proposed this explanation. But we must not forget that women are, on the average, a little less intelligent than men, a difference which we should not exaggerate but which is, nonetheless, real. We are therefore permitted to suppose that the relatively small size of the female brain depends in part upon her physi-cal inferiority and in part upon her intellectual inferior-ity.

In 1873, the year after Eliot published *Middlemarch,* Broca measured the cranial capacities of prehistoric skulls from L'Homme Mort cave. Here he found a difference of only 99.5 cubic centimeters between males and females, while modern populations range from 129.5 to 220.7. Topinard, Broca's chief disciple, explained the increasing discrepancy through time as a result of differing evolutionary pressures upon dominant men and passive women:

> The man who fights for two or more in the struggle for existence, who has all the responsibility and the cares of tomorrow, who is constantly active in combating the environment and human rivals, needs more brain than the woman whom he must protect and nourish, the sedentary woman, lacking any interior occupations, whose role is to raise children, love, and be passive.

In 1879, Gustave Le Bon, chief misogynist of Broca's school, used these data to publish what must be the most vicious attack upon women in modern scientific literature (no one can top Aristotle). I do not claim his views were representative of Broca's school, but they were published in France's most respected anthropological journal. Le Bon concluded:

> In the most intelligent races, as among the Parisians, there are a large number of women whose brains are closer in size to those of gorillas than to the most developed male brains. This inferiority is so obvious that no one can contest it for a moment; only its degree is worth discussion. All psychologists who have studied the intelligence of women, as well as poets and novelists, recognize today that they represent the most inferior forms of human evolution and that they are closer to children and savages than to an adult, civilized man. They excel in fickleness, inconstancy, absence of thought and logic, and incapacity to reason. Without doubt there exist some distinguished women, very superior to the average man, but they are as exceptional as the birth of any monstrosity, as, for example, of a gorilla with two heads; consequently, we may neglect them entirely.

Nor did Le Bon shrink from the social implications of his views. He was horrified by the proposal of some American reformers to grant women higher education on the same basis as men:

> A desire to give them the same education, and, as a consequence, to propose the same goals for them, is a dangerous chimera. . . . The day when, misunderstanding the inferior occupations which nature has given her, women leave the home and take part in our battles; on this day a social revolution will begin, and everything that maintains the sacred ties of the family will disappear.

Sound familiar?*

I have reexamined Broca's data, the basis for all this derivative pronouncement, and I find his numbers sound but his interpretation ill-founded, to say the least. The data supporting his claim for increased difference through time can be easily dismissed. Broca based his contention on the samples from L'Homme Mort alone—only seven male and six female skulls in all. Never have so little data yielded such far ranging conclusions.

In 1888, Topinard published Broca's more extensive data on the Parisian hospitals. Since Broca recorded height and age as well as brain size, we may use modern statistics to remove their effect. Brain weight decreases with age, and Broca's women were, on average, considerably older than his men. Brain weight increases with height, and his average man was almost half a foot taller than his average woman. I used multiple regression, a technique that allowed me to assess simultaneously the influence of height and age upon brain size. In an analysis of the data for women, I found that, at average male height and age, a woman's brain would weigh 1,212 grams. Correction for height and age reduces Broca's measured difference of 181 grams by more than a third, to 113 grams.

I don't know what to make of this remaining difference because I cannot assess other factors known to influence brain size in a major way. Cause of death has an important effect: degenerative disease often entails a substantial diminution of brain size. (This effect is separate from the decrease attributed to age alone.) Eugene Schreider, also working with Broca's data, found that men killed in accidents had brains weighing, on average, 60 grams more than men dying of infectious diseases. The best modern data I can find (from American hospitals) records a full 100-gram

---

*When I wrote this essay, I assumed that Le Bon was a marginal, if colorful, figure. I have since learned that he was a leading scientist, one of the founders of social psychology, and best known for a seminal study on crowd behavior, still cited today (*La psychologie des foules*, 1895), and for his work on unconscious motivation.

difference between death by degenerative arteriosclerosis and by violence or accident. Since so many of Broca's subjects were very elderly women, we may assume that lengthy degenerative disease was more common among them than among the men.

More importantly, modern students of brain size still have not agreed on a proper measure for eliminating the powerful effect of body size. Height is partly adequate, but men and women of the same height do not share the same body build. Weight is even worse than height, because most of its variation reflects nutrition rather than intrinsic size— fat versus skinny exerts little influence upon the brain. Manouvrier took up this subject in the 1880s and argued that muscular mass and force should be used. He tried to measure this elusive property in various ways and found a marked difference in favor of men, even in men and women of the same height. When he corrected for what he called "sexual mass," women actually came out slightly ahead in brain size.

Thus, the corrected 113-gram difference is surely too large; the true figure is probably close to zero and may as well favor women as men. And 113 grams, by the way, is exactly the average difference between a 5 foot 4 inch and a 6 foot 4 inch male in Broca's data. We would not (especially us short folks) want to ascribe greater intelligence to tall men. In short, who knows what to do with Broca's data? They certainly don't permit any confident claim that men have bigger brains than women.

To appreciate the social role of Broca and his school, we must recognize that his statements about the brains of women do not reflect an isolated prejudice toward a single disadvantaged group. They must be weighed in the context of a general theory that supported contemporary social distinctions as biologically ordained. Women, blacks, and poor people suffered the same disparagement, but women bore the brunt of Broca's argument because he had easier access to data on women's brains. Women were singularly denigrated but they also stood as surrogates for other disenfranchised groups. As one of Broca's disciples wrote in 1881:

"Men of the black races have a brain scarcely heavier than that of white women." This juxtaposition extended into many other realms of anthropological argument, particularly to claims that, anatomically and emotionally, both women and blacks were like white children—and that white children, by the theory of recapitulation, represented an ancestral (primitive) adult stage of human evolution. I do not regard as empty rhetoric the claim that women's battles are for all of us.

Maria Montessori did not confine her activities to educational reform for young children. She lectured on anthropology for several years at the University of Rome, and wrote an influential book entitled *Pedagogical Anthropology* (English edition, 1913). Montessori was no egalitarian. She supported most of Broca's work and the theory of innate criminality proposed by her compatriot Cesare Lombroso. She measured the circumference of children's heads in her schools and inferred that the best prospects had bigger brains. But she had no use for Broca's conclusions about women. She discussed Manouvrier's work at length and made much of his tentative claim that women, after proper correction of the data, had slightly larger brains than men. Women, she concluded, were intellectually superior, but men had prevailed heretofore by dint of physical force. Since technology has abolished force as an instrument of power, the era of women may soon be upon us: "In such an epoch there will really be superior human beings, there will really be men strong in morality and in sentiment. Perhaps in this way the reign of women is approaching, when the enigma of her anthropological superiority will be deciphered. Woman was always the custodian of human sentiment, morality and honor."

This represents one possible antidote to "scientific" claims for the constitutional inferiority of certain groups. One may affirm the validity of biological distinctions but argue that the data have been misinterpreted by prejudiced men with a stake in the outcome, and that disadvantaged groups are truly superior. In recent years, Elaine Morgan has followed this strategy in her *Descent of Woman,* a speculative reconstruction of human prehistory from the woman's point of view—and as farcical as more famous tall tales by and for men.

I prefer another strategy. Montessori and Morgan followed Broca's philosophy to reach a more congenial conclusion. I would rather label the whole enterprise of setting a biological value upon groups for what it is: irrelevant and highly injurious. George Eliot well appreciated the special tragedy that biological labeling imposed upon members of disadvantaged groups. She expressed it for people like herself—women of extraordinary talent. I would apply it more widely—not only to those whose dreams are flouted but also to those who never realize that they may dream—but I cannot match her prose. In conclusion, then, the rest of Eliot's prelude to *Middlemarch:*

> The limits of variation are really much wider than anyone would imagine from the sameness of women's coiffure and the favorite love stories in prose and verse. Here and there a cygnet is reared uneasily among the ducklings in the brown pond, and never finds the living stream in fellowship with its own oary-footed kind. Here and there is born a Saint Theresa, foundress of nothing, whose loving heartbeats and sobs after an unattained goodness tremble off and are dispersed among hindrances instead of centering in some long-recognizable deed.

15 | Dr. Down's Syndrome

MEIOSIS, THE SPLITTING of chromosome pairs in the formation of sex cells, represents one of the great triumphs of good engineering in biology. Sexual reproduction cannot work unless eggs and sperm each contain precisely half the genetic information of normal body cells. The union of two halves by fertilization restores the full amount of genetic information, while the mixing of genes from two parents in each offspring also supplies the variability that Darwinian processes require. This halving, or "reduction division," occurs during meiosis when the chromosomes line up in pairs and pull apart, one member of each pair moving to each of the sex cells. Our admiration for the precision of meiosis can only increase when we learn that cells of some ferns contain more than 600 pairs of chromosomes and that, in most cases, meiosis splits each pair without error.

Yet organic machines are no more infallible than their industrial counterparts. Errors in splitting often occur. On rare occasions, such errors are harbingers of new evolutionary directions. In most cases, they simply lead to misfortune for any offspring generated from the defective egg or sperm. In the most common of meiotic errors, called nondisjunction, the chromosomes fail to split. Both members of the pair go to one sex cell, while the other comes up one chromosome short. A child formed from the union of a normal sex cell with one containing an extra chromosome

160

by nondisjunction will carry three copies of that chromosome in each cell, instead of the normal two. This anomaly is called a trisomy.

In humans, the twenty-first chromosome suffers nondisjunction at a remarkably high frequency, unfortunately rather tragic in effect. About 1 in 600 to 1 in 1,000 newborn babies carry an extra twenty-first chromosome, a condition technically known as "trisomy-21." These unfortunate children suffer mild to severe mental retardation and have a reduced life expectancy. They exhibit, in addition, a suite of distinctive features, including short and broad hands, a narrow high palate, rounded face and broad head, a small nose with a flattened root, and a thick and furrowed tongue. The frequency of trisomy-21 rises sharply with increasing maternal age. We know very little about the causes of trisomy-21; indeed, its chromosomal basis was not discovered until 1959. We have no idea why it occurs so often, and why other chromosomes are not nearly so subject to nondisjunction. We have no clue as to why an extra twenty-first chromosome should yield the highly specific set of abnormalities associated with trisomy-21. But at least it can be identified *in utero* by counting the chromosomes of fetal cells, thus providing an option for early abortion.

If this discussion strikes you as familiar, but missing in one respect, I have indeed left something out. The common designation for trisomy-21 is Mongolian idiocy, mongolism, or Down's syndrome. We have all seen children with Down's syndrome and I feel certain that I have not been alone in wondering why the condition was ever designated *Mongolian* idiocy. Most children with Down's syndrome can be recognized immediately, but (as my previous list demonstrates) their defining traits do not suggest anything oriental. Some, to be sure, have a small but perceptible epicanthic fold, the characteristic feature of an oriental eye, and some have slightly yellowish skin. These minor and inconstant features led Dr. John Langdon Haydon Down to compare them with orientals when he described the syndrome in 1866. But there is far more to the story of Down's designation than a few occasional, misleading, and superficial similarities; for it embodies an interesting tale in the history of scientific racism.

Few people who use the term are aware that both words, Mongolian and idiot, had technical meanings for Dr. Down that were rooted in the prevailing cultural prejudice, not yet extinct, for ranking people on unilinear scales with the ranker's group on top. Idiot once referred to the lowest grade in a threefold classification of mental deficiency. Idiots could never master spoken language; imbeciles, a grade above, could learn to speak but not to write. The third level, the slightly "feeble-minded," engendered considerable terminological controversy. In America, most clinicians adopted H.H. Goddard's term, "moron," from a Greek word meaning foolish. Moron is a technical term of this century, not an ancient designation, despite the length of metaphorical whiskers on those terrible, old moron jokes. Goddard, one of three major architects for the rigidly hereditarian interpretation of IQ tests, believed that his unilinear classification of mental worth could be simply extended above the level of morons to a natural ranking of human races and nationalities, with southern and eastern European immigrants on the bottom (still, on average, at moron grade), and old American WASP's on top. (After Goddard instituted IQ tests for immigrants upon their arrival at Ellis Island, he proclaimed more than 80 percent of them feeble-minded and urged their return to Europe.)

Dr. Down was medical superintendant of the Earlswood Asylum for Idiots in Surrey when he published his "Observations on an ethnic classification of idiots" in the London Hospital Reports for 1866. In a mere three pages, he managed to describe Caucasian "idiots" that reminded him of African, Malay, American Indian, and Oriental peoples. Of these fanciful comparisons, only the "idiots who arrange themselves around the Mongolian type" survived in the literature as a technical designation.

Anyone who reads Down's paper without a knowledge of its theoretical context will greatly underestimate its pervasive and serious purpose. In our perspective, it represents a set of flaky and superficial, almost whimsical, analogies presented by a prejudiced man. In his time, it embodied a deadly earnest attempt to construct a general, causal classification of mental deficiency based upon the best biological theory (and the pervasive racism) of the age. Dr. Down played for stakes higher than the identification of some curious noncausal analogies. Of previous attempts to classify mental defect, Down complained:

> Those who have given any attention to congenital mental lesions must have been frequently puzzled how to arrange, in any satisfactory way, the different classes of this defect which have come under their observation. Nor will the difficulty be lessened by an appeal to what has been written on the subject. The systems of classification are generally so vague and artificial, that, not only do they assist but feebly, in any mental arrangement of the phenomena which are presented, but they fail completely in exerting any practical influence on the subject.

In Down's day, the theory of recapitulation embodied a biologist's best guide for the organization of life into sequences of higher and lower forms. (Both the theory and "ladder approach" to classification that it encouraged are, or should be, defunct today. See my book *Ontogeny and Phylogeny,* Harvard University Press, 1977). This theory, often expressed by the mouthful "ontogeny recapitulates phylogeny," held that higher animals, in their embryonic development, pass through a series of stages representing, in proper sequence, the adult forms of ancestral, lower creatures. Thus, the human embryo first develops gill slits, like a fish, later a three chambered heart, like a reptile, still later a mammalian tail. Recapitulation provided a convenient focus for the pervasive racism of white scientists: they looked to the activities of their own children for comparison with normal, adult behavior in lower races.

As a working procedure, recapitulationists attempted to identify what Louis Agassiz had called the "threefold parallelism" of paleontology, comparative anatomy, and embryology—that is, actual ancestors in the fossil record, living representatives of primitive forms, and embryonic or youthful stages in the growth of higher animals. In the racist tradition for studying humans, the threefold parallel meant fossil ancestors (not yet discovered), "savages" or adult members of lower races, and white children.

But many recapitulationists advocated the addition of a fourth parallel—certain kinds of abnormal adults within superior races. They attributed many anomalies of form or behavior either to "throwbacks" or "arrests of development." Throwbacks, or atavisms, represent the spontaneous reappearance in adults of ancestral features that had disappeared in advanced lineages. Cesare Lombroso, for example, the founder of "criminal anthropology," believed that many lawbreakers acted by biological compulsion because a brutish past lived again in them. He sought to identify "born criminals" by "stigmata" of apish morphology—receding forehead, prominent chin, long arms.

Arrests of development represent the anomalous translation into adulthood of features that arise normally in fetal life but should be modified or replaced by something more advanced or complicated. Under the theory of recapitulation, these normal traits of fetal life are the adult stages of more primitive forms. If a Caucasian suffers developmental arrest, he may be born at a lower stage of human life—that is, he may revert to the characteristic forms of lower races. We now have a fourfold parallel of human fossil, normal adult of lower races, white children, and unfortunate white adults afflicted with atavisms or arrests of development. It is in this context that Dr. Down had his flash of fallacious insight: some Caucasian idiots must represent arrests of development and owe their mental deficiency to a retention of traits and abilities that would be judged normal in adults of lower races.

Therefore, Dr. Down scrutinized his charges for features of lower races, just as, twenty years later, Lombroso would measure the bodies of criminals for signs of apish morphology. Seek, with enough conviction aforethought, and ye shall find. Down described his search with obvious excitement: he had, or so he thought, established a natural and causal classification of mental deficiency. "I have," he wrote, "for some time had my attention directed to the possibility of making a classification of the feeble-minded, by arranging them around various ethnic standards,—in other words, framing a natural system." The more serious the deficiency, the more profound the arrest of development and the lower the race represented.

He found "several well-marked examples of the Ethiopian variety," and described their "prominent eyes," "puffy lips," and "woolly hair . . . although not always black." They are, he wrote, "specimens of white negroes, although of European descent." Next he described other idiots "that arrange themselves around the Malay variety," and still others "who with shortened foreheads, prominent cheeks, deep-set eyes, and slightly apish nose" represent those people who "originally inhabited the American continent."

Finally, mounting the scale of races, he came to the rung below Caucasian, "the great Mongolian family." "A very large number of congenital idiots," he continued, "are typical Mongols. So marked is this, that when placed side by side, it is difficult to believe that the specimens compared are not children of the same parents." Down then proceeded to describe, with fair accuracy and little indication of oriental features (beyond a "slight dirty yellowish tinge" to the skin), a boy afflicted with what we now recognize as trisomy-21, or Down's syndrome.

Down did not confine his description to supposed anatomical resemblances between oriental people and "Mongolian idiots." He also pointed to the behavior of his afflicted children: "They have considerable power of imitation, even bordering on being mimics." It requires some familiarity with the literature of nineteenth-century racism to read between these lines. The sophistication and complexity of oriental culture proved embarrassing to Caucasian racists, especially since the highest refinements of Chinese society had arisen when European culture still wallowed in barbarism. (As Benjamin Disraeli said, responding to an anti-Semitic taunt: "Yes, I am a Jew, and when the ancestors of the right honorable gentleman were brutal savages . . . mine were priests in the temple of Solomon.") Caucasians solved this dilemma by admitting the intellectual power of orientals, but attributing it to a facility for imitative copying, rather than to innovative genius.

Down concluded his description of a child with trisomy-21 by attributing the condition to developmental arrest (due, Down thought, to the tubercular condition of his parents): "The boy's aspect is such that it is difficult to realize that he is the child of Europeans, but so frequently are these characters presented, that there can be no doubt that these ethnic features are the result of degeneration."

By the standards of his time, Down was something of a racial "liberal." He argued that all people had descended from the same stock and could be united into a single family, with gradation by status to be sure. He used his ethnic classification of idiots to combat the claim of some scientists that lower races represented separate acts of creation and could not "improve" towards whiteness. He wrote:

If these great racial divisions are fixed and definite, how comes it that disease is able to break down the barrier, and to simulate so closely the features of the members of another division. I cannot but think that the observations which I have recorded, are indications that the differences in the races are not specific but variable. These examples of the result of degeneracy among mankind, appear to me to furnish some arguments in favor of the unity of the human species.

Down's general theory of mental deficiency enjoyed some popularity, but never swept the field. Yet his name for one specific anomaly, Mongolian idiocy (sometimes softened to mongolism) stuck long after most physicians forgot why Down had coined the term. Down's own son rejected his father's comparison of orientals and children with trisomy-21, though he defended both the low status of orientals and

the general theory linking mental deficiency with evolutionary reversion:

> It would appear that the characteristics which at first
> sight strikingly suggest Mongolian features and build
> are accidental and superficial, being constantly as-
> sociated, as they are, with other features which are in
> no way characteristic of that race, and if this is a case
> of reversion it must be reversion to a type even further
> back than the Mongol stock, from which some ethnolo-
> gists believe all the various races of men have sprung.

Down's theory for trisomy-21 lost its rationale—even
within Down's invalid racist system—when physicians detected it both in orientals themselves, and in races lower
than oriental by Down's classification. (One physician referred to "Mongol Mongolians" but that clumsy persever-
ance never took hold.) The condition could scarcely be due
to degeneration if it represented the normal state of a
higher race. We now know that a similar set of features
occurs in some chimpanzees who carry an extra chromosome probably homologous with the twenty-first of humans.

With Down's theory disproved, what should become of
his term? A few years ago, Sir Peter Medawar and a group
of oriental scientists persuaded several British publications
to substitute Down's syndrome for Mongolian idiocy and
mongolism. I detect a similar trend in this country, although mongolism is still commonly used. Some people
may complain that efforts to change the name represent yet
another misguided attempt by fuzzy-minded liberals to
muck around with accepted usage by introducing social
concerns into realms where they don't belong. Indeed, I do
not believe in capricious alteration of established names. I
suffer extreme discomfort every time I sing in Bach's St.
Matthew Passion and must, as an angry member of the
Jewish crowd, shout out the passage that served for centuries as an "official" justification for anti-Semitism: Sein Blut

komme über uns und unsre Kinder—"His blood be upon us and upon our children." Yet, as he to whom the passage refers said in another context, I would not change "one jot or one tittle" of Bach's text.

But scientific names are not literary monuments. Mongolian idiocy is not only defamatory. It is wrong on all counts. We no longer classify mental deficiency as a unilinear sequence. Children with Down's syndrome do not resemble orientals to any great extent, if at all. And, most importantly, the name only has meaning in the context of Down's discredited theory of racial reversion as the cause of mental deficiency. If we must honor the good doctor, then let his name stand as a designation for trisomy-21—Down's syndrome.

16 | Flaws in a Victorian Veil

THE VICTORIANS LEFT some magnificent, if lengthy, novels. But they also foisted upon an apparently willing world a literary genre probably unmatched for tedium and inaccurate portrayal: the multivolumed "life and letters" of eminent men. These extended encomiums, usually written by grieving widows or dutiful sons and daughters, masqueraded as humbly objective accounts, simple documentation of words and activities. If we accepted these works at face value, we would have to believe that eminent Victorians actually lived by the ethical values they espoused—a fanciful proposition that Lytton Strachey's *Eminent Victorians* put to rest more than fifty years ago.

Elizabeth Cary Agassiz—eminent Bostonian, founder and first president of Radcliffe College, and devoted wife of America's premier naturalist—had all the right credentials for authorship (including a departed and lamented husband). Her *Life and Correspondence of Louis Agassiz* turned a fascinating, cantankerous, and not overly faithful man into a paragon of restraint, statesmanship, wisdom, and rectitude.

I write this essay in the structure that Louis Agassiz built in 1859—the original wing of Harvard's Museum of Comparative Zoology. Agassiz, the world's leading student of fossil fishes, protégé of the great Cuvier (see essay 13), left his native Switzerland for an American career in the late

169

1840s. As a celebrated European and a charming man, Agassiz was lionized in social and intellectual circles from Boston to Charleston. He led the study of natural history in America until his death in 1873.

Louis's public utterances were always models of propriety, but I expected that his private letters would match his ebullient personality. Yet Elizabeth's book, ostensibly a verbatim report of Louis's letters, manages to turn this focus of controversy and source of restless energy into a measured and dignified gentleman.

Recently, in studying Louis Agassiz's views on race and prompted by some hints in E. Lurie's biography *(Louis Agassiz: a life in science)*, I encountered some interesting discrepancies between Elizabeth's version and Louis's original letters. I then discovered that Elizabeth simply expurgated the text and didn't even insert ellipses (those annoying three dots) to indicate her deletions. Harvard has the original letters, and a bit of sleuthing on my part turned up some spicy material.

During the decade before the Civil War, Agassiz expressed strong opinions on the status of blacks and Indians. As an adopted son of the north, he rejected slavery, but as an upper crust Caucasian, he certainly didn't link this rejection to any notion of racial equality.

Agassiz presented his racial attitudes as sober and ineluctable deductions from first principles. He maintained that species are static, created entities (at his death in 1873, Agassiz stood virtually alone among biologists as a holdout against the Darwinian tide). They are not placed upon the earth in a single spot, but created simultaneously over their entire range. Related species are often created in separate geographic regions, each adapted to prevailing environments of its own area. Since human races met these criteria before commerce and migration mixed us up, each race is a separate biological species.

Thus, America's leading biologist came down firmly on the wrong side of a debate that had been raging in America for a decade before he arrived: Was Adam the progenitor of all people or only of white people? Are blacks and Indians our brothers or merely our look-alikes? The *polygenists*, Agassiz among them, held that each major race had been created as a truly separate species; the *monogenists* advocated a single origin and ranked races by their unequal degeneration from the primeval perfection of Eden—the debate included no egalitarians. In logic, separate needn't mean unequal, as the victors in Plessy vs. Ferguson argued in 1896. But, as the winners in Brown vs. the Topeka Board of Education maintained in 1954, a group in power always conflates separation with superiority. I know of no American polygenist who did not assume that whites were separate *and* superior.

Agassiz insisted that his defense of polygeny had nothing to do with political advocacy or social prejudice. He was, he argued, merely a humble and disinterested scholar, trying to establish an intriguing fact of natural history.

> It has been charged upon the views here advanced that they tend to the support of slavery. . . . Is that a fair objection to a philosophical investigation? Here we have to do only with the question of the origin of men; let the politicians, let those who feel themselves called upon to regulate human society, see what they can do with the results. . . . We disclaim all connection with any question involving political matters. . . . Naturalists have a right to consider the questions growing out of men's physical relations as merely scientific questions, and to investigate them without reference to either politics or religion.

Despite these brave words, Agassiz ends this major statement on race (published in the *Christian Examiner*, 1850) with some definite social recommendations. He begins by affirming the doctrine of separate and unequal: "There are upon earth different races of men, inhabiting different parts of its surface . . . and this fact presses upon us the obligation to settle the relative rank among these races." The resulting hierarchy is self-evident: "The indomitable, courageous, proud Indian—in how different a light he stands by the side of the submissive, obsequious, imitative negro, or by the side of the tricky, cunning, and cowardly Mongolian! Are not these facts indications that the different races do not rank upon one level in nature." Finally, if he hadn't made his political message clear by generalization, Agassiz ends by advocating specific social policy—thus contravening his original pledge to abjure politics for the pure life of the mind. Education, he argues, must be tailored to innate ability; train blacks in hand work, whites in mind work.

> What would be the best education to be imparted to the different races in consequence of their primitive difference. . . . We entertain not the slightest doubt that human affairs with reference to the colored races would be far more judiciously conducted if, in our intercourse with them, we were guided by a full consciousness of the real differences existing between us and them, and a desire to foster those dispositions that are eminently marked in them, rather than by treating them on terms of equality.

Since these "eminently marked" dispositions are submissiveness, obsequiousness, and imitation, we can well imagine what Agassiz had in mind.

Agassiz had political clout, largely because he spoke as a scientist, supposedly motivated only by the facts of his case and the abstract theory they embodied. In this context, the actual source of Agassiz's ideas on race becomes a matter of some importance. Did he really have no ax to grind, no predisposition, no impetus beyond his love for natural history? The passages expurgated from *Life and Correspondence* shed considerable light. They show a man with strong prejudices based primarily on immediate visceral reactions and deep sexual fears.

The first passage, almost shocking in its force, even 130 years later, recounts Agassiz's first experience with black people (he had never encountered blacks in Europe). He first visited America in 1846 and sent his mother a long letter detailing his experiences. In the section about Philadelphia, Elizabeth Agassiz records only his visits to museums and the private homes of scientists. She expunges, without ellipses, his first impression of blacks—a visceral reaction to waiters in a hotel restaurant. In 1846 Agassiz still believed in human unity, but this passage exposes an explicit, stunningly nonscientific basis for his conversion to polygeny. For the first time, then, without omissions:

It was in Philadelphia that I first found myself in prolonged contact with negroes; all the domestics in my hotel were men of color. I can scarcely express to you the painful impression that I received, especially since the sentiment that they inspired in me is contrary to all our ideas about the confraternity of the human type and the unique origin of our species. But truth before all. Nevertheless, I experienced pity at the sight of this degraded and degenerate race, and their lot inspired compassion in me in thinking that they are really men. Nonetheless, it is impossible for me to repress the feeling that they are not of the same blood as us. In seeing their black faces with their thick lips and grimacing teeth, the wool on their head, their bent knees, their elongated hands, their large curved nails, and especially the livid color of the palms of their hands, I could not take my eyes off their faces in order to tell them to stay far away. And when they advanced that hideous hand towards my plate in order to serve me, I wished I were able to depart in order to eat a piece of bread elsewhere, rather than to dine with such service. What unhappiness for the white race—to have tied their existence so closely with that of negroes in certain countries! God preserve us from such a contact!

The second set of documents comes from the midst of the Civil War. Samuel Howe, husband of Julia Ward Howe (author of *The Battle Hymn of the Republic*) and a member of President Lincoln's Inquiry Commission, wrote to ask Agassiz his opinion about the role of blacks in a reunited nation. During August 1863, Agassiz responded in four long and impassioned letters. Elizabeth Agassiz bowdlerized them to render Louis's case as a soberly stated opinion (despite its peculiar content), derived from first principles and motivated only by a love of truth.

Louis argued, in short, that races should be kept separate lest white superiority be diluted. This separation should occur naturally since mulattoes, as a weak strain, will eventually die out. Blacks will leave the northern climates so unsuited to them (since they were created as a separate species for Africa); they will move south in droves and will eventually prevail in a few lowland states, although whites will maintain dominion over the seashore and elevated ground. We will have to recognize these states, even admit them to the Union, as the best solution to a bad situation; after all, we do recognize "Haity and Liberia."

Elizabeth's substantial deletions display Louis's motivation in a very different light. They radiate raw fear and blind prejudice. She systematically eliminates three kinds of statements. First, she omits the most denigrating references to blacks: "In everything unlike other races," Louis writes, "they may but be compared to children, grown in the stature of adults, while retaining a childlike mind." Second, she removes all elitist claims about the correlation of wisdom, wealth, and social position within races. In these passages, we begin to sense Louis's real fears about miscegenation.

> I shudder from the consequences. We have already to struggle, in our progress, against the influence of universal equality, in consequence of the difficulty of preserving the acquisitions of individual eminence, the wealth of refinement and culture growing out of select associations. What would be our condition if to these difficulties were added the far more tenacious influences of physical disability. Improvements in our system of education . . . may sooner or later counterbalance the effects of the apathy of the uncultivated and of the rudeness of the lower classes and raise them to a higher standard. But how shall we eradicate the

stigma of a lower race when its blood has once been allowed to flow freely into that of our children.

Third, and of greatest significance, she expunges several long passages on interbreeding that place the entire correspondence in a different setting from the one she fashioned. In them, we grasp Louis's intense, visceral revulsion toward the idea of sexual contact between races. This deep and irrational fear was as strong a driving force within him as any abstract notion about separate creation: "The production of half-breeds," he writes, "is as much a sin against nature, as incest in a civilized community is a sin against purity of character. . . . I hold it to be a perversion of every natural sentiment."

This natural aversion is so strong that abolitionist sentiment cannot reflect any innate sympathy for blacks but must arise because many "blacks" have substantial amounts of white blood and whites instinctively sense this part of themselves: "I have no doubt in my mind that the sense of abhorrence against slavery, which has led to the agitation now culminating in our civil war, has been chiefly if unconsciously fostered by the recognition of our own type in the offspring of southern gentlemen, moving among us as negros [sic], which they are not."

But if races naturally repel each other, how then do "southern gentlemen" take such willing advantage of their bonded women? Agassiz blames the mulatto house slaves. Their whiteness renders them attractive; their blackness, lascivious. The poor, innocent young men are enticed and entrapped.

As soon as the sexual desires are awakening in the young men of the South, they find it easy to gratify themselves by the readiness with which they are met by colored [mulatto] house servants. [This contact] blunts his better instincts in that direction and leads him gradually to seek more spicy partners, as I have heard the full blacks called by fast young men. One thing is cer-

tain, that there is no elevating element whatever conceivable in the connection of individuals of different
races; there is neither love, nor desire for improvement
of any kind. It is altogether a physical connection.

How a previous generation of gentlemen overcame their
aversion to produce the first mulattoes, we are not told.

We cannot know in detail why Elizabeth chose her deletions. I doubt that a conscious desire to convert Louis's
motives from prejudice to logical implication prompted all
her actions. Simple Victorian prudery probably led her to
reject a public airing of any statement about sex. In any
case, her deletions did distort Louis Agassiz's thought and
did render his intentions according to the fallacious and
self-serving model favored by scientists—that opinions
arise from dispassionate surveys of raw information.

These restorations show that Louis Agassiz was jolted to
consider the polygenist theory of races as separate species
by his initial, visceral reaction to contact with blacks. They
also demonstrate that his extreme views on racial mixing
were powered more by intense sexual revulsion than by any
abstract theory of hybridity.

Racism has often been buttressed by scientists who present a public façade of objectivity to mask their guiding
prejudices. Agassiz's case may be distant, but its message
rings through our century as well.

5 | The Pace of Change

17 | The Episodic Nature of Evolutionary Change

ON NOVEMBER 23, 1859, the day before his revolutionary book hit the stands, Charles Darwin received an extraordinary letter from his friend Thomas Henry Huxley. It offered warm support in the coming conflict, even the supreme sacrifice: "I am prepared to go to the stake, if requisite . . . I am sharpening up my claws and beak in readiness." But it also contained a warning: "You have loaded yourself with an unnecessary difficulty in adopting *Natura non facit saltum* so unreservedly."

The Latin phrase, usually attributed to Linnaeus, states that "nature does not make leaps." Darwin was a strict adherent to this ancient motto. As a disciple of Charles Lyell, the apostle of gradualism in geology, Darwin portrayed evolution as a stately and orderly process, working at a speed so slow that no person could hope to observe it in a lifetime. Ancestors and descendants, Darwin argued, must be connected by "infinitely numerous transitional links" forming "the finest graduated steps." Only an immense span of time had permitted such a sluggish process to achieve so much.

Huxley felt that Darwin was digging a ditch for his own theory. Natural selection required no postulate about rates; it could operate just as well if evolution proceeded at a rapid pace. The road ahead was rocky enough; why harness the theory of natural selection to an assumption both unnecessary and probably false? The fossil record offered no support for gradual change: whole faunas had been wiped out during disarmingly short intervals. New species almost always appeared suddenly in the fossil record with no intermediate links to ancestors in older rocks of the same region. Evolution, Huxley believed, could proceed so rapidly that the slow and fitful process of sedimentation rarely caught it in the act.

The conflict between adherents of rapid and gradual change had been particularly intense in geological circles during the years of Darwin's apprenticeship in science. I do not know why Darwin chose to follow Lyell and the gradualists so strictly, but I am certain of one thing: preference for one view or the other had nothing to do with superior perception of empirical information. On this question, nature spoke (and continues to speak) in multifarious and muffled voices. Cultural and methodological preferences had as much influence upon any decision as the constraints of data.

On issues so fundamental as a general philosophy of change, science and society usually work hand in hand. The static systems of European monarchies won support from legions of scholars as the embodiment of natural law. Alexander Pope wrote:

> Order is Heaven's first law; and this confessed,
> Some are, and must be, greater than the rest.

As monarchies fell and as the eighteenth century ended in an age of revolution, scientists began to see change as a normal part of universal order, not as aberrant and exceptional. Scholars then transferred to nature the liberal program of slow and orderly change that they advocated for social transformation in human society. To many scientists, natural cataclysm seemed as threatening as the reign of terror that had taken their great colleague Lavoisier.

Yet the geologic record seemed to provide as much evidence for cataclysmic as for gradual change. Therefore, in defending gradualism as a nearly universal tempo, Darwin had to use Lyell's most characteristic method of argument

—he had to reject literal appearance and common sense for an underlying "reality." (Contrary to popular myths, Darwin and Lyell were not the heros of true science, defending objectivity against the theological fantasies of such "catastrophists" as Cuvier and Buckland. Catastrophists were as committed to science as any gradualist; in fact, they adopted the more "objective" view that one should believe what one sees and not interpolate missing bits of a gradual record into a literal tale of rapid change.) In short, Darwin argued that the geologic record was exceedingly imperfect—a book with few remaining pages, few lines on each page, and few words on each line. We do not see slow evolutionary change in the fossil record because we study only one step in thousands. Change seems to be abrupt because the intermediate steps are missing.

The extreme rarity of transitional forms in the fossil record persists as the trade secret of paleontology. The evolutionary trees that adorn our textbooks have data only at the tips and nodes of their branches; the rest is inference, however reasonable, not the evidence of fossils. Yet Darwin was so wedded to gradualism that he wagered his entire theory on a denial of this literal record:

> The geological record is extremely imperfect and this fact will to a large extent explain why we do not find interminable varieties, connecting together all the extinct and existing forms of life by the finest graduated steps. He who rejects these views on the nature of the geological record, will rightly reject my whole theory.

Darwin's argument still persists as the favored escape of most paleontologists from the embarrassment of a record that seems to show so little of evolution directly. In exposing its cultural and methodological roots, I wish in no way to impugn the potential validity of gradualism (for all general views have similar roots). I wish only to point out that it was never "seen" in the rocks.

Paleontologists have paid an exorbitant price for Darwin's argument. We fancy ourselves as the only true students of life's history, yet to preserve our favored account of evolution by natural selection we view our data as so bad that we almost never see the very process we profess to study.

For several years, Niles Eldredge of the American Museum of Natural History and I have been advocating a resolution of this uncomfortable paradox. We believe that Huxley was right in his warning. The modern theory of evolution does not require gradual change. In fact, the operation of Darwinian processes should yield exactly what we see in the fossil record. It is gradualism that we must reject, not Darwinism.

The history of most fossil species includes two features particularly inconsistent with gradualism:

1. *Stasis.* Most species exhibit no directional change during their tenure on earth. They appear in the fossil record looking much the same as when they disappear; morphological change is usually limited and directionless.

2. *Sudden appearance.* In any local area, a species does not arise gradually by the steady transformation of its ancestors; it appears all at once and "fully formed."

Evolution proceeds in two major modes. In the first, phyletic transformation, an entire population changes from one state to another. If all evolutionary change occurred in this mode, life would not persist for long. Phyletic evolution yields no increase in diversity, only a transformation of one thing into another. Since extinction (by extirpation, not by evolution into something else) is so common, a biota with no mechanism for increasing diversity would soon be wiped out. The second mode, speciation, replenishes the earth. New species branch off from a persisting parental stock.

Darwin, to be sure, acknowledged and discussed the process of speciation. But he cast his discussion of evolutionary change almost totally in the mold of phyletic transformation. In this context, the phenomena of stasis and sudden appearance could hardly be attributed to anything but imperfection of the record; for if new species arise by the transformation of entire ancestral populations, and if we almost never see the transformation (because species are essentially static through their range), then our record must be hopelessly incomplete.

Eldredge and I believe that speciation is responsible for almost all evolutionary change. Moreover, the way in which it occurs virtually guarantees that sudden appearance and stasis shall dominate the fossil record.

All major theories of speciation maintain that splitting takes place rapidly in very small populations. The theory of geographic, or allopatric, speciation is preferred by most evolutionists for most situations (allopatric means "in another place").* A new species can arise when a small segment of the ancestral population is isolated at the periphery of the ancestral range. Large, stable central populations exert a strong homogenizing influence. New and favorable mutations are diluted by the sheer bulk of the population through which they must spread. They may build slowly in frequency, but changing environments usually cancel their selective value long before they reach fixation. Thus, phyletic transformation in large populations should be very rare—as the fossil record proclaims.

But small, peripherally isolated groups are cut off from their parental stock. They live as tiny populations in geographic corners of the ancestral range. Selective pressures

---

*I wrote this essay in 1977. Since then, a major shift of opinion has been sweeping through evolutionary biology. The allopatric orthodoxy has been breaking down and several mechanisms of sympatric speciation have been gaining both legitimacy and examples. (In sympatric speciation, new forms arise within the geographic range of their ancestors.) These sympatric mechanisms are united in their insistence upon the two conditions that Eldredge and I require for our model of the fossil record—*rapid* origin in a *small* population. In fact, they generally advocate smaller groups and more rapid change than conventional allopatry envisages (primarily because groups in potential contact with their forebears must move quickly towards reproductive isolation, lest their favorable variants be diluted by breeding with the more numerous parental forms). See White (1978) for a thorough discussion of these sympatric models.

are usually intense because peripheries mark the edge of ecological tolerance for ancestral forms. Favorable variations spread quickly. Small, peripheral isolates are a laboratory of evolutionary change.

What should the fossil record include if most evolution occurs by speciation in peripheral isolates? Species should be static through their range because our fossils are the remains of large central populations. In any local area inhabited by ancestors, a descendent species should appear suddenly by migration from the peripheral region in which it evolved. In the peripheral region itself, we might find direct evidence of speciation, but such good fortune would be rare indeed because the event occurs so rapidly in such a small population. Thus, the fossil record is a faithful rendering of what evolutionary theory predicts, not a pitiful vestige of a once bountiful tale.

Eldredge and I refer to this scheme as the model of *punctuated equilibria.* Lineages change little during most of their history, but events of rapid speciation occasionally punctuate this tranquillity. Evolution is the differential survival and deployment of these punctuations. (In describing the speciation of peripheral isolates as very rapid, I speak as a geologist. The process may take hundreds, even thousands of years; you might see nothing if you stared at speciating bees on a tree for your entire lifetime. But a thousand years is a tiny fraction of one percent of the average duration for most fossil invertebrate species—5 to 10 million years. Geologists can rarely resolve so short an interval at all; we tend to treat it as a moment.)

If gradualism is more a product of Western thought than a fact of nature, then we should consider alternate philosophies of change to enlarge our realm of constraining prejudices. In the Soviet Union, for example, scientists are trained with a very different philosophy of change—the so-called dialectical laws, reformulated by Engels from Hegel's philosophy. The dialectical laws are explicitly punctuational. They speak, for example, of the "transformation of quantity into quality." This may sound like mumbo jumbo, but it suggests that change occurs in large leaps following a slow accumulation of stresses that a system resists until it reaches the breaking point. Heat water and it eventually boils. Oppress the workers more and more and bring on the revolution. Eldredge and I were fascinated to learn that many Russian paleontologists support a model similar to our punctuated equilibria.

I emphatically do not assert the general "truth" of this philosophy of punctuational change. Any attempt to support the exclusive validity of such a grandiose notion would border on the nonsensical. Gradualism sometimes works well. (I often fly over the folded Appalachians and marvel at the striking parallel ridges left standing by gradual erosion of the softer rocks surrounding them.) I make a simple plea for pluralism in guiding philosophies, and for the recognition that such philosophies, however hidden and unarticulated, constrain all our thought. The dialectical laws express an ideology quite openly; our Western preference for gradualism does the same thing more subtly.

Nonetheless, I will confess to a personal belief that a punctuational view may prove to map tempos of biological and geologic change more accurately and more often than any of its competitors—if only because complex systems in steady state are both common and highly resistant to change. As my colleague British geologist Derek V. Ager writes in supporting a punctuational view of geologic change: "The history of any one part of the earth, like the life of a soldier, consists of long periods of boredom and short periods of terror."

18 | Return of the Hopeful Monster

BIG BROTHER, THE tyrant of George Orwell's *1984*, directed his daily Two Minutes Hate against Emmanuel Goldstein, enemy of the people. When I studied evolutionary biology in graduate school during the mid-1960s, official rebuke and derision focused upon Richard Goldschmidt, a famous geneticist who, we were told, had gone astray. Although 1984 creeps up on us, I trust that the world will not be in Big Brother's grip by then. I do, however, predict that during this decade Goldschmidt will be largely vindicated in the world of evolutionary biology.

Goldschmidt, a Jewish refugee from Hitler's decimation of German science, spent the remainder of his career at Berkeley, where he died in 1958. His views on evolution ran afoul of the great neo-Darwinian synthesis forged during the 1930s and 1940s and continuing today as a reigning, if insecure, orthodoxy. Contemporary neo-Darwinism is often called the "synthetic theory of evolution" because it united the theories of population genetics with the classical observations of morphology, systematics, embryology, biogeography, and paleontology.

The core of this synthetic theory restates the two most characteristic assertions of Darwin himself: first, that evolution is a two-stage process (random variation as raw material, natural selection as a directing force); secondly, that evolutionary change is generally slow, steady, gradual, and continuous.

186

Geneticists can study the gradual increase of favored genes within populations of fruit flies in laboratory bottles. Naturalists can record the steady replacement of light moths by dark moths as industrial soot blackens the trees of Britain. Orthodox neo-Darwinians extrapolate these even and continuous changes to the most profound structural transitions in the history of life: by a long series of insensibly graded intermediate steps, birds are linked to reptiles, fish with jaws to their jawless ancestors. Macroevolution (major structural transition) is nothing more than microevolution (flies in bottles) extended. If black moths can displace white moths in a century, then reptiles can become birds in a few million years by the smooth and sequential summation of countless changes. The shift of gene frequencies in local populations is an adequate model for all evolutionary processes—or so the current orthodoxy states.

The most sophisticated of modern American textbooks for introductory biology expresses its allegiance to the conventional view in this way:

> [Can] more extensive evolutionary change, macro-evolution, be explained as an outcome of these micro-evolutionary shifts? Did birds really arise from reptiles by an accumulation of gene substitutions of the kind illustrated by the raspberry eye-color gene?
>
> The answer is that it is entirely plausible, and no one has come up with a better explanation. . . . The fossil record suggests that macroevolution is indeed gradual, paced at a rate that leads to the conclusion that it is based upon hundreds or thousands of gene substitutions no different in kind from the ones examined in our case histories.

Many evolutionists view strict continuity between micro- and macroevolution as an essential ingredient of Darwinism and a necessary corollary of natural selection. Yet, as I argue in essay 17, Thomas Henry Huxley divided the two issues of natural selection and gradualism and warned Darwin that his strict and unwarranted adherence to gradualism might undermine his entire system. The fossil record with its abrupt transitions offers no support for gradual change, and the principle of natural selection does not require it—selection can operate rapidly. Yet the unnecessary link that Darwin forged became a central tenet of the synthetic theory.

Goldschmidt raised no objection to the standard accounts of microevolution; he devoted the first half of his major work, *The Material Basis of Evolution* (Yale University Press, 1940), to gradual and continuous change within species. He broke sharply with the synthetic theory, however, in arguing that new species arise abruptly by discontinuous variation, or macromutation. He admitted that the vast majority of macromutations could only be viewed as disastrous —these he called "monsters." But, Goldschmidt continued, every once in a while a macromutation might, by sheer good fortune, adapt an organism to a new mode of life, a "hopeful monster" in his terminology. Macroevolution proceeds by the rare success of these hopeful monsters, not by an accumulation of small changes within populations.

I want to argue that defenders of the synthetic theory made a caricature of Goldschmidt's ideas in establishing their whipping boy. I shall not defend everything Goldschmidt said; indeed, I disagree fundamentally with his claim that abrupt macroevolution discredits Darwinism. For Goldschmidt also failed to heed Huxley's warning that the essence of Darwinism—the control of evolution by natural selection—does not require a belief in gradual change.

As a Darwinian, I wish to defend Goldschmidt's postulate that macroevolution is not simply microevolution extrapolated, and that major structural transitions can occur rapidly without a smooth series of intermediate stages. I shall proceed by discussing three questions: (1) can a reasonable story of continuous change be constructed for all macroevolutionary events? (my answer shall be no); (2) are theories of abrupt change inherently anti-Darwinian? (I shall argue that some are and some aren't); (3) do Goldschmidt's hopeful monsters represent the archetype of apostasy from Darwinism, as his critics have long maintained? (my answer, again, shall be no).

All paleontologists know that the fossil record contains precious little in the way of intermediate forms; transitions between major groups are characteristically abrupt. Gradualists usually extract themselves from this dilemma by invoking the extreme imperfection of the fossil record—if only one step in a thousand survives as a fossil, geology will not record continuous change. Although I reject this argument (for reasons discussed in essay 17), let us grant the traditional escape and ask a different question. Even though we have no direct evidence for smooth transitions, can we invent a reasonable sequence of intermediate forms—that is, viable, functioning organisms—between ancestors and descendants in major structural transitions? Of what possible use are the imperfect incipient stages of useful structures? What good is half a jaw or half a wing? The concept of *preadaptation* provides the conventional answer by permitting us to argue that incipient stages performed different functions. The half jaw worked perfectly well as a series of gill-supporting bones; the half wing may have trapped prey or controlled body temperature. I regard preadaptation as an important, even an indispensable, concept. But a plausible story is not necessarily true. I do not doubt that preadaptation can save gradualism in some cases, but does it permit us to invent a tale of continuity in most or all cases? I submit, although it may only reflect my lack of imagination, that the answer is no, and I invoke two recently supported cases of discontinuous change in my defense.

On the isolated island of Mauritius, former home of the dodo, two genera of boid snakes (a large group that includes pythons and boa constrictors) share a feature present in no other terrestrial vertebrate: the maxillary bone of the upper jaw is split into front and rear halves, connected by a movable joint. In 1970, my friend Tom Frazzetta published a paper entitled "From Hopeful Monsters to Bolyerine Snakes?" He considered every preadaptive possibility he could imagine and rejected them in favor of discontinuous transition. How can a jawbone be half broken?

Many rodents have cheek pouches for storing food. These internal pouches connect to the pharynx and may have evolved gradually under selective pressure for holding more and more food in the mouth. But the Geomyidae (pocket gophers) and Heteromyidae (kangaroo rats and pocket mice) have invaginated their cheeks to form external fur-lined pouches with no connection to the mouth or pharynx. What good is an incipient groove or furrow on the outside? Did such hypothetical ancestors run about three-legged while holding a few scraps of food in an imperfect crease with their fourth leg? Charles A. Long has recently considered a suite of preadaptive possibilities (external grooves in burrowing animals to transport soil, for example) and rejected them all in favor of discontinuous transition. These tales, in the "just-so story" tradition of evolutionary natural history, do not prove anything. But the weight of these, and many similar cases, wore down my faith in gradualism long ago. More inventive minds may yet save it, but concepts salvaged only by facile speculation do not appeal much to me.

If we must accept many cases of discontinuous transition in macroevolution, does Darwinism collapse to survive only as a theory of minor adaptive change within species? The essence of Darwinism lies in a single phrase: natural selection is the major creative force of evolutionary change. No one denies that natural selection will play a negative role in eliminating the unfit. Darwinian theories require that it create the fit as well. Selection must do this by building adaptations in a series of steps, preserving at each stage the advantageous part in a random spectrum of genetic variability. Selection must superintend the process of creation, not just toss out the misfits after some other force suddenly produces a new species, fully formed in pristine perfection.

We can well imagine such a non-Darwinian theory of discontinuous change—profound and abrupt genetic alteration luckily (now and then) making a new species all at once. Hugo de Vries, the famous Dutch botanist, supported such a theory early in this century. But these notions seem to present insuperable difficulties. With whom shall Athena born from Zeus's brow mate? All her relatives are members of another species. What is the chance, of producing Athena in the first place, rather than a deformed monster? Major disruptions of entire genetic systems do not produce favored—or even viable—creatures.

But all theories of discontinuous change are not anti-Darwinian, as Huxley pointed out nearly 120 years ago. Suppose that a discontinuous change in adult form arises from a small genetic alteration. Problems of discordance with other members of the species do not arise, and the large, favorable variant can spread through a population in Darwinian fashion. Suppose also that this large change does not produce a perfected form all at once, but rather serves as a "key" adaptation to shift its possessor toward a new mode of life. Continued success in this new mode may require a large set of collateral alterations, morphological and behavioral; these may arise by a more traditional, gradual route once the key adaptation forces a profound shift in selective pressures.

Defenders of the modern synthesis have cast Goldschmidt as Goldstein by linking his catchy phrase—hopeful monster—to non-Darwinian notions of immediate perfection by profound genetic change. But this is not entirely what Goldschmidt maintained. In fact, one of his mechanisms for discontinuity in adult forms relied upon a notion of small underlying genetic change. Goldschmidt was a student of embryonic development. He spent most of his early career studying geographic variation in the gypsy moth, *Lymantria dispar.* He found that large differences in the color patterns of caterpillars resulted from small changes in the timing of development: the effects of a slight delay or enhancement of pigmentation early in growth increased through ontogeny and led to profound differences among fully grown caterpillars.

Goldschmidt identified the genes responsible for these small changes in timing, and demonstrated that large final differences reflected the action of one or a few "rate genes" acting early in growth. He codified the notion of a rate gene in 1918 and wrote twenty years later:

The mutant gene produces its effect . . . by changing
the rates of partial processes of development. These
might be rates of growth or differentiation, rates of
production of stuffs necessary for differentiation, rates
of reactions leading to definite physical or chemical
situations at definite times of development, rates of
those processes which are responsible for segregating
the embryonic potencies at definite times.

In his infamous book of 1940, Goldschmidt specifically
invokes rate genes as a potential maker of hopeful monsters: "This basis is furnished by the existence of mutants
producing monstrosities of the required type and the
knowledge of embryonic determination, which permits a
small rate change in early embryonic processes to produce
a large effect embodying considerable parts of the organism."

In my own, strongly biased opinion, the problem of
reconciling evident discontinuity in macroevolution with
Darwinism is largely solved by the observation that small
changes early in embryology accumulate through growth to
yield profound differences among adults. Prolong the high
prenatal rate of brain growth into early childhood and a
monkey's brain moves toward human size. Delay the onset
of metamorphosis and the axolotl of Lake Xochimilco re-
produces as a tadpole with gills and never transforms into
a salamander. (See my book *Ontogeny and Phylogeny* [Harvard
University Press, 1977] for a compendium of examples, and
pardon me for the unabashed plug.) As Long argues for the
external cheek pouch: "A genetically controlled developmental inversion of the cheek pouch may have occurred,
recurred, and persisted in some populations. Such a morphological change would have been drastic in effect, turning the pockets 'wrong side out' (furry side in), but nevertheless it would be a rather simple embryonic change."

Indeed, if we do not invoke discontinuous change by
small alteration in rates of development, I do not see how
most major evolutionary transitions can be accomplished at
all. Few systems are more resistant to basic change than the

strongly differentiated, highly specified, complex adults of "higher" animal groups. How could we ever convert an adult rhinoceros or a mosquito into something fundamentally different. Yet transitions between major groups have occurred in the history of life.

D'Arcy Wentworth Thompson, classical scholar, Victorian prose stylist, and glorious anachronism of twentieth-century biology, dealt with this dilemma in his classic treatise *On Growth and Form.*

> An algebraic curve has its fundamental formula, which defines the family to which it belongs. . . . We never think of "transforming" a helicoid into an ellipsoid, or a circle into a frequency curve. So it is with the forms of animals. We cannot transform an invertebrate into a vertebrate, nor a coelenterate into a worm, by any simple and legitimate deformation. . . . Nature proceeds from one type to another. . . . To seek for steppingstones across the gaps between is to seek in vain, forever.

D'Arcy Thompson's solution was the same as Goldschmidt's: the transition may occur in simpler and more similar embryos of these highly divergent adults. No one would think of transforming a starfish into a mouse, but the embryos of some echinoderms and protovertebrates are nearly identical.

1984 will mark the 125th anniversary of Darwin's *Origin,* the first major excuse for a celebration since the centenary of 1959. I hope that our "new speaking" these few years hence will be neither dogma nor vacuous nonsense. If our entrenched, a priori preferences for gradualism begin to fade by then, we may finally be able to welcome the plurality of results that nature's complexity provides.

19 | The Great Scablands Debate

of popular guidebooks usually tout prevailing orthodoxy in its purest form—dogma unadulterated by the "howevers" of professional writing. Consider the following from our National Park Service's auto tour of Arches National Park:

> The world and all it contains is in a continuous process of change. Most of the changes in our world are very tiny and so escape our notice. They are real, however, and over an immense span of time their combined effect is to bring about great change. If you stand at the base of a canyon wall and rub your hand on the sandstone, hundreds of grains of sand are dislodged. It seems like an insignificant change, but that's how the canyon was formed. Various forces have dislodged and carried away grains of sand. Sometimes the process is "very fast" (as when you rub the sandstone) but most of the time it is much slower. If you allow sufficient time, you can tear down a mountain or create a canyon —a few grains at a time.

As the primary lesson of geology, this pamphlet proclaims that big results arise as the accumulated effect of tiny changes. My hand rubbing the canyon wall is an adequate (if anything, overeffective) illustration of rates that carved the canyon itself. Time, geology's inexhaustible resource,

194

performs all the miracles.

Yet, when the pamphlet turns to details, we encounter a different scenario for erosion in Arches. We learn that a balanced rock known as "Chip Off the Old Block" fell during the winter of 1975–76. Before and after photographs of the magnificent Skyline Arch receive the following commentary: "It remained thus for as long as man knew the arch, until, late in 1940, the block of stone fell, and Skyline was suddenly twice its former size." The arches form by sudden, intermittent collapse and toppling, not by imperceptible removal of sand grains. Yet gradualist orthodoxy is so entrenched that the authors of this pamphlet failed to note the inconsistency between their own factual account and the stated theory of their introduction. In other essays of this section, I argue that gradualism is a culturally conditioned prejudice, not a fact of nature, and I make a plea for pluralism in concepts of rate. Punctuational change is at

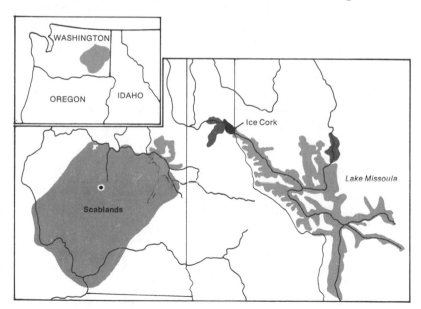

The channeled scablands of eastern Washington.

least as important as imperceptible accumulation. In this essay I tell a local, geologic story. But it conveys the same message—that dogmas play their worst role when they lead scientists to reject beforehand a counterclaim that could be tested in nature.

Flow basalts of volcanic origin blanket most of eastern Washington. These basalts are often covered by a thick layer of loess, a fine-grained, loosely packed sediment blown in by winds during the ice ages. In the area between Spokane and the Snake and Columbia rivers to the south and west, many spectacular, elongate, subparallel channelways are gouged through the loess and deeply into the hard basalt itself. These coulees, to use the local name, must have been conduits for glacial meltwaters, for they run down gradient from an area near the southern extent of the last glacier into the two major rivers of eastern Washington. The channeled scablands—as geologists designate the entire area—are puzzling as well as awesome, and for several reasons:

1. The channels connect across tall divides that once separated them. Since the channels are hundreds of feet deep, this extensive anastomosis indicates that a prodigious amount of water must once have flowed over the divide.
2. As another item favoring channels filled to the brim with water, the sides of the coulees contain many hanging valleys where tributaries enter the main channels. (A hanging valley is a tributary channel that enters a main channel high above the main channel's modern stream bed.)
3. The hard basalt of the coulees is deeply gouged and scoured. This pattern of erosion does not look like the work of gentle rivers in the gradualist mode.
4. The coulees often contain a number of high-standing hills composed of loess that has not been stripped away. These are arranged as if they were once islands in a gigantic braided stream.
5. The coulees contain discontinuous deposits of basaltic stream gravel, often composed of rock foreign to the local area.

Just after World War I, Chicago geologist J Harlen Bretz advanced an unorthodox hypothesis to account for this unusual topography (yes, that's J without a period, and don't ever let one slip in, for his wrath can be terrible). He argued that the channeled scablands had been formed all at once by a single, gigantic flood of glacial meltwater. This local catastrophe filled the coulees, cut through hundreds of feet of loess and basalt, and then receded in a matter of days. He ended his major work of 1923 with these words:

Fully 3,000 square miles of the Columbia Plateau were swept by the glacial flood, and the loess and silt cover removed. More than 2,000 square miles of this area were left as bare, eroded rock-cut channel floors, now the scablands, and nearly 1,000 square miles carry gravel deposits derived from the eroded basalt. It *was* a debacle which swept the Columbia Plateau.

Bretz's hypothesis became a minor *cause célèbre* within geological circles. Bretz's stout and lonely defense of his catastrophic hypothesis won some grudging admiration, but virtually no support at first. The "establishment," as represented by the United States Geological Survey, closed ranks in opposition. They had nothing better to propose, and they did admit the peculiar character of scabland topography. But they held firm to the dogma that catastrophic causes must never be invoked so long as any gradualist alternative existed. Instead of testing Bretz's flood on its own merits, they rejected it on general principles.

On January 12, 1927, Bretz bearded the lion in its lair and presented his views at the Cosmos Club, in Washington, D.C., before an assembled group of scientists, many from the Geological Survey. The published discussion clearly indicates that a priori gradualism formed the basis for Bretz's glacial reception. I include typical comments from all detractors.

W. C. Alden admitted "it is not easy for one, like myself, who has never examined this plateau to supply offhand an alternative explanation of the phenomena." Nonetheless, undaunted, he continued: "The main difficulties seem to be: (1) The idea that all the channels must have been developed simultaneously in a very short time; and (2) the tremendous amount of water that he postulates. . . . The problem would be easier if less water was required and if longer time and repeated floods could be allotted to do the work."

James Gilluly, this century's chief apostle of geological gradualism, ended a long comment by noting "that the actual floods involved at any given time were of the order of magnitude of the present Columbia's or at most a few times as large, seems by no means excluded by any evidence as yet presented."

E. T. McKnight offered a gradualist alternative for the gravels: "This writer believes them to be the normal channel deposits of the Columbia during its eastward shift over the area in preglacial, glacial, and postglacial times."

G. R. Mansfield doubted that "so much work could be done on basalt in so short a time." He also proposed a calmer explanation: "The scablands seem to me better explained as the effects of persistent ponding and overflow of marginal glacial waters, which changed their position or their places of outlet from time to time through a somewhat protracted period."

Finally, O. E. Meinzer admitted that "the erosion features of the region are so large and bizarre that they defy description." They did not, however, defy gradualist explanation: "I believe the existing features can be explained by assuming normal stream work of the ancient Columbia River." Then, more baldly than most of his colleagues, he proclaimed his faith: "Before a theory that requires a seemingly impossible quantity of water is fully accepted, every effort should be made to account for the existing features without employing so violent an assumption."

The story has a happy ending, at least from my point of view, for Bretz was delivered from the lion's lair by later evidence. Bretz's hypothesis has prevailed, and virtually all geologists now believe that catastrophic floods cut the channeled scablands. Bretz had found no adequate source for his floodwaters. He knew that the glaciers had advanced as far as Spokane, but neither he nor anyone else could imagine a reasonable way to melt so much water so rapidly. Indeed, we still have no mechanism for such an episodic melting.

The solution came from another direction. Geologists found evidence for an enormous, ice-dammed glacial lake in western Montana. This lake emptied catastrophically when the glacier retreated and the dam broke. The spillway for its waters leads right into the channeled scablands.

Bretz had presented no really direct evidence for deep, surging water. Gouging might have proceeded sequentially, rather than all at once, anastomosis and hanging valleys might reflect filled coulees with gentle, rather than raging, flow. But when the first good aerial photographs of the scablands were taken, geologists noticed that several areas on the coulee floors are covered with giant stream bed ripples, up to 22 feet high and 425 feet long. Bretz, like an ant on a Yale bladderball, had been working on the wrong scale. He had been walking over the ripples for decades but had been too close to see them. They are, he wrote quite correctly, "difficult to identify at ground level under a cover of sagebrush." Observations can only be made at appropriate scales.

Hydraulic engineers can infer the character of flow from the size and shape of ripples on a stream bed. V. R. Baker estimates a maximum discharge of 752,000 cubic feet per second in the scabland flow channels. Such a flood could have moved 36-foot boulders.

I could end here with a cardboard version of the story much to my liking: Perceptive hero suppressed by blinded dogmatists stands firm, expresses his allegiance to fact over received opinion, and eventually prevails by patient persuasion and overwhelming documentation. The outline of this tale is surely valid: gradualist bias *did* lead to a rejection of Bretz's catastrophic hypothesis out of hand, and Bretz (apparently) was right. But, as I read through the original papers, I realized that this good guy–bad guy scenario must yield to a more complex version. Bretz's opponents were not benighted dogmatists. They did have a priori preferences, but they also had good reasons to doubt catastrophic flooding based on Bretz's original arguments. Moreover, Bretz's style of scientific inquiry virtually guaranteed that he would not triumph with his initial data.

Bretz proceeded in the classic tradition of strict empiricism. He felt that adventurous hypotheses could only be established by long and patient collecting of information in the field. He eschewed theoretical discussion and worried little about the valid conceptual problem that so bothered his adversaries: where could so much water come from so suddenly?

Bretz tried to establish his hypothesis by toting up evidence of erosion in the field, piece by patient piece. He seemed singularly uninterested in finding the missing item that would render his story coherent—a source for the water. For this attempt might involve speculation without direct evidence, and Bretz relied only upon fact. When Gilluly challenged him on the absence of a source for the water, Bretz simply replied: "I believe that my interpretation of channeled scabland should stand or fall on the scabland phenomena themselves."

But why should an opponent be converted by such an incomplete theory? Bretz believed that the southern end of the glacier had melted precipitously, but no scientist could imagine a way to melt ice so quickly. (Bretz tentatively suggested volcanic activity under the ice, but quickly abandoned the theory when Gilluly attacked.) Bretz stayed in the scablands, while the answer sat in western Montana. Glacial Lake Missoula had been in the literature since the 1880s, but Bretz did not make the connection—he was working in other ways. His opponents were right. We still do not know a way to melt so much ice so quickly. But the premise shared by all participants was wrong: the source of the water was water.

Events that "cannot happen" according to received wisdom rarely gain respectability by a simple accumulation of evidence for their occurrence; they require a mechanism to explain how they *can* happen. Early supporters of continental drift ran into the same difficulty that Bretz encountered. Their evidence of faunal and lithological similarities between continents now widely separated strikes us today as overwhelming, but it failed in their time because no reasonable force had been proposed for moving continents. The theory of plate tectonics has since provided a mechanism and established the idea of continental drift.

Moreover, Bretz's opponents did not rest their case entirely on the unorthodox character of Bretz's hypothesis. They also marshaled some specific facts on their side, and they were partly right. Bretz originally insisted upon a single flood, while his opponents cited much evidence to show that the scablands had not formed all at once. We now know that Lake Missoula formed and re-formed several times as the glacial margin fluctuated. In his latest work, Bretz called for eight separate episodes of catastrophic flooding. Bretz's opponents were wrong in inferring gradual change from the evidence of temporal spread: catastrophic episodes can be separated by long periods of quiescence. But Bretz was also wrong in attributing the formation of the scablands to a single flood.

I prefer heroes of flesh, blood, and fallibility, not of tinseled cardboard. Bretz is inscribed on my ledger because he stood against a firm, highly restrictive dogma that never had made any sense: the emperor had been naked for a century. Charles Lyell, the godfather of geological gradualism, had pulled a fast one in establishing the doctrine of imperceptible change. He had argued, quite rightly, that geologists must invoke the invariance (uniformity) of natural law through time in order to study the past scientifically. He then applied the same term—uniformity—to an empirical claim about rates of processes, arguing that change must be slow, steady, and gradual, and that big results can only arise as the accumulation of small changes.

But the uniformity of law does not preclude *natural* catastrophes, particularly on a local scale. Perhaps some invariant laws operate to produce infrequent episodes of sudden, profound change. Bretz may not have cared for this brand of philosophical waffling. He probably would brand it as vacuous nonsense preached by an urban desk man. But he had the independence and gumption to live by a grand old slogan from Horace, often espoused by science but not often followed: *Nullius addictus jurare in verba magistri,* "I am not bound to swear allegiance to the words of any master."

My tale ends with two happy postscripts. First, Bretz's hypothesis that channeled scabland reflects the action of catastrophic flooding has been fruitful far beyond Bretz's local area. Scablands have been found in association with other western lakes, most notably Lake Bonneville, the large ancestor of a little puddle in comparison—Great Salt Lake, Utah. Other applications have ranged about as far as they can go. Bretz has become the darling of planetary geologists who find in the channelways of Mars a set of features best interpreted by Bretz's style of catastrophic flooding.

Second, Bretz did not share the fate of Alfred Wegener, dead on the Greenland ice while his theory of continental drift lay in limbo. J Harlen Bretz presented his hypothesis sixty years ago, but he has lived to enjoy his vindication. He is now well into his nineties, feisty as ever and justly pleased with himself. In 1969, he published a forty-page paper summarizing a half century of controversy about the channeled scablands of eastern Washington. He closed with this statement:

> The International Association for Quaternary Research held its 1965 meeting in the United States. Among the many field excursions it organized was one in the northern Rockies and the Columbia Plateau in Washington. . . . The party . . . traversed the full length of the Grand Coulee, part of the Quincy basin and much of the Palouse-Snake scabland divide, and the great flood gravel deposits in the Snake Canyon. The writer, unable to attend, received the next day a telegram of "greetings and salutations" which closed with the sentence, "We are now all catastrophists."

Postscript

I sent a copy of this article to Bretz after its publication in *Natural History.* He replied on October 14, 1978:

> Dear Mr. Gould,
> Your recent letter is most gratifying. Thank you for understanding.
> I have been surprised by the way my pioneer Scabland work has been applauded and further developed. I knew all along that I was right but the decades of doubt and challenge had produced an emotional lethargy, I think. Then the surprise following Victor Baker's field trip in June woke me up again. What! Had I become a semi-authority on extra-terrestrial processes and events?
> Physically incapacitated now (I am 96), I can only cheer the work of others in a field where I was a pathfinder. Again I thank you.
>
> J Harlen Bretz

In November 1979, at the annual meeting of the Geological Society of America, the Penrose Medal (the profession's premier award) was given to J Harlen Bretz.

20 | A Quahog Is a Quahog

T H O M A S   H E N R Y   H U X L E Y once
defined science as "organized common sense." Other contemporaries, including the great geologist Charles Lyell,
urged an opposing view—science, they said, must probe
behind appearance, often to combat the "obvious" interpretation of phenomena.

I cannot offer any general rules for the resolution of
conflicts between common sense and the dictates of a favored theory. Each camp has won its battles and received its
lumps. But I do want to tell a story of common sense triumphant—an interesting story because the theory that seemed
to oppose ordinary observation is also correct, for it is the
theory of evolution itself. The error that brought evolution
into conflict with common sense lies in a false implication
commonly drawn from evolutionary theory, not with the
theory itself.

Common sense dictates that the world of familiar, macroscopic organisms presents itself to us in "packages" called
species. All bird watchers and butterfly netters know that
they can divide the specimens of any local area into discrete
units blessed with those Latin binomials that befuddle the
uninitiated. Occasionally, to be sure, a package may become
unraveled and even seem to coalesce with another. But such
cases are noted for their rarity. The birds of Massachusetts
and the bugs in my backyard are unambiguous members of

species recognized in the same way by all experienced observers.

This notion of species as "natural kinds" fit splendidly with creationist tenets of a pre-Darwinian age. Louis Agassiz even argued that species are God's individual thoughts, made incarnate so that we might perceive both His majesty and His message. Species, Agassiz wrote, are "instituted by the Divine Intelligence as the categories of his mode of thinking."

But how could a division of the organic world into discrete entities be justified by an evolutionary theory that proclaimed ceaseless change as the fundamental fact of nature? Both Darwin and Lamarck struggled with this question and did not resolve it to their satisfaction. Both denied to the species any status as a natural kind.

Darwin lamented: "We shall have to treat species as . . . merely artificial combinations made for convenience. This may not be a cheering prospect; but we shall at least be freed from the vain search for the undiscovered and undiscoverable essence of the term species." Lamarck complained: "In vain do naturalists consume their time in describing new species, in seizing upon every nuance and slight peculiarity to enlarge the immense list of described species."

Yet—and this is the irony—both Darwin and Lamarck were respected systematists who named hundreds of species. Darwin wrote a four-volume taxonomic treatise on barnacles, while Lamarck produced more than three times as many volumes on fossil invertebrates. Faced with the practicum of their daily work, both recognized entities where theory denied their reality.

There is a traditional escape from this dilemma: one can argue that our world of ceaseless flux alters so slowly that configurations of the moment may be treated as static. The coherence of modern species disappears through time as they transform slowly into their descendants. One can only remember Job's lament about "man that is born of a woman"—"He cometh forth like a flower . . . he fleeth also as a shadow, and continueth not." But Lamarck and Darwin could not even enjoy this resolution, for they both worked extensively with fossils and were as successful in dividing evolving sequences into species as they were in parsing the modern world.

Other biologists have even forsworn this traditional escape and denied the reality of species in any context. J.B.S. Haldane, perhaps the most brilliant evolutionist of this century, wrote: "The concept of a species is a concession to our linguistic habits and neurological mechanisms." A paleontological colleague proclaimed in 1949 that "a species . . . is a fiction, a mental construct without objective existence."

Yet common sense continues to proclaim that, with few exceptions, species can be clearly identified in local areas of our modern world. Most biologists, although they may deny the reality of species through geologic time, do affirm their status for the modern moment. As Ernst Mayr, our leading student of species and speciation, writes: "Species are the product of evolution and not of the human mind." Mayr argues that species are "real" units in nature as a result both of their history and the current interaction among their members.

Species branch off from ancestral stocks, usually as small, discrete populations inhabiting a definite geographical area. They establish their uniqueness by evolving a genetic program sufficiently distinct that members of the species breed with each other, but not with members of other species. Their members share a common ecological niche and continue to interact through interbreeding.

Higher units of the Linnaean hierarchy cannot be objectively defined, for they are collections of species and have no separate existence in nature—they neither interbreed nor necessarily interact at all. These higher units—genera, families, orders, and on up—are not arbitrary. They must not be inconsistent with evolutionary genealogy (you cannot put people and dolphins in one order and chimps in another). But ranking is, in part, a matter of custom with no "correct" solution. Chimps are our closest relatives by genealogy, but do we belong in the same genus or in different genera within the same family? Species are nature's only objective taxonomic units.

Shall we then follow Mayr or Haldane? I am a partisan of Mayr's view and I wish to defend it with an offbeat but, to my mind, persuasive line of evidence. The repeated experiment is a cornerstone of scientific methods—although evolutionists, dealing with nature's uniqueness, do not often have an opportunity to practice it. But in this case, we have a way to obtain valuable information about whether species are mental abstractions embedded in cultural practice or packages in nature. We can study how different peoples, in complete independence, divide the organisms of their local areas into units. We can contrast Western classifications into Linnaean species with the "folk taxonomies" of non-Western peoples.

The literature on non-Western taxonomies is not extensive, but it is persuasive. We usually find a remarkable correspondence between Linnaean species and non-Western plant and animal names. In short, the same packages are recognized by independent cultures. I do not argue that folk taxonomies invariably include the entire Linnaean catalog. People usually do not classify exhaustively unless organisms are important or conspicuous. The Fore of New Guinea have a single word for all butterflies, although species are as distinct as the birds they do classify in Linnaean detail. Similarly, most of the bugs in my backyard have no common name in our folk taxonomy, but all the birds in Massachusetts do. The Linnaean correspondences only arise when folk taxonomies attempt an exhaustive division.

Several biologists have noted these remarkable correspondences in the course of their fieldwork. Ernst Mayr himself describes his experience in New Guinea: "Forty years ago, I lived all alone with a tribe of Papuans in the mountains of New Guinea. These superb woodsmen had 136 names for the 137 species of birds I distinguished (confusing only two nondescript species of warblers). That . . . Stone Age man recognizes the same entitites of nature as Western university-trained scientists refutes rather decisively the claim that species are nothing but a product of the human imagination." In 1966, Jared Diamond published a more extensive study on the Fore people of New Guinea. They have names for all the Linnaean bird species in their area. Moreover, when Diamond brought seven Fore men into a new area populated by birds they had never seen, and asked them to give the closest Fore equivalent for each new bird, they placed 91 of 103 species into the Fore group closest to the new species in our Western Linnaean classification. Diamond relates an interesting tale:

> One of my Fore assistants collected a huge, black, short-winged, ground-dwelling bird, which neither he nor I had seen before. While I was puzzled by its affinities, the Fore man promptly proclaimed it to be a *peteobeye,* the name for a graceful little brown cuckoo which frequents trees in Fore gardens. The new bird eventually proved to be Menbek's coucal, an aberrant member of the cuckoo family, to which some features of body form and leg and bill shape betray its affinity.

These informal studies by biologists have been supplemented in recent years with two exhaustive treatments by anthropologists who are also competent natural historians —Ralph Bulmer's work on vertebrate taxonomies of the Kalam people of New Guinea, and Brent Berlin's study (with botanists Dennis Breedlove and Peter Raven) of plant classification by the Tzeltal Indians of highland Chiapas, Mexico. (I thank Ernst Mayr for introducing me to Bulmer's work and for urging this line of argument for many years.)

The Kalam people, for example, use frogs extensively as food. Most of their frog names have a one-to-one correspondence with Linnaean species. In some cases they apply the same name to more than one species, but still recognize the difference: Kalam informants could readily identify two different kinds of *gunm,* distinguished both by appearance and habitat, even though they had no standard names for them. Sometimes, the Kalam do better than we. They recognize, as *kasoj* and *wyt,* two species that had been lumped incorrectly under the single Western name *Hyla becki.*

Bulmer has recently teamed up with Ian Saem Majnep, a Kalam, to produce a remarkable book, *Birds of My Kalam Country.* More than 70 percent of Saem's names have one-to-one correspondence with Western species. In most other cases, he either lumps two or more Linnaean species under the same Kalam name but recognizes the Western distinction, or else he makes divisions within a Western species but recognizes the unity (in some birds of paradise, for example, he names the sexes separately because only males carry the prized plumage). In only one case does Saem follow a practice inconsistent with Linnaean nomenclature—he uses the same name for drab females in two species of birds of paradise, but awards different names to the showy males of each species. In fact, Bulmer could only find four cases (2 percent) of inconsistency in the entire Kalam catalog of 174 vertebrate species, spanning mammals, birds, reptiles, frogs, and fishes.

Berlin, Breedlove, and Raven published their first study in 1966, explicitly to challenge Diamond's claim for the generality of extensive one-to-one correspondence between folk names and Linnaean species. They held initially that only 34 percent of Tzeltal plant names matched Linnaean species and that a large variety of "misclassifications" reflected cultural uses and practices. But a few years later, in a frank article, they reversed their opinion and affirmed the uncannily close correspondence of folk and Linnaean names. They had, in the earlier study, not fully understood the Tzeltal system of hierarchical ordering and had mixed names from several levels in establishing the basic folk groups. In addition, Berlin admitted that he had been led astray by a standard anthropological bias for cultural relativism. I cite his recantation, not to show him up, but as a token of my admiration for an act all too rarely performed by scientists (although any scientist worth his salt has changed his mind about fundamental issues):

Many anthropologists, whose traditional bias is to see the total relativity of man's variant classifications of reality, have generally been hesitant to accept such findings. . . . My colleagues and I, in an earlier paper, have presented arguments in favor of the "relativist" view. Since the publication of that report more data have been made available, and it now appears that this position must be seriously reconsidered. There is at present a growing body of evidence that suggests that the fundamental taxa recognized in folk systematics correspond fairly closely with scientifically known species.

Berlin, Breedlove, and Raven have now published an exhaustive book on Tzeltal taxonomy, *Principles of Tzeltal Plant Classification*. Their complete catalog contains 471 Tzeltal names. Of these, 281, or 61 percent, stand in one-to-one correspondence with Linnaean names. All but 17 of the rest are, in the authors' terms, "underdifferentiated"—that is, the Tzeltal names refer to more than one Linnaean species. But, in more than two-thirds of these cases, the Tzeltal use a subsidiary system of naming to make distinctions within the primary groups, and all these subsidiaries correspond with Linnaean species. Only 17 names, or 3.6 percent, are "overdifferentiated" by referring to part of a Linnaean species. Seven Linaean species have two Tzeltal names, and only one has three—the bottle gourd *Lagenaria siceraria.* The Tzeltal distinguish bottle gourd plants by the utility of their fruits—one name for large, round fruits used as containers for tortillas; another for long-necked gourds well suited for carrying liquids; and a third for small, oval fruits that are not used at all.

A second, equally interesting generality emerges from studies of folk classification. Biologists argue that only species are real units in nature, and that names at higher levels of the taxonomic hierarchy represent human decisions about how species should be grouped (under the constraint, of course, that such grouping be consistent with evolutionary genealogy). Thus, for names applied to groups of species, we should not expect one-to-one correspondence with Linnaean designations but should anticipate a variety of schemes based upon local uses and culture. Such variety has been a consistent finding in studies of folk taxonomy. Groups of species often include basic forms attained independently by several evolutionary lines. The Tzeltal, for example, have four broader names for groups of species, roughly corresponding to trees, vines, grasses, and broad-leafed herbaceous plants. These names apply to about 75 percent of their plant species, while others, like corn, bamboo, and agave, are "unaffiliated."

Often, the grouping of species reflects more subtle and pervasive aspects of culture. The Kalam of New Guinea, for example, divide their nonreptilian four-footed vertebrates into three classes: *kopyak,* or rats; *kmn* for an evolutionarily heterogeneous collection of larger game mammals, mostly marsupials and rodents; and *as* for an even more heterogeneous collection of frogs and small rodents. (Under repeated questioning by Bulmer, the Kalam deny any subdivision between frogs and rodents within *as,* although they do acknowledge [and dismiss as unimportant] the morphological similarity between small furry *as* and rodents among *kmn.* They also recognize that some *kmn* have pouches and others do not.) The divisions reflect fundamental facts of Kalam culture. *Kopyak,* associated with excrement and unclean food around homesteads, are not eaten at all. *As* are collected primarily by women and children and, although eaten by most men and collected by some, are forbidden foods for boys during their rites of passage and for adult men who practice sorcery. *Kmn* are hunted primarily by men.

Likewise, birds and bats are all *yakt,* with the single exception of the large, flightless cassowary called *kobty.* The distinction is made for deeper and more complex reasons than mere appearance—for the Kalam do recognize avian characters in *kobty.* Cassowaries, Bulmer argues, are the prime game of the forest and the Kalam maintain an elaborate cultural antithesis between cultivation (represented by taro and pigs) and the forest (represented by pandanus nuts and cassowaries). Cassowaries are also the mythological sisters of men.

We maintain similar practices in our own folk taxonomy. Edible mollusks are "shellfish," but Linnaean species all have common names. I well remember the reprimand I received from a New England shipmate when I applied the informal scientific term "clam" to all bivalved mollusks (to him a clam is only the steamer, *Mya arenaria*): "A quahog is a quahog, a clam is a clam, and a scallop is a scallop."

The evidence of folk taxonomy is persuasive for the modern world. Unless the tendency to divide organisms into Linnaean species reflects a neurological style wired into all of us (an interesting proposition, but one that I doubt), the world of nature is, in some fundamental sense, really divided into reasonably discrete packages of creatures as a result of evolution. (I do not, of course, deny that our propensity for classifying in the first place reflects something about our brains, their inherited capacities, and the limited ways in which complexity may be ordered and made sensible. I merely doubt that such a definite procedure as classification into Linnaean species could reflect the constraints of our mind alone, and not of nature.)

But are these Linnaean species, recognized by independent cultures, merely temporary configurations of the moment, mere way stations on evolutionary lineages in continual flux? I argue in essays 17 and 18 that, contrary to popular belief, evolution does not work this way, and that species have a "reality" through time to match their distinctness at a moment. An average species of fossil invertebrates lives five to ten million years (terrestrial vertebrates have shorter average durations). During this time, they rarely change in any fundamental way. They become extinct, without issue, looking much as they did when they first appeared.

New species usually arise, not by the slow and steady transformation of entire ancestral populations, but by the splitting off of small isolates from an unaltered parental stock. The frequency and speed of such speciation is among the hottest topics in evolutionary theory today, but I think that most of my colleagues would advocate ranges of hundreds of thousands of years for the origin of most species by splitting. This may seem like a long time in the framework of our lives, but it is a geological instant, usually represented in the fossil record by a single bedding plane, not a long stratigraphic sequence. If species arise in hundreds or thousands of years and then persist, largely unchanged, for several million, the period of their origin is a tiny fraction of one percent of their total duration. Therefore, they may be treated as discrete entities even through time. Evolution at higher levels is fundamentally a story of the differential success of species not the slow transformation of lineages.

Of course, if we happen to encounter a species during the geological microsecond of its origin, we will not be able to make clear distinctions. But our chances of finding a species in this state are small indeed. Species are stable entities with very brief periods of fuzziness at their origin (although not at their demise because most species disappear cleanly without changing into anything else). As Edmund Burke said in another context: "Though no man can draw a stroke between the confines of day and night, yet light and darkness are upon the whole tolerably distinguishable."

Evolution is a theory of organic change, but it does not imply, as many people assume, that ceaseless flux is the irreducible state of nature and that structure is but a temporary incarnation of the moment. Change is more often a rapid transition between stable states than a continuous transformation at slow and steady rates. We live in a world of structure and legitimate distinction. Species are the units of nature's morphology.

6 | Early Life

21 | An Early Start

P O O H - B A H , T H E Lord High Everything Else of Titipu, boasted a family pride so strong as to be "something inconceivable." "You will understand this," he said to Nanki-Poo in suggesting that a bribe would be both appropriate and expensive, "when I tell you that I can trace my ancestry back to a protoplasmal primordial atomic globule."

If human pride is nurtured by such vastly extended roots, then the end of 1977 was a bounteous time for self-esteem. Early in November, an announcement of the discovery of some fossil prokaryotes from South Africa pushed the antiquity of life back to 3.4 billion years. (Prokaryotes, including bacteria and blue green algae, form the kingdom Monera. Their cells contain no organelles—no nucleus, no mitochondria—and they are regarded as the simplest forms of life on earth.) Two weeks later, a research team from the University of Illinois announced that the so-called methane-producing bacteria are not closely related to other monerans after all, but form a separate kingdom of their own.

If true monerans were alive 3.4 billion years ago, then the common ancestor of monerans and these newly christened "methanogens" must be considerably more ancient. Since the oldest dated rocks, the Isua Supracrustals of West Greenland, are 3.8 billion years old, we are left with very little time between the development of suitable conditions for life on the earth's surface and the origin of life itself. Life is not a complex accident that required immense time to convert the vastly improbable into the nearly certain—to build laboriously, step by step, through a large chunk of time's vastness, the most elaborate machinery on earth from the simple constituents of our original atmosphere. Instead, life, for all its intricacy, probably arose rapidly about as soon as it could; perhaps it was as inevitable as quartz or feldspar. (The earth is some 4½ billion years old, but it passed through a molten or near-molten stage some time after its formation and probably did not form a solid crust much before the deposition of the West Greenland sequence.) No wonder these stories hit the front page of the *New York Times,* and even inspired an editorial for Veterans' Day musings.

Twenty years ago, I spent a summer at the University of Colorado, fortifying myself for the transition from high school to college. Amidst the various joys of snowcapped peaks and sore asses from trying to "set a trot," I well remember the highlight of my stay—George Wald's lecture on the "Origin of Life." He presented with infectious charm and enthusiasm the perspective that developed in the early 1950s and reigned as an orthodoxy until very recently.

In Wald's view, the spontaneous origin of life could be considered as a virtually inevitable consequence of the earth's atmosphere and crust, and of its favorable size and position in the solar system. Still, he argued, life is so staggeringly complex that its origin from simple chemicals must have consumed an immense amount of time—probably more time than its entire subsequent evolution from DNA molecule to advanced beetles (or whatever you choose to place atop the subjective ladder). Thousands of steps, each requiring the one before, each improbable in itself. Only the immensity of time guaranteed the result, for time converts the improbable to the inevitable—give me a million years and I'll flip a hundred heads in a row more than once. Wald wrote in 1954: "Time is in fact the hero of the plot. The time with which we have to deal is the order of two billion years. . . . Given so much time, the 'impossible' becomes possible, the possible probable, and the probable virtually certain. One has only to wait: time itself performs the miracles."

This orthodox view congealed without the benefit of any direct data from paleontology to test it, for the paucity of fossils before the great Cambrian "explosion" 600 million years ago is, perhaps, the outstanding fact and frustration of my profession. In fact, the first unambiguous evidence of Precambrian life appeared in the same year that Wald theorized about its origin. Harvard paleobotanist Elso Barghoorn and Wisconsin geologist S. A. Tyler described a series of prokaryotic organisms from cherts of the Gunflint Formation, rocks nearly two billion years old from the northern shore of Lake Superior. Still, the gap between the Gunflint and the earth's origin spanned 2½ billion years, more than enough time for Wald's slow and steady construction.

But our knowledge of life continued its trek backward. Laminated carbonate deposits, called stromatolites, had been known for some time from rocks of the Bulawayan Series, 2.6 to 2.8 billion years old, in Southern Rhodesia. The laminations resemble patterns formed by modern blue green algal mats that trap and bind sediment. The organic interpretation of stromatolites won many converts after Barghoorn and Tyler's Gunflint discoveries removed the odor of heresy from belief in Precambrian fossils. Then, ten years ago in 1967, Barghoorn and J. W. Schopf reported "algalike" and "bacteriumlike" organisms from the Fig Tree Series of South Africa. Now the orthodox idea of slow construction spanning most of the earth's history began to crumble, for the Fig Tree rocks, based on dates available in 1967, seemed to be more than 3.1 billion years old. Schopf and Barghoorn dignified their discoveries with formal Latin names, but their own characterizations—algalike and bacteriumlike—reflected their doubts. In fact, Schopf later decided that the balance of evidence stood against the biological nature of these structures.

The recent announcement of 3.4-billion-year-old life is not a startlingly new discovery, but a satisfactory culmination of a decade's debate about the status of life in the Fig

Tree. The new evidence, gathered by Andrew H. Knoll and Barghoorn, also comes from cherts of the Fig Tree Series. But now the evidence is close to conclusive; moreover, recent dates indicate a greater age of 3.4 billion years for the series. In fact, the Fig Tree cherts may be the oldest appropriate rocks on earth for the discovery of ancient life. Older Greenland rocks have been too altered by heat and pressure to preserve organic remains. Knoll tells me that some unstudied cherts in Rhodesia may range back to 3.6 billion years, but eager scientists will have to await a political denouement before their arcane concerns attract sympathy or ensure safety. Still, the notion that life has been found in the oldest rocks that could contain evidence of it forces us, I think, to abandon the view of life's slow, steady, and improbable development. Life arose rapidly, perhaps as soon as the earth cooled down sufficiently to support it.

The new fossils from the Fig Tree Series are far more convincing than the previous discoveries. "In younger rocks [they] would without hesitation be called algal microfossils," Knoll and Barghoorn claim. This interpretation rests upon five arguments:

1. The new structures are within the size range of modern prokaryotes. The earlier structures described by Schopf and Barghoorn were disturbingly large; Schopf later rejected them as biological, primarily on the basis of their large size. The new fossils, averaging 2.5 micrometers in diameter (a micrometer is a millionth of a meter), have a mean volume only 0.2 percent as large as the earlier structures now considered inorganic.

2. Populations of modern prokaryotes have a characteristic distribution of size. They can be arranged in a typical bell-shaped curve, with the average diameter most frequent and a continual decrease in number towards larger or smaller sizes. Thus, prokaryotic populations not only have a diagnostic average size (point 1 above), they also have a characteristic pattern of variation about this average. The new microfossils form a beautiful bell-shaped distribution with limited spread (range from 1 to 4 micrometers). The previous, larger structures exhibited much greater variation and no strong mean.

3. The new structures are "variously elongated, flattened, wrinkled, or folded" in a manner strikingly similar to Gunflint and later Precambrian prokaryotes. Such shapes are characteristic of postmortem degradation in modern prokaryotes. The larger, earlier structures were distressingly spherical; spheres, as a standard configuration of minimal surface area, can be easily produced by a host of inorganic processes—consider bubbles.

4. Most convincingly, about one quarter of the new microfossils have been found in various stages of cell division. Lest such a proportion caught *in flagrante delicto* sems unreasonably high, I point out that prokaryotes can divide every twenty minutes or so and take several minutes to complete the process. A single cell might well spend one-fourth of its life making two daughters.

5. These four arguments based on morphology are persuasive enough for me, but Knoll and Barghoorn add some biochemical evidence as well. Atoms of a single element often exist in several alternate forms of different weight. These forms, called isotopes, have the same number of protons but different numbers of neutrons. Some isotopes are radioactive and break down spontaneously to other elements; others are stable and persist unchanged throughout geologic time. Carbon has two major stable isotopes, C^{12} with 6 protons and 6 neutrons, and C^{13} with 6 protons and 7 neutrons. When organisms fix carbon in photosynthesis, they use preferentially the lighter isotope C^{12}. Hence, the C^{12}/C^{13} ratio of carbon fixed by photosynthesis is higher than the ratio in inorganic carbon (in a diamond, for example). Moreover, since both isotopes are stable, their ratio will not alter through time. The C^{12}/C^{13} ratios for Fig Tree carbon are too high for an inorganic origin; they are in the range for fixation by photosynthesis. This, in itself, would not establish the case for life in the Fig Tree; light carbon can be fixed preferentially in other ways. But combined with the evidence of size, distribution, shape, and cellular division, this additional support from biochemistry completes a convincing case.

If prokaryotes were well established 3.4 billion years ago, how much further back shall we seek the origin of life? I have already pointed out that no suitable (or at least accessible) older rocks are known on earth, so for now we can proceed no further from the direct evidence of fossils. We turn instead to the second front-page item, the claim of Carl Woese and his associates that methanogens are not bacteria at all, but may represent a new kingdom of prokaryotic life, distinct from the Monera (bacteria and blue green algae). Their report has been widely distorted, most notably in the *New York Times* editorial of November 11, 1977. The *Times* proclaimed that the great dichotomy of plants and animals had finally been broken: "Every child learns about things being vegetable or animal—a division as universal as the partition of mammals into male and female. Yet . . . [we now have] a 'third kingdom' of life on earth, organisms that are neither animal nor vegetable, but of another category altogether." But biologists abandoned "the great dichotomy" long ago, and no one now tries to cram all single-celled creatures into the two great groups traditionally recognized for complex life. Most popular these days is a system of five kingdoms: plants, animals, fungi, protists (single-celled eukaryotes, including amoebas and paramecia, with nucleus, mitochondria, and other organelles), and the prokaryotic monerans. If methanogens are promoted, they will form a sixth kingdom, joining the monerans in a superkingdom, Prokaryota. Most biologists regard the division between prokaryotes and eukaryotes, not between plants and animals, as the fundamental partition of life.

Woese's research group (see Fox, *et al.*, 1977 in the bibliography) isolated a common RNA from ten methanogens and from three monerans for comparison (DNA makes RNA, and RNA serves as the template upon which proteins are synthesized). A single strand of RNA, like DNA, consists of a sequence of nucleotides. Any one of four nucleotides can occupy each position, and each group of three nucleotides specifies an amino acid; proteins are built of amino acids arranged in folded chains. This, in a compressed phrase, is the "genetic code." Biochemists can now "sequence" RNA, that is, they can read the entire sequence of nucleotides in order down the RNA strand.

The prokaryotes (methanogens, bacteria, and blue-green algae) must have had a common ancestor at some time near the origin of life. Thus, all prokaryotes had the same RNA sequence at one point in their past; any current differences arose by divergence from this common ancestral sequence, after the trunk of the prokaryotic tree split up into its several branches. If molecular evolution proceeded at a constant rate, then the extent of current difference between any two forms would directly record the amount of time since their lineages split from a common ancestor—that is, the last time they shared the same RNA sequence. Perhaps, for example, a different nucleotide in the two forms at 10 percent of all common positions would indicate a time of divergence a billion years ago; 20 percent, two billion years, and so on.

Woese and his group measured the RNA differences for all pairs of species among the ten methanogens and three monerans and used the results to construct an evolutionary tree. This tree contains two major limbs—all the methanogens on one, all the monerans on the other. They chose their three monerans to represent the greatest differences within the group—enteric (gut) bacteria versus free-living blue-green algae, for example. Nonetheless, each moneran is more similar to all other monerans than any moneran is to any methanogen.

The simplest interpretation of these results holds that methanogens and monerans are separate evolutionary groups, with a common ancestry preceding the appearance of either. (Previously, methanogens had been classified among the bacteria; in fact, they had not been recognized as a coherent entity at all, but had been regarded as a set of independent evolutionary events—convergent evolution for the ability to make methane). This interpretation underlies Woese's claim that methanogens are separate from monerans and should be recognized as a sixth kingdom. Since good monerans had already evolved by Fig Tree times, 3.4 billion or more years ago, the common ancestry of methanogens and monerans must have been even earlier, thus pushing the origin of life even further back toward the beginning of the earth itself.

This simple interpretation, as Woese and his group realize, is not the only possible reading of their results. We may propose two other perfectly plausible hypotheses: (1) The three monerans that they used may not represent the entire group very well. Perhaps the RNA sequences of other monerans will differ as much from the first three as all the methanogens do. We would then have to include the methanogens with all monerans in a single grand group. (2) The assumption of nearly constant evolutionary rates may not hold. Perhaps the methanogens split off from one branch of monerans long after the main groups of monerans had branched from their common ancestor. These early methanogens may then have evolved at a rate far in excess of that followed by moneran groups in diverging from each other. In this case, the great difference in RNA sequence between any methanogen and any moneran would only record a rapid evolutionary rate for early methanogens, not a common ancestry with monerans before the monerans themselves split into subgroups. The gross amount of biochemical difference will accurately record time of divergence only if evolution proceeds at reasonably constant biochemical rates.

But one other observation makes Woese's hypothesis attractive and inspires my own strong rooting for it. The methanogens are anaerobic; they die in the presence of oxygen. Hence, they are confined today to unusual environments: muds at the bottom of ponds depleted of oxygen or deep hot springs in Yellowstone Park, for example. (The methanogens grow by oxidizing hydrogen and reducing carbon dioxide to methane—hence their name.) Now, amidst all the disagreement that afflicts the study of our early earth and its atmosphere, one point has gained general assent: our original atmosphere was devoid of oxygen and rich in carbon dioxide, the very conditions under which methanogens thrive and for which the earth's original life might have evolved. Could modern methanogens be remnants of the earth's first biota, originally evolved to match its general condition, but now restricted by the spread of oxygen to a few marginal environments? We believe that most free oxygen in our atmosphere is the product of organic photosynthesis. The Fig Tree organisms were already indulging in photosynthesis. Thus, the golden age of methanogens may have passed long before the advent of Fig Tree monerans. If this reverie be confirmed, then life must have originated long before Fig Tree times.

In short, we now have direct evidence of life in the oldest rocks that could contain it. And, by reasonably strong inference, we have reason to believe that a major radiation of methanogens predated these photosynthesizing monerans. Life probably arose about as soon as the earth became cool enough to support it.

Two closing thoughts, admittedly reflecting my personal prejudices: First, as a strong adherent to exobiology, that great subject without a subject matter (only theology may exceed us in this), I am delighted by the thought that life may be more intrinsic to planets of our size, position, and composition than we had ever dared to imagine. I feel even more certain that we are not alone, and I hope that more effort will be directed toward the search for other civilizations by radio-telescope. The difficulties are legion, but a positive result would be the most stupendous discovery in human history.

Secondly, I am led to wonder why the old, discredited orthodoxy of gradual origin ever gained such strong and general assent. Why did it seem so reasonable? Certainly not because any direct evidence supported it.

I am, as several other essays emphasize, an advocate of the position that science is not an objective, truth-directed machine, but a quintessentially human activity, affected by passions, hopes, and cultural biases. Cultural traditions of thought strongly influence scientific theories, often directing lines of speculation, especially (as in this case) when virtually no data exist to constrain either imagination or prejudice. In my own work (see essays 17 and 18), I have been impressed by the powerful and unfortunate influence that gradualism has exerted on paleontology via the old motto *natura non facit saltum* ("nature does not make leaps").

Gradualism, the idea that all change must be smooth, slow, and steady, was never read from the rocks. It represented a common cultural bias, in part a response of nineteenth-century liberalism to a world in revolution. But it continues to color our supposedly objective reading of life's history.

In the light of gradualistic presuppositions, what other interpretation could have been placed upon the origin of life? It is an enormous step from the constituents of our original atmosphere to a DNA molecule. Therefore, the transition must have progressed laboriously through multitudes of intervening steps, one at a time, over billions of years.

But the history of life, as I read it, is a series of stable states, punctuated at rare intervals by major events that occur with great rapidity and help to establish the next stable era. Prokaryotes ruled the earth for three billion years until the Cambrian explosion, when most major designs of multicellular life appeared within ten million years. Some 375 million years later, about half the families of invertebrates became extinct within a few million years. The earth's history may be modelled as a series of occasional pulses, driving recalcitrant systems from one stable state to the next.

Physicists tell us that the elements may have formed during the first few minutes of the big bang; billions of subsequent years have only reshuffled the products of this cataclysmic creation. Life did not arise with such speed, but I suspect that it originated in a tiny fraction of its subsequent duration. But the reshuffling and subsequent evolution of DNA have not simply recycled the original products; they have produced wonders.

22 | Crazy Old Randolph Kirkpatrick

OBLIVION, NOT INFAMY, is the usual fate of a crackpot. I shall be more than mildly surprised if any reader (who is not a professional taxonomist with a special attachment to sponges) can identify Randolph Kirkpatrick.

On the surface, Kirkpatrick fit the stereotype of a self-effacing, mild-mannered, dedicated, but slightly eccentric British natural historian. He was the assistant keeper of "lower" invertebrates at the British Museum from 1886 until his retirement in 1927. (I have always admired the English penchant for simple, literal terms—lifts and flats for our elevators and apartments, for example. We use the Latin *curator* for guardians of museum collections; the British call them "keepers." We, however, have done better in retaining "fall" for their "autumn.") Kirkpatrick trained as a medical student, but decided on a "less strenuous career" in natural history after several bouts with illness. He chose well, for he traveled all over the world searching for specimens and lived to be eighty-seven. In the last months of his life, in 1950, he continued to pedal his bicycle through London's busiest streets.

Early in his career, Kirkpatrick published some sound taxonomic work on sponges, but his name rarely appears in scientific journals after the First World War. In an obituary note, his successor attributed this halt in mid-career to Kirkpatrick's behavior as "an ideal public servant." "Unassuming to a fault, courteous and generous, he would spare no effort to help either a colleague or a visiting student. It was in all probability his extreme willingness to interrupt whatever he was doing to help others that prevented his completing his work."

Kirkpatrick's story, however, is by no means so simple and conventionally spotless. He did not stop publishing in 1915; instead, he shifted to private printing for a series of works that he knew no scientific journal would touch. Kirkpatrick spent the rest of his career developing what has to be the nuttiest of crackpot theories developed in this century by a professional natural historian (and keeper at the staid British Museum, no less). I do not challenge this usual assessment of his "nummulosphere" theory, but I will stoutly defend Kirkpatrick.

In 1912, Kirkpatrick was collecting sponges off the island of Porto Santo in the Madeira group, west of Morocco. One day, a friend brought him some volcanic rocks collected on a peak 1,000 feet above sea level. Kirkpatrick described his great discovery: "I examined them carefully under my binocular microscope and found to my amazement traces of nummulitic disks in all of them. Next day I visited the place whence the fragments had come."

Now *Nummulites* is one of the largest forams that ever lived (forams are single-celled creatures related to amoebas, but they secrete shells and are commonly preserved as fossils). *Nummulites* looks like the object that provided its name: a coin. Its shell is a flat disk up to an inch or two in diameter. The disk is built of individual chambers, one following the next and all wound tightly into a single coil. (The shell looks much like a coil of rope, appropriately scaled down.) Nummulites were so abundant in early Tertiary times (about 50 million years ago) that some rocks are composed almost entirely of their shells; these are called "nummulitic limestones." Nummulites litter the ground around Cairo; the Greek geographer Strabo identified them as petrified lentils left over from rations doled out to slaves who had built the Great Pyramids.

Kirkpatrick then returned to Madeira and "discovered"

nummulites in the igneous rocks there as well. I can scarcely imagine a more radical claim about the earth's structure. Igneous rocks are the products of volcanic eruption or the cooling of molten magmas within the earth; they cannot contain fossils. But Kirkpatrick argued that the igneous rocks of Madeira and Porto Santo not only included nummulites but were actually made of them. Therefore, "igneous" rocks must be sediments deposited at the ocean bottom, not the products of molten material from the earth's interior. Kirkpatrick wrote:

> After the discovery of the nummulitic nature of nearly the whole island of Porto Santo, of the buildings, wine-presses, soil, etc., the name *Eozoon portosantum* seemed a fitting one for the fossils. [*Eozoon* means "dawn animal," more on it in a moment.] When the igneous rocks of Madeira were likewise found to be nummulitic, *Eozoon atlanticum* seemed a more fitting name.

Nothing could stop Kirkpatrick now. He returned to London, itching to examine igneous rocks from other areas of the world. All were made of nummulites! "I annexed in one morning for *Eozoon* volcanic rocks of the Arctic and in the afternoon of the same day those of the Pacific, Indian and Atlantic oceans. The designation *Eozoon orbis-terrarum* then suggested itself." Finally, he looked at meteorites and, yes, you guessed it, all nummulites:

> If *Eozoon,* after taking in the world, had sighed for more worlds to conquer, its fortunes would have surpassed those of Alexander, for its desires would have been realized. When the empire of the nummulites was found to extend to space a final alteration of name to *Eozoon universum* apparently became necessary.

Kirkpatrick did not shy away from the evident conclusion: —all rocks on the earth's surface (including the influx from space) are made of fossils: "The original organic nature of these rocks is to me self-evident, because I can see the

Foraminiferal structure in them, and often very clearly indeed." Kirkpatrick claimed that he could see the nummulites with a low-power hand lens, although no one ever agreed with him. "My views on igneous and certain other rocks," he wrote, "have been received with a good deal of skepticism, and this is not surprising."

I hope I will not be dismissed as an establishment dogmatist if I state with some assurance that Kirkpatrick had somehow managed to delude himself. By his own admission, he often had to work very hard in toeing his own line: "Sometimes I have found it necessary to examine a fragment of rock with the closest scrutiny for hours before convincing myself that I have seen all the above-mentioned details."

But what version of the earth's history would yield a crust made entirely of nummulites? Kirkpatrick proposed that nummulites had arisen early in the history of life as the first creatures with shells. Hence, he adopted for them the name *Eozoon*, first proposed in the 1850s by the great Canadian geologist Sir J. W. Dawson for a supposed fossil from some of the earth's oldest rocks. (We now know that *Eozoon* is an inorganic structure, made of alternating white and green layers of the minerals calcite and serpentine—see essay 23.)

In these early times, Kirkpatrick speculated, the ocean bottom must have accumulated a deep deposit of nummulitic shells over its entire surface, for the seas contained no predators to digest them. Heat from the earth's interior fused them together and injected them with silica (thus solving the vexatious problem of why igneous rocks are silicates, while true nummulites are made of calcium carbonate). As the nummulites were squeezed and fused, some were pushed upward and tossed out into space, later to descend as nummulitic meteorites.

Rocks are sometimes classified as fossiliferous and unfossiliferous, but all are fossiliferous. . . . Really, then, there is, broadly speaking, one rock. . . . The lithosphere is veritably a silicated nummulosphere.

Kirkpatrick still was not satisfied. He thought he had discovered something even more fundamental. Not content with the earth's crust and its meteorites, he began to see the coiled form of nummulites as an expression of life's essence, as the architecture of life itself. Finally, he broadened his claim to its limit: we should not say that the rocks are nummulites; rather, the rocks and the nummulites and everything else alive are expressions of "the fundamental structure of living matter," the spiral form of all existence.

Nutty, yes (unless you feel that he had intuited the double helix). Inspired, surely. A method to his madness, yes, again —and this is the crucial point. In framing his nummulosphere theory, Kirkpatrick followed the procedure that motivated all his scientific work. He had an uncritical passion for synthesis and an imagination that compelled him to gather truly disparate things together. He consistently sought similarities of geometric form among objects conventionally classified in different categories, while ignoring the ancient truth that similarity of form need not designate common cause. He also constructed similarities out of his hopes, rather than his observations.

Still, an uncautious search for synthesis may uncover real connections that would never occur to a sober scientist (although he may be jostled to reflect upon them once someone else makes the initial suggestion). Scientists like Kirkpatrick pay a heavy price, for they are usually wrong. But when they are right, they may be so outstandingly right that their insights beggar the honest work of many scientific lifetimes in conventional channels.

Let us return then to Kirkpatrick and ask why he was on Madeira and Porto Santo in the first place when he made his fateful discovery in 1912. "In September 1912," he writes, "I journeyed to Porto Santo via Madeira, in order to complete my investigation of that strange organism, the sponge-alga *Merlia normani,*" In 1900, a taxonomist named J. J. Lister had discovered a peculiar sponge on the Pacific islands of Lifu and Funafuti. It contained spicules of silica, but had an additional calcareous skeleton bearing a striking resemblance to some corals (spicules are the small, needle-

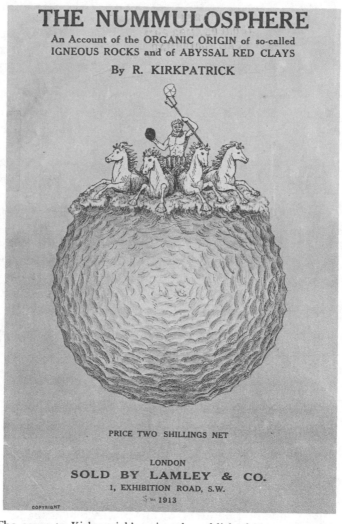

THE NUMMULOSPHERE

An Account of the ORGANIC ORIGIN of so-called
IGNEOUS ROCKS and of ABYSSAL RED CLAYS

By R. KIRKPATRICK

PRICE TWO SHILLINGS NET

LONDON
SOLD BY LAMLEY & CO.
1, EXHIBITION ROAD, S.W.
1913

COPYRIGHT

The cover to Kirkpatrick's privately published Nummulosphere. Of it, he writes: "The design on the cover represents Neptune on the globe of waters. On one of the prongs of his trident is a piece of volcanic rock in the shape of a nummulitic disk, and in his hand is a meteorite. These emblems signify that Neptune's domain is enlarged not only at the expense of nether Jove, but also at that of high Jove whose supposed emblem of sovereignty—the thunderbolt—really belongs to the Sea God . . . Neptune's bolt is poised ready to be hurled at rash and ignorant mortals of the type of the a priori would-be refuter, daring to dispute the validity of his title-deeds."

like elements forming the skeleton of most sponges). A sober man, Lister could not accept the "hybrid" of silica and calcite; he conjectured that the spicules had entered the sponge from elsewhere. But Kirkpatrick collected more specimens and correctly concluded that the sponge secretes the spicules. Then, in 1910, Kirkpatrick found *Merlia normani* on Madeira, a second sponge with siliceous spicules and a supplementary calcareous skeleton.

Inevitably, Kirkpatrick unleashed his passion for synthesis upon *Merlia*. He noticed that its calcareous skeleton resembled several problematic groups of fossils usually classified among the corals—the stromatoporoids and the chaetetid tabulates in particular. (This may seem like a small issue to many, but I assure you that it is a major concern of all professional paleontologists. Stromatoporoids and chaetetids are very common as fossils; they form reefs in some ancient deposits. Their status lies among the classical mysteries of my field, and many distinguished paleontologists have spent entire careers devoted to their study.) Kirkpatrick decided that these and other enigmatic fossils must be sponges. He set out to find spicules in them, a sure sign of affinity with sponges. Sure enough; they all contained spicules. We may be quite sure that Kirkpatrick had deluded himself again in some cases, for he included among his "sponges" the undoubted bryozoan *Monticulipora*. In any case, Kirkpatrick soon became preoccupied with his nummulosphere theory. He never published the major treatise that he had planned on *Merlia*. The nummulosphere made him a scientific pariah, and his work on coralline sponges was pretty much forgotten.

Kirkpatrick worked the same way in studying both nummulospheres and coralline sponges: he invoked a similarity of abstract, geometric form to infer a common source for objects that no one had thought to unite, and he followed his theory with such passion that he eventually "saw" the expected form, even where it manifestly did not exist. Yet, I must note one major difference between the two studies: Kirkpatrick was right about the sponges.

During the 1960s, Thomas Goreau, late of the Discovery

Bay Marine Laboratory in Jamaica, began to explore the cryptic environments of West Indian reefs. These cracks, crevices, and caves contain a major fauna, previously undetected. In one of the most exciting zoological discoveries of the last twenty years, Goreau and his colleagues Jeremy Jackson and Willard Hartman showed that these habitats contain numerous "living fossils." This cryptic community seems to represent an entire ecosystem literally overshadowed by the evolution of more modern forms. The community may be cryptic, but its members are neither moribund nor uncommon. The linings of caves and crevices form a major part of modern reefs. Before the advent of scuba diving, scientists could not gain access to these areas.

Two elements dominate this cryptic fauna: brachiopods and Kirkpatrick's coralline sponges. Goreau and Hartman described six species of coralline sponges from the fore-reef slope of Jamaica's reef. These species form the basis for an entire new class of sponges, the Sclerospongiae. In the course of their work, they rediscovered Kirkpatrick's papers and studied his opinion on the relationship between coralline sponges and the enigmatic fossil stromatoporoids and chaetetids. "Kirkpatrick's comments," they write, "have led us to compare the coralline sponges described above with representatives of several groups of organisms known from the fossil record." They have shown, quite convincingly I think, that these fossils are indeed sponges. A major zoological discovery has solved an outstanding problem in paleontology. And crazy old Randolph Kirkpatrick had known it all along.

When I wrote to Hartman to inquire about Kirkpatrick, he cautioned me not to judge the man too harshly on his nummulosphere, for his taxonomic work on sponges had been sound. But I respect Kirkpatrick both for his sponges and for his numinous nummulosphere. It is easy to dismiss a crazy theory with laughter that debars any attempt to understand a man's motivation—and the nummulosphere is a crazy theory. I find that few men of imagination are not worth my attention. Their ideas may be wrong, even foolish, but their methods often repay a close study. Few honest passions are not based upon some valid perception of unity or some anomaly worthy of note. The different drummer often beats a fruitful tempo.

23 | Bathybius and Eozoon

WHEN THOMAS HENRY Huxley lost his young son, "our delight and our joy," to scarlet fever, Charles Kingsley tried to console him with a long peroration on the soul's immortality. Huxley, who invented the word "agnostic" to describe his own feelings, thanked Kingsley for his concern, but rejected the proferred comfort for want of evidence. In a famous passage, since taken by many scientists as a motto for proper action, he wrote: "My business is to teach my aspirations to conform themselves to fact, not to try and make facts harmonize with my aspirations. . . . Sit down before fact as a little child, be prepared to give up every preconceived notion, follow humbly wherever and to whatever abysses nature leads, or you shall learn nothing." Huxley's sentiments were noble, his grief affecting. But Huxley did not follow his own dictum, and no creative scientist ever has.

Great thinkers are never passive before facts. They ask questions of nature; they do not follow her humbly. They have hopes and hunches, and they try hard to construct the world in their light. Hence, great thinkers also make great errors.

Biologists have written a long and special chapter in the catalog of major mistakes—imaginary animals that should exist in theory. Voltaire spoke truly when he quipped: "If God did not exist, it would be necessary to invent him." Two related and intersecting chimeras arose during the

236

early days of evolutionary theory—two animals that should have been, by Darwin's criteria, but were not. One of them had Thomas Henry Huxley for a godfather.

For most creationists, the gap between living and nonliving posed no particular problem. God had simply made the living, fully distinct and more advanced than the rocks and chemicals. Evolutionists sought to close all the gaps. Ernst Haeckel, Darwin's chief defender in Germany and surely the most speculative and imaginative of early evolutionists, constructed hypothetical organisms to span all the spaces. The lowly amoeba could not serve as a model of the earliest life, for its internal differentiation into nucleus and cytoplasm indicated a large advance from primal formlessness. Thus Haeckel proposed a lowlier organism composed only of unorganized protoplasm, the Monera. (In a way, he was right. We use his name today for the kingdom of bacteria and blue green algae, organisms without nucleus or mitochondria—although scarcely formless in Haeckel's sense.)

Haeckel defined his moneran as "an entirely homogeneous and structureless substance, a living particle of albumin, capable of nourishment and reproduction." He proposed the moneran as an intermediate form between non-living and living. He hoped that it would solve the vexing question of life's origin from the inorganic, for no problem seemed thornier for evolutionists and no issue attracted more rear-guard support for creationism than the apparent gap between the most complex chemicals and the simplest organisms. Haeckel wrote: "Every true cell already shows a division into two different parts, i.e., nucleus and plasm. The immediate production of such an object from spontaneous generation is obviously only conceivable with difficulty; but it is much easier to conceive of the production of an entirely homogeneous, organic substance, such as the structureless albumin body of the Monera."

During the 1860s, the identification of monerans assumed high priority on the agenda of Darwin's champions. And the more structureless and diffuse the moneran, the better. Huxley had told Kingsley that he would follow facts into a metaphorical abyss. But when he examined a true abyss in 1868, his hopes and expectations guided his observations. He studied some mud samples dredged from the sea bottom northwest of Ireland ten years before. He observed an inchoate, gelatinous substance in the samples. Embedded in it were tiny, circular, calcareous plates called coccoliths. Huxley identified his jelly as the heralded, formless moneran and the coccoliths as its primordial skeleton. (We now know that coccoliths are fragments of algal skeletons, which sink to the ocean bottom following the death of their planktonic producers.) Honoring Haeckel's prediction, he named it *Bathybius Haeckelii.* "I hope that you will not be ashamed of your godchild," he wrote to Haeckel. Haeckel replied that he was "very proud," and ended his note with a rallying cry: "Viva Monera."

Since nothing is quite so convincing as an anticipated discovery, *Bathybius* began to crop up everywhere. Sir Charles Wyville Thomson dredged a sample from the depths of the Atlantic and wrote: "The mud was actually alive; it stuck together in lumps, as if there were white of egg mixed with it; and the glairy mass proved, under the microscope, to be a living sarcode. Prof. Huxley . . . calls it *Bathybius.*" (The Sarcodina are a group of single-celled protozoans.) Haeckel, following his usual penchant, soon generalized and imagined that the entire ocean floor (below 5,000 feet) lay covered with a pulsating film of living *Bathybius,* the *Urschleim* (original slime) of the romantic nature philosophers (Goethe was one) idolized by Haeckel during his youth. Huxley, departing from his usual sobriety, delivered a speech in 1870 and proclaimed: "The *Bathybius* formed a living scum or film on the seabed, extending over thousands upon thousands of square miles . . . it probably forms one continuous scum of living matter girding the whole surface of the earth."

Having reached its limits of extension in space, *Bathybius* oozed out to conquer the only realm left—time. And here it met our second chimera.

Eozoon canadense, the dawn animal of Canada, was another organism whose time had come. The fossil record had caused Darwin more grief than joy. Nothing distressed him more than the Cambrian explosion, the coincident appearance of almost all complex organic designs, not near the beginning of the earth's history, but more than five-sixths of the way through it. His opponents interpreted this event as the moment of creation, for not a single trace of Precambrian life had been discovered when Darwin wrote the *Origin of Species*. (We now have an extensive record of monerans from these early rocks, see essay 21.) Nothing could have been more welcome than a Precambrian organism, the simpler and more formless the better.

In 1858, a collector for the Geological Survey of Canada found some curious specimens among the world's oldest rocks. They were made of thin, concentric layers, alternating between serpentine (a silicate) and calcium carbonate. Sir William Logan, director of the Survey, thought that they might be fossils and displayed them to various scientists, receiving in return little encouragement for his views.

Logan found some better specimens near Ottawa in 1864, and brought them to Canada's leading paleontologist, J. William Dawson, principal of McGill University. Dawson found "organic" structures, including a system of canals, in the calcite. He identified the concentric layering as the skeleton of a giant foraminifer, more diffusely formed but hundreds of times larger than any modern relative. He named it *Eozoon canadense,* the Canadian dawn animal.

Darwin was delighted. *Eozoon* entered the fourth edition of the *Origin of Species* with Darwin's firm blessing: "It is impossible to feel any doubt regarding its organic nature." (Ironically, Dawson himself was a staunch creationist, probably the last prominent holdout against evolution. As late as 1897, he wrote *Relics of Primeval Life,* a book about *Eozoon*. In it he argues that the persistence of simple Foraminifera throughout geologic time disproves natural selection since any struggle for existence would replace such lowly creatures with something more exalted.)

Bathybius and *Eozoon* were destined for union. They shared the desired property of diffuse formlessness and differed only in *Eozoon*'s discrete skeleton. Either *Eozoon* had lost its shell to become *Bathybius* or the two primordial creatures were closely related as exemplars of organic simplicity. The great physiologist W. B. Carpenter, a champion of both creatures, wrote:

> If *Bathybius* . . . could form for itself a shelly envelope, that envelope would closely resemble *Eozoon*. Further, as Prof. Huxley has proved the existence of *Bathybius* through a great range not merely of depth but of temperature, I cannot but think it probable that it has existed continuously in the deep seas of all geological epochs. . . . I am fully prepared to believe that *Eozoon*, as well as *Bathybius*, may have maintained its existence through the whole duration of geological time.

Here was a vision to titillate any evolutionist! The anticipated, formless organic matter had been found, and it extended throughout time and space to cover the floor of the mysterious and primal ocean bottom.

Before I chronicle the downfall of both creatures, I want to identify a bias that lay unstated and undefended in all the primary literature. All participants in the debate accepted without question the "obvious" truth that the most primitive life would be homogeneous and formless, diffuse and inchoate.

Carpenter wrote that *Bathybius* was "a type even lower, *because less definite*, than that of Sponges." Haeckel declared that "protoplasm exists here in its simplest and earliest form, i.e., it has scarcely any definite form, and is scarcely individualized." According to Huxley, life without the internal complexity of a nucleus proved that organization arose from indefinite vitality, not vice versa: *Bathybius* "proves the absence of any mysterious power in nuclei, and shows that life is a property of the molecules of living matter, and that organization is the result of life, not life the result of organization."

But why, when we begin to think about it, should we equate formless with primitive? Modern organisms encourage no such view. Viruses are scarcely matched for regularity and repetition of form. The simplest bacteria have definite shapes. The taxonomic group that houses the amoeba, that prototype of slithering disorganization, also accommodates the Radiolaria, the most beautiful and most complexly sculpted of all regular organisms. DNA is a miracle of organization; Watson and Crick elucidated its structure by building an accurate Tinkertoy model and making sure that all the pieces fit. I would not assert any mystical Pythagorean notion that regular form underlies all organization, but I would argue that the equation of primitive with formless has roots in the outdated progressivist metaphor that views organic history as a ladder leading inexorably through all the stages of complexity from nothingness to our own noble form. Good for the ego to be sure, but not a very good outline of our world.

In any case, neither *Bathybius* nor *Eozoon* outlived Queen Victoria. The same Sir Charles Wyville Thomson who had spoken so glowingly of *Bathybius* as a "glairy mass . . . actually alive" later became chief scientist of the *Challenger* expedition during the 1870s, the most famous of all scientific voyages to explore the world's oceans. The *Challenger* scientists tried again and again to find *Bathybius* in fresh samples of deep-sea mud, but with no success.

When scientists stored mud samples for later analysis, they traditionally added alcohol to preserve organic material. Huxley's original *Bathybius* had been found in samples stored with alcohol for more than a decade. One member of the *Challenger* expedition noticed that *Bathybius* appeared whenever he added alcohol to a fresh sample. The expedition's chemist then analyzed *Bathybius* and found it to be no more than a colloidal precipitate of calcium sulfate, a product of the reaction of mud with alcohol. Thomson wrote to Huxley, and Huxley—without complaining—ate crow (or ate leeks, as he put it). Haeckel, as expected, proved more stubborn, but *Bathybius* quietly faded away.

Eozoon hung on longer. Dawson defended it literally to the death in some of the most acerbic comments ever written by a scientist. Of one German critic, he remarked in 1897: "Mobius, I have no doubt, did his best from his special and limited point of view; but it was a crime which science should not readily pardon or forget, on the part of editors of the German periodical, to publish and illustrate as scientific material a paper which was so very far from being either fair or adequate." Dawson, by that time, was a lonely holdout (although Kirkpatrick of essay 22 revived *Eozoon* in a more bizarre form later). All scientists had agreed that *Eozoon* was inorganic—a metamorphic product of heat and pressure. Indeed, it had only been found in highly metamorphosed rock, a singularly inauspicious place to find a fossil. If any more proof had been needed, the discovery of *Eozoon* in blocks of limestone ejected from Mount Vesuvius settled the issue in 1894.

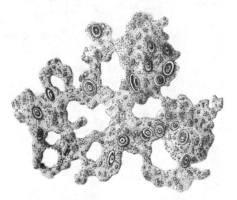

Haeckel's original illustration of *Bathybius*.
The discoidal structures are coccoliths in
the gelatinous mass.

Bathybius and *Eozoon,* ever since, have been treated by scientists as an embarrassment best forgotten. The conspiracy succeeded admirably, and I would be surprised if one percent of modern biologists ever heard of the two fantasies. Historians, trained in the older (and invalidated) tradition of science as a march to truth mediated by the successive shucking of error, also kept their peace. What can we get from errors except a good laugh or a compendium of moral homilies framed as "don'ts"?

Modern historians of science have more respect for such

inspired errors. They made sense in their own time; that they don't in ours is irrelevant. Our century is no standard for all ages; science is always an interaction of prevailing culture, individual eccentricity, and empirical constraint. Hence, *Bathybius* and *Eozoon* have received more attention in the 1970s than in all previous years since their downfall. (In writing this essay, I was guided to original sources and greatly enlightened by articles of C. F. O'Brien on *Eozoon,* and N. A. Rupke and P. F. Rehbock on *Bathybius.* The article by Rehbock is particularly thorough and insightful.)

Science contains few outright fools. Errors usually have their good reasons once we penetrate their context properly and avoid judgment according to our current perception of "truth." They are usually more enlightening than embarrassing, for they are signs of changing contexts. The best thinkers have the imagination to create organizing visions, and they are sufficiently adventurous (or egotistical) to float them in a complex world that can never answer "yes" in all detail. The study of inspired error should not engender a homily about the sin of pride; it should lead us to a recognition that the capacity for great insight and great error are opposite sides of the same coin—and that the currency of both is brilliance.

Bathybius was surely an inspired error. It served the larger truth of advancing evolutionary theory. It provided a captivating vision of primordial life, extended throughout time and space. As Rehbock argues, it played a plethora of roles as, simultaneously, lowliest form of protozoology, elemental unit of cytology, evolutionary precursor of all organisms, first organic form in the fossil record, major constituent of modern marine sediments (in its coccoliths), and source of food for higher life in the nutritionally impoverished deep oceans. When *Bathybius* faded away, the problems that it had defined did not disappear. *Bathybius* inspired a great amount of fruitful scientific work and served as a focus for defining important problems still very much with us.

Orthodoxy can be as stubborn in science as in religion. I do not know how to shake it except by vigorous imagination that inspires unconventional work and contains within itself an elevated potential for inspired error. As the great Italian economist Vilfredo Pareto wrote: "Give me a fruitful error any time, full of seeds, bursting with its own corrections. You can keep your sterile truth for yourself." Not to mention a man named Thomas Henry Huxley who, when not in the throes of grief or the wars of parson hunting, argued that "irrationally held truths may be more harmful than reasoned errors."

24 | Might We Fit Inside a Sponge's Cell

I SPENT DECEMBER 31, 1979 reading through a stack of New York Sunday papers for the last weekend of the decade. Prominently featured, as always in the doldrums of such artificial transition, were lists of predictions about "ins" and "outs" across the boundary: what will the eighties reject that the seventies treasured? what, despised during the seventies, will the eighties rediscover?

This surfeit of contemporary speculation drove my mind back to the last transition between centuries and to a consideration of biological ins and outs at this broader scale. The hottest subject of nineteenth-century biology did suffer a pronounced eclipse in the twentieth. Yet I happen to maintain a strong fondness for it. I also believe that new methods will revive it as a major concern for the remaining decades of our century.

Darwin's revolution led a generation of natural historians to view the reconstruction of life's tree as their most important evolutionary task. As ambitious men embarked upon a bold new course, they did not focus narrowly upon little twiglets (the relation of lions to tigers), or even upon ordinary branches (the link between cockles and mussels); they sought to root the trunk itself and to identify its major limbs: how are plants and animals related? from what source did the vertebrates spring?

In their mistaken view, these naturalists also possessed a method that could extract the answers they sought from the spotty data at their disposal. For, under Haeckel's "biogenetic law"—ontogeny recapitulates phylogeny—an animal climbs its own family tree during its embryological development. The simple observation of embryos should reveal a parade of adult ancestors in proper order. (Nothing is ever quite so uncomplicated, of course. The recapitulationists knew that some embryonic stages represented immediate adaptations, not ancestral reminiscences; they also understood that stages could be mixed up, even inverted, by unequal rates of development among different organs. Yet they believed that such "superficial" modifications could always be recognized and subtracted, leaving the ancestral parade intact.) E.G. Conklin, who later became an opponent of "phylogenizing," recalled the beguiling appeal of Haeckel's law:

> Here was a method which promised to reveal more important secrets of the past than would the unearthing of all the buried monuments of antiquity—in fact nothing less than a complete genealogical tree of all the diversified forms of life which inhabit the earth.

But the turn of the century also heralded the collapse of recapitulation. It died primarily because Mendelian genetics (rediscovered in 1900) rendered its premises untenable. (The "parade of adults" required that evolution proceed only by an addition of new stages to the end of ancestral ontogenies. But if new features are controlled by genes, and these genes must be present from the very moment of conception, then why shouldn't new features be expressed at any stage of embryonic development or later growth?) But its luster had faded long before. The assumption that ancestral reminiscences could always be distinguished from recent embryonic adaptations had not been sustained. Too many stages were missing, too many others discombobulated. The application of Haeckel's law produced endless, unresolvable, fruitless argument, not an unambiguous tree of life. Some tree builders wanted to derive vertebrates from echinoderms, others from annelid worms, still others from horseshoe crabs. E.B. Wilson, apostle of the "exact," experimental method that would supplant speculative phylogenizing, complained in 1894:

It is a ground of reproach to morphologists that their science should be burdened with such a mass of phylogenetic speculations and hypotheses, many of them mutually exclusive, in the absence of any well-defined standard of value by which to estimate their relative probability. The truth is that the search . . . has too often led to a wild speculation unworthy of the name of science; and it would be small wonder if the modern student, especially after a training in the methods of more exact sciences, should regard the whole phylogenetic aspect of morphology as a kind of speculative pedantry unworthy of serious attention.

Phylogenizing fell from general favor, but you can't keep an intrinsically exciting subject down. (I speak of high-level phylogenizing—the trunk and limbs. For twigs and small branches, where evidence is more adequate, work has always proceeded apace, with more assurance and less excitement.) We didn't need "Roots" to remind us that genealogy exerts a strange fascination over people. If uncovering the traces of a distant great-grandparent in a small overseas village fills us with satisfaction, then probing further back to an African ape, a reptile, a fish, that still-unknown ancestor of vertebrates, a single-celled forebear, even to the origin of life itself, can be positively awesome. Unfortunately, one might even say perversely, the further back we go, the more fascinated we become and the less we know. In this column, I will discuss one classic issue in phylogenizing as an example of the joys and frustrations of a subject that will not go away: the origin of multicellularity in animals.

Ideally, we might hold out for a simple, empirical resolution of the issue. Might we not hope to find a sequence of fossils so perfectly intermediate between a protist (single-celled ancestor) and a metazoan (multicelled descendant) that all doubt would be erased? We may effectively write off such a hope: the transition occurred in unfossilizable, soft-bodied creatures long before the inception of an adequate fossil record during the Cambrian explosion, some 600 million years ago. The first metazoan fossils do not surpass the most primitive modern metazoans in their similarity to protists. We must turn to living organisms, hoping that some still preserve appropriate marks of ancestry.

There is no mystery to the method of genealogical reconstruction. It is based on the analysis of similarities between postulated relatives. "Similarity," unfortunately, is no simple concept. It arises for two fundamentally different reasons. The construction of evolutionary trees requires that the two be rigorously separated, for one indicates genealogy while the other simply misleads us. Two organisms may maintain the same feature because both inherited it from a common ancestor. These are *homologous* similarities, and they indicate "propinquity of descent," to use Darwin's words. Forelimbs of people, porpoises, bats and horses provide the classic example of homology in most textbooks. They look different, and do different things, but are built of the same bones. No engineer, starting from scratch each time, would have built such disparate structures from the same parts. Therefore, the parts existed before the particular set of structures now housing them: they were, in short, inherited from a common ancestor.

Two organisms may also share a feature in common as a result of separate but similar evolutionary change in independent lineages. These are *analogous* similarities; they are the bugbear of genealogists because they confound our naive expectation that things looking alike should be closely related. The wings of birds, bats and butterflies adorn most texts as a standard example of analogy. No common ancestor of any pair had wings.

Our difficulties in identifying the trunks and limbs of life's tree do not record muddled thinking about methods. All major naturalists, from Haeckel on (and even before) stated their procedure correctly: separate homologous from analogous similarity, discard analogies, and build genealogy from homology alone. Haeckel's law was a procedure, unfortunately incorrect, for the recognition of homology. The goal is, and has been, clear enough.

In a broad sense, we know how to identify homology. Analogy has its limits. It may build striking external, functional similarity in two unrelated lineages, but it does not modify thousands of complex and independent parts in the same way. At a certain level of precision, similarities must be homologous. Unfortunately, we rarely have enough information to be confident that this required level has been attained. When we compare primitive metazoans with different protists as potential relatives, we often work with only a few features held in common for any contrast—too few to be sure about homology. Moreover, small genetic changes often have profound effects upon external, adult form. Therefore, a similarity that looks too uncanny and complex to arise more than once may actually record a simple and repeatable change. Most importantly, we aren't even comparing the right organisms, but only pale reflections of them. The transition from protist to metazoan occurred more than 600 million years ago. All true ancestors and original descendants disappeared eons ago. We can only hope that their essential, identifying features have been retained in some modern forms. Yet, if retained, they have surely been modified and overlain with a plethora of specialized adaptations. How can we separate original structure from later modification from new adaptation? No one has ever found an unfailing guide.

Only two scenarios have been favored for the origin of metazoans from protists: in the first (amalgamation) a group of protistan cells came together, began to live as a colony, evolved a division of labor and function among cells and regions, and finally formed an integrated structure; in the second (division), cellular partitions formed within a single protistan cell. (A third potential scenario, repeated failure of daughter cells to separate following cell division, has few takers these days.)

At the very outset of our inquiry, we come up against the problem of homology. What about multicellularity itself? Did it arise only once? Have we explained its occurrence in all animals once we decide how it arose in the most primitive? Or did it evolve several times? In other words, is the multicellularity of various animal lineages homologous or analogous?

The metazoan group usually regarded as most primitive, the sponges, clearly arose by the first scenario of amalgamation. In fact, modern sponges are little more than loosely knit federations of flagellated protists. In some species, cells can even be disaggregated by passing the sponge through a fine silk cloth. The cells then move independently, reaggregate into small clumps, differentiate and regenerate an entire new sponge in its original form. If all animals arose from sponges, then multicellularity is homologous throughout our kingdom, and it arose by amalgamation.

But most biologists regard sponges as an evolutionary dead end without subsequent descendants. Multicellularity is, after all, a prime candidate for frequent, independent evolution. It displays the two primary features of analogous similarity: it is reasonably simple to accomplish, and it is both highly adaptive and the only potential path to the benefits it confers. Single cells, ostrich eggs notwithstanding, cannot become very large. The earth's physical environment contains scores of habitats available only to creatures beyond the size limit of a single cell. (Consider only the stability that arises from being large enough to enter a realm where gravity overshadows the forces that act upon surfaces. Since the surface/volume ratio declines with growth, increasing size is the surest path to this realm.)

Not only has multicellularity evolved separately in the three great higher kingdoms of life (plants, animals, and fungi), but it probably arose several times in each kingdom. Most biologists agree that all origins within plants and fungi occurred by amalgamation—these organisms are the descendants of protistan colonies. Sponges also arose by amalgamation. May we then close the issue and state that multicellularity, although analogous both across and within kingdoms, evolved in the same basic way each time? Modern protists include colonial forms that display both regular arrangement of cells and incipient differentiation. Remember the *Volvox* colonies of high school biology labs? (Actually, I must confess that I don't. I attended a public high school in New York just before Sputnik went up. We had no lab at all, though it arrived in a flash just as I left.) Some volvoxes form colonies with a definite number of cells arranged in a regular manner. The cells may differ in size, and reproductive function may be confined to those at one end. Is it such a big step to a sponge?

Only among animals may we make a good case for another scenario. Did some animals, ourselves included, arise by division? This question cannot be answered until we resolve one of the oldest riddles in zoology: the status of the phylum Cnidaria (corals and their allies, but also including the beautiful, translucent Ctenophora, or comb-jellies). Almost everyone agrees that the Cnidaria arose by amalgamation. The dilemma resides in their relationship with other animal phyla. Almost all possible schemes have their supporters: cnidarians as descendants of sponges and ancestors of nothing else; cnidarians as a separate branch of the animal kingdom without descendants; cnidarians as the ancestors of all "higher" animal phyla (the classical view of the nineteenth century); cnidarians as degenerate descendants of a higher phylum. If either of the last two schemes can ever be established, then our issue is settled—all animals arose by amalgamation, probably twice (sponges and everything else). But if the "higher" animal phyla are not closely related to cnidarians, if they represent a third, separate evolution of multicellularity in the animal kingdom, then the scenario of division must be seriously considered.

Supporters of a separate origin for the higher animals generally cite the Platyhelminthes (flatworms) as a potentially ancestral stock. Earl Hanson, a biologist at Wesleyan University, has been a leading crusader, both for a platyhelminth origin of higher animals and for the scenario of division. If his iconoclastic view prevails, then the higher animals, including humans of course, are probably the only multicellular products of division rather than amalgamation.

Hanson has pursued his case by studying the similarities

between a group of protists known as ciliates (including the familiar *Paramecium*), and the "simplest" of flatworms, the Acoela (named for their failure to develop a body cavity). Many ciliates maintain large numbers of nuclei within their single cell. If cellular partitions arose between the nuclei, would the resulting creature be enough like an acoelous flatworm to justify a claim for homology?

Hanson documents an extensive set of similarities between the multinucleate ciliates and the acoeles. Acoeles are tiny marine flatworms. Some can swim, and a few live in water up to 250 meters in depth; but most crawl along the sea bottom in shallow water, living under rocks or in sand and mud. They are similar in size to the multinucleate ciliates. (It is not true that all metazoans are larger than all protists. The ciliates range in length from 1/100 to 3 millimeters, while some acoeles are less than 1 millimeter in length.) The internal similarities of ciliates and acoeles reside primarily in their shared simplicity; for acoeles, unlike conventional metazoans, lack both a body cavity and the organs associated with it. They have no permanent digestive, excretory, or respiratory system. Like the ciliate protists, they form temporary food vacuoles and perform digestion within them. Both ciliates and acoeles divide their bodies roughly into inner and outer layers. Ciliates maintain an ectoplasm (outer layer) and endoplasm (inner layer), and concentrate their nuclei in the endoplasm. Acoeles devote an inner region to digestion and reproduction, and an outer region to locomotion, protection, and capture of food.

The two groups also display some outstanding differences. Acoeles build a nerve net and reproductive organs that can become quite complex. Some have penises, for example, and impregnate each other hypodermically by penetrating through the body wall. They undergo embryonic development after fertilization. Ciliates, by contrast, have no organized nervous system. They divide by fission and have no embryology, although they do indulge in sex via a process called conjugation. (In conjugation, two ciliates come together and exchange genetic material. They then separate and each divides later to form two daughters. Sex and reproduction, combined in nearly all metazoa, are separate processes in ciliates.) Most prominently, of course, acoeles are cellularized, ciliates are not.

These differences should not debar a hypothesis of close genealogical relationship. After all, as I argued previously, contemporary ciliates and acoeles are more than half a billion years beyond their potential common ancestor. Neither represents a transitional form in the origin of multicellularity. The debate centers instead on the similarities, and on the oldest and most basic issue of all: are the similarities homologous or analogous?

Hanson argues for homology, claiming that acoele simplicity is an ancestral condition within the platyhelminths— and that similarities between ciliates and acoeles, largely a result of this simplicity, do record genealogical connection. His detractors reply that the simplicity of acoeles is a secondary result of their "regressive" evolution from more complex platyhelminths, a consequence of pronounced reduction in body size within acoeles. Larger turbellarians (the platyhelminth group including acoeles) have intestines and excretory organs. If acoele simplicity is a derived condition *within* the turbellarians, then it cannot reflect direct inheritance from a ciliate stock.

Unfortunately, the similarities that Hanson cites are of the sort that always produce unresolvable wrangling about homology vs. analogy. They are neither precise, nor numerous enough to guarantee homology. Many are based upon the *absence* of complexity in acoeles, and evolutionary loss is easy and repeatable, whereas separate development of precise and intricate structures may be unlikely. Moreover, acoele simplicity is a predictable result of their small body size—it may represent a functional convergence upon ciliate design by a group that secondarily entered their range of body size, not a connection by descent. Again, we invoke the principle of surfaces and volumes. Many physiological functions, including breathing, digestion, and excretion, must proceed through surfaces and serve the entire body's volume. Large animals have such a low ratio of external surface to internal volume that they must evolve internal organs to provide more surface. (Functionally, lungs are little more than bags of surface for exchange of gases, while intestines are sheets of surface for the passage of digested food.) But small animals maintain such a high ratio of external surface to internal volume that they often can breathe, feed, and excrete through the external surface alone. The smallest representatives of many phyla more complex than platyhelminths also lose internal organs. *Caecum,* for example, the smallest snail, has lost its internal respiratory system entirely and takes in oxygen through its external surface.

Other similarities, cited by Hanson, may be homologous, but so widespread among other creatures that they merely illustrate the broader affinity of all protists with all metazoans, not any specific pathway of descent. Meaningful homologies must be confined to characters that are both shared by descent *and* derived. (Derived characters evolve uniquely in the common ancestor of two groups that share them; they are marks of genealogy. A shared primitive character, on the other hand, cannot specify descent. The presence of DNA in both ciliates and acoeles tells us nothing about their affinity because all protists and metazoans have DNA.) Thus, Hanson mentions "complete ciliation" as a "permanent character significantly held in common by ciliates and acoeles." But cilia, although homologous, are a shared primitive character; many other groups, including cnidarians, have them. The *completeness* of ciliation, on the other hand, represents an "easy" evolutionary event that may only be analogous in ciliates and acoeles. The external surface sets a limit to the maximal number of cilia that may be affixed. Small animals, with high surface/volume ratios, may indulge in ciliary locomotion; large animals cannot insert enough cilia on their relatively declining surface to propel their mass. The complete ciliation of acoeles may reflect a secondary, adaptive response to their small size. The tiny snail *Caecum* also moves by cilia; all its larger relatives use muscular contraction for locomotion.

Hanson is, of course, well aware that he cannot prove his

intriguing hypothesis with the classical evidence of morphology and function. "The best we can say," he concludes, "is that many suggestive similarities are present [between ciliates and acoeles], but no rigorously definable homologies." Is there another method that might resolve the issue, or are we permanently condemned to unresolvable wrangling? Homology might be established with confidence if we could generate a new set of characters sufficiently numerous, comparable, and complex—for analogy cannot be the explanation of detailed, part-by-part similarity in thousands of independent items. The laws of mathematical probability will not allow it.

Fortunately, we now have a potential source of such information—the DNA sequence of comparable proteins. All protists and metazoans share many homologous proteins. Each protein is built of a long chain of amino acids; each amino acid is coded by a sequence of three nucleotides in DNA. Thus, the DNA code for each protein may contain hundreds of thousands of nucleotides in a definite order.

Evolution proceeds by substitution of nucleotides. After two groups split from a common ancestor, their nucleotide sequences begin to accumulate changes. The number of changes seems to be at least roughly proportional to the amount of time since the split. Thus, overall similarity in nucleotide sequence for homologous proteins may measure the extent of genealogical separation. A nucleotide sequence is a homologizer's dream—for it represents thousands of potentially independent characters. Each nucleotide position is a site of possible change.

Techniques are just now becoming available for the routine sequencing of nucleotides. Within ten years, I believe, we will be able to take homologous proteins from all the ciliate and metazoan groups at issue, sequence them, measure the similarities between each pair of organisms and obtain greater insight (perhaps even resolution) for this old genealogical mystery. If acoeles are most similar to protist groups that might achieve multicellularity by evolving cell membranes within their bodies, then Hanson will be vindicated. But if they are closest to protists that can reach multicellularity by integration within a colony, then the classical view will prevail, and all metazoa will emerge as the products of amalgamation.

The study of genealogy has been unfairly eclipsed in our century by the analysis of adaptation, but it cannot lose its power to fascinate. Simply consider what Hanson's scenario implies about our relationship with other multicellular organisms. Few zoologists doubt that all higher animals achieved their multicellular status by whatever method the flatworms followed. If acoeles evolved by the cellularization of a ciliate, then our multicellular body is the homolog of a single protistan cell. If sponges, cnidarians, plants and fungi arose by amalgamation, then their bodies are the homologs of a protistan colony. Since each ciliate cell is the homolog of an individual cell in any protistan colony, we must conclude—and I do mean this literally—that the entire human body is the homolog of a single cell in a sponge, coral, or plant.

The curious paths of homology go further back. The protistan cell itself may have evolved from a symbiosis of several simpler prokaryotic (bacterial or blue green algal) cells. Mitochondria and chloroplasts seem to be the homologs of entire prokaryotic cells. Thus, each cell of any protist, and each cell in any metazoan body, may be, by genealogy, an integrated colony of prokaryotes. Shall we then view ourselves both as a congeries of bacterial colonies and as the homolog of a single cell in a sponge or onion skin? Think upon it next time you swallow a carrot or slice a mushroom.

7 | They Were Despised and Rejected

25 | Were Dinosaurs Dumb?

WHEN MUHAMMAD ALI flunked his army intelligence test, he quipped (with a wit that belied his performance on the exam): "I only said I was the greatest; I never said I was the smartest." In our metaphors and fairy tales, size and power are almost always balanced by a want of intelligence. Cunning is the refuge of the little guy. Think of Br'er Rabbit and Br'er Bear; David smiting Goliath with a slingshot; Jack chopping down the beanstalk. Slow wit is the tragic flaw of a giant.

The discovery of dinosaurs in the nineteenth century provided, or so it appeared, a quintessential case for the negative correlation of size and smarts. With their pea brains and giant bodies, dinosaurs became a symbol of lumbering stupidity. Their extinction seemed only to confirm their flawed design.

Dinosaurs were not even granted the usual solace of a giant—great physical prowess. God maintained a discreet silence about the brains of behemoth, but he certainly marveled at its strength: "Lo, now, his strength is in his loins, and his force is in the navel of his belly. He moveth his tail like a cedar. . . . His bones are as strong pieces of brass; his bones are like bars of iron [Job 40:16–18]." Dinosaurs, on the other hand, have usually been reconstructed as slow and clumsy. In the standard illustration, *Brontosaurus* wades in a murky pond because he cannot hold up his own weight on land.

Popularizations for grade school curricula provide a good illustration of prevailing orthodoxy. I still have my third grade copy (1948 edition) of Bertha Morris Parker's *Animals of Yesterday,* stolen, I am forced to suppose, from P.S. 26, Queens (sorry Mrs. McInerney). In it, boy (teleported back to the Jurassic) meets brontosaur:

> It is huge, and you can tell from the size of its head that it must be stupid. . . . This giant animal moves about very slowly as it eats. No wonder it moves slowly! Its huge feet are very heavy, and its great tail is not easy to pull around. You are not surprised that the thunder lizard likes to stay in the water so that the water will help it hold up its huge body. . . . Giant dinosaurs were once the lords of the earth. Why did they disappear? You can probably guess part of the answer—their bodies were too large for their brains. If their bodies had been smaller, and their brains larger, they might have lived on.

Dinosaurs have been making a strong comeback of late, in this age of "I'm OK, you're OK." Most paleontologists are now willing to view them as energetic, active, and capable animals. The *Brontosaurus* that wallowed in its pond a generation ago is now running on land, while pairs of males have been seen twining their necks about each other in elaborate sexual combat for access to females (much like the neck wrestling of giraffes). Modern anatomical reconstructions indicate strength and agility, and many paleontologists now believe that dinosaurs were warmblooded (see essay 26).

The idea of warmblooded dinosaurs has captured the public imagination and received a torrent of press coverage. Yet another vindication of dinosaurian capability has received very little attention, although I regard it as equally significant. I refer to the issue of stupidity and its correlation with size. The revisionist interpretation, which I support in this column, does not enshrine dinosaurs as paragons of intellect, but it does maintain that they were not

Triceratops   GREGORY S. PAUL

small brained after all. They had the "right-sized" brains for reptiles of their body size.

I don't wish to deny that the flattened, minuscule head of largebodied *Stegosaurus* houses little brain from our subjective, top-heavy perspective, but I do wish to assert that we should not expect more of the beast. First of all, large animals have relatively smaller brains than related, small animals. The correlation of brain size with body size among kindred animals (all reptiles, all mammals, for example) is remarkably regular. As we move from small to large animals, from mice to elephants or small lizards to Komodo dragons, brain size increases, but not so fast as body size. In other words, bodies grow faster than brains, and large animals have low ratios of brain weight to body weight. In fact, brains grow only about two-thirds as fast as bodies. Since we have no reason to believe that large animals are consistently stupider than their smaller relatives, we must conclude that large animals require relatively less brain to do as well as smaller animals. If we do not recognize this relationship, we are likely to underestimate the mental

Brachiosaurus   GREGORY S. PAUL

power of very large animals, dinosaurs in particular.

Second, the relationship between brain and body size is not identical in all groups of vertebrates. All share the same rate of relative decrease in brain size, but small mammals have much larger brains than small reptiles of the same body weight. This discrepancy is maintained at all larger body weights, since brain size increases at the same rate in both groups—two-thirds as fast as body size.

Put these two facts together—all large animals have relatively small brains, and reptiles have much smaller brains than mammals at any common body weight—and what should we expect from a normal, large reptile? The answer, of course, is a brain of very modest size. No living reptile even approaches a middle-sized dinosaur in bulk, so we have no modern standard to serve as a model for dinosaurs.

Fortunately, our imperfect fossil record has, for once, not

severely disappointed us in providing data about fossil brains. Superbly preserved skulls have been found for many species of dinosaurs, and cranial capacities can be measured. (Since brains do not fill craniums in reptiles, some creative, although not unreasonable, manipulation must be applied to estimate brain size from the hole within a skull.) With these data, we have a clear test for the conventional hypothesis of dinosaurian stupidity. We should agree, at the outset, that a reptilian standard is the only proper one—it is surely irrelevant that dinosaurs had smaller brains than people or whales. We have abundant data on the relationship of brain and body size in modern reptiles. Since we know that brains increase two-thirds as fast as bodies as we move from small to large living species, we can extrapolate this rate to dinosaurian sizes and ask whether dinosaur brains match what we would expect of living reptiles if they grew so large.

Harry Jerison studied the brain sizes of ten dinosaurs and found that they fell right on the extrapolated reptilian curve. Dinosaurs did not have small brains; they maintained just the right-sized brains for reptiles of their dimensions. So much for Ms. Parker's explanation of their demise.

Jerison made no attempt to distinguish among various kinds of dinosaurs; ten species distributed over six major groups scarcely provide a proper basis for comparison. Recently, James A. Hopson of the University of Chicago gathered more data and made a remarkable and satisfying discovery.

Hopson needed a common scale for all dinosaurs. He therefore compared each dinosaur brain with the average reptilian brain we would expect at its body weight. If the dinosaur falls on the standard reptilian curve, its brain receives a value of 1.0 (called an encephalization quotient, or EQ—the ratio of actual brain to expected brain for a standard reptile of the same body weight). Dinosaurs lying above the curve (more brain than expected in a standard reptile of the same body weight) receive values in excess of 1.0, while those below the curve measure less than 1.0.

Hopson found that the major groups of dinosaurs can be

ranked by increasing values of average EQ. This ranking corresponds perfectly with inferred speed, agility and behavioral complexity in feeding (or avoiding the prospect of becoming a meal). The giant sauropods, *Brontosaurus* and its allies, have the lowest EQ's—0.20 to 0.35. They must have moved fairly slowly and without great maneuverability. They probably escaped predation by virtue of their bulk alone, much as elephants do today. The armored ankylosaurs and stegosaurs come next with EQ's of 0.52 to 0.56. These animals, with their heavy armor, probably relied largely upon passive defense, but the clubbed tail of ankylosaurs and the spiked tail of stegosaurs imply some active fighting and increased behavioral complexity.

The ceratopsians rank next at about 0.7 to 0.9. Hopson remarks: "The larger ceratopsians, with their great horned heads, relied on active defensive strategies and presumably required somewhat greater agility than the tail-weaponed forms, both in fending off predators and in intraspecific combat bouts. The smaller ceratopsians, lacking true horns, would have relied on sensory acuity and speed to escape from predators." The ornithopods (duckbills and their allies) were the brainiest herbivores, with EQ's from 0.85 to 1.5. They relied upon "acute senses and relatively fast speeds" to elude carnivores. Flight seems to require more acuity and agility than standing defense. Among ceratopsians, small, hornless, and presumably fleeing *Protoceratops* had a higher EQ than great three-horned *Triceratops.*

Carnivores have higher EQ's than herbivores, as in modern vertebrates. Catching a rapidly moving or stoutly fighting prey demands a good deal more upstairs than plucking the right kind of plant. The giant theropods (*Tyrannosaurus* and its allies) vary from 1.0 to nearly 2.0. Atop the heap, quite appropriately at its small size, rests the little coelurosaur *Stenonychosaurus* with an EQ well above 5.0. Its actively moving quarry, small mammals and birds perhaps, probably posed a greater challenge in discovery and capture than *Triceratops* afforded *Tyrannosaurus.*

I do not wish to make a naive claim that brain size equals intelligence or, in this case, behavioral range and agility (I don't know what intelligence means in humans, much less in a group of extinct reptiles). Variation in brain size within a species has precious little to do with brain power (humans do equally well with 900 or 2,500 cubic centimeters of brain). But comparison across species, when the differences are large, seems reasonable. I do not regard it as irrelevant to our achievements that we so greatly exceed koala bears —much as I love them—in EQ. The sensible ordering among dinosaurs also indicates that even so coarse a measure as brain size counts for something.

If behavioral complexity is one consequence of mental power, then we might expect to uncover among dinosaurs some signs of social behavior that demand coordination, cohesiveness, and recognition. Indeed we do, and it cannot be accidental that these signs were overlooked when dinosaurs labored under the burden of a falsely imposed obtuseness. Multiple trackways have been uncovered, with evidence for more than twenty animals traveling together in parallel movement. Did some dinosaurs live in herds? At the Davenport Ranch sauropod trackway, small footprints lie in the center and larger ones at the periphery. Could it be that some dinosaurs traveled much as some advanced herbivorous mammals do today, with large adults at the borders sheltering juveniles in the center?

In addition, the very structures that seemed most bizarre and useless to older paleontologists—the elaborate crests of hadrosaurs, the frills and horns of ceratopsians, and the nine inches of solid bone above the brain of *Pachycephalosaurus*—now appear to gain a coordinated explanation as devices for sexual display and combat. Pachycephalosaurs may have engaged in head-butting contests much as mountain sheep do today. The crests of some hadrosaurs are well designed as resonating chambers; did they engage in bellowing matches? The ceratopsian horn and frill may have acted as sword and shield in the battle for mates. Since such behavior is not only intrinsically complex, but also implies an elaborate social system, we would scarcely expect to find it in a group of animals barely muddling through at a moronic level.

But the best illustration of dinosaurian capability may well be the fact most often cited against them—their demise. Extinction, for most people, carries many of the connotations attributed to sex not so long ago—a rather disreputable business, frequent in occurrence, but not to anyone's credit, and certainly not to be discussed in proper circles. But, like sex, extinction is an ineluctable part of life. It is the ultimate fate of all species, not the lot of unfortunate and ill-designed creatures. It is no sign of failure.

The remarkable thing about dinosaurs is not that they became extinct, but that they dominated the earth for so long. Dinosaurs held sway for 100 million years while mammals, all the while, lived as small animals in the interstices of their world. After 70 million years on top, we mammals have an excellent track record and good prospects for the future, but we have yet to display the staying power of dinosaurs.

People, on this criterion, are scarcely worth mentioning —5 million years perhaps since *Australopithecus*, a mere 50,-000 for our own species, *Homo sapiens*. Try the ultimate test within our system of values: Do you know anyone who would wager a substantial sum, even at favorable odds, on the proposition that *Homo sapiens* will last longer than *Brontosaurus*?

26 | The Telltale Wishbone

WHEN I WAS four I wanted to be a garbageman. I loved the rattling of the cans and the whir of the compressor; I thought that all of New York's trash might be squeezed into a single, capacious truck. Then, when I was five, my father took me to see the *Tyrannosaurus* at the American Museum of Natural History. As we stood in front of the beast, a man sneezed; I gulped and prepared to utter my *Shema Yisrael*. But the great animal stood immobile in all its bony grandeur, and as we left, I announced that I would be a paleontologist when I grew up.

In those distant days of the late 1940s, there wasn't much to nurture a boy's interest in paleontology. I remember *Fantasia,* Alley Oop, and some fake-antique metal statues in the Museum shop, priced way above my means and not very attractive anyway. Most of all, I recall the impression conveyed in books: *Brontosaurus,* wallowing its life away in ponds because it couldn't support its weight on dry land; *Tyrannosaurus,* fierce in battle but clumsy and ungainly in motion. In short, slow, lumbering, pea-brained, cold-blooded brutes. And, as the ultimate proof of their archaic insufficiency, did they not all perish in the great Cretaceous extinction?

One aspect of this conventional wisdom always bothered me: why had these deficient dinosaurs done so well—and for so long? Therapsid reptiles, the ancestors of mammals, had become diverse and abundant before the rise of the dinosaurs. Why didn't they, rather than dinosaurs, inherit the earth? Mammals themselves had evolved at about the same time as dinosaurs and had lived for 100 million years as small and uncommon creatures. Why, if dinosaurs were so slow, stupid, and inefficient, did mammals not prevail right away?

A striking resolution has been suggested by several paleontologists during the past decade. Dinosaurs, they argue, were fleet, active, and warmblooded. Moreover, they have not yet gone the way of all flesh, for a branch of their lineage persists in the branches—we call them birds.

I once vowed that I would not write about warmblooded dinosaurs in these essays: the new gospel had gone forth quite adequately in television, newspapers, magazines, and popular books. The intelligent layperson, that worthy abstraction for whom we write, must be saturated. But I relent, I think, for good reason. In nearly endless discussions, I find that the relationship between two central claims—dinosaur endothermy (warmbloodedness) and dinosaurian ancestry of birds—has been widely misunderstood. I also find that the relationship between dinosaurs and birds has provoked public excitement for the wrong reason, while the right reason, usually unappreciated, neatly unites the ancestry of birds with endothermy of dinosaurs. And this union supports the most radical proposal of all—a restructuring of vertebrate classification that removes dinosaurs from Reptilia, sinks the traditional class Aves (birds), and designates a new class, Dinosauria, uniting birds and dinosaurs. Terrestrial vertebrates would fit into four classes: two coldblooded, Amphibia and Reptilia, and two warmblooded, Dinosauria and Mammalia. I have not made up my own mind about this new classification, but I appreciate the originality and appeal of the argument.

The claim that birds had dinosaurs as ancestors is not so tumultuous as it might first appear. It involves no more than a slight reorientation of a branch on the phyletic tree. The very close relationship between *Archaeopteryx,* the first bird, and a group of small dinosaurs called coelurosaurs has never been doubted. Thomas Henry Huxley and most nineteenth-century paleontologists advocated a relationship of direct descent and derived birds from dinosaurs.

But Huxley's opinion fell into disfavor during this century for a simple, and apparently valid, reason. Complex structures, once totally lost in evolution, do not reappear in the same form. This statement invokes no mysterious directional force in evolution, but merely asserts a claim based upon mathematical probability. Complex parts are built by many genes, interacting in complex ways with the entire developmental machinery of an organism. If dismantled by evolution, how could such a system be built again, piece by piece? The rejection of Huxley's argument hinged upon a single bone—the clavicle, or collarbone. In birds, including *Archaeopteryx*, the clavicles are fused to form a furcula, better known to friends of Colonel Sanders as a wishbone. All dinosaurs, it appeared, had lost their clavicles; hence, they

Archaeopteryx   GREGORY S. PAUL

could not be the direct ancestors of birds. An unimpeachable argument if true. But negative evidence is notoriously prone to invalidation by later discovery.

Still, even Huxley's opponents could not deny the detailed structural similarity between *Archaeopteryx* and the coelurosaurian dinosaurs. So they opted for the nearest possible relationship between birds and dinosaurs—common derivation from a group of reptiles that still possessed a clavicle, subsequently lost in one line of descent (dinosaurs) and strengthened and fused in another (birds). The best candidates for common ancestry are a group of Triassic thecodont reptiles called pseudosuchians.

Many people, on first hearing that birds might be surviving dinosaurs, think that such a striking claim must represent a complete discombobulation of received doctrine about vertebrate relationships. Nothing could be further from the truth. All paleontologists advocate a close affinity between dinosaurs and birds. The current debate centers about a small shift in phyletic branching points: birds either branched from pseudosuchians or from the descendants of pseudosuchians—the coelurosaurian dinosaurs. If birds branched at the pseudosuchian level, they cannot be labeled as descendants of dinosaurs (since dinosaurs had not yet arisen); if they evolved from coelurosaurs, they are the only surviving branch from a dinosaur stem. Since pseudosuchians and primitive dinosaurs looked so much alike, the actual point of branching need not imply much about the biology of birds. No one is suggesting that hummingbirds evolved from *Stegosaurus* or *Triceratops*.

The issue, thus explicated, may now seem rather ho-hum to many readers, although I shall soon argue (for a different reason) that it isn't. But I want to emphasize that these twists of genealogy are of utmost concern to professional paleontologists. We care very much about who branched from whom because reconstructing the history of life is our business, and we value our favorite creatures with the same loving concern that most people invest in their families. Most people would care very much if they learned that their cousin was really their father—even if the discovery provided few insights about their biological construction.

Yale paleontologist John Ostrom has recently revived the dinosaurian theory. He restudied every specimen of *Archaeopteryx*—all five of them. First of all, the main objection to dinosaurs as ancestors had already been countered. At least two coelurosaurian dinosaurs had clavicles after all; they are no longer debarred as progenitors of birds. Secondly, Ostrom documents in impressive detail the extreme similarity in structure between *Archaeopteryx* and coelurosaurs. Since many of these common features are not shared by pseudosuchians, they either evolved twice (if pseudosuchians are ancestors of both birds and dinosaurs) or they evolved just once and birds inherited them from dinosaur ancestors.

Separate development of similar features is very common in evolution; we refer to it as parallelism, or convergence. We anticipate convergence in a few relatively simple and clearly adaptive structures when two groups share the same mode of life—consider the saber-toothed marsupial carnivore of South America and the placental saber-toothed "tiger" (see essay 28). But when we find part-by-part correspondence for minutiae of structure without clear adaptive necessity, then we conclude that the two groups share their similarities by descent from a common ancestor. Therefore, I accept Ostrom's revival. The only major impediment to dinosaurs as ancestors of birds had already been removed with the discovery of clavicles in some coelurosaurian dinosaurs.

Birds evolved from dinosaurs, but does this mean, to cite the litany of some popular accounts, that dinosaurs are still alive? Or, to put the question more operationally, shall we classify dinosaurs and birds in the same group, with birds as the only living representatives? Paleontologists R. T. Bakker and P. M. Galton advocated this course when they proposed the new vertebrate class Dinosauria to accommodate both birds and dinosaurs.

A decision on this question involves a basic issue in taxonomic philosophy. (Sorry to be so technical about such a hot subject, but severe misunderstandings can arise when

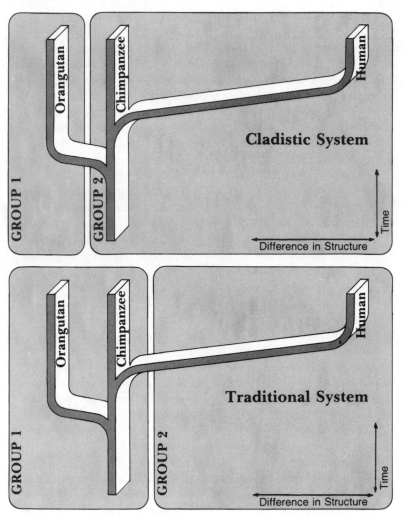

The Telltale Wishbone. With permission from *Natural History*, November, 1977. © American Museum of Natural History, 1977

we fail to sort formal questions in taxonomy from biological claims about structure and physiology.) Some taxonomists argue that we should group organisms only by patterns of branching: if two groups branch from each other and have no descendants (like dinosaurs and birds), they must be united in formal classification before either group joins another (like dinosaurs with other reptiles). In this so-called cladistic (or branching) system of taxonomy, dinosaurs cannot be reptiles unless birds are as well. And if birds are not reptiles, then according to the rules, dinosaurs and birds must form a single, new class.

Other taxonomists argue that branching points are not the only criterion of classification. They weigh the degree of adaptive divergence in structure as well. In the cladistic system, cows and lungfishes have a closer affinity than lungfishes and salmon because the ancestors of terrestrial vertebrates branched from the sarcopterygian fishes (a group including lungfishes) after the sarcopts had already branched from the actinopterygian fishes (standard bony fishes, including salmon). In the traditional system, we consider biological structure as well as branching pattern, and we may continue to classify lungfishes and salmon together as fish because they share so many common features of aquatic vertebrates. The ancestors of cows experienced an enormous evolutionary transformation, from amphibian to reptile to mammal; lungfish stagnated and look pretty much as they did 250 million years ago. Fish is fish, as an eminent philosopher once said.

The traditional system recognizes unequal evolutionary rates after branching as a proper criterion of classification. A group may win separate status by virtue of its profound divergence. Thus, in the traditional system, mammals can be a separate group and lungfishes can be kept with other fish. Humans can be a separate group and chimps can be kept with orangutans (even though humans and chimps share a more recent branching point than chimps and orangs). Similarly, birds can be a separate group and dinosaurs kept with reptiles, even though birds branched from dinosaurs. If birds developed the structural basis of their great success after they branched from dinosaurs, and if dinosaurs never diverged far from a basic reptilian plan, then birds should be grouped separately and dinosaurs kept with reptiles, despite their genealogical history of branching.

Thus, we finally arrive at our central question and at the union of this technical issue in taxonomy with the theme of warmblooded dinosaurs. Did birds inherit their primary features directly from dinosaurs? If they did, Bakker and Galton's class Dinosauria should probably be accepted, despite the adherence of most modern birds to a mode of life (flight and small size) not wonderfully close to that of most dinosaurs. After all, bats, whales, and armadillos are all mammals.

Consider the two cardinal features that provided an adaptive basis for flight in birds—feathers for lift and propulsion and warmbloodedness for maintaining the consistently high levels of metabolism required by so strenuous an activity as flight. Could *Archaeopteryx* have inherited both these features from dinosaur ancestors?

R. T. Bakker has presented the most elegant brief for warmblooded dinosaurs. He rests his controversial case on four major arguments:

1. The structure of bone. Coldblooded animals cannot keep their body temperature at a constant level: it fluctuates in sympathy with temperatures in the outside environment. Consequently, coldblooded animals living in regions with intense seasonality (cold winters and hot summers) develop growth rings in outer layers of compact bone—alternating layers of rapid summer and slower winter growth. (Tree rings, of course, record the same pattern.) Warmblooded animals do not develop rings because their internal temperature is constant in all seasons. Dinosaurs from regions of intense seasonality do not have growth rings in their bones.

2. Geographic distribution. Large coldblooded animals do not live at high latitudes (far from the equator) because they cannot warm up enough during short winter days and are too large to find safe places for hibernation. Some large dinosaurs lived so far north that they had to endure long

periods entirely devoid of sunlight during the winter.

3. Fossil ecology. Warmblooded carnivores must eat much more than coldblooded carnivores of the same size in order to maintain their constant body temperatures. Consequently, when predators and prey are about the same size, a community of coldblooded animals will include relatively more predators (since each one needs to eat so much less) than a community of warmblooded animals. The ratio of predators to prey may reach 40 percent in coldblooded communities; it does not exceed 3 percent in warmblooded communities. Predators are rare in dinosaur faunas; their relative abundance matches our expectation for modern communities of warmblooded animals.

4. Dinosaur anatomy. Dinosaurs are usually depicted as slow, lumbering beasts, but newer reconstructions (see essay 25) indicate that many large dinosaurs resembled modern running mammals in locomotor anatomy and the proportions of their limbs.

But how can we view feathers as an inheritance from dinosaurs; surely no *Brontosaurus* was ever invested like a peacock. For what did *Archaeopteryx* use its feathers? If for flight, then feathers may belong to birds alone; no one has ever postulated an airborne dinosaur (flying pterosaurs belong to a separate group). But Ostrom's anatomical reconstruction strongly suggests that *Archaeopteryx* could not fly; its feathered forearms are joined to its shoulder girdle in a manner quite inappropriate for flapping a wing. Ostrom suggests a dual function for feathers: insulation to protect a small warmblooded creature from heat loss and as a sort of basket trap to catch flying insects and other small prey in a fully enclosed embrace.

Archaeopteryx was a small animal. It weighed less than a pound, and stood a full foot shorter than the smallest dinosaur. Small creatures have a very high ratio of surface area to volume (see essays 29 and 30). Heat is generated over a body's volume and radiated out through its surface. Small warmblooded creatures have special problems in maintaining a constant body temperature since heat dissipates so quickly from their relatively enormous surface. Shrews, although insulated by a coat of hair, must eat nearly all the time to keep their internal fires burning. The ratio of surface to volume was so low in large dinosaurs that they could maintain constant temperatures without insulation. But as soon as any dinosaur or its descendant became very small, it would need insulation to remain warmblooded. Feathers may have served as a primary adaptation for constant temperatures in small dinosaurs. Bakker suggests that many small coelurosaurs may have been feathered as well. (Very few fossils preserve any feathers; *Archaeopteryx* is a great rarity of exquisite preservation.)

Feathers, evolved primarily for insulation, were soon exploited for another purpose in flight. Indeed, it is hard to imagine how feathers could have evolved if they never had a use apart from flight. The ancestors of birds were surely flightless, and feathers did not arise all at once and fully formed. How could natural selection build an adaptation through several intermediate stages in ancestors that had no use for it? By postulating a primary function for insulation, we may view feathers as a device for giving warmblooded dinosaurs an access to the ecological advantages of small size.

Ostrom's arguments for a descent of birds from coelurosaurian dinosaurs do not depend upon the warmbloodedness of dinosaurs or the primary utility of feathers as insulation. They are based instead upon the classical methods of comparative anatomy—detailed part-by-part similarity between bones, and a contention that such striking resemblance must reflect common descent, not convergence. I believe that Ostrom's arguments will stand no matter how the hot debate about warmblooded dinosaurs eventually resolves itself.

But the descent of birds from dinosaurs wins its fascination in the public eye only if birds inherited their primary adaptations of feathers and warmbloodedness directly from dinosaurs. If birds developed these adaptations after they branched, then dinosaurs are perfectly good reptiles in their physiology; they should be kept with turtles, lizards, and their kin in the class Reptilia. (I tend to be a traditionalist rather than a cladist in my taxonomic philosophy.) But if dinosaurs really were warmblooded, and if feathers were their way of remaining warmblooded at small sizes, then birds inherited the basis of their success from dinosaurs. And if dinosaurs were closer to birds than to other reptiles in their physiology, then we have a classical structural argument—not just a genealogical claim—for the formal alliance of birds and dinosaurs in a new class, Dinosauria.

Bakker and Galton write: "The avian radiation is an aerial exploitation of basic dinosaur physiology and structure, much as the bat radiation is an aerial exploitation of basic, primitive mammal physiology. Bats are not separated into an independent class merely because they fly. We believe that neither flight nor the species diversity of birds merits separation from dinosaurs on a class level." Think of *Tyrannosaurus,* and thank the old terror as a representative of his group, when you split the wishbone later this month.*

---

*This article originally appeared in *Natural History,* November, 1977.

27 | Nature's Odd Couples

From Nature's chain whatever link you strike,
Tenth, or ten thousandth, breaks the chain alike.
Alexander Pope,
An Essay on Man   (1733)

POPE'S COUPLET EXPRESSES a common, if exaggerated, concept of connection among organisms in an ecosystem. But ecosystems are not so precariously balanced that the extirpation of one species must act like the first domino in that colorful metaphor of the cold war. Indeed, it could not be, for extinction is the common fate of all species—and they cannot all take their ecosystems with them. Species often have as much dependence upon each other as Longfellow's "Ships that pass in the night." New York City might even survive without its dogs (I'm not so sure about the cockroaches, but I'd chance it).

Shorter chains of dependence are more common. Odd couplings between dissimilar organisms form a stock in trade for popularizers of natural history. An alga and a fungus make lichen; photosynthetic microorganisms live in the tissue of reef-building corals. Natural selection is opportunistic; it fashions organisms for their current environments and cannot anticipate the future. One species often evolves an unbreakable dependency upon another species; in an inconstant world, this fruitful tie may seal its fate.

I wrote my doctoral dissertation on the fossil land snails of Bermuda. Along the shores, I would often encounter large hermit crabs incongruously stuffed—big claw protruding—into the small shell of a neritid snail (nerites include the familiar "bleeding tooth"). Why, I wondered, didn't these crabs trade their cramped quarters for more commodious lodgings? After all, hermit crabs are exceeded only by modern executives in their frequency of entry into the real estate market. Then, one day, I saw a hermit crab with proper accommodations—a shell of the "whelk" *Cittarium pica,* a large snail and major food item throughout the West Indies. But the *Cittarium* shell was a fossil, washed out of an ancient sand dune to which it had been carried 120,-000 years before by an ancestor of its current occupant. I watched carefully during the ensuing months. Most hermits had squeezed into nerites, but a few inhabited whelk shells and the shells were always fossils.

I began to put the story together, only to find that I had been scooped in 1907 by Addison E. Verrill, master taxonomist, Yale professor, protégé of Louis Agassiz, and diligent recorder of Bermuda's natural history. Verrill searched the records of Bermudian history for references to living whelks and found that they had been abundant during the first years of human habitation. Captain John Smith, for example, recorded the fate of one crew member during the great famine of 1614–15: "One amongst the rest hid himself in the woods, and lived only on Wilkes and Land Crabs, fat and lusty, many months." Another crew member stated that they made cement for the seams of their vessels by mixing lime from burned whelk shells with turtle oil. Verrill's last record of living *Cittarium* came from kitchen middens of British soldiers stationed on Bermuda during the war of 1812. None, he reported, had been seen in recent times, "nor could I learn that any had been taken within the memory of the oldest inhabitants." No observations during the past seventy years have revised Verrill's conclusion that *Cittarium* is extinct in Bermuda.

As I read Verrill's account, the plight of *Cenobita diogenes* (proper name of the large hermit crab) struck me with that anthropocentric twinge of pain often invested, perhaps improperly, in other creatures. For I realized that nature had condemned *Cenobita* to slow elimination on Bermuda. The neritid shells are too small; only juvenile and very young adult crabs fit inside them—and very badly at that. No other modern snail seems to suit them and a successful adult life requires the discovery and possession (often through conquest) of a most precious and dwindling commodity—a *Cittarium* shell. But *Cittarium,* to borrow the jargon of recent years, has become a "nonrenewable resource" on Bermuda, and crabs are still recycling the shells of previous centuries. These shells are thick and strong, but they cannot resist the waves and rocks forever—and the supply constantly diminishes. A few "new" shells tumble down from the fossil dunes each year—a precious legacy from ancestral crabs that carried them up the hills ages ago—but these cannot meet the demand. *Cenobita* seems destined to fulfill the pessimistic vision of many futuristic films and scenarios: depleted survivors fighting to the death for a last morsel. The scientist who named this large hermit chose well. Diogenes the Cynic lit his lantern and searched the streets of Athens for an honest man; none could he find. *C. diogenes* will perish looking for a decent shell.

This poignant story of *Cenobita* emerged from deep storage in my mind when I heard a strikingly similar tale recently. Crabs and snails forged an evolutionary interdependence in the first story. A more unlikely combination —seeds and dodos—provides the second, but this one has a happy ending.

William Buckland, a leading catastrophist among nineteenth-century geologists, summarized the history of life on a large chart, folded several times to fit in the pages of his popular work *Geology and Mineralogy Considered With Reference to Natural Theology.* The chart depicts victims of mass extinctions grouped by the time of their extirpation. The great animals are crowded together: ichthyosaurs, dinosaurs, ammonites, and pterosaurs in one cluster; mammoths, woolly rhinos, and giant cave bears in another. At the far right, representing modern animals, the dodo stands alone, the first recorded extinction of our era. The dodo, a giant flightless pigeon (twenty-five pounds or more in weight), lived in fair abundance on the island of Mauritius. Within 200 years of its discovery in the fifteenth century, it had been wiped out—by men who prized its tasty eggs and by the hogs that early sailors had transported to Mauritius. No living dodos have been seen since 1681.

In August, 1977, Stanley A. Temple, a wildlife ecologist at the University of Wisconsin, reported the following remarkable story (but see postscript for a subsequent challenge). He, and others before him, had noted that a large tree, *Calvaria major*, seemed to be near the verge of extinction on Mauritius. In 1973, he could find only thirteen "old, overmature, and dying trees" in the remnant native forests. Experienced Mauritian foresters estimated the trees' ages at more than 300 years. These trees produce well-formed, apparently fertile seeds each year, but none germinate and no young plants are known. Attempts to induce germination in the controlled and favorable climate of a nursery have failed. Yet *Calvaria* was once common on Mauritius; old forestry records indicate that it had been lumbered extensively.

Calvaria's large fruits, about two inches in diameter, consist of a seed enclosed in a hard pit nearly half an inch thick. This pit is surrounded by a layer of pulpy, succulent material covered by a thin outer skin. Temple concluded that *Calvaria* seeds fail to germinate because the thick pit "mechanically resists the expansion of the embryo within." How, then, did it germinate in previous centuries?

Temple put two facts together. Early explorers reported that the dodo fed on fruits and seeds of large forest trees; in fact, fossil *Calvaria* pits have been found among skeletal remains of the dodo. The dodo had a strong gizzard filled with large stones that could crush tough bits of food. Secondly, the age of surviving *Calvaria* trees matches the demise of the dodo. None has sprouted since the dodo disappeared almost 300 years ago.

Temple therefore argues that *Calvaria* evolved its unusually thick pit as an adaptation to resist destruction by crushing in a dodo's gizzard. But, in so doing, they became dependent upon dodos for their own reproduction. Tit for tat. A pit thick enough to survive in a dodo's gizzard is a pit too thick for an embryo to burst by its own resources. Thus, the gizzard that once threatened the seed had become its necessary accomplice. The thick pit must be abraded and scratched before it can germinate.

Several small animals eat the fruit of *Calvaria* today, but they merely nibble away the succulent middle and leave the internal pit untouched. The dodo was big enough to swallow the fruit whole. After consuming the middle, dodos would have abraded the pit in their gizzards before regurgitating it or passing it in their feces. Temple cites many analogous cases of greatly increased germination rates for seeds after passage through the digestive tracts of various animals.

Temple then tried to estimate the crushing force of a dodo's gizzard by making a plot of body weight versus force generated by the gizzard in several modern birds. Extrapolating the curve up to a dodo's size, he estimates that *Calvaria* pits were thick enough to resist crushing; in fact, the thickest pits could not be crushed until they had been reduced nearly 30 percent by abrasion. Dodos might well have regurgitated the pits or passed them along before subjecting them to such an extended treatment. Temple took turkeys—the closest modern analogue to dodos—and force-fed them *Calvaria* pits, one at a time. Seven of seventeen pits were crushed by the turkey's gizzard, but the other ten were regurgitated or passed in feces after considerable abrasion. Temple planted these seeds and three of them germinated. He writes: "These may well have been the first *Calvaria* seeds to germinate in more than 300 years." *Calvaria* can probably be saved from the brink of extinction by the propagation of artificially abraded seeds. For once, an astute observation, combined with imaginative thought and experiment, may lead to preservation rather than destruction.

I wrote this essay to begin the fifth year of my regular column in Natural History magazine. I said to myself at the beginning that I would depart from a long tradition of popular writing in natural history. I would not tell the fascinating tales of nature merely for their own sake. I would tie any particular story to a general principle of evolutionary theory: pandas and sea turtles to imperfection as the proof of evolution, magnetic bacteria to principles of scaling, mites that eat their mother from inside to Fisher's theory of sex ratio. But this column has no message beyond the evident homily that things are connected to other things in our complex world—and that local disruptions have wider consequences. I have only recounted these two, related stories because they touched me—one bitterly, the other with sweetness.

Coenobita diogenes in the shell of *Cittarium*. Drawn from life by A. Verrill in 1900.

Postscript

Some stories in natural history are too beautiful and complex to win general acceptance. Temple's report received immediate publicity in the popular press (*New York Times* and other major newspapers, followed two months later by my article). A year later (March 30, 1979), Dr. Owadally of the Mauritian Forestry Service raised some important doubts in a technical comment published in the professional journal *Science* (where Temple's original article had appeared). I reproduce below, verbatim, both Owadally's comment and Temple's response:

I do not dispute that coevolution between plant and animal exists and that the germination of some seeds may be assisted by their passing through the gut of animals. However, that "mutualism" of the famous dodo and *Calvaria major* (tambalacoque) is an example (*1*) of coevolution is untenable for the following reasons.

1) *Calvaria major* grows in the upland rain forest of Mauritius with a rainfall of 2500 to 3800 mm per annum. The dodo according to Dutch sources roamed over the northern plains and the eastern hills in the Grand Port area—that is, in a drier forest—where the Dutch established their first settlement. Thus it is highly improbable that the dodo and the tambalacoque occurred in the same ecological niche. Indeed, extensive excavations in the uplands for reservoirs, drainage canals, and the like have failed to reveal any dodo remains.

2) Some writers have mentioned the small woody seeds found in Mare aux Songes and the possibility that their germination was assisted by the dodo or other birds. But we now know that these seeds are not tambalacoque but belong to another species of lowland tree recently identified as *Sideroxylon longifolium.*

3) The Forestry Service has for some years been studying and effecting the germination of tambalacoque seeds without avian intervention (*2*). The germination rate is low but not more so than that of many other indigenous species which have, of recent decades, showed a marked deterioration in reproduc-

tion. This deterioration is due to various factors too complex to be discussed in this comment. The main factors have been the depredations caused by monkeys and the invasion by exotic plants.

4) A survey of the climax rain forest of the uplands made in 1941 by Vaughan and Wiehe *(3)* showed that there was quite a significant population of young tambalacoque plants certainly less than 75 to 100 years old. The dodo became extinct around 1675!

5) The manner in which the tambalacoque seed germinates was described by Hill *(4)*, who demonstrated how the embryo is able to emerge from the hard woody endocarp. This is effected by the swollen embryo breaking off the bottom half of the seed along a well-defined fracture zone.

It is necessary to dispel the tambalacoque-dodo "myth" and recognize the efforts of the Forestry Service of Mauritius to propagate this magnificent tree of the upland plateau.

A. W. OWADALLY

Forestry Service, Curepipe, Mauritius

References and Notes

1. S. Temple, *Science* **197**, 885 (1977).
2. Young *Calvaria major* plants that are 9 months old or more can be seen at the Forest Nursery in Curepipe.
3. R. E. Vaughan and P. O. Wiehe, *J. Ecol.* **19**, 127 (1941).
4. A. W. Hill, *Ann. Bot.* **5**, 587 (1941).

28 March 1978

The plant-animal mutualism that may have existed between the dodo and *Calvaria major* became impossible to prove experimentally after the dodo's extinction. What I pointed out *(1)* was the possibility that such a relation may have occurred, thus providing an explanation for the extraordinarily poor germination rate in *Calvaria.* I acknowledge the potential for error in historical reconstructions.

I disagree, however, with the conclusion of Owadally

(2) that the dodo and *Calvaria* were geographically separated. There have been virtually no bones of dodos or any other animals found in the uplands of Mauritius not because the animals were never there, but because the island's topography does not cause alluvial deposits there. Catchment basins in certain lowland areas accumulated many bones of animals that were washed into these areas from the surrounding uplands. Accounts of early explorers, summarized by Hachisuka *(3,* p. 85), definitely refer to dodos occurring in the uplands, and Hachisuka makes a point of clarifying the misconception that dodos were strictly coastal birds. Early forestry records from Mauritius *(4)* indicate that *Calvaria* was found in the lowlands as well as on the upland plateau. Although native forests only occur in the uplands today, one of the surviving *Calvaria* trees is located at an elevation of only 150 m. Thus, the dodo and *Calvaria* may have been sympatric, making a mutualistic relation possible.

Taxonomic authorities on sapotaceous plants of the Indian Ocean region recognize seeds of *Calvaria major,* as well as the smaller seeds of *Sideroxylon longifolium,* from alluvial deposits of the Mare aux Songes marsh *(5),* but this has little relevance to the question of mutualism. Mutualistic species will not necessarily be fossilized together.

The Mauritius Forestry Service has only recently succeeded in propagating *Calvaria* seeds, and the unmentioned reason for their recent success strengthens the case for mutualism. Success was achieved when the seeds were mechanically abraded before planting *(6).* A dodo's digestive tract merely abraded the endocarp naturally the same way the staff of the Mauritius Forestry Service does artificially before the seeds are planted.

The reference Owadally cites *(7)* is equivocal about the age of the surviving *Calvaria* trees because there is no easy way to accurately date them. Coincidently, Wiehe, the coauthor of the paper Owadally cites, was also my source of the estimated age of over 300 years for the surviving trees. I agree that there were more trees surviving in the 1930's than today, which further suppports the notion that *Calvaria major* is a declining species and may have been so since 1681.

I erred in not citing Hill *(8)*. However, Hill does not describe how and under what conditions he induced a seed to germinate. Without these details, his description is of little relevance to the question of mutualism.

STANLEY A. TEMPLE

Department of Wildlife Ecology,
University of Wisconsin–Madison,
Madison 53706

References and Notes

1. S.A. Temple, *Science* **197**, 885 (1977).
2. A. W. Owadally, *ibid.* **203**, 1363 (1979).
3. M. Hachisuka, *The Dodo and Kindred Birds* (Witherby, London, 1953).
4. N. R. Brouard, *A History of the Woods and Forests of Mauritius* (Government Printer, Mauritius, 1963).
5. F. Friedmann, personal communication.
6. A. M. Gardner, personal communication.
7. R. E. Vaughan and P. O. Wiehe, *J. Ecol.* **19**, 127 (1941).
8. A. W. Hill, *Ann. Bot.* **5**, 587 (1941).

I think that Temple has responded adequately (even triumphantly) to Owadally's first three points. As a paleontologist, I can certainly affirm his arguments about the rarity of upland fossils. Our fossil record of upland faunas is exceedingly spotty; the specimens we do possess are generally found in lowland deposits, well worn and washed in from higher ground. Owadally was certainly remiss in not mentioning (point 3) that the Forestry Service abrades its *Calvaria* seeds before they germinate; for the necessity of abrasion lies at the heart of Temple's hypothesis. But Temple was equally remiss in not citing the local Mauritian efforts, which, apparently, predate his own discovery.

Owadally's fourth point, however, represents the potential disproof of Temple's claim. If "quite a significant population" of *Calvaria* trees were less than 100 years old in 1941, then dodos cannot have assisted their germination. Temple denies that so young an age has been demonstrated, and I certainly have no additional insight that can resolve this crucial question.

This exchange highlights a disturbing issue in the transmission of news about science to the public. Many sources cited Temple's original story. I did not find a single mention of the subsequent doubts. Most "good" stories turn out to be false, or at least overextended, but debunking doesn't match the fascination of a clever hypothesis. Most of the "classic" stories of natural history are wrong, but nothing is so resistant to expurgation as textbook dogma.

The debate between Owadally and Temple is too close to call at the moment. I'm rooting for Temple, but if Owadally's fourth point is correct, then the dodo hypothesis will become, in Thomas Henry Huxley's inimitable words, "a beautiful theory, killed by a nasty, ugly little fact."

28 | Sticking Up for Marsupials

I AM ANNOYED that the rapacious ways of my own species have irrevocably prevented me from seeing the dodo in action, for a pigeon as large as a turkey must have been something else, and stuffed, moldy specimens just don't carry conviction. We who revel in nature's diversity and feel instructed by every animal tend to brand *Homo sapiens* as the greatest catastrophe since the Cretaceous extinction. Yet I would argue that the rise of the Isthmus of Panama a mere two to three million years ago must rank as the most devastating biological tragedy of recent times.

South America had been an island continent throughout the Tertiary period (for seventy million years before the onset of continental glaciation). Like Australia, it housed a unique suite of mammals. But Australia was a backwater compared with the range and variety of South American forms. Many survived the onslaught of North American species after the isthmus rose. Some spread and prospered: the opossum moved as far as Canada; the armadillo is still making its way north.

Despite the success of a few, extirpation of the most dramatically different South American forms must be ranked as the dominant effect of contact between mammals of the two continents. Two entire orders perished (we group all modern mammals into about twenty-five orders). Think how our zoos would have been enriched with a liberal

289

sprinkling of notoungulates, a large and diverse group of plant-eating mammals, ranging from rhino-sized *Toxodon,* first exhumed by Charles Darwin on shore leave from the *Beagle,* to rabbit and rodent analogues among the typotheres and hegetotheres. Consider the litopterns with their two subgroups—the large, long-necked camel-like macrauchenids and the most remarkable group of all, the horse-like proterotheres. (Proterotheres even repeated some of the evolutionary trends followed by true horses: three-toed *Diadiaphorus* preceded *Thoatherium,* a single-toed species that outdid Man 'O War by reducing its vestigial side toes to a degree never matched by modern horses.) They are all gone forever, victims in large part of faunal disruptions set in motion by the rising isthmus. (Several notoungulates and litopterns survived well into the glacial epoch. They may even have received their *coup de grâce* from early human hunters. Still, I do not doubt that many would still be with us if South America had remained an island.)

The native predators of these South American herbivores also disappeared completely. The modern carnivores of South America, the jaguars and their allies, are all North American interlopers. The indigenous carnivores, believe it or not, were all marsupials (although some flesh-eating niches were occupied by the phororhacids, a remarkable group of giant birds, now also extinct). The marsupial carnivores, although not as diverse as placental carnivores in northern continents, formed an impresive array, from fairly small animals to bear-sized species. One lineage evolved in uncanny parallel with the saber-toothed cats of North America. The marsupial *Thylacosmilus* developed long, stabbing upper canines and a protecting flange of bone on the lower jaw—just like *Smilodon* of the La Brea tar pits.

Although it is not commonly bruited about, marsupials are not doing badly in South America today. North America may only boast the so-called Virginia opossum (actually a South American migrant), but opossums in South America are a rich and varied group of some sixty-five species. In addition, the caenolestids, pouchless "opossum rats," form a separate group with no close affinity to true opossums.

But the third great group of South American marsupials, the carnivorous borhyaenids, were completely wiped out and replaced by northern cats.

The traditional view—though I dedicate this essay to opposing it—attributes the extirpation of carnivorous marsupials to the general inferiority of pouched versus placental mammals. (All living mammals except marsupials and the egg-laying platypus and echidna are placentals.) The argument seems hard to beat. Marsupials flourished only on the isolated island continents of Australia and South America where large placental carnivores never gained a foothold. The early Tertiary marsupials of North America soon disappeared as placentals diversified; South American marsupials took a beating when the Central American corridor opened for placental immigration.

These arguments of biogeography and geological history gain apparent support from the conventional idea that marsupials are anatomically and physiologically inferior to placentals. The very terms of our taxonomy reinforce this prejudice. All mammals are divided into three parts: the egg-laying monotremes are called Prototheria, or premammals; placentals win the prize as Eutheria, or true mammals; the poor marsupials lie in limbo as Metatheria, or middle mammals—not all quite there.

The argument for structural inferiority rests largely upon differing modes of reproduction in marsupials versus placentals, bolstered by the usual smug assumption that different from us is worse. Placentals, as we know and experience, develop as embryos in intimate connection with a mother's body and blood supply. With some exceptions, they are born as reasonably complete and capable creatures. Marsupial fetuses never developed the essential trick that permits extensive development within a mother's body. Our bodies have an uncanny ability to recognize and reject foreign tissues, an essential protection against disease, but a currently intractable barrier to medical procedures ranging from skin grafts to heart transplants. Despite all the homilies about mother love, and the presence of 50 percent maternal genes in offspring, an embryo is still foreign tissue. The maternal immune system must be masked to prevent rejection. Placental fetuses have "learned" to do this; marsupials have not.

Marsupial gestation is very short—twelve to thirteen days in the common oppossum, followed by sixty to seventy days of further development in the external pouch. Moreover, internal development does not proceed in intimate connection with the mother, but shielded from her. Two-thirds of gestation occurs within the "shell membrane," a maternal organ that prevents the incursion of lymphocytes, the "soldiers" of the immune system. A few days of placental contact follow, usually via the yolk sac. During this time, the mother mobilizes her immune system, and the embryo is born (or, more accurately, expelled) soon after.

The marsupial neonate is a tiny creature, equivalent in development to a rather early placental embryo. Its head and forelimbs are precociously developed, but the hind limbs are often little more than undifferentiated buds. It must then undertake a hazardous journey, slowly pulling itself along through the relatively great distance to mother's nipples and pouch (we can now understand the necessity of well-developed forelimbs). Our embryonic life within a placental womb sounds altogether easier and unconditionally better.

What challenge can then be offered to these biogeographical and structural accounts of marsupial inferiority? My colleague John A. W. Kirsch has recently marshaled the arguments. Citing work of P. Parker, Kirsch contends that marsupial reproduction follows a different adaptive mode, not an inferior path. True, marsupials never evolved a mechanism to turn off the maternal immune system and permit a completed development within the womb. But early birth may be an equally adaptive strategy. Maternal rejection need not represent a failure of design or lost evolutionary opportunity; it may reflect an ancient and perfectly adequate approach to the rigors of survival. Parker's argument goes right back to Darwin's central contention that individuals struggle to maximize their own reproductive success, that is, to increase the representation of their own genes in future generations. Several highly divergent, but equally successful, strategies can be followed in (unconscious) pursuit of this goal. Placentals invest a great deal of time and energy in offspring before their birth. This commitment does increase the chance of an offspring's success, but the placental mother also takes a risk: if she should lose her litter, she has irrevocably expended a large portion of her life's reproductive effort for no evolutionary gain. The marsupial mother pays a much higher toll in neonatal death, but her reproductive cost is small. Gestation has been very short and she may breed again in the same season. Moreover, the tiny neonate has not placed a great drain upon her energetic resources, and has subjected her to little danger in a quick and easy birth.

Turning to biogeography, Kirsch challenges the usual assumption that Australia and South America were refugia for inferior beasts that couldn't hang on in the placental world of the Northern Hemisphere. He views their southern diversity as a reflection of success in their ancestral homeland, not as a feeble effort in peripheral territory. His argument relies upon M. A. Archer's claim for close genealogical relationship between borhyaenids (South American marsupial carnivores) and thylacines (marsupial carnivores of the Australian region). Taxonomists have previously regarded these two groups as an example of evolutionary convergence—separate development of similar adaptations (as in the marsupial and placental saber-tooths, mentioned previously). In fact, taxonomists have viewed the Australian and South American radiation of marsupials as completely independent events, following the separate invasion of both continents by primitive marsupials pushed out from northern lands. But if borhyaenids and thylacines are closely related, then the southern continents must have exchanged some of their products, probably via Antarctica. (In our new geology of drifting continents, southern hemisphere lands were much closer together when mammals rose to prominence, following the dinosaurs' demise.) A more parsimonious view imagines an Australian center of origin for marsupials and a dispersal to South America following the evolution of thylacinids, rather than two separate marsupial invasions of South America—borhyaenid ancestors from Australia, and all the others from North America. Although the simplest explanations are not always true in our wondrously complex world, Kirsch's arguments do cast considerable doubt on the usual assumption that marsupial homelands are refugia, not centers of origin.

Yet I must confess that this structural and biogeographical defense of marsupials falters badly before one cardinal fact, prominently featured above: the Isthmus of Panama rose, placental carnivores invaded, marsupial carnivores quickly perished, and the placentals took over. Does this not speak for clear competitive superiority of North American placental carnivores? I could sneak around this unpleasant fact by ingenious conjecture, but I prefer to admit it. How then can I continue to defend marsupial equality?

Although the borhyaenids lost big, I find no scrap of evidence to attribute defeat to their status as marsupials. I prefer an ecological argument predicting hard times for any indigenous group of South American carnivores, marsupial or placental. The real victims happened to be marsupials, but this taxonomic fact may be incidental to a fate sealed for other reasons.

R. Bakker has been studying the history of mammalian carnivores throughout the Tertiary. Integrating some new ideas with conventional wisdom, he finds that the northern placental carnivores experienced two kinds of evolutionary "tests." Twice, they suffered short periods of mass extinction, and new groups, perhaps with greater adaptive flexibility, took over. During times of continuity, high diversity of both predators and prey engendered intense competition and strong evolutionary trends for improvement in feeding (quick ingestion and efficient slicing) and locomotion (high acceleration in ambush predators, endurance in long-distance hunters). South American and Australian carnivores were tested in neither way. They suffered no mass extinctions, and the original incumbents persisted. Diversity never approached northern levels, and competition remained less intense. Bakker reports that their levels of morphological specialization for running and feeding lie far below those of northern carnivores living at the same time.

H. J. Jerison's studies of brain size provide an impressive confirmation. On northern continents, placental predators and prey evolved successively larger brains throughout the Tertiary. In South America, both marsupial carnivores and their placental prey quickly plateaued at about 50 percent of brain weight for average modern mammals of the same body sizes. Anatomical status as marsupial or placental seems to make no difference; a relative history of evolutionary challenge may be crucial. If, by happenstance, northern carnivores had been marsupials and southern carnivores placentals, I suspect that the outcome of isthmian exchange would still have been a rout for South America. North American faunas were continually tested in the fiery furnaces of mass destruction and intense competition. The South American carnivores were never strongly challenged. When the Isthmus of Panama rose, they were weighed in the evolutionary balance for the first time. Like Daniel's king, they were found wanting.

8 | Size and Time

29 | Our Allotted Lifetimes

J. P. MORGAN, MEETING with Henry Ford in E. L. Doctorow's *Ragtime,* praises the assembly line as a faithful translation of nature's wisdom:

> Has it occurred to you that your assembly line is not merely a stroke of industrial genius but a projection of organic truth? After all, the interchangeability of parts is a rule of nature. . . . All mammals reproduce in the same way and share the same designs of self-nourishment, with digestive and circulatory systems that are recognizably the same, and they enjoy the same senses. . . . Shared design is what allows taxonomists to classify mammals as mammals.

An imperious tycoon should not be met with equivocation; nonetheless, I can only reply "yes, and no" to Morgan's pronouncement. Morgan was wrong if he thought that large mammals are geometric replicas of smaller relatives. Elephants have relatively smaller brains and thicker legs than mice, and these differences record a general rule of mammalian design, not the idiosyncracies of particular animals.

But Morgan was right in arguing that large animals are essentially similar to small members of their group. The similarity, however, does not reside in a constant shape. The basic laws of geometry dictate that animals must change their shape in order to work the same way at different sizes. Galileo himself established the classic example in 1638: the strength of an animal's leg is a function of its cross-sectional area (length × length); the weight that legs must support varies as the animal's volume (length × length × length). If mammals did not increase the relative thickness of their legs as they got larger, they would soon collapse (since body weight would increase so much faster than the supporting strength of limbs). To remain the same in function, animals must change their form.

The study of these changes in form is called "scaling theory." Scaling theory has uncovered a striking regularity of changing shape over the 25-millionfold range of mammalian weight from shrew to blue whale. If we plot brain weight versus body weight for all mammals on the so-called mouse-to-elephant (or shrew-to-whale) curve, very few species deviate far from a single line expressing the general rule: brain weight increases only two-thirds as fast as body weight as we move from small to large mammals. (We share with bottle-nosed dolphins the honor of greatest upward deviance from the curve.)

We can often predict these regularities from the basic physics of objects. The heart, for example, is a pump. Since all mammalian hearts work in essentially the same way, small hearts must pump considerably faster than large ones (imagine how much faster you could work a finger-sized, toy bellows than the giant model that fuels a blacksmith's forge or an old-fashioned organ). On the mouse-to-elephant curve for mammals, the length of a heartbeat increases between one-fourth and one-third as fast as body weight as we move from small to large mammals. The generality of this conclusion has recently been affirmed in an interesting study by J. E. Carrel and R. D. Heathcote on the scaling of heart rate in spiders. They used a cool laser beam to illuminate the hearts of resting spiders and drew a crab spider-to-tarantula curve for eighteen species spanning nearly a thousandfold range of body weight. Again, scaling is regular with heart rate increasing four-tenths as fast as body weight (.409 times as fast, to be exact).

We may extend this conclusion for hearts to a general statement about the pace of life in small versus large animals. Small animals tick through life far more rapidly than large animals—their hearts work more quickly, they breathe more frequently, their pulse beats much faster. Most importantly, metabolic rate, the so-called fire of life, increases only three-fourths as fast as body weight in mammals. To keep themselves going, large mammals do not need to generate as much heat per unit of body weight as small animals. Tiny shrews move frenetically, eating nearly all their waking lives to keep their metabolic fire burning at the maximal rate among mammals; blue whales glide majestically, their hearts beating the slowest rhythm among active, warmblooded creatures.

The scaling of lifetime among mammals suggests an intriguing synthesis of these disparate data. We have all had enough experience with mammalian pets of various sizes to understand that small mammals tend to live for a shorter time than large ones. In fact, mammalian lifetime scales at about the same rate as heartbeat and breath time—between one-fourth and one-third as fast as body weight as we move from small to large animals. (*Homo sapiens* emerges from this analysis as a very peculiar animal. We live far longer than a mammal of our body size should. In essay 9, I argue that humans evolved by an evolutionary process called "neoteny"—the preservation in adults of shapes and growth rates that characterize juvenile stages of ancestral primates. I also believe that neoteny is responsible for our elevated longevity. Compared with other mammals, all stages of human life arrive "too late." We are born as helpless embryos after a long gestation; we mature late after an extended childhood; we die, if fortune be kind, at ages otherwise reached by warmblooded animals only at the very largest sizes.)

Usually, we pity the pet mouse or gerbil that lived its full span of a year or two at most. How brief its life, while we endure for the better part of a century. As the main theme of this essay, I want to argue that such pity is misplaced (our personal grief, of course, is quite another matter; with this, science does not deal). Morgan was right in *Ragtime*—small and large mammals are essentially similar. Their lifetimes are scaled to their life's pace, and all endure for approximately the same amount of biological time. Small mammals tick fast, burn rapidly, and live for a short time; large mammals live long at a stately pace. Measured by their own internal clocks, mammals of different sizes tend to live for the same amount of time.

We are prevented from grasping this important and comforting concept by a deeply ingrained habit of Western thought. We are trained from earliest memory to regard absolute Newtonian time as the single valid measuring stick in a rational and objective world. We impose our kitchen clock, ticking equably, upon all things. We marvel at the quickness of a mouse, express boredom at the torpor of a hippopotamus. Yet each is living at the appropriate pace of its own biological clock.

I do not wish to deny the importance of absolute, astronomical time to organisms (see essay 31). Animals must measure it to lead successful lives. Deer must know when to regrow their antlers, birds when to migrate. Animals track the day–night cycle with their circadian rhythms; jet lag is the price we pay for moving much faster than nature intended.

But absolute time is not the appropriate measuring stick for all biological phenomena. Consider the magnificent song of the humpback whale. E. O. Wilson has described the awesome effect of these vocalizations: "The notes are eerie yet beautiful to the human ear. Deep basso groans and almost inaudibly high soprano squeaks alternate with repetitive squeals that suddenly rise or fall in pitch." We do not know the function of these songs. Perhaps they enable whales to find each other and to stay together during their annual transoceanic migrations. Perhaps they are the mating songs of courting males.

Each whale has its own characteristic song; the highly complex patterns are repeated over and over again with great faithfulness. No scientific fact that I have learned in the last decade struck me with more force than Roger S.

Payne's report that the length of some songs may extend for more than half an hour. I have never been able to memorize the five-minute first *Kyrie* of the B-minor Mass (and not for want of trying); how could a whale sing for thirty minutes and then repeat itself accurately? Of what possible use is a thirty-minute repeat cycle—far too long for a human to recognize; we would never grasp it as a single song (without Payne's recording machinery and much study after the fact). But then I remembered the whale's metabolic rate, the enormously slow pace of its life compared with ours. What do we know about a whale's perception of thirty minutes? A humpback may scale the world to its own metabolic rate; its half-hour song may be our minute waltz. From any point of view, the song is spectacular, it is the most elaborate single display so far discovered in any animal. I merely urge the whale's point of view as an appropriate perspective.

We can provide some numerical precision to support the claim that all mammals, on average, live for the same amount of biological time. In a method developed by W. R. Stahl, B. Günther, and E. Guerra in the late 1950s and early 1960s, we search the mouse-to-elephant equations for biological properties that scale at the same rate against body weight. For example, Günther and Guerra give the following equations for mammalian breath time and heartbeat time versus body weight.

$$\text{breath time} = .0000470 \ \text{body}^{0.28}$$
$$\text{heartbeat time} = .0000119 \ \text{body}^{0.28}$$

(Nonmathematical readers need not be overwhelmed by the formalism. The equations simply state that both breath time and heartbeat time increase about .28 times as fast as body weight as we move from small to large mammals.) If we divide the two equations, body weight cancels out because it is raised to the same power in both.

$$\frac{\text{breath time}}{\text{heartbeat time}} = \frac{.0000470 \ \cancel{\text{body}^{0.28}}}{.0000119 \ \cancel{\text{body}^{0.28}}} = 4.0$$

This states that the ratio of breath time to heartbeat time is 4.0 in mammals of any body size. In other words, all mammals, whatever their size, breathe once for each four heart-beats. Small mammals breathe and beat their hearts faster than large mammals, but both breath and heart slow up at the same relative rate as mammals get larger.

Lifetime also scales at the same rate as body weight (.28 times as fast as we move from small to large mammals). This means that the ratio of both breath time and heartbeat time to lifetime is also constant over the entire range of mammalian size. When we perform a calculation similar to the one above, we find that all mammals, regardless of their size, tend to breathe about 200 million times during their lives (their hearts, therefore, beat about 800 million times). Small mammals breathe fast, but live for a short time. Measured by the internal clocks of their own hearts or the rhythm of their own breathing, all mammals live the same time. (Astute readers, after counting their breaths or taking their pulses, may have calculated that they should have died long ago. But *Homo sapiens* is a markedly deviant mammal in more ways than braininess alone. We live about three times as long as mammals of our body size "should," but we breathe at the "right" rate and thus live to breathe about three times as often as an average mammal of our body size. I regard this excess of living as a happy consequence of neoteny.)

The mayfly lives but a day as an adult. It may, for all I know, experience that day as we live a lifetime. Yet all is not relative in our world, and such a short glimpse of it guarantees distortion in interpreting events ticking on longer scales. In a brilliant metaphor, the pre-Darwinian evolutionist Robert Chambers wrote in 1844 of a mayfly watching the metamorphosis of a tadpole into a frog:

> Suppose that an ephemeron [a mayfly], hovering over a pool for its one April day of life, were capable of observing the fry of the frog in the waters below. In its aged afternoon, having seen no change upon them for such a long time, it would be little qualified to conceive that the external branchiae [gills] of these creatures were to decay, and be replaced by internal lungs, that

feet were to be developed, the tail erased, and the animal then to become a denizen of the land.

Human consciousness arose but a minute before midnight on the geologic clock. Yet we mayflies try to bend an ancient world to our purposes, ignorant perhaps of the messages buried in its long history. Let us hope that we are still in the early morning of our April day.

30 | Natural Attraction: Bacteria, the Birds and the Bees

THE FAMOUS WORDS "blessed art thou among women" were uttered by the angel Gabriel as he announced to Mary that she would conceive by the Holy Spirit. In medieval and Renaissance painting, Gabriel bears the wings of a bird, often elaborately spread and adorned. While visiting Florence last year, I became fascinated by the "comparative anatomy" of Gabriel's wings as depicted by the great painters of Italy. The faces of Mary and Gabriel are so beautiful, their gestures often so expressive. Yet the wings, as painted by Fra Angelico or by Martini, seem stiff and lifeless, despite the beauty of their intricate feathering.

But then I saw Leonardo's version. Gabriel's wings are so supple and graceful that I scarcely cared to study his face or note the impact he had upon Mary. And then I recognized the source of the difference. Leonardo, who studied birds and understood the aerodynamics of wings, had painted a working machine on Gabriel's back. His wings are both beautiful and efficient. They have not only the right orientation and camber, but the correct arrangement of feathers as well. Had he been just a bit lighter, Gabriel might have flown without divine guidance. In contrast, the other Gabriels bear flimsy and awkward ornaments that could never work. I was reminded that aesthetic and functional beauty often go hand in hand (or rather arm in arm in this case).

In the standard examples of nature's beauty—the cheetah running, the gazelle escaping, the eagle soaring, the tuna coursing, and even the snake slithering or the inchworm inching—what we perceive as graceful form also represents an excellent solution to a problem in physics. When we wish to illustrate the concept of adaptation in evolutionary biology, we often try to show that organisms unconsciously "know" physics—that they have evolved remarkably efficient machines for eating and moving. When Mary asked Gabriel how she could possibly conceive, "seeing I know not a man," the angel replied: "For with God nothing shall be impossible." Many things are impossible for nature. But what nature can do, she often does surpassingly well. Good design is usually expressed by correspondence between an organism's form and an engineer's blueprint.

I recently encountered an even more striking example of good design: an organism that builds an exquisite machine directly within its own body. The machine is a magnet; the organism, a "lowly" bacterium. When Gabriel departed, Mary went to visit Elizabeth, who had also conceived with a bit of help from on high. Elizabeth's babe (the future John the Baptist) "leaped in her womb" and Mary pronounced the *Magnificat,* including the line (later set so incomparably by Bach) *et exaltavit humilis*—"and he hath exalted them of low degree." The tiny bacteria, simplest in structure among organisms, inhabitants of the first rung on traditional (and fallacious) ladders of life, illustrate in a few microns all the wonder and beauty that some organisms require meters to express.

In 1975, University of New Hampshire microbiologist Richard P. Blakemore discovered "magnetotactic" bacteria in sediments near Woods Hole, Massachusetts. (Just as geotactic organisms orient toward gravitational fields and phototactic creatures toward light, magnetotactic bacteria align themselves and swim in preferred directions within magnetic fields.) Blakemore then spent a year at the University of Illinois with microbiologist Ralph Wolfe and managed to isolate and culture a pure strain of magnetotactic bacteria. Blakemore and Wolfe then turned to an expert on the physics of magnetism, Richard B. Frankel of the National Magnet Laboratory at M.I.T. (I thank Dr. Frankel for his patient and lucid explanation of their work.)

Frankel and his colleagues found that each bacterium builds within its body a magnet made of twenty or so opaque, roughly cubic particles, measuring about 500 angstroms on a side (an angstrom is one ten-millionth of a millimeter). These particles are made primarily of the magnetic material Fe_3O_4, called magnetite, or lodestone. Frankel then calculated the total magnetic moment per bacterium and found that each contained enough magnetite to orient itself in the earth's magnetic field against the disturbing influence of Brownian motion. (Particles small enough to be unaffected by the gravitational fields that stabilize us

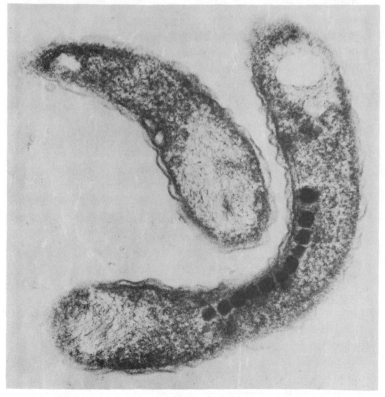

A magnetotactic bacterium with its chain of tiny magnets (X 40,000)   D. L. BALKWILL AND D. MARATEA

or by the surface forces that affect objects of intermediate size are buffeted in a random manner by thermal energy of the medium in which they lie suspended. The "play" of dust particles in sunlight provides a standard illustration of Brownian motion.)

The magnetotactic bacteria have built a remarkable machine, using virtually the only configuration that could work as a compass within their tiny bodies. Frankel explains why the magnetite must be arranged as particles and why the particles must be about 500 angstroms on a side. To work as an efficient compass, magnetite must be present as so-called single domain particles, that is, as bits with a single magnetic moment, containing opposite north- and south-seeking ends. The bacteria contain a chain of such particles, oriented with their magnetic moments north pole to the next south pole along the row—"like the elephants head to tail in a circus finale," as Frankel states. In this way, the entire chain of particles operates as a single magnetic dipole with north- and south-seeking ends.

If the particles were a bit smaller (less than 400 angstroms on a side), they would be "superparamagnetic"—a big word indicating that thermal energy at room temperature would cause internal reorientation of the particle's magnetic moment. On the other hand, if particles were greater than 1,000 angstroms on a side, separate magnetic domains pointing in different directions would form *within* the particle. This "competition" would reduce or cancel the particle's overall magnetic moment. Thus, Frankel concludes, "the bacteria have solved an interesting problem in physics by producing particles of magnetite of just the right size for a compass, of dimension 500 angstroms."

But evolutionary biology is preeminently the science of "why," and we must ask what such a small creature could possibly do with a magnet. Since a bacterium's cruising range is probably a few inches for the few minutes of its existence, I find it hard to believe that oriented motion in a north or south direction can play any role in its repertoire of adaptive traits. But what preferred direction of motion might make a difference? Frankel suggests, quite plausibly in my view, that an ability to move *down* might be crucial for such a bacterium—for down is the direction of sediments in aquatic environments, and down might lead to a region of preferred oxygen pressure. In this instance, "them of low degree" might wish to debase themselves even further.

But how does a bacterium know which way is down? With the smug prejudices of our enormous selves, we might think the question inane for its obvious answer: all they have to do is stop whatever they are doing and fall. Not at all. We fall because gravity affects us. Gravity—the standard example of a "weak force" in physics—influences us only because we are large. We live in a world of competing forces, and the relative strength of these forces depends primarily upon the size of objects affected by them. For familiar creatures of macroscopic dimensions, the ratio of surface area to volume is crucial. This ratio decreases continually as an organism grows, since areas increase as length squared and volumes as length cubed. Small creatures, insects for example, live in a world dominated by forces acting on their surfaces. Some can walk on water or hang upside down from a ceiling because surface tension is so strong and the gravitational force that might pull them down so weak. Gravitation works on volumes (or, to be more precise, upon masses that are proportional to volumes in a constant gravitational field). Gravitation rules us with our low ratio of surface to volume. But it troubles an insect very little—and a bacterium not at all.

The world of a bacterium is so unlike our own that we must abandon all our certainties about the way things are and start from scratch. Next time you see *Fantastic Voyage* on the tube, take your eyes off Raquel Welch and the predaceous white blood corpuscle long enough to ponder how the miniaturized adventurers would really fare as microscopic objects within a human body (they behave just like regular folks in the film). They would, first of all, be subject to shocks of the Brownian motion, thus making the film something of a random blur. Also, as Isaac Asimov pointed out to me, their ship could not run on its propeller, since blood is too viscous at such a scale. It should have, he said, a flagellum—like a bacterium.

D'Arcy Thompson, premier student of scaling since Galileo, urged us to set aside our prejudices if we would understand the world of a bacterium. In his masterpiece, *Growth and Form* (published in 1942 but still in print), he ends his chapter "On Magnitude" in his incomparable prose:

> Life has a range of magnitude narrow indeed compared to that with which physical science deals; but it is wide enough to include three such discrepant conditions as those in which a man, an insect and a bacillus have their being and play their several roles. Man is ruled by gravitation, and rests on mother earth. A water-beetle finds the surface of a pool a matter of life and death, a perilous entanglement or an indispensable support. In a third world, where the bacillus lives, gravitation is forgotten, and the viscosity of the liquid, the resistance defined by Stokes's law, the molecular shocks of the Brownian movement, doubtless also the electric charges of the ionized medium, make up the physical environment and have their potent and immediate influence upon the organism. The predominant factors are no longer those of our scale; we have come to the edge of a world of which we have no experience, and where all our preconceptions must be recast.

So how does a bacterium know which way is down? We use magnets for horizontal orientation so exclusively that we often forget (in fact, I suspect many of us do not know) that the earth's magnetic field also has a vertical component, its strength depending upon latitude. (We damp out the vertical deflection in building compasses because it doesn't interest us. As large creatures ruled by gravitation, we know which way is down. Only at our scale could folly be personified as not knowing "which way is up.") A compass needle follows the earth's lines of force. At the equator, these lines are horizontal to the surface. Toward the poles, they dip more and more strongly *into* the earth. At the magnetic pole itself, the needle points straight down. At my latitude in Boston, the vertical component is actually stronger than the horizontal. A bacterium, swimming north as a free compass needle, also swims down at Woods Hole.

This putative function for a bacterial compass is pure speculation at the moment. But if these bacteria use their magnets primarily to swim down (rather than to find each other, or to do Lord knows what, if anything, in their unfamiliar world), then we can make some testable predictions. Members of the same species, living in natural populations adapted to life at the equator, will probably not make magnets, for here a compass needle has no vertical component. In the Southern Hemisphere, magnetotactic bacteria should display reversed polarity and swim in the direction of their south-seeking pole.

Magnetite has also been reported as a component of several larger organisms, all of which perform remarkable feats of horizontal orientation—the conventional use of a compass for familiar creatures of our scale. Chitons, eight-plated relatives of clams and snails, live primarily on rocks near sea level in tropical regions. They scrape food from the rocks with a long file called a radula—and the tips of the radular teeth are made of magnetite. Many chitons make substantial excursions from a living site, but "home" back to the precise spot thereafter. The idea that they might use their magnetite as an orienting compass suggests itself, but the evidence so far offers no support. It is not even clear that chitons have enough magnetite to perceive the earth's field, and Frankel tells me that their particles are mostly above the single domain limit.

Some bees have magnetite in their abdomens, and we know that they are affected by the earth's magnetic field (see article by J. L. Gould, no relation, J. L. Kirschvink, and K. S. Defeyes in bibliography). Bees do their famous dance on the vertical surface of their honeycomb by converting the orientation of their flight to food in relation to the sun into an angle danced with respect to gravity. If the comb is turned so that bees must dance on a horizontal surface, where they cannot express direction in gravitational terms, they become disoriented at first. Finally, after several weeks, they align their dances to the magnetic compass. Moreover, a swarm of bees, placed into an empty hive without cues for orientation, build their comb in the magnetic direction it occupied in their parental hive. Pigeons, certainly no duffers at homing, build a structure made of magnetite between their brain and skull. This magnetite exists as single domains and can therefore function as a magnet (see C. Walcott *et al.* in bibliography).

The world is full of signals that we don't perceive. Tiny creatures live in a different world of unfamiliar forces. Many animals of our scale greatly exceed our range of perception for sensations familiar to us. Bats avoid obstacles by bouncing sound off them at frequencies that I cannot hear, although some people can. Many insects see into the ultraviolet and follow the "invisible" nectar guides of flowers to sources of food for them and pollen that they will carry to the next flower for fertilization (plants build these orienting color streaks for their own advantages, not to convenience the insects).

What an imperceptive lot we are. Surrounded by so much, so fascinating and so real, that we do not see (hear, smell, touch, taste) in nature, yet so gullible and so seduced by claims for novel power that we mistake the tricks of mediocre magicians for glimpses of a psychic world beyond our ken. The paranormal may be a fantasy; it is certainly a haven for charlatans. But "parahuman" powers of perception lie all about us in birds, bees, and bacteria. And we can use the instruments of science to sense and understand what we cannot directly perceive.

Postscript

In asking why bacteria might build magnets within their bodies, Frankel speculated cogently that swimming north could make little difference to such a tiny creature, but that swimming *down* (another consequence of life around a compass at mid to high latitudes in the northern hemisphere) could be very important indeed. This led me to predict that if Frankel's explanation be valid, magnetic bacteria in the Southern Hemisphere should swim *south* in order to swim down—that is, their polarity should be reversed relative to northern hemisphere relatives.

In March, 1980, Frankel sent me a preprint of a paper with colleagues R.P. Blakemore and A.J. Kalmijn. They travelled to New Zealand and Tasmania in order to test the magnetic polarity of southern hemisphere magnetic bacteria. Indeed, they all swam south and down—an impressive confirmation of Frankel's hypothesis and the basis of my essay.

They also performed an interesting experiment, providing further confirmation of another kind. They collected magnetic bacteria at Woods Hole, Massachusetts, divided the sample of north-swimming cells into two parts. They cultured one subsample for several generations in a chamber of normal polarity, but grew the other in a chamber of reversed polarity to simulate Southern Hemisphere conditions. Sure enough, after several weeks, north-swimming cells continued to predominate in the chamber of normal polarity. But in the chamber with reversed polarity, south-swimming cells now formed a majority. Since bacterial cells do not change polarity during their lifetimes, this dramatic change is probably the result of strong natural selection for the ability to swim down. Presumably, both north and south-swimming cells originate in each chamber, but selection quickly weeds out individuals that cannot swim down.

Frankel tells me that he is now off to the geomagnetic equator to see what happens where the magnetic field has no downward component at all.

31 | Time's Vastness

2:00 A.M., Jan. 1, 1979

I WILL NEVER forget Toscanini's last concert—the night that the greatest maestro of them all, the man who held all Western music in his infallible memory, faltered for a few seconds and lost his place. If heroes were truly invulnerable, how could they compel our interest? Siegfried must have a mortal shoulder, Achilles a heel, Superman kryptonite.

Karl Marx remarked that all historical events occur twice, first as tragedy, the second time as farce. If Toscanini's lapse was tragic (in the heroic sense), then I witnessed the farce just two hours ago. I listened while the ghost of Guy Lombardo missed a beat. For the first time in God only knows how many years, that smooth sound, that comfortable welcome to the New Year, fell apart for a mysterious moment. As I learned later, someone forgot to tell Guy about the special 61-second minute that ended 1978; he started too early and could not compensate with unnoticed grace.

This second, added for internal bookkeeping to synchronize atomic and astronomical clocks, received wide press coverage, virtually all of it in a jocular vein. And why not—good news is rare enough these days. Most reports pushed the same theme: they twitted scientists about their concern for consummate accuracy. After all, how can so trifling a

315

span of time as a single second matter?

I then remembered another figure, 1/50,000 second per year. This figure, an ant before the behemoth of a full second, is the annual rate of deceleration in the earth's rotation due to tidal friction. I will attempt to show just how important such an "insignificant" number can be in the fullness of geological time.

We have known for a long time that the earth is slowing down. Edmund Halley, godfather to the famous comet and Astronomer Royal of England early in the eighteenth century, noted a systematic discrepancy between the recorded position of ancient eclipses and their predicted areas of visibility based on the earth's rate of rotation in his time. He calculated that this disparity could be resolved by assuming a faster rotation in the past. Halley's calculations have been refined and reanalyzed many times, and eclipse records suggest an approximate rate of two milliseconds per century for rotational slowing during the past few thousand years.

Halley proposed no adequate reason for this deceleration. Immanuel Kant, a versatile fellow indeed, supplied the correct explanation later in the eighteenth century. Kant implicated the moon and argued that tidal friction had slowed the earth down. The moon pulls the waters of the earth toward it in a tidal bulge. This bulge remains oriented toward the moon as the earth rotates under it. From our point of view as earthbound observers, high tide moves steadily westward around the earth. This tide, moving continuously across land and sea (for continents have their minor tides as well), creates a great deal of friction. Astronomers Robert Jastrow and M. H. Thompson write: "A huge quantity of energy is dissipated in this friction each day. If the energy could be recovered for useful purposes, it would be sufficient to supply the electrical power requirements of the entire world several times over. The energy is actually dissipated in the turbulence of coastal waters plus a small degree of heating of the rocks in the crust of the earth."

But tidal friction has another effect, virtually invisible on the scale of our lives, but a major factor in the earth's history. It acts as a brake upon the spinning earth, slowing the earth's rotation at the leisurely rate of about two milliseconds per century, or 1/50,000 second per year.

Braking by tidal friction has two correlated and intriguing effects. First, the number of days in a year should be decreasing through time. The length of a year seems to be essentially constant relative to the official cesium clock. Its invariance is affirmed both empirically, by astronomical measurement, and theoretically. We might predict that a solar tide should slow the earth's revolution just as the lunar tide slows its rotation. But solar tides are quite weak, and the earth, hurtling through space, has such an enormous moment of inertia that the year increases by no more than three seconds per billion years. Here we finally have a figure that we can safely ignore—half a minute from the origin of the earth to its destruction by an exploding sun some five billion years hence!

Second, as the earth loses angular momentum in slowing down, the moon—obedient to the law of conservation of angular momentum for the earth–moon system—must pick up what the earth loses. The moon does this by revolving around the earth at a greater and greater distance. In other words, the moon has been steadily receding from the earth.

If the moon looks big now, low on the horizon on a crisp October night, you should have been around to see what the trilobites saw 550 million years ago. G. H. Darwin, noted astronomer and second son of Charles, first developed this idea of lunar recession. He believed that the moon had been wrenched from the Pacific Ocean, and he extrapolated its present rate of recession back to determine the time of this convulsive birth. (It does fit, but thanks to plate tectonics, we now know that the Pacific is not a permanent hole, but a configuration of the geological moment.)

In short, tidal friction induced by the moon entails two coupled consequences through time: slowing the earth's rotation to decrease the number of days per year, and increasing the distance between earth and moon.

Astronomers have long known about these phenomena in theory; they have also measured them directly over geological microseconds. But until recently, no one has known how to gauge their effects over long stretches of geological time. A simple backward extrapolation of the current rate will not suffice because intensity of braking depends upon the configuration of continents and oceans. The most effective braking occurs when tides sweep across shallow seas; the least effective when tides move with comparatively little friction over deep oceans and land. Shallow seas are not prominent features of our present earth, but they covered millions of square miles at various times in the past. The high tidal friction of those times may be matched by very slow deceleration at other times, particularly when all the continents coalesced into a single Pangaea. The pattern of rotational slowing through time therefore becomes more a geological than an astronomical problem.

I am delighted to report that my own brand of geology has yielded, albeit ambiguously, the required information—for some fossils record in their patterns of growth the astronomical rhythms of ancient times. The haughty and high-riding mathematicians and experimentalists of modern geophysics do not often take a bow toward a lowly fossil. Yet one prominent student of the earth's rotation has written: "It appears that paleontology comes to the rescue of the geophysicist."

For more than a hundred years, paleontologists had occasionally noted regularly spaced growth lines on some of their fossils. Some had suggested that they might reflect astronomical periods of days, months, or years—much like tree rings. Yet no one had done anything with these observations. Throughout the 1930s Ting Ying Ma, a somewhat visionary, highly speculative, but infallibly interesting Chinese paleontologist, studied annual bands in fossil corals to determine the position of ancient equators. (Corals living at the equator in regimes of nearly constant temperature should not show the seasonal bands; the higher the latitude, the stronger the bands.) But no one had studied the very fine laminations that often occur by the hundreds per band.

In the early 1960s, Cornell paleontologist John West Wells realized that these very fine striations might record days (slow growth at night versus faster growth during daylight, much as trees produce annual bands of alternating slow winter and rapid summer growth). He studied a modern coral with both coarse (presumably annual) and very fine banding, and he counted an average of about 360 fine lines to each coarse band. He concluded that the fine lines are daily.

Wells then searched his collection for fossil corals sufficiently well preserved to retain all their fine bands. He found very few, but they enabled him to make one of the most interesting and important observations in the history of paleontology: a group of corals about 370 million years old had an average of just under 400 fine lines per coarse band. These corals had witnessed a year of nearly 400 days. Direct, geological evidence had finally been found for an old astronomical theory.

But Wells's corals had affirmed only half the story—increasing length of day. The other half, recession of the moon, required fossils with daily and monthly banding; for if the moon had been much closer in the past, it would have revolved around the earth in a much shorter time than it does today. The ancient lunar month should have contained fewer than the 29.53 solar days of the present month.

Since Wells published his famous paper on "Coral Growth and Geochronometry" in 1963, several claims have been entered for lunar periodicities as well. Most recently, Peter Kahn, a paleontologist from Princeton, and Stephen Pompea, a physicist from Colorado State University, have argued that the key to lunar history lies with one of everybody's favorite creatures, the chambered nautilus. The nautilus shell is divided into regular internal partitions called septa. These same septa, and the beauty of their construction, inspired Oliver Wendell Holmes to exhort us, by analogy, to do better with our internal lives:

Build thee more stately mansions, O my soul,
As the swift seasons roll!
Leave thy low-vaulted past!
Let each new temple, nobler than the last,

Shut thee from heaven with a dome more vast,
Till thou at length art free,
Leaving thine outgrown shell by life's unresting sea!

I am happy to report that nautiloid septa may have extended their utility beyond Holmes's musings on immortality and O'Neill's cribbing of a title for a play. For Kahn and Pompea counted the finer growth lines on the exterior of *Nautilus*'s shell and found that each chamber (the space between successive septa) contains an average of thirty fine lines, with little variation either among shells or on successive chambers of single shells. Since *Nautilus*, living in deep Pacific waters, migrates daily in response to the solar cycle (it moves towards the surface at night), Kahn and Pompea suggest that the fine lines record days. The secretion of septa may be entrained to a lunar cycle. Many animals, including humans of course, have lunar cycles, usually tied to breeding.

Nautiloids are quite common as fossils (the modern chambered nautilus is sole survivor of a very diverse group). Kahn and Pompea counted lines per chamber in twenty-five nautiloids ranging in age from 25 to 420 million years. They argue for a regular decrease in lines per chamber from thirty today, to about twenty-five for the youngest fossils, to only nine or so for the oldest. If the moon circled the earth in only nine solar days 420 million years ago (when the day only contained twenty-one hours), then it must have been much closer. Cranking through some equations, Kahn and Pompea conclude that these ancient nautiloids saw a gigantic moon slightly more than two-fifths its current distance from the earth (yes, they had eyes).

At this point, I must confess to some ambivalence about this large body of data on fossil growth rhythms. The methods are beset with unsolved problems. How do you know what periodicity the lines reflect? Consider the case of fine lines, for example. They are usually counted as though they record solar days. But suppose they are a response to tidal cycles—a periodicity that involves both the earth's rotation and the moon's revolution. If the moon revolved in a much shorter time in the past, then ancient tidal cycles were not nearly so close to the solar day as they are now. (You should now grasp the importance of Kahn and Pompea's argument, made without direct evidence by the way, that the fine lines of *Nautilus* reflect day–night cycles of vertical migration rather than tidal effects. In fact, they explain their three exceptional cases by arguing that these nautiloids inhabited persistently shallow, nearshore waters and may have recorded the tides.)

Even if lines are a response to solar cycles, how do you assess the days per ancient month or year? Simple counting is not the solution because animals often skip a day but do not, so far as we know, double up. Actual counts generally underestimate the number of days (remember Wells's original modern corals with an average of 360, not 365, daily bands—on very cloudy days, growth during the daytime may not exceed growth at night, and bands may not form).

Moreover, to pose the most basic question of all, how can we be certain that lines reflect an astronomical periodicity at all? Too often, little beyond their geometric regularity has inspired the assumption that they record days, months, or years. But animals are not passive machines, dutifully recording astronomical cycles in all their regularities of growth. Animals have internal clocks as well, and these are often keyed to metabolic rhythms with no apparent relationship to days, tides, and seasons. For example, most animals slow down their growth rates greatly as they advance in age. But many growth lines continue to increase in size at a constant rate. The distance between septa of *Nautilus* increases constantly and regularly throughout growth. Are septa really deposited once each month, or do later ones measure longer amounts of time? *Nautilus* may live by the rule: grow a septum after reaching a regularly increasing chamber volume, not grow a septum each full moon. I am, primarily for this reason, highly skeptical about Kahn and Pompea's conclusions.

The result of these unsolved problems is a body of poorly synchronized data. Uncomfortably large differences exist in the literature. One study of supposedly lunar periodicities in corals suggests that, about 350 million years ago, the month contained three times the number of days that Kahn and Pompea would allow.

Nonetheless, I remain satisfied and optimistic for two reasons. First, despite all internal asynchrony, every study has revealed the same basic pattern—decrease in the number of days per year. Second, after an initial period of uncritical enthusiasm, paleontologists are now doing the required hard work to learn just what the lines represent—experimental studies on modern animals in controlled conditions. Criteria for the resolution of discrepancies in fossil data should soon be available.

Scarcely any geological subject could be more fascinating or more beset with juicy problems. Consider the following: if you extrapolate back through time the current recession of the moon as estimated from eclipse data, the moon enters the Roche limit about one billion years ago. Inside the Roche limit, no major body can form. If a large body enters it from outside, results are unclear but certainly impressive. Vast tides would roar across the earth and the lunar surface would melt, which, conclusively from dates on Apollo rocks, it did not. (And the recession rate estimated from modern data—5.8 centimeters per year—is much less than the average advocated by Kahn and Pompea—94.5 centimeters per year.) Clearly, the moon was not this close to us either a billion years ago or ever at all since its surface solidified more than four billion years ago. Either rates of recession have varied drastically, and were much slower early in the earth's history, or the moon entered its current orbit a long time after the earth's formation. In any case, the moon was once much closer to us, and this different relationship should have had an important effect on the history of both bodies.

As for the earth, we have tentative indications in some of our earliest sedimentary rocks of tidal amplitudes that would put the Bay of Fundy to shame. For the moon, Kahn and Pompea make the interesting suggestion that its closer position and the earth's stronger gravitational pull at that time may explain why the lunar maria are concentrated on its visible, earthward side (the maria represent vast extrusions of liquid magma), and why the moon's center of mass is displaced in an earthward direction.

Geology has no more important lesson to teach than the vastness of time. We have no trouble getting our conclusions across intellectually—4.5 billion years rolls easily off the tongue as an age for the earth. But intellectual knowledge and gut appreciation are very different things. As a sheer number, 4.5 billion is incomprehensible, and we resort to metaphor and image to emphasize just how long the earth has existed and just how insignificant the length of human evolution has been—not to mention the cosmic millimicrosecond of our personal lives.

The standard metaphor for earth history is a 24-hour clock with human civilization occupying the last few seconds. I prefer to emphasize the accumulated oomph of effects utterly insignificant on the scale of our lives. We have just completed another year and the earth has slowed down by another 1/50,000 second. So blinking what? What you have just read is what.

Bibliography

Agassiz, E.C. 1895. *Louis Agassiz: his life and correspondence.* Boston: Houghton, Mifflin.

Agassiz, L. 1850. The diversity of origin of the human races. *Christian Examiner* 49: 110–45.

Agassiz, L. 1962 (originally published in 1857). *An essay on classification.* Cambridge, Mass.: Belknap Press of Harvard University Press.

Baker, V.R., and Nummedal, D. 1978. *The channeled scabland.* Washington: National Aeronautics and Space Administration, Planetary Geology Program.

Bakker, R.T. 1975. Dinosaur renaissance. *Scientific American,* April, pp. 58–78.

Bakker, R.T., and Galton, P.M. 1974. Dinosaur monophyly and a new class of vertebrates. *Nature* 248: 168–72.

Bateson, W. 1922. Evolutionary faith and modern doubts. *Science* 55: 55–61.

Berlin, B. 1973. Folk systematics in relation to biological classification and nomenclature. *Annual Review of Ecology and Systematics* 4: 259–71.

Berlin, B.; Breedlove, D.E.; and Raven, P.H. 1966. Folk taxonomies and biological classification. *Science* 154: 273–75.

Berlin, B.; Breedlove, D.E.; and Raven, P.H. 1974. *Principles of Tzeltal plant classification: an introduction to the botanical ethnography of a Mayan speaking people of highland Chiapas.* New York: Academic Press.

324

Bourdier, F. 1971. Georges Cuvier. *Dictionary of Scientific Biography* 3: 521–28. New York: Charles Scribner's Sons.

Bretz, J Harlen. 1923. The channeled scabland of the Columbia Plateau. *Journal of Geology* 31: 617–49.

Bretz, J Harlen. 1927. Channeled scabland and the Spokane flood. *Journal of the Washington Academy of Science* 17: 200–211.

Bretz, J Harlen. 1969. The Lake Missoula floods and the channeled scablands. *Journal of Geology* 77: 505–543.

Broca, P. 1861. Sur le volume et la forme du cerveau suivant les individus et suivant les races. *Bullétin de la Société d'Anthropologie de Paris* 2: 139–207, 301–321, 441–46.

Broca, P. 1873. Sur les crânes de la caverne de l'Homme-Mort (Lozère). *Revue d'anthropologie* 2: 1–53.

Bulmer, R., and Tyler, M. 1968. Karam classification of frogs. *Journal of the Polynesian Society* 77: 333–85.

Carr, A., and Coleman, P.J. 1974. Sea floor spreading theory and the odyssey of the green turtle. *Nature* 249: 128–30.

Carrel, J.E., and Heathcote, R.D. 1976. Heart rate in spiders: influence of body size and foraging energetics. *Science.*

Chambers, R. 1844. *Vestiges of the natural history of creation.* New York: Wiley and Putnam.

Cuénot, C. 1965. *Teilhard de Chardin.* Baltimore: Helicon.

Darwin, C. 1859. *On the origin of species.* London: John Murray.

Darwin, C. 1862. *On the various contrivances by which British and foreign orchids are fertilized by insects.* London: John Murray.

Darwin, C. 1871. *The descent of man.* London: John Murray.

Darwin, C. 1872. *The expression of the emotions in man and animals.* London: John Murray.

Davis, D.D. 1964. The giant panda: a morphological study of evolutionary mechanisms. *Fieldiana* (Chicago Museum of Natural History) *Memoirs* (Zoology) 3: 1–339.

Dawkins, R. 1976. *The selfish gene.* New York: Oxford University Press.

Diamond, J. 1966. Zoological classification system of a primitive people. *Science* 151: 1102–04.

Down, J.L.H. 1866. Observations on an ethnic classification of idiots. *London Hospital Reports,* pp. 259–62.

Eldredge, N., and Gould, S.J. 1972. Punctuated equilibria: an alternative to phyletic gradualism. In *Models in Paleobiology,* ed. T.J.M. Schopf, pp. 82–115. San Francisco: Freeman, Cooper and Co.

Elbadry, E.A., and Tawfik, M.S.F. 1966. Life cycle of the mite *Adactylidium sp.* (Acarina: Pyemotidae), a predator of thrips eggs in the United Arab Republic. *Annals of the Entomological Society of America* 59: 458–61.

Finch, C. 1975. *The art of Walt Disney.* New York: H.N. Abrams.

Fine, P.E.M. 1979. Lamarckian ironies in contemporary biology. *The Lancet,* June 2, pp. 1181–82.

Fluehr-Lobban, C., 1979, Down's syndrome (Mongolism): the scientific history of a genetic disorder, unpublished manuscript.

Fowler, W.A. 1967. *Nuclear astrophysics.* Philadelphia: American Philosophical Society.

Fox, G.E.; Magrum, L.J.; Balch, W.E.; Wolfe, R.S.; and Woese, C.R. 1977. Classification of methanogenic bacteria by 16S ribosomal RNA characterization. *Proceedings of the National Academy of Sciences* 74: 4537–41.

Frankel, R.B.; Blakemore, R.P.; and Wolfe, R.S. 1979. Magnetite in freshwater magnetotactic bacteria. *Science* 203: 1355–56.

Frazzetta, T. 1970. From hopeful monsters to bolyerine snakes. *American Naturalist* 104: 55–72.

Galilei, Galileo. 1638. *Dialogues concerning two new sciences.* Translated by H. Crew and A. DeSalvio. 1914, New York: MacMillan.

Goldschmidt, R. 1940. *The material basis of evolution.* New Haven, Conn.: Yale University Press.

Gould, S.J. 1977. *Ontogeny and phylogeny.* Cambridge, Mass.: Belknap Press of Harvard University Press.

Gould, S.J., and Eldredge, N. 1977. Punctuated equilibria: the tempo and mode of evolution reconsidered. *Paleobiology* 3: 115–51.

Gould, J.L.; Kirschvink, J.L.; and Defeyes, K.S. 1978. Bees have magnetic remanence. *Science* 201: 1026–28.

Gruber, H.E., and Barrett, P.H. 1974. *Darwin on man.* New York: Dutton.

Günther, B., and Guerra, E. 1955. Biological similarities. *Acta Physiologica Latinoamerica* 5: 169–86.

Haldane, J.B.S. 1956. Can a species concept be justified? In *The species concept in paleontology,* ed. P.C. Sylvester-Bradley, pp. 95–96. London: Systematics Association, Publication no. 2.

Hamilton, W.D. 1967. Extraordinary sex ratios. *Science* 156: 477–88.

Hanson, E.D. 1963. Homologies and the ciliate origin of the Eumetazoa. In *The lower Metazoa,* ed. E.C. Dougherty et al. pp. 7–22. Berkeley: University of California Press.

Hanson, E.D. 1977. *The origin and early evolution of animals.* Middletown, Connecticut: Wesleyan University Press.

Hopson, J.A. 1977. Relative brain size and behavior in archosaurian reptiles. *Annual Review of Ecology and Systematics* 8: 429–48.

Hull, D.L. 1976. Are species really individuals? *Systematic Zoology* 25: 174–91.

Jackson, J.B.C. and G. Hartman. 1971. Recent brachiopod-coralline sponge communities and their paleoecological significance. *Science* 173: 623–25.

Jacob, F. 1977. Evolution and tinkering. *Science* 196: 1161–66.

Jastrow, R., and Thompson, M.H. 1972. *Astronomy: fundamentals and frontiers.* New York: John Wiley.

Jerison, H.J. 1973. *Evolution of the brain and intelligence.* New York: Academic Press.

Johanson, D.C., and White, T.D. 1979. A systematic assessment of early African hominids. *Science* 203: 321–30.

Kahn, P.G.K., and Pompea, S.M. 1978. Nautiloid growth rhythms and dynamical evolution of the earth-moon system. *Nature* 275: 606–611.

Keith, A. 1948. *A new theory of human evolution.* London: Watts and Co.

Kirkpatrick, R. 1913. *The nummulosphere. An account of the organic origin of so-called igneous rocks and of abyssal red clays.* London: Lamley and Co.

Kirsch, J.A.W. 1977. The six-percent solution: second

thoughts on the adaptedness of the Marsupialia. *American Scientist* 65: 276–88.

Knoll, A.H., and Barghoorn, E.S. 1977. Archean microfossils showing cell division from the Swaziland System of South Africa. *Science* 198: 396–98.

Koestler, A. 1971. *The case of the midwife toad.* New York: Random House.

Koestler, A. 1978. *Janus.* New York: Random House.

Leakey, L.S.B. 1974. *By the evidence.* New York: Harcourt Brace Jovanovich.

Leakey, M.D., and Hay, R.L. 1979. Pliocene footprints in the Laetolil Beds at Laetoli, northern Tanzania. *Nature* 278: 317–23.

Long, C.A. 1976. Evolution of mammalian cheek pouches and a possibly discontinuous origin of a higher taxon (Geomyoidea). *American Naturalist* 110: 1093–97.

Lorenz, K. 1971 (originally published in 1950). Part and parcel in animal and human societies. In *Studies in animal and human behavior,* vol. 2, pp. 115–95. Cambridge, Mass.: Harvard University Press.

Lurie, E. 1960. *Louis Agassiz: a life in science.* Chicago: University of Chicago Press.

Lyell, C. 1830–1833. *The principles of geology.* 3 vols., London: John Murray.

Ma, T.Y.H., 1958. The relation of growth rate of reef corals to surface temperature of sea water as a basis for study of causes of diastrophisms instigating evolution of life. *Research on the Past Climate and Continental Drift* 14: 1–60.

Majnep, I., and Bulmer, R. 1977. *Birds of my Kalam country.* London: Oxford University Press.

Mayr, E. 1963. *Animal species and evolution.* Cambridge, Mass.: Belknap Press of Harvard University Press.

Merton, R.K. 1965. *On the shoulders of giants.* New York: Harcourt, Brace and World.

Montessori, M. 1913. *Pedagogical anthropology.* New York: F.A. Stokes.

Morgan, E. 1972. *The descent of woman.* New York: Stein and Day.

O'Brian, C.F. 1971. On *Eozoön Canadense. Isis* 62: 381–83.

Osborn, H.F. 1927. *Man rises to Parnassus.* Princeton, New Jersey: Princeton University Press

Ostrom, J. 1979. Bird flight: how did it begin? *American Scientist* 67: 46–56.

Payne, R. 1971. Songs of humpback whales. *Science* 173: 587–97.

Pietsch, T.W., and Grobecker, D.B. 1978. The compleat angler: aggressive mimicry in an antennariid anglerfish. *Science.* 201: 369–370.

Raymond, P. 1941. Invertebrate paleontology. In *Geology, 1888–1938. Fiftieth anniversary volume,* pp. 71–103. Washington, D.C.: Geological Society of America.

Rehbock, P.F. 1975. Huxley, Haeckel, and the oceanographers: the case of *Bathybius haeckelii. Isis* 66: 504–533.

Rupke, N.A. 1976. *Bathybius Haeckelii* and the psychology of scientific discovery. *Studies in the History and Philosophy of Science* 7: 53–62.

Russo, F., s.j. 1974. Supercherie de Piltdown: Teilhard de Chardin et Dawson. *La Recherche* 5: 293.

Schreider, E. 1966. Brain weight correlations calculated from the original result of Paul Broca. *American Journal of Physical Anthropology* 25: 153–58.

Schweber, S.S. 1977. The origin of the *Origin* revisited. *Journal of the History of Biology* 10: 229–316.

Stahl, W.R. 1962. Similarity and dimensional methods in biology. *Science* 137: 205–212.

Teilhard de Chardin, P. 1959. *The phenomenon of man.* New York: Harper and Brothers.

Temple, S.A. 1977. Plant-animal mutualism: coevolution with dodo leads to near extinction of plant. *Science* 197: 885–86.

Thompson, D.W. 1942. *On growth and form.* New York: Macmillan.

Verrill, A.E. 1907. The Bermuda Islands, part 4. *Transactions of the Connecticut Academy of Arts and Sciences* 12: 1–160.

Walcott, C.; Gould, J.L.; and Kirschvink, J.L. 1979. Pigeons have magnets. *Science* 205: 1027–29.

Wallace, A.R. 1890. *Darwinism.* London: MacMillan.

Wallace, A.R. 1895. *Natural selection and tropical nature.* London: MacMillan.

Waterston, D. 1913. The Piltdown mandible. *Nature* 92: 319.

Wells, J.W. 1963. Coral growth and geochronometry. *Nature* 197: 948–950.

Weiner, J.S. 1955. *The Piltdown forgery.* London: Oxford University Press.

White, M.J.D. 1978. *Modes of speciation.* San Francisco: W.H. Freeman.

Wilson, E.B. 1896. *The cell in development and inheritance.* New York: MacMillan.

Wilson, E.O. 1975. *Sociobiology.* Cambridge, Mass.: The Belknap Press of Harvard University Press.

Wynne-Edwards, V.C. 1962. *Animal dispersion in relation to social behavior.* London: Oliver and Boyd.

Zirkle, C. 1946. The early history of the idea of the inheritance of acquired characters and pangenesis. *Transactions of the American Philosophical Society* 35: 91–151.

Index